This Book

presented to the

CHURCH
LIBRARY
IN MEMORY OF

Bessie Martin

BY

Lottie Livesay &
Nita Charles

Code 4386-23, No. 3, Broadman Supplies, Nashville, Tenn. Printed in USA

ALL THE
DIVINE NAMES
AND TITLES
IN THE BIBLE

ALL THE DIVINE NAMES AND TITLES IN THE BIBLE

A Unique Classification of All Scriptural Designations
of the Three Persons of the Trinity

by
HERBERT LOCKYER, D.D.

"The immortal names,
That were not born to die."
Fitz-Greene Halleck,
1790-1867

ZONDERVAN
PUBLISHING HOUSE OF THE ZONDERVAN CORPORATION
GRAND RAPIDS, MICHIGAN 49506

Fifth printing 1980

Library of Congress Catalog Card Number 74-25338
ISBN 0-310-28040-0

Most Bible passages are quoted from the King James Version (KJV).
If the quoted passage is not exactly as found in the KJV and is not designated ASV
(American Standard Version), RV (Revised Version), RSV (Revised Standard Version),
or that of a named translator, it is the author's own translation.

Printed in the United States of America

To
DAVID H. THOMPSON
OF LONDON,
*who is not only my
friend and solicitor,
but a diligent student
of
the Word.*

CONTENTS

INTRODUCTION

Paul asked the question of the Corinthians, "For what man knoweth the things of a man, save the spirit of man which is in him?..." (1 Corinthians 2: 11). What the apostle implied by such a pertinent question was that man knows that he exists by his own consciousness of being, and *knows* that he knows. "From our own consciousness of will we infer a supreme originating Will; of intelligence, a supreme constructing mind; of morality, a supreme righteous Lawgiver; of affection, a supreme Father." Self-consciousness and self-determination sum up what man actually is. It is so with the Persons of the Godhead who know what each is, and who *know* what they know.

For ourselves, our knowledge of the Trinity is dependent upon the way each Person presents Himself in Scripture by designations and deeds. In its restricted sense, *theology* implies the knowledge of God. The Greek term for "God" *theos*, occurring over 1,000 times, in its truest sense expresses essential deity. *Logos* means "speech." But if we would know what God says about Himself, it is necessary to study the revelation found in the great names and titles He has given us of Himself. God alone can reveal His character and will to man. The Unknown and the Unknowable, as far as fleshly wisdom is concerned, can only make Himself fully known.

This, God, along with Christ and the Holy Spirit, have done in the many designations they have given us, all of which mirror their respective attributes and activities. George Macdonald wrote that, "The name of the Lord God should be a precious jewel in the cabinet of our heart, to be taken out only at great times, and with loving care." We would go further and say that all the names used of the Three in One should be taken out at *all* times, not merely as precious jewels to admire, but as treasure to use for our constant spiritual enrichment.

All down the ages there has been a disposition to recognize conditions of peculiar blessing as set forth in divine names, seeing that they manifest the glorious virtues of Deity, and also the ever-expanding purposes of the divine Persons themselves. In *Romeo and Juliet*, Shakespeare asks –

> "What's in a name? That which we call a rose
> By any other name would smell as sweet."

There is a great deal, however, in a name, especially if it is the Name above every other name. To the Hebrews of old, the *name* of God meant the revelation of His nature, hence the various Old Testament names are very important as showing the different conceptions of the Deity held by them in the successive stages of revelation. God jealously guarded His successive names, particularly His signature one, *I, Jehovah.*

Among the primitive people, and the ancient Jews were no exception, the name of a deity was regarded as his manifestation, and therefore was treated with the greatest respect and veneration. Among savage tribes there used to be a widespread feeling of danger of disclosing one's name, because this would enable an enemy by magic means to work one some deadly injury. We know that the ancient Greeks were particularly careful to disguise or reverse complimentary names. For instance, Eumenides, a Greek name meaning "the good-tempered ones," was the name given by the Greeks to the Furies – the daughters of night and darkness – as it would have been ominous and bad policy to call them by their right name. With the Persons of the Godhead it is different, for their names are openly published, and never given adverse meanings. They all represent the true character of these august Persons, whether the names are actual or symbolic.

No person should regard his name as simply an appendage but a possession distinctively his, and often as an expression of his character. It is so with all divine names, all of which are self-revealing. In his most valuable Bible study handbook, *Knowing the Scriptures*, Dr. A. T. Pierson has this foreword to his chapter on "Biblical Names and Titles" –

"There is a distinct science of nomenclature – a system of names – in the Word of God. Usually the prominent human names have a historic or symbolic significance, closely related to the narrative. But uniformly divine names and titles are full of meaning, and used sparingly and significantly. Upon them as a basis a whole scheme of interpretation rests; even the order in which such names occur is not accidental but designed, as constituting part of the lesson taught. The compound names of Jehovah have a particular interest and importance. The name and nature of God are uniformly used as equivalents."

That God Himself sets great store upon His names is evident from the revelation given to Moses (Exodus 6:3). That He also attached importance to His several names is found in the prohibition not to take any one of them in vain (Exodus 20:7). Further, it is only as we come to know and understand the inner meaning and message of His peerless names that we can repose our trust in Him (Psalm 9:10). As we come to classify all His glorious names, may our faith and confidence in Him be strengthened, and may our lives reflect the virtues many of them represent. Wordsworth gives us the lines –

"Yet shall Thy name, conspicuous and sublime,
Stand in the spacious firmament of time,
Fixed as a Star."

Of this we are confident, that all the grand names of Deity, conspicuous and sublime, will stand, not only in the spacious firmament of time, but also of Eternity. Such names will never be –

". . . Unsung, unwept,
Unrecorded, lost and gone."

Chapter 1

THE NAMES AND TITLES OF
GOD THE FATHER

THE NAMES AND TITLES OF GOD THE FATHER

I. PERSONAL NAMES

Moses asked God, ". . . Behold, when I come unto the children of Israel, and shall say unto them, The God of your fathers hath sent me unto you; and they shall say to me, What is his name? what shall I say unto them?" (Exodus 3:13), and Jesus asked the maniac of Gadara, "What is thy name?" And he answered, saying, "My name is Legion: for we are many" (Mark 5:9). When, reverently, we ask God, "What is Thy name?" we can hear Him say, "My names are legion"! In *King Henry IV*, Shakespeare inquires, "I would thou and I knew where a commodity of good names were to be bought!" The Bible provides us with a wonderful commodity of good names, belonging to the Father, to the Son, and to the Holy Spirit, and ours is the privilege of appropriating all that such names represent. Theirs are

"The immortal Names,
That were not born to die."

In any phase of Bible study we may undertake, it is important to bear in mind what Dr. A. T. Pierson calls, *The Law of First Mention*. It will be found that so often, the first mention of a person, or place, or a doctrine, or word, is an embryo of a feature or a fact for which there is fuller development. For instance, although Adam and Eve were earth's first sinners, the term *sin* is first found in connection with Cain's murder of his brother Abel, ". . . sin lieth at the door" (Genesis 4:7), and the rest of the Bible is the unfolding of the nature of sin, and of its dread consequences both here and hereafter. The same idea applies to almost all the divine names and titles in Scripture.

ELOHIM – *Plurality in Unity*

The fourth word in the opening of the Bible is the first mentioned name in the Bible – GOD! (Genesis 1:1). This first verse is His signature, as if to suggest that the book holy men would write under His inspiration would be His book. Just as my name is found on the cover of this book you are reading, indicating that all within it is from my pen, so God's name stamped at the beginning declares Him to be the author. The Hebrew for this very first name is *Elohim,* and it fittingly describes God in the unity of His divine personality and power. It is found some 3,000 times, and in over 2,300 of these references the term is applied to God. In other places, *Elohim* is used in a secondary sense.

For instance, it is used of –
Idols (Exodus 34:17).
Men (Psalm 82:6; John 10:34, 35).
Angels (Psalm 8:5; 97:7).
Gods-men (Genesis 3:5).
Judges (Exodus 22:8).

(In these instances, the idea of *might* and authority are contemplated. Trench, in *Study of Words,* gives a full coverage of these references.)

In the first two chapters of Genesis *Elohim* occurs 35 times in connection with God's creative power. This striking name for "God" is found most frequently in the books of Deuteronomy and the Psalms. In one psalm (68), this Hebrew word is used 26 times and practically covers all aspects of Salvation. As to its first appearance, "In the beginning God," as well as in the other references, the name is in the plural, and is a foregleam of the Trinity acting in unity.

5

"God (plural) said, Let *us* (plural) make man in our image..." (Genesis 1:26) and man's creation was the concerted act of the three members of the Godhead –

The Father (Exodus 20:11).
The Son (Colossians 1:16).
The Holy Spirit (Job 26:13).

Creative glory and power and Godhead fullness are associated with this initial name of the Bible. *Elohim*, perhaps the most comprehensive of all divine names speaks of the function of Deity in creation, judgment, deliverance, and punishment of evil-doers. *Elohim*, as the Creator, expresses the fiat of Almighty God which called the world into existence "by the Word," (John 1: 1-3), while the Spirit brooded over all till Creation was complete (Genesis 1: 2). Thus, in *Elohim*, God is the majestic Ruler, and under such a name we have the idea of omnipotence, or creative and governing power.

H. E. Govan in his work, *Discoveries of God*, says –

"That the Hebrews' name for God has a plural form, *Elohim*, offers two suggestions –
1. That He was conceived as combining in Himself all the powers and attributes, so far as they were worthy, which the heathen distributed over their numerous deities.
2. That the One God is variously and progressively apprehended under different aspects. The sacred records show us enlargement of vision from time to time, with increase of faith and consequent development of character."

Parkhurst in his *Hebrew Lexicon* under *Elohim* defines the name as one usually given in Scripture to the ever-blessed Trinity by which they represent themselves as under the obligation of an oath to perform certain conditions. "*Elohim* is a plurality in unity. Accordingly Jehovah is at the beginning of Creation named Elohim, which implies that the divine Persons had sworn when they created." Some scholars object to the idea of the Trinity being found in the word *Elohim*. It is only fair to point out that this term, with the usual ending for all masculine nouns in the plural, is sometimes used with a singular pronoun, "I am your Elohim." Yet the word in this singular form is not full enough to set forth all that is intended. Trench reminds us that when "*Elohim* is employed to designate the one true and only God, it has for the most part, the usual construction of a noun in the singular number; that is, it is joined with a verb or pronoun which is also singular. The last two letters of the title *im* represent a plural ending."

Always rendered as *God* in the KJV, "Elohim" often implies "Fullness of Might" – a name full of assurance for our faith. Without doubt a great "mystery of godliness" is latent in *Elohim*. It is a repository of truth concerning the Persons in the Godhead in essential unity, and a mode of expressing the abundance and diversity of transcendent attributes combined in Deity. Further, this first name of God in Scripture contained and shadowed forth the visions and words of sacred writers regarding the works of the blessed Trinity. If the root of *Elohim*, as a word, means "to swear," then the New Testament declaration, "Because he could swear by no greater, He sware by himself" (Hebrews 6:13), takes on added significance. "As *Elohim*, in virtue of His own nature and covenant – relationship to His creature, He can never leave it fallen as it is, till all again is very good."

Andrew Juke calls us to "mark especially that *Elohim* works, not only *on*, but *with*, the creative. This is indeed grace, most wondrous and abounding. For it is all of grace that *Elohim* should restore and save His fallen creature. It is still greater grace that in the restoration He makes that creature a fellow-worker with Himself.... The idea conveyed by *Elohim* is always that of 'One in covenant,' and implies One who stands in a covenant-relationship for the out-working of His purpose.... His words to Abram, *Elohim's* name pledges the same relationship: 'I am the Almighty God; walk before me, and be thou perfect; ... and I will establish my covenant between me and thee, and thy seed after thee in all generations ... to be a God to thee, and to thy seed, ... and I will be their Elohim,' that is, I will be with them in covenant relationship" (Genesis 17:1-8).

What comfort for our hearts can be found in this first great name of God of which Dr. G. Campbell-Morgan says, "It refers to absolute, unqualified, unlimited energy." God is ever ready to put forth His power on our behalf. *Elohim* signifies a covenant relationship which He is ever faithful to keep. "What a stimulus to faith and an inspiration to love, is found in this title of God," Dr. F. E. Marsh affirms, "for looking at it in the light of the New Testament, we find –

> The Father in the power of His love,
> The Son in the provision of His grace,
> The Spirit in the potentiality of His strength."

When God lovingly reminds us, "I will be to you an *Elohim*," may ours be the quick reply – "My *Elohim*; in Him will I trust" (Psalm 91:2).

EL – *The Strong One*

This short title (from which some scholars assert *Elohim* is derived) is the most primitive Semitic name; and its root meaning is probably "to be strong." In classical Hebrew, *El* is mainly poetical. A most common word for Deity, *El* is represented by the Arabic term for God, *Aleah*. While found throughout the Old Testament, it is discovered more often in Job and the Psalms than other books. Translated some 250 times as *God, El* is frequently used in circumstances which especially indicate the great power of God. For instance it was as *El* that God brought Israel up out of Egypt (Numbers 23:22). Moses said, "Jehovah your Elohim is God of gods, the Lord of lords, *the God (or El)* who is great, mighty, and dreadful" (Deuteronomy 10:17). *El* is likewise used in connection with the great and mighty promises God gave to Abraham and to Jacob (Genesis 17:1; 35:11). *El* is also one of the names given to the promised Messiah, "El, the mighty" (Isaiah 9:6, 7).

The first time *El* is used in Scripture is in connection with Melchizedek who is described as "priest of the most high El" (Genesis 14:18). Perhaps the most sacred and expressive use of *El* is in the Calvary Psalm where Christ appeals to *El* in His agony, "My God, My God" (Psalm 22:1). Thus in the New Testament crucifixion narrative we have Jesus crying with a loud voice, "Eloi, Eloi" (Mark 15:34). In His extreme weakness He prayed "My Strength, My Strength," for *El* denotes God as "the Strong One and first and only Cause of things, and being in the singular emphasizes the essence of the Godhead. The attributes of God are generally associated with this title, or God in the expressiveness of His character and action."

El is frequently combined with nouns or adjectives to express the divine name with reference to particular attributes or phases of His being which, by usage have become names or titles of God.

Rulers may propose, but *Jehovah-Hele-yon* can dispose. As Dr. F. E. Marsh expresses our confidence –

> "It is not without significance that this title has to do with the Most High as the Ascended One who is in the highest place, guarding and over-ruling all things and making everything work to one given end, to set His Son as the King-Priest, after the order of Melchisedec, upon His throne to rule in the millennial glory of His power and majesty."

(*See* Psalm 110:4-7; Zechariah 6:13; Hebrews 5:6; 6:20; 7:17, 21.

> Lord of all being! throned afar,
> Thy glory flames from sun and star;
> Centre and Soul of every sphere,
> Yet to each loving heart how near!

It must be borne in mind that several names that are applied to God are, at times, applied in Scripture to things and persons of this world. *Elyon,* for instance, was a name used by other nations than Israel, but "wherever it is so used, its special and distinctive sense is always that the person or thing it speaks of is the highest of a series or order of like natures. . . . When applied to God, *Elyon* or 'Most High' reveals that though He is the highest, there are others below Him endowed by Him with like natures, and, therefore in some way related to Him; that, because He is the *Highest,* He has power to rule and turn them as He will, should they be disobedient or seek to exalt themselves against Him" (Daniel 4:34, 35). A further passage in Daniel is most interesting in that it shows the connection between the glory *celestial* and the glory *terrestrial* (7:27). Commenting on this verse Walter Scott, in his *Handbook to the Old Testament,* says –

> "While the earthly dominion is committed to the Jews *on* earth, the heavenly glory and rule *over* the earth will be enjoyed by the saints risen and glorified, and immediately associated with Christ; while the connection between the heavens and the earth and the saints occupying both spheres will be blessedly maintained. This is not an arbitrary thought, as Revelation 21:12, 24, 26; Hosea 2:21-23, have a similar strain as their burden."

How privileged we are to be counted among "the children of the Most High"! If *El Elyon* is "the pledge of sure and high blessing, even to priests in virtue of their sonship," as "priests unto God," may we be found giving the "Most High" the highest place in every realm of life, so that He can fulfill His will in and through us. God has revealed Himself as *Elyon* that we may know and trust and joy in Him. Further, in all crises we may face in life, like Moses, we too, will experience what it is to have the "Most High" as our shield and exceeding great reward.

EL-ROI – *The Lord That Seeth*

The only occurrence of this title is in connection with Hagar's flight from Sarah's persecutions. Out in the wilderness of Shur, Jehovah spoke to her words of promise and cheer. The distracted woman thought there was no one nigh to help her, pregnant by Abraham as she was. But One was at hand to console and inspire hope, and she called "the name of Jehovah that spake unto her, Thou art EL ROI" – meaning, "The well of Him that liveth and seeth me" (Genesis 16:13, 14). ROI is from a root implying "that seeth" or "of sight." In the wilderness Hagar discovered her *Jehovah-Shammah,* "The Lord is there," and proved Him to be her *Jehovah-Jireh,* "The Lord will provide," and when her child was born he was called, Ishma*el*, meaning "God who hears."

EL-ELOHE-ISRAEL – *God of Israel* (Genesis 33:20)

As we are discovering the name EL is combined with other terms to represent God in His various attributes; and many of these have by their usage become names or titles, as in the remarkable phrase before us which was the name Jacob gave to the altar he erected at Shalem (Genesis 33:18-20). The Scofield Reference Bible has the footnote at this passage, "Jacob's act of faith, appropriating his new name, *Israel,* but also claiming Elohim in this new sense as though God through whom alone he could walk according to his new name. A similar appropriation was made by Abraham (Genesis 14:18-23)."

The margin of the ASV has it, "God, the God of Israel." Scholars have speculated over the exact setting and significance of the compound name as the altar's inscription, some suggesting that it should read, "He called *upon* the God of Israel." Dillmann has the reading, "He called it *the altar of El,* the God of Israel." Our position is that with a new discovery of God, as the result of his victorious struggle on that eventful night at Peniel (Genesis 32:30) an event enshrined in Jacob's new name, *Israel,* when he reared his first altar in Palestine he gave it that name of God which appeared in his own new name, further explaining it by the appositive phrases *Elohe-Israel.* Thus Jacob's altar was called, and dedicated to, *El, the God of Israel.*

It will be found that when the divine and human names are combined in this way, the bearer of the same experienced a hitherto unknown revelation of God's character and purpose. In this connection, examine the contexts where such designations as The God of Abraham, The God of Isaac, The God of Jacob, The God of Jeshurin, The God of Shem, The God of the Hebrews, The God of Daniel, and others, are found. In some special, unusual way God becomes *The God* of the person concerned. We are thrice blessed if, with the psalmist we discover how great and glorious God is, we too can say from the heart, *"This God* is our God for ever and ever: He will be our guide even unto death"* (Psalm 48:14).

EL OLAM – *God of Eternity*

While this title is more rare in Scripture than others we are considering yet it is a most important one in that it provides us with a remarkable aspect of the divine character. *El Olam* is a term describing what extends beyond our furthest vision, whether we look backward or forward till it is lost to sight, for it means "The God of Eternity," or as the KJV translates it "The Everlasting God." Approaching the significance of this assuring name are these Scriptures:

> "In the Lord Jehovah is everlasting strength" (Isaiah 26:4).
> "Our Redeemer from everlasting is thy name" (Isaiah 63:16 ASV).
> "Jehovah is ... an everlasting King" (Jeremiah 10:10 ASV).
> "From everlasting to everlasting thou art God" (Psalm 90:2).
> "The everlasting God, ... the Creator of the ends of the earth" (Isaiah 40:28).

But the first occurrence of *El Olam,* however, is heavy with spiritual significance. It is found in connection with Abraham's reproof of Abimelech over the right and use of wells. What an illuminating expression that is where Abraham says to the King of Gerar, "... God caused me to wander from my father's house ..." (Genesis 20:13). *To wander* is a strong term and is used in sheep going astray, for losing their way (Psalm 119:176; Isaiah 53:6). As an owner of sheep, Abraham often had the task of seeking and recovering straying sheep. Now he felt himself as far as the World was concerned to be as one astray. Reaching Beersheba, which marked the climax of his pilgrim course, the efforts to drive him out made Abraham deeply conscious how rootless and unanchored his earthly life was. His had been a series of unending *flittings,* to use an expressive Scotch word. His life was insecure, here today and gone tomorrow.

> From Ur to Haran (Genesis 11:31),
> From Haran to Shechem (12:5),
> From Shechem to Bethel (12:8),
> From Bethel to Egypt (12:10),
> From Egypt back to Bethel (13:3),
> From Bethel to Hebron (13:18),
> From Hebron to Gerar (20:1).

Now at Beersheba, the patriarch, with no certain dwelling place, thinks of his nomadic life of continual restlessness and change, and feels that at last he had found a spot where he and his could abide, and his flocks find rest and sustenance in the verdant pastures and living streams of Beersheba. But the men of Gerar felt otherwise about this pilgrim and stranger and sought to oust him. A new discovery of God was to check any further depressing sense of insecurity – *El Olam, God the Everlasting!* Oppressed with the sense of earth's instability Abraham needed a further unveiling of divine sufficiency and it came in the name assuring him of the fact of God's eternity. *El Olam,* the God without a beginning, the God who never will cease to be, the God who will never grow old, the God to whom eternity is what present time is.

Have we learned how to place over against our changing earthly pilgrimage the secure attachment of eternity? How

true it is that, "the eternity of God is the rock on which faith can repose in view of the mutability of man." The Prophet would have us remember that waiting upon the Everlasting God imparts into one's life the everlasting vitality, the everlasting strength so necessary for the changing events and experiences of our pilgrimage. How blessed we are to have this "God who liveth for the ages of ages," as our God even unto death! We conclude with Andrew Juke's observation that "it will be found that in all places where this name *El Olam* occurs, there is always a reference, sometimes more hidden, sometimes more open, to the distinct stages of God's dealings with His creatures." May it be so with ourselves! Names, often unnoticed, wait to teach us the secrets of God's wise purpose, often hidden till the time comes for its fuller revelation. This is the truth Abraham learned when, amid the changing vicissitudes of his earthly lot, he discovered the Everlasting God as his true home.

> With me, whereso'er I wander,
>   That great Presence goes –
> That unutterable gladness,
>   Undisturbed repose;
> Ever with me, glorious, awful,
>   Tender, passing sweet,
> One upon whose Heart I rest me,
>   Worship at His feet.

For the believer such a One is the Eternal Son, "the same yesterday, today, and for ever."

El Shaddai –
The Almighty, All-Sufficient God

We have now come to one of the most potent and precious among divine names, revealing as it does, "the sweet omnipotence of love," and likewise so eloquent of the truth of God in the sufficiency of His grace, goodness and government. *El Shaddai* means "Almighty God." The first mention of this sublime name appears on an especially solemn occasion when Jehovah appeared to Abraham, and opened His message to the patriarch with the declaration, "I am the Almighty God" (Genesis 17:1). The same title was used when God appeared to Jacob and to Isaac, to bless them. In Him, all fullness dwells, and out of His constant fullness His own receive all things.

Altogether *El Shaddai* occurs 8 times in the Old Testament, and *Shaddai,* meaning "Almighty," is found some 31 times in the Book of Job, and 9 times in other parts of the Old Testament. Equivalent expressions appear about 10 times in the New Testament. For instance, God is called –

> *Lord Almighty* (2 Corinthians 6:18).
> *The Almighty* (Revelation 1:8).
> *Lord God Almighty* (Revelation 4:8).
> *God Almighty* (Revelation 16:14).
> *Lord God Omnipotent* (Revelation 19:6).

Paul, referring to Christ who said, *"All power* is given unto Me," speaks of "His mighty power," and "the power of His might" (Ephesians 1:19; 6:10). In all of these New Testament references there is the idea of the All Powerful One, the Absolute Sovereign. Throughout Scripture the term *Almighty* is used about 60 times, and is applied to God only – often in contrast to the impotence of heathen gods. To Abraham, the pilgrim and stranger called out from an idolatrous world to walk with God, His revelation as *Almighty God* must have assured the heart of the patriarch of a sure and all-sufficient resource in every time of need.

The Lord revealed this name to the Israelites through Moses as

> *God Almighty,* in His grace;
> *Almighty* in His sustaining power

and divine resources, and for the arm of flesh to lean on, Exodus 3:15; 6:3.

The first occurrence of *Almighty God* (Genesis 17:1) tells of His all-sustaining power and grace for pilgrims; the last reference reveals God under the same title as all-consuming in wrath and judgment upon those who ultimately despise His grace and mercy (Revelation 19:15). Professor W. G. Moorehead observes that *El Shaddai,* The Infinite One, expresses a double truth, namely –

1. God's almightiness, His power to fulfill every promise He has made His people.
2. His faithfulness in performing every word He has spoken. *See* Genesis 17:1, 2; 48:3, 4; 49:25.

Jacob said to Benjamin in reference to Joseph, "El Shaddai give you tender mercy before the man!" (Genesis 43:14). In his final, prophetic blessing of Joseph, Jacob said –

> "From *El* of thy father there shall help be to thee,
> And with *Shaddai* there shall blessings be unto thee" (49:25).

El set forth God's almightiness, and *Shaddai* His exhaustless bounty, so that together the double name expresses *The All-Bountiful One.* What a stimulus to faith it is to know that we serve a God who is all-sufficient, and who is strong enough to overpower, able to overcome all obstacles, and equal to every occasion! "Is there anything too hard for the Lord?" He can remove mountains even "when the order of nature offers no prospect of it and the powers of nature are inadequate to it. God is not fettered by the laws of nature; He is supreme over them, and free to intervene upon them," as many of His miracles prove.

One scholar writes that, "*Elohim* is the God who creates nature so that it is, and supports it so that it continues, *El Shaddai* the God who compels nature to do what is contrary to itself." With this all-sufficient God undertaking for us we can sing with Charles Wesley –

> Faith, mighty faith, the promise sees,
>   And looks to that alone,
> Laughs at impossibilities
>   And cries, It *shall* be done!

All things are possible to those whose faith is rooted in Him who is the Lord God Almighty. In a remarkable way the psalmist combines God's *eternity* with His supremacy and sufficiency –

> "He that dwelleth in the secret place of *El Elyon*, shall abide under the shadow of *El Shaddai* . . . From everlasting to everlasting, Thou art God" (Psalm 90:2; 91:1).

It was undaunted faith in this almighty God that made saints like George Mueller and Hudson Taylor the mighty men of faith they were. To them, such *almightiness* was not only the power of doing anything or everything, but the ability to carry out the will of a divine nature. When ultimately we reach heaven, there we shall find, "The Lord God Almighty and the Lamb shall be the glory and the light" of His abode.

It is most profitable to take the term *Shaddai* by itself, seeing it is so rich in spiritual significance. It occurs 48 times in the Old Testament and is translated *Almighty*, and comes from the root *Shad*, which means a breast, and is so rendered in its first occurrence, "The blessings of the breasts" (Genesis 49:25). This singular form *Shad* appears as *breast* some 18 times in the ASV, and as "pap" and "teat," and supplies us with a delicate yet precious metaphor, seeing it presents God as the One who nourishes, supplies, and satisfies. Dr. G.

Campbell-Morgan in his most valuable *Expositions* says –

> "The name or title *El Shaddai* is peculiarly suggestive, meaning quite literally, 'the mighty One of resource or sufficiency.' We miss much of the beauty by our rendering 'God Almighty.' The idea of almightiness is present, but it is not fully expressed in the word *El*. The word *Shaddai* goes further, and suggests perfect supply and perfect comfort. We should reach the idea better by rendering, 'God All-Bountiful,' or 'God All-Sufficient' . . . To gather sustenance and consolation from the bosom of God is to be made strong for all the pilgrimage."

Shaddai, then, presents God as "The Breasted One," or as Dr. Parkhurst expresses it, "The Pourer or Shedder-forth" that is, of blessings, temporal and spiritual." Why, then, should we fret when we have such an All-Bountiful God, an unfailing supply of spiritual nourishment? How sufficient a mother's breast is to quiet and satisfy her crying, restless child! Physicians assure us that breast-fed children are the better fed. Our *Shaddai* says, "Open thy mouth wide and I will fill it." There is, therefore, no reason for our spiritual impoverishment when we have such a *Pourer-Forth*. As Andrew Jukes applies the metaphor –

> "His Almightiness is of the breast, that is, of bountiful, self-sacrificing love, giving and pouring itself out for others. Therefore He can quiet the restless, as the breast quiets the child; therefore He can nourish and strengthen, as the breast nourishes; therefore He can attract, as the breast attracts, when we are in peril of falling from Him."

How weak we become when we fail to

nestle near to Him who is "girt about the paps with a golden girdle" (Revelation 1:13)! Has He not invited us to come unto Him and drink? (John 6: 53-57).

ADON-ADONAI – *Jehovah Our Ruler*

Adonai, an intensive plural of *Adon,* meaning "lord," is another of the vigorous names of God expressing divine dominion. *Adonai* sometimes occurs in prophecy and poetry as a substitute for JHVH – Jehovah. It is a title that heathen nations applied to their gods, such as the *Adonis* of the Phoenician Tammerly. It is found compounded with Jehovah as a proper name as, for instance, in Adoni-jah, which means, "Jehovah is LORD." *Adonai,* meaning master or owner, is occasionally united with *Jehovah* – Jehovah and LORD (Ezekiel 16:8, 30), and combined thus suggests that God was the master and husband of His people Israel. *Adonai* is akin to *Baal,* which also implies master or owner.

While we think of *Baal* as the title of the Canaanite local gods, in earlier times it was used by worshipers of Jehovah. Thus was one of Saul's sons called *Ishbaal.* One of David's men of war was known as *Baaliah* which means, "Jehovah is Baal." When this title came to have degrading associations, obnoxious proper names were changed and *Baal* became *bosheth,* which was substituted as in Ishbosheth. A further feature careful readers of Scripture have noticed is that when *Jehovah* and *Adonai* appear together, it is easy to distinguish which name has precedence. *Jehovah* is always in small capitals – LORD – while Adonai is printed as Lord. "The Lord GOD" (Ezekiel 16:8) in the original is Adonai Jehovah. Preb. Webb-Peploe has an illuminated paragraph on this fact in his helpful work (published in 1901 on "The Titles Of Jehovah," and long out of print) –

> "Twice over it is said, 'He that blasphemeth the name of the LORD, he shall surely be put to death ...' (Leviticus 24:16). Every Jew, therefore, became so much alarmed at the danger connected with the pronouncing, or writing of this wonderful name, that he dared not give expression to it for fear that the stroke of God might come upon him for uttering, and possibly blaspheming, the incomprehensible, or, what might be called, THE name of his God. The consequence was that after a certain time, there was no knowledge of the way in which *Jehovah* should be pronounced; and when the scribes were writing out the Scriptures, and came to the name of *Jehovah,* The Awful One, they would lay down their pens, in most cases, and would not write it as originally given, but would write the less awful Name of *Adonai,* meaning, *My Ruler.*"

It is because of this that wherever the word *Jehovah* occurred, we find the substitution of *Adonai,* except when the latter is joined to the former, as in *Adonai Elohim.* A striking illustration of this is found in the phrase, "The LORD said unto my Lord" (Psalm 110:1). Here, *Jehovah* speaks to *Adonai* words that are properly applied to Christ. *Adonai* first occurs in the phrase, "And Abram said, Lord" (Genesis 15:2). As the master owner of the patriarch, the Lord revealed to him how He would fulfill His promise to make him the head of a great nation. Several features are associated with the use of *Adonai.* For instance, we have:

1. *Authority.* Over 200 times in Ezekiel we have the expression, "Saith the Lord GOD," or *Adonai-Jehovah.* Behind

the prophet as he proclaimed the divine message was the authority of the Great Jehovah as Lord and Master.

2. *Power.* "In the LORD JEHOVAH is everlasting strength" (Hebrews 3:19). See also Isaiah 61:1; Ezekiel 8:1, all of which imply power for life and service.

3. *Deity.* David gives us the combination, "My God – *Elohim,* and my Lord – *Adonai*" (Psalms 35:23; 38:15). These were the very words falling from the lips of Thomas as he recognized the Deity of the Master, "My Lord and my God" (John 20:28).

4. *Reverence.* In Daniel's confession of national sin, he appealed to the Lord as Adonai, suggesting a holy reverence as he approached the Throne of Grace. In his innermost heart, Daniel recognized the lordship of Jehovah (9:19).

5. *Relationship.* David's expression of faith is found in the exclamation, "O my soul, thou hast said unto Jehovah, Thou art my Adonai" (Psalm 16:2). What union and intimacy there are between the Master and the servant!

6. *Responsibility.* Once Isaiah had been cleansed by Jehovah, he heard "the voice of Adonai saying, Whom shall I send and who will go for us?" (Isaiah 6:8). The prophet responded to the call, and receiving the message he was to deliver said, "Adonai, how long?" (6:11). Cleansed and commissioned, Isaiah was ready to face all the responsibilities of service.

The double title LORD God occurs for the first time in connection with God's creative work (Genesis 2:4). In chapters 2 and 3, LORD God is found 20 times and implies man's place as one of conscious intelligent relationship to his Creator, hence flows his accountability to God. As a name of Deity, *Adonai,* used some 300 times in the Old Testament, emphasizes divine sovereignty (Isaiah 7:7), and is closely related to the *Kurios,* or Lord, of the New Testament.

Almost always the name is in the plural and possessive, meaning, *my Lords,* and confirms the idea of a trinity found in the name *Elohim.* The same original word for Adonai is also used of men some 215 times and translated variously as Master, Sir, Lord, Master. The expression, "Lord of Lords" (Deuteronomy 10:17) could be rendered, "Master of masters."

For ourselves, this name, when used of God, implies His ownership and mastership and that, as Girdlestone put it, "Indicates the truth that God is the owner of each member of the human family, and that He consequently claims the unrestricted obedience of all." The question is, Do I honor and obey and love Him as my *Adonai?* Hudson Taylor was wont to say, "If He is not Lord of all, He is not Lord at all." Our Lord Himself pronounced severe judgment upon those who called Him, Lord, Lord! but never recognized His lordship in their lives. *Adonai* expresses a personal relationship, involving rights of lordship and possession. Thus, if redeemed by the blood, we are "not our own" (1 Corinthians 6:19, 20). The great mark of the saved is that they "know the Lord," and reverence and serve Him as such. All that know such a name put their trust in the One who bears it and their trust in Adonai is never confounded.

> My Lord and my God!
>   All praise and adoration,
> To the glorious Lord
>   Who came to bring salvation.

JAH – *The Independent One*

This sublime title is found in Psalm 68:4: "Extol him that rideth upon the heavens by his name JAH, and rejoice before him." The same Hebrew word, however, occurs over 40 times in Isaiah, the Psalms, and Exodus but is translated "the Lord" in our English Bible. It is to be regretted that the various titles of God have not been given their Hebrew signification. Often, they are indifferently translated, much to our loss.

JAH is a shortened form of *Jehovah*, which, "though compelled to mention such a name, the transcribers dare not write it in full." Pronounced *yä*, this name signifies, *He is*, and can be made to correspond to I AM, just as *Jehovah* corresponds to the fuller expression I AM THAT I AM. The name *Jah* first occurs in the original, in the triumphal Song of Moses, Exodus 15:2. Among the references, the one of Isaiah is suggestive, "Jehovah is *Jah*, the rock of ages" (Isaiah 26:4), implying that "Jehovah is what is meant by Jah, the ever-living, eternal one, and so, an everlasting refuge and defence." This song of salvation proves God to be a present and a perpetual support and security.

"Trust ye in Jehovah for ever;
For in JAH JEHOVAH is the Rock of Ages!"

Three times over in Isaiah *Jehovah* is compounded with *Jah*. In one case the names of God are duplicated, and in another, triplicated. In the reference to Miriam's song we have the combination, "JAH JEHOVAH is my strength and my song," for both present and future deliverance are implied (Isaiah 12:2). Then in Hezekiah's lament as he faces death we have the repetition "I shall not in the land of the living see JAH JAH" (Isaiah 38:11). Such a sigh implies that the king, in the experiences of a present daily life would behold this present God. It is affirmed that as JAH is the *present* tense of the verb "to be," it suggests Jehovah as the PRESENT LIVING GOD – the *Presence* of God in daily life, or His *present* activity and oversight on behalf of His own.

JAH, the short form of the ineffable name, JEHOVAH, is interwoven like other divine names, with human names, and always with a particular purpose and meaning. Many more names contain JAH at the end than at the beginning, probably in accordance with Jewish habits of reverence to assign the divine name the less rather than the more prominent position. So we have Abi*jah*, meaning "whose father is Jehovah." Then we have *Jahaziah*, *Jahzeel*, etc. The oft-repeated exclamation "Praise ye the Lord," is "Praise ye Jah," or "Halleлu*jah*." From the manifold use of JAH in the Psalms we find God extolled as the One who rideth upon the heavens, Father of the fatherless, and Judge of widows, and to the destitute and desolate, an ever-present helper. JAH is ever "a very *present* help in trouble" (Psalm 46:1).

I fear no foe, with Thee at hand
    to bless;
Ills have no weight, and tears no
    bitterness;
Where is death's sting? where, grave,
    thy victory?
I triumph still, if Thou abide with me.

JEHOVAH – *The Eternal, Ever-Loving One*

Among all the divine names none is so sublime and solemn as the one we are now to consider. Rabbinical writings have distinguished *Jehovah* by various euphemistic expressions as "*The* Name," "The Great And Terrible Name," "The Peculiar Name," "The Separate Name," "The Unutterable Name," "The Ineffable Name," "The Incommunicate Name," "The Holy Name," "The Distinguished Name." It was also known as "The Name of Four Letters" because from the Hebrew it is spelled YHVH, in English. This name is often called *Tetragrammaton,* or "four-lettered name." Such is Jewish reverence for this august name that even today they refrain as much from writing it, or pronouncing it. Scholars are not sure as to the exact pronunciation of the Hebrew for *Jehovah*. Leading Hebrew translators agree that probably it is *Yahveh*, or *Yahve*, or *Yahweh*. They also agree that *Jehovah* is not an altogether correct rendering of the Name, but seeing it has become so familiar the translators refuse to substitute a strange form. It is a wonderful name beyond a mere definition.

The name *Jehovah* occurs about 7,000 times in the Old Testament. In the Psalms alone, it is used some 700 times. The name is generally printed in some capitals, LORD, and is thus distinguished from the other Hebrew words translated *Lord*. LORD, *Lord* and *lord* convey different shades of thought both in Hebrew and Greek. LORD, however, is only applied to Him who is known as Jehovah – The Self-Existing One: but *Lord* is also applied to Jehovah. Commendably, the American Revisers gave the personal name Jehovah in the ASV wherever it occurs in the Hebrew. About 800 times in the KJV, it is rendered God.

As to the meaning of this ancient name, said to be whispered only by the high priest in the Holy of Holies once a year, Newbery defines its significance as "He that always was, that always is, and ever is to come." This absoluteness of the divine Being, who is independent, self-existing is found in the declaration, "I am Alpha and Omega, the beginning and the ending saith the LORD – Jehovah – which *is* and which *was*, and which is *to come*, the Almighty" (Revelation 1: 8).

"Which *is*" – the ever-existing One – His relation to the present.

"Which *was*" – His relation to the past – the One who always was.

"Which *is to come*" – His relation to the future – who always will be.

When Moses asked for God's name, He replies, I AM THAT I AM, or I AM WHAT I AM – a title expressive not only of self-existence, but of unchangeableness of character. He always was what He is, He is what He was; He will ever be what He was and is, with Him there is no variableness (James 1:17). No wonder, "This name JEHOVAH, in all significance, is God's memorial, God's 'forget-me-not,' " as H. E. Govan puts it. "Let our faith treasure it and hold it fast against all the World's attempts to filch it from us. He is the God of the blank cheque; we shall never be confronted by a claim that He cannot meet. Through all life's years, with all their needs, His wealth is open to our demands if only these are made within the terms of His will. Eternity itself will furnish us with· ever-new discoveries of His sufficiency."

Further, JEHOVAH is a name of covenant relationship. Both man and Israel were placed by Him in distinct moral relationship with Himself – Israel, of course, in special covenant relationship. Perhaps it is not too much to say that JEHOVAH is God entering into history in His redemptive relations with His people. *See* Exodus 3:14, 16; 6:3. As the *covenant* name, it covers the conception of God as the Immutable One, whose purpose and promise are as unchanging as Himself who is, "the same yesterday and today and forever." Dr. A. T. Pierson suggests that this name, which one rabbi declared that whoever dared to pronounce this name would forfeit his place in the world to come, can mean "the ever*loving* One, being connected with grace and salvation that have their origin in an eternal past, their outworking in progressive present, and their perfect goal in an eternal future."

One whole psalm is addressed to JEHOVAH, whose name occurs 8 times in it, Psalm 102. The remarkable feature is that the magnificent tribute to the eternity and immutability of JEHOVAH the Creator and Covenant God, in this great psalm, is applied to His SON. Listen to Him as He says, "For I JEHOVAH, I change not" (Malachi 3:6 ASV).

This name is derived from the Hebrew verb, *Havah*, meaning "to be, or being," and reveals God as the Being who is absolutely self-existent, and who, in Himself, possesses essential life and permanent existence. While we read of the *living* God, we never have the living JEHOVAH, for we cannot conceive of Him as other than living. His other names are associated with His works, but this unique one teaches plainly and unequivocally the *substance* of God. In JEHOVAH we have the fountainhead of the spiritual blessings for man, as distinguished from God's operations in nature. Under this title throughout Scripture He is set forth in His essential, moral, and spiritual attributes. When we have the combination of the two names JEHOVAH ELOHIM, the thought of the majestic, omnipotent God, the Three in One, is implied. "In the name JEHOVAH the personality of the Supreme is distinctly expressed." God possesses unchanging consistency of nature and will, and being the fixed and constant and absolute One, will never be found wanting, never out of time, never out of character.

> Change and decay in all around
> I see,
> O Thou Who changest not, abide
> with me.

A part of the divine name is woven into various personal names like *Jehu, Jehiel, Jehoahaz, Jehoiada, Jesus*, etc., each of which have the prefix of *JEHOVAH*, as for instance *Jehu*, meaning "Jehovah is He." (See the writer's volume on *All the Men of the Bible*). While among English speaking peoples the names of JEHOVAH and JESUS are considered too sacred for human beings, yet there are other parts of the world,

where the people have no compunctions against using Jesus as a Christian name.

There is much more that could be said regarding the general force of *"the* Name." Again and again, God brought His people into conditions and circumstances into which it was declared to them afresh in some specific combination which threw new light upon it. For a helpful coverage of the places where it is used, the reader is referred to the great work by Andrew Jukes. In the sections to follow we shall examine some of the combinations in order to bring out some new vision of the inexhaustible sufficiency of our God.

> Jehovah reigns, exalted high
> O'er all the earth, o'er all the sky.
>
> Jehovah reigns, His throne is high,
> His robes are light and majesty.
>
> Jehovah reigns, He dwells in light,
> Girded with majesty and might.
> —*Isaac Watts*

As it takes many rays to make up the pure light of the sun, so it takes various descriptions to give us a true conception of the being and glory of God. No man is able to receive the whole revelation of His majesty at once. Only one part at a time can be comprehended yet such is sufficient to give great joy and satisfaction. This is why it was the special purpose of the Great High God, who is One, to reveal Himself to saints of old in the development of their spiritual life in different names and titles of His nature and purpose. In connection with JEHOVAH, there are relative titles given, which together proclaim the manifold service of His grace and provision. As one comes to examine these *Jehovah* rays, he finds himself with an embarrassment of heavenly riches. It is to be regretted that very few Christians know about the Person of God as He is revealed in His names, even though He has specially "revealed them unto us by His Spirit."

JEHOVAH-ELOHIM –
The Majestic Omnipotent God

Having previously discussed the significance of *Jehovah* and *Elohim,* which are combined for the first time in the Creation narrative, and express man's relationship to God as his Creator, we are not devoting much further space to a consideration of these divine names, both of which present remarkable manifestations of Deity, far beyond our feeble grasp. *Jehovah* is the spiritual I AM, and is rich in the idea of majesty and power and glory; while *Elohim,* as the Creator, expresses the fiat of Almighty God. Combined, then, "the two names provide the truth of the majestic, omnipotent God, the Three in One, deigning to call into existence one creature called man, who, while made in the likeness of *Elohim,* should also possess moral and spiritual power to apprehend Jehovah." How blessed we are if we can look up and speak to Him as the LORD GOD – *Jehovah Elohim,* Creator and Ruler.

A fact that must be borne in mind is that while these two names are often combined (Zechariah 13:9; Psalm 118:27), yet these are not interchangeable. In *Jehovah* the personality of the great I AM is distinctly expressed, and wherever found it is a proper name denoting the Person of God. Ancient Jews could say "*the* Elohim," the true God, in opposition to all false gods; but they would never say "*the* Jehovah," for such is the name of the true God *only.* They could speak of *the Living God,* but never of the Living Jehovah, for they could never conceive of Jehovah other than living. The French version of the Bible translates LORD or JEHOVAH as *the Eternal.* May we be found appropriating for our needy hearts all that is treasured up for us in Him who is our LORD and

GOD! If all the words in all languages were names, the whole countless multitude could not possibly exhaust the greatness, goodness, and grace of God. *Jehovah Elohim* is sufficient to set us out along the avenue of a developing acquaintance with the mind and character of the Bearer of such august, initial names.

JEHOVAH-HOSEENU –
The Lord Our Maker
(Psalm 95:6)

We are indebted to the psalmist for this union of titles to be found in his invitation to approach the Mercy Seat. "O come, let us worship and kneel before *Jehovah* our *Maker.*" Parkhurst informs us that the Hebrew word *asah* is used of God in a variety of ways in speaking of God as our *Maker.* For instance it is applied variously as:

To produce a tree "*yielding* fruit" (Genesis 1:11).

To prepare a meal, as when Manoah, "*made* ready a kid" (Judges 13:15).

To observe an ordinance, as when Israel was told to "keep the Passover" (Exodus 12:47).

To *pare* the nails, when one dresses them (Deuteronomy 21:12).

To consecrate, as when Israel was commanded *to do* all divine commandments (Deuteronomy 28:1).

To fashion, as when the things of the Tabernacle were *made* according to the divine pattern (Exodus 36:10-38).

When the term *asah* is applied to Jehovah as our Maker, the reference is not to His work at Creation, when He caused things to come into being – He spake and it was done – but to His ability to fashion something out of what already exists. Abraham looked for "a city which hath foundations, whose builder and maker is God" (Hebrews 11:10). At present, He is preparing a spiritual Tabernacle made up of those redeemed by the blood. As *Jehovah,* the Immutable One, He is fashioning out of such poor material His habitation (Ephesians 2: 22). Paul reminds us that "we are His workmanship." It is from the Greek word for "workmanship" that we have our English term *poet.* Thus, in effect, "We are God's poem." The question is, "As such, do we read well, and are we expressive of the feelings of His heart?" How necessary it is to be submissive to Him who is our Maker, that He might shape and fashion us according to the pattern given on the Mount!

JEHOVAH-JIREH –
The Lord Will Provide
(Genesis 22:14)

Mohammed declared that he received from Gabriel 99 divine names, sufficient for him to present the whole Being of God, which he utterly failed to do. Here is a further compound name, and one of the most precious among all of God's scriptural titles. Although Abraham knew God as his Friend, he continued to make fresh discoveries of Him, and as memorials coined new names so *Jehovah-Jireh* stands as a monument of a great discovery and of a remarkable deliverance, the full story of which is found in Genesis 22. The margin of our Bible tells us that this name means "The Lord will see" or "The Lord will provide." That there is a good deal of difference between these two meanings as far as man is concerned, is seen in the fact that to *foresee* is one thing, but to *provide* is another. But when we come to deal with God the two are found to be one and the same.

Are not our hearts comforted as we remember that His *pre*-vision means His *pro*-vision, which is what is meant by His combined name that Abraham gave to the place where he found the ram provided as a substitute for Isaac. What an expression of wondrous fullness and meaning is *Jehovah-Jireh!* Because of His omniscience and perfection of character, He is able to provide for, or supply, the need whatever it may be. We may foresee a need that may arise, yet be incapable of making any provision at all for the need. What He foresees, He can furnish. A comparison of renderings is profitable. For instance in the KJV, we read, "In the mount of the LORD, *it* shall be seen," the margin of the RSV reads, "*He* will be seen." The KJV has "In the mount of the LORD, *It* shall be provided" – the RV "*He* shall be provided."

Further, these alternative readings become more emphatic as we connect them with *Moriah,* which, in the Hebrew, is a kindred word to *Jireh,* taken from "Jehovah seeing," and can be translated, "seen of JAH" or, "the vision of Jehovah." Thus, there is a far deeper and more solemn application of *Moriah* than we realize!

> "In the mount of the LORD, or in Moriah (that is, where Jehovah shall see) It or He (Jehovah) shall be seen."

Immediately we ask, who is the infinite power and love of Jehovah that shall be seen upon Mount Moriah making provision, by substitutionary sacrifice, for all the demands of Almighty GOD-Elohim? "*Jehovah* shall provide" – "*Jehovah* shall be seen"? As *Elohim* GOD demanded the sacrifice of Isaac, but as *Jehovah* He made complete provision of a substitute for the son Abraham willingly offered. What God commanded, He supplied. Augustine expressed it, "Command what Thou wilt, then give what Thou commandest." Paul puts it, "Faithful is He that calleth you, who also will do it" (1 Thessalonians 5:24).

Abraham's faith endured many trials, but that of Moriah was the summit of them all. But out of the severe test the patriarch emerged with a new name and seal,

The Lord Will See to It.

Abraham evinced a growing faith in God, which He himself cultivated, and now he came to learn in a new way the truth of God's all-sufficiency. Hence his reply to Isaac's question as to the animal for sacrifice, "The Lord will see to it that there is a lamb for the burnt offering." Even if he had to plunge his knife into Isaac, Abraham believed that God was able to raise his son from the dead. His faith was willing to go to the limit, for he knew that, "The Lord will see to it" (Hebrews 11:19).

The three interpretations of the name Abraham gave to the place God brought him to, are worthy of comparison –

> *The Lord shall appear,* an allusion to the divine interposition by which Isaac was saved from death.
> *The Lord shall see,* in the sense of looking out and selecting the offerings that should afterwards be presented in the Temple.
> *The Lord shall provide.* Here we have a backward glance to Abraham's answer, "God will provide Himself the lamb for the burnt-offering" (Genesis 22:8).

The latter interpretation, as given in the ASV, suggests at least three aspects of spiritual import, namely:

1. A Memorial of Divine Intervention.
2. A Mirror of the Lamb of Glory.
3. A Message of God's Goodness to Mankind in General, and to the Saints in Particular.

First of all, then, we think of Moriah the *place* as being commemorative of Abraham's deliverance. The interesting thing is that this is the first recorded instance in Scripture of the naming of a place after a divine interposition or manifestation; a practice afterwards frequently observed as by Jacob at Bethel and Peniel, and Moses at Rephidim. Surely, if ever a spot was worthy of remembrance by a special designation it was Mount Moriah, not so much, however, as Dr. Thomas Whitelaw, in his *Jehovah-Jesus* published in 1913, points out –

> "In order to consecrate the spot or invest it with peculiar sanctity, as if discerning with the eye of faith the sacred uses to which in the distant future it should be put, not merely to assist Abraham's own remembrance of the awful experiences through which he had passed on his journey to the mount and in his transactions there with his son and his God – these things, one can imagine would never pass from the patriarch's recollection, rather would be engraven on his memory with an iron pen and lead in the rock for ever – but to magnify the grace of God which had wrought out for him so marvellous a deliverance."

We cannot enter into the agony of Abraham's heart staggering under the heavy load of sorrow at having to slay his own son, the son of promise for whom he had waited for 25 years. This fine lad was dearer to the aged patriarch than life, and when asked the innocent question, "Father, where is the lamb for a burnt-offering?" his soul must have been lacerated to the very quick. What grief and overwhelming horror of soul darkness must have descended upon Abraham when the mount was reached, the altar prepared and Isaac bound upon it, and the knife uplifted to plunge into the lad's heart!

But God's obedient friend was to prove that in a paradoxical way, what had been divinely commanded was never intended; that the call to such a supreme sacrifice was only intended to test the reality of faith, which God vindicated. Abraham went through the dread transaction most obediently up to the last act, when suddenly his uplifted hand was stayed, and a substitute provided in "the ram caught in the thicket." So strong faith prevailed – Isaac was spared, and Abraham prevented from slaying his son. And it was to commemorate such a divine intervention that he named the place *Jehovah-Jireh* – THE LORD WILL PROVIDE.

While Abraham believed that God would not suffer His promise to be defeated, and would thus raise Isaac from the dead, the deliverance from death in the nick of time was unexpected, as most of God's deliverances are. In such an hour as they are not looked for they appear. "Man's extremity is God's opportunity." Surely that intervention is one of the most dramatic in Scripture! How startled Abraham must have been as he heard the divine voice say, "Abraham! lay not thine hand upon the lad," especially after hearing the same voice command, "Take thine only son, whom thou lovest, and offer him for a burnt-offering." Dr. Whitelaw remarks, "Ah! there is no actor like God. When He steps upon the stage, all human actors are put into the shade."

In the second place, there is the *typical* value of that grim scene on Mount Moriah. Isaac asked the question, "Behold the fire and the wood, *but where is the lamb?*" Two thousand years later John the Baptist answered this question, "Behold the Lamb of God!" We read of Abraham and Isaac that they went together to "the place of which God had told him," and once again we behold the two going forward together to Mount Calvary in holy consent and unison. "*God* so loved the World that He gave *His only begotten Son*" (John 3:16). But what a difference between Moriah and Calvary! Isaac was about to be offered but spared at the last moment and a ram sacrificed in his stead. The knife, however, was not stayed at Calvary, but was plunged deep into the heart of God's only begotten Son. The Father did not produce a substitute for His Son at the final moment. "He *gave* His only begotten Son," because He, as the Holy Ram, was to be the Substitute for sinners who deserved to die. "He gave Himself for – on behalf of – our sins."

Calvary was not a tragedy that could be avoided as the one at Moriah was. "The place called Calvary" was seen afar off even from the foundation of the world. When, in a past eternity, Love drew salvation's plan, the Father and the Son went forward deliberately until the "green hill far away without a city wall" was reached, where the Father gave – gave to the uttermost for our redemption. Perhaps the Crucifixion Day was the day our Lord spoke of to the Jews, "Your father Abraham rejoiced to see My day, and he saw it and was glad" (John 8:56), which He had in mind as He thought of Moriah. The Son, typified by Isaac, acquiesced in the sacrifice. The aged patriarch could never have captured and bound his agile, strong son without his consent. At Calvary, Christ's life was not *taken* by force, it was willingly given.

The answer of Abraham to Isaac's question as to where the lamb was coming from for the sacrifice gathers added significance as we think of the provision God has made for the deepest need of sinners. "God will provide *Himself* a lamb." God *Himself* in the

Person of His Son provided "the Lamb without blemish and without spot," for our deliverance from sin's curse and dominion. At the Cross, He became the universal Provider of redemption, providing life for our death, atonement for our guilt, strength for our weakness, Heaven for our Hell. Because God spared not His own Son, but delivered Him up for all, in virtue of the Lamb of Calvary, He stands ready to "freely give us all things" (Romans 8:32). Now, the sinner can do nothing whatever for his salvation. The Lord has seen to it, both for time and eternity.

Thirdly, we have the promise and assurance of God's goodness in *Jehovah-Jireh.* In the matter of temporal provision for mankind in general, God daily proves Himself to be the unfailing Provider. "The eyes of all – man and beast – wait upon Him, for He giveth them their meat in due season."

> He daily spreads a glorious feast,
> And at His table dine,
> The whole creation – man and beast,
> And He's a friend of mine.

For those of us redeemed by the blood of the Lamb, we have the promise, "My God shall supply all your need according to his riches in glory by Christ Jesus" (Philippians 4:19). These words of Paul are the New Testament version of *Jehovah-Jireh,* and the *all* means ALL, whether our needs are spiritual, physical or material. Food, clothing, and the sustenance of life, are nothing to Him to provide who never forgets to feed the sparrows (Matthew 6:25-34).

When Jesus sent forth the Seventy He knew all about the need that would face them, and when they returned it was with the confession that they lacked *nothing* (Luke 22:35). The heart of the Lord is as large as His power is infinite, and as we cast all our care upon Him, we experience how deeply He cares for

us, and is at hand to provide when need arises.

> Say not, my soul, "From whence can
>   God relieve my care?
> Remember that Omnipotence hath
>   servants everywhere.
> His methods are sublime; His heart
>   profoundly kind;
> God never is before His time,
>   and never is behind.

When faced with a legitimate, pressing need, faith can say, *The Lord will see to it.* The *seeing* implied here is a kindly, friendly, interested seeing, a seeing that cares and sympathizes and provides for the need it sees, and God's *vision* issues in *provision.* Trials, sorrows, and disappointments may be ours, but in all situations we can prove that it is true that God will provide.

> Tho' troubles assail and dangers affright
> Tho' friends should all fail and
>   foes all unite;
> Yet one thing secures us, whatever
>   betide,
> The Scripture assures us,
>   "The Lord will provide."

JEHOVAH-ROPHI – *The Lord, The Physician*

Humanity, collectively and individually, stands in dire need of a Physician, and He has been provided in Him who "healed them all" (Matthew 12:15). From Abraham at Moriah we learned that in times of need God provides. He is our *Jehovah-Jireh.* From Israel we further learn that in times of sickness God heals, for He is our *Jehovah-Rophi.* "I am Jehovah, thy Healer." Rotherham renders this verse as "The Lord the Physician." The word *heal* means "to mend" as a garment is mended, "to repair" as a building is reconstructed, and "to cure" as a diseased person is restored to health. The Hebrew word for "heal" is translated as *physician* in Jeremiah 8:22.

Further, the term *healeth* is used –

To express God's grace in restoring spiritual life – ·"He healeth all our diseases," spiritual as well as physical (Psalm 103:3).

To heal the broken in heart (Psalm 147:3).

To recover the backslider from his backslidings (Jeremiah 3:22).

To indicate removal of bodily infirmity (Genesis 20:17; 2 Kings 20:5).

As to wholeness in spirit, soul and body, such is ours through Him by whose "stripes we are healed." *Provision* came to Abraham in answer to his faith and obedience. *Healing* was Israel's as they "hearkened to the voice of the Lord, doing that which was right in His sight." If we believe and obey God, He will reveal Himself to us in all the fullness of His power and grace. Karl Barth in his volume, *The Word of God and the Word of Man*, reminds us that –

> "We live in a sick old world which cries out of its deepest need: Heal me, O Lord, and I shall be healed! In all men, whoever and wherever and whatever and however· they may be, there is a longing for exactly this which is here within the Bible."

Jehovah-Rophi is ever ready to heal those who have need of healing, as the experience of many in Scripture proves. Every man is conscious of his need of healing, and rejoices to hear of true healers. Scripture only uses the word *healer* once, and then hardly in a good sense. "I will not be a healer" (Isaiah 3:7). *Jehovah* alone can cover all the healing we require in our bodily, moral, and spiritual natures. "I am the Lord that healeth thee." Let us not miss the chief force resident in this revelation of God. "Healeth *thee*" – not only the bitter waters without, but "that healeth

thee." It is man himself who needs to be healed, because out of the treasure of the heart proceed all the streams that either minister life or death to the man himself and to all that are around; and it is *Jehovah-Rophi* alone who can heal the fountainhead of those streams.

As there is a wonderful and significant order in the compound names of Jehovah as they appear in Scripture, indicating as they do a progressive revelation of Himself to meet every need of His redeemed people, it is but fitting to follow the circumstances leading up to God's unveiling of Himself as *Jehovah-Rophi*. Suddenly and in a miraculous way, Israel was delivered by the Lord's own hand from the long and bitter bondage in Egypt. Freed from Pharaoh and from death by the Passover Lamb, and emancipated forever from their slavery and burdens by the passage through the Red Sea, doubtless the people felt that they had left all their troubles behind. Now, as the redeemed of the Lord they were free to go forward and enjoy their life of liberty in every possible sense of the word.

But no sooner had they sung their song of gratitude and rejoicing than unknown needs and new difficulties arose. No sooner had the chorus of deliverance left their mouths, than the people lost heart wondering how they would be able to satisfy their natural thirst. The water of the Red Sea was too salty to drink, so they hastened on to Marah, in the hope of finding fresh water there to meet their pressing need. There could be no life without water, and Marah was their only hope. Alas! however, the waters were bitter, hence the name of the place for Marah means "bitter." Death seemed to threaten the people when they came to face the Red Sea, and now a more terrible form of death was before them, an agonizing death from thirst. So they cried, "What shall we drink?" Moses, leader and intercessor of Israel cried to the Lord, *Jehovah-Jireh*, to provide for the needs of the people, and He revealed Himself as *Jehovah-Rophi*, by guiding Moses to a certain tree, telling him to cast it into the waters. This was done, and immediately bitterness turned to sweetness, deadly water had now life-giving properties, and the people drank and gained strength and went forward confident that the Lord had delivered them, once again from death. They came to Elim where there was an abundance of fresh water and fruit.

The promise was given not to smite His people with any of the diseases God brought upon Egypt, if only they would live as unto Him, and obey His statutes. Even if they came again to "a dry and thirsty land where no water is," He would be there as their *Jehovah-Rophi*. They could rely upon Him to sweeten any bitter waters they encountered. He promised, nay pledged Himself, to be their Healer on condition of their obedience to His word and will. Doubtless there was no magical or medicinal quality in the wood cast into the bitter waters. The miracle was attributed to Jehovah's interposition, and was meant to illustrate His intention to be the health and wholesomeness of Israel's life if only the nation would trust and obey Him. If the people lived as unto Him, He would ever be the health of their countenance (Psalm 43:5).

At Moriah there was illustrated a parable of Calvary. *Jehovah* showed Moses a tree which he cast into the bitter waters and they were made sweet. As it was with Israel, thus is it with ourselves – the LORD has revealed to us another tree, even the one *Jehovah – Jesus*, Himself hung upon, "Who his own self bare our sins in his own body on the tree, that we, being dead to sins, should live unto righteousness: by whose

stripes we are healed" (1 Peter 2:24). May we never forget the purchase-price of our spiritual health! Here, salvation from sin's guilt and power is referred to as healing, which is one of the meanings of the term "salvation." In earlier times, the idea of health and healing had a much larger content, covering the complete wholeness and wholesomeness of existence, both for individual life and for the whole world. Both Wycliffe and Tyndale use the word suggestively in Christ's affirmation to Zaccheus, "This day is *health* come to thine house" (Luke 19:9). The Anglican Prayer Book observes the same implication of a health that is more than physical –

> "We have left undone those things which we ought to have done, and we have done those things which we ought not to have done, and there is *no health in us*."

Such spiritual health comes from the Tree cast into the bitter waters of sin. Deliverance from the burden and bondage of iniquity is ours through the death and resurrection of Him who died on that Tree. Waters, which were by nature corrupt, engendering death for all who taste of them, have, through the Cross, been exchanged for "the rivers of living waters." At the outset of man's history, it was by a *tree* that he should have been saved from death and live for ever. It was "the tree of the knowledge of good and evil, and the tree of life." At Marah, Israel learned the sweetening and life-giving qualities of a God-chosen tree. In the Eternal State, there is another "tree of life," designed for the perpetual health of the nations.

Attention must be drawn to the fact, however, that as the tree itself which Moses flung into the bitter waters had no healing properties, the miracle of healing the waters being of God Himself, so the mere wooden tree on which

Jesus died had no saving virtue in itself, even though in our hymns we attribute accomplishments to a Cross which are Christ's alone. For instance, we often sing the well-known words —

> The Cross! *it* takes our guilt away,
> *It* holds the fainting spirit up;
> *It* cheers with life the gloomy day,
> And sweetens every bitter cup.

But the emphasis should be on *he,* not *It.* All that the Cross represents, namely, the voluntary, substitutionary death of Christ, can alone "sweeten every bitter cup." When He died upon the tree, He became the Life of the world. By entering into the water of death Himself on behalf of lost sinners, dying of spiritual thirst, He took away all "the bitterness of death," from the earth. As Webb-Peploe puts it —

> "As it was the first man — Adam — who embittered the waters of earth by sin, so was it necessary that the second man — Christ Jesus — should pass into the waters of death, and, by the omnipotence of that *Jehovahship* which lay hidden within Him, should become a true life-power for all the nations of the World."

What a blessed Gospel it is to take to the poor, sorrowful, sin-stricken hearts of men and women, "He healeth the broken in heart"! "I will heal their wounds and diseases." The precious blood the Saviour shed is the only healing balm for lives embittered by sin.

There is still another application of those bitter waters sweetened by a tree. A footnote in the *Scofield Reference Bible* at Exodus 15:25 reads —

> "These bitter waters were in the very path of the Lord's leading, and stand for the trials of God's people, which are educatory and not punitive.... When our Marahs are so

taken we cast the *tree* into the waters" (Romans 5:3, 4).

Sooner or later on our pilgrimage through the wilderness of this world we come to our *Marahs,* to those experiences so bitter and distasteful. There are blasted hopes, broken promises, wounds that ache, injuries that deeply hurt, sores that fester in the memory, accusing voices keeping conscience in a storm of mental anguish. Often we come, all athirst to a pool we hope will satisfy us, but when we stoop to drink there is only bitterness in it.

> I tried the broken cisterns, Lord,
>   But, ah, the waters failed!
> E'en as I stooped to drink they fled,
>   And mocked me as I wailed.

Setting out on our journey heavenward we anticipate that all will be sweet and pleasant, with no thought that a bitter cup may be ours to drink. Things go wrong, circumstances appear to be against us, and the bitterness of the well at Marah becomes a reflection of our own heart's bitterness. The refrain that, "Ills have no weight, and tears no bitterness," seems most unreal. The ancient Bard hopelessly asks —

> Canst thou not minister to a mind
>   diseased?
> Plucked from the memory a
>   rooted sorrow,
> Raze out the written troubles
>   of the brain,
> And with some sweet oblivious
>   antidote
> Cleanse the stuff'd bosom of that
>   perilous stuff
> Which weighs upon the heart?
> If thou canst . . . find her disease
> And purge it to a pure and
>   pristine health,
> I would applaud thee to the echo
> That should applaud again.

But the court physician Shakespeare describes had no cure for such an embittered heart. Saints, however, have a Great Physician they can applaud to an echo, because His touch has still its ancient power, and no matter what Marah may be theirs, in His mercy He can heal the waters, and sweeten the bitter cup. "Exactly as it was with the people of Israel, so the LORD God Almighty will reveal to us a Tree, which, being cast into the waters, shall make them all sweet, whether they be the waters that meet us in the pathway of life, or the bitter pools of our own inner existence."

When Naomi returned to Bethlehem a soured widow and mother because of the three graves she had left behind in Moab, her old-time neighbors met her with the query, *Is this Naomi?* or "Is this the one we knew as Naomi?" – the name Naomi meaning pleasant, agreeable, attractive. But she replied in a forlorn tone –

> "Call me not Naomi (pleasant) call me Mara (bitter) for the Almighty hath dealt very bitterly with me. I went out full, and Jehovah hath brought me home again empty; why then call ye me Naomi, seeing Jehovah hath testified against me, and the Almighty hath afflicted me? (Ruth 1:19, 20).

The Jewess erred in that she blamed God for the sorrows and losses she had experienced when it was the wrong turning she and her husband took when, with their two sons, they left Bethlehem for Moab. Although the Almighty permitted the trials endured in territory forbidden for Jews, He was not responsible for them, and Naomi erred in blaming Him for her change from a pleasant woman into an embittered one. How apt we are to charge God for the Marahs we encounter, which are of our own creation! But in Ruth, who became an ancestress of our Lord, Naomi's bitter waters were sweetened. In her grandson, Obed, she found a restorer of her life (4:15). Thus she came to experi-

ence, what Faber has taught us to sing that –

> Ill that He blesses is our good,
>   And unblest good is ill;
> And all is right that seems most wrong,
>   If it be His sweet will.

Finally, in the Great Physician whose miracles of healing dominate the four Gospels we have *Jehovah-Rophi* manifest in human form. Declaring that the Old Testament divine Healer had commissioned Him to undertake a similar ministry, "He hath sent me to heal" (Luke 4:18). "Jesus came into this sick world as Healer," says R. F. Horton "He was Himself perfectly healthy. We have no hint that He was ever ill or suffered physical pain – until they crucified Him. It was said in the words of the prophet that He bore our diseases but that was only in the sense that He bore our sins; He did not suffer the diseases nor did He commit the sins; He took both upon Himself, that He might heal our diseases, and take away our sins."

All through His earthly ministry, His acts of healing never ceased. Wherever He went He healed "all manner of sickness and all manner of diseases among the people," and His miracles, proof of His Deity and mission, constantly amazed those who either witnessed or experienced them (Matthew 11:4, 5 John 5:36). But as with *Jehovah-Jireh* of the Old Testament, so with the Great Physician of the New Testament, physical healing was only incidental to His chief mission, namely, the healing of the souls of man. Did He not declare that He came to seek and to save the lost True, He was the Physician needed by humanity, and had, not only the healing balm, but the skill as well, and willingness to use it. Yet His primary task was to shed His blood as the only balm for the spiritual maladies of a sin-sick world.

Said a grateful patient of his physician, "I like him better than any other doctor I have seen. He is so frank." Was it not so with the Healing Christ? He was always frank with those who sought His aid; never brusque and harsh, but sympathetically candid, and always able to lay His finger on the place and say, "The trouble is here." Is this not borne out when the sick man was brought to Him by his friends for the healing of his palsied body? Strange though it seemed to all concerned, Jesus first addressed Himself to the worse malady of the afflicted man for Jesus knew the man's secret, and so said, "Thy sins be forgiven thee." Many physical disorders are the result of a moral and spiritual cause, some condition of heart and mind, some inner disease requiring the service of the Saviour-Physician who deals first with the cause then with the effect. What would have been the use of merely healing the palsied man, if after taking up his bed, he walked right back into the sin probably responsible for his disease?

Coming as the Great Physician, Jesus fully recognized man's need for accepting His rule of self-estimates. He said, "They that are whole have no need of a physician, but they that are sick." He also said of the woman who had suffered from a hemorrhage for 12 years that "she had suffered many things of many physicians, and had spent all that she had, and was nothing bettered, *but rather grew worse*" (Mark 5:25, 26). How different it was with all who sought the aid of the heavenly Physician! None were ever the worse after touching the hem of His garment.

But while Jesus healed all who came His way as He walked among men, the problem exercising many today is the extent of His healing ministry. There are those, like Paul of old, who suffer grievously in the flesh and seek healing from the Lord, but freedom from pain is denied. The only answer they receive is, "My grace is sufficient for thee: for My strength is made perfect in weakness." Paul himself, who had healed others, had to leave Trophimus behind at Miletus because of sickness. The apostle could also do nothing for Epaphroditus who was sick unto death, or for Timothy's "often infirmities." Scripture does not answer the question why it is not always God's will to grant deliverance to the afflicted. He did not spare His only begotten Son from the terrible, excruciating pain and agony of the Cross.

In this age of Grace, it is not for us to claim the special earthly blessings conferred on Israel of old, or to expect every physical disease to be healed by a word as in the time of our Lord's sojourn on earth. Under the higher dispensation of the Holy Spirit, spiritual blessings are far higher than physical and we should not therefore lay too much stress on our bodily troubles, or ask unreservedly for the healing of the flesh, especially as it might result in our spiritual ruin if granted by God. With regard to our physical and temporal trials "we have no right to go one step further than Jesus did when, on that awful night in the Garden of Gethsemane, when the deep agony of death was upon His soul, He cried for the first time, so far as it is recorded of Him –

> "Not my will, but thine, be done" (Luke 22:42). "O my Father, if it be possible, let this cup pass from me: nevertheless not as I will, but as thou wilt." (Matthew 26:39).

The all-important lesson we learn from that dark night the Lord passed through is that we must leave it to God as our all-wise Father to decide what is best for us. As *Jehovah-Rophi*, He can heal all our diseases, but whether He will is His secret. From experience we know that often it pleases Him to raise up His children from sickness in response to the prayer of faith, but that in other cases He does not grant the healing requested – and that in spite of the holiness of the afflicted one seeking relief. It seems to be the philosophy in some professed faith-healing quarters, that, for a believer to suffer from some physical malady is evidence that he is out of fellowship with God, seeing that any form of sickness is the result of sin. Such reasoning is not only false, but an infringement upon God's permissive will.

Further, there are those who claim to have healing powers they can exercise in many ways even through the blessing of handkerchiefs of the afflicted, seeking help sent through the post to the self-styled healer. But no man is able to heal. Even physicians and surgeons confess they have no power to heal, that all they can do is to diagnose the sickness and suggest means. Of this we are confident, that Paul was greatly helped, physically, by the advice of his constant companion, Luke, the beloved physician. Our *Jehovah-Rophi* is able to heal immediately or gradually, without any human agency. He also uses the medical and surgical ministry of those who are qualified to care for the sick and diseased. In the last resort, however, the sufferer is dependent upon Him who said, "*I* am the Lord that healeth thee" (Exodus 15:26). And, praise Him, when ultimately He arises as the Sun of Righteousness with healing in His wings, all sickness, pain and disease will have vanished.

> Heal us, Jehovah we are here,
>   Waiting to feel Thy touch;
> Deep-wounded souls to Thee repair,
>   And, Saviour, we are such.

Jehovah-Nissi – *The Lord Our Banner*

Because banners, or flags, have ever expressed the intangible loyalties of the soul, men have been prepared to defend a particular standard with their last breath. The surrender of their flag would have meant dishonor, for as it fluttered in the wind it seemed to say on behalf of the fighters, "Here we stand, and this is the position we are prepared to defend to the death." As Shakespeare puts it –

> Hang out our banners on the
>   outward walls;
> The cry is still, "They come."
>   Our castle's strength
> Will laugh a siege to scorn.

Countless have perished to keep flags flying, content to die, so long as their colors were still up. In the moral realm, valiant souls were prepared to die rather than lower the standard, because they knew the lower the standard, the lower the living. David, the warrior, could say, "In the name of our God we will set up our banners" – banners to "be displayed because of the truth" (Psalms 20:5; 60:4).

While Amalek fought with Israel in Rephidim, and Joshua was conspicuous in the conflict, Moses and Aaron and Hur were on the top of the hill. When Moses held up his hand, holding the rod of God, Israel prevailed; and when weary, he let his hands drop, Amalek prevailed. To avoid defeat, Aaron and Hur stayed up with Moses, propping his hands, until Israel defeated their enemies, and God gave them the victory. To celebrate this glorious deliverance from Amalek, "Moses built an altar, and called the name of it Jehovah-Nissi" or Jehovah My Banner, "for he said, Because the Lord hath sworn that the Lord will have war with Amalek from generation to generation" (Exodus 17:15, 16). An expositor of the past century comments –

> "Moses took care that God should have the glory of this victory. In-

stead of setting up a trophy in the honour of Joshua – though it had been a laudable policy to put marks of honour upon him – he builds an altar to the honour of God. . . . What is most carefully recorded is the inscription upon the altar, Jehovah-Nissi: *The Lord my Banner.* . . . The presence and power of Jehovah were the banner under which they enlisted, by which they were animated and kept together."

The word *Nissi* itself has some interesting implications and is rendered *standard,* ensign (Isaiah 5:26; 49:22; 62:10); as *sign* in Numbers 26:10, and as *pole* in connection with the brazen serpent lifted up upon it to give life to Israel. Our Saviour was lifted up upon the *pole* and by all He accomplished upon it we have victory over the world, flesh, and the devil. The Lord Himself is the Victory over the Amalek of our foes, and He is our Banner leading us always in triumph. As Dr. F. E. Marsh so convincingly states it –

"The Lord in His death for us is our Banner in victory – our Standard in life – our Ensign in testimony – our Sign to all that He is the Triumphant Lord."

What Moses added after he named the altar, *Jehovah-Nissi,* in literal Hebrew means, "A hand upon the throne of *JEHOVAH! JEHOVAH* will have war with Amalek from generation to generation." Amalek's hand had dared to assault Jehovah's throne to overturn it and so He gave Israel the authority and power of that throne to overwhelm Amalek – the uplifted hands of Moses symbolizing such. Here we have an illustration of the hand of faith outstretched in prayer. In the sacred name God had given Moses was the pledge of infinite resource for every emergency,

with Jehovah Himself going on before His people.

After Israel had passed through the Red Sea, she sang "JEHOVAH is a Man of war!" and now in His war with Amalek although unseen by outward eye He was near to prove Himself the Victor. Is this faith ours in the conflict against the dark forces of hell?

Thrice blest is he to whom is given
The instinct that can tell
That God is on the field when He
Is most invisible.

Joshua, who came to the front as a fearless and courageous captain in God's war against Amalek, had a name which in its Hebrew form means JESUS – "I will be Salvation." Isaiah prophesied that, "A root of Jesse which shall stand for an ensign of the people" and one around which the Gentiles and Israel would rally (Isaiah 11:10, 12). And it is *Jesus,* our heavenly Joshua, who came as "a root of Jesse," who must command our forces if there is to be conquest. Does not His very name pledge Him peculiarly to the task of routing the Amaleks of hell who tried to usurp God's throne? With the Captain of our salvation as our leader and commander, our place is up the hill, laying hold of the promise of His victory, pleading in importunate prayer until the victory falls to *His* arms.

Although this new name, *Jehovah-Nissi,* appears only here on the memorial altar, the truth it expresses is found running through Scripture. In different ways we are constantly reminded that "The battle is the Lord's," and that victory is His alone. This does not infer that God evinces any interest in the dreadful battles of modern times – wars for conquest, revenge, commerce, extension of territory, or even for the defense of religion. In World War II, Britain claimed God was on its side – so did the Germans! God was opposed to both parties and on the side of neither. The one war He eternally participates in and expects us to fight in beneath His banner, is that of light against darkness, truth against error, good against evil, holiness against sin, His Church against the World.

> We praise Thee, O Jehovah!
> Our banner gladly raise;
> *Jehovah-Nissi!* rally us
> For conflict, victory, praise.

God means His redeemed people to fight with Him and for His fellow-fighters in resisting the satanic foe. In the war with Amalek, *Jehovah* could have done without Israel, but Israel could not have done without *Jehovah*.

> "Jehovah could as easily have defeated Amalek as He drowned the Egyptians: Amalek could as easily have swallowed up Israel in the absence of Jehovah, as the sea swallowed up the hosts of the Egyptians," say William Whitelaw. "One man with Jehovah could have chased a thousand: without Jehovah a thousand could have chased one man. Hence, while Joshua went down into the valley to fight, Moses went up the hill to pray."

In all our battles against the World, Flesh and the Devil, it is so necessary that God is before us, and with us as our *Jehovah-Nissi*. No matter how strong the enemy, or continuous his attacks, He is with us, girding us with strength, teaching our hands to war (Psalm 18: 32, 34), and that his banner over us is *Love* (Song of Solomon 2:4). Actually, the term *Banner* has the idea of something which gleams conspicuously from afar. If we are secret disciples, shrinking from "nailing our colors to the mast" in open acknowledgment of our Lord, we can hardly look for victory over the principalities and powers arrayed against us.

> There's a royal banner given for display
> To the soldiers of the King;
> As an ensign fair we lift it up today,
> While as ransomed ones we sing –
> Marching on! Marching on!
> 'Neath the banner of the Cross!

> Though the foe may rage and gather
> as the flood,
> Let the standard be displayed!
> As beneath its folds, as soldiers of
> the Lord,
> For the truth be not dismayed!

JEHOVAH M'KADDESH – *The Lord Doth Sanctify*

Living, as we do, in a world ruled by a satanic god and which is therefore characterized by dens of infamy, haunts of vice, retreats of poverty, cells of misery, shameless profligates, dishonest traders, callous murderers, senseless wars, appalling crime, and moral filth, it is hard to think of a nation having *holiness* as its dominant characteristic, yet this was God's ideal of the Israel He had created to be a Holy Nation.

> "Ye shall be . . . a holy nation" (Exodus 19:5, 6).

Such a divine purpose is suggested by the further, solemn title of *Jehovah M'Kaddesh*, which is ever most precious to those who rightly appreciate their "high, holy, and heavenly calling" (Exodus 31:13).

The term *holiness* is from the Hebrew "Kodesh," and is allied to "sanctify," the Hebrew of which is translated by other English words, such as, dedicate, consecrate, hallow, and holy. It appears in its various forms, about 700 times, and used in the name before us, expresses, more than any other divine name the character of Jehovah and of His design for His people. More than ever may we know Him as our Jehovah M'Kaddesh – *Jehovah Who Sanctifies!* But while *sanctify* is one with *hallow* (when we meet with the one word we automatically think of the other), yet there is a distinction to be preserved. When *sanctify* is used with reference to God, it cannot mean to "make holy," as it does in reference to man, for God *is* absolutely and forever holy. It can only mean "to think of, or to treat as holy." When the term is applied to the Sabbath, God's name, or to anything that is essentially and inherently holy, it implies to *hallow* or to recognize its true character, or to treat it as God would have it treated.

So often in Scripture, *hallowing* or *sanctifying* is used in connection with God's people, for sanctification presupposes regeneration, and when applied thus indicates the idea of being "set apart for God's service," and carries the same positive meaning it bears in relation to God, namely, "that its expressive active as well as positional properties – qualities of character and conduct, as well as dedication to certain uses: that no born-again believer can sanctify himself is borne out by the unspeakable value of the divine word and wish, "Sanctify yourselves: for I am the LORD which sanctify you." Having been set apart from God, we must willingly take Him as our Holiness. Positionally, we have been sanctified. The Corinthian believers, not altogether spiritual in life were reminded by Paul that they had been *washed, sanctified,* and *justified*" (1 Corinthians 6:11). Our obligation – and sanctification is not something we can please ourselves about, take or refuse according to fancy, but *obligatory* – is to allow the Holy Spirit to translate *position* in the heavenlies into *practice* here below, perfecting, thereby, holiness in the fear of the Lord.

The first occurrence of *sanctify* is in connection with Creation which God completed in six days and on the seventh day He rested and sanctified this day as the Sabbath, that is, He set it apart from the other six days (Genesis 2:3). *See* Exodus 20:8, 11. The point at issue is the declaration, "I am *Jehovah M'Kaddesh*" – "The LORD that doth sanctify you." Exodus 31:13 speaks of the keeping of the Sabbath, "Verily, my sabbaths ye shall keep." Thus, as Dr. John Macbeth points out –

> "The Sabbath was given to Israel for a perpetual gift. That was one reason for its observance. God dowered mankind with this hallowed day, hallowed by divine example, by divine considerateness towards man's necessities, and by divine gift for man's good. Moreover, it was to be a sign between God and His people throughout the generations. Its observance was to be a token of remembrance, of reverence and obedience. . . . It was to be hallowed, sanctified; to be set apart from all common pursuits, a day of sacred interest and worship, that ye may know that I am the Lord that doth sanctify you."

But this term, heavy with the thought of moral and spiritual purity, is likewise used of the great feasts and fasts of Israel, which were "holy convocations," of places, things, nations, and men. Some individuals were set apart for God before, or at, their birth. The first-born of Israel was "set apart" (Exodus 13:2). Such dedication of the first-born was a figure of all Israel, and accepted in behalf of all Israel – the nation God separated from all other nations to be a people of His own possession, reflecting His holiness to surrounding nations. It is here that we can appreciate the Book of Leviticus which sets forth the holy way a holy God expected His people to follow. Already redeemed by blood and power, the people must walk worthy of their calling by the grace of their *Jehovah M'Kaddesh.* This is why this appealing title occurs seven times in Leviticus with several connections:

Sanctified to Obey

"Ye shall keep my statutes and do them: I am the LORD which sanctify you" (Leviticus 20:8).

The measure of our sanctification is gauged by our obedience to the will and word of the thrice holy One who deigns to make us holy.

Sanctified to Purity

A priest unto the Lord was prohibited from marrying an impure woman for the two-fold reason, "he is holy unto God" and "for I am the LORD, which sanctify you, am holy" (Leviticus 21:7, 8). "Be ye holy, for I am holy."

Sanctified to God

No priest must "profane his seed among his people: for I the LORD do sanctify him" (Leviticus 21:15). Others could marry a widow, or a divorced person, but not a priest. Sanctified unto the Lord, and therefore wholly His, he could not do what was allowable in others.

Sanctified to Healthiness

Any bodily blemish prohibited a man from filling the office of priest for the two-fold reason, ". . . because he hath a blemish; that he profane not my sanctuaries: for I the Lord do sanctify them" (Leviticus 21:23). Unless sanctified in body, as well as in spirit and soul, we are not fit to serve the Lord.

Sanctified to Diet

Those who were set apart to minister in holy things could not eat anything they liked. No animal "which died of itself" or was torn by beasts was allowed for consumption because of the blood in them. Likewise a diseased, or violently seized beast was forbidden. Thus, in food habits, the priest had to

remember that he belonged, JEHOVAH M'KADDESH. Sanctified souls cannot feed upon the diseased and dead things of the world (Leviticus 22:8, 9).

Sanctified to Instruct

The sacred record says that if a person should unwittingly eat of the holy bread which was for the priest and his family, then the priest had to tell him his fault, and advise him what to do, for such were not to "profane the holy things of the children of Israel, which they offer unto the LORD; Or suffer them to bear the iniquity of trespass, when they eat their holy things: for I the LORD do sanctify them" (Leviticus 22:15, 16). Our Lord had something to say about giving that which was holy unto dogs.

Sanctified to Remember

How loving yet forceful was the plea, "I am the LORD which hallow you, That brought you out of the land of Egypt, to be your God"! (Leviticus 22:32, 33). Israel had been redeemed by Jehovah, and now as their *Jehovah M'Kaddesh*, He had every right to claim their full allegiance. Thus, in every phase of her life, Israel should never forget that –

> The cause of God is holy,
> And useth holy things.

That God is not less particular concerning holiness of life in the lives of those redeemed by the blood of Jesus than He was with Israel, is evident from the New Testament insistence on sanctity of life and living. Because of the tremendous price paid for our redemption, God has a still greater demand for our separation unto Himself. "Redeemed . . . ye are not your own." Judged from the New Testament standpoint, *Jehovah M' Kaddesh* has a fullness of meaning, a largeness of hope, a certainty of fulfilment beyond anything that Israel could have known of old. Through the death and resurrection of Christ, justification and sanctification are effectual in, and for us through the communication of the Holy Spirit. It would seem from some passages that we are to cleanse, purge, sanctify ourselves – "Keep yourself pure" – but we are unable to reach and purge all impure springs within. From our side we are to recognize and acknowledge all that hinders our complete separation unto God, and in humble confession express to our heavenly Sanctifier our utter willingness to be cleansed and then dedicated to His service. The results flowing from such an intensely real and definite crisis are immeasurably great in the consecrated labor we undertake.

The whole purpose of sanctified persons and things rests upon, and arises from, the character of our *Jehovah M' Kaddesh.* Because of His holy nature, He desires only association with holy people, who can only be made holy by His patient grace. "Sanctify yourselves, and ye shall be holy; for I am holy." If we are to be "without spot and blameless," it can only be so by His power. "Be ye holy; for I am holy" (1 Peter 1: 15, 16). Here we have a positive command concerning our sanctification. But one of the blessed things about the Lord is that His commands are His enablings. The divine name, then, *I Am the Eternal Who Hallows You,* contains, not only a manifestation of the divine nature, a revelation of divine intention, but also holds a declaration of divine help.

Further, it is necessary to remember that our sanctification is not only positional yet practical, but progressive and expansive, going forward unto the perfect day. Life is growth in the spiritual realm as in the natural and physical and so we are to grow up in Him in all things. Daily we grow in grace and in the knowledge of our Lord, striving to wear sanctity's dress – the white robe of a blameless life.

My heart be daily cleansed from sin
And closer drawn to Thee.

Upon the furniture of the Temple of old, and upon the bells of the horses was written, *Holiness Unto the Lord!* Holiness toward God and faithfulness in the common round of life are complementary parts of our life. "A sanctified workman sanctifies all the labour that he does: his tools may be as consecrated as the utensils and furniture of the ancient Temple." In a remarkable passage Paul informs us what sanctification is in a practical sense when he tells us that man has a tripartite being, composed of body, soul and spirit, and that in each of these spheres he must be hallowed.

"And the very God of peace sanctify you wholly; and I pray God that your whole spirit and soul and body be preserved blameless unto the coming of our Lord Jesus Christ" (1 Thessalonians 5:23).

Dr. Arthur Way's translation of this verse is helpful –

"Now may God Himself, the Author of Peace, hallow you in all your powers. May your immortal spirit, your mortal nature, your very body, be preserved unimpaired, so as to be found flawless in the Day of the Coming of our Lord."

1. *The Hallowed Spirit.*

The *spirit* part of us is the organ of *God-consciousness,* reason and conscience as receptive of and responsive to divine revelation. By the *Spirit,* we are linked on to Him who is "God the Spirit," and therefore capable of communication with Him. We are wholly sanctified in our immortal spirit when, through the possession of the Holy Spirit, it faithfully represents the divine voice, and the will is faithfully responsive to His voice that charms us most. When hallowed, the spirit becomes the ruling center with reference to the rest of our nature. Primarily, however, prayer, worship, adoration, meditation and praise are associated with the spirit.

2. The Hallowed Soul.

The *soul* is the seat of our natural emotions, affections, desires, and imaginations; and of the active *will,* the self, standing thereby, for *self-consciousness.* When wholly sanctified, the soul uses understanding as a help to the keeping of divine precepts: desires and affections are divinely regulated and purified and tempered; there is a ready memory of the blood of God and a readiness to call up holy thoughts. A sanctified soul implies that the imagination is filled with Christ and the Christian ideal and the Christian prospect; that this part of our nature does not assert its independence of the spirit above it, but is able to resist the charms of bodily senses below. Holding the central position in our being, the soul can swing the balance either way.

3. The Hallowed Body.

Our *body* is the seat of the senses, and by its members connects us with the world without and around, and so represents *world-consciousness.* God calls for the body to be sanctified and dedicated to Him, and for its various members to be used as instruments of righteousness – eyes, ears, lips, hands, feet and other physical faculties hallowed and controlled by His will. When thus honored as His temple, the body does not aspire to rule the soul, or frustrate the upreach of the spirit, but becomes the medium of blessing to the outside world. "Out of his belly shall flow rivers of living water."

This, then, is what is meant by the wholeness of sanctification in the integrity of our nature. But such a lofty ideal seems to be beyond us altogether, and left to ourselves it is utterly unobtainable. Happily we are not left to produce what God proclaims, for this entire sanctification is of His own providing. "Faithful is he that calleth you [to the hallowing of the spirit, soul, and body] who also will do it" (1 Thessalonians 5:24), or as Way translates it, "Faithful is He who is calling you to Himself: He will so hallow you, so keep you." Thus, what He summons us to, He graciously supplies. Augustine prayed, "Give what Thou commandest, then command what Thou wilt." Daily, through trust and obedience we maintain openness of communication with the divine Source of life and victory, and come to experience the glorious reality of having God as our *Jehovah M'Kaddesh* – "The Lord Who Sanctifies."

> He will sanctify thee wholly;
>   Body, spirit, soul shall be
> Blameless till thy Saviour's coming
>   In His glorious majesty!
> He hath perfected for ever
>   Those whom He hath sanctified;
> Spotless, glorious, and holy,
>   Is the Church, His chosen Bride.

As to the agents used in our sanctification, they appear to be of a seven-fold nature:

We are sanctified by God the Father (Jude 1). *Through* His love and mercy He separates the believer for Himself.

We are sanctified by God the Son. He has been made unto us *sanctification* (1 Corinthians 1:30), and we are "sanctified in Christ Jesus" (1 Corinthians 1:2). Here we have the standing of the saint.

We are sanctified by God the Spirit. Power and progress are ours when we are "being sanctified by the Holy Ghost" (Romans 15:16).

> Sanctified by God the Father,
>   And by Jesus Christ His Son,

And by God the Holy Spirit
Holy, Holy, Three in One.

We are sanctified by the Blood. "He might sanctify the people with His own blood" (Hebrews 13:12; *see also* 10:10, 14). Because of all Christ endured on our behalf we must be not only separated *from* sin, but separated *unto* God.

We are sanctified by the Truth. The cleansing and separating influence of the Word was recognized by Jesus when He said, "Now are ye clean through the word I have spoken unto you" (John 15:3); and prayed that His own might be sanctified in the truth (17:17, 19 ASV). *See also* Psalm 119:9; 1 Timothy 4:5.

We are sanctified by Faith. ". . . Sanctified by faith that is in me" (Acts 26:18). Faith is the channel through which all divine blessings become ours.

We are sanctified by Prayer." . . . Sanctified by . . . prayer" (1 Timothy 4:5). Prayer represents consciousness of need, and divine ability to meet that need. "Ask, and ye shall receive."

Finally, Jesus not only preached that we should be holy, and prayed for the sanctification of His people, but practiced what He taught, and sought for others. In His High-Priestly Prayer we find Him saying, ". . . for their sakes I sanctify myself" (John 17:19). With us, there are negative and positive sides in sanctification. First of all, there must come separation *from* sin and all that hinders a spiritual walk, and then the more positive aspect of separation *unto* God for service. But with our Lord, there was no negative side, no sin to be separate from, for He was "holy, harmless, undefiled, separate from sinners." He was without sin, and challenged His foes to convince Him that He had sin within Him. Therefore, with Him, sanctification meant the entire dedication of all that He was and had to His heavenly Father that those redeemed by His blood might be sanctified through the truth.

"Never was there a life so united within itself to one clear end," says Dr. John Macbeth. "Undivided and undistracted He moved toward His goal, resisting every temptation to disturb the consistency of His devotion. Neither fear of foe or flattery of friend tempted Him aside. The surrender of His life was not merely His final act in the article of death, it lasted through all the years. Life was one consecrated whole, one surrendered piece. . . . In this sense 'Christ is made unto us Sanctification.' He is the pattern and power of the pure heart and the perfect life."

What an example to follow! Can we say that we are as self-dedicated to the glory of God and the service of mankind? Jesus suffered nothing to enter into competition with His vow of consecration. Do we? Must we not confess that too often we succumb to the fatality of giving a foothold to the foe, and fail in our desire to be wholly separated unto God? Yet He has left no place in His program for sinning saints. He offers Himself as our *Jehovah M' Kaddesh* – The Lord who alone can sanctify us! May we ever be "partakers of His holiness"!

O Thou of purer eyes than to behold
Uncleanness! Lift my soul, removing all
Strange thoughts, imaginings fantastical,
Iniquitous allurements manifold!
Make it a spiritual ark, abode
Secretly sacred, perfumed, sanctified,
Wherein the Prince of Purities may abide –
The Holy and Eternal Spirit of God!

There are three further *Jehovah* combined names which, although somewhat similar, yet carry different implications. Briefly they are these –

Jehovah-Eloheenu – *Lord Our God*

Nineteen times over this exression is found in the Book of Deuteronomy and is a title suggesting the commonwealth of God's people in Him (Psalm 99:5, 8, 9). From references in Deuteronomy to this expressive Jehovah compound name, the preacher could discourse on –

What He is (6:4). The ever-existing, all-sufficient One.
Where He is (4:7). Prayer and obedience bring Him near.
What He said (1:6, 19; 2:37; 5:25, 27). Inspired precepts and promises.
What He did (2:33, 36; 3:3; 23:14). Deliverances and blessings.
What He gave (1:20, 25). His givings are the secret of our living.
What He has (29:29). Secrets waiting to be revealed.
What He shows (5:24). The glory of Himself.

Jehovah-Eloheka – *Lord Thy God*

This kindred title to the one just considered likewise occurs frequently in Deuteronomy, being found in one chapter 20 times, chapter 16. (*See* 2:7). Taking its use from the Book of Exodus where it is often used, 20:2, this divine name denotes Jehovah's relationship to His people, and their responsibility to Him, and is somewhat more personal than the previous name. There are at least four truths associated with this revelation of God –

Redemption by the Lord (Exodus 20:2). Redeemed by blood and power.
Relationship to the Lord. This implies relationship through redemption.

Responsibility to the Lord (20:5, 7, 10). Relationship brings responsibility.
Reward by the Lord (20:12). Obedience brings its own reward.

Jehovah-Elohay – *The Lord My God*

This attributive name can be linked to a similar one Adhon, or Adhonay, a personal name meaning *My Lord,* and likewise emphasizing divine sovereignty (Judges 6:15; 13:8). ELOHAY, however, points to the personal pronoun as being expressive of a personal faith in the God of power (Zechariah 14:5). Wherever the title is used it is in the individual sense, and not a general one as in "the Lord Our God." Taking a few of the places where it is found, we have –

The Language of Faith (Psalm 7:1).
The Outlook of Faith (Psalm 18:28).
The Testimony of Faith (Psalm 30:2).
The Worship of Faith (Psalm 30:12).
The Consecration of Faith (Joshua 14:8).
The Stay of Faith (Ezra 7:28).
The Hope of Faith (Zechariah 14:5).

How privileged and blessed we are if we can look upon Jehovah as if He were our own exclusive possession! True, He is the God of His people, but to separate oneself from the rest, and meditating upon all He is in Himself, and of all He waits to bestow, and out of an adoring heart say, "This God is *my* God," is an experience angels would covet.

> Heaven above is softer blue,
>   Earth around is sweeter green;
> Something lives in every hue
>   Christless eyes have never seen:
> Birds with gladder songs o'erflow,
>   Flow'rs with deeper beauties shine,
> Since I know, as now I know,
>   *I am His, and He is mine.*

JEHOVAH-SHALOM –*The Lord Our Peace*

As the word *peace* and its cognates appear some 400 times in Scripture, it is not only one of its most precious terms, but also fundamentally pivotal, seeing that any blessing from God depends upon being at peace with Him. *Peace* is the prerogative of Deity (Judges 6:24). The Father is "the God of Peace" – the Son is "Our Peace" – the Holy Spirit produces "the fruit of ... Peace." Something of the uniqueness of the word *Shalom* can be gathered from its manifold renderings. For instance, it is translated –

Welfare (Genesis 43:27); *good health* (Genesis 43:28); *all is well, safe* (2 Samuel 18:28, 29); *prosperity* (Psalm 35:27); *favor* (Song of Solomon 8:10); *rest* (Psalm 38:3); *whole* (Deuteronomy 27:6); *finished* (1 Kings 9:25; Daniel 5:26); *full* (Genesis 15:16); *make good* (Exodus 21:34); *restitution* or *repay, well or welfare* (Exodus 22:5, 6; Genesis 43:27; 2 Samuel 20:9); *pay* or *perform* in the sense of fulfilling or completing obligations (Psalm 37:21; 50:14; Deuteronomy 23:21). In some cases it is translated *requite* and *recompense* (Deuteronomy 32:35). Several times it is given as *perfect* (1 Chronicles 29:19), the idea being wholeness or in harmony with God.

As can be seen from these various translations, the basic idea underlying this one Hebrew word, *Shalom*, is "a harmony of relationship or a reconciliation passed upon the completion of a transaction, the payment of a debt, the giving of satisfaction." Therefore the word is most often and most appropriately translated *peace* some 170 times. It expressed the deepest desire and need of the human heart. It represented the greatest measure of contentment and satisfaction in life.

Grant us Thy Peace throughout our earthly life,
Our balm in sorrow, and our stay in strife!
Then, when Thy Voice shall bid our conflict cease,
Call us, O Lord, to Thine eternal Peace!

The first time *Shalom* appears in the Bible is in connection with "eternal peace." "Thou shalt go to thy fathers in peace" (Genesis 15:15). In Israel "Peace be unto thee" (Judges 19:20), *Shalom!* was, and still is the most common form of greeting, just as we, in the West say "Good morning!" Entering a home, a visitor would utter the benediction: "Peace be to thy house" (1 Samuel 25:6). The occasion of God's revelation of Himself as *Jehovah-Shalom* came more than 200 years after He had revealed Himself to His people as *Jehovah M'Kaddesh*. But after the death of Joshua, Israel forgot their "Jehovah who sanctifies," and turned to the gods of surrounding heathen and corrupted themselves with idolatrous abominations. The people forgot they had been set apart for Jehovah's service and there came periods of declension and apostacy.

The Book of Judges presents alternating periods of sin, slavery and sorrow. The people were forever sinning and repenting, then young Gideon came upon the scene during the nation's suffering under the Midianites which lingered on for seven years. When the clear call came to Gideon to undertake the deliverance of Israel, he was in the fields threshing wheat. Gideon pleaded his unfitness to undertake such a task, seeing he was not a military man like Joshua, but when God assured him that He would be with him and lead him to victory, he accepted both the promise and the challenge, and in commemoration of such a wonderful interview built an altar and called it JEHOVAH-SHALOM, "Jehovah is, or sends, peace," which implied that peace for the individual and for the nation could be found only in returning to Jehovah, and that Jehovah alone was the Author and the Giver of Peace – yea, that Jehovah Himself was Peace. In confidence Gideon went forth comforted by the divine word – "Peace be unto thee; Fear not" (Judges 6:24).

Coming to the New Testament we find that Gideon's name for Jehovah, implying that *peace* is not something but *Someone,* not a virtue but a *Person,* is applied both to God and to the Lord Jesus.

> "The God of Peace" (Romans 15:33; Hebrews 13:20).
> "The very God of peace" (1 Thessalonians 5:23).
> "He is our peace" (Ephesians 2:14).

Here we have a striking evidence of the personification of peace. Christ not only preached peace, and made peace by His shed blood, but He *Himself* is peace. Peace, for us, then is not a feeling, experience, or possession, though having Christ as our Peace is the fount of sweetest feeling, but the lordship of Him who came as the living embodiment of peace. Thus, when He says, *"My peace* I give unto you," He gives us not merely an attribute but *Himself.* Wrestling Jacob has been represented by the poet as crying at Peniel –

> Wilt Thou not yet to me reveal
>   Thy new, unutterable Name?
> Tell me, I still beseech Thee, tell!
>   To know it now resolved I am.
> Wrestling, I will not let Thee go
> Till I Thy Name, Thy nature know.

What do we know of the new name God gave to Gideon, and of the nature such an inspiring name reveals? Is Jehovah-Shalom our "Peace, Perfect Peace"? Have we discovered that peace is God's wish and His gift, nay, *Himself,* and that His designs for our hearts are those of peace? Emerson was wrong when he said, "Nothing can bring peace but yourself." A Greater than Emerson said, "My peace I give unto you." The peace we need to garrison our hearts from all foes is not of ourselves but is His peace, *Jehovah-Shalom* on the throne of our life. "The Lord *is* Peace" is how the RV margin translates the name Gideon gave the altar he built unto the Lord (Judges 6:24).

What different lives ours would be if only we could appropriate by faith all that the august titles of Jehovah reveal!

> If we believe in Him as *Jehovah-Jireh,* "The LORD will provide,"
> If we have realized *Jehovah-Rophi,* "The LORD my healer,"
> If we have taken in the force of *Jehovah-Nissi,* "The LORD my Banner,"
> If we have experienced Him as *Jehovah* M'Kaddesh, "The LORD my Sanctifier,"

then surely we ought to be able to say with all boldness. He also is my *Jehovah-Shalom,* "The Lord my Peace." Cowper assures us that no one and nothing can rob us of tranquility if our heart and mind are stayed on Him who is our Peace –

> They may assault, they may distress:
> But cannot quench Thy love to me,
> Nor rob me of the Lord my Peace!

Such "Peace, sweet peace, the gift of God's love" is wrapped up for us in the blessed Trinity, for –

> Peace is provided by the Father (Isaiah 45:7).
> Secured for us by the Son as the result of Calvary (Ephesians 2:15).
> Applied by the Holy Spirit as we

repent and believe (Romans 14: 17; Galatians 5:22).

A mind at perfect peace with God: —
O what a word is this!
A sinner reconciled through blood: —
This, this, indeed is peace!

F. E. Marsh, dealing with the comprehensiveness of the word *Shalom* by Isaiah as he spells out what Jehovah is as our Peace, has this serviceable outline which the enterprising preacher can develop —

He is *the Procurer of Peace* (53:5).
He is *the Personification of Peace* (9:6).
He is *the Publisher of Peace* (52:7).
He is *the Perfection of Peace* (26:3).
He is *the Power of Peace* (26:12).
He is *the Promise of Peace* (32:17).
He is *the Perpetuator of Peace* (9:7).

When Jesus left the ivory palaces and wrapped Himself around with the garment of our humanity, taking upon Himself frail flesh to die, it was that there might be "Peace on earth, and goodwill toward men." But the nations of the earth today, armed to the teeth as they are, have no desire or place for an altar with its inscription, Jehovah-Shalom. Peace? Where is this Godlike virtue to be found among the powers spending colossal sums on weapons of destruction? The United Nations was conceived to outlaw war and establish peace among nations. Alas! however, there has been nothing but a succession of wars since its inception, and today is utterly impotent to quell wars, and threats of war. Rulers are incompetent to rule. Among the nations and the politicians, in the industrial realm and even among religious denominations, there is the absence of good will. Revolt of children against parents, students against authority, workers against masters, rob

society of peace. The shadow of a more discordant age to come as predicted by our Lord covers the world —

"...upon the earth distress of nations, with perplexity; [or, no way out] the sea and the waves [symbolic of turbulent forces] roaring: Men's hearts failing them for fear" (Luke 21:25, 26).

John Milton embodied in poetic form the rejection by the nations and men of God's proffered peace —

O shame to man! Devil with devil
        damn'd
Firm concord holds, — men only
        disagree
Of creatures rational, though under
        hope
Of heavenly grace: and — God
        proclaiming Peace —
Yet live in hatred, enmity and strife
Among themselves, and levy cruel
        wars,
Wasting the earth, each other to
        destroy
As if — which might induce us to
        accord —
Men hath not hellish foes enow
        besides,
That day and night for his
        destruction wait!

Is it possible for us to experience a world of quietude greater than Gideon knew, giving *Jehovah-Shalom* a richer content than Israel's deliverance imagined possible? Is there a peace passing all understanding, and misunderstanding also, for your heart and mine, a peace in spite of the human passions of lust and envy and callous selfishness surrounding us? Yes, it is the peace of Him who stilled the raging sea with the words — *Peace, be still!* There is nothing so tranquil as the restful heart Jesus can create. Listen to the benediction of Paul, "Now the Lord of peace himself give you peace *always* by *all* means" (2 Thessalonians 3:16)!

Until He comes as the long promised

Jehovah-Shalom to cover the earth with peace and righteousness, may ours be the inner calm and serenity nothing can disturb or destroy!

> Peace, perfect peace, in this dark
> world of sin?
> The blood of Jesus whispers peace
> within.
>
> Peace, perfect peace, with sorrows
> surging round?
> On Jesus' bosom nought but calm
> is found.
>
> It is enough; earth's struggles soon
> shall cease,
> And Jesus call us to Heaven's
> perfect peace.

JEHOVAH-TSEBAOTH — *The Lord of Hosts*

This further Hebrew name is given as *Jehovah-Sabaoth* in Romans 9:29 and James 5:4, *Sabaoth* meaning host or hosts, with special reference to warfare or service, and often appears as *The* LORD of hosts (1 Samuel 1:3; Jeremiah 11:20). It is an appellation of the Lord as controller of all created agencies, and ruler over all. *Sabaoth* combines the ideas of divine Maker and divine Controller. The Hebrew TSEBAOTH is also rendered *armies* (Numbers 1:3), *the service* (Numbers 4:23), *appointed time* (Job 14:14). The prophets had a peculiar regard for this *Jehovah* name (Isaiah 47:4; 48:2). Isaiah and Jeremiah each employ the term sixty or seventy times. In Haggai's two brief chapters it appears 14 times, and Malachi uses it 24 times. Altogether this phrase of long-standing usage, occurs 260 times in the Old Testament. The word *sabaoth* itself is first employed to designate the heavenly bodies, "Thus the heavens and the earth were formed and all the *host* of them" (Genesis 2:1). In Zechariah, *the* LORD *of hosts* occurs 53 times, and is of great interest seeing it is connected with God's action in judgment and blessing upon Israel. The frequent formula of expression, "Thus saith the LORD of hosts," implied divine revelation and divine authority. A phrase like, "holiness unto the LORD of hosts" (Zechariah 14:21), describe the climax of millennial blessing. When the Lord, as Ruler, is in possession, every possession has the name of *Jehovah* stamped upon it.

Sabaoth must not be confused with the somewhat similar word "Sabbath."

Sabaoth occurs 250 times in the Old Testament, and was first used by Samuel as "The LORD of hosts." It is found in another form when the hordes of Israel came out of Egypt and were spoken of by Moses as "The hosts of Jehovah," implying that they were as an army marching under His command. When the conquest of Canaan was about to begin, an unknown warrior with naked sword stood before Joshua, and was challenged, "For us, or for our adversaries?" Back came the reply, "I am Prince of the host of Jehovah," and Joshua humbly surrendered his sword to *Jehovah Sabaoth*. A fact that we must not forget is that no hosts or divine armies would be called into action if there were not "spiritual hosts of wickedness." In his *Personal Names of The Bible*, W. F. Wilkinson says of this name of the true God, *Jehovah Sabaoth*, rendered *Lord of Hosts* that —

> "Perhaps the ordinary conception of the meaning of this divine title is, that it represents God as ordering in His providence, or, as in the case of Israel, by His special direction, the operations of armies and the events of war. Thus, it is rendered in the French version *L'eternel des armées,* The Eternal God of armies.' It is probably this notion which originated the phrase *God of Battles*, which is found in most modern European languages,

as is doubtless received by man as a Scriptural title of God, whereas no such phrase exists in Scriptures. ...In a celebrated passage Shakespeare adopted this title, found in the prayer of Henry V before the battle of Agincourt –

'O God of battles, steel my soldiers' hearts!' "

Rudyard Kipling fostered this idea in his most expressive *Recessional* –

God of our fathers, known of old,
Lord of our far-flung battle-line,
Beneath whose awful hand we hold
Dominion over palm and pine –
Lord, God of Hosts, be with us yet;
Lest we forget – lest we forget!
The tumult and the shouting dies;
The Captains and the Kings depart:
Still stands Thine ancient sacrifice,
An humble and a contrite heart,
Lord God of Hosts, be with us yet,
Lest we forget – lest we forget.

Although there are a few references where *Jehovah Sabaoth* is associated with human wars (1 Samuel 17:45; Psalm 24:10; Isaiah 13:4), in the great majority of passages where the title is found there is no allusion to war. While God called the people of Israel, "mine armies" (Exodus 7:4), we are not to understand them as we regard an army of military nature. The term is almost identical with *tribes*, or "the hosts of Jehovah" (Exodus 12:41), signifying God to be Jehovah Sabaoth or Ruler of the congregation, or tribes, or families of Israel. It is thus equivalent to the designation of Jehovah as Head of His Church or in Paul's language, "Head over all things to His Church." The title then seems to point to the relation of God to His people when gathered together for service or worship. *See* 1 Samuel 1:3; Isaiah 6:3. *Jehovah-Tsebaoth*, then, is a *gathering title*. Our Lord spoke of those who "gather in His name," and His name alone should be our gathering Name.

Let party names no more
The Christian world o'erspread;
Gentile and Jew, and bond and free,
Are *one* in Christ their Head.

In our spiritual work and warfare we are helpless without Him who came as the Jehovah of the Old Testament in human form. "GOD manifest in flesh." Without Him we can do, and are, nothing.

Did we in our own strength confide,
Our striving would be losing;
Were not the right man on our side,
The Man of God's own choosing:
Dost ask who that may be?
Christ Jesus it is He;
Lord Sabaoth His Name,
From age to age the same,
And He must win the battle.

Amid catastrophic experiences, and raging nations, the psalmist was confident that *Jehovah Tsebaoth* was with His people. "The LORD of hosts is with us" (Psalm 46:7). Do you not love the plural *hosts*? His sway is not limited, for "His kingdom ruleth over all" (Psalm 103:19). What *hosts* are these He is the absolute Commander of? Did not Daniel have a glimpse of God's supreme sovereignty when he said that –

"...he doeth according to his will in the army of heaven, and among the inhabitants of earth: none can stay his hand, or say unto him, What doest thou?" (Daniel 4:35).

The comment of C. H. Spurgeon on the phrase, *The LORD of hosts is with us*, is arrestive and assuring –

"The Lord rules the angels, the stars, the elements, and all the hosts of Heaven; and the Heaven of heavens is under His sway. The armies of men though they know it not are made to subserve His will. This Generalissimo of the forces of the land, and the Lord High Admiral of the seas, is on our side – our august Ally: woe unto those who fight against Him, for they shall flee like smoke before the wind when He gives the word to scatter them."

If the name *Jehovah Sabaoth* means anything it certainly declares Him to be the one, eternal, self-existent Being, who created, and controls, all powers that be, throughout the universe. It represents Him as *Lord of all power and might,* material or spiritual, Lord of Heaven and Earth, sole God and Ruler of the world, *the Lord of powers – the Lord all-possessing, all-controlling.* We miss the mark immeasurably then, if we regard the term *hosts* as representing mere earthly armies enrolled under Jehovah's command. Other forces than material, forces unseen and supernatural, multitudes of celestial beings, are at the disposal of Him who is high over all. The whole of His creation is under His control, and obeys His sovereign command, willingly or otherwise. He is:

1. *Lord of All Angelic Hosts.*

Angels, or the inhabitants of the higher world, are repeatedly described as "The Hosts of Heaven," or "God's host." Micaiah, the inspired prophet, relating his vision of *Jehovah* seated on His throne, saw Him surrounded by "all the host of heaven standing by him on his right hand and his left" (1 Kings 22:19). The psalmists frequently refer to angels as His *hosts,* "ministers ... that do his pleasure" (Psalm 103: 21). See Psalm 148:2. Nehemiah says "the host of heaven worshippeth thee" (9:6). Assemblages of heavenly beings, represented as an accessory to the divine glory, can be found in passages such as, Deuteronomy 33:2; Psalm 68: 17; Daniel 7:10; Matthew 25:31; Jude 14. As we examine these various representations of vast companies of celestial beings, we realize that they con-stitute the exhibition of the state and majesty of Jehovah, as the Lord of Angels.

No matter how great the odds against us, and no matter how devoid of earthly help we may be, there are invisible and invincible divine forces engaged on our behalf for "the chariots of God are twenty thousand, even thousands of angels" (Psalm 68:17). Having created the innumerable company of angels, God is able to control their movements, and through them carry out His purpose. Did He not stand ready to send twelve legions of angels for the defense and preservation of His beloved Son? (Matthew 26:53).

Good King Hezekiah experienced what mighty things God was able to accomplish through only *one* angel. A defiant, threatening letter had been received from Sennacherib, King of Assyria, by the hand of Rabshakeh. Hezekiah was not perturbed by what he read. He spread the letter before the Lord, and in a prayerful, relaxed frame of mind, left the matter of his deliverance in higher hands. "O Lord our God, save us from his hand, that all the kingdoms of the earth may know that thou art the Lord, even thou only" (Isaiah 37: 20). When Hezekiah awoke the next morning, he looked upon a destroyed Assyrian host for in the night *one* angel smote 185,000 Assyrians and the king beheld their "dead corpses." If God could do that with only one angel what is He not able to do with twelve legions, or 72,000 angels?

2. *The Lord of All Stellar Hosts.*

The starry host of the heavens was of God's direct creation for at His bidding the sun and moon, and the stars also came into being (Genesis 1:16). In fact, the first time *Sabaoth* is found in Scripture is in connection with God's act in garnishing the heavens. "Thus the heavens and the earth were finished, and all the *host* of them" (Genesis 2:1). Then there is the magnificent tribute of Isaiah –

> "Lift up your eyes on high, and behold who hath created these things, that bringeth out their *host* by number: he called them all by names by the greatest of his might, for that he is strong in power; not one faileth" (Isaiah 40:26). *See also* Psalm 147:4; Genesis 15:5.

What a lovely touch the prophet gives us! *Not one faileth*. Every one in the multitudinous galaxy obeys the Creator when its name is called. The heathen of old recognized heavenly forces associated with the starry host above, so innumerable and clear in the oriental sky, and worshiped them instead of their Maker and Ruler. In days of spiritual declension, Israel became guilty of the same form of idolatry (Deuteronomy 4:19; 17:3; 2 Kings 17:16).

Joseph Addison extols the obedience of the planets to their Creator –

> In Reason's ear they all rejoice,
> And utter forth a glorious Voice,
> For ever singing as they shine,
> "The Hand that made us is Divine."

Did not God command the stars in their courses to fight against Sisera and did they not obey? (Judges 5:20). Joshua knew what it was for God to cause the sun to come to his aid. To complete his victory over the Amorites he needed more light, and Jehovah hearkened to his voice, and commanded His brilliant hosts, "Sun, stand thou still upon Gibeon; and thou, Moon in the valley of Ajalon. And the sun stood still, and the moon stayed, until the people had avenged themselves upon their enemies" (Joshua 10:12, 13). The sign God gave Hezekiah that he would recover was the putting of the sun ten degrees backward (Isaiah 38:8). Then who could it have been but God who led the wise men to see that particular star in the East which was to guide them to the Babe? (Matthew 2:2).

3. *The Lord of All the Feathered Hosts.*

The sacred record tells us that God created "every fowl of the air," and the feathered hosts stand ready to obey His behest. Did He not rule in the flights of the raven, and the return of the dove when the Flood subsided? (Genesis 8: 6-12). Did not the same God command the ravens to feed Elijah with bread and flesh at the brook Cherith? How pleased they must have been as they acted as two black waiters feeding God's hungry prophet! (1 Kings 17:2-7).

4. *The Lord of All the Animal Hosts.*

Scripture provides us with many wonderful instances of God's control of "every beast of the earth" He created. The cattle upon a thousand hills are His, and with all other animals spring into action at His command. Daniel proved this when, in defiance of the king's decree, he kept his window open toward Jerusalem and prayed to his God. The penalty for such defiance was death, and so Daniel was cast into the lion's den. That night the king could not sleep, fearing the worst had befallen the prophet he revered – even though he had said to Daniel, "Thy God whom thou servest continually, He will deliver thee." What the king did not know was that the lions knew how to serve Him as well. "God sent His angel and shut the lions' mouths" – and opened them again to devour Daniel's enemies.

God's similar use of the animal hosts is seen in the miracle of speech given to Balaam's ass. The same control over God's dumb creatures can be seen in the way He cared for the lost asses young Saul sought for. Presently the majority of beasts are wild and ferocious, bent on destroying each other, and man. But He who fashioned them can refashion them and in the millennial reign of our Lord "The wolf also shall dwell with the lamb, and the leopard shall lie down with the kid; the calf and the young lion and the fatling together; and a little child shall lead them" (Isaiah 11:6).

5. *Lord of All the Human Hosts.*

Nations may rage, and cast off all divine restraints, but "He that sitteth in the heavens shall laugh," for He knows that He can do according to His will among the inhabitants of earth. Why, to Him, "the nations are as a drop of a bucket, and are counted as the small dust of the balance" (Isaiah 40:15). Scripture is replete with records of how God can raise up one nation and cast down another. He knows how to thwart the evil designs of the godless, and bring to naught the schemes of rulers who flout His will. He can make the wrath of man to praise Him.

Godless, inhuman dictators may arise to rob multitudes of their personal liberty, even that of worshiping God, but the day is coming when He will have them in derision. He who created man, exhorts us not to fear him seeing his breath is in his nostrils, and can be withdrawn at any moment by the One who gave him breath. Think of those who strutted across the world's stage with all their pomp and power, and defiance of divine decrees – Napoleon, Hitler, Stalin, Mussolini, and others, the majority of whom died dishonored deaths. Our *Jehovah-Tsebaoith* is the supreme Lord of history, ordering men and movements after the counsel of His own will. Those who seek to rule, either by force or consent, forget that God has the prerogative to overrule in the destinies of nations.

6. *Lord of the Satanic Hosts.*

Paul reminds us of these unseen, dread foes who, with all their evil stratagems are marshalled against us.

> "We have to close in grapple not with human flesh and blood alone, But with Principalities, with Powers, With the Lords of Darkness whose present sway is worldwide, With the spirit-host of Wicked Beings that haunt the upper air. Therefore, take up the God-given panoply" (Ephesians 6:12, Way's translation). tion).

We are apt to forget this aspect of divine sovereignty, namely that Satan, and his hellish host, are subservient to the will of God. The teaching of the Book of Job is that Satan is like a dog on a leash, able to go so far but no farther. When God gave Satan permission to test His servant Job, He set the limit beyond which Satan could not go. At Calvary, he became a defeated foe, for when Jesus cried, "It is finished," He implied a complete victory over the unseen rulers of the darkness of this world. Christ robbed them of their authority, and now by faith, we can resist the devil, and bruise him under our feet, and become more than conquerors.

In the days of His flesh, the Master was triumphant over Satan, and often manifested power over the demons Satan commanded. Did not one of these denizens of Hell say to Jesus, "We know thee who thou art"? Yes, they knew Him as the Lord of all hosts, even satanic ones! Are we not emboldened and assured as we contemplate all that is wrapped up in this powerful name, *Jehovah Sabaoth*? Just before Jacob met his brother Esau, he was consoled by a vision of the angels of God, and said, *"This is God's host,"* and all the *hosts* of God can be used by Him as "ministering spirits" for "the heirs of salvation." Therefore, let us be found resting in all that God is in Himself.

The One who said, "All power is given unto Me in heaven and in earth," is alive for evermore, and is at hand to manifest such power on our behalf. May we never doubt His supremacy for to do so is dishonoring to Him who reigns without a rival to oust Him. With such an omnipotent God as our heavenly Father, why should we charge our souls with care? Why fuss and fume, mope and despair and mistrust when things go wrong and trials come, acting as if the God we profess to believe in is no bigger than the needs, trials and adversities we fear? Confessed Job, "I know that thou canst do everything" – and being the Lord of all hosts, He can!

We praise Thee, blest Redeemer, the
Lord of Hosts Thy Name,
In dying Thou didst conquer death,
and host of hell o'ercame;
Now, whosoever calls on Thee shall
ne'er be put to shame,
Yet is salvation free to all who
come in Thy blest Name:
By Thy blood hast redeemed to God,
this is our precious claim.
Glory and adoration be unto the
Lamb once slain,
Chosen in Thee for ever, Lord!
with Thee to live and reign;.
Here, journeying on, the Lord of
Hosts to strengthen and sustain.

JEHOVAH-ROHI – *The Lord My Shepherd*

Our meditation upon the titles of Jehovah reveals how exactly the Holy Spirit met the needs of God's people by unfolding a new phase of the divine resources at the time in their spiritual experience when it was most required. These majestic titles appear exactly in that order in which each one was necessary for the guidance and soul-instruction of a pilgrim people. Already we have witnessed the unveiling of God –

As *Elohim*, the Creator and Ruler of mankind.
As *Jehovah Elohim*, offering life to all in need of it.

As *Jehovah-Jireh*, with provision saints and sinners alike.
As *Jehovah Rohi*, able to supply physical and spiritual healing.
As *Jehovah Nissi*, the Commander we follow and fight for.
As *Jehovah M'Kaddesh*, the One who is our Sanctifier.
As *Jehovah Shalom*, who personifies and provides peace.
As *Jehovah Sabaoth*, the All-Sovereign One.

While the people magnified the LORD for life, healing, victory, holiness, peace and protection, they were still pilgrims and were in dire need of divine provision in their wilderness journey with all its weariness and wants, duties and dangers and difficulties. Thus there came the revelation of God as their *Jehovah-Rohi*, the One whose shepherd love, care, and resources they could depend upon in all the untrodden and unknown pathways of the future. No matter what the unseen days may produce, whether their needs will be temporal or spiritual – needs they would be utterly powerless in supplying at every turn of the way, their faithful Shepherd would be at hand to relieve and undertake.

As a pastoral people Israel knew all about the features and functions of a true shepherd, and therefore could appreciate to the full all that this further title of *Jehovah-Rohi* held for their hearts. Having been a shepherd himself, and one who knew all such a vocation involved, David must have had deep feeling of soul when he wrote, "*Jehovah* is my Shepherd," which is the way the American Revised Version opens the much-loved Shepherd Psalm, which begins and ends with *Jehovah* in this version (Psalm 23:1, 6). Like so many other Hebrew words, this English term "Shepherd" – which occurs about 80 times in the Bible – has several meanings, all of which are suggestive of the many-sidedness of Jehovah's shepherd office. It is translated as –

> *feeder, keeper* (Genesis 4:2, see margin); *companion* (Proverbs 28:7); *friend* (Judges 14:20); *pastor* (Jeremiah 17:16); *herdsman* (Genesis 13:7); *shepherd* (in Psalm 23:1 and elsewhere).

Thus the LORD is the Feeder to provide, Keeper to protect, Companion to cheer, Friend to help, Pastor to comfort, Herdsman to gather, Shepherd to lead. How full, then, of both spiritual and practical significance is this most choice and consoling designation of God we are now to examine! The facets of truth emphasized by this most suggestive and appropriate symbol of the relationship existing between the Lord and His people may be studied under the captions, *Revelation* and *Relationship*.

Revelation.

The conspicuous number of shepherds in Old Testament days from Abel down, prepared Israel for the manifestation of their *Jehovah* as *the* Shepherd. The people saw in the defenseless sheep and lambs which require someone stronger than themselves to guard them from adversaries without and their own natural frailties, mirrors of themselves as needing someone to shepherd them. Human instinct and intuition told them that they could not live as sheep without a shepherd. Thus, there came about the unveiling of the Lord God Almighty as the One who could feed them as His flock, and gather them within His arms, and carry them in His bosom.

The figure of the shepherd was used to illustrate the close relationship between a leader and his people. For instance, the tribes of Israel could say to David, "Thou wast he that leddest out

... Thou shalt feed my people Israel" (2 Samuel 5:2). *Jehovah* Himself could say of Cyrus, King of Persia, "He is my shepherd, and shall perform all my pleasure" (Isaiah 44:28). Priests and prophets were likened unto "pastors" – the same word in Hebrew for *shepherd* (Jeremiah 3:15; Ezekiel 34:2, 8, 10). It is in *Jehovah-Rohi*, however, that this relationship finds its highest and tenderest expression. No other divine title has the same tender, intimate touch as this. In His august holiness as JEHOVAH He is awful and unapproachable, as Moses realized (Exodus 33:20). But as *Shepherd* He comes so near to us, as His frequent revelation as such proves –

> "Give ear, O Shepherd of Israel, thou that leadest Joseph like a flock" (Psalm 80:1).
> "He shall feed His flock like a shepherd" (Isaiah 40:11).
> "As a shepherd ... I will feed them in a good pasture" (Ezekiel 34:11-16).
> "Jehovah is my shepherd, I shall not want" (Psalm 23:1 ASV).
> "The God which fed me all my life long" (Genesis 48:15).
> "The mighty God ... the shepherd" (Genesis 49:24).
> "We are ... the sheep of His pasture" (Psalm 100:3).

Coming to the New Testament, no Old Testament title of God is more beautifully pictured and personified than that of *Jehovah-Rohi* in the life and labors of Him whose wondrous birth was first announced to shepherds seeing He came as the Good Shepherd to seek and save the lost. Later on, we shall think of Him as the One portrayed as the *good, great and chief* Shepherd. The apostles loved this designation of their Master because they had often seen His shepherd heart melt with compassion over the multitudes who were as sheep having no shepherd.

Peter speaks of Him as "the Shepherd and Bishop of your souls" (1 Peter 2: 25).

John reminds us that Jesus will ever be our *Jehovah-Rohi* for when ultimately we see Him in Glory it will be as the Lamb as the Shepherd (Revelation 7: 17 RV). May grace be ours, then, to rest in the joy of all that He is in Himself as our loving Shepherd "whose goodness faileth never"!

Relationship.

How important it is to think of the correlation of this wonderful title of Jehovah! The term *shepherd* implies sheep, and once the two are brought together the relationship becomes close, the sheep learning to obey and follow the shepherd who guards the sheep from straying off with the boar or wild beast of the field (Psalm 80:13). These are enemies of the flock. Those who claim the LORD as their Shepherd, know that He is set against those who deliberately serve the world, the flesh, and the devil, and are thus "enemies of His Cross," and therefore not numbered among His flock.

David affirmed that he had made *Jehovah* his Shepherd, so we have the personal pronoun of possession – one of many in his ancient psalm – "Jehovah is *my* shepherd" (23:1). While the psalmist knew that He was "The Shepherd of Israel," he had a unique way of expressing a collective ownership of the Shepherd – MY, as if He was all His, and His flock having but one sheep and that himself. The psalmist knew a great deal about the distinctive and individual attention, love, and care of his very own Shepherd.

There is a vital connection between Psalms 22 and 23. Psalm 22 is the Psalm of the Saviour – the Calvary Psalm.

Psalm 23 is the Psalm of the Shepherd – the Psalm of the Rod and Staff. We cannot live in Psalm 23 unless we have experienced all that is involved in Psalm 22. The Crucified One must be received as a personal Saviour, before He can be recognized as the Shepherd, for His sheep are those redeemed at heavy cost to Himself when as a Lamb He was led to the slaughter. "*His own sheep*" are only those who have been recovered out of the hand of Satan, through the sacrifice of Himself. These alone are those who are one with Him, being knit into such a holy relationship through the obedience of faith.

Are we confident that we are among His own sheep He knows *by name,* and who also in turn know Him (John 10: 14)? Not everyone has the right to call you by your name. Such a privilege only belongs to those who know you. Like a true shepherd our *Jehovah-Rohi* knows the *number* of His sheep as well as their names. Is this not the lesson we learn from His own parable about the numbered sheep and the one that was lost, sought for and found (Luke 15:3-7)? Intimately connected then, with His flock, He holds Himself responsible for its safety, and our confidence of eternal security rests upon His own assurance – "those that thou gavest me I have kept and none of them is lost" (John 17:12). Judas was lost, for the simple reason he had never been truly found. "The sheep follow him . . . a stranger will they not follow" (John 10:4, 5). Obedience is ever the test of discipleship.

> The LORD my Shepherd is,
> Salvation, life, He gives;
> None can pluck me from His hand,
> Secure in Him I stand.
> Laud, promise, and adoration be,
> My Shepherd, Lord, Who died
>   for me.

The three qualifying terms that are used of Jesus as the Shepherd – *good, great* and *chief* – cover the three great truths of *redemption, resurrection,* and *rewards.*

1. *The Good Shepherd* – REDEMPTION

The characteristic feature of a good shepherd was his willingness to lay down his life for the sheep, and applying such sacrifice to Himself, Jesus said, "I lay down My life for the sheep" (John 10:11, 15). By *sheep* here, we are to understand not only those who received Him as Messiah in the days of His flesh, and whom He called "My sheep," but a world of sinners lost and ruined by the Fall, who, like sheep had gone astray, turning every one to his own way (Isaiah 53:6). Their iniquity was laid upon Him who, as the *Good Shepherd,* bared His breast to receive the sword of judgment (Zechariah 13:7).

My Shepherd is the Lamb
The living Lord who died:
With all good things I ever am
By Him supplied.

We will never know all that was involved in the laying down of His life that we might be counted among those bearing the blood-mark of His sheep. None of the ransomed will ever know what He passed through ere He found the sheep that was lost. "It pleased Jehovah to bruise him," and He willingly subjected Himself to His Father's will, and made "his soul an offering for sin" (Isaiah 53:10). Psalm 23 and Isaiah 53 have their counterpart in John 10. Christ was the only one *good* enough to die as the Lamb of God.

There was no other good enough
To pay the price of sin,
He only could unlock the gate
of Heaven,
And let us in.

2. *The Great Shepherd* –
RESURRECTION

Had Jesus remained dead, He would not have been able to function as our Shepherd, but as He Himself declared, "I am he that liveth, and was dead; and, behold, I am alive for evermore, Amen!" (Revelation 1:18). Thus, in the apostolic benediction of his epistle to the Hebrews, the author has the thought that, while the Shepherd was *good* in that He was willing to die for the lost that they might be sheep of His fold, He became the *Great* Shepherd in that He rose again.

"Now the God of peace, that brought again from the dead, our Lord Jesus, that great shepherd of the sheep, through the blood of the everlasting covenant. . ." (Hebrews 13:20).

What an arrestive phrase that is – *brought again from the dead!* Who brought Him forth? Jehovah-Shalom – LORD of Peace. Now, as the living Christ, He cares for His own, making them to lie down in green pastures, and to muse by the waters of stillness. He knows our every need, and as all power is His, He *can* and *does* care for us as the greatest Shepherd ever.

Lord, Jesus, the Great Shepherd
of the sheep,
Through the eternal covenant of
blood,
Thou wilt from evil Thy redeemed
ones keep,
Presenting each one perfect
before God.

3. *The Chief Shepherd* – REWARDS

Writing to the elders of the Church, Peter exhorted them to "Feed [or *shepherd*] the flock of God, . . . being ensamples to the flock. And when the *chief Shepherd* shall appear, ye shall receive a crown of glory that fadeth not away (1 Peter 5:2-4). The *and* treats this verse as a simple natural consequence of what the apostle had just said about the elders being under-shepherds feeding the flock, God's heritage, and not lording it over them in any tyrannical fashion. Peter reminded those who had the oversight in the Church that he also was an under-shepherd, being commissioned by the Good Shepherd to "Feed my sheep" (John 21:15-17). Erroneously the Roman Catholic Church misapplies the title of *Chief Shepherd* to Peter, but the last thing Peter could have dreamed of as possible would be its application to himself or his so-called successors. *See also* Acts 20:17, 28.

What a beautiful description of Jesus this was that Peter conceived – *Chief Shepherd!* And, as Ellicott comments – "How could an office be more honoured than by speaking of Christ as the chief bearer of that office?" Those who had been called to shepherd the flock were brought into partnership with the Great Shepherd, and all faithful under-shepherds, striving, not for rewards here, but the approbation when their *Chief* returns, will receive the unfading, immortal crown of glory. The garlands of leaves which victors received in heathen games, soon faded and withered. But the conqueror's crown for loyal and consecrated care of God's flock will be imperishable. All who have any opportunity and responsibility in shepherding others are eligible for this glorious reward. Paul looked upon his converts in Thessalonica as being his glory, his crown of rejoicing at the coming of the Chief Shepherd. Will such a crown be yours?

> The Chief Shepherd hath promised
> a crown of glory
> To those who feed the flock of God;
> The time is but short to recount
> the story
> Of Him who shed His precious
> blood.
> Faint not, but work on, tho' your
> hair be hoary,
> Willingly feed the flock of God,
> Reward is assured by the Word.

Returning, in conclusion, to David's Shepherd Psalm which was probably written in his sunset years and which reflected his early experiences as a shepherd of his father's flock, it is most interesting to observe, as Dr. John Macbeth suggests, that it presents a cluster of the compound names and titles of *Jehovah*, comprehending as they do, every circumstance and appropriate to all conditions of life.

1. *Jehovah-Rohi* (Psalm 23:1). "Jehovah is my shepherd."

Such a confession of individual faith testifies to a personal relationship. The one absolute and eternal Being was the same One undertaking the defense and care and guidance of a single life. "*My* Shepherd."

2. *Jehovah-Jireh* (Psalm 23:1). "I shall not want."

The old Scotch lady read it, "What more do I want!" Does not this simple affirmation re-echo the assurance of Abraham, "The Lord will provide, or see to it"? As the Great Shepherd He is able to supply our every need according to His riches in glory.

3. *Jehovah-Shalom* (Psalm 23:2). "He maketh me to lie down in green pastures. He leadeth me beside the still waters."

"The Lord is Peace." While labor and service are part of the privilege and discipline of life, the other necessary side is rest, composure, and meditation. We have to learn how to rest in the Lord, as well as toil for Him.

4. *Jehovah-Ropheka* (Psalm 23:3). "He restoreth my soul."

The divine Shepherd is likewise the divine Physician whose healing ministry includes healing of soul, and also the healing of the heart. He is our Solace as we face the final trial of walking through the valley of the shadow of death.

5. *Jehovah-Tsidkenu* (Psalm 23:3). "He leadeth me in the paths of righteousness for His name's sake."

His name's sake! What name? *Jehovah-Tsidkenu* – "The LORD is righteousness." He does not drive or force us to take the road leading to likeness to His own nature, but *leads* us. May we never dishonor such an honored Name by unrighteous acts!

6. *Jehovah-Nissi* (Psalm 23:5). "Thou preparest a table before me in the presence of mine enemies."

We might well ask, What has a banner to do with a table? Well, "banners and banquets are a suggestive combination: 'He brought me into His banqueting house and His banner over me was love.' In our human way the banquet follows the battle, and successful leaders and victorious troops are entertained and feasted. But here is loftier conduct. The banquet is spread before the battle because the banner is already victorious." Even though we live in the midst of foes ours is the joyful privilege of living in fellowship with Him who is our Banner, our Defense.

7. *Jehovah M'Kaddesh* (Psalm 23:5). "Thou anointest my head with oil."

Under the Levitical system one of the rites of sanctifying, or setting apart as priest or king for his particular office, was the anointing with oil. Perhaps the direct interpretation here is that of the custom of the eastern shepherd who carried a small cruse of oil or ointment to relieve the cuts and bruises of the sheep. But a warranted application of the oil-anointed head is that of our Lord's reminder about the omission of the accustomed treatment of a guest,

"My head with oil they did not anoint." Anointing with "the oil of joy for mourning," is ever a phase of the ministry of our *Jehovah M'Kaddesh.*

8. *Jehovah-Shammah* (Psalm 23:4). "Thou art with me."

This title of the Presence may well be the title of the whole psalm. Every thought and every phrase are of the most intimate character. "The LORD is there." Whether it be in the pastures, by the waters, amid enemies, through the valley, the Shepherd is ever near. *Thou art with me!* Under any circumstance this is the language of the faithful trusting heart. He is always at hand *all* the days of our life, and when we reach His dwelling place above, He'll be the unseen Presence no longer. Thus, as our *Jehovah-Shammah*, he fills all time, and eternity as well.

> So shall it be at last in that bright
>   morning
>   When the soul waketh and the
>   shadows flee;
> Oh in that hour, fairer than daylight
>   dawning,
>   Shall rise the glorious thought,
>   *I am with Thee.*

JEHOVAH-TSIDKENU –
The Lord Our Righteousness.

With all the august titles we are considering, it will be found to be most enlightening to examine references to the same in the light of the context where they are used. For instance, when Jeremiah uttered his prophecy the *Righteous Branch* who was to appear whose name was to be known as *Jehovah our Righteousness*, the Kingdom of Judah was hastening to its fall. The people had sinned most grievously against Jehovah, and the prophet predicted the captivity of Judah in Babylon. But such judgment would not defeat His declared purpose and promise to establish One out of Judah to sit on David's throne for ever

1 Kings 2:4). Jehovah would raise up . Righteous Branch, a King who would eign justly over the earth and bring peace and security to Israel whose name vould be *Jehovah our Righteousness* Jeremiah 23:5, 6; 33:16).

The somewhat rhythmic and most ignificant word *Tsidkenu*, which can- ot be adequately translated by any one English word, is derived from *Tsedsk*, neaning straight or right, and repre- ents God's dealings with men under he ideas of righteousness, justification nd acquittal. As *Jehovah M'Kaddesh*, He demands separation from sin, and eparation unto Himself. As *Jehovah- 'sidkenu*, He commands right and just elationships among ourselves. "Ye shall lo no unrighteousness in judgment . . . n weight, or in measure. Just balances, ust weights . . . shall ye have: I am Je- lovah your God" (Leviticus 19:35, 36). o, although His people, they were not o be so heavenly minded as to be of lo earthly use. They had to be careful n giving the right weight or measure. n fact, practiced righteousness was one of the conditions of Israel's prosperity nd stay in their land (Deuteronomy 5:15).

Justice is represented as a female lolding a pair of balanced scales in her hand. *See* Job 31:6; Psalm 62:9 which peak of scales and balances. But the Hebrew term *TSEDEK* is also used of . full weight or measure toward God in he spiritual sense. Appearing well over ,000 times in Scripture it comes to us s right, righteous, righteousness, and lso as just, justify, and declared inno- ent. As Dr. Nathan Stone reminds us –

> "Human language is at best insuf- ficient to convey the full compre- hension of the ideas of righteous- ness and justification contained in this word. It is only as we see it exhibited in God's character and acts that we see it clearly."

As we seek to classify the teaching of the Bible on this all-important theme, our effort might be helped by the adop- tion of four key words.

1. *Proclaimed.*

Righteousness, divine and human, is like a river, gathering volume and strength as it flows through the whole of Scripture. *Jehovah Tsidkenu* is be- fore us everywhere as the motto and watchword of His sway. Israel and the Church alike are reminded that by Him and in Him we learn and confess Him to be our righteousness – LORD, to be the only LORD. A paraphrase of this promi- nent title reads, "The LORD is the author of our prosperity; or, more strictly, of the justification of our claims in the sight of our enemies." And this remark- able description appears on almost every page of Holy Writ. It is the chain of truth which opens out in depth and force compelling our attention, not only because of its Messianic nature, but be- cause of personal, practical implications.

In the Old Testament proclamation of the LORD as *Jehovah-Tsidkenu* there is evident revelation of Israel as being the one nation of antiquity seeking after righteousness, and that in its own pas- sionate desire for *Righteousness* the peo- ple discovered their own unrighteous- ness. Thus they became the people of the penitential psalm, seekers after hearts of purity, after communion with God in holiness. The Greeks sought after wisdom. The Romans sought after pow- er and world dominion. But there was ever the remnant in Israel who sought after God and the keeping of His laws. To the devout in Israel, goodness and character were of greater value than the wealth, wisdom and ways of the world. Placarded, then, across the pages of the Old Testament is the fact that out of this search after righteousness, or pant- ing after God, there developed the expectation of One whose name would be *Jehovah-Tsidkenu* – The Lᴏʀᴅ our Righteousness. This, then, is the ever-expanding revelation and proclamation in the Word of righteousness.

2. *Prescribed.*

Righteousness is enjoined upon man because he has neither the character nor conduct of his own to lay before a just God, and knows that His demand upon him is for absolute righteousness by which alone he can stand before those who would accuse him. Helpless and hopeless to produce the required righteousness then, what a relief to learn that by His magnificent name of *Jehovah-Tsidkenu,* He provides what He commands. As Karl Barth expresses it in his volume *The Word of God and the World of Man,* "Oppressed and afflicted by his own unrighteousness and the unrighteousness of others man – every man – lifts up from the depths of his nature the cry for righteousness, the righteousness of God. . . . This is the reason that such prophets as Moses, Jeremiah and John the Baptist are figures never to be erased from the memory of humanity. They uncovered to men their deepest need; they made articulate their conscience within them; they wakened and kept awake the longing within them for the righteousness of God. They prepared the way of the Lord."

A perfectly righteous Creator has every right to decree righteousness on the part of His creatures. It is His fiat that they should be righteous even as He is righteous. He makes it clear, however, that "there is none righteous, no, not one," even though there are those who are "righteous in their own eyes." The righteousness which is a universal need is capable of meeting men's deepest longing. Among the different forms of righteousness, Martin Luther, in his famous *Commentary on Galatians,* distinguishes four –

"A *political* or *civil righteousness* which emperors, princes of the world, philosophers and lawyers deal withal.

A *ceremonial righteousness* which the traditions of men teach.

A *righteousness of the law,* or of the Ten Commandments which Moses teacheth.

A *righteousness of faith* or *Christian righteousness* which must be carefully discerned from the fore-rehearsed."

Such discernment is imperative seeing that one may observe political, civil, and ceremonial righteousness and yet not be righteous before God. *Evangelical righteousness* goes beyond civil codes and a mere outward morality. This, alone, is the righteousness that can bring the sinful soul, who has violated God's law and incurred condemnation, into the condition of righteousness before Him. True righteousness is imputed and imparted to the sinner as he receives by faith the One who at Calvary became in very deed his *Jehovah-Tsidkenu.*

One of the greatest stumbling blocks in the way of the sinner needing salvation is the idea that righteousness can be attained by his own efforts. Christ had to condemn the artificial righteousness the Pharisees paraded because it was of their own manufacture. Paul, when Saul of Tarsus, went about trying to establish "his own righteousness." A person may be sincere in the observance of a strict code of morality, yet be a lost sinner in the sight of God. Staupitz, Martin Luther's friend, said to the renowned reformer one day, "I have vowed above a thousand times that I would become better, but I have never performed that which I vowed. Hereafter I will make no such vow, for I have learned from experience that I am not able to perform it." The righteousness God desires and demands of man cannot be produced by man. Unholy in the sight of a thrice-holy God, man is absolutely helpless to work out a justifying righteousness for himself, capable of satisfying the claims of Him whose "Justice . . . is the habitation of His throne." Observance of the Law and good works cannot save.

> No hope can on the law be built
>   Of justifying grace;
> The law that shows the sinner's guilt
>   Condemns to his face.

3. *Provided.*

To the glory of the Gospel is that *Jehovah-Tsidkenu* became flesh, and was made unto us righteousness (1 Corinthians 1:30). A righteous God pronounced *death* as the penalty of sin. "The soul that sinneth it shall die" — "The wages of sin is death." No sinner could possibly escape such a penalty. The express revelation of Scripture, however, is the blessed evangelical truth that the righteous God, demanding death for sin, sent His Son — The Righteous Branch — to taste that death for every sinner, and provide the righteousness, transferred and imputed to the repentant, believing sinner whereby he could be accepted before God. This is the only way a sinner, destitute of any righteousness, can obtain the righteousness God desires. *See* Romans 3:22; 5:18; 10:4; Philippians 3:9. Acceptable righteousness, then, is not *attained* but *obtained*.

Webb-Peploe tells the story of a girl, twelve years of age who lay dying, and whose mother asked of her —

> "Are you afraid, my darling to go and meet God?"
> "Oh no," she replied, "I am not afraid, I look to the justice of God to take me to Heaven."

The mother thought her child must be wandering, so she said —

> "My darling, you mean His pity, His love."
> "No, mother," she replied, "I mean His justice; He must take me to Heaven, because Christ is my Righteousness, and I claim Him as my own; I am as He is now in God's sight, and God would never reject His own child."

As the result of Calvary, the sinner is "made the righteousness of God in Christ," for it was there that "righteousness and peace kissed each other." Christ became Righteousness personified. The righteousness of Deity, was one of His absolute prerogatives for He "knew no sin," and so suffered as "the Just for the unjust." Unflecked holiness was a prerequisite of His efficacious death. Had he not obeyed the precepts of the law without sin, He would not have been qualified to suffer the penalty of sin, which is death, and cancel the sinner's death. But because no man could convict Him of sin, and He obeyed His righteous Father's every wish and word, by dying as the sinner's substitute, He acquired for all sinners a title to eternal life. Now, as Isaac Watts has taught us to sing —

> When I am filled with sore distress
>   For some surprising sin,
> I'll plead Thy perfect righteousness,
>   And mention none but Thee.

When the sinner regards his own personal righteousness as a filthy rag (Isaiah 64:6), and that in himself is no good thing, and cries, "O wretched man that I am!" what a blessed deliverance he experiences as he turns to *Jehovah-Tsidkenu* without one plea save that His blood was shed to provide the necessary garment of righteousness. Christ came as man's security, and voluntarily placed Himself under the law that He might finish the transgression, make an end of sin, and bring in an everlasting righteousness for all who receive Him as Saviour.

> Thy righteousness is mine – my robe
> Resplendent now before the throne;
> In Thee I stand accepted there –
> In Thee, O Son of God, *alone.*"

Said Seneca, the Roman philosopher, "None of us has strength to rise. Oh, that someone would stretch out a hand." A blood-stained Hand is stretched out to us from the Cross bidding us arise from our dead selves, and accept the scroll of cancelled sin it offers. John Bunyan heard a voice saying, "Thy righteousness is in Heaven," and he found peace of soul as with "the eyes of my soul I saw Jesus Christ at God's right hand." There are only two ways conceivable of obtaining righteousness, namely, by personal merit or through Christ's merit. As God utterly condemns the first way we are shut up to the second way, and we become saved with an everlasting salvation as we renounce self-righteousness, and by faith accept Christ who was made righteousness for all who believe.

Robert Murray McCheyne, the Scottish divine, and one of the saintliest men of his time, who died at the early age of 29, wrote a poem of seven verses around the title of *Jehovah-Tsidkenu,* three verses of which we cite –

> I once was a stranger to grace and
>   to God,
> I knew not my danger, and felt
>   not my load;
> Though friends spake in rapture of
>   Christ on the tree,
> Jehovah-Tsidkenu was nothing to me.
>
> When free grace awoke me, by light
>   from on high,
> Then legal fears shook me, I
>   trembled to die;
> No refuge, no safety, in self could
>   I see;
> Jehovah-Tsidkenu my Saviour
>   must be.

> My terrors all vanished before the
>   sweet name;
> My guilty fears banished, with
>   boldness I came
> To drink at the fountain, life-giving
>   and free;
> Jehovah-Tsidkenu is all things to me.

4. *Practice.*

If "the Lord our Righteousness" has become all things to us, then we should become, in all things, what He expects of us. With our *positional* righteousness in heaven assured, there must come a *practical* righteousness on earth. Out of a heart made righteous by the blood Jesus shed there should issue a righteous life. As He lived among men as "the Branch of righteousness," Jesus kept Himself unspotted from the world, and as "He is, so are we in this world." Being made righteous before God involves the exacting demands of integrity and uprightness in our life among men. This is the practical effect of the bestowal of the gift of divine righteousness. Having put on the new man created in righteousness, we must, by the aid of the Holy Spirit, become "the servants of righteousness." There must be no contradiction between our *standing* in Christ and our *state* in the world. We must hate iniquity and love righteousness, or living right in conduct, conversation, money, transactions and business obligations. What we are in Christ must never be divorced from what we do in the wear and tear of life. The prophet spoke of *holiness* being found upon the kitchen pots!

> A little vessel lying there,
> Midst pots and pans, just anywhere,
> Yet close to Thee, my Lord, in prayer,
> O fill and use me everywhere.

With the Judgment Seat in view, Paul spoke of "the crown of righteousness" he would receive for loving the truth of Christ's appearing (2 Timothy 4:8). This particular reward was not only a diadem he had earned, but "a condition of life to be at last attained." In his Galatian epistle, Paul has only one reference related to the Second Coming of Christ – a truth so prominent in his other epistles. Here it is –

> "We through the Spirit wait for *the hope of righteousness* by faith" (5:5).

This cannot imply the perfect righteousness we have in Christ. We do not *wait* for this, seeing it is ours already, being received as a gift. What then is the *hope* of righteousness the Spirit inspires us to *wait* for? Is it not "the crown of righteousness"? What a reward it will be to see Him face to face as our eternal *Jehovah-Tsidkenu!* Ere long, ours will be the rapture of those who, clothed in His righteousness, transported will rise to greet Him in the skies.

JEHOVAH-MAKKEH –
The Lord Shall Smite Thee.

The American Standard Version translates the passage,

> "Ye shall know that I, Jehovah, do smite" (Ezekiel 7:9).

This apparently contradictory name for a God of love, *Jehovah that smiteth*, must be studied in the light of the narrative where the prophet's new discovery of God resulted in learning that beyond so-called "second causes," His hand could be discerned in the blows that often fall upon human lives. God has set Israel in the midst of heathen nations as His witness but instead of revealing and glorifying Him she changed His judgments into wickedness greater than all the nations she was supposed to influence for God. Therefore He said,

> "Behold I, even I, am against thee; and I will execute judgments in the

midst of thee in the sight of the nations" (Ezekiel 5:8 ASV). "I will judge thee according to thy ways and thine abominations that are in the midst of thee; and ye shall know that I am *Jehovah-Makkeh*" (Ezekiel 7:9).

God had dealt graciously with His people, but they had despised His grace. They refused to walk in His statutes, and to keep His judgments. Because of the gross sin of the people He had to deal with them in judgment, and, sad to say, He had to begin at the Sanctuary (Ezekiel 9:5,6) – a solemn judgment reminding us of Peter's phrase, "The time is come that judgment must begin at the house of God" (1 Peter 4:17). If in "the place of righteousness," the Lord beholds that "iniquity is there," unconfessed before Him, then, "the Lord shall judge His people." Was it not to the church at Pergamos that the divine warning came –

> "Repent, or else I will come unto thee quickly, *and will fight* against them with the sword of my mouth" (Revelation 2:16).

Ezekiel presents God in the character of *Jehovah-Makkeh* – unless there is repentance He will smite – "I will fight against them." In a later chapter in which the sins of Israel are enumerated we have the divine condemnation, "Behold, therefore I have smitten mine hand at thy dishonest gain which thou hast made, and at thy blood which hath been in the midst of thee" (22:13). The last word of the Old Testament, from which the Jew turned uneasily, is a threat to come and smite the earth with a *curse* (Malachi 4:6). Some 60 times in Ezekiel, the expression occurs, "Ye shall know that I am JEHOVAH," in an absolute sense. For instance, He is known and presented as –

The Sanctifier (20:12).
The Covenant-Maker (16:62).
The Judge of the Heathen (39:7).

Prominent, however, is the idea that Israel was to know Jehovah as the cause of their captivity, or were to recognize Him to be *Jehovah the Smiter,* causing blows to fall upon them because of their unfaithfulness to His covenant, for the purpose of recalling a sinning people to rightness of relationship with Himself.

From Paul's teaching it appears as if there are three distinct aspects of judgment –

Self-judgment. We are "to judge ourselves, that we be not judged of the Lord." A philosopher of old taught, "Man, know thyself."

Church-judgment. If we judge ourselves in the light of God's Word, then the Church is kept clear, but if we fail to walk in the light, and evil breaks out, then the Church must judge it.

Divine-judgment. What the Church fails to do, God must assuredly deal with. The solemn thought is that if He deals with His people thus – if "judgment begins at the house of God," if the righteous scarcely be saved, what shall be the end of them that obey not the Gospel of God? If men die in their sin they must stand before a God of judgment, and be smitten by Him who is *Jehovah-Makkeh.* How terrible it will be to be smitten by Him with the tragic word – "I know you not whence ye are; depart from me, all ye workers of iniquity" (Luke 13:27).

The only hope of those who are under the rod of divine judgment because of their rejection of divine requirements is to turn to the One who was "stricken, *smitten* of God, and afflicted." At Calvary, God as *Jehovah-Makkeh* caused His beloved Son to be "wounded for our transgressions, bruised for our iniquities." How blessed it is to know, experientially, that "the chastisement of our peace was upon him; and with his stripes we are healed"! (Isaiah 53:4, 5). At the Cross, the sword awoke against the Good Shepherd, and *Jehovah-Sabaoth* said, "Smite the shepherd, and the sheep shall be scattered" (Zechariah 13:7).

> Jehovah lifted up His rod,
>   O Christ it fell on Thee!
> Thou wast sore stricken of Thy God
>   There's not one stroke for me.
> Thy tears, Thy blood, beneath it
>   flowed;
> Thy bruising healeth me.

There is yet another application we can make of this title, *Jehovah smiteth.* The sacred writer would have us remember that, "Whom the Lord loveth he chasteneth, and scourged every son whom he received" (Hebrews 12:6). If we are among the number loved and saved by the Lord, then His ministry as Jehovah-Makkeh is both necessary and salutory. We are not to *despise* His chastening, or smiting, or ignore or deny any divine intention in our chastisement, or blame the instrument that inflicts the blow; nor *faint* under the rod of correction, or lose heart and faith and hope, abandon the conflict, and cherish hard thoughts of the divine love and wisdom permitting the suffering. When the blows fall, whether in the form of sickness, physical disability, bereavement, disappointment of earthly hopes, unfaithfulness of friends, loss of prosperity, we must remember that God means us to be better, spiritually, for the trials and sufferings besetting us. And, at all times, let us bear in mind that the Jehovah-Makkeh, "The Lord who smites," is our loving heavenly Father.

When smitten of the Lord, to feel the blow keenly is not wrong, if only we retain faith as above the feeling, believing that "not a shaft can hit, till the

God of love sees fit." Our Father in Heaven never makes a mistake in the ordering of our lives, is never careless or undiscerning in His treatment of us. "He knows His medicines discriminately, proportions the burden to our strength." His is the hand that –

> . . . . Will never cause
> His child a needless tear.

Ours is a new discovery of God when we find a blessing in the smiting He permits, and like the Saviour, learn obedience by the things we suffer. *Jehovah-Makkeh,* "Jehovah that smites," is not feared when we can ask of Him concerning present chastisement –

> What wouldst Thou have this evil
>   do for me?
> What is its mission? What its ministry?
> What golden fruit lies hidden in
>   its husk?
> How shall it nurse my virtue,
>   nerve my will,
> Chasten my passions, purify my love,
> And make me in some goodly
>   sense like Him
> Who bore the cross of evil while
>   He lived,
> Who hung and bled upon it when
>   He died,
> And now in glory wears the
>   victor's crown?

JEHOVAH-GMOLAH –
The God of Recompenses.

The so-called "Weeping Prophet," Jeremiah, provides us with a prophetical account of God's judgment upon Babylon in the fifty-first chapter of his prophecy. The reason for this severe judgment is given in the opening verse. "Thus saith Jehovah: Behold I will raise up against Babylon, and against them that dwell in the midst of them *that rise up against me. . . ."* Then the character of the judgment is stated, "Babylon hath been a golden cup in Jehovah's hand, that made all the earth drunken: the nations have drunken of her wine; therefore the nations are mad. Babylon is

suddenly fallen and destroyed" (51:7, 8). So we have the action of God described, "Jehovah is a God of recompenses, he will surely requite" (51:56 ASV). He is *Jehovah El of recompenses.*

William Cowper has the line, "Heav'n awards the vengeance," and this agrees with Scripture's declaration that recompense or vengeance is meted out by the righteous Recompensor of heaven and earth who rendered unto Babylon all the evil it had done (51:25). While *Jehovah-Gmolah* may withhold His judgment, fixed vengeance ultimately overtakes all who flout His authority. "To me belongeth vengeance, and recompense" Deuteronomy 32:35. What must be borne in mind is that vengeance belongs to God, *not unto us.* For the Christian, the instruction is plain, "Recompense to no man evil for evil. . . . avenge not yourselves, but rather give place unto wrath; for it is written, Vengeance is mine; I will repay, saith Jehovah." *See* Romans 12:17-21.

Solomon, whose name means *peaceable,* gave us this peaceable advice, "Say not thou, I will recompense evil; *but wait on Jehovah, and He will save thee"* (Proverbs 20:22). Ancient heathens reckoned revenge a part of justice, and ranked it among their virtues. The corrupt nature of man today practices personal revenge, and finds it contrary to duty not to do so. People must be paid back in their own coin, and be given as good as they give. When one is shamefully treated, misjudged, wrongly condemned, blamed when innocent it may be hard not to take up the cudgels and revenge ourselves, and leave our reputation to God, yet this is the way He would have us go. If we leave the matter to Him, He will right our cause, and deal with those who treat us unjustly. Vengeance is His, and He has promised to repay. Thus, with faith in our Jehovah-Gmolah we can sing –

> Should earth and hell with malice
> burn,
> Still thou shalt go, and still return
> Safe in the Lord: His heavenly care
> Defends thy life from every snare.

JEHOVAH-SHAMMAH – *The Lord Is There*

Added luster sparkles from this jewel of a divine name when we look at it in its setting. It also proves that with a new experience there was a discovery of a new name of God. "The name of the city from that day shall be, *Jehovah Shammah,* meaning *Jehovah is there*" – a significant and most fitting name with which to climax the Old Testament revelation of God (Ezekiel 48:35). Ezekiel, the priest in a prophet's mantle, had a somewhat strange vision – a land without inhabitants, a city without citizens, a temple without priests, a ritual without worshipers. In his God-given visions Ezekiel saw the glory of God, and recorded its departure from the Temple because of Israel's idolatry and iniquity. He likewise saw judgment upon Jerusalem, and the setting up of *the Prince,* the second David, as the channel of Israel's future blessing – the judgments upon Gog and Magog – the setting up of an ideal city with the restoration of the Temple within it. The name of this ideal commonwealth or kingdom is to be *Jehovah-Shammah* – "The LORD is there" – so called because of the manifest presence and power of Jehovah therein.

Here, then, in this consoling title, the last of Jehovah's titles, in the order of their Old Testament occurrence, and the consummation of His progressive self-revelation in same, He designates Himself as the Dweller from beyond space in the millennial city of Jerusalem. In the past, Tabernacle and Temple alike were His dwelling places, but in the future a wider sphere is to be His. During the millennium there will be the Temple and the City. In the New Jerusalem, however, there is no Temple, but the LORD Himself, as *Jehovah-Shammah.*

> We praise Thee, O Jehovah!
> Thou wilt for Israel care!
> *Jehovah-Shammah,* the precious
> thought!
> Henceforth The LORD is there.

Of old, the uniqueness and glory of Israel's faith as contrasted with the religious beliefs of surrounding idol-worshiping nations, was the presence of a holy God dwelling in the midst and the assurance of the continuation of divine Presence as they remained faithful to the covenant to be a holy people obeying a holy God. From the time of Moses, God's promised Presence was real and felt. The people were brought out of the bondage of Egypt "with His presence" (Deuteronomy 4:37 RV). But the people sinned and sinned, and the consciousness of divine Presence was lost and the people became as "a city forsaken." When they repented of their gross idolatry, because of His love and pity, "the angel of his presence" redeemed them (Isaiah 63:9).

When Jehovah chose Zion for His habitation He said, "Here will I dwell; for I have desired it" (Psalm 132:8, 13, 14). But there is a wider significance or fuller meaning of the expressive name – *Jehovah-Shammah.* While He made the Tabernacle, Temple, and city of old His abode, giving to Israel visible manifestations of His Presence, all that is implied by this name was not exhausted in any earthly habitation. "The heaven of heavens cannot contain thee; how much less this house that I have builded" (1 Kings 8:27). Apart, then, from the historical content of the name Ezekiel called the city, what are some of the ways by which we can apply it? Dr John Macbeth, writing on the larger meaning of this name, asks –

"Where is that Presence to be found, and under what circumstances may men find it and cultivate it? It may come to men in some ambushed hour, when least expected; it may be encountered in some bleak spot far removed from temple or shrine; it may be mediated through our friendship, looking at us with human eyes and touching us with human hands, creating for us the experience of the name *Jehovah-Shammah*, 'The Lord is there.'"

Jacob had the experience of finding God where he least expected to. Forced to flee from home because of his trickery, the patriarch came to Luz, a wild and inhospitable region of sand, stones and desolation. Tired out after a long day's flight, he slept on a stone as a pillow, and while he slept, he had a vision of angels journeying between heaven and earth. Waking up in astonishment, he exclaimed, "Surely Jehovah is in this place, and I knew it not." Believing that he was alone and unknown, the revelation came to him of One whose dwelling place is all space, and who was at hand, even in the desert, to share his loneliness.

While the woman at the well did not seek the solitariness of the unusual place like Jacob, she yet sought out the solitariness of the unusual hour – the sixth hour, about twelve noon, the quietest time of the day. This was not the usual time for women to resort to the wells to draw water, and the unusualness of the hour is seen in that only one woman was at Samaria's well. This unnamed woman because of her shady past, had reproach to hide, and thus evaded company. But that sixth hour was "her ambushed hour, for all unexpectedly she met the Son of man and in that hour she drew water out of the wells of salvation. She found her *Jehovah-Shammah* to whose presence no place is inaccessible, no time is inconvenient."

It is impossible to list all the experiences of those who discovered God in the most unlikely places and under the most unlikely experiences. A traditional saying of Jesus reads, "Raise the stone, and there thou shalt find Me, cleave the wood and there am I." What a blessed omnipresent God is our God! To Moses He said, "Lo, I come unto thee in a thick cloud, that the people may hear when I speak with thee, and believe thee for ever" (Exodus 19:9). As for David he tells us that Jehovah made darkness His secret place (Psalm 18:11), and that darkness cannot hide anyone or anything from Him who created the darkness and waits to give us the treasures of darkness (Psalm 139:12; Isaiah 45:3). What an assuring truth for our hearts this is! As we pass through the dark, mysterious hours of life, our *Jehovah-Shammah* to whom the darkness and the light are alike is our companion, "The Lord is there."

The psalmist wondered where he could flee to from the divine Presence. If he ascended up to heaven, or made his bed in the place of the dead, Jehovah would be found there, or if he took the wings of the morning to dwell in the uttermost parts of the sea, it would only be to know that He had gone before him, and would be on hand to greet him when he arrived (Psalm 139). Jonah came to know that when he fled from the presence of the Lord to the sea in which, in a most unlikely place, the belly of a great fish, he cried unto *Jehovah* and He heard and answered the runaway, frightened prophet in what he called, "the belly of hell." Jonah learned that *Jehovah-Shammah* cannot be limited to any fixed locality, but that His presence fills the whole of His creation. No matter where we may go by choice or compulsion, we can never journey to any place He cannot reach. The atheist may affirm, *God is no-where!* The believer can take the same phrase and by separating the last word declare his faith in *Jehovah-Shammah* – "God is *now-here.*"

The continuous experience of those saints whose lives are full, either of constant movement or of a fixed abode, is that of the sense of the guiding and guarding Presence of Jehovah. Brother Lawrence amid the menial tasks of the monastery kitchen could practice, "The presence of God." David Livingstone, the famous missionary-explorer took as his motto the promise of Jesus, "Lo, I am with you alway even unto the end of the world." And, as he was wont to say, "That's the word of a perfect gentleman, and that's the end of it." When utterly worn out, he struggled out of his hard, crude bed one night in Africa, to pray his last prayer, and was found early the next day with his head resting upon his clasped hands, his *Jehovah-Shammah* was at hand to carry His honored servant to Glory.

Mary Slessor, the Dundee jute worker who became the "Uncrowned Queen of Calabar" once said, "If I have ever done anything it is because He always went in front." When Daniel found himself in the furnace of Babylonian torture, he discovered that there is always One more than the visible number, for he saw "a form like unto the Son of man." A fiery oven could not exclude Him who made the elements. When John Bunyan found himself in Bedford prison for his faithful witness, he confessed that his Saviour came into his cell and that every stone shone like jasper. In Communist lands, like China, from which all missionaries were expelled, and Bibles banned, and all forms of Christianity stamped out, the one thing those who cruelly enforce their atheistic

philosophy cannot do is to exclude God from entering their land. Even in godless China, now a mighty giant among the nations, "The Lᴏʀᴅ is there" in those persecuted saints who dare to maintain traffic with heaven.

Coming to ourselves what a blessed life would be ours if we could but realize that the presence and smile of *Jehovah-Shammah* is upon all our doings? Not knowing what may await us as the day commences in home or business how prepared we are for the expected, or unexpected, if we remember "Jehovah is there": that He is ahead of us to bless, guide, and undertake. The same applies as we set out to worship with the saints in the sanctuary. How ready we are to meet Him as we say to our heart, "He is there waiting to meet with us."

> Dear Lord! we come, for *Thou art here;*
>   Enrich each memory!
> Thy faithful promise brings Thee near,
>   And *gathers us* to Thee.

Further, what strength we have for the trials of life as we remember that as we pass through the rivers and walk in the fire we have His promise, "I will be with thee" (Isaiah 43:2). Has not Jehovah promised to be in the midst of His own, even amid all the turbulent forces that may surround them? He is there, a very present help in trouble (Psalm 46). Then there is the added declaration, "He hath said, I will never leave thee, nor forsake thee" (Hebrews 13:5). Do you know that this is the only portion of Scripture you can read backwards and it means the same – "Thee forsake, nor thee leave never will I"? What a gracious *Jehovah-Shammah* He is!

When ultimately we come to pass "through the valley of the shadow of death," we need fear no evil for "Jehovah is there." Had not the psalmist the assurance that his *Jehovah-Shammah* would be there waiting to translate him from the dusty lanes of earth to the golden streets above? "I will be with thee ... I shall dwell in the house of Jehovah for ever" (Psalm 23). What may lie before us in eternity we do not know in detail for now we know only in part, but sufficient for us is that the name of the Holy City is, and eternally shall be "The LORD is there"; that as the Lamb is in the midst of the throne He will be our Shepherd guiding us unto the waters of life and drying all our tears (Revelation 7:15-17). Perfect life and communion will be ours uninterrupted by the sins and limitations of our present earthly life because of the presence of our *Jehovah-Shammah*. Then will be realized to the full the precious word of Zephaniah, "Jehovah is in the midst of thee; thou shalt not fear evil any more" (3:15 ASV).

The mystery and marvel of the Incarnation was the erection of Jesus Himself as a "tabernacle" among men (John 1:14), through whom was the manifestation of the Shekinah-cloud of the divine Presence. Men "beheld His glory," and thus, over Him who came as Jehovah manifest in flesh, can be written the superscription – *Jehovah-Shammah* for His person was the shrine of God. His name was called "Immanuel" meaning, *God with us.* His death and ultimate ascension did not remove Him from us, but only resulted in His coming nearer to His own for through the coming of the Holy Spirit a spiritual union was established between those regenerated by the Spirit and the Saviour whose full efficacy they can now experience. Thus, over every true redeemed heart can be inscribed the inspiring title – "The LORD is there."

While among His disciples, Christ often revealed Himself as the One, always at hand in the hour of crisis or need. Caught in a wild and vicious storm, the disciples faced great peril out on the raging sea, but across the angry waves there came that Presence, those fear-stricken men thought to be some kind of ghost or apparition. But when the unrecognized object spoke and said, "Be of good cheer, it is I, be not afraid." the response was immediate – *"It is Jehovah!"* By walking over the troubled sea and calming it He confirmed Himself as *Jehovah-Shammah* in the flesh. Likewise those heavy-hearted travelers on the Emmaus road who were sad beyond comfort because they believed that the body of the Master they loved and saw crucified was still reposing in Joseph's new tomb. A Stranger, however, accosted them, and they found His presence and conversation so consoling that when they came to their village, they invited Him in to share the evening meal, and seeing His nail-pierced hands, that night the village was changed for them to Jehovah-Shammah, "The LORD is there."

Returning to Ezekiel's description of the Temple within the City, can we not think of the true Church of God as His sanctum or shrine in any city or nation? Paul declared that the redeemed as a body form "the temple of God," and that every individual believer is the temple of the Holy Spirit (1 Corinthians 3:16). The apostle further describes the Church as "a habitation of God" – "a house of God" – "the building, growing unto an holy temple in the Lord." The question is, Does the glory of Jehovah fill Jehovah's house, and are we members of that house uttering His glory? (Psalm 29:9, margin). *Jehovah-Shammah*, "The LORD is there," is a privilege and a blessing to be realized by each separate believer in his own spiritual experience. A church from which the Lord is absent – if such a congregation can be called a church –

is spiritually dead, in spite of its ceremonial splendor. A disciple whose
heart is not the Lord's throne – if such
a person can be called a disciple – is
one who cannot say of his life, "The
LORD is there." May each of us be
found living for God in such a Christ-
exalting way that those around will be
forced to say, "Surely God is in that
life!" May ours be the ever-expanding
vision and experience of Him as our
personal *Jehovah-Shammah!*

> Jehovah-shammah, the Lord is there,
> All in the city this stamp will bear;
> What glorious times, with nought
>   to alloy,
> When Jehovah-shammah alone will
>   give joy.

When ancient Jews met, or came to
part, their salutation would be, just as
we are in the habit of saying, "God bless
you," or "God bless!" –

> "The blessing of Jehovah be upon
> you; We bless you in the name of
> Jehovah" (Psalm 129:8 ASV).

As He remains the same faithful, unchangeable, everlasting Jehovah, let us
trust Him wholly and come to the end
of the road confessing "Hitherto hath
Jehovah led us." May grace be ours to
appropriate all the glorious truths the
combined Jehovah names suggest!

> If our experience is to meet *poverty*,
> in any form, may our trust be in
> *Jehovah-Jireh,* "The LORD pro-
> vides."
> If we are called upon to bear sick-
> ness or disease, let us put our-
> selves in the care of the Great
> Physician – *Jehovah-Rophi,* "The
> LORD who heals."
> In our battle with the world, the
> flesh, and the devil, it is essential
> to keep our eye on *Jehovah-Nissi,*
> "The LORD our Banner."
> If Satan tempts us to dishonor

God by sins of omission or commission, then let us remember
our *Jehovah M'Kaddesh,* "The
LORD who sanctifies."
If trouble overtakes us, and the tendency to agitation of heart and
mind appears, let us whisper *Jehovah-Shalom,* "The LORD my
Peace."
If we are privileged to gather with
the saints, let it not be to meet
man, but God who is *Jehovah-
Tsebahoth,* "The LORD of Hosts."
If tempted to wander from the
"green pastures" of the Word,
may we quickly retrace our steps
to *Jehovah-Rohi,* "The LORD my
Shepherd."
If it be in private communion or
public service may we be found
with our eyes on *Jehovah-Hele-
yon,* "The LORD Most High."
If tempted to depend on our own
righteousness forgetting that we
are complete in Christ, may we
see Him anew as *Jehovah-Tsidkeenu,* "The LORD our Righteousness."
If persecuted, ill-treated, let us not
recompense evil for evil, but leave
our reputation with our *Jehovah-
Gmolah,* "The LORD our Recompense."
If unconfessed sin is upon our conscience, let us seek immediate
cleansing for it lest we meet *Jehovah-Makkeh,* "The LORD who
smites."
If our sphere is at home or abroad,
wherever we are and whatever
we do, may we remember *Jehovah-Shammah,* "The LORD is
there."

As we seek to live, walk, worship and
serve in unbroken fellowship with our
Great Jehovah, peace, joy, comfort, and
blessing will be ours. He is the immuta-

ble One, "Who is, and was, and is to come."

Jehovah! His counsel it standeth
  eternal,
The thoughts of His are ever the
  same;
Oh! bléssed the people whose God is
  Jehovah!
The people He doth for His
  heritage claim.

FATHER – *Distinguishing Title of the New Testament*

In all the divine names or titles already considered there is no revelation of the fatherhood of God, His beloved Son had in mind when He taught His disciples to pray, "Our Father which art in heaven, Hallowed be thy name" – as *Father* (Matthew 6:9). To Israel, He was revealed principally as *Jehovah*, while the Patriarchs revelled in triumphant designations like *God Almighty, Lord of Heaven and Earth,* etc. But God is never mentioned as *Father* in the sense the New Testament reveals Him. Certainly He had a Father's heart and loved His only begotten Son, and is "The Father of earth's first father." Yet spare references to His fatherhood in Old Testament Scriptures are merely figurative, and used by way of illustration such as the psalmist's assuring word, "Like as a father pitieth his children so the LORD pitieth them that fear him" (Psalm 103:13). It is in this way that He also likens Himself to a *mother.* "As one whom his mother comforteth, so will I comfort you" (Isaiah 66:13). Job asked, "Hath the rain a father?" Yes, God as Creator.

The several meanings of the term *father* are evident. For instance –

1. The immediate male parent or grandfather or even a more distant relative (Genesis 17:4; 28:13; 42:13).

2. The pioneer of some craft or occupation (Genesis 4:21).

3. The mayor or provost of a town (1 Chronicles 2:51).

4. A courtesy title for one who had acted like a benevolent father (Genesis 45:8).

5. An aged and revered teacher (1 Samuel 10:12).

6. As a prophetic title of Christ, the coming Messiah, as "The everlasting Father" (Isaiah 9:6).

Further, there may be glimpses of God's solicitation for His redeemed people as in the song of Moses where we have the question, "Is not he thy father that hath bought thee?" (Deuteronomy 32:6). Then He speaks of Himself as "a father to Israel" (Jeremiah 31:9). He also refers to Israel as His "son ... firstborn," "... child" (Exodus 4:22; Hosea 11:1). But as Herbert F. Stevenson points out, "The relationship expressed in the term *father* was regarded as an analogy only, not an actual fact." "Father," which occurs singly, or in connection with other titles about 300 times in the New Testament, is His distinguishing title in this body of Holy Writ, and is one expressing a peculiar relationship founded on an accomplished redemption. We read and hear a good deal about the fatherhood of God and the brotherhood of man. God, however, is not the Father of all men, except in the matter of creation as Malachi indicates, "Have we not all one father? hath not one God created us?" (Malachi 2:10). Jesus called sinners, "children of the devil," and as belonging to their father the devil. In like manner, apart from a natural relationship, all men are not brothers. No man is my brother in the New Testament sense of the term if he has not shared my personal experience of the saving grace of Christ. If he has, then he is my brother in the Lord.

Thus, what the modernist preacher has missed is the middle link in the chain, namely, the Saviourhood of Christ through whom alone we can lay claim to the fatherhood of God and realize the true brotherhood of man. When we address God as our Father, we know that a blood-relationship is involved, for no man can approach God as Father save through the mediation of all His Son accomplished at Calvary. "No man cometh unto the Father, *but by me*" (John 14:6). *Father,* then, is the cry of the Spirit of the Father in the believer (Romans 8:15), and the language of the babe in Christ (1 John 2:13), and a name only fully known and enjoyed by the practically separated saint (1 John 2:15, 16). Is this not the truth Coleridge has embodied in his poem? –

> God's child is CHRIST adopted –
>   Christ my all –
> What that earth boasts were not
>   lost cheaply, rather
> Than forfeit that blest name, by
>   which I call
> The HOLY ONE, the ALMIGHTY
>   GOD, my FATHER?
> Father! in CHRIST we live, and
>   CHRIST in THEE –
> Eternal THOU; and everlasting WE!
> The heir of Heaven, henceforth I
>   fear not death;
> In CHRIST I live! In CHRIST I
>   draw the breath
> Of the true life!

It is a most profitable exercise to discover the varied ways in which Christ and His apostles employ the most precious relationship title of *Father.* Of all the divine names there is none more full of comfort or more touching to the heart than that of the one before us. Julian Huxley, the English biologist, conspicuous also for his agnosticism once wrote to Charles Kingsley, English cleric and novelist, "I cannot see one shadow or tittle of evidence that the great unknown underlying the phenomena of the universe stands to us in the relation of a Father – loves us and cares for us, as Christianity asserts." Truly, there are none so blind as those who will not see. Poor Huxley could not see beyond "Nature red in tooth and claw with ravening." He was blind to the known Father the Bible reveals and to Him who came as "The only begotten of the Father, full of grace and truth" (John 1:14).

Taking first the gospels we find that *Matthew* mentions "The Father" 44 times; *Mark,* 5 times; *Luke,* 17 times; *John,* 122 times. John's is especially the gospel revealing the Father, and a definite aspect is emphasized in each chapter where this Name is mentioned, as Dr. F. E. Marsh elaborates on in his volume on *The Structural Principles of the Bible.*

The eight distinguishable terms used by the Son of God are *The Father, Father, My Father, Your Father, Our Father, Holy Father, Righteous Father.* Added to these we have several relative expressions in the epistles which, along with those found in the gospels, emphasize the many-sidedness of the fatherhood of God.

> *A Father* (2 Corinthians 6:18; Hebrews 1:5). Here we have God's relationship to His Son and to the sons of God.
>
> *God the Father* (2 Timothy 1:2; 2 Peter 1:17). A reference to His exclusive relationship.
>
> *God our Father* (Ephesians 1:2). The saints' commonwealth and confidence in Him.
>
> *God and Father of our Lord Jesus Christ* (Ephesians 1:3). The relationship between Christ and His own, and the Father.
>
> *Father of mercies* (2 Corinthians 1:3). The plural reveals Him as the LORD God, merciful and gra-

cious, and plenteous in mercy (Exodus 34:6; Psalm 86:5).

Father of spirits (Hebrews 12:9). The writer has been speaking of the Lord as "He who chastens as a father," and passes on to the contrast between our natural parents and their correction and "The Father of spirits" – a phrase adapted from the Old Testament – "The God of the spirits of all flesh" (Numbers 16:22; 27:16). The Creator of all spirits, who is the Giver of life to all, who knows the spirit which He had made is the best one because of His fatherly concern to discipline His own by chastening.

Father of lights (James 1:17). The most worthwhile interpretation of this further description of God as father is that given by Bishop Wordsworth –

"God is the Father of all lights – the light of the natural world, the sun, the moon, the stars, shining in the heavens; the light of reason and conscience; the light of His Law; the Light of Prophecy, shining in a dark place; the Light of the Gospel shining throughout the World; the Light of Apostles, Confessors, Martyrs, Bishops and Priests, preaching that Gospel to all nations; the Light of the Holy Spirit shining in our hearts; the Light of the heavenly city; God is the Father of them all. He is the everlasting Father of the everlasting Son, who is the Light of the World."

Father of glory (Ephesians 1:17). The fine translation of this delineation by Arthur Way reads, "The Father glory clad." We have similar phrases like, "the King of glory" – "the God of glory" – "the Lord of glory," but "the Father of glory" is that God is so called as the incarnate Deity in Jesus

Christ who came with the glory of the only begotten Son of the Father (John 1:14). The glory of God the Father was seen in the person of His Son (2 Corinthians 4:6).

1. *The Father* (1 John 1:2; 3:1; 4:14).

As the article *the* is emphasized in this title, God's own personal glory as *Father* is the thought it conveys wherever it is used, the exclusiveness of His being and behavior as our heavenly Father is prominent. John, in his gospel, refers to it several times as illustrating the Father as the One above all other fathers as the source of all things.

The Exclusiveness of His Being – "He that hath seen me hath seen *the Father*" (14:9).

The Sovereignty of His Grace – "No man can come to me, except *the Father* . . . draw him" (6:44).

The Claims of His Deity – "Worship *the Father*" (4:21).

The Revelation of His Love – "The only begotten of *the Father*, full of grace and truth" (1:14).

The Holiness of His Love – *"The Father* loveth"* (3:35; 16:27).

The Power of His Spirit – "Whom *the Father* will send in my name" (14:26).

The Character of the Son's Service – *"The Father* which sent me" (12:49; 14:24).

Luthardt expressed community of action in his comment –

"The work belongs to the Father in so far as it proceeds from Him; to the Son, in so far as it is accomplished by Him in the world. There are millions of natural fathers, and of figure-heads known as fathers – Founding Fathers, City Fathers, and so on, but our God is THE

FATHER – the perfection of paternity in love, discipline, care and provision."

2. *Father*

While Jesus often spoke about God, He only once addressed Him as such, "My God, My God" (Matthew 27:46). Apart from this exception He directly addressed Him as *Father* – the single, filial term speaking of the most intimate relationship existing between the Father and the Son. "The name *Father*," says Westcott, "is indeed the sum of Christian revelation." This renowned theologian also reminds us that, "As *the Son of God* Jesus knew the Father perfectly. As *the Son of Man*, He revealed the Father perfectly." His first use of it, as far as the sacred record goes, was at the age of twelve when He said to Joseph and Mary, "Wist ye not that I must be about my Father's business?" (Luke 2:49). The last occasion was on the Cross, where His last prayer was, "Father into thy hands I commend my spirit" (Luke 23:46). *See also* 22:42; 23:34; John 17:1. Then we have His exclamation *O Father!* (Matthew 11:25; John 17:5). In the dying instructions of Christ, found in those much-loved chapters of John 13 to 17, His mind is given us for consolation and profit during the whole period of this present interval of grace, and thus the name *Father* occurs in this section with its pronouns upwards of 100 times.

As a son, Christ ever obeyed His Father's will. "I do always the things that please my Father." There was never a cloud to mar the holy intimacy which had existed from a past Eternity. Further, God was His *only* father. Paradoxical though it may seem, while Jesus had a human mother He did not have a human father. He was "born of a woman," not of a woman and a man. He was born of a *virgin* – the one who

had never known man. For 30 years, He was *supposed* to be the son of Joseph (Luke 3:23), and Joseph and Mary are spoken of as His "parents" (Luke 2:41). True, Mary said to her Son, "Thy father and I have sought thee sorrowing," because Joseph was the foster-father of Jesus, caring for Him through His earlier years and teaching Him the craft of carpentry. But Jesus asserted, however, that He had only one Father. "I must be about *my* Father's business" (Luke 2: 48, 49). The mystery of the Incarnation is that Jesus was "conceived of the Holy Spirit, and born of the Virgin Mary"; that He came as the Son of man, but not as *a* son of man. He was God's only begotten Son.

3. *My Father*

Spoken only by Jesus, the pronoun of personal possession – *my*, expresses not only an eternal relationship, but also a two-fold relationship, namely, in the fellowship of their mutual love or service, and their mutual action on behalf of believers.

a. *Mutual Service* – "*My* Father worketh hitherto, and I work" (John 5:17). There was never any conflict of aims or plan between Father and Son. They were true divine fellow-laborers. As F. E. Marsh says –

"The sphere of His service – the authority for His action – the plan He followed, the business in which He was engaged, and the fellowship of His work were all begun, continued and ended from, in, through, with, and to the Father."

b. *Mutual Sacrifice* – "This commandment have I received of *my Father*" (John 10:18). Christ was referring to His death and resurrection. The righteous requirement of the Father was met by the ransom of the Son. We read that Abraham and Isaac went *both together* to the place of sacrifice. It was likewise true that Father and Son went *both together* to Calvary, for "God gave his only begotten Son," and the Son gave Himself for our salvation (John 3:16; Galatians 2:20).

c. *Mutual Security* – "Neither shall any man pluck them out of my hand. . . . No man is able to pluck them out of my Father's hand. I and My Father are one" (John 10:28-30).

With such a double, divine grip what else can the believer be but eternally secure? All power and authority are represented by those joined hands. As heaven is a prepared place for a prepared people, only those redeemed and preserved can lay claim to the promise – "In *my Father's* house are many mansions" (John 14:2). For other pertinent occurrences of *my Father, see* Luke 24: 49; John 14:20-23; 15:10.

4. *Your Father*

Fourteen times in Matthew's gospel alone this couplet occurs, and if traced by means of a concordance will show that the central thought embedded in the words is that of responsibility to the Lord and to others. The privilege of being God's children through the finished work of Christ brings a corresponding obligation, and by divine ability we can fulfill all that is required of us. "Let your light so shine before men, that they may see your good works, and glorify [not *you* but] your Father in Heaven" (5:16).

It is important to bear in mind that while the endearing title – *Father* – is one which, perhaps above all His other names, stirs our feelings and awakens the tenderest emotions of the heart, that such a name is only fully declared after divine wrath upon sin had spent itself in the sacrifice of His Son on the Cross. Thus after His resurrection from the dead by the glory of the Father, the risen Lord commissioned Mary of Magdala to announce to the disciples, His brethren, the *new* relationship: "I ascend unto *my* Father, and *your* Father; and to my God and your God" (John 20:17).

5. *Our Father*

In response to the request of His disciples, "Lord, teach us to pray" He gave them a pattern to follow, commencing with, "Our Father which art in heaven" (Matthew 6:9). But this was not the language of Jesus *and* His disciples, speaking of a joint relationship. If a husband and his wife jointly own a house they rightly speak of it as *our* house. But here the *our* – the possessive plural form of the personal pronoun I – refers to believers only as a body. Then Jesus, in the prayer He taught His disciples to pray, prefaced it by saying, "When *ye* [not *we*, that is, Jesus *and* His disciples] pray say, *Our* Father in heaven." This is a prayer for the family of the redeemed, and not a prayer that Jesus Himself prayed. There are some phrases in this prayer He could not pray as the sinless Son of God. He had no evil to be delivered from and no trespasses to be forgiven.

6. *Holy Father*

In His high-priestly prayer, as recorded in John 17, Jesus used the tender title *Father* in three different ways corresponding to the three distinct divisions of such a holy, heart-moving utterance. First of all, He repeated the single, filial term *Father* four times (17:1, 5, 21, 24), and there was no need of any addition. This favorite form of expression revealed the unbroken intimacy that existed between the everlasting Father and His everlasting Son. In the first part of His intercessory prayer, Jesus is found speaking to God about His past glory, present life and sacrifice, and future glory, and *Father* was the most appropriate form of address.

But with verse 9, there is a change, for if the first part of the prayer is *personal* (vv. 1-8), this second section (vv. 9-15) is *particular,* "I pray [not for Himself now] for them." Then the exclusion, "I pray *not* for the world, but for them which thou hast given me; for they are thine" (v. 9). Who are these upon whom Jesus focused prayer? Why, those redeemed by His blood which was the work the Father had given Him to do (v. 4). What was His burden in this part of His prayer? It was that His redeemed ones might be kept from evil in the world. He interceded for their sanctification, and so the term *Holy Father* was most fitting. It seems to say, "My Father because Thou art all-holy, I desire these My very own to be transformed into Thy likeness. Make them holy as Thou art holy." And this is the mission of Him who came as the *Holy* Spirit. Daily He seeks to sanctify us through the truth which He Himself inspired.

The next and last section of our Lord's intercessory commences with the phrase, "Neither pray I for these alone," namely, His own, His Church which He just prayed for in verses 9-19. From verse 20 to the end of the chapter His petition becomes *general* for He looks away down the vista of the ages and thinks of the multitudes in the world who will come to believe in Him through the witness of His own and thus intercedes for them using a different form of address and approach, namely –

7. *Righteous Father*

Why "O righteous Father" (17:25), and not "Holy Father" (v. 11)? This further couplet corresponds to the burden of His prayer in this remaining section. Had it not been for Calvary where divine righteousness was manifested, vindicated, satisfied, there would never have been a Gospel for His own to proclaim to a needy world. By His death and resurrection Christ was made unto us *Righteousness* and on such a basis guilty sinners can venture nigh and be saved. Further, is it not blessed to know that we have a heavenly Father who ever acts righteously and justly? In His dealings with His own redeemed children, yes, and with the multitudes who are not His, He can never act contrary to His own nature. In all His disciplinary dealing He is, and can never be anything else, but "righteous in all His ways." In the last verse of this most remarkable prayer ever prayed, Jesus said, "I *have* declared unto them thy name, and *will* declare it" (17:26). As a whole, the prayer supposes Calvary, and our Lord's ascension to heaven, as already accomplished. The *have* refers to the *past* unfolding of His Father's name (20:17). *Will* points to the *future* declaring of God's wondrous name from the coming of the Holy Spirit and on, throughout the age of Grace.

8. *Abba Father*

Abba, a term of simple affection is an Aramaic word for *Father,* found in Mark 14:36; Romans 8:15; Galatians 4: 6, approximates to a personal name, in contrast to *Father,* with which it is always joined in the New Testament.

> In us Abba, Father! cry;
> Earnest of our bliss on high;
> Seal of Immortality,
> Comforter Divine.

In Jewish and old-Christian prayers, it was a name by which God was addressed, then in oriental churches it became a title of bishops and patriarchs. The clerical term, *Abbot,* is a derivation of Abba. Slaves were not permitted to use this term in addressing the head of the family. W. E. Vine observes that, "*Abba* having practically become a proper name, Greek-speaking Jews added the Greek word *pater,* 'father,' *from* the language they used."

> *Abba* is the word framed by the lips of infants, and betokens unreasoning truth:
>
> *Father* expresses an intelligent apprehension of the relationship. The two together express the love and intelligence and confidence of the child.

> My God is reconciled,
>   His pardoning voice I hear;
> He owns me for His child,
>   I can no longer fear;
> With confidence I now draw nigh,
> And "Father, Abba, Father!" cry.

There are several more definite titles we can include under this section of *Actual or Personal Names.*

LORD OF ALL THE EARTH

Micah describes Him as, "The Lord of the whole earth" (4:13).

This imposing title declares God's authority and proprietorship of the world He created. Such a designation is implied in Jeremiah's testimony, "Forasmuch as there is none like unto thee, O Jehovah; thou art great, and thy name is great in might. Who would not fear thee, O King of Nations?" (10:6, 7). Twice in Joshua the above title is found (3:11-13), and once in Zechariah (6:5). Walter Scott remarks, "In taking possession of 'all the earth,' of which Canaan was the earnest and Joshua a type of the Lord in the taking of the inheritance, God selected this easily understood and fitting title, and under it the people crossed the Jordan and undertook the conquest of the land. When, however, the highly favored people would dare to connect God's blessed name and presence with their evil and idolatry, God could but leave the earth, had no longer a home or throne in it; thus the glory – the divine majesty and

divine presence – is witnessed by the prophet slowly passing away from Jerusalem to its native home (Ezekiel 1-11:11)."

Had God remained in the defiled temple on earth, or sanctioned the iniquity of the throne, Ezekiel depicts (chapter 8), He would have acted contrary to His holy character and tarnished His glory as God. But *such* was impossible. So long as His people were in captivity because of their iniquity and idolatry, He could not sanction by His *presence* their estimation of Him as "Lord of all the earth." Both Daniel and Nebuchadnezzar extol Jehovah as "God of Heaven," but *not* the "Lord of all the earth." This august title will be taken up when Israel's place of supremacy in the earth and amongst the nations is being made good during the millennium when the Lord will say of her, "Israel my Glory!" The last book of the Bible unfolds God's assertion of His right and title to the whole earth. Even the wicked, inspired by fear of divine judgment praise Him as the "God of heaven" (Revelation 16:11). He has every right to dwell and govern there, but when He assumes His power, and makes "the kingdoms of this world, His world-kingdom," and sets up His rule here below, then with the knowledge of His reign covering the earth, as the waters cover the sea, His title as "God of the earth" will be undisputed.

Yet there is a sense in which God has never relinquished His right as "Lord of the whole earth." Nations have divided the earth among themselves by war or annexation, and seek to rule the parts of it they possess, but He overrules for it is still *His world.* And He accomplishes His will, not only among the army of heaven, but the inhabitants of earth. It is still true that "the most High ruleth in the kingdom of men, and giveth it to whomsoever He will, and setteth up over it the basest of men" (Daniel 4:17). "Thy God *reigneth!*" Amid the sin and chaos of this blood-soaked earth, let us not lose sight of the present tense of such an affirmation. Yes, Daniel, we too believe that "the heavens do rule" (4:26).

GOD OF HEAVEN

Such a designation, occurring about 20 times in Scripture, 8 of these in Ezra, and twice only in the New Testament, namely in *the Revelation*, deserves to be particularly noted. Walter Scott reminds us that in the post-captivity books of the Old Testament, "God is owned as the *God of Heaven*, and as such He is. The expression *Kingdom of Heaven*, which occurs in the New Testament, and only in the Gospel of Matthew (about 30 times), has its root in Daniel 4; it is an important phrase in connection with the title *God of Heaven*. This divine, and to us exceedingly important title covers the period of time from the scattering of Judah by the first imperial power, until God again takes up the cause of the Jew."

Nebuchadnezzar, as well as Daniel, lauded the *God of Heaven;* but not the *Lord of all the earth* – a title only being taken up when Israel's place of supremacy in the earth and amongst the nations is being made good. The central part of the Book of Revelation is God's assertion of His right and title to earth; the consequence being days of wrath and terror upon man, especially upon apostate Judaism and Christendom. Such will be the fear which these judgments will inspire in the wicked that they will give glory to the *God of Heaven* (Revelation 11:13).

The frequency of this title in the Book of Ezra was a reminder to the returned remnant of Israel, returned from captivity in Babylon, that God who had permitted their sufferings, was indeed

caring for and watching over them. Secretly and providentially He had been and was undertaking for the remnant, if not actively "on their behalf from His throne in Jerusalem in *power*, not from His Temple in their midst in *grace*, then from His dwelling place above, hence, the appropriateness of the title, *God of Heaven.*" God acts *in* and *from* heaven, not *on* earth, save providentially, yet directs and controls all for the blessing of His own. When He begins to act publicly on behalf of Israel, He will do so under His Jehovah-title, "LORD of all the earth."

Presently men flout both the existence and authority of a God in heaven. In fact, there is a graveyard theology asserting that "God is dead!" But while the multitudes of earth live and act as if there were no God in heaven to fear, worship, love and obey, amid the casting away of all divine restraints we go back to the psalmist's daring assertion that God has a good laugh over man's effort to get rid of Him–

> "He that sitteth in the heavens shall laugh: The Lord shall have them in derision" (Psalm 2:4).

Faith finds consolation in the fact that, in one sense,

> "God's in His Heaven,
> All's right with the world."

The Book of Esther, in which the name of God in any shape or form does not once occur, reveals the secret actings of God; that He is in the shadows watching o'er His own. Although unseen as "the God of Heaven," nevertheless He is causing all things to work together for the present blessing of His own, making His hand felt, not only in the personal circumstances of your life and mine, but also in the governments and powers of our time. The world may be in a turmoil, with iniquity abounding, but our hearts repose in the call –

> "Be still, and *know* that I am God:
> I will be exalted among the heathen,
> I will be exalted in the earth"
> (Psalm 64:10).

Our "strength is to sit still" (Isaiah 30: 7). He is still "the God of Heaven" with His divine government being providentially exercised on earth.

> Be still, my soul: thy God doth
>   undertake;
> To guide the future as He has
>   the past.
> Thy hope, thy confidence let nothing
>   shake;
> All now mysterious shall be
>   bright at last,
> Be still, my soul: the waves and
>   winds still know
> His voice who ruled them while
>   He dwelt below.

JEALOUS

One can imagine eyebrows being raised at the inclusion of such an adjective relating to a somewhat disturbing human emotion among divine names and titles. Tragic forms of this hateful passion must have been in the mind of Charles Reade when he wrote, "The jealous always thirst for blood." Perhaps there is no word in our language more indicative of the ignoble, the ugly, the malign than *jealousy* which represents "a morbid sensitiveness lest we be deprived of something to which we suppose ourselves entitled, a painful solicitude lest we be outshone by the genius, beauty, or fortune of another." Dr. W. L. Watkinson goes on to say, "The word immediately suggests an exaggerated egotism, a readiness to infer the worst concerning man, a disposition to interpret trifles ungenerously, to begrudge the success of comrades, to taste a secret satisfaction in their failure."

Solomon, who knew all about jealous intrigues in court and harem, would have

us remember that, "A tranquil heart is the life of the flesh; but envy is the rottenness of the bones" (Proverbs 14:30 ASV). This emotion, when base, feeds upon itself and grows into intense venom and misery. Such a passion becomes fatal poison. To quote Solomon again, "Jealousy is cruel as the grave" (Song of Solomon 8:6). It can transform the noble into a monster, and is no respector of persons. Even clerics are vitiated by such poisonous venom. Yet this is the word God takes to Himself as a *name – Jehovah, whose name is Jealous* (Exodus 34:14).

Frequently in the Pentateuch, or the first five books of the Bible, God is given the title, *Jealous*. But its use in passages like Exodus 20:5; 34:14; Deuteronomy 5:9, does not bear the evil meaning we have just expressed. It signifies a righteous "zeal," Jehovah's zeal for His own name or glory. Thus we have Isaiah's phrase, "The zeal of Jehovah" (9:7). *See also* Zechariah 1:14; 8:2. To quote Dr. Watkinson again, "The jealousy of God is a solicitude for truth, purity, justice, righteousness. He is alive with a sensibility to holiness altogether beyond our utmost conception. . . . The Ten Commandments are so many definitions of the noble perfection of jealousy as it exists in Him. He is of too pure eyes to behold iniquity. He is concerned lest the darkness should invade His light, or dim the glory and joy of His children."

The Apostle Paul, who knew much about the mind of God, had the nobler aspect of jealousy in his thoughts when he wrote to the carnal Corinthians, "I am jealous over you with a godly jealousy," or, as the margin puts it, "with a jealousy of God" (2 Corinthians 11: 2, 3). Here Paul dares to say that his jealousy was *like that* of God. Meyer translates this Pauline phrase, "I am jealous over you with a jealousy *which*

God has; which is no human passion, but an emotion belonging to God, which I therefore have in common with Him." Can we say that the same motive that made Paul jealous for the faith and for the purity of the Church is ours? God is not jealous of another, for to Him there is no other. His name is *Jealous,* because He is concerned for His redeemed people lest they forfeit glory and peace through forsaking Him. In this respect the jealousy of Paul was a transcript of that of God. He shared the divine jealousy found in Zechariah's prophecy, "I am jealous for Jerusalem and for Zion with a great jealousy" (1: 14). May this "godly jealousy" which is love's purest, intensest flame be ours! John Donne, Christian poet of the 16th century in his *Holy Sonnets,* wrote –

> As Thou
> Art jealous, Lord, so I am jealous now,
> Thou lov'st not, till from living more,
> Thou free
> My soul: whoever gives, takes liberty:
> O, if Thou car'st not whom I love
> Alas, Thou lov'st not me.

II. SYMBOLIC DESIGNATIONS

A prominent characteristic feature of Scripture is the appealing way it has of clothing, with the garment of symbolism, its persons and precepts. Thus it abounds in types, symbols, emblems, or striking figures of speech, as helpful volumes like Bullinger's figures of Speech and Wilson's *Dictionary of Bible Types,* clearly prove. One reason why Scripture is highly figurative may be that it was written in the East where language is still somewhat picturesque. Another explanation may be that God, because of His infinitude, had to condescend to expressions of speech finite minds could understand, in order to make clear and plain His being, revelation, and purpose. This is why the prophets and our Lord had to speak

to people in parables (Ezekiel 17:2; 20:49; Matthew 13:24). And what is a *parable* but an earthly story with a heavenly meaning, just as symbols are as windows letting in spiritual light.

As designations of Deity are most numerous, all that we can do in this work is to briefly expound a selection of some that are used directly of God. Some of these have a double application, being employed to describe both God and the Lord Jesus as, for instance, in the figure of a *king.* What must be guarded against is the tendency to let imagination run riot, and find symbols where they don't actually exist, a practice common in the Middle Ages. Among attributes, figurative names, or designations expressing the power, the majesty, and the providence of God we have these –

ANCIENT OF DAYS (Daniel 7:9, 13, 22)

What a grandeur there is about this name of Deity which Daniel repeats three times over as if to stress the importance of thinking about it! The narrative describes a central throne shaped like a chariot with wheels as burning fire upon which the Judge sat whose name was "The Ancient of days." The prophet had been outlining the nature of four succeeding empires and then presents Jehovah as contrasted with "the ephemeral transitoriness of these four successive world powers, stable as they seemed for a time," but not as enduring as the *Ancient* One, the Judge of the whole world.

The Hebrew word used here for *Ancient* means advanced, that is, in age; hence old, aged, and used in connection with God it is not meant to suggest the existence of God from eternity. What was uppermost in Daniel's mind was the venerable appearance of old age. Thus, literally, the phrase "Ancient of Days" implies "a very aged man" – the attribute of age expressing the majestic figure of the Judge. "God . . . abideth of old" (Psalm 55:19). As the scholar, Keil says, "What Daniel sees is not the eternal God Himself, but an aged man, in whose dignified and impressive form God reveals Himself."

This One Ezekiel saw on a throne like a sapphire stone upon which there was "the likeness as the appearance of a man" (1:26). This same prophet refers to "ancients of the house of Israel" (8:12). *See* Jeremiah 19:1. Above the fleeting phases of life there sits One who remains eternally the same (Psalms 90:1-3; 102:24-27). The hair being white and pure as wool bespeaks of its owner as One who is holy and venerable, and coincides with John's vision of the glorified Jesus whose head and hairs were "white like wool, as white as snow" (Revelation 1:14).

Dazzling white raiment and beautiful white hair suggest the eternal being and age, the long existence of the honorable Occupant of the throne before whom an innumerable host stood in awe and adoration. These are characteristics of Christ, as the One, "the same yesterday, today, and forever" and "The Ancient of days" whom Daniel depicts. Identified, as they are, in action and character, it is not easy to distinguish them. Comparing the feature of the white head and hair, Walter Scott says, "The identification of Jesus with Jehovah; of the wearied Man, John 4:6, with the unwearied Creator, Isaiah 40:28 is a subject of profound interest. Divine wisdom in absolute purity seems, in the main, the thought intended by the dazzling white of the head and hair. In Daniel's passage, the whiteness of the head is not mentioned. In John's description the head is uncovered. Personal attributes are in question, and not official or relative glories, which latter are found in Revelation 1:16." Jesus the

Son of man is identified with *The Ancient of days* (Daniel 7:9; Revelation 1:13-16).

When Christ as the Son of man appears crowned and with a sickle to reap the harvest of earth He is depicted as One sitting on a cloud, and in this character He bears the attributes and moral glories of the Ancient of days (cf. Daniel 7:13 with Revelation 1:13, 14; 14:14). May we ever gratefully sing of Him who is –

> The Ancient of Days,
> Positioned with splendour,
> And girded with praise.

ROCK – *God in His Strength and Permanency*

As already indicated, the Bible was written in the East by men of the East and, therefore, many symbols used in Scripture were suggested by sights these men were accustomed to see in eastern lands. The mountains round about Jerusalem with their refreshing shade and shelter afforded travelers relief from the scorching heat of the desert sun. Prophets and psalmists, then, familiar with the protection value of rocks, would see more in God as their Rock than many of us can who probably have never seen a huge rock.

The American Standard Version margin translates Isaiah's description of God under this figure thus, "In Jehovah, even Jehovah is a rock of ages" (26:4). Doubtless it was this that prompted Toplady's great hymn (although another reason is given) –

> Rock of Ages, cleft for me,
> Let me hide myself in Thee.

In his song, Moses rebuked Israel for their idolatry in the words –

> "Of the Rock that begat thee thou art unmindful, and hast forgotten God that formed thee" (Deuteronomy 32:18).

In fact, in this notable chapter Moses speaks of the Rock five times –

> "The Rock of his salvation" (32:15) – The Source of Grace.
> "The Rock that begat thee" (32:18) – The Source of Life.
> "Their Rock that sold them" (32:30) – The Source of Ownership.
> "Their rock is not as our Rock" (32:31) – The Source of Perfection.
> "Their rock in whom they trusted" (32:37) – The Source of Failure.

Old Testament references to *Rock,* as a symbol of God's strength and stability occur frequently as the Bible concordance shows. The psalmist had a peculiar affection for it, "Thou art my rock" (Psalm 72:3); "He is my rock" (Psalm 92:15). *See* 62:5-8. This impressive figure of speech reveals God in His permanency and unchangeableness. The original word for *rock* is also translated as *strength.* "O LORD my strength" (Psalm 19:14) is given in the ASV as, "O Jehovah, my rock." The RV also has "rock." This unshakeable One was "The *strength* of Israel," and is "our strength" (Psalm 46:1). The saints of every age have proved Him to be the unchangeable and unchanging One amid all the changes life may bring. When we come to names and titles of Christ, fuller attention will be given to the spiritual significance of Him as *the Rock.* May we ever be found under our divine Rock in the weary land of this world!

> Thou art my Rock; when kingdom and nation,
> Ruler and Crown, have crumbled to dust;
> Thou shalt remain my Rock of salvation,
> Rock everlasting, Thee will I trust.

COVERT – *God as Our Protector and Comforter*

Alexander Pope, in *An Essay On Man,* wrote –

> Together let us beat this ample field,
> Try what the open, what the covert yield.

Let us try to find out what the figure of God as our *covert* can yield. We read that King Ahaz removed "the covert for the sabbath that they had built in the house" (2 Kings 16:18). The ASV gives "the covered way." Opinions differ as to what *covert* actually means here. A gallery belonging to the temple, the place where the king stood or sat during the Sabbath services, a public place for teaching, the way by which the priest entered the sanctuary on the Sabbath are some of the explantions given. The word itself, from which we have *cover* means a shelter of any kind (Isaiah 4: 6). It is used of a hiding place (Job 38: 40); a place of secrecy (1 Samuel 25: 20; Isaiah 16:4); a den, or lair (Jeremiah 25:38).

Applied to God, the symbol is a touching picture of His protection and loving care of those who rest in His presence, "I will take refuge in the covert of thy wings" (Psalm 61:4 ASV). Isaiah's double reference to this figure is suggestive – "Jehovah . . . a covering . . . a covert from storm and rain" (Isaiah 4: 5, 6 ASV). Perhaps this is a prophecy of Christ who is to come as "the branch of Jehovah" (4:2), just as "A man shall be as a hiding place from the wind, and a covert from the tempest" (Isaiah 32: 2). In Him, as our "place of secrecy" there is comfort, safety, rest, and care. Says Matthew Henry, "God is to all that seek Him and fly to Him an impenetrable Shelter."

> O God, our help in ages past,
> Our hope for years to come,
> Our shelter from the stormy blast,
> And our eternal home.

REFUGE – *God Is Our Haven from the Avenger*

Edmund Waller, a 16th century poet in describing Britain wrote –

Whether this portion of the world
　　were rent
By the rude ocean, from the continent,
Or thus created, it was sure designed
To be the sacred refuge of mankind.

The Pilgrim Fathers failed to find it a "sacred refuge" and the present, large immigration of Britishers to other parts of the world would seem to refute such a reputation of the country. No, the only "sacred refuge of mankind" is God, hence, the constant reference to Him as our REFUGE. The original Hebrew words for *refuge* are given as "High Tower," "Shelter," "Hope" (Psalm 9:9 ASV; 61:3 KJV; Jeremiah 17:17 KJV). In the marvelous promise, "The eternal God is thy refuge, and underneath are the everlasting arms" (Deuteronomy 33:27), the RV has "dwelling place" for *refuge*. This promise emphasizes a double safety for the saints. Not only is the everlasting God our Refuge, but His everlasting arms are around us. The margin at Joel 3:16 gives us "harbor" for "hope" or "refuge."

As the first reference to *refuge* in Scripture is in connection with the "six cities of refuge" Joshua set up as places of asylum cared for by the Levites to protect those who had shed blood unwittingly, perhaps we should interpret the figure of a *refuge* to God in the light of such a provision. "From time immemorial in the East, if a man were slain the duty of avenging him has lain as a sacred obligation upon his nearest relative." It was from such an avenger that the sought one fled to the city of refuge nearest him for protection. Here is a designation full of spiritual instruction (Numbers 35:9-15).

These asylums of safety were appointed by God (Isaiah 26:1). At every crossroad on the east and west of Jordan there was the notice REFUGE, and the manslayer knew that this was the place of appointed protection (Isaiah 30:21;

Zechariah 9:12). In like manner God is our only safety from the avenger. In Him we are secure from the judgment of the law. Through Christ's finished work, the safety of the believer is eternally secure (Zechariah 3:2; Galatians 3:3; Romans 8:1, 35-39). Other cities, of apparently greater strength, might have been nearer for the manslayer to flee to, but in them was no safety. It could only be found in those cities of refuge, divinely appointed. *See* Psalm 142:4, 5.

Other Refuge have I none,
Hangs my helpless soul on Thee.

Further, no "blood-money" could be paid in compensation for the murder committed, in settlement of the avenger's claim; nor could the refugee be ransomed, so that he might "come again to dwell in the land," until the death of the high priest (Numbers 35:22). God is our Refuge from the accusations and revenge of the satanic avenger, whoever seeks to devour us. How long are we secure from machinations to destroy us? All the time our Great High Priest lives! How long will that be? *For ever,* because He is alive for evermore.

O Rock Divine, O Refuge dear,
　　A Shelter in the time of storm!
Be Thou our Helper ever near,
　　A Shelter in the time of storm!

FORTRESS – *God as Our Defense Against the Foe*

How assuring is this further attributive title! "Jehovah is ... my fortress" (Psalm 18:2 ASV). "Jehovah . . . is a stronghold in the day of trouble" (Nahum 1:7 ASV). A fortress suggests war and conflict, and a defense from the foe. The names *Strong Tower* and *High Tower* as applied to God express a similar provision and purpose (Psalm 61:3; 144:2).

Why should I fear the darkest hour,

Or tremble at the tempter's power?
Jesus vouchsafes to be my Tower.

Under the image of a fortress often high up and inaccessible affording perfect safety from enemies and persecutors, the psalmist in particular, delighted to declare his trust and confidence in God. Jehovah, in virtue of His righteousness and righteous judgments, was indeed a *high tower* to the oppressed, and the place of security for all troubled hearts (Psalm 9:9 ASV).

Some 13 times in the Psalms, God is exalted as our fortress, or high tower, and a perusal of these references shows that when the writer exults in the protecting care and power of God, he multiplies designations to utter his confidence in divine security.

> " I love Thee, O Jehovah, my strength, Jehovah is my rock and my fortress ... my High Tower" (Psalm 18:1, 2).

Fortified though a city might be, Hosea predicted the destruction of fortresses by invading foes (Hosea 8:14; 10:14). Our divine Fortress, however, ever remains impregnable and indestructible for who is able to vanquish the Creator? When we come to Paul's teachings we find him often drawing upon methods of warfare, with which he was so familiar because of his close contact with the Roman army, to illustrate spiritual conflict and victory. The apostle would have us know that the ultimate object of our campaign against spiritual foes is the pulling down of *strongholds* (2 Corinthians 10:3-5). The Greek word used here is equivalent to the Hebrew for *fortress*. Abiding in Him who is our Fortress we have power to cast down imaginations, and every high thing that exalted itself against the knowledge of God. *See also* Ephesians 6:10-19.

A mighty Fortress is our God,
A Bulwark never failing:

Our Helper He, amid the flood
Of mortal ills prevailing.

SHIELD – *God a Preserver and Protector of His Children*

As we are discovering, Scripture furnishes us with a rich variety of impressive names and graphic pictures to reveal who and what our Lord actually is in regard to the protective safety and positive security of His redeemed children. Dr. C. J. Rolls, eminent Bible expositor, would have us know –

> "What wonderful assurance is derived from knowing that in all circumstances and under all conditions we have a Protector, a Provider, and a Preserver, an ever-present Shield and Defender, the ancient of days, pavilioned in splendour, environed in grandeur, exalted in honour, and enthroned in Glory. All power resides in the hand of this Potentate . . . David portrays Deity as the bastion of his defence in a score of ways ... My Strength, my Rock, my Fortress, my Deliverer, my Buckler, my Salvation, my High Tower, my Defence, my Habitation, my Refuge, my Shepherd."

From among these most descriptive figures of divine ability, we choose the *Shield* as being most impressive. Jehovah came to Abraham with this new revelation of Himself which the psalmist confirms –

> "I am thy shield, and thy exceeding great reward" (Genesis 15:1).
> "Thou, O Jehovah art a Shield about me" (Psalm 3:3 ASV).
> "Jehovah God is a . . . shield" (Psalm 84:11 ASV).
> "Thou art my hiding place and my shield" (Psalm 119:114).
> "A people saved by Jehovah, the shield of thy help" (Deuteronomy 33:29 ASV).

The RV gives "shield" for *buckler*. (Proverbs 2:7).

Though hot the fight, why quit the
field?
Why must I either fly or yield
Since Jesus is my mighty *Shield*.

The shield, the most ancient and universal weapon of defense, was in two varieties. The large shield, worn by heavy-armed artillery, adapted to the form of the human body, was made oval or in the shape of a door, hence the Greek name for shield, meaning "a door." Then there was the light, round hand-buckler, as those the men of Benjamin in Asa's army carried (2 Chronicles 14:8). The two kinds are often mentioned together (Psalm 35:2; Ezekiel 23:24). In his pride of wealth, Solomon boasted of having 200 shields of beaten gold, and 300 hand-bucklers of beaten gold made for himself, to hang in the forest house at Lebanon (1 Kings 10: 16, 17).

Shields were most necessary for use against besiegers who employed darts and stones and blazing torches to overcome the besieged (Isaiah 37:33; Ezekiel 26:8). Paul, in the description he gives of the panoply of the Christian soldier, spoke of *faith* as the large Greek-Roman shield, well able to quench the fiery darts of hellish forces. A shield was the part of a soldier's armor that not only warded off sword thrusts or all objects hurled against it, but was the means of defense between the soldier and his foe. Is it not blessed to know that as our *Shield*, God is between the enemy and ourselves, and that therefore no trial can overtake us apart from His permissive will?

Not a fiery dart can hit,
Till the God of love sees fit.

Behind Him as our *Shield*, the antagonisms of Satan, and accusations of men cannot injure us. May we ever gratefully sing of Him who is our "Shield and Defender" and

Our Maker, Defender,
Redeemer and Friend.

In Roman times, a perfectly plain shield was given to a young warrior in his maiden campaign, and was known as "The Shield of Expectation." As he achieved glory, his deeds were recorded or symbolized on it. God is ever "The Shield of Expectation" of His warriors, who fight the good fight of faith, and their names are inscribed upon His heart, just as the high priest in Israel bore the names of the tribes on his breast. Charles Wesley would have us sing –

Leave no unguarded place,
No weakness of the soul;
Take every virtue, every grace,
And fortify the whole . . .

But above all lay hold
On faith's victorious shield;
Armed with that adamant and gold,
Be sure to win the field:
If faith surround your heart,
Satan shall be subdued;
Repelled his every fiery dart,
And quenched with Jesus' blood.

SUN – *God Is the Source of Light
and Life*

There is no more graphic symbol used in Scripture to illustrate all that God is in Himself.

"For Jehovah God is a sun" (Psalm 84:11 ASV).
"The sun of righteousness shall rise, with healing in its wings" (Malachi 4:2 RSV).
"O Jehovah . . . let them that love him be as the sun when he goeth forth in his might" (Judges 5:31 ASV).
"I am the light of the world" (John 8:12).

If it were not for the sun, all the

other planets, including our own, could not exist. It is in the sun that the moon and the stars and our Earth live and move and have their being. The sun is the source of light, heat, and power, and the features pertain to Him who is the divine sun. The natural sun is the king of the planets, and its Creator is king or chief in all humanity and in all human affairs, and without His provision we could not exist. He is the source of our life and sustenance, as well as our salvation. Without Him we have nothing, are nothing, and can do nothing.

> I looked to Jesus, and I found
> In Him my Star, my Sun:
> And in that light of life I'll walk,
> Till travelling days are done.

By his remarkable mechanical inventions and indomitable courage man has conquered space, reached the moon and walked on its rugged surface, and is now ambitiously planning to gain a foothold on Mars. The sun, the great center of a vast aerial system, some 95,-000,000 miles from the earth in comparison with the moon's 240,000 miles, will ever remain beyond man's reach. With its diameter of almost 900,000 miles, the sun, which could easily contain our earth a million times over, is therefore a fitting simile of Him who presents Himself as a SUN. Man, with his finite mind, cannot possibly explore divine immensity for God's ways are beyond him and past finding out.

Among the many comparisons and contrasts we could make between the divine sun, and the one that governs the planets in their orbits, is the one our Lord drew attention to, namely, the abiding impartiality of the sun, the Creator made to shine by day. "God maketh His sun to rise on the evil and on the good" (Matthew 5:45). It is no respector of persons but provides its illuminat-ing, warming rays and life-giving properties for saint and sinner alike. God sheds forth His love in the same impartial beneficence, and His redeeming Gospel is the power unto salvation to everyone that believeth. His grace and mercy are for the worst as well as the best for He so loved the world of lost sinners as to give His Son to die for their redemption.

As wonderful vigor and vitality are dispensed by the heat and energy of the sun, may we be found constantly basking in Him who is our only source of spiritual light and power. May our hearts be daily quickened by the healing beams of the Sun of Righteousness! An essential feature of the sovereign rule of the sun above us is its exercise of sufficient strength capable of subduing all other authority and power, and an illumination exceeding the glow of all other luminaries in relation to earth. It is spoken of three times as being made *to rule* (Genesis 1:16-18). It is thus with Jehovah, our SUN for He is able to subdue all things unto Himself in the minor planets of your life and mine.

During the millennium, the Messiah will be seen as the Sun of Righteousness having healing beams benefiting the whole world. Then the prophecy of old will reach fulfillment, "His seed shall endure for ever, and his throne as the sun before me" (Psalm 89:36).

> We know the Sun of Righteousness,
> With healing in His wings
> Will rise, His chosen seed to bless,
> And reign as King of kings.

CROWN AND DIADEM – *God in His Sovereignty and Radiance*

What a precious designation of God Isaiah gives us in the chapter describing the woe of Ephraim when taken captive by the Assyrians! Twice over the prophet speaks of "the crown of pride," and also of "the refuge of lies," as being responsible for the fate of Ephraim (Isaiah 28:1, 3, 15, 17). But to the residue, the godly remnant among the godless, Isaiah says that "Jehovah of hosts (Jehovah-Sabaoth)" shall become "a crown of glory, and a diadem of beauty" unto the residue of his people (28:5 asv). "The crown of pride" was trodden under foot, and Ephraim's "glorious beauty" became "a fading flower" (28:3, 4), but for the faithful the Lord was to be as a glorious crown, and as a diadem of unfading beauty.

What a charming combination Isaiah gives us of Jehovah renowned for His luster and loveliness. A "crown of glory" is fitting for Him who is the "King of Glory," and whose righteousness is "radiant with excess of glory" (2 Corinthians 3:9-11 [Way]). as for His being "A Diadem of Beauty," His is the perfection of *beauty*. "How great is His beauty" (Zechariah 9:17). In the *crown*, there sparkles His excellence, worth, sovereignty and glory. In the *diadem*, His radiance, attractiveness, and fascination. Truly, He is incomparable! To whom can we liken Him? The wonder is that, greatly desiring our beauty, He waits to make us the recipients of all that He is in Himself. In His intercessory prayer, Jesus prayed that His God-given glory might adorn our lives (John 17:22). Do we wear such a crown? Is ours the unceasing determination to live and labor for the glory of God? Then, when the psalmist expressed the wish that the beauty of the Lord might be upon us, he was not referring to any physical beauty that can be impaired by disease or age, but to the radiancy, charm of character, His gracious Spirit alone can impart. How ugly and despicable are our vaingloriousness and sins of the flesh when contrasted with Him, whose price is above rubies!

I cannot gaze enough on Thee,
　Thou Fairest of the fair;
My heart is filled with ecstasy,
And in Thy face of radiancy
　I see such beauty there.

WALL OF FIRE – *God Who Compasseth Our Path*

The prophet Zechariah is the one who gives us a most forceful title of our God, who is a consuming fire.

"For I, saith Jehovah, will be unto her a wall of fire round about, and I will be the glory in the midst of her" (2:5 asv).

A "wall" is frequently used in Scripture as being figurative of protective forces surrounding us. Abigail learned that the men of David were gracious to the servants of churlish Nabal. "They were a wall unto us both by night and day, all the while we were with them keeping the sheep" (1 Samuel 25:16). And here is the prophet presenting the LORD as "a wall of fire" around His own. What a solemn promise of divine protection and preservation this is! Many were the trials and tribulations overtaking a covenant people in their city without walls between the days of Zechariah and the coming of Christ. But although hemmed in on every side by foes, abundant proof was given that God had not forgotten His promise to shield Jerusalem and His remnant within it. The Christ-glorifying hymn reminds us –

He'll never, never leave me, nor yet
　forsake me here,
While I live by faith, and do His
　blessed will;
A wall of fire about me, I've nothing
　now to fear,
With His manna, he my hungry soul
　shall fill.

Does not the psalmist declare that God compasseth our path and our lying down, and at the same time compasseth us about with songs of deliverance?

(Psalm 32:7; 139:3). What comfort and assurance are here for our hearts if alien forces are ganging up against us! In his valuable exposition of *Zechariah,* Dr. F. B. Meyer has the comment, "The image of 'a wall of fire' is probably borrowed from the camp-fires with which hunters surround themselves at night to scare off beasts of prey. Imagine what that means! Just as no pestilence, and certainly no intruder, could break through a cordon of flame, so the unseen but almighty presence of God would be a bulwark on which all the powers of earth and hell would break to their own undoing."

This is a sure promise the saints of God can claim no matter where they may be, even though it be in atheistic China or Russia where there are saints who gather in secret for fear of hostile foes. You may feel that you are like an unwalled town with nothing between you and poverty, or misfortune, or the attacks of false friends. Do not lose heart! If you are His redeemed child then you dwell within the devouring fire of God's presence, and are surrounded by the everlasting burnings of His protection. Has He not declared that "no weapon that is formed against thee shall prosper"? (Isaiah 54:17). With His protection and presence how blessed we are!

REFINER, PURIFIER – *God as the Remover of Dross*

What expressive titles these are that Malachi uses of God's sanctifying work, "He shall sit as a refiner and purifier of silver" (3:3). Silver represents atonement money (Leviticus 5:15), and as those who have received the atonement Christ made possible by His death and resurrection, we are indeed His sons, and as such in need of His refining ministry. Such precious ore as silver requires careful, delicate handling, hence,

the sitting posture of the refiner. God is never guilty of undue haste, and takes time to make us holy. Patiently He sits at the crucible of your life and mine removing all that is alien to His holy mind and will.

But note the double process of the silversmith. First, he is the *refiner,* tempering the fire so that all dross in the silver is separated and forced to the surface. Well, if the scum is left there, the silver would be pure. Secondly, then, the refiner becomes the *purifier,* as with a small ladle, the patient watcher skims the surface of the molten mass and removes the dross as it appears. When does the silversmith know when his silver is thoroughly refined and purified? Why, when he can see the reflection of his own face on the silvery surface! Is this not how the heavenly Refiner and Purifier works? Would that He could see His face more clearly reflected in our lives!

> Work on, then, Lord, till on my soul
>   Eternal light shall break,
> And, in Thy likeness perfected,
>   I "satisfied" shall wake.

HUSBAND – *God in His Providential Role*

Here we have a striking illustration of God, condescending to use a human relationship to express a further revelation of His nature, namely, His providential care. "Thy Maker is thy husband; Jehovah of hosts is his name" (Isaiah 54:5 ASV). The prophet provides us with a twofold glimpse of our *Jehovah-Sabaoth.* First, He is our Maker. "All things were made by Him." We often speak of "self-made men," but actually there are none for He it was who made and makes us and not we ourselves. As the Creator, He made man. Jesus said to His disciples, "Follow me, and I will make you ..." and in His service there are no self-made Christians – they are all Christ-made. Would that multitudes who forget their Maker knew how to bow before Him, allowing Him to fashion them after His will!

But then Jehovah is likewise a *Husband.* The reference is related to Israel who is often depicted as the "wife" of Jehovah (Hosea 2). How unfaithful she proved to be, going after other lovers, becoming guilty of whoredom, but her divine Husband is shown, striving to win back His faithless wife to His side, and woo her from all her evil wanderings! (Isaiah 54:5-10). Yet there is another side, is there not, to God's husbandhood? Does He not say through Jeremiah, "Leave thy fatherless children, I will preserve them alive; and let thy widows trust in me"? (49:11). This was the promise D. L. Moody's dear mother marked in her Bible, the day she lost her husband, and commenced a grim struggle to care for her children.

God imposed certain obligations upon Israel regarding widows, as did Paul in the early Church.

> "Jehovah . . . relieveth the fatherless and the widow" (Psalm 146:9).
> "I was a husband unto them, saith Jehovah" (Jeremiah 31:32 ASV).

Heaven alone will reveal how many godly widows proved God to be their Husband, when death robbed them of a human, loving, provident husband! Has death taken your dear partner and provider, and are heart and home vacant, and children left fatherless? Take courage, sorrowing one, for the Lord offers to fill that dear one's place with more of His own abiding presence, and be more to you than an earthly husband could ever be. May you prove Him to be as a husband in your widowhood!

(*See also* under BRIDEGROOM, chapter 2).

> Jesus, my Shepherd, *Husband,* Friend,
> My Prophet, Priest, and King,

> My Lord, my Life, my Way, my End
> Accept the praise I bring.

GOVERNOR – *God Who Rules by Love*

As we look at the distressed, troubled, and revolutionary world we live in it does not appear that God is ruling as its Governor. In fact, He is excluded from international and national councils. Yet here in the present tense is the commanding title the psalmist gives to Him who "doeth according to His will among the inhabitants of earth" –

> "For the kingdom *is* Jehovah's;
> And he *is* the governor [ASV gives 'ruler'] over the nations" (Psalm 22:28).

The term "governor" is from the original meaning "to rule" and is the same word used for Joseph whom Pharaoh appointed, "governor over all Egypt" (Genesis 42:6), and his history proves how just and fruitful his governance of the land was. The tragedy of human government today is that we have rulers who are incompetent to rule. Alexander Pope wrote about, "The right divine of kings to govern wrong," but we live in an age when those in positions of national government seem to have so little power to curb the rising tide of evil in so many forms. Philip Massinger in *The Bondsman* says, "He that would govern others, first should be the master of himself." Perhaps this is the reason why so many governors today cannot govern? They are not masters of themselves. How true are the lines of old John Fletcher of the 16th century –

> 'Tis virtue, and not birth that makes us noble:
> Great actions speak great minds, and such should govern.

God alone is the perfect Governor for His is the perfect mind, and His alone is the divine right to govern the nations with all their wrongs. When we come to the sections dealing with the names and titles of Christ, we shall find how the promises of divine governorship made to Israel are fulfilled in Him who was born to govern (Matthew 2:6). Presently we cling to the revelation that in spite of world chaos, *Jehovah reigns;* that "He is the Governor of the nations." Human governors may appear to rule, but He overrules for it is still *His* world. Ask yourself the personal questions, Does He govern the little world of my life? As God, is He my Governor whose rule I obey?

> Lord, what a holy blesséd reign
> Will encompass all the earth,
> When Thou shalt take Thy right
>   supreme.
> And Thy will be done on earth.

REDEEMER – *God Is the Emancipator of the Captives*

"Redemption" implies the bestowal of freedom, an entire change of state or condition, and therefore differs from "purchase" which intimates a change of masters. You may purchase a slave, but that is not deliverance from the state of slavery. When God speaks of His redemption of Israel, He made possible for her both a change of condition and masters.

"Their Redeemer is strong" (Proverbs 23:11 ASV), and it was because He was EL "the strong One" that He was able to plead the cause of His people against their foes. The margin of the ASV gives *vindicator* in Job's confession, "I know that my Redeemer liveth" (19:25). Isaiah gives a combination of divine titles in his confident assertion –

> "Our Redeemer, Jehovah of hosts is his name, the Holy One of Israel" (47:4).

The word "redeem" first appears in Scripture in connection with Jacob's blessing of his son Joseph, where the verb is in the present tense, "The Angel that redeemeth me from all evil" (Genesis 48:16). *Goel*, the Hebrew term for "redeem" came to be used as a description for the nearest blood relative, whose duty it was to avenge a murder. Jacob used it in its wider sense as a deliverer or saviour. *See* Exodus 6:6; Isaiah 59:20. The patriarch testifies that a divine Presence constantly guarded him, and was ever near as his Redeemer or Deliverer. A fuller significance, however, is associated with the word "redeem," when we come to Israel's deliverance from the bondage of Egypt. "Thou in thy mercy hast led forth the people which thou hast redeemed" (Exodus 15:13). In such a wonderful redemption causing Moses to sing, "Jehovah . . . hath triumphed gloriously," four aspects are notable –

1. *Its Source.*
Israel's redemption was wholly of God. "Jehovah said . . . I am come down to deliver thee" (Exodus 3:7-14; 6:7). It was with this announcement that there came the revelation of the august name JEHOVAH – I AM THAT I AM.

2. *Its Channel.*
Moses was the divinely chosen medium of such a deliverance, being divinely preserved for the task of Israel's emancipation (Exodus 3:11-14).

3. *Its Seal.*
God said on the last night of Israel's bondage, "I am Jehovah, and the blood shall be to you for a token upon your houses where ye are: and when I see the blood I will pass over you" (Exodus 12:12, 13, 21, 27).

4. *Its Power.*
When God responded to the prayer of Moses and promised, "I will redeem you with a stretched out arm, and with great judgments" (Exodus 6:6), He assured the leader of the demonstration of

His power. When the hour of judgment struck for Egypt, Israel was delivered, "By strength of hand the Lord brought us out from Egypt, from the house of bondage" (Exodus 13:14). When we study the titles of Christ we shall see how that in the redemption He provided by His death and resurrection, the same four features can be found. Unable to pay the price of our redemption from sin's penalty and power, "in His love and in His mercy He redeemed us."

> Redeemed! Creation joyful brings
> Its tribute to the King of kings:
> Redeemed! earth's million voices raise,
> One sounding anthem to His name.

KING – *God in His Unequaled Majesty*

That kings and kingdoms dominate the Bible can be seen from the fact that the term *king* occurs some 2,400 times, and *kingdom,* some 350 times. (See author's volume on *All the Kings and Queens of the Bible*). The first "kingdom" to be mentioned was that of Nimrod which he named *Babel* (Genesis 10: 10), and the first king of the Bible was a heathen, Amraphel, king of Shinar, grouped with other kings in Genesis 14: 1. Fascinated by the pomp and splendor of surrounding kings with their courts and palaces, Israel became dissatisfied with her theocratic state, serving and obeying an invisible sovereign. She wanted a visible, titular head, some autocratic and authoritative king to lead her. Thus the request was made to Samuel "Give us a king to judge us" (1 Samuel 8:6).

Such a request or demand meant that the people had not rejected Samuel who had acted as God's representative, but as Jehovah said, "They have rejected me, that I should not reign over them" (1 Samuel 8:7). Explicit was the condemnation of Israel, "When ye saw that Nahash the king of the children of Ammon came against you, ye said unto me,

Nay; but a king shall reign over us: when Jehovah your God was your king" (1 Samuel 12:12). Thus Saul became Israel's first king by her choice and by God's permissive will, "The king whom ye have chosen . . . Behold, Jehovah hath set a king over you" (1 Samuel 12:13).

Thereafter, as a monarchy with its successive kings as a united, and then divided, kingdom, God is more frequently mentioned as King. In the second Psalm, "The Psalm of the King," God said that over against the kings and rulers of earth, He would enthrone His King in the holy hill of Zion (Psalm 2:6) – a prophetic reference to Christ as we shall presently discover. The psalmist, although a king himself, loved to dwell upon the kingship of God. For instance, here are a few of his tributes –

> "Hearken to the voice of my cry, *my King,* and my God: for unto thee will I pray (5:2).
> "The Lord is *King* for ever and ever" (10:16).
> "For God is *my King* of old" (74: 12).
> "O LORD of hosts, *my King,* and my God" (84:3).

Solomon, the most glamorous king Israel ever had, said of Jehovah –

> "By me kings reign, and princes decree justice. By me princes rule, and nobles, even all the judges of the earth" (Proverbs 8:15, 16).

When King Uzziah, who did that which was right in the sight of Jehovah, died, Isaiah the prophet, who had had a deep regard for him, was sorely grieved. But through the royal grave there came the transforming vision, "I saw also the Lord sitting upon a throne high and lifted up, and his train filled the temple" (Isaiah 6:1). Earthly kings come and go, but God is "An everlasting king" (Jeremiah 10:10). He is "the King eternal, immortal, invisible, the only wise God," worthy of "honour and glory for ever and ever" (1 Timothy 1:17). He is also the august Sovereign Paul reminded Timothy of, "The blessed and only Potentate, the King of kings, and Lord of lords; who only hath immortality, dwelling in light unapproachable; whom no man hath seen, nor can see: to whom be honor and power eternal" (1 Timothy 6:15 asv).

The term *Potentate,* the only time in Scripture God is thus called, implies His almightiness, His inherent ability to perform anything and His power to accomplish His purpose no matter how thwarted by foes. Michael Drayton (who died in 1631) wrote in *The Barrons Wars* —

> The mind is free, whate'er afflict
>   the man;
> A King's a King, do Fortune what
>   she can.

Shakespeare in *King Lear* speaks of one who was "every inch a king." Because of all God is in Himself, and all His works He is indeed in "every inch" the King who merits and demands unquestioning obedience from His subjects.

> Oh, worship the King,
>   All-glorious above;
> Oh, gratefully sing
>   His power and His love:
> Our Shield and Defender,
>   The Ancient of Days,
> Pavilioned in splendor,
>   And girded with praise.

Doubtless there are other symbolic designations of God we might have cited as, for example, His likeness to a *lamp, friend, horn, stay, mountain,* etc., but a sufficient number have been dealt with to prove the inexhaustible fullness to be found in Him for our hearts today. As "the King of the ages" (Revelation 15:3), He is *the* King for our age with all its perplexing problems and governmental ineptitude. Would that the rulers

of the nations could be found recognizing Him as the King of the nations and be united in making known the glory of the majesty of His everlasting kingdom! (Psalm 145:11-13).

"Happy is the people whose God is Jehovah" (Psalm 144:15 asv).

It is to be hoped that our coverage of the great names and titles of God has proven beneficial to the reader as a revelation and manifestation of Him, whom to know is life eternal. Taken together they designate His various relations to men, and are but different facets of the glory of His being. As Professor W. G. Moorehead expresses it —

> "My father is a man; he is likewise a citizen, an office-bearer, and a man of affairs. But he is especially my father, without ceasing to maintain his other relations. God is Creator, Sovereign and Judge; but He is the Father of believers without ceasing to be all that is implied in the other titles He takes."

SUMMARY OF DIVINE NAMES AND TITLES IN ALL OLD TESTAMENT BOOKS

Well over 90 years ago there appeared a set of small volumes known as *The Bible Student* which were made up of studies for intercommunication on biblical subjects amongst young Christians, and produced by the then editor of a magazine called *The Young Believer.* For over half a century students have found these wonderful studies of great value in searching the Scriptures. In Volume One of the series, there is one section setting forth the result students arrived at in the classification of divine names and titles in the Old Testament. Attention was drawn to the fact that it was found practically impossible fully to classify the names and titles of Jehovah, especially when looked at as applying to Christ because although the New Testament shows us that it is the Son who ever carries out the Father's will, and that this Son is the same as the *I AM*, or Jehovah of the Old Testament, inasmuch as Father, Son and Holy Spirit as one is a revelation distinctive of New Testament Christianity, the difference between God the Father and God the Son is not generally brought out in the Old Testament.

It is God who acts but often as JEHOVAH God – LORD God – so that while the names and titles of Christ can be satisfactorily worked out, those of God cannot be so clearly defined. A cited list is given of the more remarkable titles of Jehovah given in each book of the Bible, which are doubtless applicable to Christ. What must be borne in mind is that *titles* and *types* are quite distinct. Feeling that the comprehensive survey given might be helpful to present day students of the Word, we have adapted somewhat the list given in *The Bible Student*, Volume 1. Titles of Christ are more fully dealt with in our next section.

GENESIS
Titles of Christ – The Woman's Seed, Abraham's Seed, The LORD (chap. 18), Shiloh, Shepherd of Israel, Stone of Israel.
Titles of God – The God of Bethel, The Lord and Judge of all the Earth, Him That Liveth and Seeth, The Lord Will Provide.

EXODUS
Titles of Christ – No titles, but types can be found.
Titles of God – The Lord God of Your Fathers, The God of Abraham, of Isaac, and of Jacob, I AM THAT I AM, The Lord God of the Hebrews, Jehovah, The

Lord God, the God of Israel, The Lord My Banner.

LEVITICUS
Titles of Christ – None, but various types.
Titles of God – LORD, printed in capital and small capitals throughout the book is consistently given as JEHOVAH by the American Standard Version, and as the God of Holiness, He dominates its pages.

NUMBERS
Titles of Christ – Star, Sceptre, He That Shall Have Dominion.
Titles of God – No particular ones apart from LORD – JEHOVAH.

DEUTERONOMY
Titles of Christ – Prophet. Also Types.
Titles of God – Rock of His Salvation, The Rock, LORD of Lords, The Shield of Help, The Sword of Excellency.

JOSHUA
Titles of Christ – Captain of the Lord's Host.
Titles of God – LORD GOD-JEHOVAH ELOHIM, The LORD God of Israel (repeated), The Lord Our God, The Lord Your God (repeated).

JUDGES
Titles of Christ – None, unless He is "the Angel of Jehovah."
Titles of God – The Lord God of Israel, The Lord the Judge, The Lord Sends Peace.

RUTH
Titles of Christ – None, but types – Kinsman, Redeemer.
Titles of God – The Lord God of Israel, The Almighty.

1, 2 SAMUEL
Titles of Christ – None, but several types.
Titles of God – The Lord of Hosts,

The Lord God of Israel, The Lord Strength of Israel, Rock, Fortress, Deliverer, Shield, Horn of My Salvation, High Tower, Refuge, Saviour, Lamp, Tower of Salvation.

1, 2 KINGS
Titles of Christ – None, but various types.
Titles of God – Lord of Hosts, Lord God of Israel, The Lord the God of David.

1, 2 CHRONICLES
Titles of Christ – Chief Ruler and types.
Titles of God – Lord God of Israel, Lord of Hosts, Lord God of Abraham, Isaac, and Israel, Lord God of Heaven.

EZRA
Titles of Christ – None.
Titles of God – Lord God of Heaven, Lord God of Israel.

NEHEMIAH
Titles of Christ – None.
Titles of God – Lord, Lord God of Heaven, The Great, the Mighty, and Terrible God, LORD Their God.

ESTHER
No Titles of God or Christ, yet typical.

JOB
Titles of Christ – Redeemer, Daysman.
Titles of God – Maker, Holy One, Preserver of Men, The Almighty.

PSALMS
Titles of Christ –
First Section, 1-41.
The Lord's Anointed, My King, My Son, The Son, Man, The Son of man, Thine Holy One, Head of the Heathen, Seed of David, A Worm, No Man, A Reproach of Men, The Afflicted, King of Glory, The Lord Strong and Mighty, The Lord Mighty in Battle, The Lord of Hosts, A Reproach Among All Mine Enemies, A Fear to Mine Acquaintance,

Thy Servant, The Righteous, This Poor Man.

Second Section, 42-72.
The King, Mighty, God, Most High, Lord of Hosts, A Great King, A Stranger, An Alien, Servant.

Third Section, 78-150.
The LORD, A Priest for Ever, The Stone, The Head Stone of the Corner.

Titles of God – Lord of Hosts, Shepherd of Israel, Lord God of Israel, Lord God of My Salvation, Lord Our Maker, Lord of lords, Refuge, Strength, Fortress, Most High, Habitation, Defence, Jehovah, High Tower, The Lord Our Shield, Holy One of Israel, God, Their Rock, The High God, Their Redeemer, Sun, Shield.

PROVERBS
Titles of Christ – Wisdom, Friend.
Titles of God – Jehovah, Maker, Redeemer.

SONG OF SOLOMON
No titles of Christ or of Jehovah.
Types of Christ – The King, Bundle of Myrrh, A Cluster of Camphire, My Beloved, A Roe or Young Hart, Him Whom My Soul Loveth, The Chiefest Among Ten Thousand, My Friend.

ISAIAH.
Titles and Types of Christ – The Lord, Immanuel, Child, Son, Wonderful, Counsellor, The Mighty God, The Everlasting Father, The Prince of Peace, A Rod, A Stem, A Branch, Holy One of Israel, Crown of Glory, Diadem of Beauty, A Foundation, Branch of the Lord, Redeemer, The King, Arm of the Lord, Man of Sorrows, Righteous Servant, A Covenant of the People, A Light of the Gentiles, A Witness of the People, A Leader and a Commander to the People, Ensign, My Servant, Mine Elect, A Polished Shaft, Angel of His Presence, Glory of the Lord, Zion's Salvation.

Titles of God – Holy One of Israel, Redeemer, Saviour, The First, The Last, A Sure Foundation, Holy One of Jacob, The Ring, Creator of the Ends of the Earth, Feeder of Israel, Husband of Israel, King of Jacob, Mighty One of Israel, Judge, Lawgiver, Creator of All Things, Hope of Israel, Everlasting God, Creator of Israel.

JEREMIAH; LAMENTATIONS

Titles of Christ – A Righteous Branch, A King, David Their King, Branch of Righteousness.

Titles of God – The Lord Our Righteousness, Their Redeemer, King, Hope of Israel, Saviour, Strength, Fortress, Refuge, Holy One of Israel, The Lord the Enemy.

EZEKIEL

Titles of Christ – My Servant David, A Prince, A Shepherd, Plant of Renown.

Titles of God – Holy One of Israel, Lord GOD, The Almighty, God of Israel, Jehovah.

DANIEL

Titles of Christ – A Stone Cut Out Without Hands, Prince of Princes, The Most Holy, Messiah the Prince, Messiah, One Like Unto the Son of God, One Like the Son of Man.

Titles of God – The King of Heaven, God of Heaven, The Great God, God of gods, God of Shadrach, Meshach, and Abednego, The Most High God, God of Daniel, The Living God, The Ancient of Days, The Great and Terrible God.

HOSEA

Titles of Christ – David their King, Redeemer from Death.

Titles of God – Lord Most High, Maker, Holy One, Saviour King, Lord Their God, A Lion, A Young Lion, A Leopard, Lord God of Hosts.

JOEL

Titles of Christ – None.

Titles of God – Hope of His people, The Strength of Israel, Lord Your God.

AMOS

Titles of Christ – None, but probably types.

Titles of God – Lord God, God of Hosts, Jehovah Is His Name.

OBADIAH

Titles of Christ – None.

Titles of God – The Lord God.

JONAH

Titles of Christ – None, but typical.

Titles of God – God of Heaven, Lord His God, Lord God.

MICAH

Titles of Christ – Ruler in Israel.

Titles of God – Tower of the flock, Judge of Israel, Lord of Hosts, God of Judah, A God Like Unto Thee.

NAHUM

Titles of Christ – None. Type in 1:15.

Titles of God – God Is Jealous, The Lord of Hosts.

HABAKKUK

Titles of Christ – None.

Titles of God – Holy, Lord of Hosts, Lord my God, Holy One, Lord God my Strength.

ZEPHANIAH

Titles of Christ – None.

Titles of God – Just Lord, Lord of Hosts, King of Israel, Lord God, God of Israel, Lord Thy God.

HAGGAI

Titles of Christ – Desire of All Nations.

Titles of God – Lord God, Lord of Hosts, Lord Their God.

ZECHARIAH

Titles of Christ – My Servant, The Branch, A Priest, My Shepherd, The Man, My Fellow, Zion's King.

Titles of God – Lord of Hosts, King, Lord of Whole Earth, Lord Your God, Lord My God.

MALACHI
Titles of Christ – Messenger and Covenant, Refiner of Silver, Sun of Righteousness.

Titles of God – Lord of Hosts, God of Israel, God of Judgment, Great King, Father-Creator, The Lord Changing Not.

Truly the mind is staggered at such a plethora of divine names and titles all of which are necessary to reveal the might and majesty of Him who is greater than them all. "Great is our Lord, and of great power: his understanding is infinite" (Psalm 147:5). Describing those of imperishable memory Wordsworth wrote –

> Methinks their very names shine
>   still and bright;
> Apart – like glow-worms on a
>   summer's night.

Although given millenniums ago, the "victorious names" of God still shine bright amid the gathering darkness of the world, and for the child of God are constant reminders of all that He is in Himself, and all that He is able to accomplish in and through the lives of them who, knowing His names, put their trust in Him. Rotherham's translation of Solomon's affirmation reads –

> "A tower of strength is the name of Jehovah, there into runneth the righteous and is safe" (Proverbs 18:10).

May we be found running into all of Jehovah's expressive names proving that as "is His name, so is He"! In *King Henry IV*, Shakespeare asks, "I would thou and I knew where a commodity of good names were to be bought." Scripture alone tells us where a commodity of good names can be found, but not bought, for all they represent is ours for the asking and appropriation.

Chapter 2

THE NAMES AND TITLES OF
GOD THE SON

THE NAMES AND TITLES OF GOD THE SON

HIS NAMES AND TITLES

Coming to the New Testament we find the absence of the variety and number of names of Deity so characteristic of the Old Testament. Two prominent ones corresponding to the many we have considered are God and Lord. The most frequently used is *God,* occurring over 1,000 times in the 27 books forming the New Testament, and is the equivalent of *El,* "The Strong One," and *Elohim,* "the title of the Creator and Ruler of the world, as such, and indicating the power and majesty of that Being to whom every creature owes his existence, his daily life, and his habitation."

The Greek word used for *God,* is *theos,* from which the term "theology," meaning the science or knowledge of God, is derived. Dr. E. Bullinger, commenting on the appearance of *theos* says, "The Greek language, being of human origin, utterly fails – and naturally so – to exhibit the wonderful precision of the Hebrew inasmuch as the language necessarily reflects, and cannot go beyond the knowledge, or rather the lack of knowledge, of the divine Being apart from revelation."

In its true sense *Elohim* expresses essential Deity, and as expressive of such it is applied to the Son and to the Father. "My Lord and my God" (John 20:28). "Christ...who is over all, God blessed for ever" (Romans 9:5).

Then the ever-recurring title *Lord* is likewise largely employed by New Testament writers of the Son of God. Five times over the translation of one of the original words for *Lord* – "despotes," from which *despot* is derived, is used. "*Lord,* now lettest thou thy servant depart in peace" (Luke 2:29). *See also* Acts 4:24; 2 Peter 2:1; Jude 4; Revelation 6:10. Each case emphasizes sovereignty, and corresponds to *Adonai,* the possessive plural of *Adon* which means, "The Absolute Owner of All." But the most common Greek word for *Lord* is Kúrios, occurring upwards of 600 times in the New Testament, and which corresponds to *Jehovah* and *Adonai,* of old. This particular word is applied to Christ equally with the Father and the Holy Spirit, revealing that "the Messianic hopes conveyed by the name *Jehovah* were, for New Testament writers, fulfilled in Jesus Christ; and that in Him the longed-for appearance of *Jehovah* was realized."

Other actual and attribute names of God find a mention such as "Most High"; "The Highest"; "The Almighty"; "Father"; "King"; "King of kings." But the dominant name in the New Testament is *Jesus,* "the *only* name under heaven given among men, whereby they can be saved." While we do not have the array of fascinating names and titles revealed to the ancient prophets, Jesus became *God-Elohim* – manifest in the flesh."

Veiled in flesh the Godhead see:
Hail th' Incarnate Deity.

The *Jehovah* of the Old Testament revealed Himself in the person of His Son, Jesus Christ the Lord. As H. Webb-Peploe says, "We have but to look upon the Lord Jesus Christ as *Jehovah,* and endeavour to realize Him in all His beauties and perfection, to see that every one of the Old Testament titles is to be embodied in Him." This goes to prove that –

The New is in the Old contained,

The Old is by the New explained.

The Bible presents us with a formidable list of titles of God the Son, describing the various aspects of His life, redemptive work, and millennial reign. There are prophetical and figurative designations of His character and mission; metaphorical titles descriptive of His divine and human natures. Perhaps all of these could be grouped around Pre-Incarnation Titles and Names; Incarnation Titles and Names as used by and of Christ while on the earth; Post-Incarnation Titles and Names, or those employed by the apostles in the Acts, the epistles, and the Revelation. All the names and titles used of Christ represent the different *relationships* which are sustained by Him, and are most varied as we shall see. The solemn symbolism of these designations forges the Old and the New Testaments into one book, for no sooner do we open the New Testament than we read its first name *Jesus,* or *Jah, Hoshea* – "Jehovah, my Saviour" (Matthew 1:1, 21). He likewise comes to us as *Elohim* – His name shall be called "Emmanuel, *God-Elohim,* with us." Christ came as the personal and full revelation of all that God's designations implied in the past. Now "every tongue should confess that Jesus Christ is *Jehovah,* to the glory of God the Father" (Philippians 2:11).

Apart from the above classification of Christ's names and titles, several other classifications are given by different writers, as a comparison of works like Dr. B. B. Warfield's *The Lord of Glory, The Name Above Every Name* by Dr. Charles J. Rolls, and *Titles of The Triune God* by Herbert F. Stevenson will show. Among our own envelope notes and cuttings on names, we came across the following tabulation but alas! cannot remember where it was clipped from,

many, many years ago. As it is a somewhat unique and suggestive arrangement we insert it here for the benefit of students –

The Names, Titles, and Characteristics of the Son of God, Jesus Christ Our Lord, in their Variety as Found in the Scriptures.

"They are they which testify of Me."

The headings are designed to direct the mind to various aspects of the Person, and glories of the Lord. Examine each text with the context, to find proof that the Son of God is the speaker, or the One spoken of.

1. *And Simon Peter answered and said, Thou art the Christ the SON of the living God* (Matthew 16:16).

The Son ....1 John 4:14.
The Son of God ....John 1:34.
The Son of the Living God ...Matthew 16:16.
His Only Begotten Son .....John 3:16.
The Only Begotten Son of God ..John 3:18.
The Son of the Father ....2 John 3.
The Only Begotten of the Father .....John 1:14.
The Only Begotten Son Which Is in the Bosom of the Father .....John 1:18.
The First Born of Every Creature ....Colossians 1:15.
His Own Son ....Romans 8:32.
A Son given ....Isaiah 9:6.
One Son (His well beloved) Mark 12:6.
My Son ....Psalm 2:7.
His Dear Son (or the Son of His Love) .....Colossians 1:13.
The Son of the Highest .....Luke 1:32.
The Son of the Blessed ....Mark 14:61.

Testimony borne to the SON by the Father, by Jesus Himself, by the Spirit, by Angels, Saints, Men, and Devils.

My Beloved Son, Matthew 17:5 ......
    God the Father.

I Am the Son of God, John 10:36 .....
    Jesus Himself.

The Son of God, Mark 1:1 ...The Spirit
    in the Word.

The Son of God, Luke 1:35; 2:11 .....
    Gabriel.

This Is the Son of God, John 1:34 .....
    John the Baptist.

The Christ the Son of God, John 20:31
    .....Apostle John.

He Is the Son of God, Acts 9:20 ......
    Apostle Paul.

Thou Art the Son of God, Matthew 14:
    33 .....Disciples.

Rabbi, Thou Art the Son of God, John
    1:49 .....Nathanael.

The Christ Is the Son of God, Acts 8:37
    .....Ethiopian Eunuch.

Truly This Was the Son of God, Mark
    15:39 .....Centurion.

Thou Art the Son of God, Mark 3:11
    .....Unclean Spirits.

Thou Son of the Most High God, Mark
    5:7 .....The Legion.

2. *Unto the Son He saith, Thy throne,
    O God, is for ever and ever* (He-
    brews 1:8).

God ...John 1:1; Matthew 1:23; Isaiah
    40:3.

Thy Throne, O God, Is For Ever and
    Ever ....Hebrews 1:8.

The Mighty God ....Isaiah 9:6.

The True God ....1 John 5:20.

My Lord and My God .....John 20:28.

God My Saviour ....Luke 1:47.

Over All, God Blessed Forever, Amen
    .....Romans 9:5.

The God of the Whole Earth ...Isaiah
    54:5.

God Manifest in the Flesh ....
    1 Timothy 3:16.

Our God and Saviour (*marg.*) ....
    2 Peter 1:1.

The Great God, and Our Saviour Jesus
    Christ .....Titus 2:13.

Emmanuel, God With Us ....Matthew
    1:23.

The God of Abraham, The God of Isaac,
    The God of Jacob .....Exodus
    3:2, 6.

The Highest ....Luke 1:76.

As to the angel of the Lord who
spake as the God of Abraham being the
Son of God, compare Judges 13:18-22,
(*marg.*) with Isaiah 9:6; also Daniel
3:25, 28.

3. *Verily, verily, I say unto you, be-
    before Abraham was, I AM* (John
    8:58).
    *Holy, Holy, Holy is JEHOVAH
    of hosts* (Isaiah 6:3).

Jehovah ....Isaiah 40:3.

The Lord Jehovah ....Isaiah 40:10.

Jehovah my God ....Zechariah 14:5.

Jehovah of Hosts ....Isaiah 6:3;
    John 12:41.

The King Jehovah of Hosts .....Isaiah
    6:5.

Jehovah, Mighty in Battle ....Psalm
    24:8.

The Man, Jehovah's Fellow ...Zechariah

Jehovah-Tsidkenu (the Lord Our Righ-
    teousness) .....Jeremiah 23:6.

The Lord .....Romans 10:13; Joel 2:32.

The Lord of Glory ...1 Corinthians 2:8.

The Same ....Hebrews 1:12; Psalm
    102.27.

I am (before Abraham was) .....John
    8:58.

I am (whom they sought to kill) .....
    John 18:5, 6.

I am (the Son of Man lifted up) .....
    John 8:28.

I am (the Resurrection and the Life)
    .....John 11:25.

4. *He is before all things, and by
    HIM ALL things consist* (Colos-
    sians 1:17).

The Almighty, Which Is, and Which

Was, and Which Is to Come ...
Revelation 1:8.

The Creator of all things ....Colossians 1:16.

The Upholder of All Things ...Hebrews 1:3.

The Everlasting Father (or Father of Eternity) ....Isaiah 9:6.

The Beginning ....Colossians 1:18.

The Beginning and the Ending ....
Revelation 1:8.

The Alpha and the Omega ....
Revelation 1:8.

The First and the Last ....
Revelation 1:17.

The Life ....1 John 1:2.

Eternal Life ....1 John 5:20.

That Eternal Life Which Was with the Father .....1 John 1:2.

He That Liveth ....Revelation 1:18.

5. *No man hath seen God at any time, . . . he hath DECLARED HIM* (John 1:18).

The Word ....John 1:1.

The Word Was with God ....John 1:1.

The Word Was God ....John 1:1.

The Word of God ...Revelation 19:13.

The Word of Life ....1 John 1:1.

The Word Was Made Flesh .....John 1:14.

The Image of God ...2 Corinthians 4:4.

The Image of the Invisible God ....
Colossians 1:15.

The Express Image of His Person ....
Hebrews 1:3.

The Brightness of His Glory ...Hebrews 1:3.

Wisdom ....Proverbs 8:12, 22.

The Wisdom of God .....1 Corinthians 1:24.

The Power of God ....
1 Corinthians 1:24.

My Messenger ....Isaiah 42:19.

The Messenger of the Covenant ......
Malachi 3:1.

The Angel of Jehovah ...Genesis 22:15.

The Angel of God ...Genesis 31:11, 13; Exodus 14:19.

The Angel of His Presence .....Isaiah 63.9.

6. *Thou hast made Him a LITTLE LOWER than the angels* (Hebrews 2:7).

The Man ....John 19:5.

The Man Christ Jesus ...1 Timothy 2:5.

A Man Approved of God ....Acts 2:22.

The Second Man, the Lord from Heaven .....1 Corinthians 15:47.

The Son of Man ....Mark 10:33.

The Son of Abraham ....Matthew 1:1.

The Son of David ......Matthew 1:1.

The Son of Mary ....Mark 6:3.

The Son of Joseph (reputed) .....John 1:45.

The Seed of the Woman ......Genesis 3:15.

The Seed of Abraham .....Galatians 3: 16, 19.

Of the Seed of David ....Romans 1:3.

7. *Lo, I COME to do thy will, O God* (Hebrews 10:9).

The Babe ....Luke 2:12.

The Child ....Isaiah 7:16.

The Young Child ......Matthew 2:20.

A Child Born ....Isaiah 9:6.

The Child Jesus ....Luke 2:43.

Her First Born Son ....Luke 2:7.

The Sent of the Father ....John 10:36.

The Apostle ....Hebrews 3:1.

A Prophet ....Acts 3:22, 23.

A Great Prophet ....Luke 7:16.

The Prophet of Nazareth .....Matthew 21:11.

A Prophet, Mighty in Deed and Word .....Luke 24:19.

A Servant ....Philippians 2:7.

The Servant of the Father ....Matthew 12:18.

My Servant, O Israel .....Isaiah 49:3.

My Servant, the Branch .....Zechariah 3:8.

My Righteous Servant ...Isaiah 53:11.
A Servant of Rulers ....Isaiah 49:7.
A Nazarene ....Matthew 2:23.
The Carpenter ...:.........Mark 6:3.
The Carpenter's Son (reputed) ......
Matthew 13:55.

He humbled Himself unto death.

A Stranger and an Alien ...Psalm 69:8.
A Man of Sorrows ....Isaiah 53:3.
A Worm, and no Man .....Psalm 22:6.
Accursed of God, or the Curse of God
(*marg.*) ....Deuteronomy 21:23.

8. *God hath ... given Him A NAME which is above every name* (Philippians 2:9, 10).

Jesus ....Matthew 1:21.
Jesus Himself ....Luke 24:15.
I, Jesus ....Revelation 22:16.
A Saviour, Jesus ....Acts 13:23.
The Saviour of the World ...1 John 4:14.
A Saviour, Which Is Christ the Lord ...
Luke 2:11.
Jesus Christ ....Revelation 1:5.
The Lord Jesus Christ ...Colossians 1:2.
Our Lord Jesus Christ Himself ....
2 Thessalonians 2:16.
Jesus the Christ ....Matthew 16:20.
Jesus Christ our Lord ...Romans 5:21.
Jesus Christ the Righteous ...1 John 2:1.
Jesus Christ, the Same Yesterday, and Today, and Forever ...Hebrews 13:8.
Jesus of Nazareth ....Acts 22:8.
Jesus Christ of Nazareth .....Acts 4:10.
Lord Jesus ....Acts 7:59.
Christ Jesus ....1 Timothy 1:15.
Christ ....Matthew 23:8.
Messiah, Which Is Called Christ ......
John 4:25.
Anointed ....Psalm 2:2; Acts 4:26.
Christ, the Lord ....Luke 2:11.
The Lord Christ ......Colossians 3:24.
The Christ of God ....Luke 9:20.

The Lord's Christ ....Luke 2:26.
The Christ, the Son of the Blessed ...
Mark 14:61.
The Christ, the Saviour of the World ...
John 4:42.

9. *Worthy is the LAMB that was slain to receive Power, and Riches, and Wisdom, and Strength, and Honor, and Glory and Blessing* (Revelation 5:12).

The Lamb of God ....John 1:29.
A Lamb Without Blemish and Without Spot ....1 Peter 1:19.
The Lamb That Was Slain ...Revelation 5:12.
A Lamb As It Had Been Slain ....
Revelation 5:6.
The Lamb in the Midst of the Throne
Revelation 7:17.
The Lamb (the Bridegroom) .....Matthew 9:15; Revelation 21:9.
The Lamb (the Temple of the City) ...
Revelation 21:22.
The Lamb (the Light of the City) ....
Revelation 21:23.
The Lamb (the Governor) ...Revelation 7:14.

10. *I will set up ONE SHEPHERD over them, and he shall feed them* (Ezekiel 34:23).

One Shepherd ....John 10:16.
Jehovah's Shepherd ....Zechariah 13:7.
The Shepherd of the Sheep ....Hebrews 13:20.
The Way ....John 14:6.
The Door of the Sheep .....John 10:7.
The Shepherd of Israel .....Ezekiel 34:23.
The Shepherd and Bishop of Souls ...
1 Peter 2:25.
The Good Shepherd (that laid down His Life) ....John 10:11.
The Great Shepherd (that was brought again from the dead) ......Hebrews 13:20.
The Chief Shepherd (that shall again

appear) ....1 Peter 5:4.

11. *The TREE OF LIFE which is in the midst of the paradise of God* (Revelation 2:7).

The Root of Jesse ....Isaiah 11:10.
The Root of David ....Revelation 5:5.
The Root and Offspring of David .....
    Revelation 22:16.
A Rod Out of the Stem of Jesse ...Isaiah 11:1.
A Branch Out of His Roots ....Isaiah 11:1.
The Branch ....Zechariah 6:12.
The Branch of the Lord ....Isaiah 4:2.
The Branch of Righteousness ....
    Jeremiah 33:15.
A Righteous Branch ....Jeremiah 23:5.
The Branch Strong for Thyself ....
    Psalm 80:15.
The Vine ....John 15:5.
The True Vine ....John 15:1.
The Tree of Life ......Revelation 2:7.
The Corn of Wheat ....John 12:24.
The Bread of God ....John 6:33.
The True Bread from Heaven .....John 6:32.
The Bread Which Came Down from Heaven ....John 6:41.
The Bread Which Cometh Down from Heaven ....John 6:50.
The Bread of Life ....John 6:35.
The Living Bread ....John 6:51.
The Hidden Manna ...Revelation 2:17.
A Plant of Renown .....Ezekiel 34:29.
The Rose of Sharon ...Song of Solomon 2:1.
The Lily of the Valleys .....Song of Solomon 2:1.
A Bundle of Myrrh ...Song of Solomon 1:13.
A Cluster of Camphire ...Song of Solomon 1:14.

12. *I am the LIGHT of the World; he that followeth Me ... shall have the Light of Life* (John 8:12).

The Light ....John 12:35.

The True Light ....John 1:9.
A Great Light ....Isaiah 9:2.
A Light Come into the World ....John 12:46.
The Light of the World ....John 8:12.
The Light of Men ....John 1:4.
A Light to Lighten the Gentiles ...Luke 2:32.
A Star ....Numbers 24:17.
The Morning Star ....Revelation 2:28.
The Bright and Morning Star ...Revelation 22:16.
The Day Star ....2 Peter 1:19.
The Dayspring from on High ...Luke 1:78.
The Sun of Righteousness .....Malachi 4:2.

13. *The Name of the Lord is a STRONG Tower* (Proverbs 18:10).

The Strength of the Children of Israel .....Joel 3:16.
A Strength to the Poor ....Isaiah 25:4.
A Strength to the Needy in Distress ...
    Isaiah 25:4.
A Refuge from the Storm ..Isaiah 25:4.
A Covert from the Tempest .....Isaiah 32:2.
The Hope of His People, or Place of Repair (*marg.*); or Harbour of His People (*marg.*) ...Joel 3:16.
A Horn of Salvation ....Luke 1:69.

14. *They drank of that Spiritual ROCK that followed them and that Rock was Christ* (1 Corinthians 10:4).

This Rock ....Matthew 16:18.
My Strong Rock ....Psalm 31:2.
The Rock of Ages (*marg.*) .....Isaiah 26:4.
The Rock That Is Higher Than I .....
    Psalm 61:2.
My Rock and My Fortress ..Psalm 31:3.
The Rock of My Strength ...Psalm 62:7.
The Rock of My Refuge ...Psalm 94:22.

A Rock of Habitation (*marg.*) ....
Psalm 71:3.
The Rock of My Heart (*marg.*) ....
Psalm 73:26.
The Rock of My Salvation ....2 Samuel
22:47.
My Rock and My Redeemer (*marg.*)
Psalm 19:14.
That Spiritual Rock .....1 Corinthians
10:4.
The Rock That Followed Them ....
1 Corinthians 10:4.
A Shadow from the Heat ...Isaiah 25:4.

15. *Other FOUNDATION can no
man lay than that is laid, which
is Jesus Christ* (1 Corinthians 3:
11).

The Builder ....Hebrews 3:3;
Matthew 16:18.
The Foundation ....1 Corinthians 3:11.
A Sure Foundation ......Isaiah 28:16.
A Stone ....Isaiah 28:16.
A Living Stone ....1 Peter 2:4.
A Tried Stone ....Isaiah 28:16.
A Chief Cornerstone ......1 Peter 2:6.
An Elect Stone ....1 Peter 2:6.
A Precious Stone ....1 Peter 2:6.
The Head Stone of the Corner ...Psalm
118:22.
A Stone Cut Out Without Hands .....
Daniel 2:34, 35.

But unto them which are disobedient –

A Stone of Stumbling .....1 Peter 2:8.
A Rock of Offence ....1 Peter 2:8.

16. *In his TEMPLE EVERY WHIT
of it uttereth His Glory* (Psalm
29:9 [*marg.*]).

The Temple ....Revelation 21:22.
A Sanctuary ....Isaiah 8:14.
The Minister of the Sanctuary and of
the True Tabernacle ...Hebrews
8:2.
Minister of the Circumcision ...Romans
15:8.
The Veil (His Flesh) ...Hebrews 10:20.

The Altar ....Hebrews 13:10.
The Offerer ....Hebrews 7:27.
An Offering ....Ephesians 5:2.
A Sacrifice ....Ephesians 5:2.
A Ransom (His Life) .....Mark 10:45.
The Lamb ....Revelation 7:9.
The Lamb Slain .....Revelation 13:8.

Within the Veil –

The Forerunner (for us entered, even
Jesus) ....Hebrews 6:20.
The Mercy-Seat (or Propitiation) ....
Romans 3:25.
A Priest ....Hebrews 5:6.
The High Priest ....Hebrews 3:1.
A Great High Priest ....Hebrews 4:14.
The Mediator ....1 Timothy 2:5.
The Daysman ....Job 9:33.
The Interpreter ....Job 33:23.
The Intercessor ....Hebrews 7:25.
The Advocate ....1 John 2:1.
The Surety ....Hebrews 7:22.

17. *A GIFT is as a precious Stone in
the eyes of him that hath it;
whithersoever it turneth, it pros-
pereth* (Proverbs 17:8).

The Gift of God ....John 3:16;
John 4:10.
His Unspeakable Gift ....2 Corinthians
9:15.
My Beloved, in Whom My Soul Is Well
Pleased ....Matthew 12:18.
Mine Elect, in Whom My Soul Delight-
eth ....Isaiah 42:1.
Thy Holy Child Jesus ......Acts 4:27.
The Chosen of God ....Luke 23:35.
Thy Salvation ....Luke 2:30.
The Salvation of the Daughter of Zion
.....Isaiah 62:11.
The Redeemer ....Isaiah 59:20.
The Shiloh (Peace Maker) ....Genesis
49:10.
The Consolation of Israel ...Luke 2:25.
The Blessed ....Psalm 72:17.
The Most Blessed Forever .....Psalm
21:6.

18. *Who was FAITHFUL to him that appointed him* (Hebrews 3:2).

The Truth ....John 14:6.
The Faithful and True .....Revelation 19:11.
A Covenant of the People .....Isaiah 42:6.
The Testator or Covenantor .....Hebrews 9:16, 17.
The Faithful Witness ...Revelation 1:5.
The Faithful and True Witness ..Revelation 3:14.
A Witness to the People ...Isaiah 55:4.
The Amen ....Revelation 3:14.

19. *He that is HOLY, He that is TRUE* (Revelation 3:7).

The Just ....1 Peter 3:18.
The Just One ....Acts 7:52.
Thine Holy One ....Acts 2:27.
The Holy One, and the Just .....Acts 3:14.
The Holy One of Israel ....Isaiah 49:7.
The Holy One of God .....Mark 1:24.
Holy, Holy, Holy ....Isaiah 6:3; John 12:41.

20. *That in All Things He might have the PREEMINENCE* (Colossians 1:18).

The Beginning of the Creation of God .....Revelation 3:14.
My Firstborn ....Psalm 89:27.
The Firstborn from the Dead .... Colossians 1:18.
The First Begotten of the Dead ...... Revelation 1:5.
The Firstborn Among Many Brethren Romans 8:29.
The Firstfruits of Them That Slept ... 1 Corinthians 15:20.
The Last Adam ...1 Corinthians 15:45.
The Resurrection ....John 11:25.
A Quickening Spirit .....1 Corinthians 15:45.
The Head (Even Christ) ...Ephesians 4:15.

The Head of the Body, the Church ... Colossians 1:18.
The Head Over All Things to the Church .....Ephesians 1:22.
The Head of Every Man .....1 Corinthians 11:3.
The Head of all Principality and Power .....Colossians 2:10.

21. *Gird thy SWORD upon thy thigh, O Most Mighty, with thy Glory, and thy Majesty* (Psalm 45:3).

The Captain of the Host of the Lord ... Joshua 5:14.
The Captain of Salavtion .....Hebrews 2:10.
The Author and Finisher of Faith .... Hebrews 12:2.
A Leader ....Isaiah 55:4.
A Commander ....Isaiah 55:4.
A Ruler ....Micah 5:2.
A Governor ....Matthew 2:6.
The Deliverer ....Romans 11:26.
The Lion of the Tribe of Judah ...... Revelation 5:5.
An Ensign of the People ...Isaiah 11:10.
The Chiefest Among Ten Thousand (in an army) or Standard Bearer (*marg.*) ...Song of Solomon 5:10.
A Polished Shaft ....Isaiah 49:2.
The Shield ....Psalm 84:9.

22. *All POWER is given unto Me in heaven and in earth* (Matthew 28:18).

The Lord ....1 Corinthians 12:3.
One Lord ....Ephesians 4:5.
God Hath Made that Same Jesus Both Lord and Christ ......Acts 2:36.
Lord of Lords ....Revelation 17:14.
King of Kings ....Revelation 17:14.
Lord Both of the Dead and Living ... Romans 14:9.
Lord of the Sabbath ....Luke 6:5.
Lord of Peace ...2 Thessalonians 3:16.
Lord of all ....Acts 10:36.
Lord Over all ....Romans 10:12.

23. *Him hath God exalted ... to be a PRINCE and a SAVIOUR* (Acts 5:31).

The Messiah the Prince ...Daniel 9:25.
The Prince of Life ....Acts 3:15.
A Prince and a Saviour .....Acts 5:31.
The Prince of Peace .... Isaiah 9:6.
The Prince of Princes .....Daniel 8:25.
The Prince of the Kings of the Earth ... Revelation 1:5.
A Prince (among Israel) .....Ezekiel 34:24.
The Glory of Thy People Israel ...Luke 2:32.
He That Filleth All in All ...Ephesians 1:23.

24. *He shall REIGN for ever and ever* (Revelation 11:15).

The Judge ....Acts 17:31.
The Righteous Judge ...2 Timothy 4:8.
The King ....Zechariah 14:16.
King of Kings . .....Revelation 19:16.
Lord of Lords ......Revelation 19:16.
A Sceptre (out of Israel) ....Numbers 24:17.
The King's Son ....Psalm 72:1.
David Their King .....Jeremiah 30:9.
The King of Israel ....John 1:49.
King of the Daughter of Zion ....John 12:15.
The King of the Jews (born) .....Matthew 2:2; Mark 15:2.
The King of the Jews (crucified) ..... John 19:19.
The King of Saints, or King of Nations Revelation 15:3.
King Over All the Earth ....Zechariah 14:4, 5, 9.
The King of Righteousness ...Hebrews 7:2.
The King of Peace ....Hebrews 7:2.
The King of Glory ....Psalm 24:10.
The King in His Beauty ...Isaiah 33:17.
He Sitteth King Forever ...Psalm 29:10.
Crowned with a Crown of Thorns .... John 19:2.

Crowned with Glory and Honour ..... Hebrews 2:9.
Crowned with a Crown of Pure Gold ... Psalm 21:3.
Crowned with Many Crowns ...Revelation 19:12.

Before we come to an exposition of the New Testament names and titles of Christ under the letters of the alphabet, the following numerical facts might prove useful. Numbers given with each name can be quickly traced under each name in a Bible concordance. These charts which we have adapted from *The Bible Student*, Vol. I, and which are based on the Authorized King James Version, should be compared with those given by Dr. W. Graham Scroggie in his most valuable handbook, *A Guide To The Gospels*, which no Bible student should be without.

NAMES AND TITLES OF CHRIST IN THE NEW TESTAMENT

Names used in the narrative

| | Number of times repeated | | | | |
	Matt.	Mark	Luke	John	Acts
Jesus	160	90	94	242	17
Jesus Christ	2	2	..	1	1
Christ	3	..	1	1	1
Mary's First-born Son	1	..	1	..	..
Son of God	..	1	..	1	1
The Lord	..	2	11	6	38
The Lord Jesus	..	..	1	..	6
The Christ	..	..	..	1	6

Used in quotations

My Son	1	..	..	..	1
The Lord	1	1	1	2	..
Thy King (of Sion)	1	..	..	1	..

The Stone (which the builders rejected become the head of the corner)	1	1	1	..	1
The Shepherd	1	1	..	..	..
My Lord	..	..	1	..	1

Used by the Lord Himself in direct teaching and in parables

Son of Man	32	15	26	9	..
The Bridegroom	5	2	2	..	..
The Master of the House	1	1	..	..	..
The Son	2	1	3	12	..
The Lord	4	2	1	..	..
The Lord of the Sabbath	1	1	1	..	..
Sower	3	2	1	..	..
The Master	1	1	1	..	..
The King of the Jews	1	1	1	..	..
Christ	3	1	2	..	..

Used by God

Jesus	1	..	1	..	..
My Beloved Son	2	3	2	..	..

Used by Others

Lord	21	3	25	26	23
King of the Jews	3	5	1	6	..
Master	10	14	18	10	..
Jesus	3	2	..	5	13
Son of God	3	2	..	4	..
This Man or Fellow	6	..	7	3	..
Son of David	7	2	2	..	..
The Christ, the Son of the Living God	1	..	..	1	..
Christ	1	1	..	5	3
Jesus of Nazareth	1	4	2	4	3
Holy One of God	..	1	1	..	..
Son of the Most High God	..	1	1	..	..
Son of Joseph	..	..	1	2	..
My Lord	..	..	1	2	..
Jesus Christ	..	..	..	1	5
The Christ	..	..	..	5	2
Son of Man	..	..	..	2	1

Names the Lord said others gave Him

Lord	5	..	4	..	..
Gluttonous Man	1	..	1	..	..
Wine bibber	1	..	1	..	..
Friend of Publicans and Sinners	1	..	1	..	..
Beelzebub	1	..	..	..	..

Number of Times Repeated in One Book Only

MATTHEW

Used in the narrative
  The Young Child – 4
  Son of David – 1

Used in quotations
  Emmanuel – 1
  A Governor – 1
  A Nazarene – 1
  My Servant – 1
  My Beloved – 1
  Him That Was Valued – 1

Used by the Lord of Himself
  King's Son – 2
  This Stone – 1
  Jesus the Christ – 1
  A Man – 4
  A Merchantman – 1
  A Certain King – 3
  Householder – 1
  Christ the Son of God – 1

Used by God
  The Young Child – 2

Used by others
  The Young Child – 1
  Your Master – 2
  Carpenter's Son – 1

The Prophet of Nazareth
and Galilee — 1
Jesus of Galilee — 1
Jesus Which is Called Christ — 2
That Just Man or Person — 2
Jesus the King of the Jews — 1
That Deceiver — 1

MARK

Used by the Lord of Himself
A Man's Son — 1
The Christ the Son of the
Blessed — 1
Used by others
The Carpenter — 1
Son of Mary — 1
Christ the King of Israel — 1

LUKE

Used in the narrative
The Babe — 1
Child — 2
The Consolation of Israel — 1
The Lord's Christ — 1
The Child of Jesus — 2
Used by the Lord of Himself
The Stronger Man — 1
A Certain Nobleman — 1
The Son of God — 1
Used by God
The Son of the Highest — 1
That Holy Thing — 1
Son of God — 1
Used by others
An Horn of Salvation — 1
Prophet of the Highest — 1
Dayspring From on High — 1
A Saviour — 1
Christ the Lord — 1
The Babe — 1
Thy Salvation — 1
A Light to Lighten the
Gentiles — 1
The Glory of Thy People
Israel — 1
One Mightier Than John
the Baptist — 1
A Great Prophet — 1
The Christ of God — 1

Good Master — 1
The King That Cometh in the
Name of the Lord — 1
A Prophet, Mighty in Deed
and Word — 1

JOHN

Used in the narrative
The Word — 4
God — 1
Light — 5
Only Begotten of the Father — 1
The Son — 3
Used by the Lord of Himself
Only Begotten Son — 1
His (God's) Son — 1
Son of God — 5
Light — 7
Messiah — 1
The True bread — 1
The Bread of God — 1
The Bread of life — 2
The Bread Which Came Down
From Heaven — 1
He Which Is of God — 1
The Living Bread — 1
The Light of the World — 2
I Am — 7
A Man That Hath Told You
the Truth — 1
The Door of the Sheep — 2
The Good Shepherd — 3
The Resurrection and the Life — 1
The Way — 1
The Truth — 1
The Life — 1
The True Vine — 1
The Vine — 2
Thy Son — 2
Jesus Christ — 1
A King — 1
Used by others
The Lamb of God — 2
Messias — 2
King of Israel — 2
Bridegroom — 1
A Prophet — 1
Saviour of the World — 1
That Prophet — 1

A Teacher From God — 1
A Good Man — 1
The Very Christ — 1
The Prophet — 1
The Master — 1
A Malefactor — 1
The Man — 1
Your (the Jews') King — 2
The Lord — 3
My God — 1

ACTS
Used in the narrative
   The Lord Jesus Christ — 1
Used in quotations
   Thy Holy One — 2
   A Prophet — 2

His Christ — 1
Used by the Lord of Himself
Jesus — 3
Used by others
Lord or the Lord Jesus — 7
A Man — 3
Jesus Christ of Nazareth — 2
God's Holy Servant Jesus — 2
The Just One — 2
Our Lord Jesus Christ — 2
God's Servant Jesus — 2
The Holy One and the Just — 1
Prince of Life — 1
A Prince and a Saviour — 1
A Saviour Jesus — 1
Lord of All — 1

NAMES AND TITLES OF CHRIST USED IN THE EPISTLES

NAMES AND TITLES	Romans	1 Corinthians	2 Corinthians	Galatians	Ephesians	Philippians	Colossians	1 Thessalonians	2 Thessalonians	1 Timothy	2 Timothy
Christ	35	43	37	25	27	18	18	3	2	2	1
Jesus Christ	13	4	5	8	5	7	2	..	..	3	3
Jesus Christ Our Lord	5	3	..	..	..	..	..	..	..	1	..
The Lord Jesus Christ	3	3	3	..	1	1	1	1	3	1	2
Christ Jesus	6	4	..	5	6	8	2	2	..	4	7
The Lord	17	47	18	2	15	9	8	13	8	..	12
Our Lord Jesus Christ	6	8	3	3	5	1	1	7	8	2	..
The Lord Jesus	2	3	3	1	1	1	2	3	1	..	..
Christ Jesus our Lord	1	1	..	..	1	..	..	..	..	1	1
Jesus	2	1	5	..	1	1	..	3	..	..	..
Son of God	7	..	1	4	1	..	..	1	..	..	..
Stumbling Stone and Rock of Offence	1	..	..	..	..	..	..	..	..	..	..
His Son Jesus Christ Our Lord	..	1	..	..	..	..	..	..	..	..	..
The Lord of Glory	..	1	..	..	..	..	..	..	..	..	..
The Head	..	..	..	..	1	..	1	..	..	..	..
Master	..	..	..	..	1	..	1	..	..	..	1
Our Lord	..	..	..	..	..	..	..	..	..	1	1
God	..	..	..	..	..	..	..	..	..	1	..
Our Saviour Jesus Christ	..	..	..	..	..	..	..	..	..	..	1
Chief Corner Stone	..	..	..	..	1	..	..	..	..	..	..
King of Kings	..	..	..	..	..	..	..	..	..	1	..
Lord of Lords	..	..	..	..	..	..	..	..	..	1	..

NAMES AND TITLES OF CHRIST USED IN THE EPISTLES

NAMES AND TITLES	Titus	Philemon	Hebrews	James	1 Peter	2 Peter	1 John	2 John	3 John	Jude	Revelation
Christ	..	1	9	..	9	..	..	2	..	..	2
Jesus Christ	1	2	3	..	8	1	4	1	..	2	6
Jesus Christ Our Lord	..	..	..	..	..	..	..	..	..	..	..
The Lord Jesus Christ	..	1	..	1	..	..	..	1	..	..	..
Christ Jesus	..	2	1	..	2	..	..	..	..	..	..
The Lord	..	3	1	11	4	7	..	..	..	1	2
Our Lord Jesus Christ	..	1	..	1	1	3	..	..	..	3	1
The Lord Jesus	..	1	..	..	..	..	..	..	..	..	..
Christ Jesus Our Lord	..	..	..	..	..	..	..	..	..	..	..
Jesus	..	..	7	..	..	..	4	..	..	..	6
Son of God	..	..	11	..	..	..	20*	1*	..	..	..
Stumbling Stone and Rock of Offence	..	..	..	..	1	..	..	..	..	..	..
The Lord of Glory	..	..	..	1	..	..	..	..	..	..	..
Our Lord	..	..	1	..	..	..	..	..	..	..	1
God	..	..	1	..	..	..	..	..	..	..	..
Our Saviour Jesus Christ	1	..	..	..	..	1	..	..	..	..	..
Chief Corner Stone	..	..	..	..	1	..	..	..	..	..	..
King of Kings	..	..	..	..	..	..	..	..	..	..	2
Lord of Lords	..	..	..	..	..	..	..	..	..	..	2

*Including *the* Son

Number of Times Repeated in One Book Only

ROMANS
Jesus Our Lord — 1
Propitiation (or Mercy Seat) — 1
Firstborn Among Many Brethren — 1
Over All God Blessed Forever — 1
Deliverer — 1
Minister of the Circumcision — 1
Root of Jesse — 1
He That Shall Rise to Reign Over the Gentiles — 1

1 CORINTHIANS
The Power of God and the Wisdom of God — 1
The Foundation — 1
Our Passover — 1
Rock — 2
Head of Every Man — 1
Firstfruits of Them That Slept — 1
The Last Adam – a Quickening Spirit — 1
The Second Man – the Lord from Heaven — 1
The Son — 1

2 CORINTHIANS
Christ Jesus the Lord — 1
The Image of God — 1

GALATIANS
The Seed of Abraham — 2

EPHESIANS
The Beloved — 1

Head Over All Things to the
Church — 1
Our Peace — 1
The Head of the Church — 1
The Saviour of the Body — 1

PHILIPPIANS
The Saviour — 1
"Christ Jesus My Lord" — 1

COLOSSIANS
Christ Jesus the Lord — 1
The Son of God's Love — 1
Image of the Invisible God — 1
First Born of Every Creature — 1
Head of the Body — 1
The Beginning — 1
Firstborn from the Dead — 1
Head of All Principality and
Power — 1
Our Life — 1
The Lord Christ — 1

2 THESSALONIANS
The Lord of Peace — 1

1 TIMOTHY
Mediator — 1
Blessed and Only Potentate — 1
Our Hope — 1

2 TIMOTHY
Of the Seed of David — 1
The Righteous Judge — 1

TITUS
God Our Saviour — 3
The Lord Jesus Christ Our
Saviour — 1
Jesus Christ Our Saviour — 1

HEBREWS
Heir of All Things — 1
The Brightness of God's Glory — 1
Express Image of His Person — 1
First Begotten — 1
Son of Man — 1
Captain of Our Salvation — 1
A Merciful and Faithful High
Priest — 1
Apostle and High Priest of Our

Profession — 1
A Great High Priest — 1
A High Priest — 3
A Priest Forever After the Order
of Melchizedek — 3
Author of Eternal Salvation — 1
A High Priest After the Order of
Melchizedek — 2
A High Priest Forever After the
Order of Melchizedek — 1
A Minister of the Sanctuary and
of the True Tabernacle — 1
Mediator of a Better
Covenant — 1
A High Priest of Good Things to
Come — 1
Mediator of the New Covenant
— 2
A High Priest over the House of
God — 1
The Author and Finisher of
Faith — 1
Great Shepherd of the Sheep — 1

1 PETER
A Lamb Without Blemish and
Without Spot — 1
A Living Stone — 1
The Stone Which the Builders
Disallowed — 1
Head of the Corner — 1
Shepherd and Bishop of Your
Souls — 1
The Just — 1
The Chief Shepherd — 1

2 PETER
Our Lord and Saviour Jesus
Christ — 3
Jesus Our Lord — 1
God's Beloved Son — 1
The Lord and Saviour — 1

1 JOHN
The Word of Life — 1
The Life — 1
Eternal Life — 2
God's Son Jesus Christ — 3
Jesus Christ God's Son — 1

Advocate — 1
The Righteous — 1
The Propitiation for Our Sins — 1
His That Is from the Beginning
— 2
The Christ — 2
God's Only Begotten Son — 1
The Saviour of the World — 1
Him That is True — 2
The True God — 1

2 JOHN

The Son of the Father — 1

REVELATION

The Faithful Witness — 1
The First Begotten of the Dead
— 1
The Prince of the Kings of the
Earth — 1
Alpha and Omega — 4
The Beginning and the Ending
— 1
The First and the Last — 3
One Like unto the Son of Man
— 2
He That Liveth and Was Dead
and Is Alive Forevermore — 1
He That Hath the Keys of Hell
and of Death — 1
He That Holdeth the Seven Stars
in His Right Hand and That
Walketh in the Midst of the
Seven Golden Candlesticks — 1
He Which Hath a Sharp Sword
with Two Edges — 1
The Son of God Who Hath His
Eyes Like unto a Flame of Fire
and His Feet Like Fine Brass
— 1
He Which Searcheth the Reins
and Hearts — 1
The Morning Star — 1
He That Hath the Seven Spirits
of God and the Seven Stars — 1
He That Is Holy, He That Is
True, He That Hath the Key
of David. He That Openeth and

No Man Shutteth, and Shutteth
and No Man Openeth — 1
The Amen, the Faithful and True
Witness, the Beginning of the
Creation of God — 1
The Lion of the Tribe of Judah
— 1
The Foot of David — 1
A Lamb or the Lamb — 28
God's Christ — 2
Faithful and True — 1
Word of God — 1
King of Nations — 1
Root and Offspring of David — 1
The Bright and Morning Star — 1
Lord Jesus — 1

ALPHABETICAL EXPOSITION OF NAMES AND TITLES APPLIED TO CHRIST IN THE BIBLE

A

Adam, the Last (1 Corinthians 15:45, 47).

In his remarkable analogy of the natural body and the spiritual body, Paul connects Creation with Redemption by referring to "the first man Adam," and the "second man . . . the last Adam." The *second* man, but *last* Adam for there will never be another federal head of mankind. Paul reminds us that the Adam of Creation was "the figure of Him – the last Adam – that was to come" (Romans 5:14). The name *Adam* occurs about 30 times in Scripture. The original Adam was created in *innocence* but transgressed, and all who descended from him were born in sin (Psalm 51:5). Thus fallen, he became the head of the race tainted by his sin. "Through the offence of one many may be dead" (Romans 5:15).

But "the second man," the Man Christ Jesus, who came as "the last Adam," or Head of another race, was born holy and remained sinless, and in His victorious power over death became the

Head of the redeemed race. Innocence and Paradise forfeited by the first Adam cannot be regained; but holiness, heaven and eternal life are ours through the sacrifice of the last Adam. "The gift of grace, which is by one man, Jesus Christ, hath abounded unto many." Paul divides mankind into two companies – those who are "in Adam," and the rest who are "in Christ," but having opposite destinies. "In Adam all die . . . in Christ shall all be made alive" (1 Corinthians 15:22). The core of the Gospel is that although born in Adam and under condemnation of eternal death, we can, through grace, become new creatures in Christ Jesus having the assurance of life forevermore.

A prayer in the Anglican baptismal service reads, "O merciful God, grant that the old Adam in this child may be so buried, that the new man may be raised up in him." But this transference from the *offense* of Adam to the *grace* of Christ is related to the regenerating work of the Holy Spirit (John 3:6, 7). Ellicott's comment on Paul's comparison of the two Adams is illuminating –

> "The first Adam and the last Adam here stand as Heads of Humanity. All that is fleshly in our nature is inherited from the first Adam; in every true son of God it is dying daily, and will ultimately die altogether. All that is spiritual in our nature we inherit from Christ, it is immortal, is rising daily, will ultimately be raised a spiritual and immortal body."

In Adam all his race was lost,
  But Christ, the Lord from Heaven,
Regarding not its fearful cost,
  True life to man hath given.

In the birth records of Jesus, Matthew sets forth the Incarnation in its *Jewish* connection. It is the legal line of succession from David – royalty, and Abraham – promise, and *down* through Joseph, the supposed but foster father of Jesus. Luke relates the Incarnation in connection with the *human* family, and so gives us the *civil* genealogical tree, through the mother of Jesus, *up* to Adam whose sin necessitated the birth and death and resurrection of Him who became one of the human race minus its inherited evil tendencies for He was born "holy, harmless, undefiled, separate from sinners." Arthur Way's translation of the apostolic contrast is one of the best –

> "The first Man, Adam, came into
>   being as a living existence,
> The last Adam as a life-giving
>   spirit.
> Yet not first was the spiritual, but
>   the animal;
> Then the spiritual.
> The first man was of the earth, a
>   vessel of clay;
> The second Man is from Heaven.
> As was the vessel of clay, so are the
>   sons of clay;
> And as is the Heavenly One, so are
>   the sons of Heaven.
> And, as we have borne the image
>   of the vessel of clay,
> We shall bear also the image of
>   of the Heavenly One."

*   *   *

Advocate (1 John 2:1, 2).

Although the English word *Advocate* is only found in this passage, "We have an advocate with the Father," in our English Bible, the same Greek term is translated four times as *Comforter* in John's gospel, in reference to the Holy Spirit, John 14:16, 26; 15:26; 16:7. The difference is the name may in some measure explain the difference in the mission of Jesus and of the Spirit. The Holy Spirit *pleads with us in our hearts,* and produces peace and comfort within (Romans 8:15, 16, 26, 27). He intercedes that we might not sin.

> In us, for us, intercede,
> And with voiceless groanings, plead
> Our unutterable need,
> Comforter Divine.

But the Lord Jesus *pleads for us in Heaven,* and so advocates our cause before the throne of God against him who is "the accuser of the brethren." If we do sin, He pleads the efficacy of His precious blood shed on our behalf! He ever liveth to make intercession for us (Hebrews 7:25). Thus we are blessed with two Divine Advocates, One within, One above.

> Christ is our Advocate on high:
> Thou art our Advocate within:
> O plead the truth, and make reply
> To every argument of sin.

In the original, then, *Advocate* has a double meaning – one as in Job, "miserable comforters are ye all" (16:2). The Holy Spirit, however, is a gracious, encouraging Comforter. The other word means one who is appealed to as a proxy, or attorney (Hebrews 4:14-16), which is the continuing function of Jesus before the Father's face. Certainly, we have Him as our *Counsellor,* but His advocacy is distinct from His *counsel.* In the latter He speaks *to us,* but as the Advocate, He pleads for us *with God.*

If we were in trouble about any matter of the law, we should first require the opinion of a *counsellor* to make our case clear (Proverbs 12:15; Psalm 16:7). Then an advocate would be necessary to plead our cause (Job 16:21). To plead our own cause would be folly (Job 9: 2-4). Further, confidence is ours as our attorney is one well acquainted with the ways of the court, and at the same time is thoroughly interested in, and able to undertake, our case (Isaiah 59: 1). How privileged we are to have such an Advocate in Jesus! "O Lord, Thou hast pleaded the causes of my soul" (Lamentations 3:58).

Other points, familiar to us in the work of an earthly advocate, and enabling us to appreciate more fully the unceasing advocacy of Jesus in Heaven, are these –

1. He must be a wise and learned person in the court of judicature – this our heavenly Advocate is (Colossians 2:3).

2. He must belong to the Law, which is the rule for him in practice. Christ satisfied the Law for us by His death (Galatians 3:13; 4:4), and likewise fulfilled the Law for us by His obedience (Romans 5:19).

3. He must have the Judge's ear more than others, having full authority to speak, which Jesus has (John 11:42). The ground of His pleading is Calvary, which gives Him all-prevailing power with the Judge of all the earth.

4. He must be careful to keep up the honor of the Judge, to prevent any contempt of Court. In His high-priestly prayer of John 17, our heavenly Advocate illustrated this feature.

Because of all they are in themselves, God the Son and God the Spirit are alone qualified to intercede *in* and for *us,* and they are our only Intercessors. Mary the mother of our Lord, nor any so-called Saint, have no access to God on our behalf. We have only one Advocate in the presence of God, namely, the Lord Jesus Christ, and God's ears are open to our every plea presented on our behalf by the Advocate above, inspired by the Advocate below.

* * *

Almighty (Revelation 1:8; 15:3).

Apart from Paul's solitary use of this term (2 Corinthians 6:18), it is peculiar to the last book of the Bible in the New Testament. It occurs some 8 times in Revelation, indicating that the almightiness of Deity has been a rock of strength to afflicted saints in all ages. *The Almighty* is not simply the witness of omnipotent power, as Walter Scott observes, but signifies *Almighty* in "sustaining resources," and is found in the Apocalypse associated with the adverse circumstances of God's people as they made demands on such a strong Name. *Almighty* is a title full of hope, strength, and consolation. After his marvelous introduction, John closes with a marvelous description of the eternity of Christ as the One "which is, and which was, and which is to come, the *Almighty*" (Revelation 18). And He has never failed as the One almighty in sustaining His redeemed children, yet equally almighty in judgment on those who blatantly reject His claims. It is because of His almightiness that He is able to do exceeding abundantly above all we could possibly ask or think. May grace be ours ever to rest in Him who is Lord of all power and might!

> Oh, tell of His might,
> Oh, sing of His grace!

❧   ❧   ❧

Alpha and Omega (Revelation 1:8; 22: 13).

Among the numerous and impressive divine titles in Revelation, none is arrestive as this one the divine Speaker announces of Himself, "I am Alpha and Omega, the beginning and the ending"; "I am Alpha and Omega the beginning and the end, the first and the last." All authority is Christ's to announce His own titles and glories. *Alpha* and *Omega* are the first and last letters of the Greek alphabet, just as *A* and *Z* are the first and last in the English one.

As *Alpha*, our Lord is the Source, the Beginning of all revealed truth, of all promise given, and of all testimony committed to men. This title can intimate His relationship to Creation. He is the Spring from which the River of Grace flows. Is He our Alpha? Do we begin every phase of life with Him? "All my springs are in Thee."

As *Omega*, He is also our End, with His glory as our goal. "Man's chief end is to glorify Him, and to enjoy Him forever." Everything in life finds its answer in Him who is "the first and the last."

> God's perfect Alphabet art Thou,
>   Of truth, the kernel and the crown;
> Eternal Word to whom we bow,
>   The Lord of glory and renown,
> The First and Last, oh wondrous sight!
>   The First and Last of love and light.
>
> The Alpha and Omega true,
>   Inclusive this of all between,
> Sum total of the Old and New,
>   Of things invisible and seen.
> The First and Last, oh precious
>   thought,
>   The First and Last who sought and
>   taught.
>   —C. R. Rolls.

All our testing as we sojourn here below is between Him as our *Alpha* and *Omega*. "To Him as the end all gravitate. On *our* hands the threads are broken; in *His* hands they have never been rent. In the midst of failed and failing circumstances, and the Church ecclesiastically, a ruin amidst the wrecked testimony of the ages, God's voice is heard above the din and strife. The beginning of all testimony is in God, and the end, too, centers in Him. In Him as the Omega is finished what as the Alpha He began."

The writer of Hebrews reminds us that the warriors of old prevailed because their faith was in Him who was the Author and Perfecter of such faith. To them He was A and Z, and all in between – the Center and Circumference of all things, with past, present, and future all under His control. How the strain goes out of living when we rest in the joy of all Christ is in Himself! Whether we think of creation, revelation, redemption, history, or personal experience, Christ is "the beginning and the end." None is before Him; none is to follow. How expressive are the lines of T. W. H. Myers –

> Yes, through life, death, through
>   sorrow and through sinning,
> He shall suffice me, for, He hath
>   sufficed:
> Christ is the end, for Christ is the
>   beginning,
> Christ the beginning, for the end
>   is Christ.

Can we truthfully confess that He is everything from A to Z in our lives? When it comes to our desires, plans, ambitions, is He the First and the Last? Is every phase of life inspired by His Spirit and marked by His glory? "In the beginning *God*." What tranquillity is ours, and how life is made radiant with His favor when Christ is all and in all our hearts! To have Him answer to the whole alphabet of life is to spell out the language of Heaven.

> I am the First and I the Last,
>   Time centres all in Me;
> Th' Almighty God, Who was, and is,
>   And evermore shall be.

                    *   *   *

Amen (Revelation 3:14).

Occurring over 80 times in Scripture, this interjection and expression of solemn ratification, or of approval, is only once used as a personal name as John records, "These things saith the Amen, the faithful and the true witness, the beginning of the creation of God." In ancient times *amen* to make the word more emphatic (Numbers 5:22). Our Lord, the true *amen*, had a unique habit of starting a sentence with an *amen* instead of ending it. The Word "verily" is another translation of the Greek word for *amen*. The Hebrew form is "truly." As an affirmative response, it implies the soul's assent to the truth of what is uttered. Used as a substantive, it signifies truth, "The God of *truth*" (Isaiah 65:16), or "The God of amen" as the margin has it. "The faithful God" (Isaiah 49:7) can be expressed as "The amen God."

When employed as a title of Christ it is because He is "faithful and true," and the One through whom the purposes of God are established (2 Corinthians 1:20). The oft-repeated phrase Jesus used, "Verily (Amen) I say unto you," usually introduced a new revelation of the mind of God (Matthew 16:28; Mark 9:1). In the Old Testament the Israelites used the amen to indicate their assent to a law and their willingness to submit to the penalty attached to the breach of it (Deuteronomy 27:15; Nehemiah 5:13). It also expressed acquiescence to another's prayer (1 Kings 1:36), and meant "say so too." When uttered by God, *amen* meant, "It is and shall be so," and when used by men, implied, "So let it be." The early Church associated the *amen* with prayers and thanksgivings, and when personally employed expressed the individual's response, "let it be so," to the divine, "there it shall be" (1 Corinthians 14:16; Ephesians 3:21; Revelation 22:20).

Used elsewhere in the sacred volume as an adverb but by John with the definite article, "*The* Amen," is thereby added as another glorious, descriptive title to the long list our blessed Lord has. Men, and even the Church, have utterly failed to make good the promises and truth of God. Theirs has not been the fixed, true, unchangeable condition the Hebrew word for *amen* implies. But Christ is "*The* True Amen," for in Him the promises and truth of God are both secured. In His own adorable Person we have the guarantee that every promise and every truth will be *amened* – "It is and shall be so."

> "The same is true of *all* the promises of God: they are affirmed by His, 'I will,' ay, and they are sealed by His 'Amen'; and so God is glorified through our faith in His promises" (2 Corinthians 1:19, 20, Way's translation).

When Jesus prefaced His solemn utterances with "verily, verily" or "Amen, amen," He revealed Himself as the Source of all certainty and truth. With Him there was never any guesswork, conjecture, or equivocation, for He came as the One, "that is holy, and that is true" (Revelation 3:7). He ever spoke of what He *knew*, and testified to what He had *seen* (John 3:11), and was thus, "*The* faithful and true witness." Archbishop Trench suggests that three things constitute a true, reliable witness –

> "He must have an eye-witness of what He relates, He must possess competence to relate what He has seen, He must be willing to do so."

As Jesus possessed these characteristics in perfection, and combined them in Himself, He is humanity's most trustworthy Witness. He will ever remain –

The wonderful AMEN,
  Whom God the Father sealed,
Salvation brought to sons of men,
And Love Divine revealed.

*   *   *

Angel of Jehovah (Genesis 16:7-11).

The Bible has a great deal to say about the reality, nature, and mission of angels. Yet there is a lamentable knowledge among Christians as to who these heavenly beings are and why God created them. The writer may be allowed to refer to his study of angelology in his paperback volume, *The Unseen Army*. The term *angel*, meaning "messenger" –

an ev-*angel*-ist is a messenger who proclaims the same message the angels did at the Birth, "Unto you is born a Saviour" – is a term used of God, of men, as well as created spiritual beings. Our present concern is that of its application to Christ, "made so much better than the angels" (Hebrews 1:4). Only two of the angels are named, Michael and Gabriel.

From the description given of the special Angel associated with the seven angels who stood before God, Christ as the High Priest is evidently portrayed. Also, the oft-repeated expression, "the angel of Jehovah" (Genesis 16:1-13; Exodus 3:2-4), usually implies the presence of Deity in the angelic form – a pre-theophanic appearance of Christ. Isaiah has a unique phrase occurring nowhere else in Scripture, "The angel of his presence saved them" (63:9). The margin has it, "The Angel of His Face." In the context where Isaiah expresses the faith and hope of the Remnant in the day of vengeance, we have a striking evidence of the unity of the Trinity in divine actions, Isaiah 63:1-14, namely –

> *Jehovah* – repeated three times in 63:7.
> *The Angel of His Presence* (63:9).
> *The Holy Spirit* – thrice mentioned (63:10, 11, 14).

All three are here distinguished, "as three existences," as Delitzsch the renowned theologian reminds us: "an unmistakable intimation of the mystery of the Triune nature of the one God, which is revealed in historical fulfillment in the New Testament work of Redemption."

This particular Angel is not one of those who minister to the heirs of salvation (Hebrews 1:14), who, although associated with the saved, are not able to *save*. This august angelic being is the One God refers to as "Mine Angel shall go before thee" (Exodus 23:20-23) and is the *Jehovah* God spoke of to Moses as the One whose divine presence and guidance were vouchsafed to the Israelites (Exodus 13:21, 22), and who is also "*Jehovah* – the Angel of the Covenant" (Malachi 3:1).

As the word *angel* itself means "one sent" or "messenger," Jesus is described as "the *Sent* One" – "God sending His own Son" (Romans 8:3; Galatians 4:4), and He was "the Angel of God's presence," and as "the express image of His Person," the Glory of God shone in His face. It was in this way that His manifestation was comforting and assuring to saints of old like Abraham, Manoah, and Jacob (Genesis 18:22; Exodus 33:15; Judges 13:21, 22; Hosea 12:3-5). The glory of the Gospel, however, is the fact that a *human* presence is far superior to that of an *angelic* presence, thus Jesus took upon Himself frail flesh and was seen, known, and touched by those who saw Him as the Man Christ Jesus. "Which we have heard, which we have seen with our eyes, which we have looked upon, and our hands have handled, of the Word of life" (1 John 1:1). But corporeally He could only be in one place at one time (John 20:13). Now, by His Spirit, the saints everywhere at every time can realize His continual presence, and indwelling, an earnest of the full enjoyment of Christ's presence in heaven with God and all the angels (Romans 8:9; 1 John 3:2).

The Angel of His Presence
Doth lead God's children on,
Till, through His loving guidance,
We stand before His throne.

❋ ❋ ❋

Anointed (Psalm 2:2).

In what is known as "The Psalm of the King," God's only begotten Son, whom He calls, "My King," is also described as *His Anointed* (Psalm 2:2).

The Hebrew word, *Messiah,* means "anointed," just as the corresponding Greek word "Christ" does (Daniel 9:25, 26). *See under* CHRIST. The word *Messiah* was applicable in its first sense to anyone anointed for a holy office or with holy oil (Leviticus 4:3, 5, 16). Then it came to stand for an expected prince, as the references in Daniel, indicate, who would redeem the chosen people from their enemies, and fulfill completely all the divine promises for them, which Christ, God's Anointed, did when He became a "Light to lighten the Gentiles and the glory of His people Israel."

Prophets, priests, and kings in ancient history were anointed for their particular office, and Christ, at once Prophet, Priest, and King, became the Center of all prophecy, and the Antitype of all priesthood, and Source and End of all kingship (Luke 4:18; Acts 4:27; 10:38). Thus, He was anointed with the Holy Spirit from the womb, and then at His baptism, thereby marking Him out as *the* Messiah of the Old Testament (John 1:32, 33, 41; Acts 9:22). And what He is, His redeemed people are, His messiahs, or "anointed ones," by union with Him and through the unction of the Holy Spirit (Zechariah 4:14; 2 Corinthians 1:21; 1 John 2:20). Would that we could experience to the full all it means to be among "the Lord's anointed"!

O Thou the Anointed One,
Who left Thy Father's throne
To suffer, bleed, and die,
And Satan's hosts defy –
A song of worship, praise,
To Thee, my Lord, I raise.

❋ ❋ ❋

Apostle (Hebrews 3:1).

The word "apostle" itself literally means "one sent forth" and was the title Jesus chose for the Twelve. He called and trained and then sent forth to witness for Him (Luke 6:13; 9:10). It is also the title given to the Lord Jesus to indicate His relation to God as the One He sent forth from heaven to take away our sins, "The only true God, and Jesus Christ, whom Thou hast sent" (John 17:3). "Consider the Apostle and High Priest of our profession, Christ Jesus" (Hebrews 3:1). In his speech on the choice of a successor to Judas, who degraded his apostleship, Peter made clear the qualifications of one chosen to be an apostle. He must be one –

> "Which have companied with us all the time that the Lord Jesus went in and out among us.
> Beginning from the baptism of John, unto that same day that he was taken up from us, must one be ordained to be a witness of the resurrection" (Acts 1:21, 22).

Although Paul did not match up to this necessary qualification, yet he became the mighty Apostle to the Gentiles, in that He was commissioned directly by the risen, ascended Lord Himself to witness so wonderfully in His name (Acts 9:1-17). When the Lord is referred to as *The Apostle,* it is in contrast to angels and others before Him sent forth by God for specific purposes. Thinking of Him as "The Apostle of our profession," three distinguishing marks of His perfect apostleship can be noted –

1. *Christ was sent directly from, and by, God.*

In one of his biographical sketches, Paul reminds us that this is the first great characteristic of an apostle.

> "Paul, an apostle, (not of men, neither by man, but by Jesus Christ, and God the Father . . .)" (Galatians 1:1). *See* Galatians 1:15, 16.

The Apostle Paul constantly spoke of his commission to preach and teach as being received directly from the pierced hands of his Master, who likewise constantly urged concerning Himself, that He was the One sent by God, to become the Saviour of the World (John 5:23; 6:44). The mission He undertook from, and for, the Father was not taken reluctantly, or against His own will, for He could confess, "I delight to do Thy will, O God!" In the parable of the householder, Jesus used the phrase of Himself –

> "Last of all he sent unto them his son, saying, They will reverence my son" (Matthew 21:37).

How grateful we are that God sent His Son who, although reverenced by a few, was rejected by the majority! "He was despised and rejected of men," and through His sacrifice we have been redeemed and are among His sent ones (Matthew 28:18-20).

2. *Christ was anointed by the Holy Spirit.*

The anointing with the Spirit was a further mark of an apostle. "Be filled with the Holy Spirit" (Acts 9:17). *See also* Acts 13:2, 4. The prophet of old declared that such an anointing would be evident in Christ when He appeared (Isaiah 61:1), and as He entered His public ministry, He declared the fulfillment of such a prophecy concerning Himself (Luke 4:16-31; John 1:32; 3:34). As for Him, so with ourselves, such an anointing for service is of God (2 Corinthians 1:21). From an old Latin hymn of the 9th century we have the prayer –

> Thy blesséd Unction, from above
> Is comfort, life, and fire of love;
> Enable with perpetual light
> The dullness of our blinded sight.

3. *Christ gave miraculous proof of His mission.*

For a fuller coverage of all that was involved in apostleship, the reader is referred to the writer's volume on *All the Apostles of the Bible*, in which a whole chapter is given to a consideration of Christ as *The* Apostle. Under this section we observe that a further distinguishing feature of an apostle was that of the miraculous in his ministry. Thus Paul could affirm of himself –

> "Truly the signs of an apostle were wrought among you in all patience, in signs, and wonders, and mighty deeds" (2 Corinthians 12: 12).

Christ appealed to His miracles as evidence of His divine authority, as well as His Deity. "The works which the Father hath given me to finish, the same works that I do, bear witness of me, that *the Father hath sent me*" (John 5: 36; Matthew 11:4, 5). It was also to His miracles that the apostles pointed as evidence of One sent, and approved by God (Acts 2:22).

Yes, we must "Consider the Apostle of our profession, Christ Jesus" because of what He means to us today –

> His word is that of God Himself speaking to our hearts (John 12: 48-50). His word is brought by the Holy Spirit for our reception and sanctification (John 14:26; 16:14; 17:17). His word comes with a miraculous power to the soul (Hebrews 4:12).

The prophet God said, "Advise and see what answer I shall return to him that sent me" (2 Samuel 24:13). If among the saved and sent of the Lord, what answer are we to return to Him at the judgment seat for our apostleship? L. H. S. poems on "The Names, Titles, Types, or Attributes of God our Saviour, and the Lord Jesus Christ," under the title of *His Glorious Name,* and pub-

lished back in 1906, is a work we are indebted to for many of the apt verses quoted. Under *Apostle*, L. H. S. has the following appropriate lines –

> The Great Apostle, sent of God,
>   His mercy to make known,
> Was faithful over all His house,
>   The *well-belovéd Son.*
> Consider Him, and courage take
>   He knoweth well our frame;
> Strength for the duty He will give
>   To those who love His name.

* * *

Arm of the Lord (Isaiah 51:9; 53:1).

This symbolic title associated with the human body is one of the most comforting of all our Lord's names. Christian poets have used this symbol of the "Glorious th' almighty stretch'd-out arm" most effectively. Christopher Smart in the 17th century wrote in his poem *Song to David* –

> He sung of God – the mighty source
> Of all things – the stupendous force
>   On which all strength depends;
> From whose *right arm,* beneath whose eyes,
> All period, pow'r, and enterprize
>   Commences, reigns, and ends.

Isaac Watts, in his remarkable paraphrase of Psalm 90, wrote –

> Beneath the shadow of Thy Throne,
>   Thy saints have dwelt secure;
> Sufficient is *Thine arm* alone,
>   And our defence is sure.

In what Polycarp called, "The golden passional of the Old Testament," Isaiah asked, "To whom is the arm of the Lord revealed?" (Isaiah 53:1). It was to this *Arm* that he appealed to awake and reveal its strength (51:9). The expression, "The arm of God" is frequently used in Scripture to signify the active, saving energy of the Most High. Its first occurrence is in God's message to Moses concerning the deliverance of Israel from Egyptian bondage, "I will redeem them with a stretched-out arm."

Often it is used in Deuteronomy, and was a favorite simile with the poets and prophets of Israel who wrote of such an *arm* as being holy, able to redeem, glorious, and bared to protect.

The *Arm* cannot be separated from the *head* and *fingers* of the body. The *head* plans what is to be done; the *arm* receives those plans; the *fingers* display the ability and agility of the *arm* to carry out the dictates of the *head,* or mind. God is likened unto the Head – "The *Head* of Christ is God" (1 Corinthians 11:3). All originates in Him. Christ is prophesied as the Arm – "To whom shall the *arm* of the Lord be revealed?" (Isaiah 53:1). The Holy Spirit was likened by Christ as the Finger – "If I with the finger of God cast out devils"; "If I cast out devils by the Spirit of God." Compare Luke 11:20 with Matthew 12:28.

In this dispensation of divine grace this is the mode of divine operation. Since Pentecost the *Finger of God* has been manifesting the power the *Arm of the Lord* gained on the Cross as He fulfilled the plan of Redemption conceived by the *Head – God,* in a past eternity. Even a child knows the use and power of an arm whether its own or another's. Arms are referred to in Scripture in several ways, all of which can be used to illustrate all we have in Him as our *Arm.*

1. *Arms can embrace.*

Jesus took children up in His arms and blessed them (Mark 9:36; 10:16). Underneath and around us are the Everlasting Arms (Deuteronomy 33:27). Christ is the Arm of God's love by which He embraces His people, and such a wonderful embrace is eternal safety (Romans 8:38, 39; John 10:29). What a blessed day that was when we looked unto Him for salvation and He threw His loving arms around us.

Come and rejoice with me!

For I was wearied sore,
And I have found a mighty Arm
Which holds me evermore.

2. *Arms can support.*

How often you have said to one – aged or weak or helpless, "Here, take my arm!" How sustaining is the support of a strong arm! "The Lord God will come with a strong hand, and his arm shall rule for him" (Isaiah 40:10). His Arm can bear any weight placed upon it, and give rest to those who "labour and are heavy laden." The strength of such a divine Arm is everlasting (Isaiah 26:4). Do you not love that precious phrase of Isaiah concerning *Jehovah* – "Be thou *their arm every morning*" (Isaiah 33:2)?

Is it not consoling to know that as we step out every new morning with all the cares, trials, needs, disappointments, decisions, and sorrows the day may hold for us that the Lord is saying, in effect, "Here take my arm and lean on me, and I'll sustain you through the day"?

What have I to dread, what have I to
    fear,
  Leaning on the everlasting arms?
I have blessed peace with my Lord
    so near,
  Leaning on the everlasting arms.

3. *Arms can defend.*

Mary in her *Magnificat* extolled God her Saviour, because, "He hath shewed strength with his arm" (Luke 1:51). The psalmist rejoiced because "God's holy arm, hath gotten him the victory" (Psalm 98:1). Jeremiah reminds us that God used His arm in Creation (27:5). He who made the worlds sent His Son to be our Arm of Salvation, and also Heir of All Things (Hebrews 1:2). Does not God often speak of His arm *against* His enemies and *for* His people? (Exodus 6:6; Jeremiah 21:5). May ours be the happy assurance that He has set us as a seal upon His heart, and as a seal upon His arms, and whose love for us is as strong, nay, stronger than death (Song of Solomon 8:6).

> Arm of the Lord! Thou hast redeemed
> Thine own from death and sin;
> Thy pitying love salvation brought,
> The victory Thou didst win.

* * *

Author (Hebrews 5:9; 12:2).

Apart from our accustomed acceptance of the term "author" as the original writer of a book, the dictionary gives us two meanings of it, namely, one who brings anything into being, and a beginner of any action or state of things. This English word came to us from the Latin through the French and signifies, to produce, or to increase. In the KJV "author" appears three times, twice in Hebrews, and then in 1 Corinthians 14:33 where we read that "God is not the author of confusion, but of peace." As can be seen *the author* is in italics, implying that the word is not in the original. Thus the RV translates, "God is not a God of confusion but of peace."

The word, as used in the other two references in the KJV, carries a two-fold interpretation. In the phrase, where Christ is described as "the *author* of eternal salvation unto all them that obey him" (Hebrews 5:9), the Greek word implies "that which causes something." The margin of the RV gives *cause* for "author." In all that Christ accomplished by His death and resurrection He became the personal mediating Cause of a salvation of which all the conditions, attainments, privileges, and rewards transcend the conditions and limitations of time.

W. E. Vine remarks that it is difficult to find an adequate English equivalent to express the meaning of *Author* here. "Christ is not the merely formal cause of our salvation. He is the concrete and active cause of it. He has not merely caused or effected it, He is, as His name,

Jesus, implies, our salvation itself" (Luke 2:30; 3:6). He, *Himself,* is Salvation. "Behold, God *is* my salvation." Such a gift is not something but *Someone.* But when we turn to the other reference to Jesus as "The author and finisher (RV, perfector) of our faith" (Hebrews 12:2), *author* here carries a different meaning. This word is given as "Prince" in Acts 3:15, where the margin has "author" or "captain." Jesus is not only *Prince* or *Author* of life but also "Prince (same word in original for *Author*) and Saviour" (Acts 5:31).

The particular word used here "primarily signifies one who takes a lead in, or provides the first occasion of, anything," and is associated with the chief or head of a tribe or family. For *head* in Numbers 13:3 the RV gives "prince." A "captain" or "leader" or "originator" is suggested by the word *author* in this instance, and is a word suggesting a combination of the meaning of a leader with that of the source from whence a thing proceeds. That Christ is the Prince of Life, signifies, as Chrysostom says, that "the life He had was not from another; the Prince or Author of life must be He who has life from Himself."

The title, "The Author and Finisher of Our Faith," is an impressive one with its twofold designation of Christ. First of all, it is necessary to observe that *our,* as given in the KJV, is not in the original, and should be simply *faith,* or the *faith,* and not our personal Christian faith, but faith absolutely, as exhibited in the whole range of believers down past ages as given in Hebrews 11. "Christ cannot be called the *author* or *originator* of faith, since the faith here treated existed and worked before Christ. Christ is the *leader,* or *captain* of faith, in that, He is the *perfecter* of faith. In Himself, He furnished the perfect development, the supreme example of faith, and in virtue of this He is the *leader* of the whole believing host of all time."

Having explained what *faith* is (11:1), the writer goes on to illustrate its working in the saints of old –

> Abel in offering the lamb (Genesis 4:4, 5; Hebrews 11:4). Noah in building the ark (Genesis 6:14-22; Hebrews 11:7). Abraham in seeking the land (Genesis 12:1-4; Hebrews 11:8-10). Moses in making his choice (Exodus 2:10, 11; Hebrews 11:23-29).

These and others mentioned reveal the working power of faith – the true character of the godly man's life (Habakkuk 2:4; Galatians 2:20). For us, however, who are running the race there is the higher, nobler example than all, even JESUS, the perfect Personification of Faith, and therefore worthy to be the *Leader* and *Perfecter* of the faith once delivered to the saints (Jude 3). Let us think of Him in this two-fold capacity –

1. As the Leader.

The writer of Hebrews represents Christ as One who takes precedence in *faith,* and is thus the perfect Example of it. In the days of His flesh He trod undeviatingly the paths of faith, and as the *Perfecter* has brought it to a perfect end in His own person. Thus He is the leader of all others who tread the path of faith.

HE WAS THE PERFECTION OF TRUST IN GOD. We have His own personal affirmation in the confession, "I will put My trust in God" (Hebrews 2:13), and His entire life was a manifestation of such a life of faith (John 5:30).

> His prayers expressed His trust (Luke 3:21; 5:16; 6:12).
> His sufferings could not shake His trust (Matthew 26: 39, 53; Job 13:15).

> His death was triumphant because of His trust (Luke 23:46).
> His enemies testified to His trust (Matthew 27:43).

HE WAS THE PURCHASER OF THE SPIRIT OF FAITH. Faith is part of the fruit of that blessed Holy Spirit Jesus promised and sent to His redeemed ones (Galatians 5:22). Joy and Peace come through such faith (Romans 15:13).

HE WAS THE PUBLISHER OF THE RULE OF FAITH. As Jesus commenced His public ministry He emphasized the necessity of repenting, and believing His Gospel (Mark 1:15). He it was who made known "the obedience of faith," which is the secret of all blessings from His bountiful hand (Romans 16:26). Thus in every way Christ is the Leader of Faith, and the Perfect Example of unshaken and unshakeable trust in God (John 5:19).

2. As the Perfecter.

The great object of the entire life of Jesus here on earth was to be the Fulfiller and the Fulfilling of the Word of God. Thus, He could expound in all the Scriptures the things concerning Himself (Luke 24:27, 44). Constantly, He acted all that was written of Him – "The Son of man goeth as it is written of him" (Matthew 26:24). Because the written Word and the living Word became one (John 1:1), all divine promises are sure in Him (2 Corinthians 1:20), and all divine prophecies are transparent in Him (Romans 15:8).

Our Lord is likewise the *Perfecter,* in that He finishes the work of faith in His own. "The Lord will perfect that which concerned me" (Psalm 138:8). Does not Paul assure us that, "He which hath begun a good work [even the work of faith (1 Thessalonians 1:3]) in you will perform it until the day of Jesus Christ" (Philippians 1:6)? Further, as the Leader and Perfecter of Faith, He will be the Judge and Rewarder of faith (2 Corinthians 5:10).

B

Beginning and End – (*See* under *Alpha* [Revelation 22:13].)

*   *   *

Beginning of the Creation of God (Revelation 3:14).

In His letter to the church in Laodicea, the worst spiritually of all the churches, Christ commences with a remarkable triad of His august titles.

"The Amen,
The Faithful and True Witness,
The Beginning of the Creation of God."

Four Headships are ascribed to our Saviour in Scripture. These are –

Headship of the Body, the Church (Ephesians 1:22, 23).
Headship of regenerated Jews and Gentiles (Galatians 3:28).
Headship of Creation (Colossians 1:15).
Headship of every man (1 Corinthians 11:3).

The headship Christ Himself referred to when He called Himself, "The beginning of the creation of God" is the same one Paul gives Him when he described Him, as "the image of the invisible God, the first born of every creature." Both passages involve Christ's headship. Of the four headships, Walter Scott says –

United *to* Christ give the thought of the first;
in Him is involved in the second;
dignity is covered by the third;
lordship, in the fourth.

Adam is the head, or beginning, of the human race, "the first man," but Christ's beginning precedes that of Adam, for the "Creation" He spoke of was the original one, "the extensive and magnificent system of things, celestial and terrestrial, animate and inanimate, of which Christ as man is here termed 'the Beginning.'" As the *Amen,* the Securer of Truth and Promise, and *the Faithful and True Witness,* we know that He will bring to a glorious consummation "the creation of God," of which He is "the Beginning."

For He shall have dominion
O'er river, sea, and shore,
Far as the eagle's pinion
Or dove's light wing can soar.

*   *   *

Beloved (Matthew 12:18).

Addressing the multitudes that followed Him, Jesus declared Himself to be the Servant of Jehovah portrayed by Isaiah (42:1-4). "Behold my Servant, whom I have chosen; my Beloved, in whom my soul is well pleased." We will never be able to plumb the depth of affection in the title, *My Beloved!* All God's counsel was known to Him from a past eternity, and He ever delighted to accomplish His Father's will. Perfect love made the Father and Son one. The epithet is to be recognized as a Messianic title in the divine commendations of the Son (Mark 1:11; 9:7). In the Parable of the Householder, many slaves were sent one after another to the rebellious husbandmen but only one son, who is called "the beloved one" (Mark 12:6). United to the ascription of Sonship was the additional Messianic title of endearment "My Beloved," or my "sole, unique Son." The "beloved son" the lord of the vineyard sent was also his "heir," differentiated by such from all the servants in the parable.

Paul also uses this title of Christ, expressing as it does, a unique filial consciousness for he speaks of the redeemed as being made "accepted in the beloved" (Ephesians 1:6). Here the epithet appears in its simple majesty without any qualification – *Beloved*. But as Benjamin Warfield points out – "Here the epithet meets us without defining accompaniments: Jesus Christ is in full simplicity set forth as by way of eminence 'The Beloved,' in and through whom God has communicated His grace to me. This designation makes us feel the greatness of divine grace. But it does this only by making us feel the greatness of the Mediator of this grace. It is only at the cost of the blood of the *Beloved* that God redeemed us."

Dr. Warfield goes on to describe a parallel passage Paul has in his sister epistle, Colossians, where he speaks of the Saviour as "The Son of his love" (Colossians 1:13 asv). The combination of epithets, *Saviour, Son of God*, and *Beloved* is unique.

> *Saviour* is His designation from the point of men.
> *Beloved* tells us what He is from God's viewpoint – His own unique One, the Object of His supreme choice, who stands related to Him in the intimacy of appropriating love.
> *Son of God*, stands in closest relation with Beloved. "This is my Son, the Beloved, in whom I am well pleased." It is only in connection with the idea of *Son*, that *Beloved* comes to its rights.

Reminding the saints of the declaration of the Father and the Transfiguration of Christ, Peter affirms that He was "God's Son," "God's Beloved," with profound and reverential satisfaction (2 Peter 1:17). If asked, "What is thy Beloved more than another beloved?" there is no other reply we can give than that of the Bride herself, "My Beloved is white and ruddy, the chiefest among ten thousand" (Song of Solomon 5:9, 10).

> Oh! Christ is my Belovéd,
>   I am for ever His;
> Nought from His love can sever,
>   This, even here, is bliss.
> But soon I shall behold Him,
>   Where faith gives place to sight;
> There dwell with God's Belovéd
>   In Heaven's unclouded light.

❖   ❖   ❖

Beloved Son (Matthew 3:17; Luke 3:22).

In this title all we need to add to the previous examination of *Beloved* is that such an eternal and blessed and unbroken relationship was testified to by both Father and Son. When the court convened, and the High Priest presided, charges were brought against Christ by false witnesses whose witness failed to agree. The High Priest put the question to Jesus, "Art Thou *the* Christ, the Son of the Blessed?" There could be no denial of such a designation, only a straight, fearless confession of His sonship, heirship, power, and coming glory. Under the further title of *Son*, consideration will be given to the various aspects of sonship. As those, having received the adoption of sons, can we say that we are always pleasing to God, as His own unique, only begotten Son was?

❖   ❖   ❖

Blessed and Only Potentate (1 Timothy 6:15).

The translation by Arthur Way of Paul's doxology-chant in his first letter to Timothy is impressive –

> That blessed and only Potentate,
> King of all that reign, Lord of all who
>   bear lordship,
> Who alone hath immortality,
> Who dwelleth in light
>   unapproachable,

Whom none of men hath seen,
  nor can see,
Unto Him be honour and might
  eternal!
    Amen!

The title used here, *Potentate,* is from the Latin "potent," meaning to have power. *Potential* is that which is coming into power, power existing in possibility, not in actuality. Thus *Potentate* is a Sovereign or Monarch wielding great power, and therefore, fittingly describes Him who is "King of all that reign." This is the only occurrence in the Bible of this title, depicting our Lord as the "All Powerful One." What limitless power is His, which will be manifested to the full when He takes unto Himself His power to reign! Then, none will dispute His authority, nor resist His power as He appears as *Potentate* over all the earth with might eternal.

O the joy to see Thee reigning,
  Thee, my own, beloved Lord!
Ev'ry tongue Thy name confessing,
Worship, honour, glory, blessing,
  Brought to Thee with one accord;
Thee, my Master and my Friend,
Vindicated and enthron'd,
Unto earth's remotest end
Glorified, adored, and own'd.

      ✿ ✿ ✿

Branch (Zechariah 6:12).

This prophetic title of Christ, as suggested by Dr. C. I. Scofield, is used in a fourfold way in Scripture, and is consistently descriptive of Him who came forth from the Father, just as a branch or stem grows out of the trunk of a tree.

1. *The Branch of Jehovah* (Isaiah 4:2).
This is the *Emmanuel* character of Christ – "God with us" (Isaiah 7:14), to be fully manifested to restored and converted Israel after His return in divine glory (Matthew 25:31).

2. *The Branch of David* (Isaiah 11:1; Jeremiah 23:5; 33:15).
This aspect speaks of the Messiah who came of "the seed of David according to the flesh" (Romans 1:3), and who will be revealed in His earthly glory as King of kings, and Lord of lords. Jeremiah describes Him as the *Branch of Righteousness,* therefore qualified to execute judgment and righteousness in the earth when He sets up His rule.

3. *The Branch, Jehovah's Servant* (Zechariah 3:8, 9).
This august One predicted by Zechariah would remove iniquity in one day. This One who grew up before Jehovah as a tender plant, is no other than the Messiah whose humiliation and obedience unto death for the iniquity of us all was according to the prophetic Scriptures (Isaiah 52:13-15; 53; Philippians 2:5-8). It was most appropriate for the populace to cut down branches to carpet the way of Christ's entry into Jerusalem seeing He came as the Branch of Jehovah, and as the Branch of David to die on the branch of a tree for man's sin.

4. *The Branch, Name of the Man* (Zechariah 6:12, 13).
In the symbolic crowning of Joshua, "The man whose name is The BRANCH; and he shall grow up out of his place," is none other than the Man Christ Jesus, in His character as Son of Man, the "last Adam," the "second Man" (1 Corinthians 15:45, 47), when He comes to reign as Priest-King, over the earth in the dominion given to and lost by the first Adam. He came as "the Stem of Jesse's Rod." Then, "In Him the sons of Adam boast more blessings than their father lost."

Matthew is the gospel of *The Branch of David.*
Mark is the gospel of *Jehovah's Servant, the Branch.*

Luke is the gospel of *The Man Whose Name Is the Branch.*
John is the gospel of *The Branch of Jehovah.*

In the figure of Himself as *The Vine,* Jesus graciously describes His own as *branches* who can only be fruitful as they continually take in spiritual sap from Him as parent tree. How slow we are to learn that we cannot bear fruit of ourselves! Without, or apart from, Him we can do nothing, have nothing, and are nothing (John 15:5).

❊   ❊   ❊

Bread (John 6:41).

Among the symbolic designations of Christ none is so expressive and understandable as *bread,* a symbol so full of spiritual suggestions. Mentioned 10 times by John, such a figure was apt in reference to Israel, and arose out of her Feast of the Passover and of Unleavened Bread, as well as from the notable miracle Jesus performed in supplying bread for the hungry multitude (6:1-14). The Jews who heard our Lord's marvelous discourse on "The Bread of Life" would readily understand His application of the symbol both to Himself and to themselves. James Martineau, English theologian of the 18th century, wrote that —

> "The Israelitish tradition of the Manna in the wilderness left behind it a long bequest of imagery and doctrine. To the nation whose romantic history it enriched, this *angel's food* became the favourite emblem of the providing care of God; first of the affluence of His natural supplies; then the fulness of His spiritual grace."

There were also other references to bread in the Old Testament beside the manna which would come to the mind of the instructed Israelite, as he listened to the Master's sermon on *Bread.*

There was the bread which was to be earned by Adam by the sweat of his brow, and which was therefore associated with the curse that was brought upon humanity by reason of sin (Genesis 3:19).

There was the bread brought by Melchizedek to Abram and presented to him with the first priestly benediction Scripture records, and which foreshadowed the life and sustenance found in "The Bread of Life" (Genesis 14:18).

There was the bread stored by Joseph in the Egyptian granaries, and in due course distributed to the famine-stricken, a graphic prophecy of the plenteousness of the provision of the Gospel, and the unleavened shew-bread, symbolizing Him who would stand in the presence of God for those who feed upon Him, and also how all their needs are fully met in Him (Exodus 40:23). The *twelve loaves* speak of Christ for the communion of Israel — twelve being the expression of her unity (Leviticus 24:3-9), just as the *One Loaf* represents Christ for the communion of His Church — one being the expression of her unity.

The occasion of our Lord's sermon on the Staff of Life was that of His miracle by which He fed a great multitude in a desert place cut off from ordinary sources of food. Then the people asked for a sign of Christ's authority for His assertion that men should labor not for food that perished, but which endured for ever. Then came His reference to the manna of old, which, although divinely provided, was not spiritual food. The souls could not be fed upon material matter. Neither could such manna preserve from corruption for although the Israelites "did eat the bread of the mighty," they yet perished in the wilderness.

Then Jesus came to the divine reality

that He, Himself, was infinitely better than the miraculous manna of old in that He was not a lump of matter but a *Person*. "I am the bread of life" (6: 35). The frequent use by John in his gospel of this great I AM emphasizes the Deity of Jesus. As God the Son, He is the Bread upon which men must feed if they are not to perish eternally. Several pregnant phrases are used to describe all that He is as Bread.

1. *The Bread of God* (6:33).

We can put this definition another way, "The Bread which is God." He claimed Deity, and was therefore able to satisfy the cravings of human souls — a feat impossible for ordinary bread to accomplish. When He used the mysterious I AM of Himself, He knew it contained the great, ineffable name *Jehovah* to which no other creature could lay claim. He would not have used such an august title if He had not been conscious that He was the Eternal Son of the Eternal Father. The living Bread is the living God, and those who appropriate such Bread, live forevermore.

2. *The Bread From Heaven* (6:33).

Where the manna of old was made or came from is God's secret. All the Israelites knew was that it was divinely provided and eaten, and satisfied their hunger. But with God the Son it was different. Seven times over in this sixth chapter of John, He speaks of coming down from heaven, which proved that He lived before He was born of Mary. In regeneration, we become the recipients of a divine nature which can only be fed and nourished by divine food, even though a meal of the bread of tears may be ours.

> Bread of Heaven! Bread of Heaven!
> Feed me till I want no more.

3. *The Bread of Life* (6:35).

It was nothing less than arrogant as-

sumption to stand and say, "I am the bread of life; he that cometh to me shall never hunger; and he that believeth on me shall never thirst," if He were not Very God of Very God. Ordinary bread is a substance that has been formed by life. Life is in the seed we get from the harvest. Life is in the wheat by which human beings may be fed and sustained. Life can only be sustained by that which has been produced by life. If this is true of our physical life, it is likewise true of our spiritual life which can only be derived from One who has such life in perfection. Christ has "life in himself" (John 5:26), and possesses the ability to impart this life to others. He "quickeneth whom he will" (5:21). Westcott defines "The Bread of Life," as food of which "life is an endowment which is capable of communicating." Well might we cry with those who heard Christ's sermon, "Lord, evermore give us *this* bread."

4. *The Bread of Sacrifice* (6:51).

Among the mystic sayings of Jesus none is so wonderful as the one about Himself as Living Bread from Heaven coming down to earth to die. "The bread that I will give is my flesh, which I will give for the life of the world" (6: 51). This astounding declaration surely points to Calvary, where the Bread was broken. But not only was His body bruised, battered and bloodied, but He shed His ruby blood that He might give life to the world (6:53-58). It was by His death for sinners that He became the Bread of Life to sinners.

What must be noted, however, is our Lord's teaching about Himself as the Bread of Life in that He was to be appropriated by faith, which eating His flesh and drinking His blood symbolizes. The sinner must come to Him, believe on Him, eat and drink of Him (6:35, 37, 44-48), and all who partake of Him are richly blessed with everlasting life (6: 47). Death may assail the body which has been nourished by material bread, but the believer himself is assured that Christ "will raise him up at the last day" (6:40), to feast eternally upon Him, and hunger no more.

Thou bruised and broken Bread,
  My lifelong wants supply;
As living souls are fed,
  O feed me, or I die.

* * *

Bridegroom (Matthew 25:1-10; Mark 2:19, 20; John 3:29).

Among the manifold titles of our Lord none is so closely associated with our human life and rich in spiritual significance as the one we are now to consider. The metaphor of the marriage bond is a familiar one in Scripture. The figure of the bridegroom is found some 14 times in the New Testament, and the adoption of this title by Jesus identified Him with the Jehovah of the Old Testament where He is represented as the *Husband* of Israel, His wife – a figure of speech expressive of His covenant-relationship with His people.

As the *Bridegroom,* He decked Himself with ornaments that bridegrooms wore on the day of their espousals (Isaiah 61:10; Song of Solomon 3:11).

As the *Bridegroom,* He rejoiced over His Bride, and vowed to cherish and protect her, and delight in her (Isaiah 62:4, 5; 65:19; Jeremiah 32:41; Zephaniah 3:17).

As the *Bridegroom,* He comes out of His chamber rejoicing as a strong man to run a race, having His creation to glorify Him (Psalm 19:1-6). Nothing is hid from the warm love of His heart.

While we deem *bridegroom* and *husband* kindred terms, one wonders whether there is a shade of difference between the two. The moment a man is married, of course, he becomes a *husband.*

But by a *bridegroom* we understand a man newly married, or about to be married. Whereas by *husband* we usually think of one who has been united to his wife for awhile. Both names, however, are used to symbolize the relationship between God and His own, and also between Christ and His Church.

As the "Bridegroom" *God* could say of Israel, "I have betrothed thee to Me in righteousness" (Hosea 2:19), and His is the call of the Bridegroom (Jeremiah 7:34), or the voice of the Beloved whose love is better than wine (Song of Solomon 1:2). Then God promised to be a "Husband" to the widow, and to pity His children as an earthly father loves and cares for his offspring. (*See* more fully under *HUSBAND,* under "Titles of God.")

As the "Bridegroom" Christ presents Himself to His own. Precious to Him, His Church – "with His own blood He bought her" – is His Bride. Yet He is also referred to as her "Husband." Paul could write to the Corinthians –

"I have espoused you to one husband, that I may present you as a chaste virgin to Christ" (2 Corinthians 11:2).

The same relationship of "Husband" is implied by the apostle when he wrote of the believer having one dead husband, the Law, and married to another even Christ (Romans 7:4). *See also* Ephesians 5:25-33.

In the Old Testament, then, Jehovah's relationship to Israel is presented under the figure of Bridegroom and Husband (Isaiah 54:5; Jeremiah 31:32), and as such He was jealous over her (Exodus 20:5). To His sorrow, however, she played the harlot, and her straying love for idols is referred to as "whoredom" (Jeremiah 2:20). But although she forsook Him for others, He still loved her, even as she suffered for breaking her wedlock (Ezekiel 16:57-59). Yet, pacified, He was willing to take His unfaithful people back.

The most heart-moving illustration of God's disappointment over Israel's desertion for other lovers is to be found in the Book of Hosea – a book that thrills with power and emotion, and flames with light throughout. The prophet's own experience of a broken heart and home over his wife's infidelity enabled him to enter into fellowship with God's anguish over Israel's adultery and idolatry. As Dr. G. Campbell Morgan expresses it in his study of *Hosea* –

"The prophet declared to the people of God that the relation existing between them and God was most perfectly symbolised in the sacred relationship of marriage; and therefore that their sin against God was that of infidelity, unfaithfulness to love. The prophet learned the truth through the tragic and awful experience of his own domestic life. He entered into fellowship with God when his own heart was broken. Then there came to him the unutterable and most appalling sorrow that can befall the spirit of man. What the sin of Israel meant to God, Hosea learned by the tragedy of his own home and heart; and with fierce, hot anger he denounced kings, priests, and people alike.... Through the infidelity of his wife Hosea entered into understanding of the sinfulness of sin; so by God's command to him, and his obedience thereto, he entered into understanding of how God loves even in spite of sin – and loves amazingly." (Read Hosea 3 and 4.)

The truth for the Church is that Christ's adaptation of the titles of Bridegroom and Husband, particularly *Bride-*

groom, identifies Him with the Jehovah of the Old Testament, which title sets Him forth Messianically. From the early days of His ministry, Christ identified His coming with that of Jehovah, the Husband of Israel and of mankind (Hosea 2:19). Dealing with His own employment of the figure of the *Bridegroom* with reference to Himself and His relations to God's people, Dr. Warfield observes that –

"Christ thus declared His people to be His Bride, as the people were currently represented as the Bride of Jehovah in the Old Testament. In this remarkable title ... we have evidence not only that Jesus regarded His ministry as a mission He had come to perform, and already knew that it involved His death, but that He conceived this mission as Messianic and the Messiaship as a divine function, so that His coming was the coming of Jehovah, the faithful husband of his people.... In complete harmony with this portrait He is represented as calling Himself, *Bridegroom*, charged as that term was with Old Testament associations with Jehovah" (Mark 2:19, 20).

An examination of the passages setting forth marital relationship symbolized by the *bridegroom* and the *bride*, may enable us to understand their spiritual application to our own hearts. As each of the four gospels have references to Jesus as the *Bridegroom*, let us take them in order.

Matthew, in his record of our Lord's answer to the question of the Pharisees about the fasting habits of His disciples, gives the reply –

"Can the children of the bride-chamber mourn, as long as the bridegroom is with them? but the days will come, when the bridegroom shall be taken away from them, and then shall they fast" (9:15).

As Jesus was speaking to those around Him, the phrase, "As long as the Bridegroom is with them," intimates His bodily presence, and such nearness with the manifestation of His love, power, and glory kept fear and doubt away from His own. But when He went on to say, "The Bridegroom shall be taken away," He had Calvary in mind when, after His death, resurrection and exaltation, the disciples found themselves in a hostile world and had to rely, not on the omnipotence of One they could see and touch, but on the assurance of His inner and spiritual presence (Matthew 28:18-20; Mark 16:19, 20).

Then we come in Matthew to the Parable of the Marriage Feast for the King's Son, and see the way those who were bidden to the wedding slighted the invitation. Some who refused murdered the servants of the king who had brought them the royal invitation. "The wedding is ready, but they which were bidden were not worthy" (22:1-14; Luke 14:16-24). Many a Gospel sermon has been preached on this great parable with its warning as to neglect of calls of mercy and of the judgment overtaking the abuse of the offered privileges. None but Christ Himself dared to represent divine mercy so sublime nor depict human guilt so wicked. Dr. Warfield says of this striking parable, that it suggests that, "the fate of men hangs on their relation to Christ; that men all live in reference to Him; and it is He that opens and shuts the door of life for them."

But while we dwell upon the infinite mercy of God, the joy of the King must not be lost sight of. How happy He was when He saw the wedding furnished

with guests *good and bad (Jews and Gentiles).* We can compare this feast with the Marriage of the Lamb (Revelation 19:7). The great joy of Christ, of God the Father and of man, springs from the King's Son's marriage with His Bride, the Church.

Further, there is the Parable of the Ten Virgins, which formed part of our Lord's Olivet discourse (Matthew 25:1-13). Again, Jesus designates Himself the *Bridegroom,* who holds in His hands the issues of life. While it is permissible to make spiritual applications of this somewhat dramatic parable, it must not be forgotten that it has a definite future implication – "Behold, the Bridegroom cometh!" This is a parable of judgment describing the impressions and results of the Second Advent.

The image before us is supplied by the marriage usages of Eastern lands, which require the bridegroom to go in procession to the house of the bride and fetch her back to his own. As he returns, at various points on the route friends of bride and bridegroom join in the procession and *go in* to the marriage feast. Thus, when we read of the midnight cry, "Behold, the bridegroom cometh," the Bride was *also* with Him. Moffat quotes the Latin and Syriac version of this verse as being, "They went out to meet the bridegroom and the bride" (Matthew 25:1). Moffat has the footnote at this verse, "The omission of 'the bride' may have been due to the feeling of the later church that Jesus as the Bridegroom ought alone to be mentioned."

Mark, who devoted his gospel to enforce the impression that Jesus' life and manifestation were supernatural through and through, also records His reply about the children of the bridechamber being happy and contented while the Bridegroom was with them. *See* under Matthew 9:15. The only difference in detail between these two accounts is that in Matthew the disciples of John are more definitely specified as being the questioners. When *Luke* records this same incident (5:33-35), he is less definite than Matthew and Mark were in stating who the questioners were. Mark only states who the two classes were to whom the question referred.

John has a portrait of the Bride and Bridegroom all his own (John 3:29, 30). In this instance there is no reference to the death of Christ, the Bridegroom, as is found in the first three gospels.

Thus, as we have sought to show, the relation between Jehovah and His people set forth in the Old Testament under the figure of the Bridegroom and the Bride is likewise used to illustrate the union between Christ and His Church (Ephesians 5:30-32). The Bride awaits the consummation of marriage which is the glorious hope the Apostle John so vividly describes (Revelation 19:7-9), and which will take place when "the voice of the bridegroom and of the bride shall be heard no more in Babylon" (18:23). The presentation of the Glorious Church (Ephesians 5:27), by the Bridegroom to Himself will be an unforgettable occasion, "Come hither, and I will shew the the bride, the Lamb's wife" (Revelation 21:9). Then, "the Bride eyes not her garment, but her dear Bridegroom's face." We close with Tennyson's memorable lines –

He lifts me to the golden doors,
    The flashes come and go;
All Heaven bursts her starry floors,
    And straws her light below,
And deepens on and up! The gates
    Roll back, and far within
For me the Heavenly Bridegroom waits,
    To make me pure of sin.
The Sabbaths of Eternity!
    One Sabbath deep and wide –
A light upon the shining sea –
    The Bridegroom and His Bride!

*   *   *

Bright and Morning Star (Revelation 22:16).

The Messianic tone is especially prominent in the many designations John gives us of Jesus. For instance, what a captivating title is the one of Him as "The Bright, the Morning Star." It was by the leading of a star – "His Star," as it is called – that God manifested His Son to the Gentiles (Matthew 2:9, 10).

It is interesting to discover that stars are emblematically used within Scripture in several ways. For example, they typify:

1. *The Greatness of Abraham's Seed.*
   "Tell the stars . . . so shall thy seed be" (Genesis 15:5).
2. *The Angelic Host.*
   "When the morning stars sang together, and all the sons of God shouted for joy" (Job 38:7).
3. *The Deities of the Heathen.*
   "Star of your god" (Acts 5:26; Acts 7:43; Deuteronomy 4:19).
4. *Men of Renown.*
   "Cast down . . . some of the stars" (Daniel 8:10).
5. *Faithful Soul-Winners.*
   "Shine as the stars forever" (Daniel 12:3).
6. *Pastors and Teachers.*
   "The seven stars" (Revelation 1: 16, 20; 3:1).
7. *Severe Judgments.*
   "Stars fall from heaven" (Isaiah 13:10; Ezekiel 32:7; Matthew 24: 29).
8. *False Teachers.*
   "Wandering stars" (Jude 13).
9. *Satan's Past History.*
   "Lucifer, son of the morning" (Isaiah 14:12). The word for "Lucifer" is the same as *Venus*, and is suggestive of glory, brilliance, high position, all of which Satan had in the past.

10. *The Lord Jesus Christ.*

There are four passages we can combine as we think of a star symbolizing Christ and His work. In Numbers 24: 17, which is a direct prophecy of Christ, the star is used as a symbol of honor, dignity and authority. "There shall come a Star out of Jacob." Peter has the word: "Until the day dawn and the day star arise in your hearts" (2 Peter 1:19). What Christ will be for the world, namely, a light rising upon its darkness, that He is for each of us, rising in our hearts. It is not yet full day with the Church or the world; twilight lingers around and there are shadows within the souls of men. But here is the promise of the Rising Star, the arising of which is a token and a promise of the perfect day which is at hand.

And then, twice over in Revelation we read of *"the Morning Star."* One of the rewards given to overcomers is the Morning Star (2:28). Well, as Christ is this Star, He is to give us Himself, and what greater reward could we possibly have than the full enjoyment of Christ Himself?

"One thing I know, I cannot say Him nay
  One thing I do, I press towards my Lord;
My God, my glory here from day to day,
  And in the glory there my great Reward."

Further, Christ presents Himself as "Jesus ... the bright and morning star" (22:16), or, as a modern translation has it, "the bright Star of the morning." In order to understand the full application of this glorious metaphor to Christ, we must give some consideration to the splendor of this sparkling planet in the dawning skies, ever proverbial for brightness and beauty. As this glorious Star, He is the Heart of Prophecy.

1. The Star Itself. By the bright and morning star we are to think of Venus, the brightest of the planets, and conspicuous for its wonderful brilliancy

and beauty. The ancients knew this star under two aspects. First, as *Phosphorus,* or "Light-Bearer," the morning star. Then as *Hesperus,* meaning "Evening," seeing that it is an evening star as well. Some connected it with the Sun-god, Apollo.

2. The Symbolism of the Star. Under this striking figure Christ gives us an earnest of the sovereignty of light over darkness when, with the children of the day, He will be manifested. Let us trace one or two characteristic features of this renowned star, which is a sun itself.

a. *It Is the Forerunner of the Day!* The morning star is the harbinger, a prophecy, a messenger of light and life. Christ sustains the same relation to His people as this star does to the world. It succeeds the darkness of night and ushers in another day, mingling its rays with the morning light. It heralds the approach of a new period of time and is therefore a fitting type of Him who is to lead us on to Eternal Day. Ere long Christ is to chase away the dark night of sin and deliver His own from a world of gloom. The morning star is a harbinger of the greatest natural joy, namely, the rising of the sun, and Christ is the Harbinger of great joy to all nations. As His first coming heralded a new day, "The dayspring [sunrising] from on high hath visited us" (Luke 1:78), so His second coming is to usher in the longed-for Day (Isaiah 60:1-3; Romans 13:12). And, giving most light just before the break of day, we have in this fact a thought we can apply as to the bright witness of the Church, which she ought to bear as she nears Daybreak.

The morning star is likewise a terror to evil men and thieves, for when they see this sun of the morning rising they haste away to hide themselves, lest the light of day overtake them and they are discovered. "Men love darkness rather than light because their deeds are evil." It is thus Christ is a terror to the wicked. Godless men would like to pluck this revealing star out of the divine firmament.

The morning star possesses an honorable name. It is called "son of the morning." And Christ is the true Son of the Morning. Lucifer is a counterfeit. Twilight may linger, but Dayspring is at hand. As the Light of the World, the Son of God is coming to banish its darkness.

Dan Crawford used to tell about his Africans: when they were on the march and night was coming on, they would lie down to sleep; but, before dropping off to sleep there would pass from group to group around the fires the word *Lutanda* (morning star). It was the laconic agreement to be up and ready to move when the morning star appeared.

> He is coming, coming for us;
>   soon we'll see His light afar,
> On the dark horizon gleaming,
>   as the bright and morning star,
> Cheering every waking watcher,
>   as the star whose kindly ray
> Heralds the approaching morning,
>   just before the break of day.
> Oh! what joy as night hangs round us,
>   'tis to think of morning's ray;
> Sweet to know He's coming for us,
>   Just before the break of day.

The morning star shines on although it may be obscured by mists, fogs, clouds and misty vapors. It is constantly in motion; nothing can stay its circuit or shining. How suggestive all this is of Christ! Nothing demons or men can do will ever deter His progress. He will appear according to His promise.

b. *It Is the Guide of Mariners!* This notable, beautiful star serves many great and beneficent purposes. It is esteemed as a useful guide to mariners across the ocean. By its light, travelers are able to direct their course. And Christ is highly esteemed as a Guiding Star. Sailing homewards, we can steer a right course and avoid all the rocks and ultimately arrive in the heavenly port, when our eyes are on Jesus. What a blessed thing it is that light came into the world in the person of Him who is the Bright and Morning Star! Shipwrecked souls, distressed and storm-tossed, can depend upon the Lord to guide them into a desired haven.

3. SUGGESTED CONTRASTS. As we come to the study of metaphor, we must be careful to mark contrasts as well as comparisons, seeing we can be taught by both. We must also guard ourselves against straining the many features presented. The best metaphor falls short of perfection. It takes all the best to depict Him who exceeds and excels all language.

a. *The Morning Star Is Distinct from the Sun!* The sun and the morning star are two distinct bodies, the latter being inferior to the former, yet dependent upon it. Christ, however, fulfills both types. He has a twofold relationship of which we must never lose sight.

In His character as the Sun of Righteousness, He is connected with Israel whom He is to heal and bring into blessing.

In His character as the Morning Star, He is associated with the Church and for her eye He rises as the Sun.

As the Sun of Righteousness, He is to arise with noonday glory and splendor for Israel's future bliss.

As the Morning Star He is to appear for His Bride at least seven years before the millennium dawn. The morning star appears just before the day and is seen only by watchers and early risers. If we would shine as a morning star here, we must bask in the light of Him who, as the Morning Star, will burst upon a dark world.

b. *The Morning Star Gives External Light Only!* This glorious star can only reflect visible light to a visible world. What it constantly receives, it transmits. It has no light of its own. The little boy said that the stars were gimlet holes to let the glory through. But Christ imparts the eternal light, seeing He is the True Light (John 8:12), and His glory radiates now, and will remain even when the stars are no more.

c. *The Morning Star's Glory Becomes Dim in the Daytime!* Venus is brightest at night. As day dawns, and the sun rises, this star loses its brilliance. Not so Christ! He is ever the same, day and night, summer and winter. Darkness and light are both alike to Him (Isaiah 60:20; John 1:5).

d. *The Morning Star Awaits Destruction!* Peter tells us that the heavens, which include all the planets, are to be destroyed. God tells us that the heavens, in spite of their glory, are not clean in His sight. But Christ is absolutely pure, indestructible and eternal.

In conclusion, it must be observed that as the Morning Star, Christ is the pledge of the coming day, both for His own and for the ungodly, who love darkness because of their evil deeds. He is the earnest of the sovereignty of light over darkness, when the children of the day are manifest, and shine as the stars forever and ever.

I SHALL SEE THY STAR

I've seen Thy star in the morning,
   When I ran with childish feet
Through the misty, dewy meadows,
   O the early flowers were sweet!

I've walked in Thy sun at noontide,
   When my heart was young and strong,
I've pressed the flowers to my bosom,
   O life was a glad, sweet song!

I creep to Thy shade at even;
   I am weary now and worn;
I would rest me in Thy twilight,
   O life has many a thorn.

I will rest me 'till Thy daybreak,
   'Till again my waking eyes
Shall see Thy star in the morning,
   I shall see it and arise.
                Margaret M. Rankin

❀   ❀   ❀

Brightness of the Father's Glory (Hebrews 1:3).

Arthur Way's translation of the phrase, "The brightness of his glory" reads, "He is to God as the rays are which reveal to us all we know of the sun." For "brightness," the RV gives "effulgence," a shining forth not of a reflected brightness, but of inherent glory. The Greek word used here implies the brightness coming from a luminous body. The marvel of the Godhead is that the glory of God was seen in the face of Jesus Christ (2 Corinthians 4:6). Glory was His before the foundation of the world (John 17:24), and in the days of His flesh there were times when He radiated this glory. "We beheld His glory," was the confession of the three disciples who witnessed His transfiguration on the mount. But contsantly, in His life and works, there was the shining forth of God. In ancient times when the Ark was removed the glory of the Lord departed (1 Samuel 4:22; Psalm 78:61), but with Him who is our Ark of Salvation, the glory ever abides.

Brightness of the Father's Glory,
   Showing forth His truth and grace;
Who can tell the wondrous story
   Of His love, who brought full peace.

❀   ❀   ❀

Captain of Our Salvation (Hebrews 2:10).

Under *Author*, we saw that the Greek word can also mean captain, prince, chief, leader. Christ is not only the

Author, Cause, Origination of our Salvation but Leader – Leader of our Faith (Hebrews 12:2). He, Himself, has trodden the pathway over which our feet should pass. Thus, as Dr. E. Schuyler English says, the best rendition here of "Captain" is *Leader*. He is the Leader of His saved sons He brings unto Glory. "The whole work of salvation and of bringing sons of God unto Glory has been committed to the Son, that is, this *Jesus* of whom the author is treating. A leader goes before those whom he leads. He is the guide along the way. He sustains and strengthens them. He subdues opposing forces. He suffers with them. He comforts them. And he takes them through to the end. Such a leader is the Captain of our Salvation. And it became God the Father to make Him *perfect through sufferings*."

It was Jesus Himself who appeared to Joshua of old as the Captain of the Lord's host (Joshua 5:13-15), and in Israel's leader we have a type of what the Captain of Our Salvation is. He was marked by these three virtues –

1. By his faith and decision for God (Joshua 14:8; 24:15).
2. By his uncompromising warfare against God's enemies (10:28-40).
3. By his strict adherence to the guidance of God's Word (1:7, 8).

As soldiers in the army of the Divine Captain are these not virtues we may lay well to heart? Philippians 3:16, 17).

> Our Captain, Thou, to nerve us now
> With strength for every hour;
> In Thee to quell the assaults of Hell
> By Thine Almighty Power.

❖ ❖ ❖

Carpenter (Matthew 13:55; Mark 6:3).

A very large percentage of the some 31,173 verses that go to make up the Bible are in the form of questions – questions Deity asks of men, and men of Deity. Among these numerous questions, some are asked but not answered, like the pertinent question asked somewhat sneeringly, "Is not this the carpenter's son?" In his record of the occasion when this question was asked, Mark is more personal, "Is not this the carpenter?" Well, Jesus was both the supposed son of Joseph, the carpenter at Nazareth, and also the carpenter, for according to Hebrew custom the firstborn son followed the trade represented by the father of the household.

Christ followed the honorable trade of carpentry. Like any Jewish lad, He would attend the synagogue school until He was about 15 years of age, and then leave to become an apprentice to His foster-father. As He was 30 years old when He left the Nazareth home to enter upon His public ministry, that means that for about 15 years He labored at the bench earning His own bread by His own skill and labor. In that humble shop adjacent to the home we have the toil of divinity, revealing the divinity of toil. Dean Farrar commenting on the question, "Is not this the carpenter?" says that the designation "throws the only flash which falls on the continuous tenor of the first 30 years, from infancy to manhood, of the life of Christ."

Of this, we are confident, that this illustrious Son of a humble carpenter through His 15 years at the bench, never made anything shoddy, but put the very best into necessary making and mending of tools and utensils. The shop was renowned around the countryside for its good and honest work. When, finally, Jesus left His profession to become a preacher, He returned to His old home to teach in the synagogue there, and the religious leaders were astonished and scornful. Spitefully, they ask two questions. First, "Whence has this man these mighty works?" Where were His academical and ordination papers to prove that He was qualified to teach and to do mighty works? Second, "Is not this the carpenter's son?" In this, His scorners and rejectors upbraided Him for the meanness and poverty of His home relations, with which they were fully acquainted.

Willfully blind, as they were, those spiteful leaders failed to see that it was no disparagement to Jesus that He was reckoned to be the son of an honest, and honored tradesman and, in turn, to be a tradesman Himself. Though a carpenter, Jesus was a person of honor for He was of the house of David, His royal ancestor who left sheep to become a sovereign. (In the writer's volume, *All the Trades and Occupations of the Bible,* the reader will find a fuller treatment of Jesus the Carpenter.)

A world, so badly broken by its sin, violence, crime, and wars, needs to find its way also to the same Carpenter whose pierced hands can alone make it whole again. For the most of His life, Jesus was accustomed to wood and nails, and cruel men saw that He had them when He died. But it is only through those nail-torn hands of the Carpenter that lives, broken by sin, can be reshaped, and a shattered world remade into a thing of beauty. To right its wrongs and woe, a distracted age like ours does not need a commander of uncanny ability – only this once lowly Carpenter of Nazareth. If He is our personal Saviour, then we are in the hands of One who knows how to shape our life aright.

> Thus fashioning a workman rare,
> O Master, this shall be Thy fee;
> Home to Thy Father Thou shalt bear
> Another child made like to Thee.

✿   ✿   ✿

Chief Cornerstone (1 Peter 2:6; Isaiah 28:16).

Throughout Scripture the stone is symbolic of many things. It is figurative of Christ, of the believer, and of the Word itself. At times, it represents glory and beauty, at other times, solidity and permanence. Peter not only describes Christ as "A living stone," and as "A chief corner stone" (1 Peter 2:4, 6), but those redeemed by His blood as "lively stones" (1 Peter 2:5). They are as "chips off the old block" as it were, partaking of His appearance and character. To them, He is precious, as "the Chief Corner Stone," but to those who see no beauty in Him that they should desire Him, He is "a stone of stumbling," "a rock of offense" (1 Peter 2:8). Upon the rejectors, He will fall as the Stone and crush them.

In any building, the cornerstone is of fundamental importance. It is called *corner* because it forms part of a corner or angle in a wall, and is usually laid at the formal inauguration of the erection of a building. No edifice is reckoned complete until it has received this *headstone* (Zechariah 4:7). It is under the figure of a building that the formation of the Church is described (Ephesians 2:19-22; Jude 20).

The *foundation* of the Church Christ is building has been laid strong and deep, in the eternal counsels of God (Isaiah 28:16; 1 Corinthians 3:11; 1 Peter 1:20).

The *materials* forming this "spiritual house" are stones of a piece with the foundation stone, chosen by the Builder, brought together and shaped by Him (Isaiah 51:1; Ephesians 1:4; 2:22).

The *style* of the building as it rises is of a piece also with the foundation. The divine Builder brings His pattern from heaven (1 Chronicles 28:11, 12; Hebrews 8:5), and builds according to His own image (Colossians 3:10). As the Building advances, though in a measure hidden by scaffolding and rubbish that are about it now (Romans 8:18-23), it is going on to completion (Ephesians 4:11-13), its completion being reached when the Cornerstone crowns the edifice, and the Builder becomes all in all (1 Thessalonians 1:10; 1 Corinthians 15:23, 24).

The *duration* of the Building is for eternity. It will never crumble nor decay. What the Builder does is forever. "Whatsoever God doeth it shall be for ever" (Ecclesiastes 3:14). Christ, then, as "the Chief Cornerstone" is what the Church needs, and what her every member needs (Romans 8:23); Hebrews 10:13). What a glorious completion awaits the Church He said He would build! (2 Peter 3:14).

> In Zion is the Corner-Stone,
>   Which precious is, and tried;
> Thus is the costly Building one
>   In Christ, the Crucified.

✤   ✤   ✤

Chiefest Among Ten Thousand (Song of Solomon 5:10).

Although divine names and titles cannot be found in the Song which is Solomon's, nevertheless, ardent saints all down the ages have found in this love-idyll glimpses of the divine Bridegroom and of His heavenly Bride. (See under previous section at *Song of Solomon* in Old Testament tabulation of divine names and titles.) The margin gives us "a standard bearer" for *Chiefest*. As a standard-bearer is an officer who is in front of his branch of the army he represents and holds aloof the standard or flag of his regiment, so the Lord is our *Jehovah-Nissi*, the Divine Standard, or Banner, Himself, at the head of 10,-000 He commands. The number 10,000 symbolizes a vast unnumbered host (Revelation 5:11).

The adulation of the Beloved by the Bride came as the result of the question put to her by those who wondered what she could see in her Lover to seek him so ardently, "What is thy beloved more than *another* beloved?" Then came the heart-felt reply, "My Beloved excels all others being 'fairer than the children of men,' brighter than 'the morning stars' that celebrated His birth, 'the first and the last,' the *first* and none before him, the *last* and none after him, none like, none second, none next, none other. This My Beloved, 'the chiefest among ten thousand.' "

The most spiritual and exhaustive commentary on "The Song of Solomon" is that by A. Moody Stuart, which he wrote in Edinburgh, Scotland in 1857. This remarkable work has formed the basis of many of the commentaries dealing with the spiritual aspect of the Song published since Stuart's day. When this author comes to the Chieftainship of the Beloved, here is the way he graphically describes it –

> Among ten thousand kings He is the One Anointed King, "the King of kings";
> Among ten thousand lords, "the One Lord over all, the Lord of lords";
> Among ten thousand leaders, "The One Leader and Commander of the people";
> Among ten thousand captains in the Lord's host, He is the one "Captain of Salvation";
> Among ten thousand conquerors, with palms in their hands, the One Conqueror over sin, death, and Hell, who proclaims "I have overcome";
> Among ten thousand holy ones, He is "the Holy One of God";
> Among ten thousand shepherds, He is "the Good Shepherd, the Great Shepherd, the Chief Shepherd of the sheep";
> Among ten thousand priests unto

God, He is "the One High Priest, consecrated for evermore";

Among ten thousand prophets, the One Prophet "that Prophet of whom Moses wrote";

Among ten thousand first-born in the general assembly, He is the One "First-born of the Father";

Among ten thousand born out of death, "the First-born from the dead";

Among ten thousand holy creatures, "the First-born of every creature";

Among ten thousand risen ones, He is "the Resurrection";

Among ten thousand living He is "the Life";

Among ten thousand names in Heaven or in earth, His is "the one Name by which men must be saved";

Among ten thousand brothers, He is the "Brother born for adversity";

Among ten thousand friends, the "Friend that sticketh closer than a brother";

Among ten thousand kinsmen, "the Kinsman Redeemer, the next of kin";

Among ten thousand advocates, He is "the one Advocate with the Father";

Among ten thousand judges, "the Judge of the World is righteousness";

Among ten thousand physicians, He is "the Physician of the sick for whom there is no healer";

Among ten thousand deliverers, He is "the Saviour of the lost";

Among ten thousand philanthropists, the Philanthropic One, "the Friend of sinners";

Among ten thousand counsellors He is "the Wonderful, the Counsellor";

Among ten thousand orators, it is

He that "spake as never man spake";

Among ten thousand true witnesses, He is "the True and Faithful Witness";

Among ten thousand martyrs, the Martyr who "witnessed a good confession";

Among ten thousand meek and lowly, He is "the meek and lowly one";

Among ten thousand valiant ones, He "stood alone in the breach" in the day of battle;

Among ten thousand wise, He is "the Wisdom of God";

Among ten thousand just, He is "that Just One";

Among ten thousand mourners, He is "the Man of Sorrows";

Among ten thousand joyful souls, He is "Anointed with gladness above His fellows";

Among ten thousand stars, He is "the Sun shining its strength";

Among ten thousand trees of righteousness, "the one True Vine";

Among ten thousand branches, "the Branch of the Lord";

Among ten thousand roses, "the Rose of Sharon";

Among ten thousand lilies in the midst of thorns, "the Lily of the Valleys";

Among ten thousand sheep, "the Lamb of God";

Among ten thousand faithful servants, He is "the Servant of the Father";

Among ten thousand children, He is "the Father's Only-Begotten and Well-Beloved Son."

Truly, in our beloved Lord all fullness dwells, and in all things He has the preeminence, and the marvel is that this Chieftain is our Friend! Paul, looking back over his guilty past, saw himself as being preeminent in sin, "the chiefest among ten thousand" in sin, for he confessed, "Jesus Christ came into the world to save sinners, of whom *I am chief.*" So, if the chiefest sinner has been saved, there is hope for all other sinners. Thus, as Stuart puts it –

> "The greatness of salvation and the greatness of transgression, by their very contrast suit each other; the chief of sinners needing the Chief of saviours – the Chief of saviours sufficient for the chief of sinners, and condescending, as it were, to need an amount of loss in us corresponding to the amount of salvation in Him."

What a glorious Gospel this is to preach! To face ten thousand times ten thousand transgressors, lovers of pleasure rather than lovers of God, ten thousand earth worms grovelling in the dust, and tell them that the Father sent His well-beloved Son, "the Chiefest among ten thousand" in heaven and on earth to save sinners, even the chiefest of them. How blessed we are if out of a redeemed heart we can sing –

> In sorrow He's my comfort, in
> trouble He's my stay;
> He tells me ev'ry care on Him to
> roll.
> He's the "Lily of the Valley," the
> "Bright and Morning Star"
> He's the fairest of ten thousand
> to my soul.

* * *

Child (Isaiah 9:6; Luke 2:27, 43; Acts 4:30).

In his foregleam of Bethlehem, Isaiah announced, "Unto us a child is born – unto us a son is given," and thereby declared the fusion of Deity and humanity in the One who was to be born outside the inn. As a child, Jesus was *born* of a woman, and by such took upon Himself the likeness of our flesh. But as a Son,

He was *given*, meaning that He came as God's well-beloved Son. "God so loved the world that he gave his only begotten Son" (John 3:16). Thus, when Mary was "great with child," within the womb, the Holy Spirit was active as the Love-Knot binding into one the two natures of our Lord, so that He could appear as the God-Man, "God manifest in flesh," or as the Christmas hymn expresses it, "Veiled in flesh the Godhead see."

Several times over, in his Birth narrative, Luke uses the term of relationship, *child*, the original of which means a little child, an infant, and also a term of endearment. As Mary's first-born, Jesus must have been very precious to her heart. There is something very tender about the language Luke the beloved physician used, *the Babe, the Young Child, the Child Jesus.* This sign was given to the shepherds who were the first humans to receive from angelic heralds the announcement of the coming of the Good Shepherd into the world. The angels said that this sign would guide the shepherds to the birthplace of the Saviour, who was Christ the Lord – "Ye shall find the babe wrapped in swaddling clothes, *lying in a manger*" (Luke 2:12).

It was an ordinary matter to see a babe wrapped in infant's clothing, but that a newborn child should be found, not in a cradle, but in a stable cattle used was strange, and it was still stranger that that Babe born in such crude circumstances should be Heir of the House of David. This was indeed a sign, a sign of humiliation and condescending love. Mary, listening to all the wonderful tributes being paid to her Child, kept them in her heart and pondered over them. The Virgin herself knew that her first-born was not a child like others. There were many things she did not know about Him, but faith was hers that

He was, in some sense, the Son of God and the Hope of Israel.

Mary also knew that although she was the mother of our Lord, that Joseph her espoused husband was not His father. Luke makes it clear that Jesus is the only Babe who had a human mother but not a human father (Luke 1:34-38). We speak about Christ's miraculous birth, but the formation of His body within the womb and then His birth were perfectly natural. The miraculous element was in the conception. When Gabriel said to Mary, "Thou shalt conceive in thy womb," the language implies *forthwith conceive,* and such a supernatural conception took place as the Holy Spirit came upon Mary, and the power of the Highest overshadowed her (Luke 1:35).

The Birth, then, was a virgin one, in that Mary was still a virgin when her Son was born. We cannot explain the *Virgin* Birth. If we try to, we lose our reason. If we deny and discredit such a Birth we lose our soul, for no one can be a Christian after the New Testament norm who rejects the fundamental truth of the Incarnation. The wonder of wonders is that He who created the first woman was born of one; that the Ancient of Days became a Babe; that He who fashioned the world deigned to be born in poverty, not wealth, in a stable, not a palace, with lowly shepherds as the witnesses of His birth, and not princes; that He who had pavilioned the heavens with splendor was found girded with cheap infant clothes.

The God who planned childhood when He created Adam and Eve, and told them to "multiply and replenish the earth," became a Child, and the Saviour of all children. Early in life, in Sunday school, the children learn to sing –

I know 'twas all for love of me
   That He became a Child,
And left the heavens so fair to see,
   And trod earth's pathway wild.

Thus, Saviour, who was once a Child,
   A child may come to Thee;
And oh, in all Thy mercy mild,
   Dear Saviour, come to me.

Peter and John in their remarkable ministry at Jerusalem used the phrase twice over in their fearless preaching of the Gospel – "Thy holy child Jesus" (Acts 4:27, 30) – with which we can combine the statement of Gabriel to Mary, "That holy thing which shall be born of thee" (Luke 1:35). From Adam down, all children born into the world were "born in sin," which does not mean being born out of wedlock, but because of Adam's transgression were born with inherited evil tendencies. Thus a child is a sinner by birth, and becomes a sinner by practice. But Jesus was "separate from sinners," in that He had no inherited tendencies toward evil. He was born "holy, harmless and undefiled" (Hebrews 7:26). He knew no sin, and never committed sin (1 Peter 2:22). The blood He shed at Calvary was never tainted. It was "innocent blood."

Conceived of the *Holy* Spirit, Jesus was born *holy,* and we cannot account for the remarkable life He lived, the miraculous ministry He exercised, and the efficaciousness of His death, if we deny His sinlessness. But born holy, and remaining perfectly holy in a corrupt world, He alone could die as the Saviour of sinners. He had no need to "perfect holiness in the fear of the Lord" as we have to do, He was perfectly holy, not only as a *Child,* but as the *Man* Christ Jesus. Certainly, sin was *on* Him for God "laid upon Him the iniquity of us all," but never *in* Him. He was made *sin* for us, but was never a *sinner.* He ever remained the "Holy Child Jesus."

There was no other good enough,
   To pay the price of sin,
He only could unlock the gate
   Of Heaven, and let us in.

* * *

Christ (John 6:69).

The wonderful triad of names – *Lord, Jesus, Christ* – are moved around in most interesting ways. Sometimes they are taken separately and the Saviour is exalted as *Lord,* or as *Jesus,* or as *Christ.* Then we have such combinations as, *Lord Jesus, Jesus Christ, Christ Jesus, Christ Jesus our Lord, Christ the Lord, the Very Christ.* As *Christ* is the most familiar of all the titles of our Lord, and especially coupled in the epistles with the name given Him before He was born, *Jesus,* let us try to consider the implications. No Messianic title is more often met with in the narrative of the gospels than the simple *Christ.* In his incomparable translation of the epistles, Dr. Arthur Way always used *Messiah* for Christ, for two reasons –

"1. Because *Christ* is to modern readers a proper name, nonsignificant, and so conveying nothing of what was implied in *Christos.*

2. Because the essence of Paul's preaching was that the promised *Messiah* of the Old Testament had now come, that He had come for the Gentiles as well as for Jews."

The Hebrew word *Messiah* and the Greek one, *Christ,* both mean "Anointed." Thus in Psalm 2:2, He is spoken of as "his anointed" (*See* under *Anointed*). This was His official designation and occurs in the four gospels about 50 times, and is usually given with the article prefixed, "*The* Christ." It is unfortunate that in many instances the article, found in the original, is not given in the English Bible, because its use formed a vital part of our Lord's testimony to the Jews, who knew of the claims of false Messiahs. But in Christ, *the* Messiah – the burden of the Old Testament – had come and offered Himself as "*the* Christ," the Deliverer of the Jews, not only from Gentile rule but from their sin (Luke 1:67-79).

It will be found that the general use of *Christ* is associated with the Old Testament prophecies (Matthew 22:42; 23: 8, 10; John 7:26, 27, 31). As the priests, kings, and prophets of old were anointed to their respective offices, and were thus reckoned as God's anointed ones, we can readily understand why *Christ* – The Anointed One – should be chosen to express the fact that Jesus of Nazareth was the Prophet, Priest, and King of whom Moses and the Prophets gave witness. Through grace, the name *Christ* is no longer exclusive Jewish property, but has become the cherished name of *Christians,* who take their name not from Jesus, but from *Christ* (1 Peter 4:16). In the early history of the Church, among the heathen, Christ often became *Chrest,* meaning, benign in acknowledgment of the Christlikeness of their character.

It would seem from Peter's declaration that the title *Christ* is connected in a peculiar manner with the outpouring of the Holy Spirit on the historic day of Pentecost –

"Let all the house of Israel know assuredly, that God hath made that same Jesus, whom ye have crucified, both Lord and *Christ*" (Acts 2:36. *See* John 7:37-39).

It is the Holy Spirit who communicates to us all the blessings represented by all the names of the Saviour. He it is who presents the Lord in His threefold office –

As the Anointed Prophet, that we might have His teaching (John 14:26; 16:13).

As the Anointed Priest, that we might partake of His sacrifice and intercession (John 16:24; Hebrews 7:25).

As the Anointed King, that we might enjoy His gifts and largesses (Ephesians 4:8).

With Christ's ascension on high His *new* place as the risen, glorified Lord measures our place in the glory He entered, and fixes such a position before God. Thus, while His official title as Christ occurs about 50 times in the four gospels, it is associated with His exaltation in the Acts about 20 times, and the epistles upwards of 300 times where it is used to define our privileged *position* or standing before God. Thus, as believers we are *in Christ*, whether alive or dead (1 Corinthians 15; 2 Corinthians 12:2). It is *Christ*, who is the Head of His body the Church, as well as the Head of every man (1 Corinthians 11:3). That Christ and His redeemed children are inseparable is seen in the remarkable passage where Paul calls the Body joined with the Head, *The Christ* (1 Corinthians 12:12, 27). In this divine name, then, we see expanded in a full and glorious way in His Resurrection and Ascension all the potential that lay hidden in His own sweet name, *Jesus*.

Jesus Christ.

The combinations given of His full and majestic appellation *Lord Jesus Christ*, are profitable to study. For instance, the double title "Jesus Christ" occurs some six times in the gospels, but more frequently in the epistles. Paul uses it some 66 times, and Peter, 12 times, and John in his three epistles, about 9 times. In the union of the two names herewith described, the former, *Jesus*, is emphatic by its position, the second, *Christ*, being subsidiary and explanatory. In the gospels, this union of names means, *Jesus the Messiah,* while in the epistles it implies Jesus who humbled Himself, but is now exalted and glorified as *Christ*. This fact shows

that care must be taken to examine the various combinations. All He *was* as "Jesus," He *is* as "Christ," and thus the sufferings of earth and the glories of heaven are wondrously linked in the divine order of these two names *Jesus Christ*. Jesus the humbled Man, Christ the risen Lord, together tell all the story of "the sufferings of Christ and the glories that follow."

Christ Jesus

This converse of the previous combination denotes the now exalted One, who once humbled Himself. While "*Jesus* Christ" is a title common enough to all the epistles, "*Christ* Jesus" is almost wholly confined to Paul. Peter uses it twice in his second epistle, but Jude does not use it, neither does John in his epistles, and Revelation. Walter Scott notes that, "The Apostles and writers of the New Testament were converted when Jesus was on earth, save Paul, whose first acquaintance with Christ was formed in the glory (Acts 9), hence he and they speak of Jesus as they knew Him. In this way we account for the rare occurrence of Paul's favourite title, *Christ Jesus,* in other than Pauline writings. Peter, John and the others *first* knowing Jesus on earth, speak and write of Him as '*Jesus* Christ'; while Paul *first* knowing Jesus in glory, uses the expressive title, not found in the gospels, '*Christ* Jesus.'"

Christ the Lord.

The only occurrence of the phrase is in connection with the angelic announcement of the birth of Jesus – "Unto you is born this day in the city of David a Saviour, which is *Christ the Lord*" (Luke 2:11). The Holy Spirit used a similar phrase when he assured godly Simeon that he would not die until he had seen "the *Lord's Christ*" (Luke 2:26), or "the Anointed of Jehovah." It was this same phrase David used of King Saul when he called him, "the Lord's anointed" (1 Samuel 24:6). Peter, in his sermon at Pentecost, declaring that the Resurrection proved Jesus to be both Lord and Christ said, "Know assuredly, that God hath made that same Jesus, whom ye have crucified, both Lord and Christ" (Acts 2:36). While the consummation of these two names, *Lord* and *Christ,* became His as the result of His Resurrection and Ascension, the angel messenger at His birth affirmed that He was *born* a Saviour, *born* Christ, *born* Lord. For a fuller exposition of His lordship see under title – *Lord.* Paul expressed his gratitude for his ministry to "Christ Jesus our Lord." Can I say that He is *my* Lord? As *Jesus* He died for me, and as *Christ* rose again and ascended on high that He might be *Lord* of my life. Am I sanctifying Him as *Lord* in all things?

Christ of God (Luke 9:20).

Each evangelist gives Peter's confession of the Master's Deity differently:

> Matthew has it – "The Christ, the Son of the living God" (16:16).
> Mark simply says – "The Christ."
> Luke calls Him – "The Christ of God" (9:20).

While we have come to regard *Christ* as a proper name, and use it without the article, in the Gospel narratives, the article *the* is habitually used. Thus, in Peter's confession as given by Matthew the emphatic and definite force of the article is prominent, as well as the emphatic position of the pronoun *Thou* – "*Thou* art *the* anointed, *the* Son of *the* God, *the* living." The precise form of expression, "The Christ of God," is peculiar to Luke, and agrees substantially with "The Lord's Christ" (Luke 2:26).

Christ, the Chosen of God (Luke 23:35; 1 Peter 2:4, 5).

The twin reference to our Lord, as being "Chosen of God" has a significance all its own. W. E. Vine says that the term *chosen* "signifies to take, with the implication that what is taken is eligible or suitable; hence, to choose, by reason of suitability" (Matthew 12:18). It is in this sense that it is used as expressive of God's delight in Christ as His *Chosen.* When it came to the redemption of a lost world, God looked around the courts of heaven, and said, "Whom shall I send, and who will go for us?" His choice fell upon His beloved Son, who willingly acquiesced in the choice, and replied, "Here am I, Jehovah, send Me." God chose Him because of His perfect suitability to die as the Saviour of the world. Thus He was not only "chosen of God," but at Calvary, "afflicted of God."

Christ, the Son of God (Acts 9:20).

One of the marvelous features of Paul's conversion was the immediate recognition of the Messiahship and Deity of the Jesus he had formerly persecuted (Acts 9:5). Soon after his miraculous transformation he was in the synagogues preaching that Christ was the Son of God. He had received spiritual insight that the Nazarene was indeed the Messiah. Under the caption *Son,* further material will be found of this divine relationship.

Christ, Son of the Blessed (Mark 14:61).

Both Matthew and Luke in their separate accounts of Christ's silence before the High Priest have simply, "The Son of God"; but the use of *the Blessed* as a name of God in doxologies and other solemn ritual was a common practice. Paul wrote to young Timothy of "the glorious gospel of *the blessed God,*" and of "the blessed and only Potentate" (1 Timothy 1:11; 6:15). He is "God blessed for ever" (Romans 9:5). Applied to God, *blessed,* One worthy of praise, or to celebrate with praises, acknowledging His goodness thereby. One meaning of *blessed* is "happy," and so ours is the Gospel of "the Happy God." Jesus often spoke of His *Joy,* and in such revealed Himself to be a true Son of "The Happy God."

The Very Christ (Acts 9:22).

We are told that Paul confounded the Jews at Damascus as he proved that the One he preached was "*the* very Christ." There had been others called "messiahs," or anointed ones (1 Chronicles 16:22; Psalm 105:15). Cyrus is described as "the LORD's anointed" because he was brought to the throne to deliver the Jews out of captivity (Isaiah 45:1). Christ, however, as "*the* [article emphasized in the original] very Messiah." He alone fitted all the Messianic prophecies of the Old Testament.

Lord Jesus Christ.

This majestic title graces the introductory of the Pauline Epistles. Paul slightly alters it in Second Timothy 1:2, but concludes the epistle with "The Lord Jesus Christ be with your spirit" (4:22). Dr. Warfield reminds us that –

> James speaks of our Lord by name only twice, and on both occasions he gives Him the full title of reverence – "The (or our) Lord Jesus Christ" (1:1; 2:1) – coupling Him in one case on equal terms with God, and in the other adding further epithets of divine dignity in contexts which greatly enhance the significance of the term. When James speaks of Christ as *the Lord of glory* (2:1), the "glory" seems to stand here in opposition to the name, "our Lord Jesus Christ," further defining Him in His majesty.

We magnify Him when we use this full written title the apostle gives Him. How complete a title it is!

We have His *authority* in LORD, His *manhood* in Jesus, His *glory* in CHRIST. Together this trio of names reveals that His power is indissolubly linked with His humanity and present exaltation (Matthew 28:18-20).

* * *

Consolation of Israel (Luke 2:25).

Satisfied in seeing and receiving Christ, the aged, godly Simeon spoke of Him as the One he had waited for as "the consolation of Israel" (Luke 2:25, 28-30). While it is true that He came to impart "consolation," or "to bind up the broken-hearted" (Isaiah 61:1-3), yet what Simeon implied was that Christ Himself was the *Consolation* of His covenant people. When He came to His public ministry, He promised the Holy Spirit as a Comforter, and a comforter's work is to give consolation. The early Church walked in "the comfort of the Holy Spirit" (Acts 9:31). The consolation He imparts, and also *is in Himself,* is the comfort, faith, hope, love, joy and peace whereby we can stand up against all satanic attacks.

Christ is precious to the hearts of the saints because every spiritual blessing is wrapped up in Him (Ephesians 1:3). No matter what our need may be He is there to meet it. Alas! there are multitudes who find no consolation in Christ now. "Ye will not come unto Me that ye might have life." For all such, if they die in their sin, will find no consolation hereafter (Revelation 6:16). How we need to echo forth anew the message of the prophet, "Comfort ye, comfort ye, my people, saith your God" (Isaiah 40:1). Does not Paul exalt Him as "The God of all comfort" (2 Corinthians 1:3), and "our consolation also aboundeth by Christ" (1:5)? A Jewish formula of blessing was, "May I see the consolation of Israel." It was an adjuration also: "May I not see it, if I speak not the truth!" Bless the Lord, He is ever our *Strong Consolation* (Hebrews 6:18).

> Consolation of Israel! all praise to
> Thy name,
> A strong consolation Thy Word doth
> proclaim
> To all sinners renouncing all other
> claim,
> On eternal life lay hold in Thy
> blessèd name.

❁   ❁   ❁

Counsellor (Isaiah 9:6).

In his remarkable prophecy of a divine Child as Israel's only hope, Isaiah gives a cluster of marvelous names we are to consider in alphabetical order. Before us is the second of these names – "His name shall be called . . . Counsellor." Scripture has much to say about counsellors, good and bad; and about counsel, true and false. Solomon would have us know that "Where no counsel is, the people fall: but in the multitude of counsellors there is safety" (Proverbs 11:14; 24:6). But if one has many counsellors, and their counsel does not agree, there won't be much safety. One might become "wearied in the multitude of their counsels" (Isaiah 47:13). What the Christian must guard against is "walking in the counsel of the ungodly" (Psalm 1:1). Moses hearkened unto the voice of his father-in-law when he said, "I will give thee counsel," and sound, practical counsel it was! (Exodus 18:19-27). Alas! Moses had to say of the nation he led that it was "void of counsel" (Deuteronomy 32:28); and Joshua, his successor, blundered when he "asked not counsel at the mouth of the Lord" (Joshua 9:14).

The Lord, however, stands out as the Counsellor per excellence, for His "counsels of old are faithfulness and truth" (Isaiah 25:1), and He ever "worketh all things after the counsel of his own will" (Ephesians 1:11). His counsel is immutable (Hebrews 6:17). The psalmist could say, "I will bless Jehovah, who hath given me counsel," and was confident that He would "guide him with His counsel" (Psalm 16:7; 73:24). Because sin and unbelief have warped the mind of man, he is in constant need of guidance and advice from above (1 Kings 3:7-10). What a relief to know that there is a Counsellor able to answer our questions, solve our riddles, and relieve us of our perplexity!

Such a *Counsellor* is *Christ,* who has a guiding mind to think for all, a guiding heart to feel for all, a guiding hand to act for all. Problems and enigmas are not insoluble to Him who is omniscient. But His unerring counsel is one thing, the right use of it by us is another thing. Generally speakng, in our society there are two kinds of counsellors:

There are Counsellors of State. These are qualified, wise men of the first rank, who sit in the council or cabinet with the sovereign or president, to fashion and establish laws. Such an efficient counsellor was Daniel (6:1-3).

There are Counsellors at Law. These are legally trained men whose work and business it is to unfold and make known the law to those who require its protection. It would seem as if Tertullus was one of these (Acts 24:2). Christ offers Himself in both of these respects as the Counsellor for His people. For instance – in the eternal counsels of the Father, Christ was a member of cabinet (Trinity), when it came to establishing laws for mankind (Genesis 1:26; Proverbs 8:30; Romans 11:34).

In His capacity as Counsellor at Law, He has a perfect knowledge of its nature and requirements, and is able to give counsel to His people concerning God's mind and will (Revelation 3:18).

There are, at least, three ways by which His counsel is imparted.

1. *By Scripture.*

In the Word of God we have the mind of God, and if ours is the mind, or thinking faculty, of Christ, then we will come to know His thoughts on all matters. The psalmist could say, "Thy testimonies also are my delight and my *counsellors*" (119:2). Scripture is the best, and only infallible rule of life for our daily guidance, seeing that it –

> Reveals most fully the designs of Satan, and the end of the wicked (Psalm 9:17).
>
> Manifests all the fulness of God's grace for us (Ephesians 1:3-14).
>
> Teaches us how to live and labor (Titus 2:11-14).
>
> Provides us with the best example in living (1 Peter 2:21).

2. *By Providence.*

Concurrently with Scripture, divine providences come in to help to guide us. We must, however, be unselfish and honest in interpreting these providences, and not allow ourselves to be led contrary to our convictions, into courses that seem to promise most. We receive true counsel, and are directed aright when, as children, we watch our Father (Psalm 32:8, 9). All who sincerely desire heavenly counsel receive it as they believe that –

> A divine Hand controls and governs everything (Colossians 1:16, 17).
>
> A divine Voice assures the heart that all is well (Proverbs 1:20, 21; Hebrews 3:7, 8).
>
> A divine Word is in exercise, providing assurance (Job 36:22; Romans 8:28).

3. *By the Spirit.*

Paul firmly believed that we can be "led by the Spirit" (Romans 8:14); that He was speaking in different ways to different ages, different dispositions. If ours would be the guided life, the promise is ours, "He will guide thee continually" (Isaiah 58:11). Have we not the assurance that when Christ entered the heavens, that He sent the Holy Spirit to give counsel to the redeemed? (John 16:13). Ours is the privilege of having an inward monitor to teach us, as well as to assure us of pardon and sonship (John 14:26; Romans 8:16; 1 John 5:10). All other counsel, apart from that which the heavenly Counsellor will give us is false, and ruinous. King Saul died a tragic death because he not only forsook the Lord, but asked counsel of one that had a familiar spirit, the witch of Endor (1 Chronicles 10:13).

> In counsel Thou art mighty,
>   Lord! keep me ever near;
> May Thine own presence guide me,
>   Then I have nought to fear.
> Now, deign my Counsellor to be,
> And may I love my will in Thee.

❋   ❋   ❋

Covenant (Isaiah 42:6).

From Scripture we discover that a covenant not only represents an agreement between persons or parties, but is also used as a divine title. In his prediction of Christ, the Servant of Jehovah, Isaiah is found saying, "Behold my servant . . . mine elect . . . I will give *thee* for a *covenant* of the people, for a light to the Gentiles" (Isaiah 42:1-7). What a unique designation of Christ this is! The context, of course, makes it clear that such a title is not limited to Israel, but that the Servant-Covenant would also be as a *Light* to lighten the Gentiles. Christ was to be in Himself not only the Mediator of the covenant, but *the* Covenant, the meeting place between God and man, just as He is *the* Peace, as well as the *Peacemaker* (Micah 5:5; Ephesians 2:14). "The words of Isaiah may well have furnished a starting-point for the *new covenant* (Jeremiah 31:31) and the whole series

of thoughts that have grown out of it."
See Isaiah 49:6; Luke 2:32.

> A Covenant of the people, Lord!
> Alone we could not keep Thy word;
> In Christ, the Covenant, we stand,
> Thro' Him we reach the better land.

D

David, Perfect King (Jeremiah 30:9; Hosea 3:5).

That Jeremiah and Hosea were not referring to David, the second king of Israel, is evident from the fact that he was long dead when these two prophets were active. Further, in both cases the future tense is used, "They shall serve Jehovah their God, and David their king, whom I will raise up unto them." "The children of Israel shall return and seek Jehovah their God, and David their king." By the phrase, *David their king*, the meaning is that of a predicted representative of the Davidic dynasty. Rehoboam and his house are spoken of as *David* (1 Kings 12:16). Zerubbabel also is described as being, in measure, another partial representative of David, the son of Jesse (Haggai 2:21-23). But Zerubbabel never claimed the title of *king*.

The mode of speech used, however, suggests that the name of the old hero-king of Israel is to appear as that of the new representative of the house who will restore the kingdom – a second David for Israel, a true King answering to the ideal David, the sweet psalmist of Israel, imperfectly represented. Hosea's reference to the distant future, "In the later days," shows that on the horizon of the seer's gaze, the fulfillment of his prophecy of *David their King* would be in His Messianic reign. *See* Ezekiel 34:23, 24; 37:24. As no king of David's seed has held the sceptre since the Captivity, *The Son of David*, Messiah, must therefore be meant (Isaiah 55:3, 4). That the original *David* made a tremendous impact upon Jewish and biblical history is evident from the fact that his name occurs about 1120 times in Scripture.

David, God's choice of a king to succeed Saul, was the *only* king to be born in Bethlehem, the birthplace also of Jesus, the Son of David; and the only type of Jesus in His coming millennial conflict and successful warfare. The New Testament often refers to Jesus as "The Son of David," "The Seed of David," "David's Greater Son," and as One who will yet occupy "The Throne of David," and hold the "key of David," (Revelation 3:7). As "the Root and Offspring of David," He will be God's Perfect King (Revelation 22:16). When Jesus argued with the Scribes over the significance of the title "Son of David," He had in mind His own Messiahship, and asserted the claim that He was greater than Israel's past David. The Person thus described by Mark (12:36, 37), as "the superior and sovereign of David and his house and of all Israel, could not possibly be David himself, nor any of his sons and successors except One who by virtue of His twofold nature was at once his Sovereign and His Son."

Our Lord did not deny that He was David's Son, but asserted that as David's Lord, His sonship was derived from a higher source than David, and that therefore He was preeminently the Son of God rather than that of David (Mark 12:35). When Paul represented Jesus as "the seed of David," it was only on one side of His being, the apostle calls "according to the flesh." But the two sides of His being were well understood by Paul so when he calls Jesus "The Son of God," He was such "according to the Spirit of Holiness." His human nature had a historical beginning as "the Son of David," but His divine nature was eternal in its substance. He was *made*, or came to be, "the Seed of David" according to the flesh, but He was designated, or marked out, "the Son of God" by resurrection from the dead. Paul had a remarkable insight into our Lord's two natures (Romans 1:3, 4; 9:5).

To return then, to the prophetic title, *David their King*, the Messianic ideal of a perfect King, the prediction of a Davidic king who will reign for ever and ever over His people, will be fulfilled in Jesus who was born *King*. (*See* further under *King*.)

> David's Lord, and David's Son,
> Thine is an eternal throne:
> Over all Thou yet wilt reign;
> Come, Lord Jesus, come – Amen!

❋   ❋   ❋

Dayspring (Luke 1:78).

"Dayspring" is not to be confused with "Day-Star" the Greek form of which gives us the English word *phosphorus,* meaning, light-bearing, and is used of the morning star as the light bringer. As used by Peter "it indicates the arising of the light of Christ as the personal fulfillment, in the hearts of believers, of the prophetic Scriptures concerning His coming to receive them to Himself" (2 Peter 1:19). (*See* under *Bright And Morning Star*.)

> The Day-Star hath risen, the night-
>   clouds have flown;
> No longer in sadness I wander alone;
> Its beams in the valley reflected I see
> The Day-Star hath risen – it shineth
>   on me.

"Dayspring" is from a word meaning, "a rising up," and is used of the rising of the sun and stars. The word *east* (Matthew 2:1), also means the same. It also has a further meaning of "a shoot," and so the KJV margin (Luke 1:78) gives us *branch.* The symbolic title Dayspring therefore implies One through whom light came into the world,

shining immediately on Israel, to dispel the darkness which was upon all nations. Then it is from the *east,* the quarter of the sun's rising that the Glory of God came (Ezekiel 8:16; 43:1, 2). "The *east* in general stands for that side of things upon which the rising of the sun gives light." Ellicott observes that "The English word expresses the force of the Greek very beautifully. The dawn is seen in the East rising up, breaking through the darkness." Job reminds us that it is God who caused "the dayspring to know his place" (38:12). With prophetic insight he personalized the *Dayspring.*

The phrase suggesting "on high" occurs six times in the New Testament (Luke 1:78; 24:49; Ephesians 3:18; 4:8; James 1:9; Revelation 21:16), and reveals the origin of the *Dayspring,* even Christ Himself who came from "on high" as "the Sun of Righteousness" arising on a dark world (Isaiah 60:19). Wycliffe translates Luke's phrase, "*He* (Christ) springing up from on high." The word for *dayspring* is also used of the rising of a heavenly body. The purpose of our heavenly Dayspring is that He might "give light" (Luke 1:79). The Hebrew for *dayspring* signifies *Branch,* as in Jeremiah 23:5 and Zechariah 3:8 where the word means springing, or rising up. Both meanings are combined in the prophecy of Zacharias (Luke 1:78), for Jesus came both as the *Branch* and as the *Light.*

> Dayspring! Thou heavenly source
>   Of each returning day;
> And each one in its course
>   Still points to Thee, the Way,
>   To everlasting day
>   For all who Thee obey.

❋   ❋   ❋

Deliverer (Romans 11:26).

In his prophecy of Israel's national salvation, Paul, quoting from David, wrote, "There shall come out of Sion *the* Deliverer" (Psalm 14:7; Romans 11:26). Used as a noun and name of Christ, *Deliverer* proclaims Him to be One who rescues us from sin and destruction and preserves from such. Paul also reminds us of the threefold deliverance secured for us (2 Corinthians 1:10) – *past, present*, and *prospective*. How perfectly Christ answers to the question, "Shall the prey be taken from the mighty, or the lawful captive delivered?" Such a question was answered of old (Isaiah 49:25, 26). He is *the* Deliverer (Psalm 91:14-16).

He delivers us from the *guilt of our sin*, that separated us from God (Isaiah 59:2). Then He assures us that in receiving Him as our Saviour from the penalty of sin, that the past has been cast into the depths of the sea (Micah 7:19). Can any words more fully assure us of the completeness of deliverance from our guilty past?

He delivers us also from the *power and dominion of sin*. Although saved from the *guilt* of sin, we need to be daily delivered from the *government* of sin, for there is a constant warfare against satanic forces (Romans 7:23, 24; Ephesians 6:11-13). But in living union with the Deliverer, and with the indwelling Holy Spirit we can be more than conquerors (Galatians 5:17, 18; Romans 8:37). The omnipotence of the Deliverer is pledged to us (Philippians 4:13).

He likewise delivers us from the entire *presence* of sin when He returns. Now we live in the presence of sin. It is within in the possession of the old nature, and sin is all around us in a corrupt world. But when Jesus comes the Church will be saved to sin no more, and she will be caught up out of a sinful world to be with Him in the land where nought that defileth can enter. What a complete Deliverer then He is! He has done all

for us; He *is* doing all for us; He *shall* yet accomplish all for us (Hebrews 2:15).

Our Christ is the Deliverer
  From sin, from Hell, from ev'ry fear;
And Israel shall gathered be
  By Him whose love is full and free.

* * *

Desire of All Nations (Haggai 2:7).

While Haggai's prophecy concerning the Messiah, "the *Desire* of all nations shall come," received a fulfillment in the Incarnation, a wider fulfillment is to be understood by the prophet's declaration. The word for *desire* can be given as "hope," and Jeremiah describes *Jehovah* as "The Hope of Israel" (14:8; 17:13). Paul tells us that he was a prisoner in chains for "the hope of Israel" (Acts 28:20). The shaking of the nations – not their conversion – but the turmoil, agitation, and universal unrest is to precede the coming of the One who alone can usher in world peace. Alas! today the Messiah is not desired by all nations for to the vast majority of men He is as "a root out of a dry ground" having no beauty that they should desire Him (Isaiah 53:2). While the nations do not presently desire Him, yet He is the only One who can satisfy the yearning desires within the heart of man.

But Christ is not only the Desire or Hope of all nations, He is the Hope of His redeemed Church. Does not Paul describe the Rapture of the Church at Christ's return as "the Blessed Hope" (Titus 2:13)? We could not live without hope. Robert Bridges called it, "Sweet Hope – Bearer of dreams." Christ's promised return is certainly "the salt and sinew" of our life in Him (John 14:1-3). Because He cannot lie we know that He will come again as He said He would.

"Upheld by hope" in darkest days
  Faith can the light descry:

The deepening glory in the east
Proclaims deliverance nigh.

❈   ❈   ❈

Door (John 10:7, 9).

What marvelous truths are embodied in the glorious I Am's of Christ! Here we have one easily understood by a child, *I am the Door!* As soon as the youngest can grasp the meaning of things, they know that a door can both admit and exclude. Christ is the *Way In* to the fold, with all its blessed privileges, both for shepherds and sheep (John 14:6; Ephesians 2:18). Taken with the opening verses of our Lord's allegory of Himself as the Good Shepherd it would seem as if the phrase, "I am the door of the sheep" implies not a "door for the sheep" but the "door to the sheep" – "the door into the sheepfold" (John 10: 1, 2). Such a Door can never be narrowed to the fold, nor widened (Revelation 22:18, 19).

A door is also used to describe a divine opening and liberty for the Master's service (1 Corinthians 16:9; Revelation 3:8), as well as liberty for communion with Christ (Revelation 3:20), but its relevance to Christ as the Shepherd is what presently concerns us. Sinners in their spiritual blindness grope for the door, but there is only access through Jesus who proclaimed Himself *the* Door (Genesis 19:11; Ephesians 2:18). Having removed the barrier of iniquity and guilt, He became the exclusive entrance into *His* Church. No statement of His is more explicit than the one declaring that "no man cometh unto the Father, *but by Me*" (John 14:6). All who dismiss His mediation have no access to God.

Man must stoop to enter this Door. Everything of self and the world and man-conceived methods of access to God, such as *Mariolatry*, must be cast away (Philippians 3:7, 8). Further, man can never enter if he doubts that the Door is not wide enough for him to enter by (Hebrews 3:18, 19). Jesus said that if we come to God in the way directed, namely, through His finished work, "we shall be *saved*" (Isaiah 12: 1-3). After this great blessing greeting us on the threshold, then we "*shall go in and out and find pasture*" (John 10: 9). This is "the glorious liberty" Paul writes of (Romans 8:21). All necessary *pasture* is found – every need is supplied – for the one who has entered the Door is "blessed with *all* spiritual blessings in heavenly places" in Him who offered Himself as the only entrance into such wealth.

But while a door admits, it can also exclude. The most moving sentence in our Lord's Parable of the Marriage Feast is the one describing those who were invited to the wedding and when the door was wide open, were not ready to enter, and then when they did arrive *the door was shut*. Although they cried, "Lord, Lord, open to us," the only reply they received was "I know you not" (Matthew 25:1-13). Did Jesus not also warn those who rejected Him as the Door that if they died in their sin they would not be with Him in Glory. "Whither I go, ye cannot come" (John 8:21-24)? What a glorious hope is ours if we have the assurance that we have entered the right and only Door into the sheepfold.

> One Door, and only *One*,
> And yet its sides are two –
> Inside and Outside,
> On which side are *you*?

E

Elect (Isaiah 42:1).

The divine Servant who was to come as a "light to lighten the Gentiles, and the glory of His people, Israel" is described by Isaiah as "*mine elect,* in whom my soul delighteth" (42:1-7). The RV gives us "chosen" for *elect*. The prophet also called Israel by the same name, "Israel mine elect" – RV chosen – (45:4; 65:9, 22). The angels also are spoken of as God's *elect*, but neither the angels nor Israel are said to be chosen *in Christ* and *before* the world began (Ephesians 1:4, 5). This honor hath all the saints – and saints alone! As God's *elect* they were chosen in Christ before the world began and they know that they are God's election (1 Thessalonians 1:4), because they were chosen in Christ in a past eternity.

> "God's *purpose* in Eternity infallibly makes good in time and for ever the salvation of the elect; while God's eternal *grace* in Christ characterises the blessed nature of that salvation" (*See* 2 Timothy 1:9).

For all sinners outside the household of faith, the Gospel of free, full, unlimited grace to *all* should be presented; while election and the sovereign grace of God are precious truths most comforting to the *saint*. It will be observed that this election refers to *individual* believers not to the Church collectively. The phrase "The *church* that *is* at Babylon, elected together with you" (1 Peter 5:13), may seem to contradict such a statement. But, *church* is in italics implying it is not in the original. It is the feminine definite article that is used, and implies an individual sister of the Church, "*She* that is elected together with you," probably Peter's own wife, or some prominent saintly woman in the church.

Returning to Christ, as Jehovah's *Elect*, He is described thus as the One chosen by God for the accomplishment of His purposes on behalf of Israel and the earth. He is also the *Elect* as a Foundation-Stone on which to *rest,* and the Cornerstone in which to glory (1 Peter 2:4-7). Christ was selected by God before the foundation of the world, for our atonement (1 Peter 1:20; Revelation 13:8). Redemption was no afterthought to remedy an unforeseen disaster. "Before the disease, God provided the remedy." Thus Jesus came as the Lamb slain *before* the world began (Romans 16: 25, 26; Ephesians 3:9, 11; Titus 1:2, 3). Matthew uses *Mine Elect* with *My Beloved* (12:18), and *election* and the *love of God* are inseparably bound together. If the original of *elect* has the idea of being "picked out from others," we can understand why God gathered out those of high angelic rank for administrative association with God for service in heaven, and among men. The greater wonder is that He picked out His beloved Son from the whole army of heaven to be the Mediator between Himself and men. As Jesus hung upon the cross, the mocking Jews flung in His face His claim to be "the Christ of God, *His Chosen* – His Elect." He was indeed the One whom God had "separated out, equipped, and dedicated to His service," even the death of the cross. As "The Elect, Consecrated One" we have a tribute to the unique loftiness of His Messianic office. Truly the Saviour was –

> Elect to do Thy Father's will
> In spotless holiness;
> And thus the perfect law fulfil,
> And bring in life and peace.

* * *

Emmanuel (Matthew 1:23).

This meaningful name the angel of the Lord gave to Jesus before His birth, is found three times in Scripture, namely, Isaiah 7:14; 8:8, and then in the above New Testament verse, where the Hebrew significance of Emmanuel is given – *God with us*. The Old Testament references were fulfilled in Christ. Dr. Warfield says this name is "a testimony to the essential deity of the virgin-born Child. . . . The very name *Jesus* as truly as that of *Emmanuel* itself, is thus freighted with an implication of the Deity of its Bearer; and this sense of the supreme majesty of the great personality whose life-history as the promised Messiah Matthew has undertaken to portray."

Although Isaiah applied this name to Ahaz it was by no means exhausted in him. The prophet furnishes us with a comment on the Hebrew meaning of the name Emmanuel – *God is with us,* to protect and save, in the verse, "Devise a device, but it shall come to naught; speak a word, but it shall not stand, for *with us is God*" (Isaiah 8:10). The promise of this precious name by Jesus is His helpful and saving presence with His people in their sorrow, their conflict with sin, and their facing of death, "Lo, I am *with you* alway" (Matthew 28:20). "Thou art with me" (Psalm 23:4). It is in this character as the ever-present Companion, that the living bond and most intimate fellowship between God and man was summed up in one word – *Emmanuel.*

> Law declares that God is *against* us (Romans 3:19, 20).
> Grace shows us that God is *with* us (Luke 2:10, 11).

Certainly God was with His people of old, for He walked and talked with Enoch, Noah, and Abraham. Then His word to Israel long ago was, "Fear not, for I am with thee." But the marvel of Bethlehem was when, in the little earthen framework of a helpless Babe, Very Man and Very God became One – "God manifest in flesh." God and man, one Christ. *As the Man,* He understands all about our human emotions, needs, and temptations; and *as the God* He can meet every one of them.

While Paul clearly taught the abiding presence of Christ, he loved to dwell on Christ *within* the believer. "Christ *in you* the hope of glory." One of the old divines wrote of the believer as "a mysterious cabinet of the Trinity."

> He is *before* us, and will be our Guide; He is *behind* us, so no ill can betide; He is *beside* us to comfort and to cheer; He is *around* us, then why should we fear? He is *within* us, as Companion and Friend.

* * *

Ensign (Isaiah 11:10, 12).

Being in capitals, LORD means Jehovah as the American Standard Version uniformly shows. "A root of Jesse" is a prophecy of Him who would come as "the Son of David," and stand permanently and prominently as a banner lifted up to be the rallying-point of Jews and Gentiles alike. (*See* more fully under *Jehovah-Nissi,* The Lord our Banner.)

* * *

Everlasting Father (Isaiah 9:6).

The ASV gives the Hebrew significance of this remarkable name as "Father of Eternity." "His name shall be called . . . Everlasting Father." When a Roman citizen had done some brave, beautiful deed of infinite value and of noble self-denial, while soldiers raised him on their shields and maidens threw garlands of flowers at his feet, the populace would hail him in their shouts and songs as *Pater Patriae* – Father of his country.

Such an honorable title given to men can illustrate the idea associated with the words rendered *Everlasting Father.* Christ was certainly, *The Father of His Country,* for while on earth He declared that He came from heaven where He had been through the eternal past. For Him, whose Fatherland was the universe, and whose age is eternity, the glory is that He is the Christ of all ages. The mystery our finite minds cannot understand is that although the Everlasting *Father,* He became a *child.* Further, earthly fathers leave the world after reaching their allotted span, but this *Father* will never die, but ever live to bless with fatherly love and provision. The Septuagint and Vulgate versions translate the prophetic name as, "Father of the age to come."

Some may feel that this fourth name in the cluster Isaiah gives "confounds the persons," and makes the names of the Father and the Son as interchangeable. But the prophet used "Father" of the coming *Prince of Peace,* because no other seemed to express the true idea of loving and protecting government. Job speaks of himself as being "a *father* to the poor" (29:16). Isaiah referred to Eliakim as "a father to the inhabitants of Jerusalem" (22:21). Such is the idea resident in Isaiah's use of *Father.* "If the kingdom was to be 'for ever and ever,' then in some very real sense He would be in that attribute of Fatherly government, a sharer in the eternity of Jehovah."

O Everlasting Father, God!
Sun after sun went down, and trod
Race after race the green earth's sod,
Till generations seemed to be
But dead leaves from a deathless tree.
But Thou hast come, and now we know
Each wave hath an eternal flow,
Each leaf a life-time after snow.

F

Faithful and True (Revelation 19:11).

As we know, the Revelation abounds in elaborate descriptive titles of Him which this final book of the Bible magnifies. Among these are those designations extolling Jesus for His trustworthiness and reliability. He is called –

"The Faithful and True" (19:11).
"The faithful witness" (1:5).

"The faithful and true witness" (3:14).
"He that is true" (3:7).

Christ was not only faithful to the truth always, and faithful in its application, whether in promises of blessing or cursing, He was the personification of Truth. "I am *the . . . truth*" (John 14:6). Pilate asked, "What is truth?" How blind he was to the fact that *Truth* stood before Him, who was ever "faithful and true." In His person and ways He was the perfect embodiment of these attributes. "Faithful in the performance of every promise and every threat, while every word and act bears the stamp of absolute truth." As the coming King of nations, His ways will be "righteous and and true" (Revelation 16:7).

Lord! The Faithful and the True,
    Thou wilt yet come again;
In judgment wilt make all things new,
    And take Thy right, and reign.

※　※　※

Faithful Witness (Revelation 1:5; 3:14).

First of all, let us try to understand what a true witness is. The Bible has much to say about false witnesses, those who are not truthful. They lie in the evidence they give. But a faithful witness is one who furnishes evidence or proof from having known or actually seen something. In the Greek, the word *witness* is "martyr" – one that gives testimony to the truth at the expense of life. It has been pointed out that the word *witness,* in its noun or verb form, is found not less than 72 times in the writings ascribed to John. It is his characteristic word. In His *salutation* (Revelation 1:5) to the seven churches in Asia, John has a triad of names covering the past, present, and prospective ministry of our Lord:

"The Faithful Witness" – *past,* public ministry.

"The First begotten of the Dead" — *present,* alive for evermore.

"The Prince of the Kings of the Earth" — *future,* millennial reign.

The first title is the one presently concerning us, and is one embracing the whole of our Lord's life from the cradle to the cross. Such a comprehensive title is in marked contrast to all preceding witness for God. "The path of human testimony is strewn with wreck and ruin. He alone passed through earth in His solitary and rugged path of unswerving devotedness to God, without break or flaw in all His holy separateness to God." In declaring His credentials He could say, "To this end was I born, and for this cause came I into the world, that I should bear witness unto the truth" (John 18:37).

There are at least three things which go to the making of a faithful witness, and such are evident in the life, and ministry of our Lord.

1. *Experience.*
An effective witness is one who has a personal realization of the truth he seeks to testify to. Christ is the only One who has seen and known God, and with such a qualification He must be listened to as He speaks about His Father (Luke 10:22; John 1:18). Like Him, we are only true witnesses as we speak the things which *we* have seen and heard (Acts 4:20).

2. *Certainty.*
If there is anything of a doubtful character about a witness, the people will not pay much heed to his testimony. Life and lips must ring true. Christ always declared the truth with authority and certainty, because He was *The Truth.* Behind the witness of His lips was the faithfulness of life (John 8:40-46; 1 Corinthians 14:7-9). He said of His own, "Ye are My witnesses," and

like Him we should be able to proclaim the truth with assurance and confidence because of obedience to the truth (Ephesians 1:13; 2 Timothy 1:12). *See* 1 Kings 17:24.

3. *Boldness.*
A testimony has greater effectiveness when it is proclaimed with courage. Light must not be hid under a bushel. We are told that the people marvelled at. the *boldness* of Peter and John as they witnessed to the reality of Christ's resurrection (Acts 4:13). The Master never shrank from telling the truth He had come from heaven to announce. Even in the face of the greatest danger and opposition, He never failed to declare the whole counsel of God (John 6:66; 8:59). May ours be the spirit, not of fear, but of power to present the testimony of the Lord (2 Timothy 1:7, 8)! May we never fail to declare by word and deed, the truth received from God (Proverbs 14:25)! Think of the reward if we emulate the example of Him who is "The Faithful Witness" (Matthew 10:32)!

> Faithful in all, Lord Jesus,
>   To Him Who called Thee;
> And Thou wilt deign to bless us,
>   In granting constancy.

*   *   *

Finisher of Faith (Hebrews 12:2). (*See* under *Author of Faith*).

*   *   *

First and Last (Revelation 1:11; 22:13).

*   *   *

Applied to Christ as eternal and supreme. (*See* under *Alpha and Omega.*)

*   *   *

First Begotten (Hebrews 1:6).
Arthur Way translates the passage,

"What time He shall again bring His First-born Son into the world," and in a footnote connects this with the Second Advent (2 Thessalonians 1:7).

The term "firstborn" implies a title of dignity, not necessarily of birth (Psalm 89:27; Colossians 1:15). The designation, used of Christ without qualification means that as God's *Firstborn* He takes rank above all other existing beings; even all the angels shall do Him reverence. *Firstborn* and *Heir* are equal in honor with *Son*. God's *Firstborn* is also naturally God's *Heir,* an Heir whose inheritance embraces the universe, and whose tenure stretches to eternity. "All these declarations are bound very closely together in their common relation to the fundamental conception of our Lord's Sonship."

The term *firstborn* was used in its natural sense of Christ as Mary's firstborn (Luke 2:7). It is also employed in a literal sense of the firstborn of men and animals (Hebrews 11:28). But when used of Christ Himself, the title implies that in His incarnation He was brought into the world as God's Firstborn, and therefore should be honored and obeyed by "the church of the firstborn who are enrolled in heaven" (Hebrews 12:23). Primogeniture gave princedom and priesthood in patriarchal times. The eldest son in all Israelite families was regarded as sacred to God, because Israel's firstborn were exempted from the stroke which destroyed all the firstborn of Egypt on that first Passover night (Genesis 49:3; Exodus 4:22, 23; 1 Chronicles 5:1; Hebrews 12:16).

Christ is the Firstborn, and as the laws and customs of all nations show that to be *firstborn* means, not only priority in time, but a certain superiority in privilege and authority, so used of Christ the designation means that He, too, has the full rights of primogeniture, hence the divine proclamation –

"When God *shall* bring in *again* the First-begotten into the world, He shall be deemed worthy of no less honour for – He saith (Psalm 97:7), Let all the angels of God worship Him" (Hebrews 1:6 – *Greek*).

Thus, His being "brought into the world" – the inhabited world – as the theater of His power, mainly applies to His second appearance to usher in His millennial reign.

Associated with Christ as God's *Firstborn* is the avowal of His sonship and kingship involving His universal dominion as indicated by the psalmist as the decree of Jehovah –

"Yet I have set my king
Upon my holy hill of Zion.
I will tell of the decree:
Jehovah said unto me, Thou art my son;
This day have I begotten thee" (Psalm 2:6, 7 asv).

Here we have the solemn recognition of eternal Sonship – "Thou *art* my son." From the dateless past Christ has been God's only begotten Son. What then is the significance of the assertion, "*This day* have I begotten thee"? Paul, in his synagogue sermon at Antioch, takes this Old Testament quotation and links it to the Resurrection of Christ (Acts 13:29-37). Then, in a wonderful way He was begotten as the Son, "alive for evermore." But there is the larger fulfillment of the psalmist's prophecy for the risen Christ was promised "the sure mercies of David." Jehovah said He would set His Eternal Son as King upon His holy hill of Zion, and the day this takes place He will be begotten as *King* claiming the nations for His inheritance as He reigns from David's throne.

❦　❦　❦

First Begotten of the Dead (Revelation 1:5; Colossians 1:18).

By this further designation of Christ we are not to understand that He was the first to rise from the grave. There were resurrections in the Old Testament, and He Himself while here among men raised Lazarus and two young people from the dead. As He died upon the cross, many graves were opened, and "the saints which slept arose," to herald the resurrection of Him, whose veil of flesh had been rent in 'twain, resulting in their return to earth (Matthew 27: 52). In what sense, then, was He the "Firstborn of the dead," or out from among the dead? In his Magna Carta of the Resurrection, Paul refers to Christ as "the firstfruits of them that slept" (1 Corinthians 15:20-23), and He is both *Firstborn* and *Firstfruits* of the blessed dead. If there is any distinction between these two descriptions –

Firstborn is the title signifying that He is first in *rank* of all the saints who will rise from the dead, for this title suggests supremacy, preeminent dignity, and not one of time or of chronological sequence (Psalm 89:27). He became the Prince of Life.

Firstfruits intimates that He is first in *time* of the coming harvest of those who sleep in Him, and who, at the return of Christ in the air, will undergo a change equivalent to the raising of the dead (Philippians 3:21; 1 John 3:2). As the *Firstfruits*, Christ is the pledge of the resurrection of the dead in Him.

As the Federal Head of a new race, namely, the redeemed of all ages known as His Body, His Church, who are to be raised from the dead and caught up to meet Him at His return, it was essential for Him to rise again and ascend on high as the Captain or Leader of their salvation. He is the Firstborn out from the dead, who died in Him (Colossians 1:18). Thus Paul outlines the order of the resurrection of the Head and the Body –

"Every man in his own order:
    Christ the firstfruits;
    Afterward they that are Christ's
    at His coming" (1 Corinthians 15:23).

In what he calls the "Hymn of the Resurrection and Exaltation" Arthur Way has this most expressive translation of the passage dealing with the Resurrection of Christ and His Church –

"Messiah *has* been raised from the dead! and (since one resurrection disproves the impossibility)

He is the first sheaf of a great Harvest,
Of all who have 'been hushed to death's sleep . . .'

Yet must each come in his befitting rank – Messiah the firstfruits,
Then, in the Day of His Coming, Messiah's Own,
Then shall be the end."

❋   ❋   ❋

Firstborn Among the Brethren (Romans 8:29).

"He should have many brothers, Himself the first-born." The gathering home of the Elect will witness the consummation of God's grace. Then Jesus will see of the travail of His soul, and with joy exclaim, "Behold, I and the children which God hath given me" (Hebrews 2:11-13). He is the Pattern, as well as Lord of those He is not ashamed to call His brethren, who were "foreordained to be conformed to His image" (*see* Romans 8:20). As the *Firstborn*, He has eternal priority, yet He condescended brotherhood with those redeemed by His blood, or participants of the salvation through His sufferings (Hebrews 2:10).

Lord, how wonderful! surpassing
    human ken

Is Thy condescension to the sons
of men;
Thou art not ashamed to call us
brethren,
Making us one with Thee and heirs
of Heaven.

❋   ❋   ❋

Firstborn of Every Creature (Colossians 1:15).

In his hymn of Messiah Supreme, Paul rises to great heights in his exalted description of Christ who rescued us from "the tyranny of darkness, and transferred us into the Kingdom of the Son of His love."

First-born before all created things
is He.
For in Him were all things created –
Things in the heavens and on the
earth;
The things visible, the things invisible.

Christ is not only prior to Creation in time, but above it in power and authority. As Lightfoot in his most valuable commentary on *Colossians* states it, "He is sovereign Lord over all creation by virtue of primo-geniture." In this solemn designation of Deity, "First born of all creation," Paul makes it clear that "all things have been created through Him, and unto Him" (Colossians 1:16; John 13:16). Such a title denotes "Christ's status and character not His origin; the context does not admit the idea that He is a part of the created universe." Seeing that He was "long before every creature," He cannot be a creature Himself but the Creator. The Head of every man is Christ (1 Corinthians 11:3).

❋   ❋   ❋

Forerunner (Hebrews 6:20).

This meaningful name signifies one who goes in advance to make observations or act as a scout, especially in military matters, or one sent before a king to see that the way is prepared (Isaiah 40:3; Matthew 11:10). Used of Christ it implies that He went in advance of His own to prepare a place for them, so that when He returns for them they can be with Him according to His wish (John 14:2, 3; 17:24). This is the only place in the Bible where the term *Forerunner* occurs, and is most fitting of Him who is the *Pioneer* of His redeemed ones, their *File-Leader,* who goes before them to prepare a way for them, to open up the gates of heaven by His atoning blood and priestly intercession.

Christ is the heavenly Joseph who went before to prepare a home and provisions for His brethren (Genesis 45:26-28; 50:19-21). It will be enough for us when we see that He is alive forevermore. When He left for His home on high, He assured His own that He would not leave them as orphans before He returned for them, but that He would send Another like Himself to console their hearts, and keep alive in them the hope of His return (John 14:18, 26). As John the Baptist was Christ's forerunner on earth, so Christ is ours in heaven. Chrysostom, church father of the 3rd century, the most eloquent preacher of the early Church, and often called "golden-mouthed" because of a legend that when he was a baby a swarm of bees settled on his mouth," has this comment –

"The First-Fruits of our nature has ascended, and so the rest is sanctified. Christ's ascension is our promotion: and whither the glory of the Head has preceded, thither the hope of the body, too, is called. We ought to keep the festal day, since Christ has taken up and set in the heavens the first-fruit of our lump, that is the human flesh."

Our Great Forerunner, Jesus,
Has entered in for us;
The veil is rent, the way is clear,

Our Great High Priest is there.

❋　❋　❋

Foundation (1 Corinthians 3:11).

Roman Catholicism errs in its claim that because Peter's name means *rock,* that when Jesus said, "Upon this rock I will build my church" (Matthew 16: 16-18). He implied that it would be built upon Peter. So, impulsive Peter is claimed as the first Pope. Peter would have been the very first to admit that he was very poor material to build on. By the *rock,* Jesus meant the words Peter had said as the result of a heavenly revelation, "Thou art the Christ, the Son of the Living God." Thus Jesus Christ Himself is the only Foundation of His Church, and no man can lay another.

> The Church's one Foundation,
> Is Jesus Christ her Lord;
> She is His new creation
> By water and the Word.

Had He meant Peter as such a Foundation, He would have said, "Thou art Peter, and on thee will I build My Church." But what Christ said suggests an implied contrast—

> "Thou art the Rock-Apostle; and yet not *the* Rock on which the Church is to be built. It is enough for thee to have found the Rock, and to have built on one Foundation."

All who build upon the Rock of Ages are indeed wise, for founded upon such a Rock, their house cannot fall (Matthew 7:24). (*See* further under *Cornerstone.*)

> On Christ, the solid Rock, I stand:
> All other ground is sinking sand,
> All other ground is sinking sand.

❋　❋　❋

Fountain (Zechariah 13:1).

The Bible has frequent references to fountains, or the natural bursting of waters from the ground (Deuteronomy 8:7; 11:11). As a figure of speech *fountain* is applied in many different ways —

> Of God (Psalm 36:9; Jeremiah 2: 13).
> Of wisdom and godliness (Proverbs 13:14; 14:27).
> Of good wives (Proverbs 5:18).
> Of obedient children (Deuteronomy 33:28; Psalm 68:26).
> Of prosperity (Psalms 107:35; 114: 8; Hosea 13:15).
> Of the physical heart (Ecclesiastes 12:6).
> Of life everlasting (Revelation 7: 17; 21:6).

Zechariah, however, was given a vision of Calvary when he prophesied that the day would come when "a fountain would be opened to the house of David, and to the inhabitants of Jerusalem for sin and for uncleanness." While there is an obvious reference here to Israel, yet it carries the wider implication of divine pardon and purification for all who repent and believe. The tragedy is that although such a Fountain was opened when the hands, feet and side of Jesus were pierced, the vast majority do not have opened eyes to the Well of Life at their disposal in Him. Hagar was ignorant of the refreshment divinely provided for her until her "eyes were opened" (Genesis 21:19). The Cross is a *Fountain* ever flowing, and not a laver needing constantly to be replenished. Justification and sanctification both flow from the blood of Christ, not from ceremonial sacrifices (1 Corinthians 1:30; Hebrews 9:13, 14).

> There is a Fountain filled with blood,
> Drawn from Emmanuel's veins;
> And sinners plunged beneath that flood,
> Lose all their guilty stains.

❋　❋　❋

Friend (Proverbs 18:24; Matthew 11: 19).

It was Tacitus, the Roman philosopher, who said that, "nothing can be purchased which is better than a firm friend." What firmer Friend, then, can we have than Jesus who offers Himself as the Friend sticking closer than a brother, and who ever remains a Friend of sinners (Luke 15:1, 2). The Bible has much to say about friends and friendship, whether beneficial or baneful. For instance, Solomon's references to the qualifications of a true friend are profitable to observe: "A friend loveth at all times, and a brother is born for adversity" (Proverbs 17:17).

Christ is both Friend and Brother and in His friendship clings closer than a brother (Proverbs 18:24). He loves us in adversity, as well as in prosperity. "A friend in need is a friend indeed," and He is ever with us in time of need, just as when we are satisfied. A maxim said to have been used by Francis Bacon in advice to students was, "Friends are thieves of time." But our heavenly Friend is never a thief of our time, but ever enriches it with His presence, and provision.

Seneca once wrote, "Friendship is ever serviceable; love has at times also the property of being hurtful." It is so with our heavenly Friend who chastens those He loves. His sharpest reproofs are from an upright and loving heart. "Faithful are the wounds of a friend" (Proverbs 27:6). Ever faithful in the performance of all friendly offices, He reproves and rebukes when there is anything alien to His holy will in the lives of those to whom He extends friendship.

"Ointment and perfume rejoice the heart; so doth the sweetness of a man's friend by hearty counsel" (Proverbs 27:9). By such counsel as comes from the very heart of our divine Friend, we are refreshed, gladdened and given a heavenly aroma. A similar thought of benefit is found in Solomon's further

word that, "Iron sharpeneth iron, so a man sharpeneth the countenance of his friend" (27:17). Our very faces come to reflect the spiritual initiative we receive from fellowship with the Friend above the best of friends. A saying of Cicero's was, "A friend is, as it were, a second self." Christ is not our "second self," but our very life.

It is interesting to seek out those to whom heavenly friendship was extended, and are named as being friends of Him who ever desires to be at peace with men. The coveted title, "The Friend of God," was one principally given to Abraham, "God's friend for ever" (2 Chronicles 20:7). "Abraham my friend" (Isaiah 41:8). James likewise speaks of the patriarch as "The friend of God." Such a designation was given Abraham, not only because God frequently appeared to him, and revealed His secrets to him (Genesis 18:17), but also because He entered into a covenant of perpetual friendship with Abraham and his seed forever (Genesis 12:2, 3). A further reason was the renewal of the covenant upon the willing sacrifice of Isaac when the patriarch came into a closer degree of friendship and communion with his Friend (Genesis 22:16, 17). It was for this willing sacrifice and obedience that James says that he came to be called, *the* friend of God."

Coming to the New Testament, we have the Master calling those He had chosen as apostles, *His friends.* "I have called you friends" (John 15:15). Then He adds the reason naming them thus. "For all things that I have heard of my Father, I have made known unto you." We sometimes say that there should be no secrets between true friends. What a marvelous revelation of Himself He gave to the disciple He loved, which is found in the last book of the Bible! All that is necessary for salvation, instruction, service and comfort He ever reveals to His friends. "He that hath friends must show himself friendly" (Proverbs 18:24). Jesus is never anything else but friendly towards His friends.

> Not a Friend but Jesus
> Fully understands;
> All the secret lieth
> In His holy hands.

That He was the perfect Friend even when those who professed to be His friends hurt Him is seen in His treatment of Judas in his act of betraying his Friend. Judas kissed Jesus but it was not the greeting kiss of a true friend but the heartless kiss of a traitor. Yet Jesus greeted him, "*Friend,* wherefore art thou come?" (Matthew 26:50). There is no irony in the Master's voice, as if He meant the contrary to what the name meant. It came from a loving heart smitten with sorrow over the action of such a professed apostle and friend. What a sting that name *friend* must have left behind in the conscience of Judas who knew himself to be the reverse of what Jesus had called him!

In one of His matchless parables, Jesus used the term *friend* freely (Luke 11:5-8). James warns us that "the friendship of the world is enmity with God" (4:4). If we are among His friends then it is incumbent upon us to love what He loves, and hate what He hates. The marvel is that He offers Himself as "the Friend of publicans and sinners." But as such He does not condone their sins, or shut His eyes to their iniquities. When we were His enemies, He loved us and died for us. When He feasted with sinners, it was not to show Himself as a fellow well-met, or good mixer, but as a Friend who loved their souls and sought to love them out of their sin to Himself. May we be brought into a fuller realization of what it means to have this Beloved as our Friend (Song of Solomon 5:16)!

> What a Friend we have in Jesus
> All our sins and griefs to bear.
> What a privilege to carry
> Everything to Him in prayer!

G

Gift of God (John 4:10).

It was at Jacob's well in Sychar that Jesus gave Himself the title of "the Gift of God," for to the woman who came to draw water He said, in reply to her question, "If thou knewest the gift of God, and who it is that saith to thee, Give me to drink; thou wouldest have asked of him, and he would have given thee living water" (John 4:10). Jesus had asked the women for a gift of water, not only because He was weary and thirsty, but that He might prepare the way to speak of the gift He had to bestow, namely, Himself. Truly there is no greater Gift man can receive.

We are often reminded that Jesus came as God's unspeakable Gift to a lost world. "God so loved the world that he *gave* his only begotten Son" (John 3:16). As the Giver was the Gift, He willingly acquiesced in the giving, and "gave Himself for us" (Galatians 2:20). One of two things can be done with a gift – it can be received or rejected. What great reward there is for all who receive the Saviour as God's Gift (John 1:12). How blessed we are when, having received the Gift, we live for the glory of the Giver! Having received the Gift of eternal life ours is the obligation of living as those who, being heaven-born, are heaven-bound.

> Thy life was given for me,
> Thy blood, O Lord, was shed,
> That I might ransom'd be,
> And quicken'd from the dead;
> Thy life was given for me;
> What have I given for Thee?

❖ ❖ ❖

Glory (James 2:1).

It is practical James who gives us the

unique epithet, "our Lord Jesus Christ, *the glory.*" The words "the Lord" in the KJV are in italics, meaning that they are not in the original. Certainly, He is *the Lord of Glory* (1 Corinthians 2:8), but that is not what James had in mind. *The Glory* stands in apposition to "Our Lord Jesus Christ" and both titles define Him in His deity and majesty. The apostle saw in Him the fulfillment of the promise, "For, I, saith Jehovah, will be unto her a wall of fire round about, and I will be *the glory* in the midst of her" (Zechariah 2:5 ASV).

While we would like to elaborate and deal with all aspects of the Glory of Deity, fascinating as they are, we are confining ourselves to the noun used of Jesus, as *the Glory,* but there are yet one or two relevant features we can speak of in passing. First of all, there is the root meaning of the term *glory,* in reference to divine beings. The Hebrew word for same means "weight" or "laden," or "heaviness," and in its primary uses conveys the idea of some external physical manifestation of dignity, preeminence or majesty. Paul alluded to the original significance of the term when he wrote, "our lightness of affliction worketh out of us a *weight* of glory" (2 Corinthians 4:17) – a weight exceeding beyond all measure the affliction.

When the sons of Laban said of Jacob that when he had taken away "that which was our father's hath he gotten all this *glory*" (Genesis 31:1), "glory" here means laden with material wealth, represented by the cattle, camels, asses, and servants Jacob had amassed (Genesis 30:43). In the same way, "tell my father of all my *glory* in Egypt" (Genesis 45:13), refers to the way Joseph was laden with honor, power and authority as governor of the land. When Moses requested, "Shew me thy glory," he implied, "show me thyself, all the honours with which thou art laden" (Exodus 33:

18). He wanted to witness the whole blaze of divine majesty. Evidently the patriarch was permitted to catch a passing glimpse of the glory of Jehovah as a physical manifestation (*see* Exodus 34:5). While the brightness of His face was not seen, spiritual glory was revealed in the proclamation of the name of Jehovah, full of compassion and gracious.

One of the marvels of the Incarnation is that the supreme revelation of the glory of Jehovah was manifest in His beloved Son, a glorious truth John declares in the opening of his gospel, "we beheld *his glory*, the glory as of the only begotten of the Father, full of grace and truth" (John 1:14). He came to manifest the infinite perfections of His Father. So, to quote Paul's affirmation, as given by Arthur Way's translation –

"God . . . has kindled a flame in my heart, to make me a world's beacon of the knowledge of the glory of God as revealed in the face of Jesus the Messiah" (2 Corinthians 4:6).

Thus, although "the heavens declare the glory of God," something more was needed for mankind than divine glory as revealed in the ample sweep of earth and sky. But while God's skill and power are revealed in nature, the sublime character of God is fully revealed in His Son, Jesus Christ, in whom the Glory of God became *personal*. While no man had fully seen God at any time, the Son of His bosom declared Him, and became the perfect, permanent, and final revelation of the Father. "He that hath seen Me hath seen the Father."

On the Mount of Transfiguration there was the outflashing of Christ's inherent glory, as *the Glory*, of which Peter testified when he said of James, John and himself, that they had been "eyewitnesses of his majesty" (2 Peter 1:16). Dr. John Macbeth, dealing with the miracles Jesus performed, and His death and resurrection as being further expressions of divine glory, thereby making the invisible God visible says that —

> "A whole world of progress lies between these two points of expression — 'The heavens declare the glory of God,' and 'The glory of God in the face of Jesus Christ.' The one indicates greatness, the other expresses grace. The first exhibits power, the second presents personality. The former is material, the latter is spiritual."

Christ, then, as *The Glory*, is the manifest excellence of God. Paul referred to "the glory of the incorruptible God" (Romans 1:23), and such is the essential nature of Christ as the sinless One who, therefore, was like God, "the Lord of glory" (1 Corinthians 2:8). The apostle likewise named God as "the Father of glory" (Ephesians 1:17), a title inferring that He is the Source from whom all divine splendor and perfection proceed in their manifestation in Him whose grace and power were weighted with glory. Further, Pauline phrases like — "the praise of his glory" (Ephesians 1: 12, 14) and "the might of his glory" (Colossians 1:11 asv) — acknowledge the exhibition of Christ's attributes and actions, and the might which is characteristic of His Gospel.

But as *The Glory*, Christ will be the wonderful embodiment of "the God of Glory," when in the Glory-land, the redeemed see Him in all "wisdom, power, honour, glory, and blessing" — humanity's dust glorified, worthy to receive "glory, and honour and power" (Revelation 4:11; 5:12).

The Head that once was crowned with
    thorns,
  Is crowned with glory now;
A royal diadem adorns
  The mighty Victor's brow.

The highest place that Heaven affords

Is His by sovereign right:
The King of kings, and Lord of lords,
  He reigns in glory bright.

Jesus is *The Glory*, then, because it is to Him glory belongs as to the One described as "the effulgence of the glory of God" (Hebrews 1:3 asv). As Dr. Warfield comments, "He is *the Glory* of God, the Shekinah: God manifest to men. It is thus that James thought and spoke of his own Brother who died a violent and shameful death while still in His first youth. Surely there is a phenomenon here which may well awaken inquiry."

The Lamb is all *the Glory*,
  In Emmanuel's land.

* * *

Glory of Israel (Luke 2:32).

How fascinating it is to watch how Old Testament predictions are fulfilled in Christ! (*See* further the writer's volume on *All the Prophecies of Christ in the Bible*.) For instance, God is referred to as glory in the midst of Israel (Zechariah 2:5), and as "the God of Israel, the Saviour" (Isaiah 45:15) and the Babe born in Bethlehem came as the King of Israel, and as "the glory of thy people Israel" (Luke 2:32). Jehovah named Himself "*The Glory* of Israel" because He was the proudest possessor of His people. Alas! they prostituted their *Glory* (1 Samuel 4:21, 22; Jeremiah 2:11).

Glory, then, is the possession and characteristic of Jehovah, and was given by Him to His people or to anything connected with Him (Isaiah 60:7; 1 Chronicles 29:11). Jesus became the physical manifestation of divine glory to Israel. It will be noted that godly Simeon in his prophetic insight into the character and ministry of the Babe he held in his arms, proclaimed Him as the universal Saviour in a twofold way —

> "A *Light* to lighten the Gentiles,
> The *Glory* of Thy people Israel."

Naturally, as a devout Jew he had waited for "the consolation of Israel," but Simeon knew that Jesus was born the Saviour of the world. "Mine eyes have seen Thy salvation, which Thou hast prepared before the face of *all* people."

To the *Gentiles,* Jesus came as the *Light,* for they were in spiritual darkness and ignorance and needed the promised enlightening or the revelation by unveiling and manifestation of the One to lighten their darkness (Isaiah 25:7; Matthew 12:21).

For Israel, Jesus came as *The Glory.* She had the *Light* as *His* people, and she has yet to have the glory, which will be fulfilled and realized in the millennium when the Lord will say of her, "Israel my glory!" Having received *light* by the revelation of God through the Law and the Prophets, such light will expand into glory through Him, then Israel can attain her true and highest glory. It will be noticed that this "swan-like song of Simeon, bidding an eternal farewell to this terrestrial life" takes a more comprehensive view of the Kingdom of Christ than that of Zacharias, though the Kingdom they sing of is one (Luke 1:67-80).

> Israel will yet rejoice in Thee, her Lord
>   and God,
> And Thou wilt be her glory, as
>   promised in Thy Word;
> Eternal in Thy covenant, in Thy
>   goodness planned,
> Thy Glory will be dwelling in,
>   covering the land.

* * *

God (Mark 2:7, 10; John 10:28-30).

Many of the numerous names and titles of Christ we are considering testify, either directly or indirectly, to the fact of His Deity, as can be seen from our coverage of designations like, "The Lamb of *God*"; "Lord"; "Mighty *God*"; "Only Begotten"; "Power of *God*"; "Son

of *God.*" Warfield remarks that this Sonship to God is "essentially consubstantiality with God." In these, and other titles, passing references can be found to specific statements as to Christ's inclusion in the Godhead, and now we come to examine them more particularly. We start with the premise that it is in the Bible alone that we have the only authentic record in the world of God revealing Himself and of the various responses of human beings to such a progressive revelation, which culminates in the revelation of Jesus who came as "*God* manifest in flesh." As James L. Low expresses it in his *Dictionary of the Bible* —

> "The writers of the books of the Bible have been like artists trying to paint a picture. The portrait changes with the passing years. The Genesis portrait is not Isaiah's portrait. Till at last in Jesus comes the portrait that remains because it cannot be improved. Every attempt to improve it results merely in one of the earlier portraits emerging. When the Christian thinks of God he thinks of his own mental and spiritual portrait of Jesus and asks for nothing more because he knows there is none better."

That "the mental and spiritual portrait of Jesus" as depicted by the apostles is superb, no honest reader of the New Testament can deny for they all saw in Him God the Son, who was their Lord and their God (John 20:28). That Paul is preeminently the herald of the Deity of Christ is clearly evident from his writings. How he exalted Him as One who, having essential equality with God, yet stooped to the death of the cross (Philippians 2:6-8). When the apostle exalts Christ as Lord, "the whole majesty of Christ lies in this predicate." For Paul the recognition of His Lordship, or

Deity expresses the essence of Christianity (Romans 10:9; 2 Corinthians 4:5).

It is Paul who provides us with the most solemn ascriptions of the proper Deity of Jesus Christ discoverable in the whole compass of the New Testament. The apostle never leaves us in any doubt as to his Christ being of the same substance as God. Think of these remarkable epithets – "the great God and our Saviour," or "our great God and Saviour" – "God our Saviour" (1 Timothy 1:1; Titus 2:13; 3:4).

Had Deity not been His, His death would have had no efficacy to save from sin. But He is mighty to save because the blood He shed, was "the blood of God" (Acts 20:28). When the apostles identified Jesus with *Jehovah* and called Him LORD, they used a title charged with associations of Deity. When Paul called Him "the Lord of glory" (1 Corinthians 2:8), he had a clear and strong conception of Him who claimed equality with God (Philippians 2:6). Whether he thought of Jesus as *Saviour* or *Lord*, the same were to Him standing epithets of God (Titus 1:3).

In his synopsis of Israel's privileges Paul depicts Christ as the God who ruleth over all things "Christ came, who is over all, God blessed for ever" (Romans 9:5). Then, in his letter to the Colossians, he makes it clear that Christ as God was not in any sense inferior to God the Father, or that He possessed "a merely delegated authority," but that in "him dwelleth all the fulness of the Godhead bodily" (Colossians 2:9, 10). Here the term *bodily* means in bodily fashion, or as "the form of a body," and implies an organic whole. The fullness of the Godhead existed in all its completeness in Christ. Although He came as "the image of God" (Colossians 1:15), He was not only an invisible God made visible, but in Himself, the *great God* (Titus 2:13). Paul's epistles are strewn

with affirmations of Christ's Deity because everywhere he "thinks and speaks of Christ as very God."

To the apostle, his Lord was not in His real nature merely God's Son who loved him (Galatians 2:20), but the One consubstantial with the Father. *God* as well as Saviour, and *Saviour* because He was God. That Peter shared a like faith in the Deity of Christ, is evident in his presentation of Him as "God and Saviour" (2 Peter 1:1; 3:2, 18). It will be found that when Peter mentions the title *Christ*, he couples it with another designation (2 Peter 1:11; 2:20; 3:18).

As for John who is notable for his remarkable designations of Him whose bosom he rested on, in his gospel and epistles, as well as in Revelation, he loved to magnify the Saviour as *the True God* (1 John 5:20). The Apostle of Love never tired of reminding his readers of the divine dignity of Christ. "So closely is He associated with God the Father (1 John 1:3; 3:23), that to deny Him is to deny the Father (2:23), and to confess Him is to confess the Father (2:23; 4:15), and to abide in Him is to abide in the Father (2:24; 1:3). Obviously to John the *Son of God* is Himself God."

That Christ shared and manifested the attributes of the Godhead can be seen not only in the miracles He performed in the days of His flesh, but in the works assigned to Him in eternity. This is borne out by the marvelous description given of Him in Hebrews which, if Paul did not actually write, he had a great deal to do with. Made "Heir of all things" by the Father, Christ was also the Agent in Creation, "by whom also he made the worlds" (Hebrews 1:2). Creative energy is an attribute of Deity, as is the "upholding" or continuing to control and sustain what is created (Hebrews 1:3).

The RV gives us "the very image of

His substance." *Image* is the Greek word for "character" (*See* under title *Image*), and implies "substance," and is equivalent to "nature" or essence." In no single trait does the Son differ from God. He is the exact reproduction of the divine essence, and counterpart or facsimile of the Father. Is it any surprise therefore that when God spoke of His Son, He said, "Thy throne, O God, is for ever and ever" (Psalm 45:6). Christ, then, stands infinitely above every creature just because He is *God* Himself.

R. W. Gilder would have us sing –

> If Jesus Christ be a man,
>   And only a man, I say,
> That of all mankind I will follow Him,
>   And to Him will cleave alway.
>
> If Jesus Christ be a God,
>   And the only God, I swear,
> I will follow Him through Heaven,
>   or Hell,
> The earth, the sea, the air.

That Christ is a divine Being clothed with all the divine attributes is summarized in a brief but instructive way by Professor Swete in his sketch of Christology in the Book of the Revelation. Identifying Christ with God, the writer says –

"1. *He has the prerogatives of God.*
    He searches men's hearts (Revelation 2:23).
    He can kill or restore life (Revelation 1:18; 2:23).
    He receives a worship which is rendered without distinction to God (Revelation 5:13).
    His priests are also priests of God (Revelation 20:6).
    He occupies one throne with God (Revelation 22:1, 3).
    He shares one Sovereignty (Revelation 11:15).
2. *He receives the titles of God.*
    He is the Living One (Revelation 1:18).

He is the Holy and True (Revelation 3:7).
    He is the Alpha and Omega, the First and the Last, the Beginning and the End (Revelation 22:13).
3. *He has applied to Him without hesitation, Old Testament passages relating to God.* Compare –
    Deuteronomy 10:17 with Revelation 17:14.
    Proverbs 3:12 with Revelation 3:19.
    Daniel 7:9 with Revelation 1:14.
    Zechariah 4:10 with Revelation 5:6."

Is it not comforting to know that as we continue to walk the dusty lanes of earth that as *Emmanuel*, He is "God *with* us" in all that life may hold for us. How apt are the lines of William J. Barnes –

> Paul names His Mediator,
>   Job's Daysman is found.
> A Man, tho' our Creator,
>   Upon God's Throne sits crowned.
> As God, God's rights maintaining
>   From that bright throne on high.
> As Man, our new place gaining,
>   Blest with Himself, so nigh.

✻   ✻   ✻

Good Master (Matthew 19:16, 17).

To the diligent student of Scripture, the personal, private conversations of Jesus with those who crossed His pathway are full of absorbing interest. It will be found that they contain some of the most sublime truths to leave His holy lips. He did not reserve His greatest messages for the crowds, but preached them when alone with individuals who came seeking spiritual light. A case in point is that of the rich young ruler who sought out Jesus for a private talk on how he could obtain eternal life. The seeker's question was,

"Good Master, what good thing

shall I do, that I may have eternal life?"

The Master's reply was clear, concise and conclusive –

> "And he said unto him, Why callest thou me good? there is none good but one, that is, God: but if thou wilt enter into life, keep the commandments."

Parallel passages in Mark and Luke are almost identical in wording as Matthew (Mark 10:17-30; Luke 18:18-30). Compare another who came to Jesus with a similar question as the young ruler's (Luke 10:25-30).

Cynically, Nathanael asked, "Can any *good* thing come out of Nazareth?" Philip replied, "Come and see" (John 1:46). The rich youth, who called forth the love of Jesus, came and saw the *Good Master*, who came out of Nazareth. The word "good" denotes a quality whether physical, moral, or spiritual. As for "master," the term means teacher, schoolmaster, and is from a root signifying, to teach. The Greek has other meanings, but *teacher* is to be understood in the majority of cases in the gospels where "master" is used. *Rabbi* – Rabboni, a Galilean title meaning "My Master," was used out of respect to Jewish teachers. Dalman, the Greek scholar, says –

> "Christ forbade His disciples to allow themselves to be called *Rabbi*, on the ground that He alone was their Master (Matthew 23:8). In reference to Himself the designation was expressive of the real relation between them. The form of *Good Master* He, however, refused to allow (Mark 10:17, 18) . . . in the mouth of the speaker it was mere insolent flattery . . . the Lord was unwilling that anyone should thoughtlessly deal with such an epithet; and here, as always, the

honour due to the Father was the first consideration with Him. . . . The primitive community never ventured to call Jesus *Our Teacher* after He had been exalted to the Throne of God. The title *Rabbi*, expressing the relation of the disciple to the teacher, vanished from use; and there remained only the designation *Maran*, the servant's appropriate acknowledgment of his Lord."

Among his many qualities the young ruler had *reverence* for he named Jesus "Good Master"; and there was also *spiritual hunger* for he wanted eternal life. Alas! the title "Good Master" was only a compliment from one who wanted instruction from the Teacher sent from God. There was no sense of sin behind his approach to Jesus. He came with the preconceived idea that he could win heaven, not knowing that eternal life cannot be won, but is *given*, and *grown* in those who receive Jesus, as the Saviour, who is Christ the Lord.

What a strange reply the ruler received! Jesus rejected the compliment, for to Him *Master* was not acceptable from the lips of one who would disobey the instruction given; nor could He accept "*Good* Master" from one who would not be "good" in obedience and renunciation for His sake. As cast in the KJV, the language of the reply of Jesus has presented a difficulty to some lovers of Scripture.

> "Why callest thou me *good?* there is none good but one, that is, God."

This cannot mean that only God is good, and that His beloved Son was not. Had Jesus not been good as well, He could never have gone about "doing good" (Acts 10:38). Did He not come as the *Good* Shepherd? The RV has the rendering –

"Master, what good thing shall I do, that I may have eternal life? And He said unto him, Why askest thou Me concerning that which is good? One there is Who is good."

Phillips in the New Testament in Modern English has the translation –

"Master what good thing must I do to secure eternal life?"
"I wonder why you ask me about what is good?" Jesus answered him. "Only one is good. But if you want to enter that life you must keep the commandments."

The phrase, "Why callest thou me good," should be, according to the original form, "Why askest thou me concerning the good?" Thus, the emphasis is shifted from the two Persons, to the eternal life as the "good thing." Jesus had but one object in His reply to the rich young ruler, namely, to raise his ideas of Himself, and not to be classed merely with other "good masters," and declining to receive this title *apart from* the One who is essentially and only *good*. This indeed is but distantly hinted; but unless this is seen in the *background* of His words, nothing worthy of Him can be made out of them. The name GOD, used by Jesus in His reply is equivalent to *Elohim* of the Old Testament, which in its plural form expresses essential Deity and is applied to the Son as well as to the Father (John 20:28; Romans 9:5).

The tragedy of the rich young ruler was that he had everything which would permit or promote contentment of soul yet failed to realize his deepest need. But the sacrifice Jesus demanded was too high for the youth to make. Choosing Calvary for Himself, He prescribed sacrifice for others. He was willing to accept him as a disciple and promised him treasure in heaven, but he could not give up his earthly treasures for what Jesus offered and so there came the great refusal for he "went away sorrowful." It is thought that Dante described one like the ruler whom neither hell nor heaven would have, in the lines –

I looked, and I beheld the shade of him
Who made through cowardice the great refusal.

What a commentary this conversation between Jesus and the young ruler is on Paul's marvelous picture of the complete renunciation of Him who called for the complete surrender of all the youth had (2 Corinthians 8:9)!

❊ ❊ ❊

Governor (Matthew 2:6).

To those who desire to present a seasonable message at a Christmas service, the various names and titles given to Jesus at His birth, and found in the birth-narratives of Matthew and Luke, will provide an impressive study. Among these is the predicted title of *Governor* –

"Out of thee shall come a Governor, that shall rule my people" (Matthew 2:6).
"Out of thee shall he come forth unto me that is to be ruler in Israel, whose goings forth have been from of old, from everlasting" (Micah 5:2).

Isaiah in his cluster of Messianic names implies that of *Governor* in the description of Christ's millennial reign –

"Of the increase of His government and peace there shall be no end ... the government shall be upon his shoulder" (9:7, 6).
"I will commit thy government into His hands" (22:21, 22).

In Roman parlance a "governor" was

the superintendent of a province, responsible for the collection of the imperial revenues, and also entrusted with magisterial powers for decisions of questions relative to the province. Usually he was a person of high social standing. After Judea became a province, procurators or governors, were sent there from Rome. Pontius Pilate was the Roman governor at the time when Christ was crucified.

But in biblical usage many different Hebrew and Greek words are behind the English word *governor*. Ignorance of varied details of the government of ancient oriental nations makes it difficult to distinguish between such titles as *deputy, duke, judge, lawgiver, overseer, prince, ruler*. In the New Testament, *governor* also represents a variety of Greek words, but the words chiefly used are derived from roots meaning to drive, to lead, to rule. Vincent in his *Word Studies* suggests that "the word *governor* is in harmony with the idea of shepherding, since the Greek word originally means one *who goes before*, or *leads the way*, and suggests Christ's words about the good shepherd, 'He calleth his own sheep by name, and leadeth them out . . . He goeth before them, and the sheep follow him' (John 10:3, 4). . . . The word for *shepherd* implies 'shall rule,' and involves his whole office – guiding, guarding, folding, as well as feeding. Hence appropriate and often applied to the guides and guardians of others." Homer calls kings "*the shepherds of the people*."

This is why Phillips translates the prophecy of Isaiah quoted by Matthew,

"For out of thee shall come forth a
    governor,
Which shall be *shepherd* of my
    people Israel."

The margin gives *feed* for "rule." Coupled, then, with administrative ability is compassionate love and care in the divine use of *Governor* as applied to Christ, whose governance is connected with promises made to God's ancient people. By the Holy Spirit, Jacob made the prophecy that "The sceptre *or* leadership shall not depart from Judah, nor the ruler's staff from between his feet until Shiloh [the Messiah, the Peaceful One] comes to Whom it belongs" (Genesis 49:10, *Amplified Bible*). "Judah is My sceptre and My lawgiver" (same word in original given as Governor) (Psalm 60:7).

An outstanding illustration of Jesus as *Governor* can be found in the history of Joseph, who was made governor of all Egypt. He typifies the governorship Jesus holds in the Kingdom of His Father (1 Corinthians 15:23-28) –

1. *Joseph had a rough road to travel before he became second to Pharaoh, controlling the food of Egypt.*

He was beloved of his father – so was Jesus (John 3:16).

He was hated by his brethren without a cause – so was Jesus (John 15:25).

He was sent by his father to his brethren – so was Jesus (Hebrews 10:7).

He was conspired against, and threatened with death – so was Jesus (Acts 3:14, 15).

He was betrayed and sold – so was Jesus (Matthew 26:15, 56).

He was triumphed over for a time – it was so with Jesus (Psalm 22:1).

2. *Joseph proved himself worthy and capable of governorship for even in his profound humiliation these characteristics are prominent –*

He honored God (Genesis 39:9; 41:16).

He did his best for his distressed fellow men (40:6, 7).

Commendable features, such as these, led to his exaltation –

"See, I have set thee over all the land" (Genesis 41:41).

What a mirror this is of the ultimate governorship of Jesus who, when He returns to earth, will reign where'er the sun doth its successive journeys run (*See* Psalm 2:6-8). "*Wherefore* God hath highly exalted Him" (Philippians 2:5-11). All power is His (Matthew 28:18). He is able to bless (Hebrews 7:25). He has authority to destroy (Revelation 6:16).

We live in an age of impotent government, for rulers are not able to rule, and those who try to govern us are utterly incapable of solving national crises and problems. Our disorganized, revolutionary world needs the firm control of Him who came into the world as *the* Governor able to rule the nations. And make no mistake about it, He is on His way to clear up the mess of earth and cause peace and righteousness to cover it. When He does appear with the government on His shoulder, then of the increase of such perfect government there will be no end.

The real governor of the marriage feast at Cana was not "the one who tasted the water that was made wine," but Jesus who performed the miracle and greatly contributed to the happiness of the occasion. Mary the mother of Jesus recognized her Son's right to governorship when she said, "Whatsoever He saith unto you, do it" (John 2:1-12). In all that happened that day Jesus manifested His glory as One able to meet the crisis. The practical, personal question is, "Have I made Him the Governor of my life, and is there the daily increase of His government over every part of my being?"

True, "He *is*, and will yet be, Governor among the nations" (Psalm 22:28), but is He *the* Governor of the little world of my life? Because of His Shepherd love, His rule is ever benign and beneficent, with commands that are never grievous.

When the Governor came to
   Bethlehem
There was found no room for Him
   in the inn –
For the mighty God – clothed in
   human form:
But the ends of the world shall yet to
   Him turn,
And Him as Governor and Lord adore,
Whose mercies are infinite as of yore.

H

Head (Revelation 19:12).

As a mode of expression, *head* implies a preeminent, authoritative position, and is used symbolically of Jesus in several ways. Upon His head rest many diadems.

1. *He is Head of every man* (1 Corinthians 11:3).

Christ "filleth all in all," and as the Creator, Preserver, and Governor of the world, constituted by God (Colossians 1:16), *fills* the "universe of things *with all* things and beings. The Greek puts it, Filleth *for Himself*." Alford has the phrase, "Fills all creation with whatever it possesses."

Jesus is the Head of the whole human race and of all things. "By Him were all things created" – "He is the Head of all principality and power" (Colossians 1:16; 2:10). As Co-Creator of man, he was made for His pleasure. In the chapter, however, where Paul speaks of Jesus as "the Head of every man" (1 Corinthians 11), he is not dealing with Creation but with the Church, and was referring to men praying with covered heads.

2. *The Head of the Church* (Ephe-

sians 1:22, 23; 5:23; Colossians 1:18-20).

As the Founder of the Church He purchased with His own ruby blood, He is its worthy Head. The true Church is not a machine composed of various parts automatically controlled, but a Body consisting of various members, subordinate to the Head. A member is not an isolated irresponsible atom, but a part of an organic whole. A body severed from its head is a lifeless trunk, and apart from Christ the Head, the members can do nothing (John 15:5). As the head rules, guides, directs, and has full sympathy for the rest of the body, so is it with Christ and His Church (1 Corinthians 12:14-27). Because He is the Head the Body is sure of safekeeping. "He that keepeth Israel shall neither slumber nor sleep" (Psalm 121:4; 1 Peter 4:19). Blessed to know that "He is Head over all things to the *Church*"! As "He is over, or far above, all things," why should His members have any fear?

Head not only implies dominion, but union: therefore if we look upon Christ at the right hand of God, we see ourselves in heaven, with nothing able to sever the union. Without the Head, the Body ceases to be the Body, and the Head ceases to be the Head. But the life of the risen Head is the life of the Body, and such life cannot cease.

3. *The Head of the Corner* (Matthew 21:42). (*See* under *Cornerstone*)

* * *

Heir of All Things (Hebrews 1:2; Romans 8:16, 17).

Under the Mosaic Law there were most implicit instructions regarding heirs and inheritances. The principle of inheritance was acknowledged already in Abram's time, when he replied to God's promise to be his exceeding great reward –

"Behold to me thou hast given no seed; and, lo, one born in my house is mine heir" (Genesis 15: 1-18).

The term *heir* is also used symbolically of Christ, and of those who, through a blood-relationship, have a glorious inheritance.

"You have accepted a Spirit which gives you the status of sons in the rapture of which we cry, 'My Father, my own dear Father!' This very Spirit adds its testimony to that of our own spirit, telling us that we are God's children. If we are His children, it must follow that we are His heirs – yes, heirs to God's wealth, co-heirs with the Messiah!" (Romans 8:16, 17, Way's translation).

The application of the figure of speech to Christ, however, is most profitable to observe – "God has made His Son *the Heir* who takes for His inheritance the universe. Nay more, it was through His agency that God created all cosmic systems" (Hebrews 1:2). A Latin proverb has it, "God makes the heir, not man." It was so with Christ whom "God has made Heir of all things." A further proverb speaks of "heir by right of representation," which is also true of Him who came as the perfect representation of the Father (John 14:9). The word *appointed,* and given as "ordained" in John 15:16, means *to set in order,* and is used in the sense of *appointing* one to fulfill the divine purpose.

God eternally predestined His Son to be the Possessor and Sovereign of all things and confirmed such an appointment in the prophecy, "my covenant shall stand fast with him" (Psalm 89: 28). In his parable on "The Householder and the Vineyard" (Mark 12:1-12), Christ describes in parabolic language

His rejection and death as the Heir to the Vineyard. Even as the only, well-beloved Son, He was not reverenced. Considering Him as "Heir of all things" we first of all ask the question, *What exactly is an heir?* Generally, it is one who succeeds to some possessions or property at the death of their owner. Christ, however, cannot be the Heir of God in this way, since God is deathless.

But the term also denotes one who becomes a possessor of anything received as a portion or property. For example, Paul says that the promise God made to Abraham that "he should be the heir of the World (earth) was not to Abraham, or to his seed, through the law, but through the righteousness of faith" (*See* Romans 4:15, 16). It is thus that Christ is Heir who, as the Son of God, could say, "All things that the Father hath are mine" (John 16:15; Acts 10:36). It is part of the wondrous covenant between the Father and the Son, that the latter should be "Heir of all things" (Isaiah 53:10-12). What vast resources and unsearchable riches form the inheritance of the Son! They are like an ocean whose waters are unfathomable.

> There is *Life* – John 5:26; 1 Corinthians 15:45.
> There is *Dominion* – Daniel 7:14; Matthew 28:18.
> There is *Glory* – John 17:24.

The rich inheritance of Christ is sure and everlasting and is thus compared to the treasure laid up for those redeemed by His blood (Psalm 31:19; Colossians 1:5). Commenting on Christ's heirship, Vincent remarks that –

> "Christ *attained* the messianic lordship through resurrection. Something was acquired as the result of His incarnation which He did not possess before it, and could not have possessed without it. Equality with God was His birthright; but out of His human life, death, and resurrection came a type of sovereignty which could pertain to Him only through His triumph over human sin in the flesh, through His identification with men as their brother (Hebrews 1:3). Messianic lordship could not pertain to His pre-incarnate state: it is a matter of function, not of inherent power and majesty. He was *essentially* Son of God; He must *become* Son of Man."

A wonder of wonders is that through grace we are made sharers of the riches of Christ's inheritance for as God's children we are "heirs; heirs of God, and joint-heirs with Christ" (Romans 8:16). "Wherefore thou art no more a servant, but a son; and if a son, then an heir of God through Christ" (Galatians 4:7). Heirship goes with sonship, thus the necessity of a spiritual relationship on the basis of a spiritual inheritance. "*If*, a son, then an heir." Only those who have been the recipients of God's abundant mercy have the title deed to an "inheritance incorruptible, and undefiled, and that fadeth not away, reserved in heaven for you" (1 Peter 1:4).

To whatever Christ is Heir, we share with Him. In Him, we overcome and inherit all things (Revelation 21:7). The term "joint-heir" or "co-inheritor" is used of several in Scripture –

> Of Isaac and Jacob as participants with Abraham in the promises of God (Hebrews 11:9).
> Of husband and wife who are united in Christ (1 Peter 3:7-9).
> Of Gentiles who believe, as participants in the Gospel with Jews who believe (Ephesians 3:6).
> Of all born-again believers, who will share a new order of things to be ushered in when Christ returns and makes us participate with

Him in His glory as recompense for participation in His sufferings (Romans 8:17).

The Lord Jesus, He is Heir,
    And we joint-heirs with Him;
Thus made free from every care,
    We may look up and sing.
A glorious and broad expanse.
Is this God-given inheritance.

*   *   *

High Priest (Hebrews 3:1; 4:14; 7:23, 24).

Among the prominent types of our Lord none is so precious to the child of God as that of the *Priesthood*. This is the reason why we are called to consider Christ Jesus as "the Apostle and High Priest of our profession," as our "Great High Priest," as One who has "an unchangeable priesthood." We have already thought of Him as *The Apostle*. Now we give attention to the One of whom the writer speaks as our *Great High Priest*. "Consider the High Priest." Truly we ought to give the most prayerful and careful consideration to Him who exercised His high-priestly function when He "put away sin by the sacrifice of himself" (Hebrews 9:26).

In our volume on *All the Prophecies of Christ in the Bible*, a full coverage will be found of the prophetic and symbolic significance of the Tabernacle, and its priestly services. That the entry of Israel's high priest into the Holy of Holies was typical of Christ's ascension *into*, and intercessory ministry *in* Heaven is borne out by the statement, "a great high priest, that is passed into the heavens, Jesus the Son of God" (Hebrews 4:14). *See* Leviticus 16:12, 20, 21; Psalm 68:18. The constant work of the priests in their daily application of blood that was shed at the altar is symbolic of the efficacy of the shed blood of Christ (1 John 1:7; Exodus 24:8). Ancient priests were responsible for offering up animal sacrifices, but Jesus gave Himself as the one sacrifice for our sins. "He gave himself for me" (Galatians 2:20). When He once offered Himself to bear the sins of many (Hebrews 9:28), He became our *Propitiation,* or "mercy-seat," as the word implies (Romans 3:25), or "place of communion" (Exodus 25:21, 22). *See* Hebrews 4:14-16; 1 John 2:2.

The general teaching of Hebrews is that the *whole priesthood* of Israel was symbolic of our one Great High Priest, in whose crucified, risen and exalted Person is centered *every priestly power,* and whose finished work at Calvary gathered up *every sacrificial act* (Hebrews 9:11-14). To consider all that was associated with priesthood is beyond our present range. We could, for example, pay regard to –

The *"garments* for glory and for beauty"* (Isaiah 59:17).
The various *anointings* (Acts 10:38).
The different *sacrifices* or offerings (Hebrews 7:26-28).

Sufficient for our present purpose is the way the writer marks out *three distinct appearings* in connection with Him who is our Great High Priest (Hebrews 9:24-28).

1. *Past Appearing* (Hebrews 9:24).

On the morning of the Day of Atonement the high priest of old *appeared before the people,* and who did they behold?

One taken from among themselves (Hebrews 5:1)! Is this not what happened when Christ was born, as bone of our bone, and flesh of our flesh? He appeared to put away sin by the sacrifice of Himself.

One who could sympathize with them in everything (Hebrews 2:17, 18; 5:2). The conspicuous difference between Israel's high priest and Christ, the Great High Priest, is that the high priest had need to make atonement for his own sin, but Christ was without sin, and needed no cleansing for Himself.

One chosen by God to offer sacrifice for all (Numbers 16:40; 2 Chronicles 26:18). Any daring to usurp the priestly function was severely dealt with. Christ is the divinely chosen Priest who offered a sacrifice for all (Isaiah 53:4-8; 2 Corinthians 5:21; Hebrews 5:4).

2. *Present Appearing*, Hebrews 9:24.

After appearing before the people, the next act of the high priest was to enter the Holy of Holies with the blood of the sacrifice, and thus *appear before God* for the people, bearing their names collectively on his shoulders, and individually in his heart (Exodus 28:12-29; Leviticus 16:14, 15). All of this was but "a figure of the true High Priest for Christ entered into Heaven itself, to appear in the presence of God for us." His present ministry in God is to intercede for those saved by His blood, and whose names are in His heart (Hebrews 7:25; Romans 8:34; 1 John 2:1, 2).

3. *Prospective Appearing* (Hebrews 9:28).

When his priestly ministry in the Most Holy Place was finished, the high priest came out from the unseen compartment and once more *appeared before the people* to assure them that their sin had been put away, and that pardoned, future blessing would be theirs (Numbers 6:23-27). "Christ . . . shall appear the second time without sin unto salvation." By His death at His first appearing He made possible salvation from the past *penalty* of sin. By His present intercession in heaven, He provides His own with a daily salvation from the *power* of sin. By His return for His own, He will bless them with salvation from the *presence* of sin forever.

May we be found constantly considering Him who, as the Great High Priest, was chosen of God –

> *Has* appeared to man and died for their sin (John 1:14, 29).
> *Is* appearing before God in intercession for the redeemed (Romans 8:34; Revelation 5:6).
> *Shall* appear from heaven for His own (John 14:1-3; 1 Thessalonians 4:13-18).

How apt are the lines of Keble on the present unceasing ministry of Him who is the High Priest of good things to come (Hebrews 9:11).

> The golden censer in His hand,
> He offers hearts from every land,
> Tied to His own by gentlest hand
> Of silent love:
> About Him winged blessing stand
> In act to move.

* * *

Holy One (Psalm 16:10; Daniel 9:24).

David had a prophetic insight into the nature of the Messiah as *the Holy One,* who because He was holy would not, and could not, see corruption. Even demons recognized Him as the spotless Son of God for when He cast them out of a man they had possessed they said, "Let us alone . . . I know thee who thou art; the Holy One of God" (Luke 4:34). Peter, in his second sermon after Pentecost rebuking the leaders of Israel, condemned them for their denial of Jesus as "The Holy One" (Acts 3:14). (*See* John 6:69 rv). Daniel exalted Him as "The Most Holy" (9:24).

The "Holy Thing" born of Mary, lived among men as the only Man to be "holy, harmless, undefiled, separate from sinners." He alone is excluded from the declaration that "*all* have sinned, and come short of the glory of God." There was never the least stain upon His character. The Holy Son of a Holy God,

Jesus, whom none could convict of sin, was intrinsically holy. We have constant need to pray, "more holiness give me." With Christ, however, there was no development in holiness, for He was perfect in holiness before He was born, and perfect in every way as He tabernacled among men, never having any need to "take time to be holy." And it is only as we seek to live in the white scorching light of His holiness that we discover all that is alien to His holy mind and will. It was as the "Holy One of Israel" that He promised to help the worm Jacob (Isaiah 41:14. See 54:5). Through grace, the *Holy* Spirit is ever with us to transform us into the holiness the Lord desires and demands, "Be ye holy, for I am holy."

> The cause of God is holy,
> And useth holy things.

❖   ❖   ❖

Hope of Glory (Colossians 1:27).

Under *Desire*, we considered various aspects of "hope," yet space must be given to Paul's marvelous designation of Christ as "The Hope of Glory." The original uses the emphatic article, "Christ in you the hope of *the* glory." He who "dwells in our hearts by faith" (Ephesians 3:17) is our *Hope* in Glory. It will be noticed that we frequently refer to Dr. Arthur Way's translation and we make no apology for doing so, seeing that we deem his *Letters of St. Paul*, published in 1935, to be the most illuminative extant work of its kind on the Epistles. A most gifted Greek scholar, it was he who translated all the Greek classics into English. Here is Dr. Way's rendering on the portion before us.

> "Yes, to them was it God's will to make known what is the wealth of glory of this mystic secret pro-

claimed among the Gentiles. That secret's essence is that

> 'Messiah is living within you,' which means for you the hope of the glorious vision of God. This Coming I now proclaim" (Colossians 1:26, 27).

Dr. Way has a like translation of Paul's affirmation, "Christ liveth in me" – "It is Messiah whose life is in me." In the apostolic designation we have two thoughts, namely,

> *Presence*, "Messiah is living within you," or "Whose life is in me."
> *Prospect*, "The hope of the glorious vision of God."

The *presence* is the basis, pledge, guarantee of the *prospect*. How dynamically different life would be if only we could live under the impact of God's mystic secret that "Messiah is living with us"! In his study of Colossians, Dr. A. T. Pierson reminds us that the substance of the teaching of this epistle is that in Christ Jesus we have "the pleroma of God, and that this idea is inwrought into the structure of the epistle and curiously into its language."

Pleroma – "filled" (Colossians 1:9) – is an untranslatable word, and means more than *fullness*. It was a term Paul borrowed from philosophic writers of his time "who claimed to know the secret of something that filled up all human deficiency – a plentitude of knowledge and power. Paul claims that in Christ the true pleroma is found: that He as the Son of God has all the plentitude of the Godhead in Him, in full measure, and running over – and so, if we are in Him, all that divine pleroma becomes ours." What a staggering thought this is! Our finite minds cannot grasp the significance of having this Perfection of power, strength, wisdom, love and holiness living with *us!*

Further, it is this One in whom it pleased the Father that all the *pleroma* should dwell (Colossians 1:19), who is not only our representative before God, and God's representative before us, but who is our assurance of "the glory" or, as Way puts it, "the glorious vision of God." When we speak of *glory* we imply that surpassing excellence belonging to certain things. There is an *earthly glory*, after which the prominent on earth strive, but it is only of a transitory character, and used by Satan for the destruction of those who seek it (Daniel 4:30; 2 Timothy 4:10; 1 Peter 1:24).

But then there is also *heavenly glory*, for which God's children look, and which is real in character (Psalm 73:24; I Peter 4:13; 5:1, 10). This is "the hope of *the* glory," and includes not only beholding the glory of Christ according to His own prayerful wish (John 17:24), but being with Him in His eternal abode, for heaven is referred to as *Glory*.

While beyond all human description we know that *Glory* has been procured for us, and that it is so great that present afflictions are not worthy to be compared to it (John 17:22; Romans 8:18; Hebrews 2:10). Although we can conceive nothing like it, and it passes our understanding, naturally, God by His Spirit, grants us a glimpse of it, and assures us that His beloved Son is our confidence that *the* Glory will be ours (1 Corinthians 2:9, 10; Job 19:25-27). As we linger amid the shadows may ours be the full realization of the *Presence* – "Christ in you"; and the constant inspiration of the *Prospect* – "The Hope of the Glory."

> No radiant beams from sun or moon
> Adorn that land so fair;
> For He Who sits upon the throne
> Shines forth resplendent there.

* * *

Horn of Salvation (Luke 1:69).

Are we not truly amazed at the great variety of symbols chosen to set forth all that Christ is in Himself? It would seem as if every realm is ransacked for fitting designations of Him whom no man can fully describe. All the names and titles given Him in Scripture are but broken arcs and cannot fully reveal Him who is beyond all human comparison. "To whom will ye liken God?" (Isaiah 40:18). Zacharias in his song at the birth of John the Baptist, chose a common object familiar to people in Old Testament times to describe Him whose way John was to prepare – it was a *horn*.

> "The Lord God . . . hath raised up a horn of salvation for us in the house of his servant David."

Zacharias also used other symbols to portray Him who was to be born in Bethlehem as the Saviour of the world. The figure of the *Horn* is taken from those animals whose *strength* is in their horns (Psalms 18:2; 75:10; 132:17), and so "Horn of Salvation" implies "Strength of Salvation," or "Mighty Salvation" meaning Jesus Himself, whom Simeon called "Thy Salvation" (Luke 2:30). Because the "horn" was once the instrument of the oxen's strength, it became the symbol of *power* (1 Kings 22:11). On Egyptian and Roman coins, and in Assyrian sculptures, are figures of gods with horns symbolic of their prowess, and our God and Saviour came as a *Horn*, or mighty instrument of salvation.

Daniel represents Darius and Alexander as a goat and ram running violently at each other with their powerful horns (Daniel 8:3-6). Mighty nations were styled in prophecy as *horns* (Zechariah 1:18). It may be that Zacharias, conversant with Old Testament claims and promises, had verses like –

> "Mine horn is exalted in the LORD" (1 Samuel 2:1);

"The LORD . . . shall exalt the horn of his anointed" (1 Samuel 2:10)

in mind when he described Jesus as "The Horn of Salvation."

When God exalts the horn of a man it is a sign of favor and manifested power (Psalm 89:24).

When a man exalts his own horn, it is a sign of arrogance. In modern jargon, "He likes to blow his own trumpet" (*See* Psalm 75:4, 5). An old proverb has it, "He had better put his horns in his pocket than blow them."

When horns were fixed to an altar they became projections to which sacrifices were bound and to which those who needed protection could cling (1 Kings 2:28; Psalm 18:2; 118:27; Amos 3:14). Pursued by the enemy of souls we can cling to Him who is our "Horn of Salvation" and who will protect us.

If Jesus is your "Horn of Salvation" then all strength is His to keep you saved and safe. A modern writer says that, "Most Chinese believe that if you save someone's life, you are forever responsible for that person." Whether this is true we cannot say, but we do know that if we have laid hold on Him who came as the "Horn of Salvation," then He will be eternally responsible for us. None can ever sever us from Him who is God's anointed Horn (John 10: 28-30). He is not like the Grecian king described as "the great horn that was broken" (Daniel 8:8, 21, 22). Nothing or no one can break our indestructible *Horn.*

> I hide beneath my Horn of strength,
>   For I am weak and frail,
> And rest in Thee until, at length,
>   (Thy might can never fail) –
> I reach the land of light and love,
> And sing to Thee with saints above.

I

I Am (John 8:58).

To the religious leaders who disputed Christ's claim that He was the Son of God, and proceeded from His Father, the astounding declaration was given them – "Verily, verily, I say unto you, Before Abraham was, *I Am.*" He presented Himself as Jehovah-Jesus, adopting the very name God gave to Moses: "Say unto the children of Israel, *I AM* hath sent me unto you" (Exodus 3:14). It is in Jesus that all Jehovah promised to be to His people finds full realization. Coming to us in the New Testament in plain human form He constantly surprises us with His I AM in an absolute sense, and also with a complementary substantive –

> "*I Am* the bread of life" (John 6: 35).
>
> "*I Am* the light of the world" (John 8:12; 9:5).
>
> "*I Am* the door of the sheep" (John 10:7).
>
> "*I Am* the good shepherd" (John 10:11).
>
> ."*I Am* from above . . . *I Am* not of this world" (John 8:23).
>
> "*I Am* the resurrection and the life" (John 11:25).
>
> "*I Am* the way, the truth, the life" (John 14:6).
>
> "*I Am* the true vine" (John 15:1, 5).
>
> "*I Am* the root and offspring of David (Revelation 22:16).

When He said, "*Before Abraham was, I Am*" He asserted His pre-existence as the Eternal Son. Declaring His name to be *I AM,* He meant by such that He possessed and could exercise divine prerogatives and functions, and could be to us what the *Jehovah* of the Old Testament proposed to be to His ancient people. Ere His bodily presence was withdrawn from His disciples, His parting word was a kind of paradox considering He was leaving them, and was another I AM –

"Lo, *I Am* with you alway, even unto the end of the age" (Matthew 28:20).

That great unchangeable I AM. The King of Glory and of Grace.

Truly, the Saviour is our *Jehovah Shammah* – The Lord is there. He did not say to those who took up stones to stone Him for His assertion of eternal existence, "I *was*," but "I *AM*" implying all He is in the present, as well as what He was in the past. The Greek version of I AM THAT I AM (Exodus 3:14) reads, "I am HE WHO IS." All that He was, He is, and will be for evermore A. F. H. Faber sings –

Backward our thoughts through ages
    stretch,
Onward through endless bliss –
For there are two eternities, and
    both alike are His.

       ❈ ❈ ❈

Image (Hebrews 1:3).

Paul had a profound regard for this noun as a name for the Master he dearly loved and so loyally and sacrificially served.

"Christ who is the image of God" (2 Corinthians 4:4).
"Who is the image of the invisible God" (Colossians 1:15).
"The express image of His Person" (Hebrews 1:3).

The apostle speaks of man as "the image and glory of God" (1 Corinthians 11:7; Genesis 1:26) and of the new man in Christ as "the image of him that created him" (Colossians 3:10). Way's translation of the KJV "Who being the brightness of his glory, and the express image of his person" (Hebrews 1:3) reads –

"He is to God as the rays which reveal to us all we know of the sun:

He is the Image that bodies out for us the essential being of God."

The word *Image* implies one who represents, or is very much like another. In the family circle, as a child takes on facial characteristics it is common to say, "My, isn't he like his father!" Coleridge speaks of one who "was his Maker's image undefaced." Man, made in his Maker's image, defaced the likeness, but Jesus ever remains as God's "image undefaced." He came as the culmination of the revelation of God, hence His affirmation, "He that hath seen Me hath seen the Father" (John 14:9). The Greek for "of his person," implies "of His substantial essence."

God said to Moses as he sought a new vision for a new task –

"Thou canst not see my face: for there shall no man see me, and live" (Exodus 33:20).

No created being could gaze upon His dazzling glory and live, but what God is like in all His eternal splendor is revealed in the face of Him who came as the impress or image of God.

The Son of God in glory beams
    Too bright for us to scan;
But we can face the light that streams
    From the mild Son of man.

The description *Express Image* has the original meaning to *engrave,* or *inscribe,* as with a graving tool, and signifies the *impression* made by the die or stamp or graver. Thus a *mark, impress, stamp* as the image on a coin indicates its nature and value, and the symbol as used of Christ indicates that "the essential being of God is conceived as setting its distinctive stamp upon Christ, coming into definite and characteristic expression in His Person, so that the Son bears the exact impress of the Divine nature and character." If, then, we want to know what God is like all we have to do is to meditate upon His ways, works and words while here among men. In character and conduct, He was the perfect expression of God's being – the unblemished engraving of His Father.

> In Thee most perfectly expressed,
>   The Father's glories shine;
> Of the full Deity possessed,
>   Eternally divine!

The heart-searching personal question is, To what degree does my life manifest the marked traits of God? Paul could humbly confess that He bore on "his very body the brands which proclaimed him Jesus' bondsman" (Galatians 6:17). Are we so committed to, and controlled by Him who indwells us that He is able to reveal His personality through ours? Can we say that we are "the express image of His person" having a Christlikeness produced by the Holy Spiirt causing those around to see Jesus in all His beauty?

> Then with the gift of holiness
>   within us;
> We not less human, but made
>   more divine;
> Our lives replete with Heaven's
>   supernal beauty,
> Ever declare that beauty, Lord,
>   is Thine.

J

Jesus (Matthew 1:21).

Many names are dear, but the dearest one which grows more dear with the passage of time is the simple yet sublime name – *Jesus*. Paul had such a profound respect for it that he called it the "name which is above every name" (Philippians 2:9). It is the name the angel announced before Christ was born, and represented Him as a gift from heaven who, in His person, would fulfill the promise of Jehovah to save His people. "Jehovah . . . shall redeem Israel from all his iniquities" (Psalm 130: 7, 8). Expressly given by divine command, in a sense *Jesus* is His only name, all others being titles. This *personal* name of One born into the world (Matthew 1:21; Luke 1:31) is not only a preeminently human one given to Him as man, but likewise preeminently divine seeing it proclaimed the Babe as God over all, blessed forever. The double significance of this simple yet sublime name is borne out in its construction.

JE – This first syllable *Je,* or *Jeho,* or Jah – *Jehovah* – this name of God, speaks of the divine authority that Jesus came as the great I AM. The syllable tells us of His eternal Godhead, of His covenant relations, and of His mighty power and condescending love. All the virtues dimly seen in the Jehovah of old became manifest in Him who came from heaven.

SUS – This other syllable is associated with the name *Oshea, Hosea,* or *Houshaia,* meaning "help," which was the name of one of the spies sent out by Moses, but which he changed to *Jehoshua,* signifying "Jehovah our Saviour," or "Deliverer," or "The help of Jehovah" (Numbers 13:16). Jesus is the Greek form of *Joshua,* which itself is a contraction of *Jehoshua.* Thus in this second part of Je-*sus,* we are assured of pardon and peace, of deliverance from sin and hell. Eusebius, early church father, of the third century said, "The name of Jesus means the Salvation of God. For *Houshaia* among the Hebrews is salvation, and among the Hebrews, is called Joshua – 'Salvation of God,' or 'God the Saviour'." The two Joshuas of old were remarkable types of Jesus as saviours in Israel (Joshua 1:1, 2; Zechariah 3:9).

The matchless name *Jesus,* therefore, expresses the *relation* of Jehovah to Him in incarnation, by which "He humbled Himself, and became obedient un-

to death, even the death of the cross"
(Philippians 2:8), as the twin syllables
of the name knit together imply. Occasionally in Scripture the *object* is put
for that which pertains or relates to it
as, for instance, where Paul puts *Jesus*
for His *doctrine* – "For if he that cometh [whether from any of the other apostles or from the Council at Jerusalem]
preacheth another *Jesus*" – meaning a
different doctrine or teaching concerning Jesus (2 Corinthians 11:4). See
Galatians 1:6-9.

Further, the power of this divinely
given name *Jesus* was prominent in
apostolic days in many ways –

In healing (Acts 4:10; 16:18).
In praying (John 16:23).
In daily walk (Colossians 3:17).
In conversation (Acts 9:5).
In future bliss (Philippians 2:10,
11).

That our Lord was spoken of more
commonly in the gospels by the simple
name *Jesus* is evident from the fact that
out of the some 700 times it is quoted in
the New Testament, upwards of 600 of
these are found in the gospels alone.

In *Matthew*, it is found about 170
times.
In *Mark*, around 100 times.
In *Luke*, almost 100 times.
In *John*, about 250 times.
In *Acts*, it is not of frequent occurrence.
In the *epistles*, about 30 times only,
yet *Christ*, His title as the Exalted, Glorified One, appears upwards of 200 times.

The constant use of the name *Jesus*
by the apostles testifies to the supreme
position He occupied in their minds,
and of the high reverence they had of
His varied glories. To them, such a
precious name proclaimed *who* and
what He is. All down the ages the name

of Jesus has been so sweet in the believer's ear. To hymnists and poets it has
ever been a favorite name – the fragrance of Christian song for over 18
centuries, and as long as the world en-
dures it will be the

Sweetest sound in seraph's song,
Sweetest note on mortal tongue,
Sweetest anthem ever sung.

Quaint George Herbert, English divine
and poet, of the sixteenth century wrote
a verse containing a deep and true insight into the virtue that lies in the name
of *Jesus* –

Jesus is in my heart, His sacred
name
Is deeply carved here; but th' other
week
A great affliction broke the little
frame,
Ev'n all to pieces; which I went to
seek:
And first I found the corner where
was *J*,
After, where *ES,* and next where *U*
was graved.
When I had got these parcels,
instantly
I sat me down to spell them and
perceived
That to my broken heart, He was *I
ease you*
And to my whole is *JESU.*

If we are among the number who
have heard the joyful sound that "Jesus
saves," and have experienced His saving, emancipating power, our obligation
is to proclaim, "Jehovah our Salvation"
to sinners far and wide for "neither is
there salvation in any other; for there
is none other *name* under heaven given
among men, whereby we must be saved"
(Acts 4:12). Signs and wonders can
only be accomplished "by the name of
thy holy child *Jesus*" (Acts 4:30). The
disciples rejoiced because they discovered that demons were subject unto
them through that all-powerful name
(Luke 10:17). In his most valuable
Sourcebook of Poetry, Al Bryant in-

cludes a most expressive poem on *The Name,* by Henry W. Frost —

> There is a name, a wondrous name,
> Of infinite and endless fame,
> Of God beloved, by saints revered,
> By angels and archangels feared,
> Ordained by God ere world began,
> Revealed by angels unto man,
> Proclaimed by men, believed, adored
> By hearts in prayer and praise
>   outpoured.
> The theme of prophet, priest, and
>   king,
> The word of which sweet psalmists
>   sing,
> By pilgrims blessed, by suff'rers sung,
> The last work breathed by martyr's
>   tongue,
> The name most precious and sublime,
> Supreme in space, supreme in time,
> Destined to live and conquer all
> Till all knees everywhere shall fall
> And tongues confess — what God
>   proclaims —
> This name to be the Name of names,
> The name which in high heaven
>   will be
> The One Name of eternity;
> Then, O my soul, its praise forthtell,
> *Jesus* — the Name ineffable!

(See further under *Christ*)

*   *   *

Jesus of Nazareth (John 18:5, 7; 19:19; Mark 1:24).

While the simple, single name *Jesus* was constantly used as a narrative name, His contemporaries distinguished Him in different ways. For instance as —

> "A man that is called *Jesus*" (John 9:11).
> "Jesus, the son of Joseph" (John 6:42); Luke is careful to add "Being (as was supposed) the son of Joseph (3:23).
> "Jesus of Nazareth" (John 18:5, 7; Mark 1:24; Luke 18:37).
> "Jesus of Nazareth, the King of the Jews" (John 19:19).
> "Jesus, the King of the Jews" (Matthew 27:37).

The title "Jesus of Nazareth" identifies Him with the Galilean town where Joseph and Mary had their home and in which Jesus lived for the first 30 years of His life. That He was held in high esteem in this place of His earthly origin until He started His public ministry is evident from passages like Luke 2:51, 52; 4:16, 28-31. Evidently the town cannot have been of much size or importance, seeing it is not mentioned in the Old Testament. It stood on an eminence in a valley of lower Galilee, some 90 miles from Jerusalem. Because of its insignificance and failure to produce anyone of importance, when Philip sang the praises of Christ as "Jesus of Nazareth," Nathanael contemptuously replied, "Can any good thing come out of Nazareth?" (John 1:45, 46).

*   *   *

Jesus the Nazarene

While not so full in form as the previous title, the one before us occurs frequently. Once it is used as a description of Jesus by Himself. "I am Jesus of Nazareth" (Acts 22:8). The Jews, describing with some contempt the great claims made by His followers, spat out the phrase, "*this* Jesus of Nazareth" (Acts 6:14). Twice the full name "Jesus Christ the Nazarene" is used as "a solemn designation throwing up for observation His entire personality in all its grandeur" (Acts 3:6; 4:10). Frequently the apostles spoke of Him as "Jesus the Nazarene" (Acts 2:22; 6:14; 26:9).

When Matthew wrote of Jesus, "He shall be called a Nazarene" (2:23), he doubtless had in mind the prophecy of Isaiah who spoke of Him as a *netger* (or "rod"), relative word of Nazareth, "out of the stem of Jesse" (11:1; 60:21). Those who came to follow Jesus were nicknamed, *Nazarenes* (Acts 24:5). While ordinarily *Nazarene* meant one born in, or a native of, Nazareth, it took on a different meaning after the lowly Nazarene became a conspicuous figure. It is necessary to stress that *Nazarene* has no connection with *Nazirite* who was a person who placed himself completely at the disposal of God, by vow, for a stated period, and underwent abstentions (Numbers 6:1-21).

But *Nazarene* was a title that would come to signify shame and humiliation. Men came to speak of the term with scorn, simply because of Nazareth's obscurity and poverty. We have no record that the small town had any notoriety for evil. The presence of the Holy Child Jesus in it for 30 years sanctified the place in which He grew up, went to school, learned a trade, helped to support the home. Godly parents were His, and His labor at the bench developed His physical power and provided contact with those around. He early cultivated the art of not being ministered unto, but ministering. Time was His to study Scripture and nature, both of which revealed their secrets to His Spirit-possessed mind.

✿ ✿ ✿

Jesus of Nazareth, King of the Jews (John 19:19).

This extension of the title associated with His earthly origin and home is further proof that the "Good Thing" born of Mary and brought up in such a humble home, came out of Nazareth as the Person who would change the world. To many of His friends and critics it was unthinkable that the King of kings could come out of a town of no renown. But there over His cross, upon which He died only some 3½ years since leaving Nazareth for good, Pilate wrote the title, so expressive of Christ's supreme royalty in spite of His lowly circumstances. A King out of Nazareth? Yes, God knows the best training ground for

those He desires to use for a world-wide ministry!

The hierarchy of the Jewish party were incensed over such a title. The phrase, "the chief priests of the Jews" which only occurs in the New Testament is found only here, and perhaps was used by John in contrast to the inscription, "King of the Jews" which Messianic title they scorned. Had not those Jewish rulers affirmed in accomplishing the death of Jesus – "We have no king but Caesar"? To them, who looked for a King to come from a royal background and with all associated pomp and glory, it was an insult to give such national honor to One who came out of a humble village like Nazareth.

Pilate turned a deaf ear to the appeal of the chief priests, "Write not, The King of the Jews; but that he said, I am King of the Jews" (John 19:21). This, then, was the only supposed crime for which He was being crucified. He pronounced Himself as "Jesus the King of the Jews." Yet He was that, and more – King of the human heart; Lord of all. Had not Nathanael declared, once He came to know Jesus as King of his life – "Rabbi, thou art the Son of God, thou art the King of Israel" (John 1:49)?

The Kingship of the poor Peasant of Nazareth is a fascinating study. First of all, He was *born*, not only "the Saviour which is Christ the Lord" (Luke 2:11), but also *King*. "Where is He that is born King of the Jews?" (Matthew 2:2; John 18:37). It will be observed that Matthew denotes Christ's supremacy as King among kings by giving Him the capital *K*, and Herod the small *k* as king (Matthew 2:2, 3). Christ was *born King* for the simple reason that He was King *before He was born* (Psalm 2:6; 1 Timothy 1:17). Matthew's gospel is preeminently one of the King and His kingdom.

When Jesus left His native town as

"the Prophet of Nazareth of Galilee," His Kingship was uppermost in His teaching as His "Kingdom Parables" prove. The time came when the populace was ready to crown and acclaim Him as King. "They would come and take Him by force, to make Him a King" (John 6:15). With His entry into Jerusalem, there came the application to Himself of the prophecy of Zechariah of the King coming lowly riding on an ass (9:9). "Behold, thy King cometh unto thee, meek, and sitting upon an ass" (Matthew 21:5).

Rejected as King of the Jews by their chief priests, the time drew near for Him to be crucified as *King*. Asked Pilate of the religious leaders, "Shall I crucify your King?" They replied that they only recognized one king – Caesar. In His last hours, one of the most memorable incidents was Pilate's interrogation of our Lord which ended in Pilate's testifying of the complete innocence of the charge brought against Him (John 18:38).

> "Pilate therefore said unto Him, Art thou a king then? Jesus answered, Thou sayest that I am a king. *To this end was I born*, and *for this cause* came I into the world" (John 18:37).

Also in His good confession before Pontius Pilate (1 Timothy 6:13, 15), Jesus described the difference between His Kingship and that of earthly rulers –

> "My kingdom is not of this world: if My kingdom were of this world, then would my servants fight, that I should not be delivered to the Jews: but now is My kingdom not from hence" (John 18:36).

A glorious era awaits this earth, which earthly kings and rulers have ravaged by countless wars, when Jesus of Nazareth reveals Himself as "King of kings, and Lord of lords", and as "The Prince of the kings of earth" (Revelation 19:16). Appearing as "King of nations" (not *saints* as in KJV) (Revelation 15:3; Jeremiah 10:7), the iron, rebellious will of the peoples will be broken, and His reign in righteousness will be universally acknowledged. "King of kings, and Lord of lords" (Revelation 19:16) – the order is reversed in Revelation 17:14 – is a royal title expressive of universal dominion. As the ruling monarch or emperor, all lesser ruling authorities will be under His control. Then the sacred Head once crowned with thorns will be crowned with glory. "Jesus is publicly, officially, and intrinsically King of kings and Lord of lords," says Darby in his *Synopsis of the Books of the Bible*.

Jesus was *born* and *died* a King that He might be our Sovereign as well as our Saviour. Paul speaks of the believer as one not only delivered from "the power of darkness," but "translated into the Kingdom of the Son of God's love" (Colossians 1:13 margin). The apostle further counsels us to walk worthy of God, who has called us into His kingdom and glory, or glorious kingdom (1 Thessalonians 2:12). Jesus was born a *Saviour*, and we believe that He has saved us from a guilty past, but He was likewise born a *King* and as such claims our complete submission and loyalty. As *sinners* we need Him as Saviour. As *subjects*, the King expects our willing and loving allegiance. Have we brought forth the royal diadem and given Him His coronation as King of our lives?

> King of my life, I crown Thee now,
>   Thine shall the glory be;
> Lest I forget Thy thorn-crowned
>   brow,
>   Lead me to Calvary.

* * *

Judge (Acts 10:42; 17:31).

In his remarkable sermon delivered in

the house of Cornelius (Acts 10:34-48), Peter declared that his Risen Lord was the One "ordained by God to be the Judge of Living and dead" (Acts 10:42). What a comprehensive title this is! Jesus is a judge, not wholly by an external creation, but by an internal right, and the divine declaration and designation endorsed and proclaimed that right. God who ordained His Son to be *Judge* is likewise referred to as "God the Judge of all" (Hebrews 12:23), a phrase implying that He who is the Judge of His people is at the same time their God. God is often referred to as Judge whether of men or nations, saints or sinners (Genesis 18:25). But Peter calls us to consider Jesus in such judicial capacity, for He it was who said –

> "The Father judgeth no man, but hath committed *all* judgment unto the Son: That *all* men should honour the Son, even as they honour the Father" (John 5:22, 23).

It may seem as if Christ's divinely ordained Judgeship is contradicted by His own explicit statement – "I came not to judge the world, but to save the world" (John 12:47). There was the day a follower came with the request, "Master, speak to my brother, that he divide the inheritance with me." But Jesus answered, "Man, who made me a judge or a divider over you?" (Luke 12:13, 14). (See Exodus 2:14). This would seem as if He shrank from exercising the functions of a judge. What our Lord implied, however, was that He had not been designated *Judge* to deal with family disputes which ordinary judges of the law were qualified to settle.

Further, when He said He came not "to judge the world," it was the world of unbelievers He had in mind who had rejected the truth and were reminded that He would not Himself pronounce judgment upon them, but that *His word* was a Judge before whose tribunal they already stood. "The word that I have spoken, *the same* shall judge him in the last day" (John 12:48). As the breath leaving the mouth has the double effect of cooling a bowl of hot soup or warming cold hands, so the same truth which Jesus taught can save the sinner, and if rejected, will eternally condemn the lost. The Judgment to which Peter says Christ was designated or marked out, is not in the spiritual sense of saints and sinners, but a literal one of all generations, past, present, and to come. See 1 Peter 4:5. It is the general Judgment Paul likewise mentioned in his powerful sermon on Mars' Hill when he declared that Christ was *the Man* set apart by God to judge the whole human race, the proof of such being the fact of His resurrection from the dead.

> "Because He hath appointed a day, in the which He will judge the World in righteousness by that man whom he hath ordained" (Acts 17:31).

This will be a righteous judgment by a righteous Judge, and likewise an impartial judgment by One who created all things, who knows all things, and who is therefore qualified to act as a holy, unerring Judge. "*In righteousness,* implies not merely righteously or justly, as an epithet of quality or manner, but in the actual and active exercise of righteousness or justice as a moral attribute or trait of character."

Some confusion has arisen over Paul's statement, "Do ye not know that saints should judge the world?" (1 Corinthians 6:2, 3). Such a question has been thought to imply that God's people are to be *assessors* with Christ in the judgment of the whole human race, but Scripture never states that they shall judge with Him. The saints themselves are to be judged by Christ, and, further, no fallible being is competent to function in a universal judicial capacity. Such an act, as one writer expresses it –

"Requires *omniscience* and *omnipresence* to comprehend and witness all that has been thought, said and done by every creature; also *infinite justice* and *entire freedom from all partiality,* as well as an *inherent right* to fix the eternal destinies of undying souls. These attributes are possessed by God alone. They are His glory, and 'His glory will He not give to another.' "

What, then, are we to understand by Paul's declaration? The verse should be read in the *present,* and not in the *future* tense, as the next phrase indicates – "If the world is judged by you?" Thus, the verse can be translated, "Do ye not know that the saints (now) judge the world, and if in you the world is judged are ye unworthy to judge the smallest matters?" By the use of the verb *crino* "to judge" means here, as in other New Testament references "to condemn" (Luke 19:22; John 16:11). This last reference, "Of judgment, because the prince of this world *is* judged," coincides with the correct significance of Paul's question, namely, that the saints, by the moral influence of their faith and daily holy life, *judge,* that is, *condemn* the world.

The present moral influence which the spiritually and consistent deportment of Christians exert on the minds of an unbelieving world is suggested by our Lord's symbol of them as "the salt of the earth." What a solemn obligation is theirs to exhibit the influence of the Gospel in every phase of life so that the ungodly "may see their good works, and glorify – not them for such, but – their Father who is in Heaven." By their testimony to the efficacy of the finished work of Christ at Calvary, and to the regenerating, transforming power of the Holy Spirit, they *condemn* the world for its unbelief. See Matthew 12:41, 42. This same interpretation is relevant to what Paul goes on to say about judging angels.

Such *present* judgment does not imply that the saints will ultimately assist their Lord in the governmental control of all things. Reigning in their hearts, theirs will be the honor of reigning with Him. See Matthew 19:28. "If we suffer, we shall also reign with him" (2 Timothy 2:12). Paul goes on to use the same phrase as Peter, concerning the Lord Jesus Christ as "the Judge of the living and the dead" (2 Timothy 4:1), but goes on to make a distinction between these two companies, giving to each class its particular judgment.

"To judge the *living* . . . at His appearing – To judge the *dead* . . . at His kingdom."

Among the Judgments of Scripture there are two at which Christ is the august Judge.

1. *The Judgment Seat of Christ* (Romans 14:10; 1 Corinthians 3:12-15; 2 Corinthians 5:10).

This judgment of the saints, and saints only, is related to their service and earned rewards. "Every man's *work* shall be tried by fire of what sort it is." Christ's reward will be with Him, ready to present to those who have been faithful to Him and to His cause (Revelation 2:10). What an incentive this is to holy living and sacrificial service! When He appears this second time, what a reward it will be to hear Him say, "Well done, good and faithful servant, enter thou into the joy of thy Lord." God forbid that we should stand before the Judge at that day with a saved soul, but a lost life – nothing to our credit!

2. *The Great White Throne* (Revelation 20:11-15).

This dread judgment with the Christ of Calvary as the righteous Judge is for the wicked dead, and the wicked dead only, and is associated with His final Kingdom rule. Divine justice requires such a just judgment. It must be borne in mind, however, that the accused are not arraigned before this final assize to have their sinful and guilty past examined and judged upon. As sinners, before they died, they *were* condemned (John 3:18, 36). The wicked dead are raised for the ratification of their condemnation and to hear the pronouncement of their eternal doom. Relationship to Christ as Saviour here determines the particular Judgment hereafter.

Thou Holy Judge of quick and dead,
And to Thy Church the Living Head;
When Thou in glory shalt appear,
With all Thy saints to Thee so dear,
Thou wilt award the meek, the crown,
To each and all who overcome.

❋   ❋   ❋

Just One (Acts 7:52).

In his defense before the Sanhedrin, Stephen, the first martyr of the Christian Church, condemned its leaders with the crime of history when he declared that they had murdered Jesus, the *Just One*. Being unjustly tried, condemned, and then to be stoned to death, this Spirit-filled deacon was willing to sacrifice himself for the Lord he loved knowing that He was just and righteous in all His ways. As the Just One, He never acted contrary to His own nature or attributes. This Righteous One had been unjustly tried and condemned to death Himself, although before the law of God or man He was innocent of the crime He was charged with, because of intrinsic righteousness. Wycliffe translates the term, *The Rightful Man*.

Peter, in his sermon to the men of Israel charged them with having denied *the Holy One and the Just* (Acts 3:14). Here the double title tended to aggravate the guilt of those who had killed the Prince of life, in whose place the killers preferred the murderer, Barabbas (Matthew 27:21). *Holy and Just* are epithets not only of Christ's innocence before the law (Matthew 27:19, 24), but in a higher sense of His peculiar character and mission as the Holy One of God, who Himself is "Just and Justifier of all who believe." The *Just* or *Righteous One* is a common description of Christ in the New Testament (Acts 22:14; 1 John 2:1; 1 Peter 3:18).

Evidently Pilate's wife had a most disturbing dream over Jesus whose fate her husband had to decide. Bravely she said to Pilate, "Have thou nothing to do with that *just man*" (Matthew 27:19). Yielding to the clamor of the crowd thirsting for the blood of this Righteous One, Pilate washed his hands of the whole matter saying, "I am innocent of the blood of this *just person*: see ye to it" (Matthew 27:24). Thus the Saviour was sacrificed to a bad man's diplomacy. Pilate's injustice is seen in that although he pronounced Jesus guiltless, he yet adjudged Him to an unjust death.

How grateful we are that we serve One who is essentially just and righteous, and the fountain of justice in all those who are His! "Just and right is he" (Deuteronomy 32:4). Mingled, however, with His inflexible justice is His mercy. He is "a just God and Saviour" (Isaiah 45:21). By His amazing grace we are justified (Titus 3:7).

O Christ! The Holy and The Just,
Thy love is worthy of all trust;
The Just One for the unjust died,
The Lord of Life was crucified.
Now, all who come are justified,
Pardoned through Thy most precious
    blood;

Thou, Thou hast made our peace with God.

K

King (Luke 19:38).

One of the grandest of ancient prophecies was that of a King who would come having Salvation, and who, although meek and lowly, would found a vast empire of redeemed hosts (Zechariah 9:9, 10). "Men have strange glimpses afforded them of the Divine," says Richard Glover, "and visions of hope come to eyes that look. The *advent of a saving King* is a vision which many religions have enjoyed and all mankind shall find fulfilled." (See under section *Jesus of Nazareth – King of the Jews* for material on the Kingship of Christ.)

*   *   *

King of Glory (Psalm 24:7-10).

The psalmist makes it plain that only those who ascend the hill of the Lord, and have clean hands and a pure heart are fit enough to behold Christ as the *King of Glory,* as Heaven's gates open to reveal Him. That the *King of Glory* was the *Lord of Glory,* cruel men crucified (1 Corinthians 2:8), but who at His Ascension found the everlasting doors open to receive Him, is clearly evident from the language of this *glory* psalm. Kings of ancient times, when they returned from battles, conspicuous victories, entered their capitol in triumph and gave largesses to the people. It was so with the One who came from Glory and was *born* a King.

> He was the King appointed of God (Psalm 2:6; 89:18-21).
>
> He was completely victorious over the enemies of God (Colossians 2:15); over Satan (Hebrews 2:14, 15); over the grave, sin,

and death (Acts 2:24; 1 Corinthians 15:54-57).

He was humiliated, but afterwards exalted (Philippians 2:9).

He endured the Cross, but is now crowned with many diadems (Hebrews 12:2).

He entered His heavenly capitol in triumph, and gave gifts unto men (Psalm 68:18; Acts 2; Ephesians 4:8).

He will be manifested in all His Glory when He returns as King.

> The King shall come when morning dawns,
>   And light and beauty brings;
> Hail, Christ, the Lord! Thy people pray,
>   "Come quickly, King of kings."

*   *   *

King of Kings (Revelation 19:16).

This was a title well known in the East, being assumed by Persian and Assyrian monarchs, and indicating one of supreme power. Thus Artaxerxes was called, "king of kings" (Ezra 7:12). A ruler bearing this title had many kings subject to him. For instance, Ben-hadad, king of Syria, had 32 kings under his command (1 Kings 20:1). Applied to Jesus, the designation points to the time when "the kingdom of this world becomes the world-kingdom of our Lord, and He shall reign for ever and ever" (Revelation 11:15; 12:10). Then "*every knee* will bow, . . . and every tongue confess Jesus Christ is Lord, to the glory of God the Father" (Philippians 2:10, 11). (See under section *Jesus of Nazareth – King of the Jews.*)

*   *   *

King Over All the Earth (Zechariah 14:9).

A similar title, expressing universal dominion, is given by Isaiah, "Thy Redeemer the Holy One of Israel: The

God of the whole earth shall he be called" (54:5). The earth is His, so He comes to take possession (Psalm 19:1). Such a prophecy implies that this is to be the consequence of Israel being again recognized by God as His own people (Daniel 2:44; Revelation 11:15). (For further material see under title, *Lord of the Whole Earth.*)

L

Lamb (Revelation 5:6).

It is a most fascinating study to follow the evolution of the lamb in Scripture from its first mention in Genesis to its last reference in Revelation (Genesis 21:28; Revelation 22:3).

The lamb chosen for sacrifice had to be a faultless male, in keeping with established estimate of animal perfection (Malachi 1:14).

The sacrificial lamb had to be under one year old, meek, gentle, having a tractable nature.

The offered lamb had to be kept whole, not a bone broken, and roasted (Exodus 12:46; Psalm 34:20; John 19:36).

The lamb was the symbol of unity – unity of the family, unity of the nation, unity of God and His people, whom He had taken into relationship with Himself.

The offering of a lamb by a sinning Israelite could never result in redemption from sin. Such an offering was accepted by God in virtue of the sacrifice of His own Son as *the* Lamb who would take away the sin of the world. Thus, the question of Isaac, "Where is the Lamb?" is answered by John the Baptist as he gazed upon the Saviour, "Behold the Lamb of God!" (Genesis 22:7; John 1:29). Several references can be found to Jesus as *the* Lamb, especially in the last book of the Bible where some 27 times He is given this name.

We are not only to think of Jesus as the Lamb in respect to the example He left as such in meekness (2 Corinthians 10:1); in *patience* (Isaiah 53:7); in *submission* (1 Peter 2:23), but above all in *sacrifice* (Hebrews 9:22; 1 John 1:7). John saw Christ as the Lamb that had been newly slain (Revelation 5:6). As God's Lamb, Jesus was ordained for blood-shedding before the world was (1 Peter 1:19, 20) and it is His shed blood that gives the spirit to the "new song" only the redeemed can sing (Revelation 5:9). It is not difficult to follow the *minute particulars* concerning the Lamb of God –

He was to be chosen *out of the flock* (Exodus 12:5; Hebrews 2:14).

He was to be *without blemish* and *without spot* (Hebrews 7:26, 27; 1 Peter 2:22).

He was to be roasted with fire (Leviticus 9:24; Hebrews 12:29).

His blood *must* be sprinkled on every house for safety (Hebrews 9:20).

His flesh *must* be eaten according to the ordinance of God (John 6:53-55).

With us, lambs are reared to provide two things. First, *clothing*. What a warm covering their wool provides! Thus it is with God's Lamb (Romans 8:7; 13:14; Galatians 3:27; Ephesians 1:6). Second, *food*. How the lamb we eat nourishes and sustains life! What sustenance there is for our souls in the Divine Lamb! (John 6:56, 57). Our obligation is to see that the blood of the Lamb has cleansed us, and that we are covered with "the robe of righteousness" (Isaiah 61:10; 2 Corinthians 5:3; Revelation 7:14), and that we daily feed upon the Lamb for our necessary spiritual nourishment (John 21:15, 16; 2 Peter 3:18; Psalm 34:8).

> Lamb of God! Behold Him ready
>   To be offered, waiting there,
> Dwelling in a human body,
>   Son of God, to Heaven heir!

*   *   *

Lamb of God (John 1:36).

We return to the twice repeated exclamation of John the Baptist, "Behold, the Lamb of God," not merely to indicate that the audience of the forerunner of Jesus would be familiar with the figure of the lamb because lambs were daily offered in the Temple, and every year in connection with the Passover, but because of who the One exalted as *the* Lamb actually was. Previous verses describe Him as "the Word made flesh," as the One who came as "the glory as of the only begotten of the Father," as "the only begotten Son, which is in the bosom of the Father," as "the Son of God" (John 1:1, 14, 18, 34) – titles which have a direct bearing on the quality of the blood He was to shed as the Lamb of God.

It is taken for granted that in Christ as *the* Lamb there was the fulfillment of a notable prophecy (Isaiah 53:7), and that the lambs slain on Jewish altars pre-figured the atoning work of the Saviour; and that John's declaration, "Behold the Lamb of God who beareth away the sin of the world" can be regarded as the first clear presentation of the doctrine of the Cross in New Testament times; and that, as F. B. Meyer put it, "The Gospel glistens in it as the whole sun in a single dewdrop." The question we ask is, "Why was not all the blood of beasts able to give the guilty conscience peace, or wash away the stain?" The answer is, Because they were only innocent unblemished lambs. This is why we go on to sing –

> But Christ, the heavenly Lamb,
> Takes all our sins away;
> A sacrifice of nobler name
> And richer blood than they.

But what actually constituted this *richer blood*, so efficacious in bearing away the world's sin? If Christ was *only a man* who, because of His innocence, meekness, and submission merited the name of Lamb, His shed blood would have had no more power to give peace to guilty consciences and remove sins than a perfect dumb animal sacrificed on an altar was able to do.

Who, then, was this *Lamb* John extolled whose blood had such marvelous power? He was not only "the Lamb of God" that is, the One ordained and sent by God as such, but "the Lamb who was God"! This was why His poured-out blood "atoned for all the race," and those "five bleeding wounds" of His continue to "pour effectual prayers." When He died, it was not only as the "Saviour mild," but as the Mighty Monarch." Charles Wesley caught something of the mysterious quality of the blood of the Lamb when he wrote –

> Amazing love! how can it be
> That Thou, *my God,* should die
>   for me?
> 'Tis mystery all! *The Immortal* dies!
> Who can explore His strange design.

In his heart-moving farewell message to the elders of Ephesus, Paul gave utterance to a truth of tremendous import when he spoke of the Church being purchased by "the blood of God." Urging those overseers of the flock, to "feed" the Church of God," or "Church of the Lord," the apostle went on to say "which he [God] hath purchased with *his* own blood" (Acts 20:28). This is the Church, God the Son said He would build (Matthew 16:18), and the blood He shed to make this Church His own, is associated with His Deity. Thus "the blood of God" – a phrase found in several of the earliest Christian writers — is the blood of Christ who, though He became man, was divine. Thus, the transcendent sacredness of the Church of Christ rests upon the dignity and Deity of her Lord, and upon the precious, intrinsic character of the blood He shed to make her His.

Within the womb of Mary there took place the mingling of Deity and humanity, the Holy Spirit being responsible for the love-knot of our Lord's two natures, making possible the coming of Jesus, not as God exclusively, nor man exclusively, but as the marvelous combination of two — the *God-Man,* or "God manifest in flesh." So, although with our finite minds we cannot explain the mystery, we believe the fact that the blood shed on Calvary was the blood of the *God-Man;* and that the mingling of Deity and humanity in that blood gave it its unceasing efficacy to wash away our stains, make us acceptable to God, and secure for us eternal life. Had it not been for the shedding of such precious, unique blood there would never have been remission of sins, and

"ten thousand times ten thousand, and thousands of thousands, Saying with a loud voice, Worthy is the Lamb that was slain to receive power, and riches, and wisdom, and strength, and honor, and glory, and blessing" (Revelation 5:11, 12).

* * *

Leader (Isaiah 55:4).

In his unique description of the beneficent merchant inviting all those who had no money to come to his market, and paradoxically buy wine and milk without money and without price, Isaiah was referring primarily to the historic David. In the triad of titles he uses under divine inspiration he gave us a prophecy and picture of Him who offers us blessings silver or gold cannot buy. Christ also fully realized in Himself the three designations of *Witness, Leader, Commander* (Isaiah 55:1-4).

1. *A Witness.* He alone is the perfect faithful and true Witness (John 15:27; Revelation 1:5; 3:14). Jesus bore witness even unto death for God, to His law, claims, and plan of redeeming love and grace. Revelation is a *testimony* because it is propounded to be received on the authority of the Giver, and not merely because it can be proved by arguments.

2. *A Leader.* The original word for *leader* is variously translated as author, prince, or captain. The writer to the Hebrews reminds us that God made His Son to be "the Leader of our salvation perfect through sufferings" (2:9, 10). The word itself means first in a file of men, and therefore their leader and commanding officer. In His resurrection Jesus is "the first in a long procession of souls whom He is leading up from the grave, with its darkness and corruption, through the steeps of air, past principalities and powers, to the very throne of God." How precious are the words from the Shepherd Psalm — *"He leadeth me"* (Psalm 23:2, 3).

3. *A Commander.* Barnes gives us Lawgiver, and Jesus is "the one lawgiver" (James 4:12). See Isaiah 33:22. Canon Horsley translates "Commander" as *Preceptor* — an instructor or schoolmaster. Yet, somehow, we prefer the KJV word, for Jesus has earned the right to the title of *Commander,* and likewise the authority to command our loving obedience and implicit trust.

He leadeth me! O blessed thought,
O words with heavenly comfort
 fraught,
Whate'er I do, where'er I be,
Still 'tis God's hand that leadeth me.

* * *

Life (John 14:6).

In the trio of titles Jesus uses of Himself, the third, "I am . . . the life," is fundamental to the other two – *way, truth*. "In him was life" (John 1:4). He is *the* Life, or Life personified, and perfect in Himself (John 11:25). Paul, appropriating Him whose "life is the light of men," could say, "Christ, who is our life" (Colossians 3:4). There are various ways of thinking of Him as "the Life." For instance –

> In His preexistence, life was perfect (John 3:13).
> In His birth, life was manifested (John 1:14).
> In His days, life was consecrated (John 8:29).
> In His death, life was offered (John 10:15).
> In His resurrection, life was accepted (Acts 3:15).
> In His glory, life is shared (John 14:19).

This was the *Life* that was manifested (1 John 1:2). When a sinner accepts Him as Saviour, he becomes one with Him, and derives life from Him, as the stem, leaves, and fruit receive their life or sap from the vine (John 15:1-8; Galatians 2:20). Spiritual life can only be derived from being in union with Him who is *the Life* (1 Corinthians 15:45). He alone is "the Living Way."

LIFE, then, is not something but *Someone*, as John makes clear when he says, "This life is in His Son," or "this life *is* His Son." Then comes the warning –

> "He that hath the Son hath life,
> He that hath not the Son of God
> hath not life" (1 John 5:11, 12).

A person may be physically and mentally alive, yet spiritually dead. There are those in the world who speak about their desire to see *life,* but what they seek for brings spiritual and eternal death.

> "She that liveth in pleasure is dead while she liveth" (1 Timothy 5:6).

Christ described those in the church at Sardis who had a name that they lived, but were *dead* (Revelation 3:1). The Pharisees prided themselves on being very much alive, but Jesus called them "whited sepulchres, full of dead men's bones." If Christ is our Life, then, for us to live will be Christ, and to die, gain, seeing that death opens the gate to life in its completeness (Philippians 1:21).

> I live; not I; 'tis He alone
> By whom the mighty work is done,
> Dead to myself, alive to Him,
> I count all loss His rest to gain.

* * *

Light (John 1:7).

As a noun, this illustration from the natural world is used of God, of Christ, of the Spirit, of Scripture, of saints, and of Satan. It was God who created the light by which the earth was first illuminated, and who sent Jesus to illumine the world lost in the darkness of sin. As a pole star in a dark night, Jesus shone, and ever shines as "the Light shineth in the darkness." The tragedy, however, is that "the darkness comprehended it not" (John 1:5). The Greek reads "*overcame* it not." Christ is the Light lightening every man coming into the world. As the Author of nature (Romans 1:20), He imparted to man the instincts and intellectual faculties with which human beings are endowed with a consciousness of the existence of God and of the desirability of knowing Him.

This inherent heritage of man is one aspect of a Christ-given life, as is also the certainty of life after death. "He hath set Eternity in their hearts" (Ecclesiastes 3:11 ASV). Even in the most degraded, there is not total darkness. Sin can never succeed in extinguishing this inner light, even though the sinner may do his best to quench it. Man may hide from the sun, but he cannot put it out. When Judas sinned the sin that ruined him there was light enough left to enable him to see the tragedy of his foul deed (Matthew 27:3-5).

Christ, then, is the *Light,* and not a lamp carrying a light in it. He, Himself, is LIGHT and what John makes clear in the prologue of his gospel is that as He was the *life*-giving Word, so He is the *light*-giving Word. All truth is light, and being the sum of all truth, as *the Truth,* He is the Source of all light. Then is there not a pregnant thought in the statement — *the life is the light?* Behind the Light there was the Life. It was all Christ was *in* Himself as the Light from Heaven that expressed itself in all His words, ways, and works. Is it not so with ourselves? It is not so much what we say or do that enlightens others, but the real life behind such. The life is ever the light. Horatius Bonar taught the Church to sing —

> O Light of Light, shine in!
> Cast out this night of sin,
> Create true day within:
> O Light of Light, shine in!

* * *

Light, Everlasting (Isaiah 16:19, 20).

The prophet foretold the cessation of all natural light in the prediction John proclaimed (Revelation 21:23; 22:5).

> "The sun shall be no more thy light by day; neither for brightness shall the moon give light unto thee. . . . Thy sun shall no more go down; neither shall thy moon withdraw itself; for the Lord shall be thine everlasting light . . ." (Isaiah 60:19, 20).

Note the distinction between *"the sun"* and *"thy sun."* When Christ as the *Sun* of Righteousness shall rise with His healing rays, He will never "go down." He will be not only *an,* but *our, Everlasting Light.* The sun and moon will be no longer needed in the radiance of the greater glory of the presence of Jehovah. Now, the sun sets and the moon wanes, but when the Lamb is the Light in Glory, there will be no waning and no setting. And with the Everlasting Light, there has come everlasting joy. "Thy mourning shall be ended" (Isaiah 60:20).

> No need of the sunlight in Heaven,
>   we're told,
>   The Light of the World is Jesus:
> The Lamb is the Light in the City
>   of Gold,
>   The Light of *that* World is Jesus.

* * *

Light of the World (John 8:12).

In harmony with the symbol of Light John gives us in the introduction to his matchless gospel (1:4, 5, 7, 8, 9) where the apostle speaks of Jesus as "The Light of men" — the designation is more fully illustrated by the *Light* Himself in His discourses. In fact, *light* is one of the characteristic words of the fourth gospel, occurring some 23 times. Jesus called Himself "the light of the world" with interesting additions —

> "I am the light of the world . . . The light of life" (8:12).
> "As long as I am in the world, I am the light of the world" (9:5).
> "Yet a little while is the light with you. . . . While ye have light, believe in the light. . . . I am come a light into the world" (12:35, 36, 46).
> "Light is come into the world" (3:19-21).
> "He seeth the light of this world" (11:9, 10)

The Jewish tradition that *"Light* was one of the names of Messiah" is certainly borne out in our Lord's oft-repeated use of the figure of speech. While John's vocabulary is more restricted than, say, that of Luke, yet as Godet expresses it, "If John has only a few words in his vocabulary, these terms may be compared to pieces of gold with which great lords make payments. Among these precious, priceless words are *life, light, love,* which form the warp and woof, not only of John's gospel, but also his first epistle.

The claim of Christ to be the *Light of the world* implies that He is in relation to the souls of men everywhere just as the sun is in relation to the material world. Coming into the world as its *light,* He came as the Divine Revealer, revealing to all who comprehended Him as such –

> The character of God (John 17:6).
> The sinfulness of man (Luke 5:8).
> The beauty of holiness (1 Peter 2:21, 22).
> The way of salvation (John 3:16; 6:51).

The state of man by nature is described as one of *darkness* –

> "Who . . . walk in the ways of darkness" (Proverbs 2:13).
> "To turn men from darkness to light" (Acts 26:18).
> "Having the understanding darkened" (Ephesians 4:18).
> "Delivered us from the power of darkness" (Colossians 1:13).
> "Darkness hath blinded his eyes" (1 John 2:11; 2 Corinthians 3:14; 4:4).

But by no power or effort of his own could the sinner obtain spiritual illumination, which is different from the moral and intellectual light, also emanating from Christ, and which all men have (John 1:9). Scripture takes cognizance of the *Light of Nature* men have, but which cannot provide spiritual light (Romans 1:19, 20); and also of the *Light of Conscience* with similar failure (Romans 2:14, 15; 3:23). The history of the world clearly proves that the world by its own wisdom can never know God (1 Corinthians 1:21). Thus, the great need of the world, lost in the darkness of sin, was for LIGHT, not *of* this world, but *for* it. And in the fullness of time Jesus came, and now, "the true light now shineth" (1 John 2:8). The tragedy is that after almost two millennia after the coming of the *Light,* the largest part of the world is still covered with gross darkness.

Scripture declares that "God is light," and "dwells in light," and is the only source of light (1 Timothy 6:16; James 1:17; 1 John 1:5), and that as the great luminary, the sun, can only be seen by its own light, so God can only be manifested by Himself. It was thus that God the Son came to reveal Him in whom is no darkness at all (John 14:9; Colossians 1:15; Hebrews 1:1-3). It may help us to understand how Jesus functions as light, if we think of the constitution of natural light, which as we know is a combination of color rays – red, orange, yellow, green, blue, indigo, violet. These lovely rays, forming light, are figurative of combinations of divine attributes Jesus fully possessed and manifested while in the world (1 Timothy 3:16):

> There was His *love* (John 3:16; Romans 5:8).
> There was His *holiness* (Luke 1:35; Acts 3:14).
> There was His *wisdom* (1 Corinthians 1:24; Ephesians 3:10).
> There was His *justice* (Romans 3:26).

There was His *omnipresence* (John 3:13).

There was His *omniscience* (John 13:38).

There was His *omnipotence* (Matthew 28:18).

These are the glorious seven rays found in Him who came as the true *light* upon whom we are totally dependent for spiritual light and life. As things cannot live and grow without natural light, so man cannot live and grow without *the light* (John 14:19; 15:5; Colossians 3:3). Light is most unselfish in that it never shines for itself merely, but for the benefit of others. It is so with Him who is "the *Light* of men" (Matthew 4:16; Romans 15:3; Ephesians 5:2).

How grateful we should be that we can come to this *Light*, shining for us, and that "in His light we can see light" (Psalm 36:9)! The psalmist could say, "The Lord is my light and salvation" (Psalm 27:1). Can we confess the same? The *Light* has been sent out, but have we received it? (Psalms 40:3; 118:27). Are we walking under the influence of Him who is the *Light,* and living and shining as children of light, or as Paul put it, "*as lights in the world*" (Philippians 2:15)? The Greek reads, "as luminaries in the world" the implication being that as the sun and the moon – the great lights – in the firmament shine for the benefit of earth, so our lives are to function spiritually. What wonderful condescension it was when "*the Light* of the World" Himself said of His followers – "*Ye are the light of the world*" (Matthew 5:14)!

The somber and dreadful warning is that if men fail to come to the *Light* shining for them, and finally close their eyes and hearts against Him, that there is "reserved for them the blackness of darkness for ever" (Jude 13). Our message to those who "walk on in darkness" (Psalm 82:5) is an urgent and all-important one –

> Ye dwellers in darkness, with sin
>   blinded eyes,
> The Light of the world is Jesus;
> Go, wash at His bidding, and light
>   will arise,
> The Light of the world is Jesus.

✻   ✻   ✻

Light of Gentiles (Isaiah 42:6; 49:6; 60:3; Luke 2:32).

Having already dealt with the significance of godly Simeon's declaration of the Babe coming as a "Light to lighten the Gentiles, and the glory of thy people Israel," all we want to add at this point is that up until Pentecost, salvation had been of the Jews. With the conversion of Paul, however, the tide turned in favor of the Gentiles. Peter had to be brought to realize that Salvation was also for Gentile as well as Jew, and rejoiced when a company of Gentiles became believers (Acts 10:34-48). But it was to Paul that the call came to witness as an apostle to the great Gentile world.

> "I have set thee to be a light of the Gentiles, that thou shouldest be for salvation unto the ends of the earth" (Acts 13:47-49).

Out of a world population of over 3,000 million, there are only some 15 million Jews. Thus, the vast mass of earth's inhabitants are Gentiles, millions of whom are still waiting to hear of Him who is the *Light* of the enormous Gentile world today. In this age of grace, He is likewise the *Light* of Israel but rejected as such. Before He can become her *Glory* in His millennial reign her eyes must be opened to see Him whom they pierced, and mourn or repent for their long rejection of Him. Certainly, our evangelistic efforts must include the lost in the house of Israel, but when we think of the tremendous perponderance of Gentiles all over the earth, what a challenge faces the Church to function as a Light to these 3,000 million souls for whom Christ. died.

> He expecteth – but He heareth
> Still the bitter cry
> From earth's millions, "Come and
> help us,
> For we die."

* * *

Lion (Revelation 5:5).

One of the elders bade John not to weep, but dry his tears and "Behold, the Lion of the tribe of Judah," but when he looked he "beheld . . . a lamb as it had been slain" (Revelation 5:5-7). *Lion* and *Lamb* – Christ was both. A *Lamb* in His death, He was a *Lion* in His resurrection. Then He combines the qualities of both in Himself, for He exhibited majesty yet meekness, sovereignty and suffering, severity and goodness.

The figure of the *Lion* applied to the meek and lowly Jesus is indeed a forceful one. Noblest of animals, the lion has been called "the king of beasts." The reason why Jesus is called "the Lion of the tribe of Judah" is because a lion was traced on the ensign or banner of Judah, noblest of the tribes of Israel, from which He sprang. Applied to Him, the lion is symbolic of His prowess, dignity and great strength. When He comes to usher in His world-wide reign it will be as the all-powerful Lion. "In irresistible might, majesty, and sovereignty, He will secure the blessing of Israel and of the whole earth," says Walter Scott. "In His lion-like character He crushes every opposing force, and establishes His universal kingdom on the ruin of all opposition. Here worth and might are combined."

* * *

Living Bread (See under *Bread*)

* * *

Living Stone (See *Chief Cornerstone*)

* * *

Lord (Matthew 22:43, 44).

The claim by Christ of equality with the Father, as well as the assertion of Deity, are implied in the application of the psalmist's words to Himself, "The LORD said unto my Lord" (Psalm 110:1). Because of its varied, glowing facets, this is a diamond of a name for Him who was born, "Christ the LORD" and desires all who love and obey Him to sanctify Him as LORD in their hearts (1 Peter 3:15).

The angel at the birth of Jesus gave Him three separate titles which so far explain one another –

> A Saviour,
> The promised Messiah,
> The Sovereign Lord of men and
> angels (Luke 2:11).

Because the Saviour came as the promised *Messiah*, He is therefore entitled to our obedience as *Lord*. In the city of David was born a Child who was to exercise the functions of Redemption, Messiahship, and supreme Lordship, a marvelous trinity of titles! Perhaps there may be a higher significance in the term *Lord* than that of mere Messianic dignity. It is with the absorbing theme, the *Lordship* of Christ, that we are particularly concerned at this junction. The importance of such a study can be judged from the fact that "all Christian responsibility whether of a corporate, individual, or social character is directly connected with Christ as *Lord*. The various relationships of life are to be duty observed and regulated by what is due to Him in this character (Ephesians 6:1-10; Colossians 3:17-25)."

Christ's Lordship in the Church, and in the godly observance of the Lord's Supper, in connection with which the title *Lord* is used 8 times (1 Corinthians 11), is a truth largely ignored in the professing Church today. What a mighty spiritual upsurge there would be if she could get back to the recognition of Christ's *Lordship* in all her affairs (1 Corinthians 12:3-31).

Christ's title, *Lord,* is also an expression of His rights over creation and man (2 Peter 2). In his remarkable Pentecostal sermon, Peter concluded with the statement, "that God hath *made* that same Jesus whom ye have crucified, both *Lord* and Christ" (Acts 2:36). As *Jehovah,* and in virtue of His Deity and humanity, He was made *Lord,* and exalted to God's right hand, and as such He has every just claim over the Christian, over man, and over creation. Thus, as one expositor states it –

> "Our *responsibilities* are connected with the exalted Man as *Lord,* our *blessings* are connected with the exalted Man as *Christ,* thus *in Christ* defines my place before God, while the former name is directly connected with the whole range of Christian duty and responsibility, hence 'in the *Lord*' divinely regulates my place and conduct on earth."

That the whole of the New Testament breathes the air of Christ's *Lordship* can be gathered from the fact that *Lord* is used of Him about 650 times, 170 of which are to be found in the gospels with nearly 160 occurrences of this divine, august title being clearly identified with *Jehovah.* The term *Lord* does not occur once in John's three epistles, and the familiar phrase *in the Lord* is only found in Paul's epistles, save for one exception, "Blessed are the dead which die *in the Lord*" (Revelation 14:13).

Under our first section, *The Names of God the Father,* we elaborated upon the significance of the ineffable name *Jehovah,* mentioned almost 7,000 times in the Old Testament, and given as LORD, printed in capitals in the KJV, but always consistently given as *Jehovah* in the ASV. Among the Jews there were said to be seven names for God which were so sacred that they required special care, and a scribe, when writing them, was not to stop after once beginning the name until completion. If an error was made when writing one of these names, it was not to be erased. The seven names were –

Elohim – the One worshipped and adored.

El – the strong or powerful One.

Jehovah – the proper name expressing the Person of God.

Adonai – signifying *Lord.*

Ehyeh-Asher-Ehyeh – meaning *I AM THAT I AM.*

Shaddai – the Almighty or All-Sufficient One.

Zeba'ot – the armies or hosts of men.

The God to whom the Old Testament bears witness is called LORD because throughout the canon He is shown to be the sole Exerciser of power over the unwise and all mankind, as the Creator of the world and Disposer of life and death. This all-embracing title, then, conveys a summary of the faith of Old Testament saints, and, as we shall see, is likewise the climax of faith in New Testament saints. Various words, however are translated as LORD, *Lord,* and lord, both in Hebrew and Greek Scriptures, and convey shades of thought interesting to close readers. One of the most erudite studies of all phases of

Lordship is that entitled *LORD*, by Foerster and Quell.

The high title LORD, however, is only applied to Him who is known as *Jehovah*, the Self-Existing One; but *Lord*, always given in ordinary letters, and not in small capitals as LORD, is likewise applied to Jehovah, particularly in the Psalms. See Psalm 110:1 where both forms are found. Before coming to the identification of the *Lord Jesus* with the Old Testament *Jehovah* or LORD, it may help us to try to discover the meaning, uses, and significance of such a term.

In the Septuagint Version of the Old Testament, the Greek word used for the Hebrew *Jehovah*, as well as the frequent name God, is given as *Adhon*, meaning "Lord." In Syria and Egypt, *Jehovah*, and similar names of God, came to be rendered as *Kurios* in Greek, the basic meaning of which is that of "a lord who commands willing service." This predominating term used in the New Testament, then, owes much to its oriental background. The German word for "Lord" – *herr* – implies "the most common expression of a situation confined to the personal sphere of human life, and indeed of a situation which constitutes an important part of personality, the circumstances that there is such a thing as the exercise of personal power over men and things."

Foerster and Quell elaborate on the ways ancient writers and orators understood the full import of *Kurios*. It denotes "with full powers concerning"; "a person with rights to dispose of slaves"; "lord of subject people." In the treaty between Miletus and Heraclea, the legal proprietors of runaway slaves are called *kurivi*. In general the rabbis use for *Lord*, "rabba," "rabbona," "mare," the latter meaning *Lord* in the most varied used of the term – "master of a slave," "owner of property," "lord of the soul

or of passions," as "a mode of address," "a courteous address from inferiors – servants and subjects," also between equals, corresponding to *Adhon* in the Old Testament.

Coming to the New Testament, *Kurios*, properly an adjective signifying power or authority, is also used as a noun, and is variously translated, *lord, master, owner, sir*. The forceful Greek word, *despotes*, from which is derived our English term "despot," means *master* – one who possesses supreme authority. Further discussion of this particular word will be found under *Master*. At this point we are concentrating upon the uses of *Kurios*, a title of wide significance found in each book of the New Testament with the exception of Titus, and John's three epistles. Its manifold meanings and aspects are:

1. The lord and owner of a vineyard (Mark 12:9; Acts 16:16), or one who has the disposal of anything (Matthew 12:8).

2. The master of free steward, or unfree slaves – one to whom service is due on any ground (Matthew 6:24; Luke 16:3, 5; Ephesians 6:5, 9).

3. The king or emperor, or any person who controls and has to give his word whether over the harvest or the Sabbath (Matthew 9:38; Mark 2:28; Acts 25:26; Revelation 17:14).

4. The oriental courtesy addressed either to a friend or stranger (John 12:21; 20:15). Elizabeth called Mary, "the mother of my Lord" (Luke 1:43). *Kurios* is the title of respect addressed to a father (Matthew 21:30); a husband (1 Peter 3:6); a ruler (Matthew 27:63); an angel (Acts 10:4; Revelation 7:14). It was the common form of address in the approach to

Christ by the people (Matthew 8:2), and by His disciples (Matthew 8:25; John 6:68).

5. The most common Greek word for Lord – *Kurios* – represents Old Testament names of God of *Jehovah, Adon, Adonay, Elohim* (Matthew 1:22; 4:7; 22:44; 1 Peter 1:25). Quotations from the Old Testament in which *Jehovah* occurs are rendered by Kurios – *Lord!* Much of what is said of the *Lord* in the Old Testament was carried over in Jesus, and with it the term itself.

6. Christ Himself assumed the title thereby giving it its highest significance (Matthew 7:21, 22; Luke 8:39). It is applied to Him equally with the Father and the Holy Spirit showing, thereby, that the Messianic hopes conveyed by the sacred name *Jehovah* were for the New Testament writers fulfilled in Jesus, and that in Him the long-hoped-for appearance of Jehovah was realized.

7. The Resurrection and Ascension of Christ brought a richer and deeper meaning of His Lordship to the minds of the disciples. The whole of the New Testament uses *Kurios* of Jesus as the resurrected One. Paul expressly sets the confession of the Lordship of Jesus side by side with his heart's faith that God had raised Him from the dead (Romans 10:9). Most decisive was the Resurrection in the exalted conception of the disciples in Jesus as their *Lord*. Now He, as the exalted One, has all power and authority (1 Corinthians 4:19; 14:37; 16:7). As the risen and ascended *Lord*, He now exercises God's sovereignty over the world in order to lay it, and Himself, at the Father's feet, after the overcoming of all evil, opposing forces (1 Corinthians 15:28).

Kurios, then, used absolutely, expresses the comprehensive Lordship of Jesus, testifying that "the Father has given all judgment to His Son (Matthew 28:18; John 5:22). Any lower significance of *Kurios* was cancelled out for them. True, He had been their Lord and Master while He was with them in the flesh, but knowing that He was now alive forevermore, and at the right hand of God, where He was made *Lord* (Acts 2:36), and was now, *"Lord of all"* (Acts 10:36), their relationship to Him transcended all human analogies of *Kurios*, and was vitally renewed and sealed by His resurrection from the dead. To quote the comment of W. E. Vine at this point –

> "Christ's purpose did not become clear to the disciples until after His resurrection, and the revelation of His Deity consequent thereon. Thomas, when he realised the significance of the presence of a mortal wound in the body of a living man, immediately joined it with the absolute title of Deity, saying, *My Lord and my God* (John 20:28). Thereafter, except in Acts 10:4, and Revelation 7:14, there is no record that *Kurios* was ever again used by believers in addressing any save God and the Lord Jesus (Acts 2:47 with 4:29, 30). . . . The title *Lord* as given to the Saviour, in its full significance rests upon the resurrection (Acts 2:36; Romans 10:9; 14:8), and is realised only in the Holy Spirit (1 Corinthians 12:3, 11)."

8. An aspect that must be stressed is the fact that all Christ was in Himself enhanced *all* designations

ascribed to Him. Some men have titles of honor, but are not very honorable in life and living. But the names associated with Christ grow in richness of content as the New Testament unfolds. Might it not also be said that the majesty of the Master gives honor to the servant?

In the Acts "the reverential *the Lord,* becomes the ruling designation of Jesus, and the simple Jesus takes a subordinate place, both as the narrative designation and in the reports of the remarks of our Lord's followers incorporated in the narrative." Titles of honor such as *Lord* and *Lord Jesus* were used with the profoundest reverence, and were meant to be the vehicle of the highest possible ascription. He was the *God* to whom prayer could be addressed and the One who knew the hearts of all men (Acts 1:24). He was the *God* who could forgive sin, and receive His dying saints (7:59, 60). He is the Lord God (John 10:30; 20:28).

In Paul's writings "the designation of our Lord by the simple *Jesus* falls strikingly into the background," says Dr. Warfield, "while the designation of Him as Lord comes strikingly forward. The simple *Jesus* occurs in all his epistles only some 17 times, while the simple Lord, occurs some 144 or 146 times, to which may be added 95 to 97 more instances of the use of Lord in conjunction with the proper name."

Finding in Christ the *Jehovah* of the Old Testament, Paul's constant application of *Lord* to Jesus was not merely a formal mark of respect, but the definite ascription to Him of universal absolute dominion not only over men, but over the whole universe of created beings (Philippians 2:11; Romans 10:12). As Dr. Warfield states it, "On the pages of Paul's Bible — the Greek version of the Hebrew Scriptures — Lord stood side by side with *God,* as the most personal and intimate name of Deity: and then he took it and applied it to Jesus."

For appellations like *Lord Christ, Lord Jesus, The Lord's Christ, The Lord Jesus Christ, Christ the Lord,* see under titles *CHRIST* and *JESUS.* There is, however, the close association of His Lordship with what are called "The Means of Grace." The phrases the disciples used of such could not have been framed unless Jesus had been to His followers *The Lord* by way of eminence.

* * *

Lord's Word

While the usual designation of Scripture is "the Word of God" which is also one of the titles of Christ (Revelation 19:13), Paul has the phrase, *the word of the Lord* (1 Thessalonians 4:15). Arthur Way translates it, "A revelation from God." See Galatians 1:11, 12. But what the apostle probably had in mind was the actual word or promise of the Lord when He told His disciples that He would come again (John 14:1-3). Yet is not the whole Bible the revelation of Him who came as Christ the Lord? This characteristic designation of the Old Testament (Jeremiah 29:20), "Hear ye the word of the Lord," implies divine authorship and authority.

* * *

Lord's Day (Revelation 1:10).

Known as "Sunday," so named by heathen sun-worshippers, it was described by the apostles as "The Lord's Day," seeing it was the very day on which, by His resurrection, He was made both *Lord* and *Chirst.* It is a beautiful expression and a scriptural title for it is the day above all others when He claims our time and services, and seeks to fill our thoughts with Himself. There is, of course, a similar title that must not be confused with John's *Lord's*

Day, namely, "the Day of the Lord," a rightful title with a future connotation (Isaiah 2:11, 12).

* * *

Lord's Supper (1 Corinthians 11:20).

The early Christians celebrated the Lord's Supper on the Lord's Day, or "the first day of the week" (Acts 2:42; 20:7; 1 Corinthians 16:2). This feast is the memorial of His death, as the Lord's Day is of His Resurrection. Thus the sufferings and the glory are beautifully linked together on the one day. The *Lord's Supper* tells of darkness, sorrow, suffering, and death when He was crucified as "the Lord of Glory." *The Lord's Day* is full of light, power, glory, joy, triumph, and life. What a privilege is ours to have this *Supper* and this *Day,* which are both the Lord's — the one taking us by the hand back to Calvary, the other leading us on to a bright and glorious future when He will return for the resurrection of His own.

* * *

Lord's Money (Matthew 25:18).

The servant in our Lord's parable of the lord travelling into a far country, who failed in using the talent, buried it for protection. How pathetic is the fear some men have of losing what they will not use. Taking Christ's description of the talent the servant hid, "his lord's money," can we not put it as His *Lord's Money,* for after all, all money is His. "The silver is mine and the gold is mine, saith *Jehovah* of hosts" (Haggai 2:8 asv)? "What hast thou, that thou didst not receive?" Are we hiding the Lord's money or using it to the full for the extension of His cause in a world of need? If He is our *Lord,* then He has a claim upon all we have – and are!

* * *

Lord's House (Haggai 1:2; Matthew 21:13).

It is apt to be forgotten that the Greek word for *church* is related to *Kurios* – *Kryriakon,* meaning "the Lord's House." The Scotch term for *Church* is *Kirk,* which is likewise derived from *Kurios,* the Greek for *Lord.* Thus, the three titles form a trinity in unity, The Lord's Supper on the Lord's Day in the Lord's House. Paul has some very pertinent and practical counsel to offer those who hold responsible positions in the Lord's House. He instructs them on behavior and belief, knowing that belief greatly influences behavior (1 Timothy 3:14-16). Read chapters 3, 4, 5, 6. *See* 1 Peter 4:11. (See further under *Master of House.*)

We now come to an examination of some very valuable Lordship combinations, set forth as titles of Jesus, who had no hesitation in claiming for Himself the lofty dignity of Lord, because of His preexistence and supernatural origin. *Born* Lord, implies His position in the eternal Godhead, and while on earth, if any disputed His right to use what He required, His answer was, "the Lord hath need of him" (Mark 11:3). As "Lord of all" He could command all for His service.

* * *

Lord From Heaven (1 Corinthians 15:47).

This oft-repeated phrase proves heaven to be no nebulous state but an eternal place, our Lord had dwelt in from the dateless past. It was His Father's home (Matthew 6:9; John 14:1, 2). Then, the phrase is used in a two-fold way. *First,* in connection with His Incarnation, when He came from above, and "dwelt among us" (John 1:14). He, Himself, declared that "He came down from heaven" and that "coming from above, He was above all" (John 3:13, 31). As "the Bread of God" Jesus affirmed that He came down from heaven to die for the world (John 6:33). Paul spoke of Jesus as "the second man, the Lord from heaven" (1 Corinthians 15:47). The Lord *before* heaven (Psalm 110:1), He became the Lord *from* heaven. What else can we do to love and magnify Him for His willing condescension and voluntary humiliation and sacrifice that brought Him down from the ivory palaces to a world of sin and woe. From heaven He carried with Him the aroma of His eternal abode, and when near Him, people felt themselves near heaven. He ever lived in the atmosphere of heaven (John 3:13).

After His resurrection from the grave, His disciples, who were loath to see Him go, witnessed His return to heaven, and stood "gazing up into heaven" (Acts 1:8-11). What a glorious welcome He must have received as He came back as the mighty Victor over sin, death, and Satan! But He was different from what He was when He came down from heaven. As a member of the Godhead, He was of the same essence as God, who was a *Spirit* (John 4:24), and of the Holy *Spirit,* and like them had no corporeal or material body. See Luke 24:39. When the Lord came from heaven, and became the Babe of Bethlehem, a radical change took place in the composition of the Trinity.

At His Incarnation Jesus took upon Him the likeness of our flesh, and became the *Man* Christ Jesus, and when He came to ascend on high, like Enoch and Elijah before Him, He took His body with Him. Thus, from His birth, when He became the Son of Man, the Trinity has had as its "Second Person," the *God-Man.* This was the vision both Stephen and John had of Him (Acts 7:56-60; Revelation 1:12-18). An object of adoration in heaven, then, as some of humanity's dust, glorified, seated on the right hand of the majesty on high,

as the Representative of a redeemed race (Hebrews 9:24).

There is, however, a *second* aspect of this heavenly Lord we must consider. Not only had He lived in heaven from a past eternity, and in the fulness of time left heaven for earth, and then returned to heaven from earth. Scripture abounds with the truth that He is to descend from heaven the second time to gather all those with whom He has a covenant by His sacrifice unto Himself, and then to usher in His earth rule. When about to leave the earth, Jesus assured His disciples, "I will come again, and receive you unto myself" (John 14:1-3), and He prayed that His own might share heaven with Him (John 17:24). Paul affirms that Jesus is to "descend from heaven with a shout" and that we are to wait for Him as God's "Son from heaven" (1 Thessalonians 1:10; 4:16; 2 Thessalonians 1:7; Hebrews 9:28). And the glorious prospect is that when He does appear the second time, seeing Him as the Man of Glory we shall be transformed into His likeness as He changes our body into one like unto His own (Philippians 3:20, 21; 1 John 3:1-3).

> "Upheld by hope," that wondrous hope,
> That I shall see His face,
> And to His likeness be conformed
> When I have run the race.

  ❋ ❋ ❋

Lord of Glory (1 Corinthians 2:8; James 2:1).

In a way, this title is akin to the one we have just considered for *glory* is synonymous with *heaven.* Describing the return of Jesus to heaven at His ascension, Paul says, "He was received up into glory" (1 Timothy 3:16). As the Lamb, "He is all the glory in Emmanuel's land." Twice over Jesus is designated *Lord of Glory,* and this title, as all others, is illuminated when interpreted in the light of its context.

The companion titles *Father of Glory* and *Lord of Glory* are pregnant with spiritual meaning. Take the former, which reads in the original, "the Father of *the* glory," "the Father Glory-Clad" as Way puts it. The article suggests that *the* glory is preeminently the Father's, "the Father to whom *the* glory belongs," and He waits to make us the recipients of "the riches of the glory of his inheritance in the saints" (Ephesians 1:7, 18). Stephen tells us that as "The God of Glory" He appeared unto Moses (Acts 7:2). See Psalm 29:3.

As for our inheritance of "the riches of the glory," Ellicott comments that Paul gives us in these verses "a noble accumulation of genitives, setting for the inheritance on the side of its glory, and the glory on the side of its riches." Glory is the essential characteristic of salvation, and this glory is richly abounding.

Lord of Glory, the majestic title of Christ, embodies the thought that He Himself possessed glory as His native right. As used by Paul, the title implies that he had the most exalted conception of Christ as *Lord*. T. C. Edwards on 1 Corinthians 2:8 says, "The Lord to whom glory belongs as His native right. . . . Glory is the peculiar attribute of Jehovah among all the gods (Psalm 29:1). The expression . . . implies that Jesus was Lord of Glory, that is Jehovah and that the Lord of Glory died" (Acts 3:15). Paul also speaks of "the Lord's death" (1 Corinthians 11:26). The hymnist invites us to "survey the Cross, on which the Prince of Glory died." As we saw in another connection our Lord's Deity gave efficacy to His death for sinners. He is called *The Lord of Glory*, then, because glory belongs to Him as His characterizing quality and because He came as "the

effulgence of the glory of God" (Hebrews 1:3).

Paul describes how the princes of this world "crucified the Lord of glory" who was "ordained before the world unto our glory" (1 Corinthians 2:7, 8; Matthew 25:34). The glory was ever His, and He came to bestow it upon us, and to bring to us the perfection of our nature. Arthur Way translates it, "to lift us into the glory of His presence." It was only through His sacrifice, however, that He achieved this purpose (Revelation 11:8). Jesus is the Lord whose attribute is glory (Psalm 29:1; Acts 7:2; Ephesians 1:17).

The quotation from James has a different significance. Here, the words, *the Lord* are in italics, meaning they are not in the original, and so the passage should read, "our Lord Jesus Christ, the glory," or, "the Glorious One" (2:1), and is akin to the phrase, "the brightness of His glory" (Hebrews 1:3). He is the true *Shekinah*. But rich in glory, for our sakes He became poor, and the application James makes is instructive, namely, that in the presence of *Christ the Glory* earthly distinctions and glory should disappear (2:1-9). Incidentally, this is one of the rare passages in which James, the natural brother of our Lord, breaks through his habitual reserve in speaking of his brother, who had become his Master, and shows us something of his reverence and devotion. To him, Jesus was *The Glorious One*.

※　※　※

Lord of Hosts (Isaiah 44:6).

Five times Jehovah, as the Lord of Hosts, is described as *The King of Glory*, strong and mighty in battle (Psalm 24), all of which can be applied to Him described by the apostles as "Lord of [or over] all" (Acts 10:36; Romans 10:12). See under first section

– *Jehovah-Tsebaioth* and under this second chapter – *Almighty.*

❁   ❁   ❁

Lord of the Sabbath (Matthew 12:8; Mark 2:28).

Mark's quotation is somewhat fuller than Matthew's, "the Son of Man is Lord even of the Sabbath day." He is Lord of all, even of the Sabbath *too*, is Mark's thought. As the Son of Man, He brought the highest blessings to men, and arranges everything for their blessedness, even the Sabbath which He meant for their enrichment and not enslavement (Matthew 12:4-7). As "the Son of Man," He is man's Saviour and Guardian, and therefore urges man to keep the Sabbath sacred, since it was meant for his highest spiritual and physical welfare. The lesson to be learned from the teaching on the Lord's Day by the Lord Himself is – "Accept the day as a gift of love, not as a bond of slavery. Profane it not by any *work*, the motive of which is greed, but work on it like a slave, if mercy prompts you." It is still true that –

> A Sabbath well kept
> Brings a week of content,
> And health for the toils of the
>   morrow;
> But a Sabbath profaned,
> Whatsoe'er may be gained,
> Is a certain forerunner of sorrow.

❁   ❁   ❁

Lord of the Dead and Living (Romans 14:9; Revelation 1:5).

In this wonderful designation Paul which gives Christ, the context proves that he had the Christian dead and Christian living in mind. "If we die, for the Lord we die. If we live, for the Lord we live. Whether, then, we die or live, we belong to the Lord." It was the object Christ had before Him when He died, and rose again (Romans 14:7, 8). Dead, but now alive forevermore, the keys of life and death are rightly His. Bishop Handley Moule puts it, "He who to save them in both worlds, was their Master in both." The grand purpose of Christ's death and resurrection was to *acquire* absolute lordship over His redeemed, both in their living and in their dying, as His of right. How blessed we are if, resting in the assurance of faith, we know that whether we live or die we are the Lord's.

❁   ❁   ❁

Lord and Saviour (Luke 2:11; 2 Peter 1:11; 2:20; 3:18).

Paul in Titus has a kindred title to the repeated *Lord and Saviour.* He urges us to "adorn the doctrine of God our Saviour" (2:10), or "Our Saviour-God." This agrees with Peter's designation, "God and our Saviour, Jesus Christ" (2 Peter 1:1). Dr. Warfield's comment on the repeated use of *Saviour* and *our Lord* is that, "the clear note of Deity is struck in these designations. *Saviour* itself is a divine appellation transferred to Christ, to whom it is applied 15 times by Peter out of the 23 in which it occurs in the New Testament. In 2 Peter it occurs 5 times, always of Christ, and never alone, but always coupled under a single article with another designation, and so forming a solemn formula."

Our Lord became the embodiment of Old Testament promises and prophecies of "a saviour and a mighty one" (Isaiah 19:20). As the result of Calvary, "beside Him there is no Saviour" (Hosea 13:4; Isaiah 43:11). He became the "Holy One of Israel, thy Saviour" (Isaiah 43:3). These foregleams became manifest in Him who is "our Lord and Saviour Jesus Christ," and in "our God and Saviour Jesus Christ," designations perfectly similar and which must stand and fall together. The Deity of our Lord is openly asserted in both phrases, and is implied in the conjunction of *God* and

Jesus our Lord as co-objects of saving knowledge (2 Peter 1:2, 8; 2:20; 3:18), and in the ascription to "our Lord and Saviour Jesus Christ" of an eternal kingdom (2 Peter 1:11). *See* Jude 4. (*See* further under *Captain of Our Salvation.*)

* * *

Lord Our Righteousness (Romans 5:18-21; 1 Corinthians 1:30).

Under the title *Jehovah-Tsidkeenu* (which see) we dealt with the doctrine of divine righteousness. All that we would state at this point is the way Paul expounds Christ our Righteousness as an all-sufficient answer to the claim of law and justice upon us, and to our deep need. How Martin Luther revelled in Paul's teaching on righteousness by faith! One of the mighty Reformer's utterances is fitting as we think of "Christ who was made unto us – Righteousness"

> "Your menaces and terrors, domine Satan, trouble me not; for there is One whose name is called *The Lord our Righteousness* on whom I believe. He it is who hath abrogated the law, condemned sin, abolished death, destroyed hell, and is a satan to thee, O Satan."

Old John Trapp thinks this great sentence of Luther's is of so much worth that rather than be without it one should "fetch it on his knees from Rome to Jerusalem" – and we agree!

> No works of merit now I plead,
> But Jesus take for all my need;
> No righteousness in me is found,
> Except upon redemption ground.

No one studying all the aspects of Christ's *Lordship* can escape being overwhelmed by His greatness and majesty as Lord over all, and as Lord of lords, and find himself forced to ask his own heart the question, "Is this won-derful Lord, Lord of my life?" After all, is it not experience that proves the power and reality of truth?

> If Christ is not Lord of *all*,
> He is not Lord at all.

Jesus had strong condemnation for those who called Him, *Lord! Lord!* but who yet failed to obey His word (Luke 6:46). In fact, He explicitly declared that –

> "Not every one that saith unto me, Lord, Lord, shall enter into the kingdom of heaven; but he that doeth the will of my Father which is in heaven" (Matthew 7:21).

If we acknowledge His authority as *Lord*, then ours is the obligation to be subject to His control, and to do as He bids us. We say well if we call Him Lord, but such recognition means following His example as His professed servants (John 13:13-20). When Jesus revealed His purpose to suffer, die, and rise again, Peter took Him aside and remonstrated with Him over such a sacrificial decision, "Be it far from thee, Lord: this shall not be unto thee" (Matthew 16:22) – as if as *Lord*, He did not know better than Peter what to do! As those professing His Lordship, we sin against Him when we question the wisdom of His acts. "Ours is not to question why." While we may not fully understand the meaning and ministry of what He asks of us, ours must be –

> ... a joyous *Yes*,
> To every dear command of Thine.

M

Man (John 19:5; Romans 5:15; 1 Corinthians 15:47).

When Pilate exclaimed, "Behold the man!" the emphasis was on the word *behold* by which he made the bloodied appearance of Jesus the ground of an appeal for pity. Perhaps Pilate knew that the Jews had always been influenced by what they could see (Zechariah 12:10; John 1:51); but in this case prejudice blinded their eyes. In effect, Pilate said, "Look at this poor sufferer, and consider whether His condition is not such as might lead you to have compassion on Him!" Alas! however, the terrible, battered sight of Jesus only led those Jews to clamor the more for His blood. That which should have melted their hearts only hardened them, so they cried, "Crucify him!" (19:6). Turning from the direct interpretation of Pilate's forlorn appeal, "Behold the man!" in this particular section what we want to do is to behold Him as the *Man,* or to consider His evident humanity, as One born of a woman. Mary could say in a truer and fuller sense than the first woman, Eve – "I have gotten a *man* even *Jehovah*" (Genesis 4:1 margin).

Often throughout Scripture our Lord's Deity and humanity are emphasized in combined titles. The simple designation Man united with the personal names He bore all declare the fact of His manhood. He was –

> "The *man* Jesus Christ" (Romans 5:15).
> "The *man* Christ Jesus" (1 Timothy 2:5).
> "Born of a woman" – "God's own Son" (Acts 13:33; Romans 18:31, 32; Galatians 4:4) – and in some high sense *God* Himself (Acts 20:28).
> "Being a man makest thyself God" John 10:33).

Peter, in his Pentecostal sermon, constrained the Jewish rulers to give heed to the words of "Jesus of Nazareth, a *man* approved of God" (Acts 2:22). Proofs of our Lord's humanity are manifold:

1. He had a man's career because first of all He was born of a human mother (Luke 2:5, 7). As the *Man-Child* (Revelation 12:5, 13), He fulfilled the Messianic prophecies (Genesis 3:15; Isaiah 66:7).

2. He possessed, as a man, a material body and rational soul. In His physical make-up He was the same as any other man (Matthew 26:38; Luke 24:39).

3. He was subject to the laws of human development –

> He grew like every other child, in wisdom and stature, and naturally as any child (Luke 2:40).
> He grew by direct and definite effort (Luke 2:52).
> He was tempted and learned obedience (Luke 2:51; Hebrews 2:10).

4. He had the bodily and spiritual faculties and emotions of a man. We read of Him as being hungry, thirsty, weary, angry, sorrowful, compassionate, and as One "standing in the need of prayer."

5. He could hold fellowship with men, and communion with God and man. "Never man spake like this man" (John 7:46), either to man or God.

6. He suffered and died – sweated blood, and gave up His spirit as "the Man of Sorrows" (Luke 22:44; John 19:30, 34; Isaiah 53).

7. He also impressed others as being a man – they counted Him an uncommon man, but still a manly man with a real human touch (John 9:16, 24).

8. He called Himself, "A man that hath told you the truth" (John 8:40), and *the* Son of Man, but never as a son of a man, for He had no human father (Matthew 8:20; 1 Timothy 2:5).

9. He was the world's only Per-

fect Man. Free from hereditary depravity, or actual sin (John 8:46; 18:29; 2 Corinthians 5:21; Hebrews 4:15), He presented an ideal or pattern for all men in relation both to God and man to follow (1 Peter 1:21).

10. He was presented in some point of likeness or contrast with other men, namely with the world's first man Adam (1 Corinthians 15:21, 45-49), and with Solomon and others, declaring Himself to be greater than they.

11. He became – and is – the *God-Man.* The great mystery our finite minds cannot comprehend is the fact that Jesus was one Person, having a dual nature, namely, divine and human, but single consciousness. These two natures were joined yet divided, distinct yet united. In Him, God became man, or manifest in flesh (1 Timothy 3:16), and His career among men reveals two things no reader of the Gospel can miss –

First, His Deity never effaced His humanity;

Second, His humanity did not degrade or nullify the Deity, but was suppressed by a self-chosen state of manifest humiliation. The perfect harmony between His two natures is seen in some of His miracles, and likewise in His dealings with those who crossed His pathway.

As the Man, He was weary and thirsty and asked for a drink from the woman at the well. But as God, He revealed His omniscience when He unveiled the woman's dark past and yet her aspirations, so much so that she caught a glimpse of His Messiahship –

"Come, see a man which told all things that ever I did . . . this is indeed the Christ, the Saviour of the world" (John 4:29, 42).

As the Man, He was fatigued through His arduous labors, and needed necessary sleep, and found a bed in the boat belonging to His disciples. But a storm arose which had no effect on the sleeping Christ, and the disciples fearing a disaster, awake their honorable passenger with the cry, "Master, carest thou not that we perish?" There are two phrases in this incident we can combine – "The storm arose" and "He arose." With the rising of the storm, there was the rising of the Saviour, who is ever a *present* help in time of trouble (Psalm 46:1). So great was the effect of the sudden change from turbulence to tranquillity that the relieved disciples said –

> "What *manner* of *man* is this, that even the wind and the sea obey him?" (Mark 4:35-41). It had to obey Him, for He made it (Psalm 95:5; Proverbs 8:29).

These, and other instances, clearly prove that Jesus appeared as God's perfect Man, and as Man's perfect God, and that He proved Himself to be, "A man approved of God among you by miracles and wonders and signs, which God did by him in the midst of you" (Acts 2:22-24). As the Man, He knows all about our human needs, and as God, He can meet every one of them.

12. His union of a dual nature is indissoluble, because it is eternal. When Christ left earth for heaven at His Ascension, He did not shed

His humanity, and revert to the totally spiritual nature He had had from the dateless past. As already indicated, He is glorified humanity in Heaven, and well-qualified to function as Intercessor between God and man, seeing He understands both. "There is one God, one mediator between God and men, himself *man,* Christ Jesus" (1 Timothy 2:5 ASV).

* * *

Master (Matthew 23:8, 10; John 13:13).

The most common title used by others of Jesus was *Lord,* or *Master.* Altogether, there are eight distinct Greek words associated with the designation of *Master.* There is *Kurios,* meaning "Lord," which is used of Jesus, and of others, and represents one who exercises power (Luke 19:33, 34). This particular Greek word is often translated *Master,* a title of address to Christ. (See further under title *Lord.*)

Another original word implies *teacher,* which occurs 58 times, and is twice given as *rabbi,* and transliterated as *rabboni.* Yet another term denotes a commander, chief, overmaster, and occurs only in Luke. See Luke 5:8; 8:24, 25, 45; 9:33, 49; 17:13. A further word means a *guide* or *leader* from a root implying to go before, or guide, and used by Jesus of Himself three times (Matthew 23:8, 10). Then there is another word which in English means pilot, steersman of a ship, or governor (Acts 27:11; 1 Corinthians 12:28; Revelation 18:17).

But the Greek word concerning us under the title above is *Despotes,* and represents one who has absolute ownership and uncontrolled power. When used of God this term implies unlimited and despotic authority and power in heaven and on earth, and is derived from two words which mean "to

bind the foot." Demosthenes used *Despotes* 16 times to indicate a master of bound slaves. Our English word *despot* is from this Greek term, which now is usually used of a tyrant. This particular word occurs 10 times in the New Testament, and is rendered 5 times as Lord, and 5 times as *Master,* and once of the Divine Master (2 Timothy 2:21). Four times it is used of human masters.

Twice over in His portrait of a Pharisee Jesus used the phrase, "One is your Master, even Christ." The Scribes and Pharisees who loved to sit in Moses' seat, loved to be greeted as *Rabbi, Rabbi,* a grand title their ears liked to have addressed to them. But Jesus said that He only had the right to this form of address, which means "My Master," and thus declared "One is your Master [authoritative teacher], even Christ and all ye are brethren" (Matthew 23:7, 8). Then He went on to say, "Neither be ye called masters: for one is your Master, even Christ" (Matthew 23:10). The repetition in 23:8, 10 implies divine emphasis (see Luke 8:24). Thus He forbade His disciples to call themselves by titles which were His alone. A quotation from Dalman by Vine says –

"The primitive community never ventured to call Jesus 'Our Teacher' after He had been exalted to the Throne of God. The title *Rabbi,* expressing the relation of the disciples to the teacher, vanished from use; and there remained only the designation *Maran,* the servant's appropriate acknowledgement of his Lord."

Jesus spoke of Himself as *Master* eight times – three times in Matthew (10:24, 25; 26:18); once in Mark (14:14); three times in Luke (6:40; 22:11); once in John (13:14).

He was spoken of as *Master* by others,

ten times – twice in Matthew (9:11; 17: 24); once in Mark (5:35); five times in Luke (5:5; 8:24; 9:33, 49; 17:13); twice in John (11:28; 13:13).

The constant use of this title by the disciples reveals their close relation to the Master, and is an acknowledgement of Him as their Superior Officer – Chief, Commander, Leader. Jude, who called himself the *slave* of Jesus Christ (verse 1), recognized in Him his *Despotes* when he said of Him, "our only Master [Despotes] and Lord, Jesus Christ" (verse 4 ASV). He was proud to be the slave of such a heavenly Despot. Dr. Warfield remarks –

> "We cannot feel surprised that one who pointedly calls himself in the first verse of his Epistle *slave* of Jesus Christ, should apply the correlation of that term, 'Despotic Master and Lord,' to Jesus Christ, three verses later. No doubt 'no Jew could use' such a phrase 'without thinking of the one Master in Heaven': but that is only evidence that this Jew thought of his *Lord* and whose slave he recognized himself as being, as, in this eminent verse, His *Master in Heaven.*" (*See* 2 Peter 2:1).

In keeping with his lowly estimation of himself, Jude multiplies reverential titles of his divine owner – *Jesus Christ* (verse 1); *our Lord Jesus Christ* (17, 21); *Jesus Christ our Lord* (25 ASV); *the only Lord God, and our Lord Jesus Christ* (4). In the industrial realm good relations greatly depend upon the quality of the master. In Christ, we have the greatest Master in that He is perfect in His treatment of His servants – so kind, understanding, considerate, sympathetic, and liberal. Judas greeted Jesus with a heartless, "Hail, master" (Matthew 26: 49). What kind of a servant was he who could see his Master sold for the price

of a common slave? But how different was His treatment of such a professed, treacherous servant! Grace was His to greet His betrayer as *friend* (verse 50).

Do we claim Him as our Master, our Despotes? If so, does He have absolute control over all we are and have? Are we His love-slaves? Paul could call himself the *bond-slave* of the Master he dearly loved and so sacrificially served. Slaves have no claim to anything they possess – their bodies, talents, time, and labor are all to be used according to the dictates of an absolute owner. Few of us who acknowledge Jesus as our Saviour and Master are willing to accept the spiritual slavery true discipleship involves. Under the ancient Mosaic Law in the Year of Jubilee, "the year of liberty" (Ezekiel 46:17), all who were slaves, male or female, in Jewish service were offered their freedom, but if a slave so loved his master that he refused to leave his employment, then the master would take an awl and pierce the ear of the slave to the door, the branded ear becoming the mark of willing perpetual servitude – "the slave shall be thy servant for ever" (Deuteronomy 15:16, 17). Bishop Handley Moule caught the spiritual significance of this unique relationship between master and slave in his poem, *My glorious Victor* –

My Master, lead me to Thy door;
Pierce this now willing ear once more:
Thy bonds are freedom; let me stay
With Thee, to toil, endure, obey.

Yes, ear and hand, and thought and will,
Use all in Thy dear slav'ry still.
Self's weary liberties I cast
Beneath Thy feet; there keep them fast.

Before leaving this appealing title of Master, attention can be drawn to the figurative expression, *Master of the House*, found in the gospels. This extension of Despotes, *Oikodespotes* occurs 12 times, and is used in the parables by the Lord of Himself seven times, and of others thrice. It is rendered 4 times as *Householder;* 5 times as *Goodman of the House;* 3 times as *Master* (Matthew 10:25; Luke 13:25; 14:21). Twice the word is used of others than Christ (Mark 14:14; Luke 22:11). Is such a description of Christ not suggestive of a comforting truth? One has often seen the printed motto in Christian homes –

CHRIST IS THE MASTER OF THIS HOUSE,
THE WELCOME GUEST AT EVERY MEAL,
THE SILENT LISTENER OF EVERY CONVERSATION,
THE LOVING FRIEND IN ALL TRIALS.

How blest is any house bidding welcome to such a Guest and Friend!

If He is the Master or Lord of our house or home, whether it be a castle or cottage, then the thought of His oversight and control of it should calm and steady the hearts of those living beneath its roof. We should not anxiously run hither and thither like a dog without a master, but live and act rather like those that are highly trained, steadily following our heavenly Master, watching His eye, listening to His voice for all our actions.

Is He the Master of your house? Then because He has promised to meet your every need, trust and obey Him. What a relief it is in a practical Christian life to cultivate the habit of instinctively turning to the Master when needs and difficulties arise.

O Master let me walk with Thee,
In lowly paths of service free.
Tell me Thy secret – help me bear
The strain of toil, the stress of care.

* * *

Mediator (Galatians 3:20; 1 Timothy 2:5; Hebrews 12:24).

That the mediatorial ministry of Jesus is a vitally important scriptural truth for

saints – and sinners – to fully comprehend is evident from His own emphatic declaration, "I am *the* Way . . . no man cometh unto the Father, *but by me* (John 14:6). Man cannot successfully approach God in ways of his own choice. Jesus came as the culmination of the revelation of God, and is our only means of access to God. It is only through Him, by the Spirit, that we come to the Father (Ephesians 2:18).

The dictionary informs us that a mediator is "one who interposes between parties at variance to reconcile them." The Greek term for mediator means, a "go-between" or "middle-man." W. E. Vine in his most serviceable *Dictionary of New Words,* tells us that this word is used in two ways in the New Testament –

"1. As one who mediates between two parties with a view to producing peace, as in 1 Timothy 2:5, though more than mediatorship is in view, for the salvation of men necessitated that the Mediator should Himself possess the nature and attributes of Him towards whom He acts, and should likewise participate in the nature of those for whom He acts – sin apart; only by being possessed of both Deity and humanity could He comprehend the claims of the one and the needs of the other; further, the claims and the needs could be met only by One who, Himself being proved sinless would offer Himself an expiatory sacrifice on behalf of man.

"2. The Mediator is one who acts as a guarantee so as to secure something which otherwise would not be obtained. Thus, Christ is the Surety of 'the better covenant' – 'the new covenant,' guaranteeing its terms for His people (Heb. 8:6; 9:15; 12:24)."

The Old Testament term *daysman* is equivalent in meaning to *mediator*. Daysman signifies one "who gives a day" to judge and decide a controversy between contending parties. When brought together, the judge lays his hands on *both* men, in an effort to reconcile them (Job 9:33). See 1 Kings 3:16-28. Scripture presents Christ as the Ideal Daysman between God and man. As God the Son, He can act for God, and as the Son of Man, He can enter into the interests of the human race. "God was in Christ, reconciling the world unto himself" (2 Corinthians 5:19). How privileged we are to act as ambassadors of the perfect reconciliation which the heavenly Daysman effected by His death and resurrection!

Paul declares that "a mediator is not a mediator of one," by which he means, not of one party (Galatians 3:20). An effectual mediator or reconciler is a person who interposes between two other persons at variance, for the sole purpose of reconciling them. Further, the very title and office of mediator implies that a right relationship, that once existed, has been broken off or disrupted and that the severed friendship stands in need of reconciliation. In solely human relationships when two persons, once friends, part, we usually say, "Well, there are faults on both sides to be put right." But the estrangement between God and man is different, for the faults are all on the one side, namely man's. Hence the precise language of Paul that in Christ, God is found "reconciling the world unto Himself" and "reconciling all things unto Himself" (2 Corinthians 5:18, 19; Colossians 1:20-22). On God's side there is no fault whatever, and therefore no need of Him to be reconciled unto men.

Since the first Adam, man has been at variance with God in the matter of sin, alienating himself thereby from God's love and heavenly government (Isaiah 59:2; Amos 3:2, 3). Yet God never stood aloof with the air of one saying, "I'll let the sinner, who ruptured the harmony between us go his own way. If he wants to make it up between us, then he must make the first move." No, as soon as the first man sinned, God came to offer reconciliation and the manner it could be effected in the promise of "the seed of the woman" (Genesis 3:15).

The message of the Gospel of Reconciliation is that God, loving us even when we were His enemies, provided His only begotten Son, as the One to bridge the gulf separating us because of our iniquities from a thrice holy God. But guilt on our part had to be expiated, and the curse removed, and the broken law magnified, and the enmity destroyed. All of this was accomplished by the Cross at which God held out His holy, righteous hand, and a lost world stretched out its sin-stained hand and clasping the divine hand was reconciled by the blood of His cross (Isaiah 53:10; Ephesians 2:16; 1 Peter 3:18). Now, at peace with God, He makes His covenant sure to us through Jesus the Mediator (2 Corinthians 1:20-22) who is both the Mediator and the Messenger of the New Covenant (Malachi 3:1; Hebrews 12:24).

Mediation, reconciliation, and atonement which are all related to Christ's sacrificial death, are terms related to the barrier between man and God, and to its divine removal. If we take the one word *atone*, and divide it in two, we have AT-ONE, and this is what the mediation of Christ through His death makes possible. Calvary enables the sinner, through his repentance and faith, to be *at-one* with God (Romans 5:11).

Today, those who preach the Word should ceaselessly pray for

Hearts of love, and tongues of fire,
To preach the reconciling Word.

* * *

Messiah (Daniel 9:25, 26; John 1:41; 4:25).

This title, occurring 4 times in Scripture, and implying the Prince who was to come as Leader, means *the Anointed One* (see further under title CHRIST). At first the term *anointed* was applied to anyone anointed with the holy oil. For instance, it was applied to the High Priest (Leviticus 4:3, 5-16), and figuratively to Saul's shield (2 Samuel 1:21). But the designation as used both by Daniel and John especially refers to Christ who, as the Promised Prince, is to restore Israel to more than her pristine prosperity. Israel will yet see her Messiah who was "cut off, but not for himself," and mourn for Him.

* * *

Mighty God (Isaiah 9:6; Titus 2:13).

Among the galaxy of Messianic, prophetic titles of our Lord cited by Isaiah, none is more potent than the third one – *The Mighty God*. Yet liberal-minded theologians have no compunction of conscience as they tear the crown of Deity from the brow of Him who was born "Christ *Jehovah*," and rob this descriptive, correct title of its true significance by affirming that it implies, "a mighty Hero, or Ruler." The absurdity of this contention is seen when in the very next chapter, the same Hebrew expression is used again, and no one would ever dream of saying that it means there, "a mighty, or great Hero" (Isaiah 10:21). Going back we have Moses writing of "a great God, a mighty" (Deuteronomy 10:17), and Nehemiah exalting, "our God, the great,

the mighty, and the terrible God" (9:32). Jeremiah speaks of Him as "the Great, the Mighty God" (32:19). See 10:6.

Isaiah, then, using the singular for *God*, directly applies the very same title to Jehovah as other writers do. Further, that the significance of the title *God* or EL, meaning "the strong, or mighty One," as a title of Jehovah was in the prophet's mind at the time can be gathered from the further name, Emmanu-*el*, meaning "God with us" (Isaiah 7:14). Then again, the titles preceding "The Mighty God" and following it, seem to have the same suggestion of Deity. The natural meaning of the words is that the One the prophet predicted is *Mighty God*, and nothing less; that the One born for our salvation would be mighty with the might of God. All who have proved Him to be the only One, mighty to save and strong to deliver are looking for His glorious appearing as their "Great God and Saviour" (Titus 2:13). He was "The Mighty One of Israel" – "The Mighty One of Jacob" – "The One, Mighty to save" (Isaiah 30:29; 49:26; 63:1).

Scriptures abound which directly show Jesus to be "The Mighty God" Isaiah prophesied would come. As the *Word*, He not only came *from* God, but *was God* (John 1:1), and never thought it robbery to claim equality with God His Father (John 10:30; Philippians 2:6). All the prophets gave witness to Him that He was "God's fellow" whose "goings forth were from of old, from everlasting." Peter had no hesitation in naming Jesus as "God and Saviour" (2 Peter 1:1). As for Jude, one of the natural brothers of Jesus, think of him saying of his illustrious Brother, "Our only Lord God, even our Lord Jesus Christ" (verse 4). The divine might of our Emmanuel can be seen in that –

1. *He Created All Things.*

Honoring God as Creator, we must likewise honor the Son, for Father, Son and Holy Spirit were Co-Creators of the universe and of man. Says John, Creation was the work of Him who came as the *Word*, "By whom all things were made" (John 1:3). *See* Psalm 33:6. Then there is Paul's wonderful description of Christ who came as "the image of the invisible God, the firstborn of every creature" (Colossians 1:15-17). Creation, implying making out of nothing, is only possible to Deity. Man may be able to *make*, but only God can *create* (Isaiah 40:12). As the Creator, then, Jesus is the *Mighty God* for "all things were created by Him, and for Him." Marvelous though Creation was, Redemption was a far more remarkable work —

'Twas great to call a world from
  nought,
'Twas greater to redeem.

2. *He Sustains All Things.*

Every aspect of Creation is preserved and kept in perfect order by Christ who "upholdeth all things by the word of his power" (Hebrews 1:3). Paul says that "by him all things consist" or hang together (Colossians 1:17). "Excellent in power," God challenged man to show miraculous power such as He has displayed in Creation and Providence (Job 38). Had Jesus been "a mighty Hero" merely, the winds and the sea would not have acted at His bidding (Mark 4:41). All our Lord's miracles prove Him to be *The Mighty God*. (See the author's work on *All The Miracles of the Bible*.) Take the miracle of raising the dead. Only God is able to raise the dead (1 Peter 1:21). We have three instances of Jesus exerting this power (Luke 7:14; 8:54; John 11:43). But His might was most shown in raising Himself from the grave. All along He had declared that He would rise

again (Matthew 16:21; John 2:19), and exercising His power and prerogative to take up His life again, He declared Himself to be the One to whom all power had been given (Matthew 28:18; Revelation 1:8; Job 42:2).

Never in all history has there been an absolutely original character like Him who was born the King, whose Word was power. There has never been another Being like our "God and Saviour" who never did an injury, and never resented one done to Him; never uttered an untruth, nor practiced one; generous in the midst of the selfish, pure in the midst of the sensual, and wise above the wisest. There has never been His like, and never will be. As J. B. Figgis puts it in his volume, *Emmanuel*, published in 1885:

"Christ's inimitable meekness and patience never once forsook Him in a vexatious, ungrateful, and cruel sphere. He never stepped out of the humble sphere in which He had been brought up; He does not seem to have ever possessed for Himself so much as the smallest coin, and when He died had no means of providing for His mother, and could only commend her to one of His disciples. Yet His life was infinitely superior to all others. If Jesus were no more than a man or hero, why are there not more men like Him? What God did for one man, God would certainly have done for others. It is unaccountable that it has never been done. The Incarnation, when Jesus came as *The Mighty God*, alone helps us to the solution of such an enigma."

Frail children of dust,
  And feeble as frail,
In Thee do we trust,
  Nor find Thee to fail;
Thy mercies how tender,
  How firm to the end,

Our Maker, Defender,
Redeemer, and Friend.

* * *

Morning Star (Revelation 22:16).

The reference is to the Messiahship of
our Lord, as the *Star* of Balaam's prophecy (Numbers 24:17). He came as the
"Bright and Morning Star" when He
ushered in the day of grace at His birth,
and will function as the same when He
ushers in the everlasting day of glory
(Malachi 4:2). Along with *Morning
Star* is the kindred title, "*Dayspring*
from on high" (Luke 1:78). Both are
poetic presentations of the Messiah's appearance. (See more fully under *Dayspring.*)

N

Nazarene (Matthew 2:23).
(See under *Jesus of Nazareth.*)

O

Offspring of David (Revelation 22:16).
(See under *Seed of David.*)

* * *

Only Begotten (John 1:14, 18).
This repeated designation of Christ
is laden with the truth of His preexistence and Deity, as well as with His
eternal relationship with His Father.

> "Then I was by him, as one brought
> up with him: I was daily his de-
> light, rejoicing always before him;
> Rejoicing in the habitable part of
> his earth; And my delights were
> with the sons of men" (Proverbs
> 8:30, 31).

What a remarkable portrait this is of
Him who came from the bosom of the
Father to die on a wooden gibbet for
the sons of men!
The phrase *Only Begotten* in reference to Christ appears nowhere else
save in John's writings in which he em-

ploys it 5 times. With the apostle, *Son
of God* and *Only Begotten Son* described the eternal relationship between
Father and Son, with both carrying the
idea of a supernatural origin. In the
opening verse of his gospel, John describes Christ not only as *The Word,*
but says *The Word was God.* Thus,
when John goes on to add, "God only
begotten," the idea in all this phrase-
ology is not "the derivation in that beside Jesus Christ there is no other — He
is the sole complete representation of
God on earth." As Westcott, in his *Commentary on John,* puts it, "The thought
is centered in the personal Being of the
Son, and not in His generation. Christ
is the One only Son," or the *only* Son
besides whom the Father has none.
Equality with God was Christ's one
claim, and it was for this the Jews tried
to kill Him.

> "He also called God his own Fa-
> ther, making himself equal with
> God" (John 5:18 ASV).

If we take John's references to Christ
as *The Only Begotten Son* in order, not-
ing the language the apostle uses in
each case, we may be able to more fully
understand the import of such a remarkable title. It must be added, however,
that while *faith* accepts, and rests in,
Christ's eternal subsistence, and His essential nature, finite reason can fathom
all that is associated with His Eternal
Sonship.

> ". . . the glory as of the only begot-
> ten [or only born] of the Father"
> (John 1:14).

Without doubt this passage is associated with the Incarnation of Christ,
when He was made flesh, and came,
not "*of the Father,*" but "*from the Father.*" Thus, the glory the disciples beheld, probably at His Transfiguration
(2 Peter 1:16-18), was *like* or cor-

responding in nature to, the glory of an only Son sent from His Father. "It was the glory of One who partook of His divine Father's essence; on whom the Father's love was visibly lavished, and who represented the Father as His Ambassador." The phrase, "only begotten," or "only *born*," is also used of a human relationship – "The only son of his mother" (Luke 7:12). See Luke 8:42; 9:38.

In the Greek translation of the Old Testament, known as the *Septuagint*, the phrase, "only *born*" answers to –

Darling (Psalms 22:20; 35:17).
Desolate (Psalm 25:16).
Only Son (Genesis 22:2, 12; Jeremiah 6:26; Amos 8:10; Zechariah 12:10).
Only Beloved (Proverbs 4:3).

The expression, then, as can be gathered from its occurrences, suggests the thought of the deepest affection. But John only uses the phrase of Christ. "Only *born*" can be compared with Paul's "first born" (Romans 8:29; Colossians 1:15-18), which John also uses of Christ (Revelation 1:5 ASV). On the comparison of these kindred terms Vincent remarks –

"John's word marks the relation to the Father as unique, stating the fact in itself. Paul's word places the Eternal Son in relation to the universe. Paul's word emphasizes His existence before created things – John's, His distinctness from created things.

The Greek for "Only Begotten" distinguishes between Christ as the only Son, and the many children of God; and further, in that the *only* Son did not *become* such by receiving power, by adoption, or by moral generation, but *was* such in the beginning with God. . . . The statement is anthropomorphic, that

is, attributing human form and human modes of activity to God, as when we speak of the *hand,* the *face,* the *eye* of God, or of God *begetting* as here."

While the manifestation of divine glory took place on earth, the *begetting* referred to has nothing to do with Christ's Incarnation when He appeared as Mary's *firstborn.* He did not have two births, one as the Son of God, and the other as the Son of Mary, or Son of Man. He was the Son of God in His divine and eternal nature, but this Sonship effloresced into human and palpable manifestation by His being born through "the power of the Highest." Thus, we cannot conceive of two births. What John expressed was Christ's connection between His human birth and His proper personal, eternal Sonship. "The only begotten" used of Him implies an unoriginated relationship.

Bishop Handley Moule has this comment on John's unique phrase – "The begetting is not an event of time, however remote, but a fact irrespective of time. The Christ did not *become,* but necessarily and eternally *is* the Son. He, a Person, possesses every attribute of pure Godhood. This necessitates eternity, absolute being; in this respect He is not *after* the Father." Being the Eternal One, having no "beginning of days," precludes any notion that His being was derived from the Father.

"Only begotten Son which is in the bosom of the Father" (John 1:18).

This exquisitely, beautiful designation, found only here, declares the depth and tenderness of the love in which the Son ever abode with His Father. How expressive are the words of the love and dignity of such a relationship! Some of the oldest MSS read here, "Only begotten God, which is in the bosom of the

Father." Soon after the middle of the second century, the text read, "Only begotten *God*," or *"God only begotten."* While this term may seem unfamiliar to us, nevertheless it is not foreign to the thought of John in the prologue of his gospel, the central idea of which is that the *Logos* was with God, and *was* God.

This eternal Sonship is expressed, then, in the parallel descriptions, "In the bosom of the Father" and "only begotten Son." The original then is fully expressive –

"No man hath seen God at any time; only begotten God as He is, He who is in the bosom of the Father, *He* has declared Him."

The oneness of essence and of existence between Father and Son is made prominent by the natural figure of being "in the bosom" as necessary in Him who came to reveal the nature of God. John, "the disciple whom Jesus loved," is depicted as "leaning on Jesus' bosom" (John 13:23) – an indication of the holy intimacy existing between them. This may be why we come nearer to the heart of Jesus in John's writings than in those of any other writer. The phrase *is in* probably refers to the return to, and presence with the Father after the Ascension – "I go to My Father." The preposition *in* means "into," and can express the arrival back to heaven after His incarnation. "The Son who has entered *into* the Father's bosom and *is* there." Yet, the precious description, *who is in the bosom*, can express a timeless present, eloquent of the inherent and eternal relation of God to the Father, and of an unending *abiding*.

The figure of the *bosom* is essentially one of *love*, and is used at least four ways in Scripture –

The relation of husband and wife (Deuteronomy 13:6).

The bond between a father and infant child (Numbers 11:12).

The affectionate protection and rest afforded to Lazarus in Paradise (Luke 16:23).

The mutual love and trust between Jesus and John (John 13:23). Used of the Father and the Son, the figure is expressive of perfect love, "of an ever active relation, and eternal going forth and returning to the Father's bosom by the Son in His eternal work of love. He ever goes forth from that element of grace and love and returns to it. That element is His life. He is there *because He plunges into it by His unceasing action."*

God so loved the world that he gave his only begotten Son (John 3:16).

Here we have the Gospel in a nutshell, the maximum of saving truth in the minimum of words. But this glorious utterance must not be taken to mean that Christ became the Only Begotten Son by His incarnation, in order to achieve Redemption. "His Sonship was not the effect of His being given," says Vine. The value and the greatness of the Gift lay in the *eternal* Sonship of Him who was given. The language used implies that Jesus existed before He appeared on earth. The force of this most favorite verse in the Bible seems to turn on the intimacy of the relation expressed by the repeated term, *only begotten Son*, "having been already existent before the giving; otherwise how is the greatness of the love expressed in the giving to be measured?" Dr. Warfield goes on to say, "Similarly in a passage like, 'For God sent not His Son into the World to condemn the World, but that the World through Him might be saved' (John 3:16), there seems an implication of the Sonship is underlying the mission; He was sent on this mission because He was Son – He did not become Son by being sent." See Hebrews 11:17 for a type.

Sent implies that He was in the Father's presence waiting to come at His Father's bidding. Loving His Son, and committing all to Him (John 3:35), and likewise having the full revelation of His Father's redemptive plan and purpose, Jesus was ready to be sent to fulfill such (John 5:20). And "the glory of an Only Begotten of the Father" is what men saw as He came as God's Gift. He brought this glory with Him from heaven, outflashings of which His disciples saw as "eye-witnesses of His majesty" as the world's Redeemer. Paul rejoiced in the trust that "God spared not his own Son, but delivered him up for us all" (Romans 8:32).

> *He hath not believed in the name of the only begotten Son of God* (John 3:18).

In this further use of such an august name, which stands for the Person Himself, the crime of those who reject Him is accentuated by the glory and majesty of the Eternal One from heaven. Such do not have to wait till the final assize for the pronouncement of their condemnation (Revelation 20:11-15). By their unbelief they are "condemned already" (John 3:18, 19). The occurrence here, then, of the unique title, "Only Begotten," or "God only Begotten," lays stress upon the full revelation of the character, will, love, grace and purpose of God, emphasized in the name of the Son who, being in an eternal relationship with the Father, was provided by Him as the Saviour of the world, and the Object of faith.

> *God sent his only begotten Son into the world* (1 John 4:9).

Here, again, the implication is not that God sent into the world one who at His birth in Bethlehem *became* His Son. Being *sent* proves that He was God's Son already, and at hand to be sent at the appointed time. Two features are to be observed in connection with this declaration of John's –

1. The coming of the Eternal Son was a manifestation of God's love toward a sinning world. "The love of God" (1 John 4:9) can be compared with the twice-repeated phrase "God is love" (4:8, 16).

2. The purpose of the coming of the Son of His love was that "we might live through him," that He might be "the Saviour of the world" (4:9, 14).

It is John who describes the Incarnation of Christ, more frequently than any others, as *a sending*, with the use of the perfect tense, *hath sent*, which points to the abiding results of the sending. The word *sent* implies "to send under commission, as an envoy." How perfectly the heavenly Envoy carried out the commission of the One who sent Him forth! "I have finished the work which thou gavest me to do" (John 17:4). "It is the grand *proof* of God's love, His having sent *His only begotten Son, that we might live through Him*, who is our *Life*, and who has redeemed our forfeited life; and it is also the grand *motive* to our mutual love." See 1 John 4:10-13.

A kindred phrase used of Christ, *First begotten* (Hebrews 1:6; Revelation 1:5), is worthy of a brief reference. The Greek means *First Born*. Paul speaks of Christ as "The Firstborn of every creature" (Colossians 1:15). The psalmist has the prophecy of the Messiah, "my firstborn, higher than the kings of earth" (Psalm 89:27). Phrases like "He was before me" and "He is before all things" (John 1:15; Colossians 1:17) speak of priority and superlative dignity. As Fausset states it, *"Firstbegotten* marks at once His *eternal priority* and His condescending to *brotherhood with us* (Romans 8:29). *Only begotten,* marks *His relation to the Father* by generation to everlasting. Since He is 'long before any creature,' He cannot be a creature Himself but the Creator. As He is the first begotten, originating the natural creation, so He is the *firstborn* – first begotten from the dead, and therefore the 'Beginning' of the 'Church of the Firstborn,' the originating Agent of the new Creation." *See* Colossians 1:18; Hebrews 12:23; Revelation 1:5.

Connecting the phrase "the firstborn" and "heir of all things" (Hebrews 1:2, 6), Warfield says that *firstborn* and *heir* are little more than specially honorific ways of saying *son.* God's *Firstborn* as such takes rank above all other existing beings: even all of the angels shall do Him reverence. God's *Firstborn* is also naturally God's *Heir,* an heir whose inheritance embraces the universe, and whose tenure stretches to Eternity. (See further under title *Heir.*)

P

Passover (1 Corinthians 5:7; Exodus 11; 12:23:15-17).

The Holy Spirit's commentary on the first and most significant of all the seven feasts of Jehovah, namely, the *Passover,* is to be found in Paul's great evangelical proclamation, "Christ our Passover is sacrificed for us." This united feast was instituted by God Himself to commemorate Israel's deliverence when the destroying angel *passed over* their dwellings in Egypt. In the circumstances of this feast as related in *Exodus,* a peculiarity of the narrative is that, though several lambs are spoken of, the singular is used – "every man a lamb," "a lamb for an house." God said, "The

whole assembly of the congregation shall kill *IT* in the evening."

This *one* lamb that was offered up, prefigured *the one great Lamb,* even "the Lamb of God" whose blood was shed for *the whole Church,* but which must be appropriated by *each* member of the Church (Galatians 2:16; Acts 20:28). When Paul said that Christ as the Passover was sacrificed for *us,* the pronoun meant every born-again member of the Church. The lamb slain *instead* of the Israelite told out impressively that the only way of escape from coming wrath is by another bearing the judgment. The glorious truth of Substitution and its application to be believed as before God, is the grand teaching of Paul in his matchless epistle (1 Corinthians 15:3, 4).

One of the great purposes God had in view when instituting the Passover Feast was *to put a difference* between His own redeemed people and the world (Exodus 11:7; Psalm 4:3). Paul elaborates on the necessity of separation from the ways of a godless world on the part of those who form part of "the temple of the living God" (2 Corinthians 6:11-18). There are two ways in which we can think of every Israelitish home on that memorable night when redemption came through the death of the firstborn (Exodus 12:29):

From Without.
What a dreadful night of darkness and death that must have been when, by one angelic stroke, Egypt – proud, defiant Egypt – became a nation with drawn blinds! The all-searching eye of God alone could see any difference in the houses. "All things are . . . opened unto the eyes of him with whom we have to do" (Hebrews 4:13), and when He saw the blood-mark of distinction upon the homes of Israel, He was gratified. Where in the sacred volume can

we find a passage to exceed this one where the Lord is found saying –

"And the blood shall be to you for a token upon the houses where ye are: and when I [*Jehovah*] *see the blood,* I will pass over you" (Exodus 12:13).

Although it was dark, so very dark that night, God was able to see the protecting blood sprinkled on the outside of the Jewish homes. This made all the difference as God smote all the firstborn in the land of Egypt. Every Jewish home in the land was safe through the blood. Alas, Pharaoh and his hosts were ignorant of the protecting blood, and so perished!

How secure we are if we have the assurance that our sin is covered by the Blood of richer vein than that of the lamb slain that terrible night in Egypt (Psalm 32:1). To all who are sheltered by the sacrifice of "Christ our Passover," there is no condemnation, for Christ endured our decreed death (Romans 8:1). What a resting place for the wretched heart and struggling conscience of man, and a divine resting place for all who are weary and heavy laden can be found in our Heavenly Passover! Have we experienced the efficacious, delivering and protecting power of the blood He shed for our sins? (1 John 1:7; Revelation 7:14).

Jehovah bade His sword awake;
   O Christ it woke 'gainst Thee:
Thy blood the flaming blade must
      slake,
   Thy heart its sheath must be;
All for my sake, my peace to make;
   Now sleep that sword for me.

From Within.
Outside the Jewish homes there was nothing but darkness and blood. The flowing blood of countless numbers of firstborns of Egyptian families and their cattle was the blood of deserved judg-

ment for the rejection of God and His people. The shed blood of the lamb marking the door of every Jewish home was the evidence of divine favor, love, and protection. But while sorrow, anguish, destruction and death were being experienced outside, and within every Egyptian home there was nothing but fear and grief, what was the condition in every fast-closed Israelitish home at the midnight hour of doom?

Only God knew what was going on within each house and family being redeemed that night. The psalmist could say, "Thou hast visited me in the night . . . and shalt find nothing" (Psalm 17:3). It was so that night of death for all who were sheltered by the blood of the lamb, even as it is for us if God's Paschal Lamb is our Saviour. No matter how black the midnight may be outside, bless God, within us we can have praying and singing hearts (Acts 16:25).

The one thing God looked for within the blood-marked houses of His people was obedience to His command.

"They shall eat the flesh in the night . . . It is the Lord's passover" (Exodus 12:8-11).

The blood of the lamb was on the lintel and two side posts outside the house, and represented a God-required *sacrifice.* But inside the family gathered and ate the flesh of the lamb slain and the same provided sustenance. Thus, both the blood and the body of the lamb were of great service to all within the houses of the redeemed. Is not all this symbolic of what Christ our Passover accomplished for us?

Redeemed by the blood of God's Lamb, we are to feed upon His flesh. This brings us to a consideration of our Lord's discourse on Himself as *The Bread of Life* in which He gave utterance to the mystic truth about His disciples eating His flesh, and drinking His blood (John 6:51-59). The question of the unregenerate heart is, "How can this Man give us His flesh to eat?" It is only those who have come to God through Christ (John 6:47), who know what it is to feed upon Him in their hearts by faith with thanksgiving (Proverbs 9:5; Revelation 7:17). The truth expressed is that the relationship between Christ and His own is so close that the assimilation of the food we eat is not too strong a figure to illustrate it.

Eating the flesh of Christ means appropriating Him as the Sustenance of our life. Physically we cannot live without food; and spiritually we cannot exist without Him who is our daily portion (Psalm 16:5; Galatians 2:20; Ephesians 3:17). He is our Meat indeed! The word "eateth" which our Lord used here is a very strong one and literally implies the art of dividing the food by the teeth. And being in the present tense describes the process of careful eating and mastication. The only other place where this sense occurs is in the Parable of the Fig Tree where Jesus said of those before the Flood came, "they were eating and drinking" (Matthew 24:38).

Drinking the blood of Christ symbolizes the appropriation of the saving merit of His death. As the celebration of the Passover was approaching when He instituted *The Supper,* the reference may well have been to the flesh and blood of the Paschal Lamb. Although, "the life of the flesh is in the blood," here *the flesh* and *the blood* are separated – a separation suggesting His *death* He had often predicted. Says Ellicott's *Commentary* –

"The blood is spoken of as distinct from the flesh, and in this involved physical death. The eating of the flesh would itself involve the thoughts of sacrifice and of sustenance, the removal of the death-penalty attached to sin, and the strength of life sustained by food. But the spiritual truth is fuller and deeper than this; and the true element of life in the soul depends upon such communion with Christ as is expressed by drinking the blood itself; that is, by receiving into the human spirit the atonement represented by it and with this the very principle of life. They may not receive into the human frame the principle of animal life, but no man really has spiritual life who does not receive into the inmost source of his being the life-principle revealed in the Person of Christ. This is to pass through and through his moral frame, like the blood which traverses the body, hidden from sight, but passing from the central heart through artery and vein, bearing life in its course to muscle, nerve and tissue. It is to traverse the soul, passing from the Eternal Life and Love, which is the heart of the Universe, through the humanity of Christ, and carrying in its course life and energy for every child of God."

Eating the flesh, and drinking the blood, then, must be taken figuratively and not literally as the Church of Rome erroneously does in its celebration of Mass. When He spoke of His *flesh* and *blood,* He had something different in mind than the gross idea which these bare terms expressed. It is impossible to believe that for those who heard Him utter these words He meant that the *temporal* life they were then living was dependent on their eating and drinking, in this gross sense, His flesh and blood.

Yet the false and grotesque teaching of Rome is that when the wine and wafer are used in its parody of the Lord's Supper, that in the act of participation these elements are transformed into the actual flesh and blood of the Saviour. This *Transubstantiation* or *Real Presence* as Rome calls this change can be found in the *Agreed Statement* which reads —

> "Through the prayer of thanksgiving, a word of faith addressed to the Father, the bread and wine become the body and blood of Christ by the action of the Holy Spirit, so that in communion, we eat the flesh of Christ, and drink His blood. . . . In the whole action of the Eucharist, and in and by His sacramental presence, given through bread and wine, the crucified and risen Lord, according to His promise, offers Himself to His people."

What an utterly false interpretation of the Lord's Supper this is, which He only meant to be a simple, symbolic commemoration of Calvary, the bread and wine being symbols of His broken body and shed blood! Going back to the New Testament teaching regarding the Supper, no form of administration is specified, no suggestion of an altar and eucharistic vestments, no evidence of any priestly prerogative can be found. While preparing this particular section on the *Passover,* I happened to read in a London daily paper the report of a Scottish Roman Catholic priest addicted to alcoholism who is seeking to overcome his problem as a member of Alcoholics Anonymous. His greatest temptation comes when he sips the wine each time he celebrates Mass, and here is his reported confession —

> "My faith pulls me through. As a Roman Catholic Priest I am mentally geared to the fact that I am not taking wine *but the blood of Christ.* It is by thinking this way that I manage to cope."

How sacrilegious it is to teach and practice that by the observance of Mass, Catholics sacrifice Jesus Christ every time they engage in it! Scripture says that "Christ was once offered," and that as our Passover, He has been sacrificed for us, but Rome crucifies Him afresh at its Mass. At the Passover time, Jesus instituted the Last Supper, as it is called (Matthew 26:20-29), and Paul outlines for us the order and significance of this simple yet solemn service (1 Corinthians 11:23-34).

At the original Passover, as God's people were gathered together, all *leaven* had to be put away because they were redeemed people, and Paul has some strong things to say about our conduct both before and at the Lord's Table (1 Corinthians 11:27, 28). When the saints gather in His name to remember His dying love, and drink of the cup in gratitude, they think of His outpoured blood on their behalf, symbolized by the blood of the lamb sprinkled on Jewish homes. When they eat the bread, they recall His body bruised and battered and crucified, and praise Him for bearing their sins in His body broken for them, and feast upon all He accomplished thereby. Like Israel of old, in the House, they eat of the slain lamb — it is the Lord's Passover (Exodus 12:11), proclaiming redemption by blood as the foundation of all blessing and glory. We always honor Christ our Passover when we gather at His Table to remember His sacrifice and sing —

> Thy body, broken for my sake,
> The bread of heaven shall be;
> The cup of blessing I will take,
> And thus remember Thee.

* * *

Physician (Luke 4:23; Psalm 32:1).

The Gospel hymn conveys the comforting and assuring message to the hearts of all who are in need of the Master's healing touch –

> The Great Physician now is near,
>   The sympathizing Jesus;
> He speaks the drooping heart to cheer,
>   Oh, hear the voice of Jesus!

It would seem as if Jesus did not have a very good opinion of the professional physicians of His day. He recognized, of course, that those who were sick required the attention of a doctor (Luke 5:31). But He told of a woman who had suffered from a hemorrhage for 12 years, and had spent all her money on physicians but was "nothing bettered, but rather grew worse" (Mark 5:25, 26). Immediate and perfect relief, however, was received as soon as she touched the hem of the garment of the Great Physician (Luke 8:43-48). How consoling are the lines of Whittier –

> That Good Physician liveth yet
>   Thy Friend and Guide to be;
> The Healer by Gennesaret
>   Shall walk the rounds with thee.

It is interesting to find the proverb "Physician, heal thyself" in the gospel written by Luke, the "beloved physician" (Colossians 4:14). Doubtless he knew it to be a common Jewish proverb. It occurs frequently in rabbinical writings as, "Physician, heal thine own lameness," or as, "In a sad state is the city whose physician has the gout, and whose steward has one eye." What it means is, "Charity begins at home." Interpreted in the light of the context, this proverb Jesus evidently knew and quoted was aimed at the Nazarenes who were jealous because He worked miracles at Capernaum and other places before He worked any at His own hometown of Nazareth.

In effect, these grumblers were saying, "Strange rumors have reached our ears of Thy doings elsewhere; but if such power resides in Thee to cure the ills of humanity, why has none of it yet come nearer home, and why is all this alleged power reserved for strangers?" The defect of the renowned Physician from Nazareth, in the opinion of the Nazarenes, was want of consideration among those who knew Him best, especially his fellow-townsmen. Jesus replied to the one proverb by quoting another, equally familiar, "No prophet is accepted in his own country" (Luke 4: 24), which, expressed in a rougher form implies, "Too much familiarity breeds contempt." This second proverb was quoted twice by Jesus, perhaps oftener: on His first visit to Nazareth after His baptism and on His second visit (Matthew 13:57; Mark 6:4; John 4:44).

There is a curious parallel to this proverb in the life of "The Heathen Christ," Appollonius of Tyana, who is represented as saying, "What wonder is it, if, when I am esteemed by the rest of mankind like a god, and by some even as a god, my own country alone until now refuses to recognize me?" Plutarch also said, "You will find that few of the most prudent and wisest of mankind have been appreciated in their own country." Yet another ancient writer said, "All the philosophers seem to have had a hard life in their own country." Well, Jesus came to those where He was born and brought up, and they received Him not. Even His own brothers and sisters did not believe in Him (Mark 6:2, 3; John 7:5). Like them, we, too, often think lightly of what is very familiar. The blessings at our doors are those we value least.

The long residence of 30 years in Nazareth merely as a townsman had made Him *too common,* incapacitating the Nazarenes from appreciating Him as others did who were *less familiar with His everyday demeanor in private life. See* Matthew 7:6. Yet, when Jesus left the obscurity of a peasant home for His public ministry, His gift of healing was for all who came to Him believing. He was able to heal their diseases, whether physical or spiritual. There was no disease of the body or soul for which He did not have a specific remedy (Matthew 8:14-18; Luke 5:30-32).

A striking manifestation of His Deity as the Son of God with power was His ministry as the Great Physician. Yet each miracle of physical healing He wrought was a parable of His ability to deal with maladies of the soul. Actually, the world is one large hospital for the sick in body and soul, with Jesus the Physician visiting every ward.

He healed the physically sick (Mark 1:34), and offers health to all the soul-sick sons of men (Isaiah 1:4-6; Jeremiah 8:22; Matthew 11:28).

He cured the palsied who were physically incapacitated (Matthew 9:2), and waits to make those palsied by sin to work and labor for God (Isaiah 40:29; Romans 7:18, 19; Ephesians 2:10).

He gave sight to the blind (Luke 18:42, 43), and He alone by His Spirit can give spiritual sight to the blind (Isaiah 42:16; Revelation 3:18).

He cleansed the leper of his foul disease (Matthew 8:2, 3), and alone He is able to make the sinner separated from God, whiter than snow by His own blood (Isaiah 59:2; Ephesians 2:13; 1 John 1:7).

He opened the ear (Mark 7:35), and offers to open the ears of those who have been long deaf to the sweet sound of His voice (Psalm 10:17; Isaiah 36:11).

He loosed the tongue of the dumb (Mark 9:25), and ever waits to unloose the tongue of the spiritually dumb to sing His praises (Isaiah 35:6).

He raised the dead – a miracle *no* earthly physician has been able to do (John 11), and is ever ready to raise those who are dead in their trespasses and sins (Ephesians 2:1).

Healing all diseases, and forgiving all iniquities, Jesus revealed Himself as the Great Physician appointed by God (Matthew 11:3-6). As for His qualifying diploma as a physician of soul and body, He ever carries this with Him (John 5:36, 37). If we are among those who have been healed, physically or spiritually, or both, then may we be found living to the glory of God (Psalm 126:2, 3; Luke 8:39). But, if we are in dire need of His healing touch, and hear Him say, "Wilt thou be made whole?" may we seek His aid without delay (2 Kings 5:13; Luke 8:43, 44), and pray the prayer of one of old, "Lord, heal my soul, for I have sinned against thee" (See under NAMES OF GOD – *Jehovah Rophi*.)

O Saviour Christ, our woes dispel;
For some are sick, and some are sad,
And some have never loved thee well,
And some have lost the love they had:

Thy touch has still its ancient power;
No word from Thee can fruitless fall.

* * *

Plant of Renown (Ezekiel 34:29).

That this Messianic prophecy is related to the house of Israel God called "my people," "my flock," is clearly evident from the narrative (Ezekiel 34:11-31). Speaking as *Jehovah*, He declares that He will set up one *Shepherd*, even His servant David, to feed His flock (34:23). This Servant from the house of David who will be a Prince among Jehovah's people is the One who will bring them "showers of blessing" (34:26), and who, as the *Plant of Renown* will provide the flock of His pasture with all necessary food so that "they shall be no more consumed with hunger" (34:29).

By the *Plant* we are to understand the Messiah, who is the *Rod* and *Branch* (Isaiah 11:1), and the *Righteous Branch*

(Jeremiah 23:5), who shall obtain for Israel "renown." God's ancient people will yet be the planting of the Lord, and an object of "renown" when He calls them, "Israel My Glory" (Isaiah 60:21; 61:3). There are some writers however, who affirm that the "Plant of Renown" is not a reference to the Messiah, but should be read, as the ASV puts it, "plantation for renown," and so refers to the fertility of the land Israel is to possess as a plantation of peace and plenty. We prefer the interpretation that the figure refers to Him who came as "a tender plant" (Isaiah 53:2), but who will yet be the *Plant of Renown.*

Israel shall no more hunger
  When the Plant of Renown will come;
Dispersed not any longer,
  They will then be gathered home.
The Plant of Renown their boast,
The Lord alone their trust.

* * *

Potentate (See under section, *Blessed and Only Potentate*)

Power of God (1 Corinthians 1:24).

In his first letter to the Corinthians, Paul in writing about Jews and Gentiles used a double designation of Jesus in relation to both groups: "Christ, the *Power* of God – Christ the *Wisdom* of God" (1 Corinthians 1:18-25). Way's translation is helpful in that it makes clear the connection between *Jews* and *Gentiles* with *power* and *wisdom* –

"To us who have heard God's call, Jews and Greeks alike, this Messiah embodies God's power – so meeting the Jews' craving for miracles – and God's wisdom – so meeting the Greeks' desire for philosophy."

Power and *Wisdom!* What excellent qualities to possess! When they act together in perfect harmony what an irresistible influence they exert. If a man has power, but not the wisdom to direct its energies for beneficent ends, then its exercise can be disastrous. If, on the other hand, a man has wisdom, but lacks power to enforce his wise precepts, then his gift is futile. Possessing both power and wisdom in perfection, Christ knew how to make the one the handmaid of the other. Power was never manifested at the expense of wisdom nor vice versa. In Him, these attributes walked together because of the agreement between them.

The Scripture often mentions the happy union of *power* and *wisdom* in the divine character:

"Wonderful Counsellor – Mighty God" (Israel 9:6 RSV).
"Wonderful in counsel, excellent in working" (Israel 28:29).
"Great in counsel, and mighty in work (Jeremiah 32:19).
"The power of God . . . the wisdom of God" (1 Corinthians 1:18, 24).

In the passage before us, "Christ, the power of God, and the wisdom of God" (1 Corinthians 1:24), it will be observed that Paul personalizes these two qualities. Both the Power and the Wisdom are not something but *Someone,* even Christ in whom both reached perfection. At this point, we are to deal with Christ who *was* Power, and who manifested the power with which God had anointed Him (Acts 10:38). Under the latter title of *Wisdom,* attention will be given to this feature of Christ.

In *Romeo and Juliet* Shakespeare writes of –

"A greater Power than we can contradict
Hath thwarted our intents."

The gospels reveal that none could contradict Christ as a divine Power both aiding and thwarting the intents of men. Power without a knowledge of the one possessing it only produces fear. If you meet a Goliath he would terrify you, for you would not know what use he might make of his power. But if a friend who knew all about this herculean fellow assured you that with all his immense strength he was kind and good, then you would not be alarmed.

Who is this mighty Power of God? Why, the One who could say of Himself, "I am meek and gentle in heart" (Matthew 11:29). Creation reveals His "eternal power and Godhead" (Romans 1:20). Yet the greatness of this power in His created works can strike terror into the heart of man (Psalm 66:3). In grace, His power is concentrated upon the deliverance of sinners from the thralldom and tyranny of their sin. Thus, His finished work at Calvary is the power unto Salvation to all who believe (Romans 1:16; 1 Corinthians 1:18). There are, at least, four realms in which His power is manifested.

1. *In Creation.*

As everything was created by the Lord Jesus (John 1:3; Ephesians 3:9), He is able to command and control His creations. All within the universe is upheld by Him (Colossians 1:17), and obeys His will, as some of His miracles prove. He could change water into wine – and the best kind at that! (John 2:9). Having made the sea He was able to still its tempests (Mark 4:39), and walk on its storm-tossed waves (Matthew 14:25). The trees are His, He fashioned them, and so the fig-tree submitted to His command (Mark 11:20-22).

2. *Over All Flesh.*

All animate beings appeared at His bidding. "He spake and it was done." Man was the divine masterpiece, and Jesus confessed that He had received power over all flesh from the Father (John 17:2). This is seen in His dealings with men. He could give sight to the blind, cure the paralytic, cleanse the leper, restore the withered, heal the wounded. We see His power over animals: the fish (Matthew 17:27); the ass (Mark 11:2); the cock (Mark 14:30).

3. *Power to Forgive Sins.*

Jesus was always honest with people, and if they were sinners He told them so (Matthew 9:13), but at the same time He revealed His power and willingness to forgive them if they would but confess their sins. "Who can forgive sins but God only" (Mark 2:7). As God the Son He forgave women who were sinners (Luke 7:48; John 8:11) – and also men (Matthew 9:6).

4. *Prerogative to Give Life.*

John declared, "In him was life" (John 1:4), and Christ proclaimed Himself to be *The Life* (John 14:6). See John 11:25, 26. That the Father and He were one is seen in His assertion –

> "As the Father hath life in himself; so hath he given to the Son to have life *in* Himself" (John 5:26).

Power was His to lay down His life, and take it up again (John 10:18). Some of His miracles reveal His power to give life to others. Jesus was known to upset funerals, as He did in the case of a girl, of a youth, and of a friend He loved (Mark 5:42; Luke 7:15; John 11:44). As only God can raise the dead, then Jesus, as the Lord of Life, must be God (2 Corinthians 1:9).

Without doubt, then, Christ is the Power of God pledged to us and acting for us. The trinity of danger, "the lust of the flesh, and the lust of the eyes, and the pride of life" (1 John 2:16), and our presence in "the whole world that lieth in wickedness" (1 John 5:19), are beyond the frailty of our fallen nature to overcome. We need a Power, not of ourselves, to deliver us and carry us through all temptations, and such is ours only through "Christ the Power of God"

(Ephesians 3:20). May grace be ours to appropriate all we have in Him whose Power is never impoverished by giving, or enriched by withholding! The woman who touched the hem of Christ's garment and felt fresh life coursing through her afflicted body heard Him say, "I perceive that power [original for *virtue*] is gone out of me" (Luke 8:46), and she went forth in peace. (For other references to His Power see under *Almighty, Potentate, Deliverer.*)

> He, Whose Power mere Nullity obeys,
> Who found thee Nothing, formed thee for His praise.
> To praise Him is to serve Him, and fulfil,
> Doing and suffering, His unquestioned Will.
>   – Cowper

* * *

Precious Cornerstone (Isaiah 28:16). (See under title *Cornerstone*).

* * *

Priest (Hebrews 7:17). (See under title *High Priest*).

* * *

Prince (Acts 5:31).

Occurring over 300 times in Scripture, this striking title represents some 20 different Hebrew words in the Old Testament, and 3 different Greek terms in the New Testament, and an examination of these references reveals the various applications of the title, especially in the Old Testament where it is most frequently used. There are only 14 references in the New Testament where the designation, *Prince*, is found. In the majority of cases, the title is applied to human beings. Occasionally used of those of royal parentage and position (1 Chronicles 29:24), it more often indicates actual ruling power coupled with royal dignity and authority.

When God said of Solomon, "I will make him a prince all the days of his life," a term is used equivalent to that of "king" (1 Kings 11:34). The same is also true of the name given to a Jewish king (Ezekiel 12:10). (*See* also Ezekiel 32:29; 34:24; 45:21-25; 46.) The word used of David as God's choice as king – *captain* (1 Samuel 13:14) – is equivalent to ruler or prince.

While it might be profitable to continue this feature and indicate the many in different walks of life described as *prince*, we are only dealing with divine names and titles, therefore, let us discover how Scripture applies the particular title before us to Deity. That regal princedom is Christ's is evident from the several ways in which He is described as *Prince*. Of *Antony*, Shakespeare wrote –

> "... The greatest prince o'er the world,
> The noblest."

But such an acclamation is truer of our Lord Jesus Christ, who has distinctive royalty as King of Kings, and majestic authority as Lord of Lords. As Dr. C. J. Rolls says –

> "Christ is most certainly supreme in every stately position of power, and spaciously sublime in every high rank of honor . . . He is truly a Prince, buoyant in spirit, brilliant in wisdom, and beneficent in heart. The imperishable riches of His immortal love support and sustain the myriads of redeemed peoples, who have been transformed by His own inherent power."

Daniel can be looked upon as a book about princes, for its pages are full of them. With princes all around the prophet, some of whom were jealous of the princely life of Daniel, we can understand his feelings when he wrote about the Prince of Heaven.

The Prince of princes (Daniel 8:25).

Those who exercise royal or ruling power are apt to forget the assertion of Israel's illustrious ruler, Solomon, "By me princes rule" (Proverbs 8:16). With Spirit-inspired prophetic insight, Daniel predicted the coming of the Messiah, as One who would rule as "the Prince of princes," or "Prince of the kings of earth" (Revelation 1:5). Here, the highest human title in its absolute sense is applied to Christ. He was "the Prince [same word as *captain*] of the host of Jehovah," the mysterious Stranger Joshua encountered near Jerusalem. Here a high military title is applied to a superhuman being (Joshua 5:14).

Messiah, the Prince (Daniel 9:25).

In his outline of "the seventy weeks of years," Daniel refers to two princes who are as opposite in character as light is to darkness. There is Messiah the Prince, who was to be "cut off" or crucified, "but not for Himself," which literally means "shall have nothing," that is, "nothing which was rightly His" (Daniel 9:25, 26). Then we have "the prince that shall come to destroy the city and the sanctuary," whom we identify as "the Beast" of Revelation 13; 19:20. This Roman prince, or emperor, will endeavor to make war with the saints, but he is to find more than his match in "Messiah *the* Prince." The conquering prince of Daniel 11:18 has been identified as Antiochus the Great, 198 B.C., forerunner of "The Man of Sin" who, making a seven-year covenant of peace with the Jews, and becoming known as "the prince of the covenant," breaks it halfway through and reveals himself in his true diabolical character (Daniel 11:21-35).

Michael, your Prince.

In the remarkable vision of the glory of God Daniel received by the side of the great river, Hiddekel, and which he records in the tenth chapter of his prophecy, evidently "Michael, one of the chief princes [of Heaven]" who had withstood the resistance of "the prince of the kingdom of Persia" was the medium of Daniel's remarkable experience (10:13). God assured the prophet that the unfolding of the Scripture of Truth was fully understood by "Michael, your Prince" (10:21). Then Daniel goes on to describe this heavenly protector of Israel as "Michael . . . the great prince which standeth for the children of thy people" (Daniel 12:1). The reference here is to the severe persecution of the Jews during the last half of the great tribulation (Revelation 7:14). Presently, because of their rejection of God, the Jews are "without a prince" (Hosea 3: 4). A glorious transformation will be theirs when they see "The Prince of Glory" they crucified and mourn because of the sorrow which sin caused Him (Zechariah 12:10).

The Prince of Peace.

The last in Isaiah's group of Messianic titles is this glorious one, "His name shall be called . . . The Prince of Peace" (Isaiah 9:6). As this Almighty Prince was to come from the line of Judah, it was fitting that the land of Judah should be referred to as "not the least among the princes of Judah: for out of thee shall come a *Governor* [or Prince], that shall rule my people Israel" (Matthew 2:6).

While He was among men, He was the princeliest of them all.

> Our God has sanctified all ages; He,
> Not for twelve years but those
>   long thirty-three
> Dwelt in our world, the ever-undefiled;
> Loving, obedient, gentle, stainless,
>   mild,
> Exemplar He alike to sire and boy.

Born in the most humble circumstances, Christ yet came as a King, and His Kingdom is the most vast and royal realm a sovereign ever ruled. What kind of peace did this heavenly Prince bring?

Old Trapp answered, *Pacis omnimodae,* peace of every kind – peace, outward and inward, of country and conscience, temporal and eternal. Of all these aspects He is the Prince, as having full power to bestow them.

But He is not only the Prince *of* Peace, but the Prince who *is* Peace. Peace is not only a benefaction He can impart, but part of Himself. "*He* is our Peace," said Paul. In Him, Peace is personified and reaches its perfection. Thus when He left His disciples the legacy of peace, "My Peace I give unto you," He left them *Himself.* He only was princely enough to be the purchaser and procurer of peace between God and man, between man and man, between Jew and Gentile (Ephesians 2:15). Christ adorned this highest human title in its most ideal sense.

The Prince of Life.

The language Peter used seems to be contradictory. "Ye ... killed the Prince of Life" (Acts 3:15). *Life* cannot be *killed.* Man is only able to destroy the body, was what the Prince Himself said. Yet cruel men slew the *Author* of all life. The word Peter used for "Prince" means author (*see* margin), founder, or leader, and Christ is the Originator of Life – physical, spiritual, and eternal (John 1:4; 1 John 5:11, 12). (*See* further under title *Life.*)

The Prince and Saviour.

In his public discourses Peter used a wide range of names and titles to describe the One he had declared to be, "The Christ, the Son of the Living God." The designations of Him are unique, and as Dr. Warfield expresses it –

"The composite portrait which Peter presents of Jesus the Messiah as he passes freely from one of these designations to another is a complex and lofty one; what is most appar-

ent is that he conceives Him as the focus upon which all the rays of the Old Testament prophecy converge, and as exalted above all earthly limitations."

Peter was conversant with the prophets of all predictions of Christ for he could say, "To him give *all* the prophets witness" (Acts 10:43), therefore with Daniel's references to Christ, as "Prince of princes" and "Messiah the Prince" and Isaiah's prophecy of Him as "The Prince of Peace," great significance is attached to the title the apostle gives Him as *Prince and Saviour* (Acts 5:31). The Rhemish version reads, "This Prince and Saviour hath God exalted." Here, again, the word for *Prince* is captain, or author, in the original. Now, exalted on high, He is able, in virtue of His death and resurrection, to grant forgiveness to all who repent – Jew and Gentile alike.

This remarkable double title of Christ as the princely Saviour expresses that *royalty* which all Israel looked for in the Messiah; the other, the *saving* character of it which they had utterly lost sight of. Each of these features in our Lord's work enters into the other, and both make one magnificent whole (Acts 3:15; Hebrews 2:10). But what exactly happened when the Prince of Glory died at Calvary as the Saviour of the world? John reminds us that as the Prince of Life Jesus was killed that "he might destroy the works of the devil" (1 John 3:8).

Who were those princes of this world responsible for crucifying the Lord of Glory (1 Corinthians 2:8)? They were the chief religious leaders in Jewry who, alas! were ignorant of the eternal purpose of God to redeem a lost world through His Son. These officials of the Sanhedrin were "the princes of the sanctuary" (Isaiah 43:28), yet they were blind to the true identity of the Prince of Life in their midst and so plotted His death. But behind all human agents responsible for Calvary was Satan himself, for he was the one who inspired Judas to betray Jesus into the hands of those who hated Him.

Strange, is it not, that Jesus gives His satanic foe, whom He was about to "cast out" by His death, the title He Himself bore of *prince* – one first in power, authority, or dominion – "Now shall the *prince of this world* be cast out" (John 12:31). Paul calls Satan "The god of this world" (2 Corinthians 4:4). This was the one who boasted to Christ of having the kingdoms of this world to offer Him for His allegiance (Luke 4: 5-8). At Calvary, this boastful world-possessor and ruler was deposed and defeated, and faith appropriates the victory over God's and man's foe. John Milton, in *Paradise Lost*, depicts Belial thus –

> And princely counsel in his face
>   yet shone,
> Majestic through his ruin.

But no matter what original, angelic majesty he may still possess, the Prince of Life by His death destroyed the devil's power, and secured for mankind a glorious liberty from his bondage (Hebrews 2:14, 15; John 16:11). A testimony to the perfect holiness of the Prince of Heaven is seen in the fact that the Prince of Hell could find nothing of sin in Him (John 14:30).

The Pharisees gave Satan, or Beelzebub, the title of "The Prince of Devils" – or *demons*, as it should be. There is only one devil – and he is more than enough! (Matthew 9:34). A mightier Prince than this satanic lord, Jesus was able to cast out demons, thereby emancipating those in bondage to the devil (Matthew 12:22-30). Paul wrote of the *princes*, or rulers, of the darkness of this world, all of whom are under the

sway of the Prince of Darkness himself whose constant purpose it is to blind "the minds of them that believe not, lest the light of the glorious gospel of Christ who is the image of God should shine unto them" (Ephesians 6:12; 2 Corinthians 4:4). But Jesus, "The Light of the World," is more than able to banish the spiritual and eternal darkness in the lives of those who believe. For the one responsible for such darkness there is reserved "the blackness of darkness for ever" (Jude 13).

In conclusion, there is the title Paul gives Satan, namely, *Prince of the Power of the Air* (Ephesians 2:2). The word for *air* used here is the same the apostle employs to describe the saints being caught up to meet the Lord *in the air,* when He returns (1 Thessalonians 4:17). By the *air,* we are to understand "the sphere in which the inhabitants of the world live and which, through the godless and rebellious condition of humanity, constitutes the seat of Satan's authority." This is the seat and center of his evil designs upon mankind and from which he operates with "the spirit-host of wicked beings that haunt the upper air" (Ephesians 6:12, Way's translation). What a wonderful deliverance awaits the saints when their heavenly Prince returns to deliver them forever from the satanic domain!

Prince of the Kings of Earth.

It is John who gives us this last glimpse of the princely dominion of Him, God called, *My King!* (Psalm 2:6). Christ is to appear as the King of kings, and rule over all, even His greatest and most powerful enemies among kings, princes, and lords. What a tower of strength is this title of *Prince*, who is "higher than the kings of the earth," and who will yet possess the kingdoms of this world which are His by right and claim. At present His full princely rights are in abeyance, but the time is not far distant when He will shiver every imperial scepter, and break the crown of all opposing authority, and take under Himself His princely power, and reign.

What is our Prince more than any other prince? Why, He is the *Prince* of the most princely who have ever lived. As Dr. C. J. Rolls expresses it –

"He Himself is the originator, author, or prince of the treasures of truth, the riches of righteousness, the values of virtue, the merits of mediation, the resources of regeneration, the ministration of mercy, the legacies of love, and the wealth of infinite wisdom. To this Prince of princes we may attribute all that is precious, virtuous, and gracious . . . His princely rights and claims are emblazoned throughout Creation, Revelation, and Mediation."

Thou art exalted, Thou alone
Art Prince of princes, Mighty One;
Jesus, to whom all knees shall bow,
All kingdoms at Thy feet laid low.

✿ ✿ ✿

Prophet (John 7:40).

The three representative birth-names the Son of God received when He was born in Bethlehem were *Jesus* (Saviour), His human name – *Christ,* His Messianic name – *Lord,* His Jehovah name (Luke 2:11). Dr. A. T. Pierson points out that these three names have a definite *order,* and historic development –

"Up to His Crucifixion, He was conspicuous as *Jesus.*
After His resurrection and ascension, He was pre-eminent as *Christ,* the Anointed and anointing One.
When He returns, it will be the

Lord, to reign, with every tongue confessing His lordship."

When Paul uses these three names, he observes this order "Jesus Christ is Lord" (Philippians 2:11). Further, these three names indicate also His threefold office and ministry –

Jesus, suggests His career as a *Prophet,* teaching men the truth.
Christ, suggests His *Priesthood,* atoning for our sin.
Lord, suggests His *Kingship,* ruling over men and nations.

The priesthood came into full exercise when the prophetic work ended, and the kingly begins where the priestly terminates. These lines of separation are not absolute, yet they indicate general facts. These three names likewise suggest man's relation and responsibility –

Obedience to Him as *Prophet;*
Faith in Him, as *Priest;*
Surrender to Him, as *King.*

How blessed we are when with John Newton we too can sing –

My Prophet, Priest and King,
Accept the praise I bring.

Having already considered Christ's titles as *Priest* and *King* (*see* under titles *King* and *High Priest*), let us now confine our attention to Him as *Prophet.* As the three offices of prophet, priest, and king are prominent in the Old Testament and were acknowledged as foregleams of Him who would combine all three in perfection in Himself, it is necessary to discover the work of each office, and the necessary qualities of those fulfilling them, in order to see how they were figures of the true (Hebrews 8:5; 9:8, 24). What then were the marks or qualities of the prophets of old?

First of all, they were men divinely called, anointed and instructed. They were both prophets and patriots. "Patriotic fervour, and the ability to trace tendencies to their logical and inevitable end become allied qualities of the prophet." Theirs had to be a clear understanding, both of God's will, and man's need.

The prophet had to be a *patriot* for the sake of the Divine Covenant; one who wanted his nation to be in the right relationship to God, and who would foresee the inevitable results of national rebellion against God's ideals for the nation.

The patriot had likewise to be a *prophet*, believing that his vision and utterances were divinely inspired. He was one who spoke in the name and by the authority of another. Men of the highest moral character, they had to act by the inspiration of the Holy Spirit. In their declarations, they were both *fore*-tellers and *forth*-tellers. When they ministered as the latter it was to thunder forth a divine message for their own time and people. As to the former, they had the gift of God to foretell future events. Thus, they preached and predicted (1 Kings 18:46; 19:8; Amos 3:7; 1 Peter 1:11; 2 Peter 1:21), and were regarded with veneration, and looked on as men not only with superhuman knowledge but with supernatural power. It is not difficult for a lover of the Word to trace how Jesus, the Prophet of Galilee, brought to perfection in Himself those Old Testament delineations of prophets.

Coming to the New Testament we find prophecy in the strictest sense of the word continuing in saints who eagerly anticipated the coming of the Messiah as Prophet, and also as Priest and King. We have devout souls like –

> *Simeon,* who died in peace after seeing the Lord's Christ (Luke 2:25-35).

> *Anna,* the aged, godly widow who saw in the Babe the Redeemer (Luke 2:36-38).

> *John the Baptist,* who proclaimed Jesus as the Lamb of God (Matthew 14:5).

As for Jesus Himself, during His public ministry the following features emerge as to His function as a Prophet.

As the Messiah He was expected to come in the line of the prophets (Deuteronomy 18:15, 18), and He appeared as the Prophet from the midst of His brethren, as John indicates, "This is of a truth *that* prophet that should come into the world" (John 6:14; Acts 3:22).

Because of His character and conduct, words and works, people had no difficulty in identifying Jesus as "the prophet of Nazareth in Galilee" (Matthew 21:11).

Those who were nearest to Him – namely, His chosen disciples – knew Jesus better than the common people who heard Him gladly, and their testimony of Him was that He was "a prophet mighty in deed and word before God and all the people" (Luke 24:19; Mark 8:28). No evidence could be more conclusive than this!

Knowing, as He did, that He was the Prophet that Moses said would emerge from His own people, Jesus had no hesitation in applying the title of *Prophet* to himself. "A prophet is not without honor, save in his own country, and in his own house" (Matthew 13:57). So, widely acclaimed as a Prophet, He accepted the designation of Himself as such as being appropriate. He never repelled such an attribution, and with no uncertainty assumed the role of Prophet (Luke 4:24; 13:33, 34).

"Christ is unrivalled as a Prophet because of His unprecedented character and unparalleled honour. His intimate association with the Father, His inherent knowledge of all men, and His perfect insight into all future events, assured Him the highest and holiest distinction in fulfilling this function," says Dr. Rolls. "In Him we meet a Prophet whose qualities we can never estimate, whose abilities we can never calculate, and whose capacities we can never tabulate. He has told us the end from the beginning and His counsel abides (Isaiah 46:10)."

> God's Word declares that Jesus came,
> A Prophet of God's Grace,
> To cover sin "hath He appeared";
> His love redeemed the race.

R

Rabbi (John 1:49).

Scripture itself provides us with the meaning of this literary or scholastic title. Nicodemus said to Jesus, "Rabbi, we know that thou art a teacher come from God" (John 3:2). *See* John 1:38. *Rabbi* is synonymous with "teacher," or "master," thus he who came to Jesus by night actually said, "Rabbi, we know that thou art a rabbi," or "Teacher, we know that thou art a teacher." *Rabbi* was the usual expression of honor and respect used by a pupil when speaking of, or to, his instructor in Jewish schools. It was a title of dignity among doctors, teachers, and masters in Jewish circles.

Rabbi is the transliteration of a Hebrew word signifying, "my master," and used in contrast to a slave, and came to be the recognized form of address with which the learned were greeted. Derived from the Chaldean *Rab,* this appellation distinguished the chief officers of the Chaldean court (Jeremiah 39:13).

The three titles of dignity used were —

> *Rabh,* meaning "great."
> *Rabbi,* implying "greater."
> *Rabban,* signifying "greatest."

These rabbis were regarded as being infallible oracles in religious matters, and usurped not only the place of the law, but of God Himself. They were supposed to have power to settle disputes, religious and otherwise, and received the greatest homage. Coming to the gospels, we find the title applied to John the Baptist speak of Jesus followed and called *Rabbi* by his disciples. "They came to John and said . . . Rabbi." But the Baptist declared that as a teacher all the truth he taught came from heaven (John 3:26, 27).

Christ also was often addressed as *Rabbi.* The two disciples who heard John the Baptist speak of Jesus, followed Him and He asked them, "Whom seek ye?" Then in their reply we have an interpretation of the title of dignity, "Rabbi (which is to say, being interpreted, *Master*), where dwellest thou?" (John 1:38). In the same chapter we have the confession of Nathanael, "Rabbi, thou art the Son of God: thou art the King of Israel" (1:49; 6:25). The American Standard Version often gives *Rabbi* for "Master" as in Mark 9:5. "Rabbi, it is good for us to be here." See also Mark 11:21; 14:45.

Those who occupied the chief seats in the synagogue loved to be greeted in market places as *Rabbi, Rabbi* (Matthew 23:2), but Jesus forbade his disciples using such a designation of themselves. "Be ye not called *Rabbi:* for one is your teacher [Master KJV] and all ye are brethren" (Matthew 23:8 ASV). This prohibition was against adopting the title in the spirit of exercising dominion over the faith of others. Jesus did not forbid the giving of title to others when it was customary or not regarded as improper, but *they* were not to receive it. *See* Acts 26:25. The Master exhorted His disciples not to be ambitious of gaining such titles and distinctions as the Scribes and Pharisees sought after, but to look to Him only, as the perfect

Law-Giver and Teacher, and follow Him in all matters of faith and worship (Matthew 23:7-12). (See further under title *Master*.)

❊ ❊ ❊

Rabboni (Mark 10:51; John 20:16).

This Aramaic form of "rabbi" occurs only twice. It was the word the blind man used when asking Jesus for sight. The KJV has it, "Lord, that I may receive my sight," but the ASV translates it, "*Rabboni*, that I may receive my sight" (Mark 10:51). Even more respectful than rabbi, Rabboni was a title of the highest dignity, or a term of reverent love and admiration, and means "My great master."

The other occurrence of this particular title was in the garden at our Lord's resurrection when a sorrowful woman met the mention of her name, *Mary*, with "*Rabboni*."

She said unto him, "*Rabboni*, which is to say, Master" (John 20:16). Such a tender title was at once an expression of Mary's joy, and an acknowledgment of Christ as Lord and Master. When Mary saw the Risen Christ, she failed to recognize Him. Either the dark hour of the early morning, or her tear-blinded eyes, prevented her from seeing Him whom she *did not* expect to see again (Luke 24:16). But the first words the Lord uttered after His resurrection were, "Why weepest thou?" Then there came a case of mistaken identity, for Mary supposed the speaker to be the *gardener* and requested him to tell her where the body of her Lord had been taken.

Then came the utterance of her name, *Mary!* and spoken with a tenderness Jesus alone had, because of all He had accomplished for this woman, it awoke instant recognition in her of the Saviour she loved.

Oh! joy to Mary first allow'd,

When rous'd from weeping o'er His shroud.
By His own calm, soul-soothing tone,
Breathing her name, as still His own!

Immediately she cried, *Rabboni!* but this single word of transported recognition was not enough for Mary's full heart. Sibbes' comment on the mention of this one word, *Mary!* is arrestive, "One word coming from Christ and set on the heart by the Spirit of Christ, hath a mighty efficacy."

But although it was not a time for many words and all Mary had to do was to wonder and adore, yet her expression of the name so full of reverential regard was not enough for her heart, she reached out her hands to touch Him. Westcott says that the exact form here implies that "she was already clinging to Him when He spoke." Now, actually seeing Him again, she wanted to keep Him, but this could not be, seeing that He had yet to ascend to His Father. Mary tried to express by her action what words failed to convey, but she was checked and came to learn that old familiarities must now give place to new and more spiritual, yet sweeter approaches; but for these the time had not yet come.

Jesus, however, rewarded Mary for her vigil and for her love and loyalty by making her the first human herald to proclaim the glorious tidings that He who died was alive forevermore. "Go, tell my brethren." And so, as dear old Sibbes put it, "A woman is sent to be the apostle of the Apostles." Mary went and told of all she had seen and heard, and this is what Christ expects all His witnesses to do (Matthew 11:4; 1 John 1:3).

In Bickersteth's remarkable poem, *Yesterday, To-Day, and For Ever,* he has these lines in the section on "Redemption" with which we conclude —

. . . Little she reck'd

Of angel ministries who sought her
  Lord:
And when we ask'd, "Woman, why
  weepest thou?"
She utter'd her one plaint, "He is
  not here"
But turning mournfully away beheld
One whom she knew not, for the
  sluice of tears
Had drenched her eyelids: and He
  likewise ask'd,
"Woman, why weepest thou?
  Whom seekest thou?"
She answer'd; when the Stranger
  turn'd and said,
"Mary." She started, and, in one
  deep cry,
Breathing her incommunicable bliss,
"Rabboni," fell before His feet,
  and fain
Had clasp'd them.

But not now as heretofore,
The human intercourse vouchsafed
  on earth;
Nor was He to His Father's throne
  in Heaven
That hour ascending. . . .

*   *   *

Redeemer (Job 19:25; Isaiah 44:24;
  Luke 2:38).

The Cross, on which the Prince of
Glory died as our Redemption, is both
the focal and pivotal point of Scripture,
the central message of which is deliverance from sin and its fate by act or
grace of God. It is so true that

"All the light of sacred story
Gathers round its head sublime."

This is why the Scripture is a crimson
book, and crimson is the evangelical
color. We read that, "Moses . . . took
blood . . . and sprinkled . . . the book
(Hebrews 9:19), and while modernistic
professors and preachers may not like
the red word, *blood,* the Bible is a blood-
sprinkled Book. The ASV lends emphasis
to this fact for it reads "the book *itself.*"
The renowned German theologian, De-
litzel, wrote, "That Moses actually did
sprinkle the Book of the Covenant with

the sacrificial blood might be inferred
by analogy." *See* Hebrews 9:22 ASV.
Written large, then, over the whole of
Holy Writ is the divine fiat – "Without
shedding of blood is no remission" (Hebrews 9:22; 10:18).

The recurring theme of the New Testament is that the blood on Jewish altars
slain was symbolic and prophetic of the
sacrifice of Jesus, who came as the Redeemer looked for in Jerusalem (Luke
2:38). The doctrine of the atoning virtue of "the blood of Jesus Christ" which
Paul had no scruple in calling, "the
blood of God" (*see* Acts 20:28) is preeminent after the Redeemer's death and
resurrection. There is a sense in which
the *blood* is God's endorsement of His
Book, or His autograph to the Book.
Of old, the blood ratified the Covenant
contained in the Book (Exodus 24:7, 8).
God chose, then, to make the *blood* His
sign of fidelity – all of which is a parable
of the efficacy of the Redeemer's blood.
Says Dinsdale T. Young, one of the great
Evangelicals of Methodism –

"Let sneerers dub the Book as gory;
we glory in its ruby redness. To us
the Blood-besprinkledness of the
Bible is the guarantee of its everlasting veracity . . . The Blood of
Jesus streaks its every page . . . I
cannot discredit the Covenant, for
the Maker of the Covenant endorses
it with His precious Blood."

Acknowledging, as we do, that our
Redemption is an eternal mystery, we
accept by faith the sacrifice we cannot
understand, and glory in Him who redeemed us from all iniquity. That God
prepared the world for the coming of
His beloved Son as its Redeemer is evident from many Old Testament Scriptures. The redemption of Israel with a
lamb (Exodus 13:13), prefigured the
offering up of Christ, as "the Lamb of
God" for our redemption (John 1:29).

Job believed that his Redeemer was the ever-loving One, and would bring about his final transformation (19:25).

David could sing of Jehovah, as "my redeemer" (Psalm 19:14; 78:35).

Isaiah spoke of "The Holy One of Israel" as "Your Redeemer" (43:14; 44:6, 24). Then there is his great prophecy, "A Redeemer shall come to Zion, and unto them that turn from transgression in Jacob, saith Jehovah" (59:20 ASV).

In the second part of his prophecy, chapters 40-66, Isaiah uses the title of *Redeemer* some 14 times. Then the power of the Redeemer to fulfill His purpose is found in verses like these –

"Their redeemer is mighty" (Proverbs 23:11).

"Their Redeemer is strong" (Jeremiah 50:34). *See* 32:7.

That all of these foregleams became a reality in Christ is seen from Paul's teaching that the Redeemer to come out of Zion had appeared (Romans 11:26), and that all who believe, whether Jews or Gentiles, are "justified through redemption in Christ" (Romans 3:24), and that it is in Him alone that we have "redemption through His blood" (Ephesians 1:7; Colossians 1:14). Through His death, Christ "obtained eternal redemption for us" (Hebrews 9:12). He Himself was made unto us *redemption* (1 Corinthians 1:30).

The word *redeem* itself means to buy back what was sold, pledged, or forfeited (Luke 1:68), and so a *redeemer* was one who ransomed by paying a price. Usually he was the *goel*, or nearest of kin who bought back a forfeited inheritance. There are, then, two distinct features of the mission of the Redeemer to be distinguished –

1. *There was Redemption by Purchase.*

This glorious institution in Israel, appointed by God Himself reveals that a lost inheritance could be bought back, and how one who had been sold as a slave could be redeemed (Leviticus 25; 27). If the person in dire need of the redemption was unable to pay the price, the right of purchase was with the nearest of kin. It was thus that Boaz became the redeemer for Ruth (Ruth 4:4), and Jeremiah, the redeemer for Hanameel (Jeremiah 32:8).

The substance of the Gospel of Redemption is that through sin, man bartered away his magnificent inheritance (Genesis 3:23, 24), and found himself sold into bondage (Romans 7:14), and utterly unable to redeem himself, or any other sinner for that matter (Psalm 49:7, 8). But Christ, by assuming our manhood, became our *Goel*, our nearest of kin, and paid the price for our inheritance – and what a fearful price He paid! "He gave Himself a ransom for all." He became the Redeemer by purchase (Galatians 3:13), and redeemed the sons of Adam's race (Ephesians 1:7; 1 Peter 1:18, 19), and likewise paid the price for our bartered inheritance (Ephesians 1:14; 1 Peter 1:3, 4).

2. *There was Redemption by Power.*

A further aspect is that those who were kept prisoners by an enemy were brought out of their captivity without any ransom being paid, but by a strong hand (Isaiah 50:2; Jeremiah 15:21). It was in this way that God redeemed Israel from bondage in Egypt (Exodus 6:6; Deuteronomy 7:8), and promised to redeem Judah from Babylon in like manner (Micah 4:10). Jesus, our Mighty Redeemer, delivers by power.

By *purchase*, the shedding of His precious blood, He has redeemed us from the demands of God's broken law.

By power, He redeems us from the bondage of sin and Satan "the lawful captive delivered" (Isaiah 49:24; Titus 2:11-14).

Under the Mosaic law the *goel,* or redeemer had the right to avenge the death of his slain kinsman as a point of honor. Our heavenly Redeemer through death destroyed him who had the power of death, even Satan who has been man's *murderer* from the beginning (John 8:44; Hebrews 2:14, 15). In a sense, Job did not realize what we mean when we say, "I know that my Redeemer – my Vindicator, my Avenger – liveth," for He is alive forevermore to redress my wrongs on Satan their inflictor.

> I know that my Redeemer liveth,
> And on the earth again shall stand!
> I know eternal life He giveth,
> That grace and power are in His hand.

What must not be forgotten, however, is that our strong Redeemer by the price He paid for our emancipation provided not only a redemption covering the present, but one which also includes the future. I have a redeemed heart but it is still in a "body of sin," and I must have a body in harmony with my spirit. Thus, we have what Paul calls *the redemption of the body* (Romans 8:23). In an age of dim revelation this also was the hope of Job (19:25-27). The final installment of our purchased redemption, the redemption of our now weak body, and its restoration from corruption will be the grand vindication of the efficacy of the Redeemer's work. This will be the final phase of the finished transaction of the Cross (Ephesians 1:14; 4:30; Philippians 3:20, 21). What blessedness will be ours if we are found among those redeemed from among men (Revelation 14:4)!

> Free from the law, oh! happy
>   condition!

> Jesus hath bled, and there is
>   remission!
> Cursed by the law, and bruised by
>   the Fall,
> Grace hath redeemed us once for all.

* * *

Resurrection (John 11:25).

Dealing with the names and titles of our Lord as found in the gospels, Dr. Warfield observes that they fall into three general classes –

> Those that are purely designatory, such as the most natural, personal name, *Jesus.*
> Those that are generally honorific, like *Teacher, Master.*
> Those that are specifically Messianic, for instance the oft-repeated *Christ,* or *Son of Man.*

It is in this last section that we can place the impressive designation, *Resurrection,* which Jesus said He *is.* Not only did He bring about resurrections in the days of His flesh, but even before He Himself rose from the dead, He could affirm. I AM *the Resurrection,* or He is Resurrection personified. Here we have another of those personal pronouns of asserted Deity. "How wonderful," says a writer of a past century, "that there was so much of *I* without any egotism!" The repetition of this pronoun is frequent in our Lord's teaching, *I am, I am not, I come, I do, I bear record, I speak, I go* – each of which must be studied in the light of the occasion when used. I AM was the divine name by which God revealed Himself to Moses, and which Jesus appropriated as His own (Exodus 3:14). As a name it implies not merely a divine origin but a divine nature, and describes an existence which had no beginning, and will have no end.

The remarkable declaration of Himself as "The Resurrection and the Life," set in verses intoned at almost every funeral (John 11:25, 26), is not a figurative double designation of what Jesus is in Himself, but a definite statement of fact. He is both, and believing in Him as both, the dead shall live, and the living never die. It has been said that, "Any blessing that is lasting is a blessing that is contained in some new *discovery of God.*" It was so with Mary and Martha who would never have known Jesus as "the Resurrection and the Life" had it not been for the sickness and death of Lazarus, and of their tears – and the Master's own – over his passing. But theirs was an experience resulting in the delightful zest and surprise of active discovery.

Lazarus, "sick unto death," died, and was in his grave for four days when Jesus arrived at Bethany. He knew this beforehand, however, without being told (11:14). Here we have one of the frequent occurrences to Christ's omniscience to be found in John's gospel. Then there came the sorrowful meeting with the bereaved sisters, and of Martha's expressed belief in the resurrection of her brother as a far-off event at "the last day" (John 6:39, 44, 45). But Christ's reply was an emphatic assertion of His claim to be, in Himself, the power by which the dead are raised. Martha went on to say that perhaps God would raise her dead brother in answer to Christ's prayer, but Jesus replied, "I am *myself* the resurrection."

Martha had stated the resurrection of the dead as a doctrine, as a current tenet of faith. Jesus, however, stated resurrection *as a fact*, identifying it with His own person. Thus, He did not say, *I raise the dead*, which of course He did (Luke 7:12-14; 8:49, 50), or "*I perform* the resurrection," but, "*I am* the resurrection." Says Vincent, "In His own person, representing humanity, He exhibits man as immortal, but immortal only through union with Him." But He not only proved Himself to be the *Resurrec-*

tion by the dead He raised, but by His own wonderful resurrection from the grave: He also proclaimed Himself to be *The Life.*

While resurrection implies a return to life, the claim, "I am . . . the Life" suggests a larger and inclusive idea. To quote Vincent's *Word Studies* again –

> "Resurrection is involved in life as an incident developed by the temporary and apparent triumph of death. All true life is in Christ. In Him is lodged everything that is essential in life, in its origin, its maintenance and its consummation, and all this is conveyed to the believer in his union with Him. This life is not affected by death."

Had not Christ declared that all who believe in Him never die? Godet, in his commentary on John, says of this fact –

> "Every believer is in reality and for ever sheltered from death. To die with full light, in the clear certainty of the life which is in Jesus, to die only to continue to live to Him, is no longer that fact which human language designates by the name of death. It is as though Jesus had said: 'In me death is certain to live, and the living is certain never to die.'"

It is likewise profitable to connect the double designation of Christ as *Resurrection* and *Life* with the two companies of saints who are to participate in "the Rapture" when He returns for His Church (1 Thessalonians 4:13-18). Paul says, "If we believe that Jesus [as the Resurrection and the Life] died and rose again," then we must accept the glorious hope of the *living* and the *dead*. That the apostle separates these two conditions is seen in these two phrases.

"The dead in Christ shall rise first" (1 Thessalonians 4:16). In his Magna

Charta of the Resurrection, Paul declaring that by "man [the Man Christ Jesus] came also the resurrection of the dead" goes on to say that as "the First-fruits" He guaranteed the resurrection of the dead in Him, "Afterward they [the dead] that are Christ's at his coming" (1 Corinthians 15:22, 23). All who died in Him are to be "raised incorruptible" (15:52). For this section of the redeemed, Christ will be *The Resurrection*.

The other company are described as *"we which are alive and remain"* – "we shall be changed" (1 Corinthians 15:52; 1 Thessalonians 4:17). Those who are alive when Jesus comes will escape tasting death, and their bodies will be transformed into a glorious body like unto Christ's (Philippians 3:21; 1 John 3:1-3). Says Paul, "In Christ shall all be made alive" (1 Corinthians 15:22). The dead in Christ are made alive again, that is in respect to their bodies, for having eternal life they cannot die. They are with Christ and return with Him (1 Thessalonians 4:14), and their dust awakes for its redemption (Romans 8:23). For the living, who are to be changed, Christ will be, not *the cause* of the continued and enhanced life, but *the Life*, granting them life for evermore (Revelation 1:18). To them, He will not say, "I *shall* be your Life," but, "I *am* . . . your Life." All who have the Son as Saviour have life (1 John 5:11, 12). (*See* under title – *Life*.)

> I am the Resurrection and the Life,
> What blessed words of consolation;
> Earnest of Immortality and Life,
> With holy, solemn benediction.

*   *   *

Righteous (1 John 2:1).

Had Jesus Christ not been "the Righteous" He would never have been the propitiation for our sins, and also for the sins of the whole world (1 John 2:2). What He *was* gave validity and efficacy to what He *did*. One of the most noble of designations Peter assigned to Jesus was "the Holy and Righteous One" (Acts 3:14 ASV). *See* also 22:14. Over against the gross injustice of the leader of the Jewish Council, Stephen placed Jesus as "the Just One" (Acts 7:52). In the original of 1 John 2:1 there is no article, and so it reads, *Jesus Christ, righteous*.

John describes Jesus as our *Advocate*, but as such He is not a mere suppliant petitioner, but pleads for the saints on the ground of His *justice*, or *righteousness*, as well as *mercy*. It is His perfect *righteousness*, or obedience to the law, and endurance of its full penalty for us, on which He grounds His claim for our acquittal. The sense therefore is, "in that He is *righteous*," in contrast to our *sin*. Because God raised Christ from the dead and set Him at His own right hand, He accepted once and for all Christ's claim for us. This is why the accuser's charges against the saints are vain.

> Be Thou my Shield, and Hiding Place;
> That sheltered near Thy side,
> I may my fierce accuser face,
> And tell Him Thou hast died.

*   *   *

Righteous Branch (Jeremiah 23:5).

The One thus described is "THE LORD OUR RIGHTEOUSNESS" (Jeremiah 23:6). The word *branch* means "shoot," which is immediately connected with the root, and contains, as it were, the springs of life. *See* Jeremiah 33:15; Zechariah 3:8; 6:12. The same word Isaiah uses denotes *Branch* (11:1). The prediction is that of an ideal descendant of David, a King who shall reign in righteousness, and deal as wisely as David did (1 Samuel 18:5, 14). Christ will be the fulfillment of this prophecy when He comes to reign as the Righteous Ruler exercising His sovereignty marked by absolute justice. His name as such is to be the sign that God will make His people righteous. (*See further* titles, *Jehovah Tsidkenu* and *Branch*.)

Righteous Servant (Isaiah 53:11).

Had Jesus not been the ever-obedient, righteous, loving Servant of the Father, He would not have had the authority to "justify many" or *make many righteous*, as the ASV puts it. Christ makes us righteous by delivering us from the guilt and consequences of our sins through His atoning death as the One who knew no sin. That Isaiah had in mind the Messiah when he wrote of Him as "the righteous servant" is evident from his description of Him as One in whom God's soul delighted (42:1-4). It is, therefore, on the ground of His own righteousness as the Servant of Jehovah, that He can justify others who can never be justified by their own righteousness. (*See* further under title *Servant*.)

*   *   *

Righteous Judge (2 Timothy 4:8).

Whether it be at the Judgment Seat of Christ for believers, or the Great White Throne for the wicked dead, the Lord will be true to His appropriate title as *the Righteous Judge*. That Paul was referring to the former Judgment can be gathered from his expressed personal hope, "Henceforth there is laid up for *me* a crown of righteousness." As a saved man he could not have had before him the Great White Throne where no saints appear, and no crowns are bestowed (Revelation 20:11-15).

If we were to be put on trial, how eager we would be to secure a good, honorable and just judge – not one vacillating like Pilate (John 19:6), nor corrupt like Felix (Acts 24:26). Because the Judge appointed by God must be good (Genesis 18:25) in delivering all judgment into the hands of His Son, He appointed the most perfect Judge of all (John 5:27; Acts 17:31). No angel, however just and holy he might be, would be qualified to act as Judge. It must be a Man to judge His fellowman, One who knows his ways and doings (Hebrews 2:14-18). In Jesus who became the Son of Man, we have the only perfect righteous Man the world has ever known (Romans 3:5-23; 1 Peter 2:22, 23). Therefore, when as saints we stand before Him for the trial of our words to discover of what sort they are (1 Corinthians 3:1; 2 Corinthians 5:10), we can be certain of an impartial verdict. As "the Righteous Judge" He will adjudicate without favor. If a reward has been earned He will bestow it with His benediction (Matthew 24:14-30; 25:31-40).

*   *   *

Rock (1 Corinthians 10:4).

Although we lustily sing, "The Lord's our Rock, in Him we hide," it is to be questioned whether we fully understand all that Paul meant when he cited the Israelites of old drinking of the rock that followed them through wilderness, and that *that Rock was Christ* – many centuries before He was born in Bethlehem. In the chapter from which the above verse is taken, the apostle, using historical illustrations to enforce some practical advice upon the carnal Gentile Corinthians, warned them against the fate of the Israelites. Failure, through self-confidence, characteristic of a God-privileged people, was the very sin the Corinthians were committing.

Ancient Israel had been signally blessed and favored of God, yet most of them perished in the wilderness because of sin. They accepted the privilege of their high calling, but renounced its responsibility, and Paul used their fall from grace as a type of the sacramental privileges vouchsafed to the Corinthians, but which they were in danger of bartering away for idolatry, impurity, presumption, and murmurings. Paul took it for granted that his readers were familiar with the historical facts he mentioned in his epistle to them, and so used them, metaphorically, to forewarn them against a like apostasy. Emphatically, he repeats *all* five times to drive home his warning. An examination of 1 Corinthians 10:1-4 reveals the five *alls*, in the enumeration of the five favors which God had bestowed on Israel. Five times, correspondingly, they sinned (10:6-10). In contrast to the *all* stands *many* (rather "the most") of them (10:5). *All* of them had great privileges, yet *most* of them were castaways through lust, and the Corinthians, with greater privileges than Israel, were in peril of sharing the same doom.

As to Paul's description of all Israel being "baptized unto Moses in the cloud and in the sea" – the margin has it, "baptized *into* Moses" – this means that they were initiated into a spiritual union with Moses, and became, thereby, his disciples. The *cloud* symbolized God's presence. It concealed Him when He spoke to His people (Numbers 12:5). Formed as a pillar it seemed to roll before marching Israel. At night it glowed (Exodus 13:21, 22). For the believer in this age, Jesus is the accompanying cloud (Matthew 28:20). There was no actual baptismal rite as we understand it. The word *baptism* has two senses –

1. The application of water as a religious rite, in whatever mode this is performed.
2. The implication of devoting, consecrating, initiating into or bringing under obligation to.

It is the second sense we are to understand in Paul's use of Israel's baptism for by it they became *devoted* to Moses as their leader. As God's representative he enunciated God's laws, and they must obey him, and consequently find themselves under the protection and guidance by the miraculous interposition of God. Thus, passing through the cloud and the sea the people gave public recognition of being the followers of Moses and obligated to obey his laws. Initiated into his faith and surrender to God, Israel was bound to honor his divine mission, and obey his injunctions. (For a study of the significance of *The Cloud* and *The Sea*, consult the writer's volume, *All the Messianic Prophecies in the Bible*.)

We now come to consider the symbolic significance of Paul's mystic reference to the sustenance Israel received in her long journey in the wilderness from her *spiritual meat* and *spiritual drink*. The word *spiritual* implies that which was given by the Spirit, or God, as a miraculous gift. The meat and drink were called by Josephus, "divine and extraodrinary food." Such food came from heaven, and not as the result of human labor. The Greek word for *spiritual* is applied to things in the divine sphere, as well as to those in Satan's realm (Ephesians 6:12). It is put in contrast with that which is *natural* (1 Corinthians 3:1; 12:1; 15:44). Here, in 10:3, 4, *supernatural* expresses the meaning. The food and drink are called "spiritual" by Paul because such was *miraculous*, or God-given; *typical* of our sustenance in Christ; *assuring* of God's providential care whereby faith is strengthened (*see* Psalm 78:25; John 6:31).

The phrases "did all eat" and "did all drink" are in the imperfect tense denoting continued action – throughout the whole journey of the Israelites, and typical of our unceasing supply from

Him who is our Bread and Water (John 4:10; 6:35).

The phrase that seems to perplex many sincere lovers of Scripture is that where Paul says of the Israelites of old, "They drank of that spiritual Rock that followed them: and that Rock was *Christ*" (1 Corinthians 10:4). As Christ was not born until many centuries later (Luke 2:11), how could He have been there when Moses led the children of Israel through the wilderness? Was Paul right when he affirmed that that Rock *was* Christ? Some commentators affirm that at this point the apostle was using a legend allegorically. This we do not believe.

According to a rabbinic tradition a well was formed out of the spring in Horeb where Moses smote the rock and the water gushed forth (Exodus 17:6), and that the well of water gathered itself into a rock like a swarm of bees, and followed the people for 40 years; sometimes rolling itself, sometimes carried by Miriam, and always addressed by the elders, when they encamped, with the words, "Spring up, O well!" (Numbers 21:17).

But it was not the *literal* rock at Horeb that left its entrenched position there, or even a fragment of it, that accompanied the people. To think so is ludicrous. No, the Rock that followed them from place to place was *spiritual,* or of a supernatural character. Paul says that this mysterious Rock was not *something* but *someone* – even Christ. Ellicott says that we recognize here, "the mystery of a *real presence.*" So we do, for Christ the Word was with His people under the Old Covenant. *God was in Christ* here, as from the beginning. As Christ was "God manifest in the flesh in the new dispensation, so God manifest in the Rock – the Source, sustaining life – was the Christ of the old dispensation.

That the Jews were familiar with the figure of a Rock as illustrative of God's permanence and provision is evident from the numerous references to same (Deuteronomy 32:4-37; Exodus 33:15; 1 Samuel 2:2; Psalm 78:20, 35; Isaiah 28:16; 32:2). Although the people thought of the Rock poetically as God, they knew not that it was, as a manifestation which was yet to be given in the Incarnation of Christ. The word *but* (1 Corinthians 10:5) is significant. "But with many of them God was not well pleased," because they thought it only a Rock, or applied the word poetically to Jehovah, not discerning that the Rock *was* Christ. By the Spirit's illumination, Paul saw in the Rock a recognition of Christ's preexistence; the divine power which sustained the Israelites was the power of Christ working on earth *before* His Incarnation (John 7: 37, 38). (See further under NAMES OF GOD – *Rock.*)

The tragedy was that a people divinely sustained came to lightly esteem their supernatural sustenance and so perished in the wilderness, that is, all of the first generation to leave Egypt, save Joshua and Caleb who were the only two to enter the land of promise. Paul warned the Corinthians that the fate of those who despised the Bread of Heaven was an example, or sample of what befalls all who, with all their spiritual privileges, walk carelessly (1 Corinthians 10:5-33). The Blessed Redeemer is our Rock in a weary land, following us all the way and forever increasing and multiplying mercy (Psalm 81:16). May we be found drinking unceasingly of the Rock who will never leave nor forsake us! If spurned as such a beneficial Rock, then He will become the *Rock of offense* (1 Peter 2: 8). With the psalmist may we pray, "Lead me to the rock that is higher than I" (Psalm 61:2).

Hiding in Thee, hiding in Thee,
Thou blest Rock of Ages,
I'm hiding in Thee.

* * *

Root (Romans 15:12; Revelation 5:5; 22:16).

In the plant world, a root is the subterranean part of a tree or the part "provided with a growing point, and functioning as an organ of absorption, an aerating organ." In this natural sense, the word *root* is often used in Scripture (Matthew 13:6, 21). But the term is also employed symbolically of the origin, or source, of persons and ancestors (Romans 11:16-18); of that which springs from a shoot, an offspring; of things evil such as avarice, and bitterness (1 Timothy 6:10; Hebrews 12:15).

When Isaiah described the coming Messiah as *A Root of Jesse* (Romans 15:12; Isaiah 11:1, 10), he used the same word as the "rod" and "branch" growing from the root. "The new shoot of the fallen tree of Jesse is to grow up like a stately palm, seen afar off upon the heights of the 'holy mountain,' a signal round which the distant nations might rally as their centre."

Extol the Stem of Jesse's rod,
And crown Him Lord of all.

Special significance is attached to the offspring here, *of Jesse,* who was the father of David and grandson of Ruth the Moabitess through her son Obed (Ruth 4:17). Jesse died, yet his name and family would not be extinct. By the time of Christ, the line of Jesse had fallen into poverty and obscurity, yet there sprouted from the decayed or fallen tree, a royal descendant to reign over the *Gentiles* (Job 14:7). Obed, the father of Jesse, had mingled blood of Jew and *Gentile* in his veins, his father, Boaz, being a Jew and his mother, Ruth, a Moabitess.

Thus, although the Messiah, the root

of Jesse, was born of a Jewish mother, and born and recognized as a Jew from the tribe of Judah (Matthew 2:2; John 4:9), yet because of His human descent from Obed and Jesse, He likewise had the same mingled blood, just as Timothy had (Acts 16:1; 2 Timothy 1:5). Thus, the Messiah is the rallying point for both Jew and Gentile, for He is no respecter of persons, and in Him is neither Jew nor Gentile.

* * *

A Root of David (Revelation 5:5; 22:16).

John had no hesitation in applying this name signifying a royal descent to the glorified Christ. Springing from Israel's illustrious king, the reign of Christ is depicted as the return of a golden age. The *oak,* symbol of Israel in the height of her glory as a nation, and, particularly of the monarchy of the house of David, still had life remaining in it after it had been cut down, and the rod, or sucker, that would spring from its roots would flourish once again in greater glory than in David's time, through David's greater Son, Jesus, King of Kings (Isaiah 6:13; Ezekiel 17:22).

After David's passing, his name is often used as the representation of *royalty,* just as the name Moses became the expression of *law.* Thus, Christ is named as both the *Root* and *Offspring* of David for in the former He is *divine,* and in the latter, *man.* He came as the *Root* and the *Branch* (Isaiah 11:1). (*See* further under *Branch.*)

Hail to the Lord's Anointed,
Great David's greater Son!
Hail, in the time appointed,
His reign on earth begun!

* * *

Rose (Song of Solomon 2:1).

While Christ is not specifically named as a *rose,* the saints of all ages have loved to see in Solomon's description of "The Rose of Sharon" an expressive symbol of His beauty and fragrance. Poets, for instance, have made much of this designation. Matthew Bridges in his famous hymn, "Crown Him with Many Crowns," speaks of Him as

> Fruit of the mystic Rose,
> As of that Rose the Stem,
> The Root from whence all mercy
>   flows,
> The Babe of Bethlehem.

Another hymnist has the beautiful stanza –

> I cannot breathe enough of Thee,
>   O gentle breeze of love;
> More fragrant than the myrtle tree
> The Rose of Sharon is to me,
>   The Balm of Heaven above.

Then there is a Christmas hymn, "A Great and Mighty Wonder," in which we have the line, "The Rose has come to blossom, which shall for aye endure." In his eminently spiritual commentary on the Song of Solomon, Moody Stuart has a most illuminating chapter on the symbolism of "The Rose of Sharon and the Lily of the Valleys" in which he says that,

> "Amongst flowers, the rose always and everywhere, with us now and still more in the East and of old, has held the foremost rank; and amongst the roses, the Rose of Sharon was chief. In the words of an ancient author, 'If a king were set over flowers, it would be the rose that should reign over them, being the ornament of the earth, the splendor of plants, the eye of flowers, the beauty of the field.' ... Amongst the works of God on earth, flowers are most expressed for beauty and delight, apart from necessity; created for the admiring mind of man, and not for the beasts that perish."

While the exact identification of the Rose of Sharon has ever been a much-vexed question, the sweet-scented Narcissus has been voted by the majority of scholars to have been the flower Solomon had in mind when he described the Beloved as such. Evidently this was the flower the Orientals had a fondness for, with both men and women always carrying blossoms with them which they were continually smelling.

Under this figure, then, Christ is before us as an object of pure admiration and delight to those who are His, and who love Him, and as the only One who can make "the desert to rejoice and blossom as the rose" (Isaiah 35:1). As the Babe in the manger He was Sharon's opening Rosebud, and as He developed it was as the Rosebud of Sharon, the one Rosebud that ever bloomed on earth without a worm in it, or any possibility of withering away. As the Holy One of God, Jesus –

> "Expanded into Sharon's fully blossomed Rose with every leaf shining in its loveliness, every petal perfect; and then the hand of the Father plucks it and transfers it to the Paradise above whence it came – now also a flower of earth, but fairer than all the flowers of Heaven. There for ever it both perfumes and beautifies the palace of the King eternal, immortal, invisible; and, amid admiring angels and archangels, Jesus still for ever says, 'I am the Rose of Sharon.' Happy Sharon – blessed Earth, to have furnished such a flower for Heaven!"

Robed in the beauty of His holiness, none can equal our roselike Redeemer for "His inherent beauty, His intrinsic majesty, and His ineffable glory." Truly, He is the chiefest of ten thousand to our souls! The mingling of all perfections can be found in Him who is our "Preciousness" (1 Peter 2:7 margin).

Every admirable and adorable grace arises and abides complete and replete in Him, in whom dwells all the fullness of the Godhead bodily (Colossians 2:9).

> Chiefest of ten thousand, all to heart
> and mind,
> The Rose of Sharon, ever fresh
> and fair –
> In Thee all glorious beauty is
> combined,
> All uncreated excellence is here.

✿　✿　✿

Ruler (Micah 5:2).

(*See* under name of *Governor.*)

S

Sanctification (1 Corinthians 1:30).

For all who have been saved through Christ's redeeming work no theme is more *à propos* than that of *sanctification,* the root idea of which means *setting apart* towards an object (John 17:19). For us, the *setting apart* is of a twofold nature. First, there is a separation from sin, then a separation *to* God. Because our Lord was perfectly holy, He had no need of separation *from* anything alien to God's holy mind and will, but He did fulfill the second requirement of separating Himself entirely *to* God. Thus when He prayed that for our sakes He sanctified Himself, He meant that He set Himself apart, unreservedly, for the holiness of His own.

It is essential to distinguish the three aspects of New Testament *sanctification* –

1. *Absolute* sanctification, divinely provided (1 Corinthians 1:30; 6:11; Hebrews 10:14).
2. *Positional* sanctification (Hebrews 13:12).
3. *Progressive* sanctification (John 17:17; 1 Thessalonians 5:23).

Thus we *are* sanctified, and yet we are *being* sanctified. All we are *positionally* in Christ is made *practical* by the Holy Spirit who is ever active in us translat-

ing *standing* in heaven to *state* on earth. It is as we realize that *we have been* sanctified and live in its power, that a daily sanctification is produced. Both aspects must be held with an even hand.

Further, Scripture is explicit as to the media of sanctification –

1. We are sanctified by *God* (John 10:36; 1 Thessalonians 4:3; 5:9; Jude 1).
2. We are sanctified by, and in, *Christ* (1 Corinthians 1:2; 6:11; John 17:19).
3. We are sanctified by the *Spirit* (Romans 15:16; 2 Thessalonians 2:13).
4. We are sanctified by the *Word* (John 17:19; 1 Timothy 4:5).
   Cleansing and *sanctifying* are both ascribed to the Word of God – the former completely removing all blemish and refinement – the latter setting an object before the soul (Ephesians 5:26).
5. We are sanctified by our own eager effort (Leviticus 11:44; 2 Corinthians 7:1).

As it is God's will that we should be sanctified, love to Him wills what He desires, then both He that sanctifieth and they who are being sanctified are one (Hebrews 2:11). God is the Origin of sanctification, and gave His Son that such might be accomplished both *for* us and *in* us. All related to our spiritual and eternal welfare comes to us through all Christ made possible as our Salvation and Sanctification.

> Jesus calls to separation,
> And Himself hath led the way;
> His own life the explanation,
> His own life the illustration –
> Who is ready to obey?

✿　✿　✿

Saviour (Luke 2:11; 1 Timothy 2:3; Titus 3:6).

What a wealth of meaning and hope is stored up in the simple phrase, "He is able to save" (Hebrews 7:25), and such ability is His because He was born a Saviour (Luke 2:11), and consequently died as the Saviour of the world (John 4:42; 1 John 4:14). There may be matters of minor importance about which the Church of Christ is not agreed, but the instinctive conviction of all Christendom is that Jesus alone is able to save sinners from the guilt and thralldom of sin. "When other helpers fail and comforts flee," men and women almost driven to despair because of the tightness of sin's grip upon them find in Him who died for our sins a "Help of the helpless."

The phrase *save to the uttermost* is unusual in that it only occurs twice in the New Testament. There is Paul's bold declaration that because Jesus ever lives to make intercession, He is able to save to the uttermost all who come to Him in penitence and faith. He can save to the uttermost of need for in Paul He saved the chief of sinners (1 Timothy 1:15). He can also save to the uttermost of time for He saved the dying thief in the last moments of his life (Luke 23:42, 43).

The other occasion where the words "to the uttermost" are used is in connection with the poor woman who was disabled through a spirit of infirmity. The same Greek words found in Hebrews 7:25 appear in Luke's description of this wretched woman's condition, "in no wise able to lift herself up" (Luke 13:11). The Holy Spirit did not allow this to happen by chance. This daughter of Abraham was in the synagogue on the Sabbath Day, and because of her disability it was most difficult for her to get there seeing she was to the uttermost bound, to the uttermost impotent, to the uttermost depressed through her satanic bondage for eighteen years. He

is the Saviour of the body, as well as the soul (Ephesians 5:23).

Jesus knew all about those long years past as He knew the exact number of years the impotent man had been suffering when He met him at the pool of Bethesda (John 5:7). In fact the same word for *infirmity* used of the woman in Luke 13, is used of this man in John 5. But although bound to the uttermost, the woman was delivered to the uttermost for she heard the all-commanding word of the Saviour, "Be loosed from thine infirmity." The word *loosed* is the same occurring in the verse declaring that Jesus was "manifested that He might destroy [loose, or undo] the works of the devil."

The basic significance of the term "to the uttermost," however, is that of completion. Ever-living, and ever-interceding, Jesus is able to save, and when He begins His work of salvation, He never relinquishes His sacred task.

> Love perfecteth what it begins,
> His power doth save me from my sins.

Uttermost, then, does not mean simply *forever*, but that as the matchless Saviour, Jesus has power to complete our salvation which will be achieved when He returns for His Church, and saves her from a sinning world so that she will sin no more. *Uttermost* means "utterly," perfectly saved that nothing should be wanted afterwards forever.

Further, Jesus is efficacious as a Saviour because of His Deity. In the persons of judges, God gave Israel "saviours" (Nehemiah 9:27), but because they were human they were not always able to deliver the people from their foes. But besides our Jehovah-Saviour, there is no Saviour for He is unique and incomparable. Then these saviours were limited to their own nation in their delivering power, but Jesus came as "the Saviour of the world" (1 John 4:14).

Born a Saviour, He appeared as *Christ the Lord* (Luke 2:11). Mary could rejoice in Him as *"God my Saviour"* (Luke 1:47) – a designation Paul was fond of using (1 Timothy 1:1; 2:3; 4:10; Titus 1:3; 2:10; 3:4, 6). Peter, likewise, exalted Jesus as "God our Saviour" (2 Peter 1:1), and as "our Lord and Saviour" (2 Peter 1:11; 3:2). Then what a great designation is the one Jude has, "the only wise God our Saviour" (Jude 25). As we have already indicated, the finished work of Calvary has unceasing potency to save, even the worst, because the blood shed there was "the blood of God" (Acts 20:28).

> Give the winds a mighty voice,
>   Jesus saves! Jesus saves!
> Let the nations now rejoice;
>   Jesus saves! Jesus saves!
> Shout salvation full and free,
> Highest hills and deepest caves;
> This our song of victory,
>   Jesus saves! Jesus saves!

* * *

Sceptre (Genesis 49:10; Numbers 24:17).

The word for "sceptre" implies a short royal rod or staff, or wand of office, as, for instance, "the golden sceptre" (Esther 4:11). It was the symbol of authority, as is *The Black Rod,* or *Royal Mace* in governmental circles, heavenly and earthly, today. At times, the *sceptre* represented royalty (Psalm 45:6; Amos 1:5). The reed thrust into Jesus' hand was an imitation sceptre of royalty (Matthew 27:29). In ancient times the sceptre, or staff, usually adorned with carvings, was handed down from father to son. Homer often refers to "sceptres," or walking sticks, magnificently ornamented. From these there developed the glittering, golden sceptres of kings and the *batons* of field-marshalls.

The following phrase, "nor a lawgiver from between his feet, until Shiloh come," calls for attention, seeing that *lawgiver* in many old versions is given as *ruler's staff.* "From between his feet" can signify, "from among his descendants," although there was an ancient custom of planting the sceptre or staff of a prince or chieftain in the ground between his feet as he sat. As for "the rod [or sceptre] of the wicked," the same represents evil power and influence (Psalm 125:3). In Balaam's parable, the Sceptre arising out of Judah is a Messianic prophecy of Him who, descending from Jacob, shall have world dominion (Numbers 24:17-20).

When Messiah appears, all failing to obey His loving sceptre will be crushed as with an iron sceptre (Psalm 2:9; Daniel 2:34, 35, 44; Matthew 21:44). The *iron* kingdom is to be broken as clay when Messiah holds out His "right sceptre" (Psalm 45:6; Isaiah 11:3, 4). When Moses held out his staff, or rod, or sceptre, symbol of his divinely appointed leadership of Israel and of authority as God's representative, mighty things happened. Still mightier things will transpire when Jesus comes to exercise His universal dominion. Then the sceptres of earth's rulers will yield to His royal sceptre, as the authoritative rod of Aaron swallowed up the rods of the Egyptian magicians (Exodus 7:10-13).

> Empires, temples, *sceptres,* thrones,
>   May they all for God be won:
> And in every human heart,
>   Father, let Thy kingdom come!

* * *

Second Man (1 Corinthians 15:47).

When our attention is directed to Jesus as a *man* (Romans 5:15; 1 Timothy 2:5), with emphasis on His humanity, the term is associated with some point of likeness or contrast between Jesus, and that other man, Adam (Romans 5:15, 19; 1 Corinthians 15:21, 47-49). In His descriptions as "the second

Man" and "last Adam" the singleness or the superiority of Jesus as *man* is prominent. In Jesus, man is impersonated in his true ideal as God originally designed Him. Christ is the representative man, the federal head of redeemed man. (*See* further under title *Adam, Last*).

* * *

Seed (Genesis 3:15; 2 Timothy 2:8).

In Scripture the term *seed* symbolizes a "son" or posterity (Ruth 4:12). Paul's favorite phrase for Israel was, "the seed of Abraham" (Romans 11:1). John uses the word in its highest sense when he applies it to the life of God within man's divine vitality. Peter employs the term to describe Scripture (1 Peter 1:23). *See* Luke 8:11; 1 John 3:9. *Seed*, which in the plant world, is that part from which the several species are propagated (Genesis 1:11). This word is applied to Christ in a twofold way.

The Seed of The Woman (Genesis 3:15; Isaiah 7:14; Matthew 1:25).

It is vastly important to observe the first occurrence in Scripture of a particular word, prophecy, or person. This is known as "The Law of First Mention." With the first sin on earth, there came the first promise and prophecy of a Saviour from sin, and with it His first designation in Scripture, namely, "*the seed* of the woman." It was Douglas Everett, poet of the early 18th century, who gave us the lines –

Large streams from little fountains
flow,
Tall oaks from little acorns grow.

Out of the "little acorn" of this first named *Seed*, the tall oaks of all other Messianic titles grew. A large stream of revelation of who the *Seed* would be, and of what He would accomplish flowed from "the little fountain" of this

initial prophecy. In the declaration Satan received we have the sum of the whole matter –

"I will put enmity between thee and the woman, and between thy seed and her seed; it shall bruise thy head, and thou shalt bruise his heel" (Genesis 3:15).

Triumph in the struggle with satanic forces was to be gained, not by mere human strength, as Jacob overcame the angel when he wrestled with him, but by the coming of One who would be "the Seed of a Woman," and round this title the rest of Scripture groups itself. As Ellicott's *Commentary* expresses it –

"Leave out these words, 'Thy seed and her seed,' and all the inspired teaching which follows would be an ever-widening river without a fountain-head. But necessarily with the Fall came the promise of restoration. Grace is no after-thought, but enters the world side by side with sin. Upon this foundation the rest of Holy Scripture is built, till revelation at last reaches its cornerstone in Christ."

Adam and Eve, the world's first sinners, were not the first to receive the message of salvation from sin, but Satan who had tempted them to disobey God's command. Purposely and consciously he led our first parents into transgression, and as he stood there, the tempter received the divine decree of his ultimate defeat. We have no hesitation of affirming that Satan knew who the *Seed* of the woman would be, and from that hour he set out to destroy the royal Seed from which the Messiah would come. When finally He appeared, born of a woman, Satan sought to destroy Him before the Cross because he knew by His death his own power would be destroyed, and the promise given to him in the Garden of Eden would be fulfilled (Hebrews 2:14, 15).

It was the renowned theologian Anselm Archbishop of Canterbury in the 10th century who said –

"God can form man in four ways –
1. From a man and a woman, as constant custom shows;
2. From neither man nor woman, as with Adam;
3. From man without the woman, as with Eve;
4. From a woman without man, as with the Son of God."

The first Adam was supernaturally created without a woman, while the last Adam was supernaturally created without a man, which brings us to the extraordinary statement, *her seed,* in what has been called "protevangelium." How absolutely unique is this foundational prophecy of redemption in Scripture! In most instances where *seed* is mentioned the reference is to the seed of a man, such as the seed of Abraham, the seed of Jacob, the seed of David, etc. But here we have the seed of a *woman,* which can only be interpreted as a prophecy of the virgin birth of Christ, and which was fulfilled when He was born of Mary (Matthew 1:16).

A natural conception would not have been a miracle, but Isaiah wrote that this would be the *sign* or miracle that "a virgin shall conceive, and bear a son" (Isaiah 7:14). There is not the slightest evidence that the Hebrew word for virgin, *almah,* has ever meant anything else but "virgin." Dealing with the incarnation of Christ, Paul was very careful to state that when God sent forth His Son into the world, that He was *made of a woman* – not of a man and a woman. Thus as "her seed," Jesus is the only Babe who had a human mother but *not* a human father (Luke 1:31-33). While the finite mind cannot penetrate the mystery of our Lord's virgin-conception when becoming man, faith believes that to God, nothing is impossible.

The Seed of Abraham (Galatians 3: 16; Hebrews 2:16; Genesis 12:7).

Paul, a Hebrew of the Hebrews, was intimately acquainted with the Hebrew *Scriptures,* and was therefore at home in writing about Abraham, who was the first to bear the name of *Hebrew.* The epistles of the apostle are studded with references to this "friend of God." Referring to the blessings God promised to give to Abraham and his own descendants, as well as to Gentiles, Paul said, "Now to Abraham and his seed were the promises made. He saith not, And to seeds, as of many; but as of one, *And to thy seed,* which is Christ" (Galatians 3:1). Blessing is never separable from Christ, whether for Jew or Gentile. Both *literal* Israel, and *spiritual* Israel, Christ's body, the Church, are enriched through the coming of Christ as the *Seed,* who is the representative Head of literal and spiritual Israel alike. Paul regarded all who are united to Christ by faith, as the true seed of Abraham.

The further verse, "verily he took not on him the nature of angels; but he took on him the seed of Abraham" (Hebrews 2:16), is given in the ASV as "verily not to angels doth he give help, but he giveth help to the seed of Abraham." The word *took* means to lay hold of, as with the hands, and carries the idea of undertaking or helping a cause. Christ came to help not angels, but men, especially those who are Abraham's seed, because they do the work of Abraham (John 8:39, 40). That Gentiles were not excluded from Christ's delivering hand is evident from a previous verse where Christ is spoken of as having tasted death for *every man* (Hebrews 2:9). Regenerated Jews and Gentiles form the spiritual seed of Abraham and are in "the church," praising the Deliverer (Hebrews 2:12).

The Seed of David.

Christ, as the seed of the woman, appeared, not only as "the son of Abraham," but as "the son of David" (Matthew 1:1). *See* under title *Root*. It was from the lineage of Mary, His mother, that He was "the Son of David" in reality as well as in heirship (Luke 1: 32). Paul affirms that "Jesus Christ our Lord . . . was made of the seed of David according to the flesh" (Romans 1:3), and that as "the seed of David He was raised from the dead" (2 Timothy 2:8). As the Seed and Son of Abraham, Christ is associated with the covenant blessings God gave the patriarch of old (Genesis 12:1-3). As the Seed, and Son of David, Christ is related to the prophecies of royalty and sovereignty, and He will yet sit on the throne of David (1 Chronicles 17:11-14; Luke 1:31-33).

Presently, Christ as the *Seed*, holds the secret and sustenance of life. The first occurrences of "seed" afford an insight into the value of seed. "Whose seed is in itself" – "The fruit tree yielding fruit after his kind, whose seed is in itself" (Genesis 1:11, 12). Christ as the Seed assures us that He Himself is the Source of life. But in order to produce fruit the seed has to be buried in the earth, a truth Christ applied to Himself as falling into the ground and dying in order to bring forth much fruit (John 12:24). As the Holy Seed He alone is our satisfying substance (Isaiah 6:13).

Isaiah, in his prophecy of Satan bruising the heel of Christ, which means being responsible for His terrible death, and of Christ, bruising the head of Satan, or robbing him, by His death, of his power over death and dominion over the souls of men, speaks of Christ's reward for His agony –

"He shall see his seed, he shall prolong his days, and the pleasure of the Lord shall prosper in his hand. He shall see of the travail of his soul, and shall be satisfied" (Isaiah 53:10, 11).

He shall see His seed. Such a phrase declares that His supreme sacrifice was the condition of spiritual parentage. He came as the Seed of a woman, in order that all born of man might become His children by His finished work and the regenerating ministry of the Holy Spirit (John 3:1-18). Are you not overwhelmed by the thought that as a born-again one, you are the *seed* of Christ (1 John 3: 9; 5:18), and that in you, He sees of the travail of His soul and is satisfied? (Hebrews 2:13). The truest explanation of this divine satisfaction can be found in His dying promise to the dying thief, "Today thou shalt be with me in paradise" (Luke 23:43). "The refreshment *after* travail, *because* of the travail, was already present to the sufferer's consciousness."

> The Life was forfeited when Adam
>   sinned,
>   "Dying, thou shalt die," had been
>   proclaimed;
> But, Oh! the love of God to Adam's
>   race,
> The Seed of the Woman – what
>   wondrous grace –
> Should come, and bruise the serpent's
>   head,
> And on the destroyer through death
>   should tread.

* * *

Servant (Isaiah 52:13-15; Matthew 12:18).

One of the most revealing insights into the character and mission of Christ the New Testament affords is the one He Himself gives us when, in the strife among His disciples as to who among them should be the greatest, He said, "I am among you as he that serveth"

(Luke 22:27). The great I AM – the "Chief" One (Luke 22:26) yet, He doth serve! What condescension on the part of the Creator who willingly wore the apron of humility (1 Peter 5:5, 6). First and foremost Christ was the Servant of Jehovah, as Isaiah portrays Him as Co-Creator with God, He yet became His chosen Servant who through His death and resurrection received greater exaltation than He possessed before His Incarnation. Because He was the willing, obedient, sacrificial Servant, He will become the universal Sovereign with "kings shutting their mouths at him" (Isaiah 52:13-15). All through His loving servitude here below, we hear the echo of His voice, "I delight to do Thy will, O my God" (Psalm 40:8; John 8: 29; Hebrews 10:9). In *King Henry VIII*, Shakespeare makes Cardinal Wolsey say –

> Had I but serv'd my God with half
> the zeal
> I serv'd my king, he would not in
> mine age
> Have left me naked to mine enemies.

Our blessed Lord served God with all His zeal, and was never left naked to His enemies. Did He not confess, "I am never alone for my father is with me"? Cavendish, in his *Negotiations of Thomas Wolsey*, quotes the Cardinal's own words – "Had I served God as diligently as I have served the King he would not have given me over in my gray hairs." How different the heavenly King treated His chosen Servant!

Matthew's record of Christ's application of Isaiah's prophecy of the Elect, Chosen Servant to Himself (Isaiah 42: 1-4; Matthew 12:17-21), emphasizes the divine prediction of the unostentatiousness of His ministry, in striking contrast with the accepted expectations of a Messiah with all the accustomed ostentatious trappings of royalty. Christ Himself declared that He came, "not

to be ministered unto, but to minister, and to give his life a ransom" for sinners (Matthew 20:28). *King, Prophet, and Servant* were unitary titles and fittingly described Him who was all three – A King like David, A Prophet like Moses, The Servant of Jehovah. The apostles, like the prophets, never failed to see in Jesus, "The Righteous Servant of Jehovah" (*see* Isaiah 53:11).

Service is not only something reserved for heaven (Revelation 22:3), and which angels alone can render (Psalm 103:21), but which is rendered here on earth with its results following on into heaven (Revelation 14:13). God gives us an example of the service here below in which He delights (Matthew 3: 17). For a full portrait of Christ as "the Servant of God" one must study carefully Mark's gospel which is, characteristically, one of *service* (10:35-45). The name of "Servant" is applicable to Jesus in at least three ways –

1. *In His Voluntary Submission.*

As the Son of God, He had not to be pressed or forced into doing God's will, neither did He serve Him under duress or reluctantly. Divine service was a delight to Him (Psalm 40:7, 8). Paul tells us that "He *took upon him* the form of a servant" (Philippians 2:7). Something of His condescension in this act is seen when we compare this phrase with "being in the form of God." Christ surrendered the glory of Deity for the condition of a servant. Actually, the term *servant* indicates one in contradistinction from one of a higher rank, and in His Incarnation, He emptied and humbled Himself, and condescended to perform such acts as are appropriate only to those who are servants. "I am among you as he that serveth."

Like the Hebrew servant of old, Christ gave His ear for perpetual service (Exodus 21:5, 6). His was the *bored* ear (Psalm 40:6), and, therefore, ever open to hear and obey the Father's voice (Isaiah 50:5). It is this blessed character of voluntary, willing, and sacrificial service which Jesus manifested that God would have us behold (Isaiah 61:1, 2; 42:1-7).

2. *In His Entire Dependence.*

A striking feature of Christ as His Father's Servant is that although He voluntarily undertook to serve Him, yet He never did anything independently of His Father. Did He not confess, "I can of mine own self do nothing"? (John 5: 19, 30). The unceasing prayerfulness of His life testifies to His entire dependence upon God for all He required as He served Him. Every step He took as the Servant of Jehovah was taken in prayer. This is evident at His baptism, and in the choice of the Twelve, and in His High Priestly Prayer (Luke 3:21; 6:12; 9:18-20; 22:32, 44; John 17).

3. *In His Steadfast Devotion.*

Even when He was only 12 years of age, we have Christ's declared intention to give His Father's service first priority (Luke 2:49), and from first to last He never flinched from the task set before Him. Anticipating the climax of His service at Calvary, He could pray, "I have finished the work thou gavest me to do" (John 17:4). What determination was His to complete a God-given commission? Others might fall away (John 6:66), or waver (Luke 9:57-62), or become offended at Him (John 6:61), but the compelling *must* was His. "I *must* finish the work of him who sent me." His immediate followers tried to divert Him from His course (Matthew 16:22, 23), but "he stedfastly set his face" to accomplish what He had been sent to do (Luke 9:51). His eyes looked straight on (Proverbs 4:25-27). He was the perfect Plowman who had put His hand to the plow, and never looked back, and who was consequently highly exalted by Him He faithfully served (Luke

9:62; Philippians 2:9-11). May God enable us to live and labor as good and faithful servants! (Colossians 3:22-24; Revelation 2:10). How apt are the appealing lines of Wordsworth! –

God for His service needeth not
    proud work of human skill;
They please Him best who labour
    most in Peace to do His will.
So let us strive to live! and to our
    spirits will be given
Such wings as, when our Saviour calls,
    shall bear us up to Heaven.

❖   ❖   ❖

Shepherd and Bishop (1 Peter 2:25).

Having been made the recipient of an astounding divine revelation of the Messiahship and Deity of Christ it is understandable that Peter should give us many unique names and titles of Him (Matthew 16:16-18). In fact, it would make a most profitable study to group together *all* the designations of Christ Peter uttered or wrote. When he described the Master whom he declared he loved as "the Shepherd and Bishop of our souls," he doubtless had in mind the *shepherd* image of Christ. Peter had heard Him speak of Himself as "the good shepherd" about to give His life for the sheep (John 10:11), and had seen Him in His risen form as "the great shepherd" (Hebrews 13:20), receiving from Him the commission to go forth and feed His sheep and lambs. Then as a faithful under-shepherd, the apostle could write of the coming of Jesus as "the chief Shepherd" to reward all those who had fed the flock (1 Peter 5:2-4). Such, then, is the background of Peter's appeal to straying sheep to return to their divine Shepherd and Bishop who never forsakes His flock. Compare Zechariah 11:16, 17 with 13:7.

The double designation Peter gives us of Christ is most impressive, and the two names are related:

Shepherd. For a fuller consideration

of this aspect of His ministry see under the title *Jehovah-Rohi* in *The Names of God*, Chapter One.

Bishop. The original of this name means *overseer*, and may be applied to one who inspects or *oversees* anything, such as, public works, execution of treaties, inspection of wares. In the New Testament it signifies those who are appointed to *watch over* the interests of the Church, and is applied by Peter to Christ as the great Guardian and Superintendent of His Church – the title of *Universal Bishop* belonging only to Him and to no Pope.

Bishop of our souls is a beautiful expression, and implies that the soul of the believer has His peculiar care. As sheep of the Shepherd, we are objects of special interest to Him as Bishop. In fact, not only the soul, but everything associated with the sheep is of importance to Him, and has His supervision and care (2 Timothy 1:12; 1 Peter 5:7). Therefore, it is with confidence that we can commit the keeping of our souls to our Shepherd and Bishop, assured that He will honor the trust reposed in Him (1 Peter 4:19).

*   *   *

Shiloh (Genesis 49:10).

Meaning "tranquillity" or "rest," Shiloh is often mentioned in the Old Testament as a sacred place ten miles from Bethel, and is now identified as the modern *Seitan* (Joshua 18:1; Psalm 78: 60). In Jacob's dying blessing, when he comes to his son Judah, from whose tribe Jesus was to come (Hebrews 7:14; Revelation 5:5), the patriarch has the phrase, "until Shiloh come; and unto him shall the gathering of the people be" (Genesis 49:8-12). *Sceptre, Lawgiver, Shiloh* are synonymous titles of the prophesied Messiah whose reign will be one of peace and rest. This is the One whom Simeon at the coming of Shiloh

said would be "the sign which shall be spoken against" (Luke 2:34).

Some writers suggest that *Shiloh* means "sent," and as a personal name may refer to Solomon, whose name has a similar meaning, and whose reign was one of peace. Christ, however, fulfills all Jacob declared of Judah (Isaiah 9:6). We deem *Shiloh* to be a fitting title of the promised Messiah who came as the Tabernacle of God among men bringing peace (Luke 2:14), making peace (Colossians 1:20), and bestowing peace (John 14:27). The Jewish Targum paraphrases Genesis 49:10 thus, "Until the time when the King Messiah comes to whom it belongeth." Thus, the whole verse foretells that Judah would retain authority until the advent of the rightful Ruler, the Messiah, to whom all peoples would gather, which they now do in Grace, and will do internationally when He returns to earth to usher in His reign of peace and tranquillity. Then, as Isaac Watts has taught us to sing –

People and realms of every tongue
Dwell on His love with sweetest song;
And infant voices shall proclaim
Their early blessings on His name.

*   *   *

Son (Colossians 1:13; Hebrews 3:6).

Under this particular title we reach the most important aspect of Christology. "Christ as a Son" and "The Son of God's Love" are phrases which, like a diamond, have many brilliant facets. Jesus often used the abbreviated form, "the Son." He is referred to as "*a* Son" (Hebrews 3:6), and "*the* Son" (Psalm 2:12; Hebrews 1:8). In human relationships, a *son* is a human male born of a woman, and in respect to His humanity, Christ was the Son of Mary, having been born of her (Luke 1:35), but as the "Son of God" while an eternal relationship is implied, "the thought is centered in the personal Being of the Son, and not in His generation" says Westcott in his comment on John 1:14. "Christ is the Only one Son." He is the *only* Son besides whom the Father has none. Used of Christ, then, *the Son* implies the absolute relationship of Sonship to Fatherhood. Let us now try to separate the various *Son* combinations.

His Son, Jesus Christ (1 John 1:7; 3:23).

This combination of *Jesus* and *Christ* conveys the ideas of true humanity and Messiahship. In the phrase "Jesus Christ His Son" (1:7), *Christ* is not in some old versions, for the *human* name, *Jesus*, shows that His blood is avaiable for men and the *divine* name, *His Son*, shows that it is efficacious. Thus John emphasizes the necessity of faith in Jesus Christ, God's Son, "That we should believe on the *name*" (1 John 3:23 and John 1:12). The term *believe* indicates the present and continuous activity of faith, and not a mere mental assent to the scriptural truth that Jesus Christ is God's Son. To believe on, or believe in, means *into*, and thus indicates more than a mere acceptance of a statement. To believe on the Lord Jesus Christ (Acts 16:30, 31) implies more than believing the facts of His historic life, or of His saving power, but a belief *into* Him, or acceptance of Him as a personal Saviour for a present and eternal salvation.

"*Believe* on the *name*," then, expresses a definite, unequivocal surrender to Him who bears it, for *name* represents the sum of the qualities of which mark the nature and character of Him who, as God's Son, is *Jesus* and *Christ;* and faith accepts as true the revelation contained in these titles (John 20:31).

Son of the Father (2 John 3).

In this remarkable benediction we have double triads – Triad of Attributes,

grace, mercy, peace; and a Triad of Appellations –

"God the Father." A more common expression is "God our Father" (Matthew 6:9). (*See* under title *Father*.)

"The Lord Jesus Christ." The connecting "and" brings out the twofold relationship to the Father and Son. We have already seen (consult under title *Christ*) that this full written title provides a further Triad of Aspects –

Authority, as LORD
Manhood, as JESUS
Glory, as CHRIST.

"The Son of the Father." This phrase occurs nowhere else. The names *Father and Son* are brought together in this form, "the Father and the Son" (1 John 1:3; 2:22, 23; John 1:18), a phrase suggestive of the happy, perfect relationship between the two (Amos 3:3).

Son of the Blessed (Mark 14:61).

It was the high priest who asked Jesus at His trial before the Sanhedrin, "Art thou the Christ, the Son of the Blessed?" Jesus answered, "I AM." It is Mark alone who gives us this name of God, *The Blessed*, although *blessed* is used of Him in other ways. (*See* Romans 9:5; Ephesians 1:3; 1 Timothy 1:11.) Confined to God, the title *Blessed* implies praising and extolling Him for all He is in Himself and for all He is able to accomplish among men and nations. The particular Greek word used here for *blessed* is applied only to God (Luke 1:68; 2 Corinthians 1:3). Truly, He has blessed us with all spiritual blessings in His Son. In the Old Testament, *blessed* is often used of persons (Ruth 2:20).

Son of the Highest (Luke 1:32).

Among the birth-names of Jesus which Gabriel gave to Mary was this exalted one. "He shall be called the Son of the Highest." Gabriel goes on to designate the Holy Spirit as "the power of the Highest" (Luke 1:35). *Highest*, meaning ascendancy over all others, is used as a name of God, "the Highest gave his voice" (Psalms 18:13; 87:5). He is "higher than the highest" (Ecclesiastes 5:8). Those who emulate Christ's example are called by Him, "children of the Highest" (Luke 6:35). He also spoke of John the Baptist as "the prophet of the Highest" (Luke 1:76).

Son of the Most High God (Mark 5:7).

The remarkable thing is that evil lips uttered this most honorable title of God. Although this is the first occurrence of the name in the New Testament, it was the divine name used in the earliest stage of the patriarchal worship of one Supreme Deity. For instance, Melchizedek is described as the priest of "the most high God" (Genesis 14:18). Balaam and Moses employed it (Numbers 24:16; Deuteronomy 32:8), as did the psalmist and the prophets. How effective this great Name was in the exorcism of the demons from the demoniac! (See further under *The Names of God — Jehovah-Heleyon.*) Applied to God, then, *Most High* is a superlative designation implying the *loftiest* (Acts 7:48). "Lead me to the rock that is higher than I" (Psalm 61:2).

Son, My Beloved (Matthew 3:17; Mark 12:6).

The original word for *beloved* is akin to one of the Greek words for *dear*. Thus the asv renders "his dear Son" as "the Son of his love" (Colossians 1:13). Used also of, and among, believers (Romans 1:7; 1 Corinthians 4:14; 10:14), *beloved*, when applied to Jesus by His Father, expresses the deep love making them One. "Dearly beloved" and "well beloved" express the same eternal love. Such an epithet of divine commendation of the Son appears frequently. When He commenced His public ministry at His baptism, God's voice from the opened heavens proclaimed Jesus to be His beloved Son, in whom He was well pleased, inferring that all through the foregoing 30 years in Nazareth, His life had been lived in harmony with God's will (Luke 2:49; Matthew 3:14-17).

Then at the Transfiguration there was the same tribute by God as to Jesus being the "beloved Son" in whom He was well pleased (2 Peter 1:17, 18) — a tribute Peter himself heard with profound and reverential satisfaction when he had been present on that holy mount (Matthew 17:1-9). Further, there was our Lord's assertion that He was His Father's dearly beloved Son. In the Parable of the Vineyard Owner (Mark 12:1-8), many slaves were sent one after another to the rebellious husbandmen. Then at last the owner sent his only son, "his well beloved," thinking respect would be shown him, but the husbandmen killed him. Dr. Warfield says that the term "well beloved," or "beloved one," is "not so much designatory of affection as of that on which special affection is grounded, and is therefore practically equivalent to 'only begotten,' or 'unique,' or 'my sole, unique, Son.' It is possible that it is by this epithet that God designates this His Son on both of the occasions when He spoke from Heaven in order to point Him out and mark Him as His own (Mark 1:11; 9:7)." This Messianic designation, then, "This is my Beloved Son!" implies that He stands out among all others who may be called sons as in a unique and unapproached sense *the* Son of God (*see* 1 John 3:1-3).

No one can read the writings of Paul without being impressed with his deep understanding of, and gratitude for, the love of the Saviour towards him. Unceasingly he was constrained by such a love to give his utmost for the Highest. He was ever overawed by the fact that the Son of God loved him and gave Himself for his salvation (Galatians 2:20). To his mind, such love passed all human understanding, and he sought to reciprocate the love showered upon him in, and by, Christ. It was quite natural, therefore, when writing about the Lord who loved him, and whom he dearly loved, to refer to Him in terms of endearment. Thus, when the apostle came to magnifying the matchless love and grace manifested towards him, he wrote to the Ephesians, "God hath made us accepted in the beloved," or, as Way translates Ephesians 1:6 –

> "The grace that He so freely gave us
> In the person of His Belovéd."

Here, the name appears in its simple majesty without qualification – *beloved!* In his sister epistle to the Colossians, Paul speaks of his Beloved, as "The Son of God's love" (Colossians 1:13). It is only in such a perfect Son that a term like *beloved* comes to its rights. Then, as the apostle reminds us, it is only through this Object of divine love, that divine grace is communicated unto men. It was only at the cost of the blood of the Beloved that redemption for sin-bound souls was accomplished. "The epithet of *Beloved* tells us what Christ is from the point of view of God – *Saviour* is a designation of Him from the point of view of man. He is God's own unique One, the Object of His supreme choice, who stands related to Him in the intimacy of appropriating love." How blessed we are if we can sing out of a deep experience of His saving grace! –

> Oh, I am my Beloved's
> And my Beloved's mine;
> He brings a poor vile sinner
> Into His house of wine.

Son, Only Begotten (John 1:14, 18; 3:16).

(*See* under title *Only Begotten*.)

Son of the Living God (Matthew 16:16; 1 Thessalonians 1:9).

In his astounding confession of the identity of Jesus Peter went beyond what others at this time believed, namely, that he was *the Christ,* when he declared, "Thou art . . . the Son of the *living* God." We have seen how titles like *Christ* and *the Son of God* testify to the supernaturalness of His Person, the revelation of which Peter received from heaven, and was highly commended by Christ for confessing (Matthew 16:19). What impresses us about this designation is the term *living,* for God would not be *God* if He were not alive. This important addition, "The Son of the *Living God*" implies as the result of a distinct revelation from God, that Peter recognized that the essential and eternal life of God was *in* His Son: that, in contrast to the names of the *dead* prophets Jesus was thought to represent, He was the Son of the *living* God.

The term *living* was given to Him by Paul in 1 Thessalonians 1:9 as the true God to distinguish Him from lifeless idols; but as the Source of Life – temporal, spiritual, and eternal, *living* is often applied to Him in the Old Testament (Joshua 3:10; 1 Samuel 17:26, 36; Jeremiah 10:10). In his noble confession Peter not only expressed his belief that Jesus was the long-expected *Messiah,* but also in his belief in His Deity as the *Son of God,* and as the personification of Him who is the Creator and Controller of life.

Son of God (Matthew 8:29; 14:33; John 10:36).

This grand title expressing Christ's divine and personal glory occurs some 50 times in Scripture. The title is applied to the first Adam as well as to the last Adam in Luke's human genealogy of Jesus through Mary His mother – "Adam, which was the son of God" (Luke 3:38). Applied to the first man, this title was an expression of his place and dignity in Creation, as God's masterpiece. The mysterious fourth person in the fiery furnace who preserved Daniel's three friends from being burned to death had a "form like the Son of God" (Daniel 3:25). While angels are also styled sons of God" (Job 2:1; 38:7), yet no single angel is ever named *Son of God,* much less, *"The* Son of God." Angels are thus named either because they are creatures of God's creation, or being spiritual beings, they resemble God, who is a Spirit (John 4:24). Through matchless grace believers are called "the sons of God" (John 1:12; 1 John 3:1-3). Such a title becomes ours only by *adoption,* but "Son of God" belongs to the Saviour by *inherent* right.

No title of our Blessed Lord is more wonderful than "the Son of God," because it represents to us the mode of existence of the Second Person of the Trinity, and His relation to the First. Deriving His own eternal being from God the Father (John 6:57; 7:29), He is, therefore, by the gift of eternal generation rightly called the true and proper Son of God. As God's eternal Son, Jesus came as God's Representative to do God's will in the world, and the Vehicle of God's grace to guilty men. Although He frequently referred to God as His *Father,* He rarely used the title of "Son of God" of Himself (*see* John 10:36), yet when others used it of Him, He accepted it in such a way as to assert His claim to it. In the majority of occurrences of the title in the gospels it is used to describe the impression He made upon others. His was a supernatural relationship with God, revealing itself in supernatural power. His divine Sonship is related to His supernatural conception (Luke 1:35), and so when Gabriel announced to Mary that her Holy Son was to be a supernatural product, the supernatural advent was heralded by the declaration of His title

as "the Son of God," with all its Messianic implications (Luke 1:32, 33).

Further, Christ's titles as "the Son," "the Son of God," "the Son of the Most High God," all alike affirm His preexistence, supernatural origin, and Deity. To the disciples He was the omniscient, omnipotent Son of God. John's gospel, for example, carries many references to Christ as "the Son," and can be, therefore, rightly called, *The Gospel of the Deity of Christ.* The Messianic designation, "Son of God," comes fully to its rights in this gospel, as numerous references prove (1:34, 49; 5:25). To the apostle, the *Son* of God was *God* the Son. "Obviously to John the 'Son of God' is Himself God," says Dr. Warfield, "and what is thus implied in the current use of this title is openly declared by John when he declares that 'the Son of God, Jesus Christ' is 'the true God and eternal life' (1 John 5:20)."

It is also very profitable to trace the connections, proofs, and witnesses to Jesus as "the Son of God."

> *Matthew* connects with the title with the calling out of Jesus from Egypt (2:15);
> *Mark,* with the commencement of His public ministry (1:1);
> *Luke,* with the Incarnation of Jesus (1:35);
> *John* traces the Sonship of Jesus before time began (1:1, 14).

The one great end of our Lord's life as "God manifest in flesh" was to prove that He was the Son of God. Briefly consider the various events associated with "the days of His flesh" —

1. *His Birth.* At the Annunciation, what was beyond human comprehension was shown to be possible with God, namely, that as a Child, Jesus would be born of a virgin as the Son of God (Luke 1:34, 35).

2. *His Baptism.* When in the water

of Jordan, God's voice from heaven expressly declared that the One John was immersing was the Beloved Son of God – which became the ground of His temptation after the baptism (Matthew 3:17; 4:3, 6; Luke 3:21).

3. *His Ministry.* During the three years of His labors many testified while in His presence that He was indeed the Son of God with power. His teachings and miracles drew such a witness from His disciples (Matthew 16:16). They recognized His supernatural origin as God's Son and therefore His supernatural gifts and power. Further, demons knew Him to be the Son of God. As soon as they caught sight of Him, immediately they echoed the testimony of the unseen, satanic world as to his divine Sonship (Mark 3:11; 5:7; Luke 4:41). Nathanael and Mary were among others who declared Jesus to be "the Son of God" (John 1:49; 11:27).

4. *His Death.* The prime cause of His crucifixion was His claim to this title, and His death drew forth the acknowledgment that He was "the Son of God" (Matthew 27:54; John 19:7). The centurion's natural expression spoke of his awe in the presence of the supernatural. *See* 1 John 3:8.

5. *His Resurrection.* As the Son of God, Jesus is "the heir of all things" (Hebrews 1:2), even of power to raise the dead as "the Resurrection and the Life" (John 5:25; 11:25). He declared that He had power to raise Himself from the dead (John 2:19; Matthew 12:40), and His resurrection was clear proof that He was "the Son of God" (Romans 1:4). Embedded in Paul's epistles is the conception of the Deity of Christ – the One clothed with all the attributes of God. Paul saw in Christ, above all, the Son of God in the eminent sense of such a title (Acts 9:20). John, in his vision of Christ risen and exalted on high, saw and heard Him speaking to His Church,

as the Son of God, from the right hand of power (Revelation 2:18).

What are the personal and practical issues of the absorbing theme of divine Sonship?

It must be our *faith* (1 John 5:13).
It is our source of *life* (1 John 5:12).
It should ever be our *testimony* (1 John 4:15).
It is our only avenue of victory over the *world* (1 John 5:5).

The question each heart must answer is – "Dost thou believe on the Son of God?" (John 9:35). The reply given is associated with three things –

Reception of the Gospel and consequence of rejection (John 20:31).
Character of those who answer aright (Galatians 2:20).
Fellowship with God, here and hereafter (1 John 4:15; 5:20).

May we never be ashamed to be found among those who unhesitantly confess, "I believe that Jesus Christ is the Son of God"! (Acts 8:37).

Son of Man (Matthew 8:20; Mark 2:10; John 1:51; 3:13).

Altogether, this further title of Christ occurs 89 times in the New Testament. Out of this number, 85 references are to be found in the four gospels, where it is directly applied by Christ to Himself; it is not even once applied by others to Him. Outside the gospels the title occurs 4 times. Stephen saw Him in Glory as *"the Son of man* standing at the right hand of God" (Acts 7:56). It is only used once in the epistles, namely, in Hebrews 2:6 as a quotation from Psalm 8. Then, twice in *Revelation* John applies it to the glorified Lord (Revelation 1:13; 14:14).

Both Dr. Graham Scroggie and Dr.

E. Bullinger suggest that the first and last occurrences of this title present an impressive contrast, as the reader will find by turning to these references –

> Matthew 8:20 with 26:64.
> Mark 2:10 with 14:62.
> Luke 5:24 with 24:7.
> John 1:51 with 13:31.
> Matthew 8:20 ASV with Revelation 14:14 ASV.

Although the title the *Son of Man* was the favorite one of Jesus, He was not the originator because surprisingly enough, it occurs more often in the Old Testament than in the New Testament. Both Moses and Job used the term (Numbers 23:19; Job 25:6; 35:8). Then it appears in the Psalms (8:4; 80:17), which are an incomparable expression both of the lowliness and loftiness of human nature. The reference in Psalm 8 relates to the dominion of the earth. As the Possessor of it, "dominion" over it is given to Him, and as "heir of all things" in virtue of which all things are to be put under His feet (Hebrews 2:8, 9). The scene in this important Messianic psalm is that of a reign universal in extent, and grand in character, for here we have the earthly glory which Messiah takes as "the Son of Man" and which is a reign we are to share (Ephesians 1:11). Such a psalm, then, may have been in the heart of the youthful Jesus as He anticipated His emergence not only as the long-expected Messiah, but as man's perfect representative.

Actually, the designation *Son of Man* means Son of *Adam*, and it was to the "first man, Adam" that dominion was given over the works of the Creator (Genesis 1:26). "Through the Fall, however, this dominion was forfeited, and lost, and is now in abeyance; no one son of Adam having any right to universal dominion. Hence, all the chaos and conflicts between men and nations,

which must continue until He comes Whose right it is to rule in the earth (Ezekiel 21:27)." Dictators have arisen bent on world supremacy but all have failed. During "The Great Tribulation" the Antichrist will succeed for a brief period to exercise universal power but will be overthrown when "the second man" – "the last Adam" – "the Son of man" returns to take over world dominion, which has ever been His in the counsels of God.

Coming to Ezekiel, we find the title before us mentioned exactly 100 times, and always without the article *the*. When the title is used by, or of, Christ it is always with the article. Ezekiel applies the title to himself as a designation of his prophetic mission. "It expresses the contrast between what Ezekiel is in himself and what God will make of him, and to make his mission appear to him not as his own, but as the work of God, and thus to lift him up, whenever the flesh threatens to faint and fail." What an inspiration Ezekiel's references to himself as a man sustained by God must have been to the Prophet of Galilee! Bullinger observes that "Son of Man" used *without* the article denotes a human being, as descended of Adam, and that in Ezekiel, it is used in contrast with celestial living creatures, but that *with* the article, as used by Christ it denotes, dispensationally, His succession to the universal dominion "the first man" lost (Genesis 1:28; Psalm 8:4-8; Ezekiel 1).

Daniel is another prophet who employs the appellation "Son of Man" 3 times in his prophecy, and who put on record messages from the same high place in the same terms as Ezekiel. Two of Daniel's references are related to himself, and in the third to the Messiah of whom he made some remarkable predictions. Somewhat afraid of the approach of the angelic Gabriel, Daniel heard the voice "Understand, O son of man!" (8:17), and the words raised the trembling spirit of God's servant. The reference in Daniel 7:13, 14 is a remarkable foregleam of Matthew 24:30, and as we compare the words of Daniel with those of Jesus to the high priest at His trial, the echo of the past cannot be mistaken. Ere long, the tribes of earth shall see the Son of Man coming on the clouds of heaven with power and great glory. With all of these Old Testament references to the Son of Man before Christ, we can see how easy it was to borrow such a title from the prophets to express His consciousness of belonging to the same prophetic line, and of seeing in Himself the true Messiah they portrayed.

Distinctions exist between the titles "Son of God" and "Son of Man" as an examination of references proves.

1. As the *Son of God,* Christ is "heir of all things" and invested with "all power" (Matthew 28:18; Hebrews 1:2).

   As the *Son of Man,* earthly relationships and dominion over the earth are uppermost (Hebrews 2: 8, 9; Psalm 8:1-8; Ephesians 1:11).

2. As the *Son of God,* He has life and power to communicate that life both physically and spiritually (John 5:25, 26; 17:1, 2).

   As the *Son of Man,* all authority to execute judgment is given Him by the Father (John 5:27; Acts 17:31).

3. As the *Son of God,* He has a claim to Deity or equality with God, with this unique relationship constituting the only ground of His appeal to learn of God (Matthew 11:27-30).

   As the *Son of Man,* He will come in glory to Israel, and to the Gentiles on earth when He comes to rule (Matthew 13:41; 24:30; 25:31).

Under this self-designation Christ asserts for Himself –

1. Power over the religious ordinances of Israel (Mark 2:28).
2. Divine prerogative of forgiving sins (Mark 2:10).
3. Career of suffering, betrayal and death (Mark 9:31; 10:33; 14: 21).
4. Resurrection from the grave (Mark 10:34).
5. Ascension to the right hand of power (Mark 14:62).
6. Return in great power and glory (Mark 8:38; 13:26).

As employed by Jesus, *Son of Man* not only expressed His personal qualities as a man, but identified Him with the humanity He came to redeem. Dr. James Stalker, whose volume *The Teaching of Jesus Concerning Himself* is a classic on the theme of Christology, says that –

"A reason why Jesus fixed upon this title as His favourite self-designation may have been that it half concealed as well as half revealed His secret. Of the direct names for the Messiah He was usually shy, no doubt chiefly because His contemporaries were not prepared for an open declaration of Himself in this character, but at all stages of His ministry He called Himself the Son of Man without hesitation. The inference seems to be, that, while the phrase expressed much to Himself, and must have meant more and more for those immediately associated with Him, it did not convey a Messianic claim to the public ear (Matthew 16:13; John 13:31). That He was the Son of Man did not evidently mean for all that He claimed to be the Messiah."

While universal dominion and absolute sovereignty are glorious resting upon this exceedingly interesting title – one, moreover, with which every human being is concerned seeing that universal judgment and authority to execute same have been given to Jesus as "the Son of man" (John 5:22; Acts 17:31), yet it is a title He may have picked out from all others predicting Him in ancient Scriptures with which He was so familiar because it gave expression to His sense of connection with all men. He felt Himself to be identified with all as their Brother, their Fellow-Sufferer, their Representative, their Champion, and, in some respects, the deepest word He ever spoke was –

"The Son of Man also came not to be ministered unto, but to minister, and to give his life a ransom for many" (Mark 10:45 ASV).

Is it not comforting to us that Jesus has the sympathy of a common nature (Hebrews 2:14-18), and that He knew all about the trials and temptations common to man?

And He proclaims Himself in future glory no less than the universal King seated on the throne of judgment for the quick and dead (Matthew 25:31; Mark 8:38;).

There are further titles given to Jesus in respect to Sonship, all of which are associated with human relationships. For instance, He is described as –

The Son of Abraham (Matthew 1:1).

Jesus was thus named because He had been promised to Abraham (Luke 1:73; Romans 9:7, 9; Genesis 12:3; 22:18), and because he rejoiced to see the day of Jesus (John 8:56-58). Abraham was heir to the land (Genesis 15:18) – Jesus is Heir of all things (*See* further under title *Seed*).

The Son of David (Matthew 1:1; 21: 9).

This royal title is found 15 times in the gospels, and is a title more confined in its application than the broader and more comprehensive one *Son of Man* – Matthew uses it 8 times, Mark, 3 times, Luke, 3 times, John, only once.

There is a fourfold revelation of the Sonship of Jesus, exalting Him as the Immutable One –

Son of God – title of personal and divine glory;
Son of the Father – expressing an ever-abiding relationship;
Son of Man – the One who became Man, and who will be the gracious Ruler over the millennial earth;
Son of David – the Fulfiller of every gracious promise and prediction given to God's ancient people.

Christ is called "the Son of David" because He was promised directly to David (2 Samuel 7:12, 14). The illustrious name, *David*, commences the New Testament and ends it (Matthew 1:1; Revelation 22:16).

Son of Joseph (Luke 3:23; 4:22).

While scholars have difficulty in determining the exact significance of this item in the genealogy of Mary, all we want to point out is that Luke, the beloved physician, who doubtless learned from Mary herself all the particulars about the conception and birth of Jesus, was careful to say that Jesus was *supposed* to be "the son of Joseph" (Luke 3:23). Accepting, as he did, the miraculous conception of Jesus, Luke knew that Joseph was not His natural father but that God, only, was His Father. Although Jesus became the Son of Man, He was not the son of a man. He never entered the world along the avenue of natural generation for He was conceived of the Holy Spirit (Luke 1:35). Joseph himself received a divine revelation as to the conception of Jesus (Matthew

1:18-25), and from the time of His birth, acted lovingly is His foster father. *See* Luke 2:33.

It is quite true that Joseph and Mary are spoken of as His *parents* (Luke 2:41), but Luke was careful to say, "Joseph and His mother knew not" of His tarrying behind in the temple – and not "His father and mother knew not." Christ's own question to Joseph and Mary indicates His recognition of only one Father – "Wist ye not that I must be about *my Father's* business?" Yet He was ever obedient and dutiful to those who had the care of Him for we read that Jesus returned with them and was "subject unto them" (Luke 2:51), and with the return, the curtain of silence falls upon this humble family in Nazareth for eighteen years! Whenever the family is mentioned after Jesus, at the age of 30, left it, Joseph is not directly mentioned again (Mark 6:3; Luke 8:20, 21; John 2:1; Acts 1:14). The probability is that Joseph died sometime before Jesus left Nazareth for His public ministry. (*See* further under *Young Child*).

Son of Mary (Matthew 1:25; Mark 6:3).

In Matthew's account of the birth of "the Holy Child Jesus" He is named as Mary's *firstborn son,* and yet as God's Son – "Out of Egypt have I called my Son" (1:25; 2:15) – and He was both, for Deity and humanity are here combined. Mark refers to Jesus as "The son of Mary" (Mark 6:3), and Mary herself called Him her son, "Son, why hast thou thus dealt with us?" (Luke 2:48). On the cross at which Mary stood as He died, among His last words were, "Woman, behold thy son!" Then, giving His mother, who had cared for Him some 30 years, into the care of His close disciple, John, He said, "Behold thy mother!" (John 19:25-27).

While Mary was praised by Gabriel as being graciously accepted by God as

the woman to be the mother of the promised Messiah, and it was said of her, "Blessed art thou among women!" (Luke 1:28), the predominant veneration and effectual intercession of Mary in heaven as taught by the church of Rome is absolutely alien to the tenor of the New Testament. When the wise men from the East came to the house where they found "the young child with Mary his mother," they did not share their worship and gifts with both. "They worshipped *him.* . . . they presented unto *him* gifts" (Matthew 2:11). As to Mary interceding with the Lord on our behalf, such teaching is proved erroneous by such statements as, "*He* ever liveth to make intercession for us" (Hebrews 7:25). "For there is one mediator between God and men, the man Christ Jesus" (1 Timothy 2:5).

Both Joseph and Mary marveled over the wonderful things spoken of Jesus, and failed to understand the significance of the things He said about Himself (Luke 2:33, 50). Mary, however, came to trust and obey her firstborn Son after He became the mighty Prophet from Nazareth –

"Whatsoever He saith unto you, do it" (John 2:5)

The language of Jesus may seem to appear somewhat harsh in His reply to His mother's statement, "They have no wine." Perhaps, even at this point she had not discerned her Son's devotion to a Higher Parentage. The form of address, *Woman,* is equivalent to *Lady,* and in the Greek is a title of respect, used even in addressing queens. As for His gentle rebuke, Mary must learn that now His ministry as Messiah had actually begun, not even His own mother may presume to suggest or control His course of action. (*See* Matthew 12:46; Luke 11:27, 28).

While under her loving care in Nazareth, He was all an obedient Son should be, and everybody liked Him for He grew in "favor with *God* and *man*." All too few sons of men are liked by both. The arms of loving, wondering Mary were Christ's first cradle, and as He "increased in wisdom and stature," or in other words, grew up mentally and physically, because of all He *actually* was, He lived and acted as Mary's beloved Son, as well as God's beloved Son. John Keble wrote of Him that He was –

A Son that never did amiss,
That never shamed His mother's kiss,
Nor crossed her fondest prayer.

* * *

Star (Numbers 24:17).

Students of the Scriptures are deeply impressed with the variety of metaphors used to depict the aspects of Messianic predictions and how, ultimately, they all find their fulfillment in Him around whom they gather. Among the earliest symbols used of His coming into the world is that to be found in Balaam's prophecy –

"There shall come forth a star out of Jacob" (Numbers 24:17 ASV).

The verse contains twin titles of *Star* and *Sceptre* – the latter being the symbol of authority (Genesis 49:10; Psalm 110:2). (*See* under title *Sceptre*.) The former, however, is a common symbol in Scripture of a brilliant ruler (Isaiah 9:2; 14:12; Matthew 24:29).

While the prediction of the *Star* may refer in the first place to David, who was certainly of star quality in his smiting of Moab and Edom (2 Samuel 8:2, 14; Psalm 60:8), the larger application of the figure used concerns the arising of David's greater Son. From early times Jewish commentators have interpreted the prophecy of the *Star* as Messianic. Not long after the time of our Lord, a

false Messiah appeared who took the name of *Bar-cochba*, meaning "the son of a star," a designation he no doubt took from Balaam's prophecy.

The Christian interpretation is that the prophecy of Balaam was fulfilled when Jesus appeared as "a light to lighten the Gentiles." The star guiding the wise men to the feet of the Holy Child Jesus is spoken of as "*his* star" (Matthew 2:2). But *He Himself,* and not the star which the Magi saw at His birth, is the fulfillment of Balaam's prediction. An illustration of how Jesus often related prophecy to Himself is found in the naming of Himself as "the bright and morning star" (Revelation 22:16). (*See* under titles *Bright, Morning Star,* and *Dayspring.*) Jesus also used the symbol of the *Star* to describe His Church (Revelation 3:1).

That sacred symbols can be abused, or wrongly applied, is only too evident in these modern times. For instance, if a singer records a song which reaches the so-called "Top Ten" he is hailed over-night as a *star.* Yet he has not as much brilliance about him as the elusive firefly! Further, the rock-opera *Jesus Christ Super-Star* is a most irreverent and sometimes raucous dramatization of the last days of our blessed Lord. Some of the lines in this play, which drew large crowds, are not only un-Christian, but anti-Christian and blasphemous.

Without doubt, as "The Star out of Jacob" and as "The Bright and Morning Star," Jesus Christ is the *Superstar,* and likewise the *Super-Sun,* who will arise with healing in His wings, and whose *sceptre* will be one of a universal rule in righteousness (Hebrews 1:8). For the true child of God, Jesus is reverenced as the Star of Hope, the Star of Faith, the Star of Peace, the Star Divine. We repeat His name, "softly to ourselves as some sweet spell," because –

In the hour of gloom it shines before us,

Like that welcome star that gilds
the morn;
Vanish'd hope and joy it will restore us,
Till their sudden rays our soul adorn.

❊ ❊ ❊

Stone (Matthew 21:42; 1 Peter 2:8).

As the Bible was written in the East by those familiar with all its natural contours and local customs and varied characteristic features, it is understandable that much of what the writers of the Bible saw around them was used to symbolize spiritual truth. For instance, our Lord implied that He was the *Stone* the builders had rejected (Matthew 21:42). Now, Palestine was a very rocky and stony country in our Lord's day, and stones were put to all kinds of uses:

Jacob made a pillow of a stone (Genesis 28:18).
People used stone (or "flint" ASV) as knives and implements (Exodus 4:25).
In building there were foundation and corner-stones. (*See* under titles *Cornerstone* and *Foundation.*)
Stone-dressing and masonry were recognized trades (2 Samuel 5:11).
Stones were used in fighting, as Goliath experienced (1 Samuel 17:49).
Stoning to death was a common means of execution (Acts 7:58, 59).
Stone pillars, monuments, and landmarks were common (Genesis 31:45; Joshua 15:6).

With such a background it is not difficult to grasp the significance of *Stone* when used of Christ or of ourselves. Daniel prophesied that when the Messiah ushers in His universal reign that He is coming as a *Stone* to destroy the Gentile world-system in its final form by a sudden and irremediable crash (Daniel 2:34, 35). Then the *Stone* becomes a great mountain and fills the whole earth (2:35; 7:27). Did not Christ speak of Himself as the *Stone* upon which, if men fell, they would be broken (Matthew 21:44)? One commentator remarks –

"He who falls upon a great stone, is bruised indeed, but can be healed, but he upon whom a great stone falls, is ground as it were to dust."

Spiritually interpreted, those who fell upon the Stone are those who stumbled at the humiliation of Christ, but were to be recovered by His glorious resurrection. Those upon whom the Stone fell are those who did not suffer themselves to be recovered by that miracle, and so were involved in the destruction of the Jewish nation.

When Christ described Himself as the Stone rejected by the builders, the builders, of course, were the Jews who discounted His claims of Messiahship. But the despised *Stone* became the *Head Stone* of the *Corner* – the corner being the most important position in a building (Psalm 118:22; Acts 4:11; 1 Peter 2:6). Here, Christ represents Himself as the Foundation upon which His Kingdom was to be built up in spite of His rejection by the Jews. One of the early Christian writers said that –

"Christ is called the Corner-Stone, because as the corner-stone unites in itself two walls, so also Christ unites in Himself two peoples, the Jews and the Gentiles and by faith makes them one." See Ephesians 2:14-18.

Peter speaks of Christ as "A *stone* of stumbling and a rock [a form of stone] of offense" (1 Peter 2:8). To the Jews He was a "stumblingstone" . . . "a stumblingblock" (Romans 9:32, 33; 1

Corinthians 1:23). To *Israel*, at His return, He will be the "headstone" (Zechariah 4:7). To *Gentile* world-power, He will be the smiting "stone cut out without hands" (Daniel 2:34). To those who are finally lost, He will be the crushing Stone of Judgment (Matthew 21:44), because with hearts as adamant stone they could not respond to His loving overtures of mercy (1 Samuel 25:37; Ezekiel 36:26).

For those who overcome in the good fight of faith, Christ promises "a *white stone*, and on the stone a new name written, which no one knows but he that receives it" (Revelation 2:17). Sir William Ramsay, in his most illuminative volume, *The Seven Churches*, explains the white stone as a *tessera*, or a little cube of stone, ivory, or some other substance, with words or symbols engraved on one or more faces. John stresses that the important function of this "reward-stone" is simply to bear the believer's secret name. The stone is imperishable because what bears upon it is eternal. Mention is made of the secret name of God (Revelation 3:12). The thought implied is that the victorious saint is to receive a new discovery of God and an experience of new power.

A most satisfying explanation of what is to be understood by the white stone and the secret name engraven thereon is given by Walter Scott, in his most valuable *Exposition of Revelation*. Here is his comment on Revelation 2:17 –

> "A *white stone* was largely employed in the social life and judicial customs of the ancients. Days of festivity were noted by a *white* stone; days of calamity by a *black* stone. A host's appreciation of a special guest was indicated by a *white* stone with a name or message written on it. A *white* stone meant acquittal; a *black* stone con-

demnation in the courts of justice.

"Here the overcomer is promised a *white* stone with a *new* name written thereon, which none knows save the happy recipient. It is the expression of the Lord's personal delight in each one of the conquering band. It is by no means a public reward. . . . The *new* name on the stone, alone known to the overcomer, signifies Christ, then known in a special and peculiar way to each one, and that surely is reward beyond all price and beyond all telling. It is a secret communication of love and intelligence between Christ and the overcomer, a joy which none can share, a reserved token of appreciative love."

❋ ❋ ❋

Sun of Righteousness (Malachi 4:2).

(*See* under Names of God, *Jehovah Tsidkenu*, and Names of Christ, *Lord Our Righteousness*.)

❋ ❋ ❋

Sure Foundation (Isaiah 28:16).

(*See* under *Chief Cornerstone* and under *Foundation*.)

❋ ❋ ❋

Surety (Hebrews 7:22).

Before us is a further example of how Scripture adopts human functions and relationships to symbolize the varied ministry of our blessed Lord. Here we see Him in the role of a *Surety*. Well, who and what is a "surety"? He is a person who stands as guarantor of another's obligations; one who undertakes to pay the debt for one contracting party in a covenant if that party should prove faithless or insolvent. Thus the term implies one who gives security for the fulfillment of an agreement between two other parties, a guarantor, or sponsor, or bondsman (Proverbs 22:26, 27). Evidently Solomon had a bitter experience of going *surety* for a stranger (Proverbs 11:15; 17:18; 20:16).

The sacred record provides us with instances of those who were willing to act as surety –

> Judah became surety to his father for his brother Benjamin (Genesis 43:9).
> Job pleads with God to be his surety (17:3).
> Paul was willing to become surety to Philemon for Onesimus (Philemon 18, 19).

The writer to the Hebrews declares that Jesus is the *Surety* of a better testament, or covenant (Hebrews 7:22). This is the only occurrence of the term in the New Testament, and is akin to the word rendered "mediator" (Hebrews 8:6). In classical Greek *surety* implies "to give a pledge," and the underlying idea is that of putting something into the hollow of one's hand as a pledge. In Job's reference to "surety" he asks, "Who is there that will strike hands with me?" The "striking of hands" was the Hebrew sign of becoming surety for another.

Jesus became our Surety, or Guarantor, of a better covenant, even the covenant of grace (Hebrews 8:6), and in the hollow of His pierced hand there is the imperishable evidence that He paid the debt we had accumulated. It is a *better* covenant because Jesus is *our Surety*. Sins are called *debts,* and as debts oblige the debtor to payment, so sin doth the sinner to punishment. Jesus is the Covenant of Redemption, or an agreement between the Father and Himself, interposed as the Surety of sinners, and thus, as Cruden puts it in his *Concordance* –

> "Entering into this relation, He sustained the persons of sinners – for in the estimate of the law, the *surety* and *debtor* are but one person – and being judicially one with

them, according to the order of justice, he was liable to their punishment. For though the displeasure of God was primarily and directly against the sinner, yet the effects of it fell upon Christ, who undertook for him. And according to this undertaking, Christ as our *Surety* fulfilled the perceptive part of the moral law by the innocency and holiness of his life; and he underwent the penalty of the law when he offered up himself as sacrifice to satisfy divine justice and reconcile us to God.... Now the believing sinner must wholly rely upon his sacrifice for obtaining the favour of God; and Christ, by his intercession, secures to believers all the blessings of God's covenant for time and eternity."

It is only through grace that we can look up to the Saviour, and plead with the psalmist of old, "Be *surety* for thy servant for good" (Psalm 119:122). Because, in His nail-prints we have the guarantee of our redemption we know that we can trust Him, to undertake and plead our cause against all our foes, even as a *surety* receives the poor persecuted debtor from the hands of a severe and merciless creditor. If we have "struck hands" with Him, we have the assurance that He has dealt with our satanic debtor, once and for all. In *Troilus and Cressida*, Shakespeare has the lines –

> The wound of peace is surety,
> Surety secure.

As the result of Calvary where He, who came as our *Peace*, was wounded for our transgressions, our Surety from paying the debt of sin incurred was made eternally secure.

> My Surety, Lord, art Thou,
> Rest and repose are now
> Within Thy wounded, riven side,
> Securely there I hide.

T

Teacher (John 3:2).

In the four portraits of Jesus found in the four gospels, His ministry is presented as covering the three aspects of teaching, preaching, and miracle working, and all three are found in the compass of one verse —

> "Jesus went about all Galilee,
> *teaching* in their synagogues,
> *preaching* the gospel of the kingdom,
> *healing* all manner of sickness and all manner of disease among the people" (Matthew 4:23).

As the *Healer*, He was unique! No case baffled Him. Through His touch and word all who sought Him experienced His power to relieve. (*See* under title *Physician.*) As the *Preacher*, His success as such must be measured both by His personal ministry before His audiences, and by His creation of the ideals that have controlled the homiletical method in all ages. Although His oral ministry was brief, Jesus of Nazareth will ever remain the world's Master Preacher. As the *Teacher*, friend and foe alike testified to His authority and perfection as such. The pedagogy of Jesus has received abundant study and exposition both as to form and materials of teaching. In the KJV there are some 24 references to His ministry as teacher, and about 14 to His preaching. Differentation between preaching and teaching is given by A. R. Boyd in his work *The Master Teacher,* thus —

> "*Teaching* has for its purpose the instruction in principles and customs, whose acceptance may be reserved by the individual for his own convenience and deliberation — *Preaching* has to do with the public announcement of truth with the

intention to secure immediate response from the hearer."

A study of the gospels reveals that both terms, namely, preaching and teaching, are used to record the same event, the distinctions in method and ideals not being constantly observed. While both have common traits, *preaching* is, perhaps, the more comprehensive term, being described by two Greek words, meaning, "the proclamation of a herald" and "the publication of good tidings." Both as a Preacher and Teacher, Jesus was a Herald proclaiming good tidings, and the Interpreter of truth.

As we have already indicated, titles like *Teacher*, or *Master*, are Greek renderings of the title *Rabbi*, which also has its Greek representative in the designation, *Lord*. Dr. Warfield points out that in his gospel, Mark, as translated in the ASV, broadly uses *Teacher* as his standing representation of *Rabbi*.

> "Mark puts it upon the lips both of our Lord's disciples in the ordinary colloquy (Mark 4:38; 9:38; 10:35; 13:1), obviously as their customary form of addressing Him; and of others who approached Him for every variety of reason (5:35; 9:17; 10:17, 20; 12:14, 19, 32).... He instructed His disciples to speak of Him to others as *Teacher* (Mark 14:14). . . . He claimed authority above those who shared such a title (Mark 1:22, 27)"

John the Baptist was addressed as *Teacher* (Luke 3:12 ASV), and the Jewish rabbis in the Temple were called *Teachers* (Luke 2:46 ASV), but Jesus eclipsed them all. "Who teacheth like him?" (Job 36:22). His superb teaching was with the wisdom "which the Holy Spirit teacheth" (1 Corinthians 2:13). As the Teacher from God His instruction is of the highest and most profitable

(Isaiah 28:26). While no longer with us in the flesh, Jesus graciously provided us with the Holy Spirit to teach us all things (John 14:26). *See* John 11:28; 13:13, 14.

As to what the Master actually taught, one would like to have gathered all He uttered, not only in the gospels, but also in the Book of Revelation which contains all He revealed to John. In the epistles we likewise have the writers declaring those truths Jesus taught. If the student confines himself to the gospels, with the aid of his Bible concordance, he can readily discover what Jesus taught, in and out of the synagogues, about such themes as:

God, Himself, The Holy Spirit, Scripture, Man, Neighbors, Kingdom of God, Sabbath, Money, Love, Marriage, Satan, Death, Heaven, Hell, Calvary, Prayer, Faith, and Advent, First and Second.

Never a monarch, a lawgiver, a moralist, a philosopher, a friend, a prophet, spoke like this man. No wonder people were amazed at His teaching for He declared, "My doctrine is not mine, but his that sent me." He not only sought listeners, they sought Him. Some of His most striking teaching, however, was imparted to a single auditor as, for instance, Nicodemus who came to Jesus at night for His instruction, and the woman He met at the well.

O Christ, our Saviour, Who can teach
  like Thee,
For Thou dost blend most perfect
  sympathy
With knowledge all exhaustless? Thou
  dost lead
  Thy dull and weak disciples
  gently on,
With accurate perception of their need,
  Just as the shepherd guides his
  flock along.

Thy dew-like words fall softly on the
  heart,
And to the drooping spirit life impart;
Thou wilt not break the bruised reed,
  nor force

Into maturity the budding flower,
But soft and limpid from its hidden
  source
Thy doctrine comes with
  fertilizing power.

One would like to fully dwell upon the style of our Lord's teaching, but this would require several chapters. Professor James Stalker in *The Christology of Jesus* goes into this matter in a most thorough way proving that –

"no other teacher ever put so much into few words. Yet His matter is not too closely packed; all is simple, limpid, musical. . . . 'Render unto Caesar the things which are Caesar's, and unto God the things which are God's.' Sentences of this kind stick like goads and nails. . . . The style of Jesus is intensely figurative. . . . Never abstract statements or general terms, but always pictures, full of life, movement and colour. . . . The peculiarity of His language was due, in the fullest sense to Himself, – to His insight into the secret of beauty, His sympathy with every aspect of human life, and His perception of the play of natural law in a spiritual world. . . . The study of the words of Jesus as a whole make it increasingly evident that they form the constituent elements of one harmonious circle of truth."

The Teacher from God! who teacheth
  like Him?
Compared with Him all others are
  dim;
The teachable mind, grant, Lord,
  unto me,
Till, light in Thy light, I ever may see.

❀ ❀ ❀

Tried Stone (Isaiah 28:16).
(*See* under title *Stone.*)

❀ ❀ ❀

True (Revelation 19:11).
(*See* under title *Righteous.*)

* * *

True God (1 John 5:20).
(*See* under title God.)

* * *

True Vine (John 15:1-17).

Solemnity is attached to this most descriptive title taken from the fruit-bearing world, because it is intimately connected with the last symbol Jesus applied to Himself on earth. How gifted He was in the use of a natural object for the purpose of illustrating truth! The way in which the figure of speech is worked out, and the wealth of spiritual meaning that is associated with it, show how calm and trustful Jesus must have been as He entered the dark cloud of desolation to secure our redemption from sin.

Reference to the Vine may have been prompted –

> By the cup at the table containing wine from the vine (Luke 22:20; John 13:26).
> By a vine passed on the journey to the chamber (John 14:31; 18:1).
> By Gethsemane with its vines and olive trees.
> By a sight of the heraldic representation of the vine over the porch of the Temple.

Whatever suggested the use of the symbol, the expression, "I am the true vine" points indirectly to another vine. We can understand the title more fully when we bear in mind that *true* means "genuine," the Greek signifying what is *sincere, real, veracious,* as opposed to what is false and hypocritical. John loved to use this qualifying term, *true,* of his Lord and so speaks of Him as –

> The *True* Light (John 1:9).
> The *True* Bread (John 6:32).
> The *True* Witness (Revelation 3: 14).

The *True* God (1 John 5:20).
The *True* Vine (John 15:1).

Then there is the further use of the I AM – the *Jehovah* name, the personal pronoun of Deity and Authority. "I, and no other, am the True Vine!" He was the genuine Vine in contrast to Israel, the fruitless vine, of whom God said, "He looked that it should bring forth grapes, and it brought forth wild grapes" (Isaiah 5:2). Because by nature this vine was *wild* (Isaiah 5:4), it could not bear fruit. What grapes it did have were sour (Jeremiah 31:29, 30). In both cases the Father is the Husbandman (John 15:1; Isaiah 5:7), but whereas in the case of Israel there was disappointment on account of the sour fruit, in the case of the *True Vine* the fruit is abundant and of the finest quality. The designation "My Father" occurs 6 times in this chapter, and some 30 times in John's gospel as a whole.

The Jews have a tradition that the vine was first planted by God's own hands on the fertile slopes of Hebron. Well, God says that Israel was the vine He planted in His vineyard (Isaiah 5: 2; Jeremiah 11:17), but the nation proved fruitless (Hosea 10:1). Jesus was the True Vine planted by God in the garden of the world, and has yielded abundant fruit all down the ages. He refused to drink of the fruit of the vine (Luke 22:18), until He sees His seed, and the pleasure of the Lord prospers in His hand (Isaiah 53:10, 11). Those who listened to Jesus' allegory of the vine would be familiar with the illustration. Three trees in the New Testament are eloquent with Scripture truth –

> *The Olive Tree,* showing the relation to Abraham the root, and the Gentiles the Branches (Romans 11:17-24).
> *The Fig Tree, illustrating* an empty

profession of religion (Mark 11: 13).

The Vine, expressing the twin truths of union and fruitfulness (John 15:1-17):

Union, "Abide in Me, and I in you" (15:4).

Fruitfulness, "That ye bear much fruit" (15:8).

Unless there is vital union with Christ, we cannot bear the expected fruit. "without me [separated from me] ye can do nothing" (15:5). But if there is the mutual abiding then we can do all things through the sap of the divine Vine (Philippians 1:11; 4:13).

If we have been grafted into Christ, The True Vine (2 Corinthians 5:17; Romans 11:17), then the Husbandman expects us to bear – not produce – fruit. "From me is thy fruit found" (Hosea 14:8). As fruitfulness is that which determines the end of each branch, may we ever function as fruitful branches of the Vine (15:6).

> Thou true, life-giving Vine,
> Let me Thy sweetness prove;
> Renew my life with Thine,
> Refresh my soul with love.

❊ ❊ ❊

Truth (John 14:6; 8:32, 36).

When in the Garden Satan persuaded Adam and Eve to question God's command and they believed the lie instead of the divine Word, the truth of God was lost (Genesis 3:1-6; John 8:44). Since then man has sought in many ways to regain truth for himself, but failed (1 Corinthians 1:21), for *Truth* is only found in Him who came "full of grace *and truth*" (John 1:14, 17). Certainly, He came to teach men the truth (John 3:3), but His assertion is that He is, in Himself, "*The* Truth" (John 14:6). Pilate asked, "What is truth?" but was blind to the fact that *Truth* stood before him personified in Him who was about to die for telling the truth. Bacon in his *Essays* has the line – "What is truth? said jesting Pilate; and would not stay for an answer."

It would seem as if there is a contradiction in our Lord's statements in one of His discourses –

> "Ye shall know the *truth*, and the truth shall make you free" (John 8:32).
> "If the *Son* therefore shall make you free, ye shall be free indeed" (8:36).

But there is no contradiction whatever in the passages for the one is complementary to the other. The *Son* Himself is the *Truth* who sets men free from ignorance and sin.

As it is impossible for the Lord to lie, He is absolute Truth, and our active search for truth inevitably leads to Him who declared Himself to be *the Truth*.

Attention has been drawn to the trinity of titles Jesus gave to Thomas under His *Jehovah* designation of I AM, namely, "*The* Way, *the* Truth, *the* Life." In each case, the article is emphasized (John 14:6). Here we have a three-cord that can not be broken. (*See* under titles *Life* and *Way*).

> The Way – He is the one Mediator between God and men.
> The Truth – He is the One Teacher authorized to reveal the things of God.
> The Life – He is the one Author of spiritual as of natural life.

E. B. Browning connects the triad thus –

> . . . Breathe me upward, Thou in me
> Aspiring, Who art the Way, the
>   Truth, the Life –
> That no Truth henceforth seem
>   indifferent,
> No Way to Truth laborious, and
>   no Life,
> Not even this life I live, intolerable.

What a source of comfort it is to have someone on whom we can thoroughly depend, who is the personification of truth, and can be relied on to fulfill any promise he may make! For the believer, such a one is *Jesus* (2 Timothy 1:12; John 7:18). As a *true* ambassador of truth, He did not speak of Himself, but revealed the truth given Him by His Father (John 17:6-8). In a fourfold way Jesus qualified as *The Truth* –

1. *He could not lie.*

He could call the devil a liar, but of Himself He said, "I tell you the truth" (John 8:45, 46). Paul reminds us that it is impossible for God to lie (Titus 1:2). *See* 1 Samuel 15:29. He who came as *Truth* cannot break His word (John 10:35). Because of our inherent sinful nature it may be impossible to be absolutely truthful, but with God all things are possible (Matthew 19:26; Mark 12: 32).

2. *He was the summary of the truth He taught.*

In Him was hid all the treasures of wisdom and knowledge (Colossians 2: 3). It is through Jesus, and Him alone, that we can know God (John 1:18; 14: 9, 10). It is only in and through Him that we can experience every spiritual blessing (Ephesians 1:3). He would teach the truth, because *He* was its perfection.

3. *He is the guarantee for fulfilled promises.*

Paul reminds us that in Christ, all the promises of God are *Yea*, and *Amen* (2 Corinthians 1:18-20). How wonderful it is to know that all God has said concerning love, mercy, and judgment is fulfilled by Christ (Acts 10:43; Revelation 19:10)! How blessed to realize that as *The Truth*, Jesus keeps His word for

life – and for judgment! (John 5:24; 12:48).

4. *He related truth to every phase of life.*

In every way, Jesus was the fulfiller of the truth of God (Revelation 1:5). His life was framed according to it in everything (Luke 24:44). Truth permeated His daily life (Matthew 4:4; 22: 39). He obeyed every aspect of truth implicitly (Matthew 26:54; John 19:28, 36). In Him there was perfect agreement between the written and Incarnate Word (John 5:39). Thus, as we can see, He is *The Truth*, on whom we can depend (John 6:68). As for ourselves, our obligation is clear –

> We must simply take Him at His word (Mark 9:7).
> We must continue in Him who is Truth (John 8:31), and thereby experience the blessing of the Truth (John 8:32).

Bishop Walsham How exalts Jesus as *The Truth* in the lines –

> O *Word* of God incarnate!
> O *Wisdom* from on high!
> O *Truth* unchanged, unchanging!
> O *Light* of our dark day!
> We praise Thee for the radiance
> That from the hallowed page,
> A lantern to our footsteps,
> Shines on from age to age.

V

Very Christ (Acts 9:22).

When Paul preached in Damascus that Christ was "the Son of God," he proved that He was "*the* very Christ," or as the original expresses it, *The Christ*. To the apostle, there was no doubt whatever that Jesus of Nazareth was the very *Christ*, the long-promised Messiah. (*See* under title *Christ*.) A curse was upon any other claiming to be the Messiah (Galatians 1:7-9).

W

Way (John 14:6).

It is fitting that this name comes first in Christ's trio of self-designations. Unless we know Him, experientially, as *The Way*, or as the only road to God, we cannot understand what He is as *The Truth*, and realize to the full all He is as *The Life*. Thomas à Kempis in his famous *Imitation Of Christ*, dealing with our Lord's reply to Thomas, summarized it thus —

"I am The Way, the Truth, and The Life,
Without the *Way* there is no going;
Without the *Truth* there is no knowing;
Without the *Life* there is no living.
I am The Way which thou shouldst pursue;
I am The Truth which thou shouldst believe;
I am the Life which thou shouldst hope for.

Jesus had been talking about heaven which He called "My Father's house," and Thomas who had been listening most intently said, in effect — "Well, Lord, you are going Home because you know the way there, but we do not know the way to take." Then Jesus said, "*I am the Way*" to the place I am going to prepare for you. The disciples were distressed over the thought of separation from Jesus, and Thomas, ignorant of *whither* Jesus was going, showed ignorance of *the way*. Thus, as Milligan and Moulton put it, "Therefore, with loving condescension the figure (The Way) is taken up, and they are assured that He is Himself, if we may so speak, this distance to be traversed." Along the way to the Father's house they were still with Him.

The word for *way* implied a road. Thus Phillips' translation reads —

"I myself am the Road. . . . No one approaches the Father except through me." *See* 1 Timothy 2:5.

Man is lost in sin, and does not know the road back to God. Isaiah reminds us, that, "*All* we like sheep have gone astray," and in our desperation we have tried to carve out roads of our own. "There is a way which seemeth right unto a man, but the end thereof are the ways of death" (Proverbs 14:12; 16:25). When in certain circumstances, we are apt to say, "Well, that is not my way of doing this," implying a different mode of operation. But in the matter of our salvation and eternal destiny there is no choice of ways — only one *way*, even Christ, through whom alone we can receive eternal life (1 John 5:11-13).

It was because He became *The Way* personified that this title came to represent His cause, and the service of His followers after His ascension. Paul found many of *this way*, and persecuted them (Acts 9:2). Further on we read, "any that were of *the way*" (Acts 9:2; 19:9, 23). *The name* is used absolutely (Acts 5:41), like *the word* (Acts 4:4), and *the way* (Acts 9:2), for Him before whom every knee must bow (Philippians 2:9; Hebrews 1:4). With the apostles *The Way* was the new way of life, and way of salvation — the blood-red Way back to God.

Thou art the Way, the Living Way
Through Thine own precious blood
Thou leadest to eternal day,
Bringing the lost home to God.

* * *

Wisdom (1 Corinthians 1:30. *See* 1:18-31).

In the above most pungent Pauline passage, the contrast is drawn between those exulting in human wisdom, which is foolishness to God, and in the heavenly wisdom vastly superior in every way.

What a gulf there is between "the wisdom of this world" and "the wisdom of God" (1 Corinthians 1:20, 24)! E. Young, poet of the last century, asks –

> Wouldst thou know
> How differ earthly Wisdom and
> divine?
> Just as the waning and the waxing
> moon, –
> More empty worldly Wisdom ev'ry day;
> And ev'ry day more fair her rival
> shines.

When Paul comes to summarize divine attributes reaching their perfection in Christ he gives us a quartette of titles, namely *wisdom, righteousness, sanctification, redemption,* and many expositors have dealt with these as separate predicates of Christ. But it would seem as if this great verse (1 Corinthians 1:30), presents us with a Source from which *three* streams flow – *Wisdom* being the Source and the last three terms illustrating and exemplifying the first. God made Christ to be unto us *Wisdom,* and as personified in Him, it manifested itself in righteousness, sanctification and redemption. The ASV gives us this construction of the verse –

> "Who was made unto us wisdom from God, and righteousness and sanctification and redemption."

Arthur Way expresses a similar thought –

> "Jesus who became for us God-given wisdom our righteousness, our consecration, our ransom."

Actually, then, there are only three co-ordinate terms in the verse, righteousness, sanctification and redemption are subordinate to wisdom and descriptive or explanatory of it. "Christ is the true Wisdom of God, the expression of His desire for our salvation, and of His power in accomplishing it. That Wisdom is shown in Christ as He first forgives our sins and accepts us as righteous,

then goes on to make us pure and holy by His indwelling influences, and finally promises to give us ultimate victory over sin and death, and to raise us to life eternal."

Transformation of life and character solely through Christ crucified may seem to be foolishness to human wisdom, as it did in the case of the Jews to whom the idea of a crucified Messiah as the means of salvation was repugnant, just as the same truth was to the Greeks. But the wisdom of the world is folly when compared with the wisdom of God, for in Christ was both the power and wisdom, men, who in their fleshy wisdom have wandered from God, sadly need. By His death, Christ became the Power of God unto salvation and can enable the sinner to overcome His sin. Then as the Wisdom of God, He reveals the mind of God and all the practicable implications of being saved (1 Corinthians 1:18, 23-25).

Centuries before Christ, the question was asked, "Where shall wisdom be found?" (Job 28:12), and for ages God allowed man to try and answer it by himself – by his learning, his philosophy, and his science – that he might discover his deep-seated ignorance (Romans 1:21, 22). But man completely failed, and God answered the question Himself when He sent His well-beloved Son whom He "made unto us *Wisdom*" – and what a fount of wisdom He is!

> Wisdom Thou art from all eternity,
> And givest of Thy wisdom liberally . . .
> Eternal Wisdom, teach us to adore
> And praise Thee for Thy mercy
> evermore.

Paul goes on to say that in Christ are "hid all the treasures of wisdom and knowledge" (Colossians 2:3). That *wisdom* and *knowledge* are two distinct perfections is evident from the apostle's teaching on "spiritual gifts" in 1 Corinthians 12:8 –

"To one is given by the Spirit the word of *wisdom;* to another the word of *knowledge* by the same Spirit."

Although allied, what is the difference between the two?

> *Knowledge* is the apprehension of anything.
> *Wisdom* the carrying out of anything.

The knowledge of God is the understanding of all things. *The wisdom of God* is the skillful ordering of all things (Romans 11:33).

In Christ, *wisdom* and *knowledge* and *power* work in harmony, for as "the Wisdom of God" He knows, and makes known, the things of God; and as "the Power," He appoints and orders the things perfectly (Colossians 1:15-18). As Wisdom, Knowledge, and Power, Christ operated thus –

> In Creation (Psalm 104:24).
> In Providence (Colossians 1:17).
> In Redemption (Ephesians 3:10, 11, 20, 21).

The apostle's prayer for the saints is that they "might be filled with the knowledge of his will in all wisdom and spiritual understanding" (Colossians 1:9). While we may be eager in the pursuit of human wisdom (Matthew 12:42), we must never rest till we have the true wisdom from above (Daniel 2:23), which God ever liberally bestows upon those who "ask in faith, nothing wavering" (James 1:5, 6; Proverbs 2:6, 10, 11). One of the Anglican prayers, set for "The Tenth Sunday After Trinity," is one we should all pray, if we would reflect heavenly *Wisdom* and *Power* –

> "O Eternal Lord, Who art made us Wisdom,
> Righteousness, Sanctification and Redemption: give me –

> A fellow feeling for the calamities of others,
> A readiness to bear their burdens, aptness to forbear,
> Wisdom to advise, counsel to direct, and a spirit of meekness and modesty trembling at my own infirmities, fearful in my brother's dangers, and joyful in his restoration to security!"

I take Thee as my Wisdom, Lord,
  For Wisdom's sum Thou art;
Thou, Who dost choose the foolish things,
  Set me henceforth apart,
That I may speak and work for Thee
As Thou shalt work and speak in me.

* * *

Witness (John 18:37; Revelation 3:14).

The title *Witness* was a favorite with the Apostle John, proven by the fact that it occurs in his gospel and epistles 65 times, and 19 times in the Book of Revelation. Prophesied as a witness to the people (Isaiah 55:4), when He appeared among people, Jesus could confess that He came into the world to "bear witness unto the truth" (John 18:37). Then, in His final message to the churches, He could say of Himself that He was "the Amen, the faithful and true witness" (Revelation 3:14). Such a portrayal was a rebuke to the church at Laodicea, which had miserably failed as a witnessing company for the Saviour they had excluded from their life and worship (Revelation 3:19, 20).

The Church as a whole is not functioning as God's most responsible witness in the world to the treasures of His grace, of His character, and of His Word. Down the ages she has not been a faithful nor true witness. Her glorious Head, however, has never come short as God's perfect *Witness.* Commissioning His own, Jesus said, "Ye shall be witnesses unto me" (Acts 1:8), but the

Church corporate has been a disappointment to Him who in the days of His flesh bore an unceasing testimony to the truth (Revelation 1:2, 5). The ASV gives "witness" here for "record." John himself not only came, but was *sent* as a witness of Him who came as the Light of the World (John 1:7), and because of his faithful testimony was qualified to write so much about witnessing, as he did.

Christ declared before Pilate that He had been born to bear witness to the truth, and we were born anew by the Holy Spirit for the same end. From the human standpoint the reason why He was crucified was because He had been ever faithful and true as the *Witness* sent of God. In this connection it is interesting to note that the Greek word for "witness" is equivalent to our English term, *martyr,* and thus implies, not only one who can and does testify of what he has seen, or heard, or knows, but one who is willing to bear witness by his death, which Christ did. He was not crucified for *doing* things, but *saying* things. His *words,* rather than His *works,* resulted in His martyrdom. The gospels reveal that He faithfully witnessed for God, for Scripture, for His own authority as the Sent One, for truth as against error, for holiness as against sin, for heaven as against hell.

> A Witness to the people, Lord!
> Proclaiming wide the love of God,
> By life-giving signs in deed and word,
> That all without excuse may be:
> Blest Saviour, is Thy love so free
> And boundless as Eternity.

*   *   *

Wonderful (Isaiah 9:6).

This adjective meaning "marvelous," "astonishing," becomes a noun, and a name for the coming Messiah. "His name shall be called *Wonderful.*" When "the angel of the Lord" whom Manoah ad-dressed as *Jehovah* (Judges 13:8 ASV) appeared to the Danite, he was anxious to know the name of the august person bringing him the tidings that his barren wife was to have a son who would become Samson, a judge in Israel. "What is thy name?" Manoah asked, only to receive the answer, "Why askest thou thus after my name, seeing it is secret?" (Judges 13:17, 18). The word *secret* here means "wonderful" and is akin to *wondrously* in the next verse. Witnessing the marvelous ascension of this person Manoah and his wife said, "We have seen God."

The first prophetic name Isaiah gave to the coming Messiah was most apt. As a name is often a synonym for the nature of any object, or of any being, *Wonderful* was a fitting name for Him who was to prove it by His life and labors. In his most valuable volume on *The Miracles,* Archbishop Trench has this tribute –

> "It is not wonderful that He whose name is *Wonderful* does works of wonder; the only wonder would be if He did them not. The sun in the heavens is itself a wonder: but it is not a wonder that, being what it is, it rays forth its effluence of light and heat. These miracles are the fruit after its kind which the divine tree brings forth."

Was Jesus worthy of this captivating name which Isaiah gave Him? Was everything about Him *wonderful,* or did He, like the best of us, have defects? The gospels reveal that He never ceased to be a *wonder* and wonderful in all things. The term "wonderful," with its cognates, is constantly used of divine action (Exodus 15:11; Psalm 118:23).

His birth was wonderful, for, as we have already seen, although He had a human mother, He is the only babe born into the world who did not have a human father. He was conceived of the Holy Spirit within Mary (Luke 1:31, 35).

His person was wonderful, seeing that He combined Deity and humanity in Himself, and lived among men as the God-Man – "God was manifest in the flesh" (1 Timothy 3:16).

Crown Him the Virgin's Son,
The God, Incarnate born . . .

His teaching was wonderful. As people sat spellbound as He preached, they said, "Never man spake like this Man!" No scholar, sage, or philosopher has ever appeared who taught as Jesus did. He addressed mankind in many and varied capacities, but His remarkable versatility made Him equal to every occasion. After almost two millenniums His teachings still influence multitudes. There has never been a teacher or philosopher with presumption enough to declare, "My words shall not pass away." But because Jesus was the Teacher come from God He could make such a claim without any fear of challenge. He alone could say, "The words that I have spoken unto you are spirit, and are life" (John 6:63 ASV).

In all His words most wonderful,
Most sure in all His ways.

His character was wonderful for there has never been His like – and never will be! Think of it – Jesus was never converted, was never penitent because there was nothing whatever in His life to repent of! No one could convict Him of sin. He was "holy, harmless, undefiled, separate from sinners" because He was "higher than the heavens." He was a moral marvel.

His works were wonderful. What power He manifested over the forces of nature, over the devil and demons, over disease and death! The world has never had such a miracle-worker. If He had

come proclaiming Himself to be the Son of God, the Lamb of God, without *miracles*, the natural conclusion would be that He had a disordered mind. But He went about, not only doing good, but relieving all who were oppressed of the devil (Acts 10:38). Christianity was founded upon the miraculous.

His death and resurrection were wonderful. Had Jesus remained dead there would never have been a deliverance for mankind from the guilt and thralldom of sin. But He rose again, and it is through the combination of both His death and salvation that a marvelous salvation is provided for a sinning race. This is emphasized by Paul when he says, "If thou shalt . . . believe in thine heart that God *raised him* [*Jesus*] *from the dead*, thou shalt be saved" (Romans 10:8, 9).

His second advent will be wonderful. What a miraculous display of His power there will be when He returns for those redeemed by His blood (1 Thessalonians 4:13-18), and thereafter when He appears on earth as its rightful Lord and King to usher in His millennial reign (Revelation 11:15-19)!

The name is Secret, Wonderful,
Thy works and Word declare,
So full of grace, the Merciful,
And Thou dost deign to hear.

❊   ❊   ❊

Word (John 1:1; Revelation 19:13).

Over the first three verses in the prologue of John's gospel we can write *Multum In Parvo*, or "much in little," for here we have a compendium of divine knowledge. This trinity of verses, 1:1-3, offers a classic example of the maximum of truth in the minimum of words. Think of it – in the brief compass of 42 words eternity, personality, Deity, co-equality, and creatorship are ascribed to Him whom John describes in a wonderful combination of sublimity and simplicity! The full prologue takes in John 1:1-18, in which we have –

> Christ in Relation to God (vv. 1, 2, 14, 18).
>
> Christ in Relation to the Material Universe (v. 3).
>
> Christ in Relation to Human Nature (v. 14).
>
> Christ in Relation to Humanity (vv. 4, 6-9, 12, 15).
>
> Christ in Relation to the Old Testament (v. 17).

One aspect amazing us is the way John opens his Christ-honoring gospel. Looking at Romans, which Godet called "The Cathedral of Christian Faith," the opening statement of this masterly epistle reads, "Paul, a servant of Jesus Christ" (Romans 1:1). In fact, the first word in all his epistles is his own name – Paul. But with John and his unique gospel it was different for as Dr. F. B. Meyer says –

> "The writer does not stay to introduce himself, to mention his name, or give proofs of his trustworthiness. With singular abruptness, with no attempt to substantiate his own claims or the claims of this marvellous treatise, he casts it into the teeming world of human thought and life, as Jochabed launched the cradle on the bosom of the Nile. . . . The blessed Spirit, found congenial work in glorifying the Lord through the pen of His dearest friend and aptest pupil."

Our present endeavor is to discover the truth embodied in the two opening verses of John's gospel in which we have the threefold mention of Him as *The Word*, and likewise, the threefold designation – *God*. These sublime opening sentences emphasize a trinity of truth, namely – *eternity, personality* and *Deity*.

1. *Christ is co-equal with God in the duration of His existence.*

The six initial words, "*In* the beginning *was* the Word" (John 1:1), are a peculiar form of expression, and probably convey "the most exact and historical thought of Eternity found in the Bible." It is a phrase that has no reference to either date or epoch. In the opening of his first epistle, John has the phrase, "From the beginning" (1 John 1:1), but this refers to a specific event – the appearance of Christ as the God-Man to take away sin. Genesis has the majestic opening, "In the beginning *God*" (Genesis 1:1), which is linked on to His creative work for man. But John elevates the three words, "In the beginning" from any reference to time, which began for man at the Creation, and directs us to Christ's absolute preexistence before the Creation which John mentions in the third verse.

It is interesting to contrast the phrases "*In* the beginning" and "*From* the beginning." The latter is common to John's writings and has in it no thought of eternal preexistence. *See* John 8:44; 1 John 2:7, 24; 3:8. *Was* (past tense) indicates that Christ was already preexistent. He gave Himself the title, "*I am the beginning*" (Revelation 1:8), and He is the *Beginning* who had no beginning. Moses, in his grand opening of Scripture, "*In the beginning God,*" strikes the chord to descend the stream of time. John strikes it to look out on the expanse of eternity lying beyond created things but which in the *Word* was already existing. Christ came as "The King Eternal, Immortal, Invisible."

> Thou art the Everlasting Word,
>   The Father's only Son;
> God manifestly seen and heard,
>   And Heaven's beloved One.
>
> In Thee most perfectly expressed
>   The Father's glories shine;
> Of the full Deity possessed,
>   Eternally divine.

True Image of the Infinite,
>   Whose essence is concealed;
Brightness of uncreated light;
>   The heart of God revealed.

Further evidence of His preexistence can be found in statements like, "All things were made by him" (John 1:3), and "He is before all things" (Colossians 1:17). If *all* things were made by Him, He must have been before them. Christ is associated with Creation. In Genesis Creation is undoubtedly ascribed to God – "God said," "God made," "God created" (Genesis 1:3, 7, 21), but John ascribes the calling of a world from nought to *the Word of God,* that is, to Christ. To have attributed the work of God to Him would have been blasphemy had Christ not been one with God. Thus, His relation to the mutual universe is a proof of His preexistence and Deity. But He had an existence prior to any created thing, and was therefore, the Beginning of the beginning of Genesis 1:1. As Milligan and Moulton express it –

> "In Genesis 1:1 the sacred historian starts from the beginning and comes downward, thus keeping us in the course of time. Here (John 1:1) John starts from the same point, but goes upward, thus taking us into the Eternity preceding time."

Other books of the Bible may begin in time, John begins in eternity, and directs our gaze to the equality of the Son with the Eternal Father. Our finite mind staggers at the revelation of the expanse of an eternity lying beyond created things, and all that we can do is to humbly accept by faith the preexistence of the *Word,* and worship and adore Him as the Eternal One. See John 17:5; Ephesians 1:4.

We now come to an understanding of preexistent Christ as the *Word* – one of the most picturesque names used of Him in Scripture. As the spoken word reveals our invisible thought, so Christ, as the Living Word, reveals the invisible God. "No man hath seen God at any time; the only begotten Son, which is in the bosom of the Father, he hath declared him" (John 1:18). Vincent comments that this designation *The Word* is "the key-note and theme of the entire gospel, and that the original, LOGOS, implies *a collecting* or *collection* both of things in the mind, and of the words by which they are expressed. It therefore signifies both *the outward form* by which the inward thought is expressed, and *the inward thought* itself, the Latin *oratio* and *ratio:* compare the Italian *ragionare* – 'to think' and 'to speak.' "

In all probability, John had in mind the beginning of Scripture where the act of creation was effected by God's speaking. "By the *word* of Jehovah were the heavens made; and all the host of them by the breath of His mouth" (Psalm 33:6 ASV). See Job 26:13. Godet draws attention to the fact that –

> "Eight times in the Genesis narrative of Creation there occurs, like the refrain of a hymn, the words, *And God said.* John gathers up all those sayings of God into a single *saying,* living and endowed with activity and intelligence, from all which all divine orders emanate; he finds as the basis of all spoken words, *The Speaking Word.*"

As the *Word,* Jesus came as the embodiment of the divine will, and the personification of divine Wisdom (Psalm 119:105; Proverbs 8:9). Ancient Jewish teachers designated the permanent agent of Jehovah (Genesis 16:7-13), by the name *Memra* (which means *Word*) *of Jehovah.* They would substitute the name *the Word of Jehovah* for that of Jehovah, each time that God manifested Himself. They thus paraphrased, "Jehovah was with Joseph" (Genesis 39: 21 asv), as "The Memra was with Joseph." In like manner the *Memra* is the angel that destroyed the firstborn of Egypt, and it was the *Memra* that led the Israelites in the cloudy pillar. Early philosophers called the mediating principle between God and matter, the divine *Reason,* the *Logos.* But, John, inspired by the Spirit, set forth his *Logos* as a *Person,* with a consciousness of personal distinction, and not as "The Imperial Reason." To the apostle, the Messiah was *the Word* – the Living Word – uniting Himself with humanity, and clothing Himself with a human body in order to save a lost world.

As the Greek *Logos* for the English *Word* carries the double idea of *thought* and *speech,* John declares that Jesus, as the Word becoming flesh (John 1: 14), became the Revealer of the hidden thought of God, and the organ of all His manifestations to the world (Hebrews 1:3). While a *word* is an inward *conception of the mind,* it needs a *voice* to make it known, and John the Baptist said that he was such a *voice* giving expression to the inner conception of divine truth (Luke 3:4). May our voice ever ring true, uttering words the Holy Spirit reveals of Him who is "*The* Word"!

2. *Christ, the Possessor of a divine personality.*

John goes on to say that the Lord Jesus had, not only *the eternity of Being,* but that He eternally held a relation of communion with God as a separate personality – a personality itself divine for "the Word *was* with God.... The same was in the beginning with God" (John 1:1, 2). As the Eternal One, Christ was not only with God as co-eternal, but ever in active communion with Him from the dateless past. As Moulton put it, "Not simply the Word with God, but God with God." The prep-

osition *with* used here denotes a "motion towards," or "direction." The phrase "abide and winter *with you*" (1 Corinthians 16:6) implies Paul's desire to have fellowship with the saints. So, John's statement, "The Word was with God," suggests that the Son, as the divine Word not only *abode* with the Father from all eternity, but was in living, active communion with Him. "I was daily his delight" (Proverbs 8:30). Says the Puritan writer, John Owen, "The Word was God in the unity of Divine essence, and the Word was *with* God in the distinct personal subsistence."

A suggestive rendering of the phrase before us is, "The Word was *towards* God." "Face to face" is the idea in the Greek, and is significant of fellowship with, and delight in God, the personality of the Son attracted by the personality of the Father, as some flowers are attracted by the sun. Thus, as Dr. F. B. Meyer expresses it –

> "The preposition *with* means communion with and movement towards. It denotes the intimate fellowship subsisting between two, and well befits the intercourse of the distinct Persons of the one and ever-blessed God. 'The face of the everlasting Word was ever directed towards the face of the everlasting Father.' He was in the bosom of the Father. 'He makes the Divine glory shine outwardly because He is filled inwardly. He contemplates before He reflects. He receives before He gives' . . . Let us not forget that He is our Saviour, and our familiar Friend, and a distinct personality, who was before all worlds, and will be unchanged for evermore."

3. *Christ is one with God in the essence of the divine nature.*

What a tremendous phrase this is – *The Word was God!* Language has no meaning if these four words do not clearly teach that Christ is "Very God of Very God." Here, the title *God* without the article "the" implies the conception of God as infinite, eternal, perfect and almighty. Had Christ, as the *Word*, been created by God He could not have been God. He was not only a divine person, but the Source and Spring of all that is divine. He is not merely *of* God, and *with* God, He is *God*, and His Deity is one of the great themes of John's gospel. "My Father and I are one" (John 10:30) — they were one in substance and essence, and therefore the Son is to be worshipped with the same worship as is due the Father.

> 'Tis the Father's pleasure
> We should call Him Lord,
> Who from the beginning
> Was the Mighty Word.

Again and again, Jesus is called *God*, as we have already proved under titles *God* and *The Son of God* (John 5:18; 20:28; Romans 9:5; Titus 2:13; 2 Peter 1:1 — all in the ASV). It is not said that He is *the* God, for such an assertion would ascribe to a Son "the totality of the Divine Being, and contradict the doctrine of the Holy Trinity. And He is not said to be *Divine*, which would lessen the emphasis. But He is said, distinctly and emphatically, to be *God* — 'God manifest in flesh.'" Becoming Man, Christ revealed God to human beings. "He [the Word] hath declared Him" (John 1:18). Proofs of our Lord's Deity abound —

> He is declared to be the Creator. "All things were made by him" (John 1:3; Ephesians 3:9).
>
> He is represented as knowing the secrets of human lives (John 1:48; 2:25; 4:18).
>
> He is described as being in heaven while on earth (John 3:13).
>
> He appropriates over and over again

the Jehovah title — I AM (6:35).

> He received without rebuke the homage of an apostle who worshipped Him as *God* (John 20:28).
>
> His works reflected the power of God (John 9:33).

Christ, then, came not as *a* Word of God, but *the* Word — the only revelation of God to man, and He declared all God had to say to men. In Creation, He was the expression of divine power, but in His Incarnation He became the revelation of the divine character (Matthew 11:27; John 17:26). How grateful we are that the *Word* was made flesh, and made His abode among men for over 33 years (John 1:14)! He became *Emmanuel* — GOD WITH US. John tells us that he saw, heard, and handled Christ as "the Word of life" (1 John 1:1 ASV). There were those soon after Christ's time that taught that He was a mere phantom, but John gives evidence as an eyewitness that He was a living reality. Further, it is His manifestation as the Preexistent Eternal Word that determines man's relation to God (1 John 1:3; Hebrews 4:12). May He, as the Word, dwell in us richly in all wisdom (Colossians 3:16)! He is the Word, cleansing from sin, and if hid in our heart, will keep us clean (Psalm 119:9-11).

* * *

The Word of God (Revelation 19:13).

The name of the victorious Conqueror John describes is clothed with a garment dipped in blood which, by the way, is not His *own* blood, but that of His defeated foes. He is *The Word of God,* and the apostle is the only New Testament writer who applies this title to Christ, and how he loved to use it!

> As the *Word*, Christ represented and expressed God in His being,

character and work (John 1:1-3, 14).

As the *Word of Life,* He was in His persons and ways the living embodiment of life (1 John 1:1).

As the *Word of God,* He is perfectly described as executing the righteous judgment of God (Revelation 19:11-16; Hebrews 4:12).

Come, Thou Incarnate Word,
Gird on Thy mighty sword;
   Our prayer attend:
Come, and Thy people bless,
And give Thy Word success,
Spirit of Holiness,
   On us descend!

Y

Young Child (Matthew 2:8, 13; Acts 4:27, 30).

The references to Jesus as "the young child" reveal how early in life He was persecuted. There was no room for Him in the inn, and shortly after none for Him in Bethlehem or Judea. Hearing of His birth, Herod was troubled and though he pretended to want to worship Him, murder was in his heart. As a liar, Herod thought himself clever, and fancied he could outwit God, but He is able to make the wrath of man to praise Him. Joseph, guided by the angel of the Lord, fled with "the young child and his mother into Egypt." When we follow God's guidance we are safe from the cunning of the cleverest.

After the death of Herod, Joseph, Mary, and Jesus left Egypt, and settled in Nazareth where, for almost 30 years, Jesus lived an obscure life. We have only one glimpse of His childhood, but that is sufficient to reveal that He was the *Holy Child Jesus.* Mention has been made of His miraculous conception and of His lowly birth under the titles of *Child, Son of Mary.* Under this, our last designation of Him, we want to discover something of His childhood and youth.

When He came to leave Nazareth for His public ministry for some 3-1/2 years, He was a grown man of 30. Think of it, God was 30 years preparing His Son for a brief period of service! He always takes time and pains in the preparation of those He knows He can mightily use, whether their length of labor is short or long.

As Luke is the only historian of Christ's childhood and boyhood, let us examine what he has to say about such. There are only two verses that give us an insight into the growth and character of "the young child."

"The child grew, and waxed strong in spirit, filled with wisdom: and the grace of God was upon Him. ... And Jesus increased in wisdom and stature, and in favor with God and man" (Luke 2:40, 52).

Between these two highly informative verses we have the dramatic episode at the annual feast of the Passover with its only glimpse of Jesus in His God-relationship and parent-relationship from the time of His birth till at the age of 30 He set out to accomplish the mission given Him by the Father. Yet this solitary appearance is heavy with spiritual significance in that it reveals how Jesus was conscious of His Messiahship at the early age of 12, which did not make Him any more unusual than an ordinary-looking Child — even although the church of Rome in *The Madonna and Child,* always depict the Babe with a halo round His head! We likewise have the records of *The Apocryphal Gospels,* which appeared around the second century, in which Jesus is depicted as a most extraordinary child yet by no means a lovable One.

Silly fables and miracles, puerile in character, are attributed to the young child and also actions utterly inconsistent with His being and character, such as

His ordering of His parents to be subject to Him, rather than He to them. One of the miracles He was purported to have performed in the presence of the village boys was that of placing a dead, dried fish in a basin and commanding it to move about. It may be that John's statement, "This *beginning* of his signs [or miracles] did Jesus in Cana of Galilee, and manifested His glory" (John 2:11 ASV) was designed to counteract the unauthorized, reported miracles of His childhood. The transformation of water into wine was His *first* miracle.

Before Jesus Was Twelve Years of Age.

The description given of His childhood before He was twelve suggests "a period of quiet development of mind and body, of outward uneventfulness, of silent garnering of experience in the midst of the Nazareth surroundings." Luke cites four features of the young child –

"The Child grew –
Waxed strong in spirit –
Filled with wisdom –
The Grace of God was upon Him"
(Luke 2:40).

When, as the Mighty God, Jesus became a Babe, His Incarnation was a true acceptance of humanity, with all its sinless limitations of growth and development those born in sin are subject to. Although, He must have been striking in character, there is no hint of the omniscience or omnipotence imputed to Him in legends of His childhood.

1. The Child Grew.

These three simple words imply that He was a real child, and, outwardly, like all other children, sins excepted. Jesus was no unearthly child without a normal childhood. In His earliest years. He thought as a child, spoke as a child, and played as a child. Although Mary

knew in her heart that He was the promised Messiah, and the Child of Hope for all nations, and kept all His sayings and those of others in her heart, the villagers had not noticed anything unusual about "the young child." Nathanael, who lived only some two hours' walk from Nazareth, and no doubt made his rounds there selling fish, saw nothing remarkable about Jesus whom he knew as "the son of Joseph" (John 1:45), and was amazed when Philip declared Him to be the Messiah.

2. Waxed Strong in Spirit.

The ASV simply says *waxed strong.* The term "waxed" literally means to strike forward, or cut forward a way, and implies continual progress. This was true of young Jesus physically, mentally and spiritually. Every part of His being expanded. Development was never arrested. Body, mind, and soul gathered strength as day followed day. He grew in "every part" as a tender plant, upward, inward, and outward. All within Him was harmonious.

3. Filled with Wisdom.

Because of the Child He was, He must have had a fuller understanding than other children around Him. At an early age He would attend the ordinary village synagogue school. Jesus learned to read (Luke 4:17), to write (John 8:6-8), to work (Mark 6:3). As His mind unfolded, wisdom increased (Proverbs 4:1-13). Many a child grows in knowledge but not in *wisdom. See* Matthew 13:54. An ancient proverb has it, "An ounce of wisdom is worth a ton of learning." If it is true that a child is not all born till the mind is born and grows, the Holy Child Jesus was *all born.* As for His teachers, they were His Bible, His home, His heavenly Father's house – the synagogue, nature, and His daily work. He found a lesson and joy in everything. When, ultimately, Jesus became the Prophet of Nazareth, His parables and sayings proved what a lover of nature and human life He had been, and how closely He had observed all around Him, and linked what He had seen on to His great thoughts.

4. The Grace of God Was Upon Him. What a testimony this was for "the young child" to have! Divine favor was His because He was the Son of God, as well as the Son of Mary. When, at 30 years of age, Jesus was initiated into His public ministry by His baptism at the hands of John, His forerunner – and His cousin – there came the heavenly benediction, "This is My well-beloved Son, in whom I am well pleased" – a commendation covering those silent, previous years in Nazareth. Pilate said, "Behold the Man!" In this meditation we are saying, "Behold the Child!" for nothing is so delightful as the gospel of our Lord's childhood. Had He not become a Child on earth, we would never have become children of Heaven. Would that the grace of God was upon all the children in the homes of today!

When Jesus Was Twelve Years of Age.
Luke distinctly tells us that "Jesus was twelve years old" when He went to Jerusalem with Joseph and Mary for the Passover Feast (Luke 2:42). This was the age a boy in a Jewish home became known as *a son of the law,* and came under obligation to observe the ordinances of the synagogue personally. He was required after 12 years of age to appear three times a year before God (Exodus 23:14-17; Deuteronomy 16:16). As a babe He had been circumcised and presented in the Temple (Luke 2:21, 23), now at twelve, He attends the Passover, which must have given Him great delight (Isaiah 42:21; Matthew 5:17). What a strange and thrilling experience His must have been to visit hallowed sites for the first time!

Dr. James Orr in his remarkable contribution "Jesus Christ," found in *The International Standard Bible Encyclopedia,* says –

"Every relationship was for the time suspended or merged to His thought in this higher one. It was His Father's city whose streets He trod;
His Father's house He visited for prayer;
His Father's ordinance the crowds were assembled to observe;
His Father's name, too, they were dishonouring by their formalism and hypocrisy."

How absorbed this youth of twelve was by everything He saw and heard, so much so, that when the caravan bringing Him and His kinsfolk to Jerusalem left for Nazareth, He *tarried behind* (Luke 2:43). Then we know what happened, when the caravan reached the evening-halting place, Joseph and Mary discovered that Jesus was not in the company, and in deep distress returned to Jerusalem, seeking everywhere for Him save in the place where they should have sought first. After a three-day search there, they found the lad engrossed in lively discussion with the Temple rabbis who were renowned for their teaching.

Mary, His mother, saw how astonished the Temple teachers were by the penetration and wisdom of Jesus as He asked and answered questions (Luke 2:46, 47). During a pause in this remarkable confrontation Mary remonstrated with Jesus by asking, "Son, why hast thou thus dealt with us?" which evoked the memorable reply, "How is it that ye sought me? knew ye not that I must be in my Father's House?" or, "about my Father's business?" (Luke 2:48, 49). The Greek has it, "in the things of My Father." Mary did not forget such an impressive occasion (Luke 2:51). Reaching His ministry, it was His *custom* to worship in God's House (John 18:20).

Theologians have long debated the question as to when "the young child" became conscious that He was the promised Messiah. Was it at the moment in the Temple when He openly declared His relationship to God His Father, and revealed a self-consciousness of His divinity and also divine task? For ourselves, there is no problem as to when young Jesus knew that He was *the Christ*. Because of His preexistence, and equality with God, and His acquiescence in the plan and purpose of Incarnation – that He would be born the Saviour who is Christ the Lord, as soon as human consciousness was His, He knew who He was, and why He was in the world.

Mary, who had heard what Gabriel, Simeon and Anna had said about her Son, kept their sayings about the Deity and destiny of Jesus locked up in her heart, but somehow in the common intercourse of life they failed to be uppermost. The reply she got from her Son brought all she had heard back to her. Whether or not this was the first time Jesus declared that He knew He was "God manifest in flesh" we do not know. Perhaps it was His initial revelation of His inner consciousness of a higher relationship and allegiance.

It is important to notice the double reference to the relationship of fatherhood in the Temple conversation of Mary and Jesus. Perplexed over her Son's behavior she asked, "Son, why hast thou thus dealt with us? behold, *thy father* and I have sought thee sorrowing." Then came the reply of Jesus, "Wist ye not that I must be in *my Father's house?*" Mary should have known that it was more necessary to be in His house, than hers. But what should be observed is the recognition of only one *Father* and the implication of Jesus' eternal relationship with Him. As Alford states it, "Up to this time Joseph had been called father by the holy child Himself; but from this time never." (*See* further under title *Son of Joseph.*)

The Temple episode is all we have of the first thirty years of His life. How we would have liked to have had further knowledge of such a span! The design of the evangelists, however, was to give the world a detailed account of His brief *public ministry*, not His previous private life. Still, the glimpse Luke gives us of Jesus at twelve years of age corresponds entirely with what we might expect of *that holy thing* born of Mary (Luke 1:35).

After Jesus Was Twelve Years of Age.

One wonders whether He could have stayed in the Temple, as Samuel of old abode in it to assist in its services. But in spite of what did happen, Jesus went back with Joseph and Mary to Nazareth, and so we read of Him –

> "He went down . . . and was subject unto them . . . Jesus increased in wisdom and stature, and in favor with God and man" (Luke 2:51, 52).

Apocryphal literature, instead of depicting Jesus as growing in wisdom, represents Him as forward and eager to teach His instructors, and to be omniscient in His boyhood, and sometimes troublesome to the rest of His family (Mark 6:3). But never a stain clouded His vision of divine things, and never a wrong, cross word left His lips. Was He not "the holy Child Jesus"?

1. "He came to Nazareth and was subject unto them."

What a remarkable statement this is! Even though Jesus had just announced His higher obligation Godward, He left the Temple, returned home with Joseph and Mary, and became *subject* unto them. The original here denotes an *habitual, continuous* subjection. Says Bengel, the renowned commentator, "Even before, he had been subject unto them; but this is mentioned now, when it might seem that He could by this time have exempted Himself. Not even to the angels fell such an honour as to the parents of Jesus." (*See* Hebrews 1:4-8.)

In these modern, permissive times when it is felt that children should be given free, unrestricted expression, many of them cease to be subject to their parents, feeling that their parents should be subject unto their self-chosen ways of freedom. But Jesus returned to Nazareth to continue living as a faithful and obedient son for a further 18 years, thereby, leaving all children a shining example to follow. We are confident that Mary, who kept all her Son's sayings in her heart, could not impose any duty upon Him contrary to His high and holy calling. In turn, He never had anything but love and reverence for the one who gave Him birth. (*See* further under title *Son of Mary.*)

2. He increased in wisdom.

As we have seen, in the earlier period of His childhood, it is said that He was "filled with wisdom" (Luke 2:40). Now, we read that after the Temple experience He "increased in wisdom" (2:52). Of Samuel it is written that "he grew on" which was true of Jesus in a deeper, sense, since He was the Son of God. We can imagine how with an expanding mind He became more engrossed in the Hebrew Scriptures, and His later ministry reveals how His mind was steeped in every part of the Old Testament. As He pondered psalms and prophets, His youthful soul could not remain unmoved by presentiments, growing to ever-increasing convictions that He was the One in whom their predictions were destined to be fulfilled. His was an undying thirst for the wisdom of God which He came to personify (1 Corinthians 1:24, 30).

3. He Increased in Stature.

Some authorities suggest that *age* is meant by "stature." Both are correct, for as a lad of 12 He was not fully grown physically, but developed perfectly as the years went by. Without doubt, His physique became more prominent through His long years at the carpenter's bench. Like every other Jewish lad, Jesus would remain at the village synagogue school, and when about fifteen years of age leave, and according to Jewish custom follow the trade of the home. In this case Joseph, His foster father, was a carpenter and so Jesus took up this craft (Mark 6:3). For fifteen years then, He worked day in and day out in the humble, local shop making and mending yokes and plows and furniture. Legend has it that after Jesus joined the business, Joseph died and the burden of carrying on fell upon His shoulders.

Of this we are certain, that nothing shoddy ever left His hands, for like Himself, His work was perfect. In that carpenter's shop we have the toil of divinity revealing the divinity of toil. With the passage of years, constant laboring increased His stature, and by the time He was 21 years old, having a body without sin and always living for the pleasure of His heavenly Father, He must have been a most striking Man to look at. John Stuart Mill eulogized Jesus as "The one perfect life lived in Nazareth." Such a perfect life was matched by a perfect body which enabled Him to bear the stress and strain of His most arduous three years' ministry. At the end the Carpenter was given wood and nails at Calvary (1 Peter 2:24).

4. He increased in favor with God and man.

Such a feature does not suggest that Jesus ever lacked divine favor. In His earliest years, "the grace [or favor] of God was upon Him" (Luke 2:40), and had been from the moment of His conception within the womb of Mary. "That holy thing which shall be born of thee shall be called the Son of God" (Luke 1:35). What is impressive here is the fact that human favor, as well as divine, increased towards Him. Gentleness and grace of character endeared Him to all who knew Him. Samuel evidently had the same reputation for we read that as a child he "grew on, and was in favor both with Jehovah, and also with men" (1 Samuel 2:26 ASV). Both were what we might call "universal favorites."

As for Jesus, everybody liked to be near Him, to see His smile, to hear His voice, to watch His ways. The magic of His goodness attracted all to His side. His heart was always established with grace (Hebrews 13:9), and increasing grace and graciousness became His because of His humility (James 4:6). Paul reminds us that this Jesus of Nazareth has left us an example to emulate (Philippians 2:5). It was W. E. Gladstone, the great English statesman, who said of Jesus, "He is the greatest the ages have ever shown us." And so He is! The young Child became the Saviour of the world, and will yet reign as the King of kings. Presently we cannot live without Him for, as Tennyson expressed it, "What the sun is to the flower, Christ is to my soul." Our blessed hope is that ere long we shall see this Man of Nazareth in all His majesty as the Lord of Glory.

Our eyes at last shall see Him
  Through His own redeeming love,
For that Child so dear and gentle
  Is our Lord in Heaven above:
And He leads His children on
To the place where He is gone.

Having reached the end of our painstaking yet profitable and pleasurable study on the names and titles of God the Son, we find ourselves in full agreement with the sentiment expressed by Isaac Watts —

Not to our names, Thou only just
  and true,
Not to our worthless names is
  glory due;
Thy power and grace, Thy truth and
  justice claim
Immortal honours to Thy sovereign
  Name.

We have considered a great number of Christ's actual and symbolic designations found in Scripture. Some may feel that there are a few more that could be included, but sufficient have been alphabetically dealt with to prove that He who bears them all is "great, and greatly to be praised." Taken as a whole, His numerous names and titles describe, define, and declare Him so that He may be known. Further, since all His names were given under divine inspiration, they are identical with His nature, character, attributes and offices. But many though His names may be, He is greater and grander than them all. As Charles Wesley states it —

Join all the glorious names
  Of wisdom, love and power,
That ever mortals knew
  That angels ever bore;
All are too mean to speak His worth,
Too mean to set my Saviour forth.

No one can study the names of our Lord scattered, as they are, over the sacred pages of His Word, like the stars of heaven, without being impressed by the vast resources of grace and power they represent. From the great variety of His prophetic, personal, and parabolic designations we discover that in Him dwelt "all the fulness of the Godhead bodily" (Colossians 2:9). The group of names associated with Jesus is like a most lovely cluster of jewels, each precious to the believer's heart. The question is, Am I experiencing in my own life all that this grand collection of names and titles expresses? With the enormous wealth of grace they represent, there is no reason whatever for our spiritual penury. Knowing all these glorious names implies that we should be found putting our trust in Him who bears them (Psalm 9:10). Each of us must learn in deeper measure the meaning of the poet's verse –

> Fairer than all the earth-born race,
> Perfect in comeliness Thou art;
> Replenished are Thy lips with grace,
> And full of love Thy tender heart.
> God ever blest! We bow the knee,
> And own *all fulness* dwells in Thee.

(See further under Appendices – *Qualifying Attributes of Christ.*)

Chapter 3

THE NAMES AND TITLES OF GOD THE SPIRIT

THE NAMES AND TITLES OF GOD THE SPIRIT

An ancient creed has the following succinct statement, so impressive and expressive in its language, of the position of the Holy Spirit in the Godhead –

> ". . . the Third Person of the Trinity proceeding from the Father and the Son, of the same substance and equal in power and glory, and is, together with the Father and the Son to be believed in, obeyed, and worshipped throughout the ages."

Theology, from "theos," meaning *God,* is the study of all related to Him. *Christology,* from "Christos," or Christ, concerns all associated with the scriptural revelation of Him. *Pneumatology,* from "Pneuma," or "Spirit," revolves around the Spirit Himself, and His manifold ministry.

Having already considered the names and titles of God the Father and God the Son, we now come to a coverage of those given to God the Spirit. Sharing Deity – for the Spirit of God is God the Spirit – the designations of the promised Gift of Pentecost are just as important to study as those of the Father and the Son. What must not be forgotten is the fact that all the actual and symbolic names and titles of the Holy Spirit writers of Scripture gave Him, were prompted by Himself. "Men spake from God, being moved by the Holy Spirit" (2 Peter 1:21 ASV). "Every scripture is inspired of God" (2 Timothy 3:16 ASV) – this includes every part of Scripture mentioning the personality and ministry of the Spirit Himself, the Source of inspiration (2 Samuel 23:2; Acts 1:16).

We are cognizant of what Jesus said of the Spirit – "He shall not speak of Himself" (John 16:13), which some have taken to mean the trait of self-effacement, and have made much of the sentiment that the Spirit never spoke about Himself, but always exalted Jesus. But this is *not* the implication of our Lord's statement as the ASV proves in its translation, "He shall not speak *from* [not 'of'] himself." "*From* Himself" implies not on His own initiative. The truth the Spirit-inspired men set forth was not *conceived* in His own mind, but *received* from God, as the next phrase proves – "But what things soever *he shall hear,* these shall he speak" (John 16:13, 14 ASV).

On the other hand, as the Bible is full of the Spirit from the first reference to His activity at Creation (Genesis 1:2), right on till we have the last reference in connection with the Rapture of the Church (Revelation 22:17), He has had a great deal to say about Himself, as the hundreds of references to His person and power indicate. He dominates the sacred pages of Holy Writ just as the Father and the Son do. When we think of the gospels it is so charming to discover that Jesus sends us to the Spirit, and the Spirit leads us back to Jesus.

Although the term *Trinity,* in respect to the Father, Son and the Spirit, is not found in the Bible, their threefoldedness is clearly apparent in scores of passages as, for instance, in the benediction Paul gives us – "The grace of our Lord Jesus Christ, and the love of God, and the communion of the Holy Spirit, be with you all" (2 Corinthians 13:14). The Church believes in "A Trinity in Unity, and Unity in Trinity" or, as the hymn puts it – "Three in One; and One in Three." But this blessed Unity does not prevent each Member from playing a particular part, as our study of the Spirit's activities will prove. Further, as the Father and Son each have their own distinct names and titles, so the Spirit bears many potent divine names, expressive of His manifold qualities and attributes. Everywhere His prerogatives are before us, and His part in the divine economy is clearly emphasized.

What will be discovered is the fact that Scripture never stops to prove the Spirit's reality, but asserts it in the descriptions given of Him. Either from ignorance or thoughtlessness, many are guilty of applying neuter pronouns to Him, and present Him, not as a Person, but simply as an influence, or some kind of impersonal emanation from God. Imperfect views of the Spirit's personality and power make for spiritual barrenness. As Downer puts it in his volume, *The Mission and Ministration of the Holy Spirit,* "The results of deficient attention to the study and preaching of the Third Person have appeared in dryness of spiritual experience, a low level of Christian life, formalism in worship, want of discipline in the Church, want of zeal in missionary enterprise." It was Professor Beck of Tubingen who said that, "Theology without the Holy Spirit is not only a cold stone, it is a deadly poison."

Our attention is focused on the manifold designations given of the Spirit, which reveal Him as an active member of the Godhead, the direct Agent between heaven and earth in this present age in salvation and sanctification, and as the Administrator of the affairs of the Church Jesus purchased by His precious blood. Without doubt, it is part of the satanic plan to belittle the importance of the Holy Spirt and His activities, for he knows that nothing can ruin his hold upon the souls of men like a perfect

understanding of who the Spirit is, and of the almighty power He possesses.

That the Spirit's reality and Deity stand proven by the remarkable array of names and titles ascribed to Him is also borne out by C. H. MacGregor in his most helpful small work on *Things of the Spirit,* in which he says –

> "In the Scriptures we do not find that distinction between nominal and real, which is so familiar to us in the usage of ordinary life. What anything is in name, that it is in reality. The supreme example of this is found in the name of God. What He calls Himself is a revelation of what He is. Therefore, in the names of the Holy Spirit we have a rich revelation of His character and work."

1. ACTUAL NAMES AND TITLES

The very first designation of the Holy Spirit is found in the second opening verse of the Bible where we see Him as Co-Creator. *"The Spirit of God* moved upon the face of the waters"* (Genesis 1:2). Already we have stressed the necessity of observing the "Law of First Mention" of a person, word, or theme, seeing that in same there is the germ of development. In the first occurence of the Spirit's presence and work we have Him bringing beauty out of chaos, order out of confusion, and Scripture progressively unfolds His power as the Transformer in many realms. Abraham Kuyper, the great Dutch theologian, in his masterly study *The Works of The Holy Spirit,* summarized the work of the Holy Spirit in two significant propositions which His many names amplify –

1. "The work of the Holy Spirit is confined to the elect and does not begin with their regeneration; it touches every creation, animate and inanimate, and begins its op-

erations at the very moment of their origins.

2. The proper work of the Holy Spirit in every creature consists in the quickening and sustaining of life with reference to his being and talents, and, in its highest sense, with reference to eternal life which is his salvation."

As the Bible presents a progressive revelation of the character and activities of each member of the Trinity, let us now examine the ever-expanding, unfolding of the actuality and acts of the Holy Spirit as found in very many references out of the hundreds associated with Him from Genesis to Revelation.

OLD TESTAMENT NAMES AND TITLES

Although it is only as we come to our Lord's teaching on the Holy Spirit, as found in the four gospels that we have the full revelation of His nature and work in the Church, in the believer, in the world, yet in the Old Testament there are some ninety references to Him in which many different titles, falling into three groups, are to be found.

1. THOSE EXPRESSING HIS RELATION TO GOD.

R. A. Redford, in his erudite work published in 1889 on the doctrine of the Spirit as set forth in Scripture as a whole, aptly entitled his volume *VOX DEI – The Voice of God* – which is how the Spirit is presented, as the oft-repeated phrase, "the Spirit saith" indicates. From Genesis to Malachi represents a period extending well over 2,000 years, and throughout this long stretch of time, the Spirit appears as the authoritative voice of God, as the following titles prove.

The Spirit of God (Genesis 1:2).

Both the Hebrew word for "Spirit" – *ruach*, and its Greek equivalent, *pneuma*, mean "wind" or "breath," hence the combination Elihu gives us in the Book of Job –

"There is a spirit in man,
And the breath of the Almighty giveth them understanding" (32:8).

Some 13 times this particular title occurs in the Old Testament, and as the term GOD is *Elohim*, we have, in the Spirit, our *Ruach Elohim*. Although He proceeds from God, yet the Spirit is a personality distinct from Him whose voice He is. As "The Spirit *of* God" all of His activities must be interpreted by His eternal relationship in the Godhead. As already indicated, *Elohim* is a plural word suggesting the Trinity – "God said, Let *us* make man in *our* image" (Genesis 1:26). In this connection the Spirit has been called, *OSCULUM PATRIS et FILII* – "The *Kiss* of the Father and the Son" – which is a concrete expression of Paul, "The unity of the Spirit" (Ephesians 4:3; 2:18). He is ever seen as the Bond of Unity between the Father and the Son. His essential function, then, is that of *uniting*. "Eternally and temporally He is the *Unifier*."

The occasion of this first mention of the Spirit is also significant. It is in connection with Creation when, moving, or brooding, over the face of the waters, He brought life out of death. John Owen, in his classic work, *Discourse Concerning the Holy Spirit*, states –

"Without Him, all was a dead sea; a rude inform chaos; a confused heap covered with darkness: but by the moving of the Spirit of God upon it, He communicated a quickening prolific virtue."

Thus, from this initial reference to the Spirit, and subsequent ones in connection with Creation, He is related to –

Its order (Genesis 1:2).

Its design (Job 26:13).

Its life (Job 33:4; Genesis 1:26).

Its glory (Psalm 19:1; 33:6).

Further, we must take the second verse in Genesis 1 in connection with the third verse – "The Spirit of God was brooding on the face of the waters, and God said, Let there be light." From this we are led to think of the Word of God as coming forth from His Spirit, which corresponds with the exact force of the language. The Breath of God is brooding over Creation, and that Breath of God takes the shape of a direct command, becomes an external force and fact – "Let there be light, and there was light."

Before God, then, said *Let there be light,* He said, *Let there be Spirit.* Light would not have made those waters good and glad, if the Spirit of Light had not first moved upon them. There would not have been the herb of the field, the bird of the air, the fish of the sea, the masterpiece of man, if the brooding Spirit had not acted first. The Spirit came before all His gifts – before the light, before the firmament, before all the beauty and provision of nature. First of all, He moved upon the shapeless face of the waters, and then came light with its charm, the herb with its greenness, and the bird with its song. In some circles today there is a tendency to seek gifts before the Giver – to strive after healing, or tongues, and other manifestations of the Spirit, but not after the initial obligation of crowning the Person Himself as Lord of the life.

> My goal is God Himself, not joy,
>   nor peace,
> Not even blessing, but Himself, my
>   God.

May we be delivered from inverting the divine order of seeking *Light* before the Spirit, whose breath preceded all things;

of making a blessing our goal rather than the Blesser Himself!

The Spirit of the Lord (Isaiah 11:2).

This is His most frequent title in the Old Testament, occurring some 23 times, and, as with all other titles, has its own particular significance. This designation is common to the activities of the judges God raised up to deliver Israel (Judges 3:10). David said, "The Spirit of the LORD spake by me" (2 Samuel 23:2). In our coverage of *The Names and Titles of God* we saw that the title LORD whenever it appears in small capitals means Jehovah, as it is consistently translated in the ASV.

Further, as previously indicated, this sacred name, which ancient Jews were afraid to utter, declares the eternity of God, He who was, is, and will be always (*see* Exodus 3:14). He is the origin and essential of life, the only true life, the One without whom there can be no existence at all, the only One who has existence that is self-derived (John 5:26). As "The Spirit of Jehovah" the Third Person of the Trinity shares this essence and quality of Jehovah. In the claim of His authority as LORD, the Spirit claims such as His divine right (Luke 4:18).

The Spirit of the Lord God (Isaiah 61:1).

This title is but an extension of the one just considered, being a further *Jehovah* title of the Spirit as the ASV implies. "The Spirit of the Lord Jehovah is upon me; because Jehovah hath anointed me to preach good tidings unto the meek." The fact that the Lord Jesus applied this verse to Himself, and declared it was fulfilled in His spiritual ministry, leaves us in no doubt that Isaiah had the Holy Spirit in mind as the One who was the Executive of the Godhead, or God in action. He was the divine Representative of Heaven's authority and power, and therefore able to equip Jesus for His remarkable ministry (Luke 4:18; Acts 10:38). References to the Spirit in Isaiah are numerous, one of the last being that of Israel, who is said to have "rebelled and vexed the Holy Spirit of the Lord" (63:10). The people rejected His provision as God's Agent on their behalf.

The Spirit (Numbers 11:17, 25, 26).

Occurring some 14 times in the Old Testament, this plain, simple designation denotes the sum of His personal totality. The emphasis is on the article for He is THE Spirit as over against false spirits. "God is a Spirit" (John 4:24 ASV), and as breath is the vital principle of the body, so the Holy Spirit, who is of the same essence as God the Father, brings to us the inmost life of God. A further thought is that the use of the definite article declares His personality. He is, of course, spoken of with and without the article. For instance, some Ephesian disciples had not heard "whether there be any Holy Spirit" (Acts 19:2). Yet even here the ASV supplies the article. Modernistic teachers lay hold of the passages where the unpretentious, definite article is not used to affirm that the Holy Spirit is not a Person, only an emanation of life-energy from God. But even where the article is missing, the fact of His personality is not obliterated but implied in the manner of His activities found in the context containing the missing THE to His name. As Dr. G. Handley Moule puts it in connection with the plain *Holy Spirit* – "In the general light of Scripture in Divine influence are we abundantly secure in saying that this means nothing less than the Divine Person at work? A guiding principle is that where the article is used the *Person* is emphasised – where not used attention is drawn to the *Power* of the Person. It was this Power, Paul

saw lacking in those disciples at Ephesus (Acts 19:1, 2)."

The Spirit is not *something* but *Someone*, and abundant proofs of His Personality are to be found throughout the Bible. Our difficulty comes in not being able to distinguish between person and personality. We can accept the Lord Jesus as a Person, because He had a body that could be seen and handled (1 John 1:1), but the Spirit does not possess a visible body or person. Personality expresses itself through the person or outward frame, but when death attacks the body, personality continues. The person *within* the body never dies.

What are the true elements of personality expressing themselves through the human frame? They are the distinctive features of *heart, mind,* and *will* belonging to the tenant within the building. Being able to think, feel and will the Spirit possesses true personality, for such functions are not possible to an inanimate object. As we journey through all the titles of the Spirit in Scripture fuller attention will be given to these inner possessions, thus a brief synopsis at this point will suffice.

The *heart* is the seat of affection, and with it we love persons and things. Paul speaks of "the love of the Spirit" (Romans 15:30), and He is indeed the Spirit of love, inspiring love for Himself, for the Father and for the Son.

The *mind* is the source of intelligence, reason, and knowledge. With the mind we think, plan, and comprehend. Paul refers to "the mind of the Spirit" and describes Him as "The Spirit of Wisdom" (Romans 8:27; 1 Corinthians 2:10, 11). As He is the Author of Scripture what mind He must have!

The *will* is that part of personality that acts, decides, giving expression, thereby, to inner thoughts, feelings, and plans. Evidence about the will of the Spirit is found particularly in The Acts, when the apostles experienced the power of the Spirit to impose His will upon them (Acts 8:29, 39; 10:19, 20; 16:6, 7). How blessed we are if our heart, mind, and will are under the control of "THE Spirit"!

My Spirit (Genesis 6:3).

There are some 13 passages in the Old Testament where the personal pronoun MY is used by God of the Holy Spirit, and in all cases expresses the precious relationship between the Father and the Spirit, just as "MY beloved Son" implies the relationship of Jesus to God. What a pronoun of endearment this is! Yet its first occurrence in connection with the Flood is sad and tragic! It was as if God was saying, "*My* Spirit, reflecting my love, mercy, and grace will not always strive with those who persistently reject such a tender Friend!"

The terrible Flood answered the question as to whether the Spirit or the flesh should be supreme. It was not the will of the Spirit, woh acted for the loving God, that any should perish, but all, save Noah and his family, did perish. All carnality was drowned, and all worldly lust was buried in the waters from beneath and above, because the loving, pleading Spirit was spurned. If only man would learn not to strive against the Spirit who ever strives to save him from his sin and doom.

Thy Spirit (Nehemiah 9:30 ASV). Occurs 4 times.

His Spirit (Psalm 106:33). Occurs 6 times.

Both of these pronouns THY and HIS express the same truth of relationship as indicated under *My Spirit.*

2. THOSE EXPRESSING HIS CHARACTER.

Often a name is indicative of the nature of its bearer. When Abigail interceded with David for the life of her churlish husband she said —

"Regard not this man of Belial, even Nabal: for as is his name, so is he: Nabal is his name, and folly is with him" (1 Samuel 25:25).

Nabal means *a fool,* and so what Abigail actually meant was, "Pay no attention to him. He's a fool by name, and a fool by nature." There was correspondence between the evil thing he was and the name he bore (1 Samuel 25:3). The same harmony between name and nature, in a good sense, has already been pointed out in many of the divine names and titles considered and it is so with the Holy Spirit for, "as His name, so is He."

Thy Good Spirit (Nehemiah 9:20).

The qualifying adjective used here implies perfect agreement between attribute and action. As this name, so was the Spirit. Inherently good, He is ever found doing good. The stream was as pure as the source. "Thy spirit *is* good" (Psalm 143:10). Thus, as Paul reminds us —

"The fruit of the Spirit is . . . goodness" (Galatians 5:22).
"The fruit of the Spirit is in all goodness" (Ephesians 5:9).

Being "good," the Spirit showered goodness upon the Israelites as they journeyed through the wilderness. How good He was to Israel! He led them by His truth, fed them with His promises, pruned them by His discipline, inspired them by His presence, and instructed them by His acts. His teaching function occurring here only, is a remarkable anticipation of the New Testament. Yet although the people were the recipients of such daily, divine goodness, they turned against this Good Spirit. They despised His goodness (Nehemiah 9:30; Romans 2:4).

What must be borne in mind is the way God first gave Israel the Spirit, before the food and drink. Doubtless we would have expected the reverse order in a similar starving condition. But God knew that no amount of manna and water could permanently allay physical hunger as long as there was spiritual hunger. If there is discord in the soul, what is the use of the strains of beautiful music? To the afflicted man, the first word of Jesus was, "Thy sins be forgiven thee." This was a more abiding miracle than the mandate that followed — "Arise and walk."

Disease of heart was of more concern to Jesus than disease of body. To Him, the needs of the heart preceded needs of the body. Thus was it with Israel. Before God sent the manna, He gave the people His "Good Spirit" and in this first boon there was the promise and provision of lesser boons.

Thy Free Spirit (Psalm 51:12).

Instead of *free* the ASV gives us, "Uphold me with a willing spirit" making it applicable to David's spirit rather than to the Holy Spirit. The pronoun *Thy* is not in the original and is not used in the ASV. David prayed for a "right spirit," that is, a constant, firm, unyielding spirit to temptation; and also for a "willing spirit," implying a heart willing to be conformed to God's will, so that he could be preserved in a right course of action.

Yet in spite of this direct interpretation of David's prayer for being upheld by a free spirit, we love to think of the Holy Spirit as the *Free Spirit*, or The Spirit of Liberty and Freedom, as Paul says He is, "Where the Spirit of the Lord is, there is liberty" (2 Corinthians 3:17). What a wonderful Liberator He is from sin, self, the flesh, care and fear, and Satan! Then is He not the One who keeps us in the glorious liberty of the children of God? (Galatians 5:1; Romans 8:21). It is only as we live in con-

stant obedience to this divine Emancipator that we can find perfect freedom.

Thy Holy Spirit (Psalm 51:11).

His Holy Spirit (Isaiah 63:10, 11).

Although these appear to be equivalent terms, when each is examined in the light of the context, each takes on a different significance. David, heartbroken over his terrible sin in the matter of Uriah and Bathsheba, and acutely aware of his own unclean heart, pleaded with God not to take His *holy* Spirit from him. In Old Testament Scripture, He was viewed more as a Power than a Person, as One who came upon certain individuals marked out for special service, energizing them for such, and would be withdrawn when the task was completed. Still as king, David did not want the Spirit of Anointing removed from Him. But as Dr. C. I. Scofield rightly comments upon Psalm 51:11 —

> "No believer of this dispensation, aware of the promise of His abiding, John 14:16, should pray, 'Take not Thy Holy Spirit from me,' Ephesians 4:30: but, while Christian *position* is not found here, Christian *experience* in essence is."

The second passage emphasizes the sacredness of Deity. God is *holy,* and His Spirit is the same in essence, and shares the Father's abhorrence for uncleanness and unrighteousness. The prophet shows how the conduct of Israel in the wilderness was alien to the holy mind and will of the Spirit, and being *holy,* He became the enemy of the people (Isaiah 63:9, 10). Yet there was the holy remnant who earned the Spirit's benediction (Isaiah 63:14, 18). It is interesting to observe that the use of the adjective *holy* in connection with the Spirit is found some 100 times in the Bible, and He is described thus for several reasons –

1. *The Spirit is essentially holy in character.*

Holiness is not only one of His august attributes as a member of the Godhead, but a part of His being. He *is* holy, even as God could say, "I *am* holy" (Leviticus 20:7, 8; 1 Peter 1:16).

2. *The Spirit comes from and represents, a holy God.*

He would not have been qualified to function as "The Executive of the Godhead" unless He shared the unflecked holiness of the Father and the Son. Thus, coming as the Sent One by the Holy One, He bore His image, as all representatives of God must do (John 14:26; 17:11; 1 Peter 1:16).

3. *The Spirit is in the world to magnify the Holy Saviour.*

Jesus said of Him, "He shall glorify me" (John 16:7-15), and since Pentecost He has highly exalted "the Holy Child Jesus" seeing that as the "Holy Spirit" He is one with the Lord in His perfect holiness.

4. *The Spirit inspired holy men to compose Scripture.*

The Scriptures are rightly named *The Holy Bible* – the word "Bible" coming from *byblos*, meaning book. The "holy men," as Peter calls the writers of Holy Writ (2 Peter 1:21, *see* 1 Peter 1:11, 12), wrote under the inspiration and guidance of the Holy Spirit, and this is why Scripture is heavy with the air of holiness (2 Timothy 3:16, 17).

5. *The Spirit is in the world to advance holy living.*

Once He makes the repentant sinner a new creature in Christ Jesus, being *holy*, the Spirit strives to transform such a one into the divine image, and makes possible the advancement of holy living

through His indwelling and dominion. This is why Paul calls Him, "the spirit of holiness" for He is the Holy One who sanctifies the believer (Romans 1: 4; 15:16).

> Every virtue we possess,
>   And every victory won,
> And every thought of holiness
>   Are His alone.

A New Spirit (Ezekiel 11:19; 18:31; 36: 26).

Among Ezekiel's many references to the Holy Spirit, this repeated one is significant. To us, *new* means something recently made, modern – as opposed to *old*. The Spirit, as the Eternal One, is not *new* in this sense. David prayed that a right spirit might be renewed in him (Psalm 51:10), and Jeremiah speaks of God making a *new* covenant with His people (31:31). But what are we to understand by the promise of *the New Spirit?*

It would seem as if a new motive and principle of action is implied; that as *the new heart* means a transformation of the *will and affections*, so *the new spirit* indicates a changed *understanding*. But where are the new motives, new rules, new aims to come from, seeing the stony heart and the antagonistic spirit of man cannot produce them? As God the Spirit He says, "Behold, I make all things new," and it is in this sense that we know Him as "The New Spirit" who makes possible newness of life for the new creature He creates (2 Corinthians 5:17).

3. THOSE EXPRESSING HIS OPERATIONS UPON MEN.

Before we come to a consideration of the names and titles associated with the Spirit's ministry in men, this may be a fitting point to explain the use of *Ghost* in respect to His being. While this term often appears in the KJV, the ASV consistently uses *Spirit*. *Ghost* is an old

English word for *Spirit*, and because the word ghost has so changed and narrowed in meaning, and is now associated with "spooks," it is better not to use it, especially since its connection with the unreal and the inactive is so completely remote from the true meaning of Him who is no ghost, but God in action in a real world. That the Holy Spirit is active in the realm of human affairs and emotions is evident from the designations of Him now before us.

The Spirit That Was Upon Moses (Numbers 11:25, 29).

First of all, a word is necessary as to the exact meaning of the phrase about taking the Spirit upon Moses and transferring the same to the elders who had been chosen to share the burden of the leadership of Israel. This does not imply that the Holy Spirit ceased to rest upon Moses, and was given to the 70 elders, but that the gifts of the Spirit so manifest in Moses were likewise imparted to the elders. The qualities the Spirit made possible in the great leader were in no degree impaired, but the elders were endowed with a portion of the same gifts, especially of prophecy, or an extraordinary penetration in discovering hidden, and settling difficult, things (Numbers 11:25). The two elders who seemed to shrink from such an office received the same Spirit endowment (11:26-29).

There is frequent reference to the Spirit coming upon individuals in the Old Testament both for practical purposes as well as for spiritual or public ministry. He came upon Gideon and he blew a trumpet that rallied the people to conflict (Judges 6:34). He came upon several other judges. *See* Judges 11:29; 13:25; 14:6, 19; 15:14. He came upon Samuel, upon Saul, upon David, and others. The Spirit clothed these individuals with Himself for the accom-

plishment of a specific task, and then withdrew. He does not appear to have been their abiding Inhabitant, as He is in our hearts in this age of Grace. Jesus predicted that the with the advent of the Spirit at Pentecost He would *abide* with the saints forever. "He dwelleth with you, and shall be *in* you" (John 14:16, 17). Every born-again believer has the Spirit as a "perpetual Comforter and as an Eternal Inhabitant." (*See* further under title *Clothing*.)

Although Jesus was conceived of the Holy Spirit (Matthew 1:20), and possessed by the Spirit from His birth, yet as He entered His public ministry, the selfsame Spirit came upon Jesus in fulfillment of Isaiah's prediction, "I will put my spirit upon him" (Matthew 12:18). All upon whom the Spirit came, experienced a definite crisis in life and service, and signs of divine endowment followed. Receiving the Spirit's anointing, Jesus went into the wilderness to be tempted of the devil, and He certainly required a special unction for those 40 days of severe testing. After the *dove*, there came the *devil*, with the former triumphing over the latter (Matthew 4:1-11).

The Spirit of Wisdom (Isaiah 11:2; Exodus 28:3; 31:1-4).

In many respects the gifts of the Spirit, prophesied by Isaiah to be evident in the coming Messiah, sound so much like each other that confusion of thought may arise as to the special function of each. *Wisdom – Understanding – Counsel – Knowledge*, while they appear to be similar are yet different. Distinction between these gifts of the Spirit related to men can be briefly explained thus –

Wisdom, placed first in the group, can generally speaking be regarded as the gift of spiritual insight.

Understanding is entirely concerned

with the intellect, and represents power of comprehension of what is revealed.

Counsel has been referred to as "the great *social* gift of the Holy Spirit," being related to our life as social beings, or the working out of our salvation in connection with others.

Knowledge, differing from the first three attributes can be regarded as in the main concerned with the heart, the knowledge of the love of God.

First of all, we have WISDOM, as a gift of the Spirit. What is this divine endowment? It has been defined as "a certain Divine light given to the soul whereby it both sees and tastes God and Divine things." But the wisdom the Spirit supplies represents not only spiritual insight. It was also given for practical purposes. The wisehearted were filled with the Spirit of Wisdom to make Aaron's holy garments, just as Bezaleel and Aholiab were filled with the Spirit of *Wisdom, Understanding* and *Knowledge* to devise works of gold, silver, and brass for the Tabernacle (Exodus 28: 3; 31:1-6). (See more fully under title *Wisdom.*)

The Spirit of Understanding (Isaiah 11: 2).

It will be seen that Isaiah sets forth the Messianic titles in pairs – wisdom with understanding, counsel with might, the Spirit of knowledge with fear of the Lord. This was most fitting because the one title is the complement of the other. The Spirit's gift of spiritual understanding comes in varied degree because in this quality of mental power there is the greatest diversity in recipients. Such *understanding* has been defined in this expressive way –

> "It is a supernatural habit, or quality, or faculty abiding in the intellect, whereby it is elevated, and enabled, first, to understand supernatural truth with special clearness,

and, next, to penetrate into the reasons and motives for faith; and lastly, to exhibit and to prevail on others by the exhibition of the truth to believe in the same."

Daniel received this particular gift in an abundant degree, manifested in his understanding in all visions and dreams (Daniel 1:17). Along with his three friends Daniel outstripped the magicians and astrologers in understanding (1:20). A heathen queen had to confess that the Spirit of the Holy God was upon Daniel giving him "light and understanding and wisdom, like the wisdom of the gods" (5:11). The prophet was likewise given remarkable understanding or spiritual insight into God's plan of the ages (9: 22, 23). Only a Spirit-illuminated mind can fully grasp Spirit-revealed truth.

What an extraordinary insight into the inner meaning of Scripture, of the world of nature and of man the Lord Jesus possessed! That He had this gift of the Spirit as Isaiah prophesied is evident from what happened in the Temple when only twelve years of age. Of the learned men He sat among we read, "All that heard Him were astonished at His *understanding* and answers" (Luke 2:47). Because such spiritual understanding is the mortal foe of religious ignorance and superstition, how we need to pray –

> "We beseech Thee, the Spirit of Understanding, raise and illuminate our faculties to apprehend the Divine Nature, and its operations, that our hearts being enlarged, as the Mystery of the Adorable Trinity unfolds to our view, we may love as we have been loved."

Paul would have us know that no matter how keen and sharp our understanding may be there is something which, even it, cannot grasp – "The peace of

God passeth all understanding" (Philippians 4:7).

The Spirit of Counsel and Might (Isaiah 11:2).

We have these two promises of the Spirit together because the one is often linked with the other –

> "The Lord of Hosts is wonderful in counsel, and excellent in working" (Isaiah 28:29). *See* Job 36:5.
> "The Mighty God ... Great in counsel, and mighty in work" (Jeremiah 32:18, 19).

The Holy Spirit is one with God in the combination of counsel and might, for what He counsels He is able to enforce. He not only gives the needed counsel for direction, but He carries us through to the place of designation. The Spirit not only informs, but inspires. Many are good at telling us what to do when we need guidance, but are utterly unable to give us strength to carry out what they prescribe. But from the Spirit we have, not only precepts, but power to live them out. (*See* under title *Counsellor*.)

The Spirit of Knowledge and the Fear of the Lord (Isaiah 11:2).

Here again is a pair of gifts, woven together because of their relationship. The fuller our spiritual knowledge the Holy Spirit makes possible as we obey His commands, the deeper our reverential approach to Him who is thrice Holy. Paul gives us the height of knowledge in his pronounced aim in life, "That I may know him, and the power of his resurrection" (Philippians 3:10)! It is only as we come to experience His risen power, that we are able to worship and adore. The Holy Spirit holds up the lamp of knowledge found in Scripture, then hedges us around with holy awe lest we should fail to fear, love and obey the One revealed. What need we have to

pray the prayer of Job, for revelation and sanctification:

> That which I see not teach thou me: if I have done iniquity, I will do no more" (Job 34:32).

The Spirit of Grace and Supplications (Zechariah 12:10).

The KJV gives the plural, "supplications" but the ASV the singular, "supplication." Twice over the Holy Spirit is styled, "The Spirit of Grace." When Zechariah used the title he revealed Him as the Dispenser of divine favor to all men, either by conviction of sin in order to bless them by turning them away from their iniquities, or by imparting to believers spiritual life, witnessing to their adoption and perfecting their holiness. The Spirit is the Source of Grace not only in His own person, but He is the Channel through which the love of the Father and the grace of His Son are poured upon penitent sinners.

The other reference to "The Spirit of Grace" is a tragic one. The description of the guilt incurred by an apostate from Christ to Judaism is given in the phrase, "done despite unto the Spirit of grace" (Hebrews 10:29). Arthur Way's translation gives us, "Who has heaped insult on the Spirit that imparts the bounty of God." This was the summit of wickedness, the sin of all sins, the irremissible sin, namely, flagrantly insulting Him who, as the gift of grace, is called "the Spirit of Grace."

Then He is also named *The Spirit of ... Supplication*. Of the phrase as a whole Delitzsch says, "The Spirit is the Source of Grace, and the Inspirer of all true prayer." Grace comes first because unless we are saved by grace we cannot pray in the Spirit. It is only in and through the redeemed, consecrated heart, that He is able to intercede prevailingly (Romans 8:26, 27). Jude exhorts us to pray in the Holy Spirit (Jude 20).

> Pray, always pray: The Holy Spirit
>   pleads
> Within thee all thy daily, hourly
>   needs.

The Spirit of Burning (Isaiah 4:4).

God is likened unto a "Consuming Fire" and Scripture as *fire* in one's bones (Jeremiah 5:14; 20:9). At Pentecost, the Spirit came as *Fire* (Acts 2:3), giving the disciples, "Tongues of fire, to preach the reconciling Word." Isaiah uses the graphic title *The Spirit of Burning,* and divine judgment is in the mind of the prophet. Whatever God does in the universe, He does by His *Spirit,* without the hand of man (Job 34:20; Psalm 104:30). Here He is represented using His authority and power as Judge, searching and singing, manifesting His fiery baptism (Matthew 3:11, 12). The same Holy Spirit who sanctifies believers by the fire of affliction (Malachi 3:2, 3), dooms unbelievers to the fire of perdition (Revelation 20:15). May we ever experience the Spirit as the sacred fire burning up the dross of base desire! May He lighten our souls with celestial fire!

The Voice of the Almighty (Ezekiel 1: 24:10:5).

The Voice of Jehovah (Psalm 29).

We take these designations together because they are akin. The awesome name, *Jehovah,* implies His almightiness, as well as His eternal subsistence. What intrigues us is the significance of numerous references to His *voice,* the original of which means "the daughter of the voice." Often Jehovah's voice is associated with "thunder." *See* 2 Samuel 22: 14; Job 37:5; 40:9; Psalm 18:13). In Psalm 29, the phrase "the voice of Jehovah" occurs seven times. This great psalm is a perfect specimen of Hebrew poetry, giving a magnificent description of a thunderstorm in which "the voice of Jehovah" is the Voice revealed in thunder. Adam Welch says that this psalm of Jehovah in a storm always makes him think of Lord Byron's lines —

> From peak to peak, the echoing
>   crags among,
> Leaps the live thunder.

This sevenfold occurrence of the thunderous "Voice of the Lord" can be compared with the seven thunders of Revelation 10:3. But for the prophets of old, *voice* stood for the resultant inward demonstration of the divine will, by whatever means effected, given to them to declare. Further, such a *Voice* was to be distinguished from all natural sounds and voices, even where these were interpreted as conveying divine instruction as, for instance, in the Thunderstorm Psalm. And that this "Voice from Heaven" (Daniel 4:31, with Matthew 3:17) and other New Testament passages) was the symbolic way of describing the Holy Spirit, is evident from Peter's assertion that the voice of the prophets in their predictions was the Voice of the Spirit —

> "The Spirit of Christ which was in them did signify, when He *testified beforehand* the sufferings of Christ, and the glory that should follow" (1 Peter 1:11; 2 Peter 1:21).

Those Spirit-inspired prophets heard His Voice, speaking for Jehovah, as the still, small voice, and not as a thunderous one (1 Kings 19:12). Harriet Auber in her moving poem on *Our Blest Redeemer Ere He Breathed* wrote of the Spirit as a consoling Voice thus —

> And His that gentle voice we hear,
>   Soft as the breath of even,
> That checks each thought, that calms
>   each fear,
> And speaks of Heaven.

May we be found living in loving obedience to the will of the Spirit, as to be able to detect immediately "each whisper of His voice"!

The Breath of the Almighty (Job 32: 8 ASV; 33:4).

While the KJV gives us "the inspiration of the Almighty," the ASV puts it, "the breath of the Almighty giveth them understanding." The term "inspiration," however, means "God in-breathed" (2 Timothy 3:16). As previously indicated, in the original *Spirit* means breath or wind, and is often associated with the impartation of life (Genesis 2:7; Ezekiel 37:9; John 3:8). When Jesus came to send forth His disciples, He breathed on them saying, "Receive ye the Holy Spirit" – the Master's breath symbolizing the Spirit who was to possess them (John 20: 22). At Pentecost, the Holy Spirit came accompanied by a "sound as of a rushing *mighty* wind" (Acts 2:2). (*See* further under title *Wind.*)

Invisible, the Holy Spirit is yet the Energy of Creation, the activating force of the cosmos, God's Agent in the making of the world and man, as well as the Inspirer of all Scripture. As the thoughts of my mind are articulated through the action of my breath upon the vocal cords, and are transmitted in the shape of words from the inner world of my being to the outer world when I speak, so the Spirit, or Breath of God, takes the thoughts of God, as well as the inexpressible yearnings of the believer and articulates them (Romans 8: 26, 27). His familiar name, *The Holy Spirit*, carries with it the idea of a holy, moving, vitalizing breath.

The Spirit is called the Breath of the Almighty because He is His direct emanation, the manifestation of His presence in His invisible, heavenly actions. "The best symbol for the invisible, immaterial thinking agent in man is the wind or breath, that kind of matter which is the thinnest and has least of the grosser elements." As God's Breath gave life to the first man, Adam (Genesis 2:7), the same gives life to sinners (John 3:8), and to Scripture which honors the Spirit as the livingness of His divine inspiration. In the life-giving power of a breathing life, Jesus endowed His own for life and service. The Spirit-anointed Master, as the Breather of the Spirit, reveals the intimate relationship between them, and shows the Life-Giver and the *Life* imparted. This is why we pray –

> Breathe on me, Breath of God,
> Fill me with life anew,
> That I may love what Thou dost love,
> And do what Thou wouldst do.

NEW TESTAMENT NAMES AND TITLES

As there are over 260 passages in this body of Scripture in which direct reference is made to the Holy Spirit, and from which some 39 different designations are applied to Him, it can be seen that His presence pervades the 27 books forming the New Testament. In the Old Testament He is prominently associated with creation, natural forces, as well as prophecy, but in the New Testament, the accent is more on the spiritual, moral and ethical aspects of His activities. A prayerful and patient study of the quantity and quality of the Spirit's names and titles given Him by Christ and the apostles reveals what a never-failing treasury filled with boundless stores of grace this Executive of the Godhead is.

The present regret is that for the majority of Christians there is One in their midst they know not of. Through ignorance or neglect they live a life devoid of His power and gifts. If asked whether they received the Holy Spirit when they believed, they would have to reply with those disciples at Ephesus, "We did not so much as hear whether the Holy Spirit was given" (Acts 19:1, 2 ASV). What a mighty spiritual upsurge in Church life and work would be experienced if only she could rediscover the vast resources at her disposal in the Holy Spirit who enabled her, in the first century, to turn the world upside down. The Book of Acts should be called "The Acts of the Holy Spirit Through the Disciples," showing how they believed the Spirit, the Controller and Administrator of the affairs of the Church, whose spiritual barrenness today can be traced to her imperfect understanding of her spiritual heritage in the Spirit.

Dr. F. E. Marsh tells the story of a Christian woman being catechized in connection with her application for church membership. One of the questions put was, "How many persons are there in the Godhead?" The dear soul was known for her love of the truth and the love of souls, but her clerical questioner was a broad man in his thinking. To his astonishment and of those assembled, the devout woman replied, "There are two persons in the Godhead, the Father and the Son." Again, the minister put the same question, "How many persons are there in the Godhead?" and again she gave the same reply. Then the minister turned to his elders and to those assembled and said – "You see what comes of high flown zeal and hypocrisy. This woman seeks to teach others, and is herself more ignorant than a child. What ignorance! Woman, don't you know that the correct answer is, 'There are three persons in the Godhead, the Father, the Son, and the Holy Ghost'?"

"Sir," replied the woman, in the Scottish tongue, "I ken verra well that the Catechism say so, but whether am I to believe the Catechism or yersel? We hear you mention the Father, and sometimes, but *nae* aften, ye mak mention o' the Son in yer preachin', but wha ever heard you speak aboot the Holy Ghost? Deed, sir, ye never sae muckle as tauld us

whether be ony Holy Ghost, let alune oor need o' His grace!" What a rebuke that must have been for such an unctionless preacher!

It is to be feared that many preachers of the Word forget that while the Holy Spirit regenerates only through truth, making it the instrument of His activity within the soul, failure can be theirs if dependence is solely upon the saving efficacy of the truth without the Spirit's unction to make it real as it is proclaimed. Says Paul, "The letter killeth, but the spirit giveth life" (2 Corinthians 3:6). Arthur Way's translation reads, "The written ordinance denounces a death-penalty; but the Spirit thrills with a new life." When the truth is preached in the power and demonstration of the Spirit, mighty things always happen.

There is a legend to the effect that the eloquent head of a monastery died, and that while his body was lying in state before burial one of Satan's imps took possession of the corpse, raising it to seeming life, and preached an orthodox sermon through the lips of the dead abbot. The evil spirit returned to the caverns of hell and boasted of his exploit. When asked by Satan whether he did not run the risk of converting some soul by his orthodox sermon, he replied – "Sire, do you not well know that orthodoxy without the unction of the Spirit never saves, but always damns?"

If we are to have a revival of Spirit-inspired preaching of the truth, those who preach it must realize to the full the character and resources of the Spirit, and this knowledge can only come about by a study of what Scripture reveals of His personality and power. It is the fervent prayer of the writer that the following classification of the names and titles of the Holy Spirit as given in the New Testament will help in this direction.

1. NAMES AND TITLES ASSOCIATED
   WITH HIS PERSONALITY.

It is essential to commence with this group of designations, for if He does not possess all the elements that go to make up personality, then all the titles given Him are meaningless. During the third century the error arose of dealing with the Spirit in an impersonal way, and treating Him as a mere influence, an exertion of divine energy, an emanation from God, and such an error has continued in the Church, and in the position of liberal-minded theologians today. True, the impersonal pronoun is used in passages like Romans 8:16, 26 where the Spirit is mentioned as *it*, but such is corrected in the ASV to personal pronouns.

In a chapter like John 16, the personal pronouns are used some 13 times, proving that our Lord believed the Spirit to be a living and conscious exerciser of true personal will and love. Dr. J. H. Jowett reminds us that, "Our fellowship is not with a 'something' but with a *Somebody;* not so much with a 'force' but with a *Spirit;* not with an 'it' but with *Him.*" May we be preserved from dishonoring and displeasing the Spirit by lack of recognition! It is as true of Him, as of the Father and the Son, "They that honor Me, will I honor." As. Dr. R. A. Torrey says –

"It is of the highest importance that we decide whether the Holy Spirit is a Divine Person worthy to receive our adoration, our faith, our love, and our entire surrender to Himself, or whether it is simply an influence emanating from God or a power or an illumination God imparts to us. If the Holy Spirit is a Person, and a Divine Person, and we do not know Him as such, then we are robbing a Divine Being of the worship and the faith and the love and the surrender to Himself which are His due."

Further, our conception of the Spirit determines our attitude toward Him. If we think of Him merely as an emanation or energy from God then our attitude will be an active one – a striving and struggling to have more of such power. But if we believe the Spirit of God to be God the Spirit then our attitude will be a passive one, for yielded and still our daily quest will be, "How can He have more of me?" Although He is not a mere influence or the sum or series of influences, the Spirit yet possesses divine influence as Harriet Auber expresses in her renowned hymn –

He came, sweet influence to impart,
A gracious, willing Guest.

Proofs of the personality of the Spirit abound, and the appellations and actions ascribed to Him cannot be the expression of a *thing*. Already we have indicated that He possesseses the true elements of personality, namely, *heart* with which to love; *mind* with which to think and reason; *will* with which to act and decide (Romans 15:30; 1 Corinthians 2:10, 11; 12:11). Other evidences are as follows –

1. Jesus accepted the Spirit as a Person, and repeatedly used the masculine pronouns, *He, Him, Himself* to describe His activities (John 14:16, 17; 15:26; 16:7, 8, 13, 14).

2. Mistreatment of Him proves His personality.
   He can be lied against (Acts 5:3).
   He can be tempted, like Jesus was (Acts 5:9).
   He can be resisted (Acts 7:51).
   He can be grieved (Ephesians 4:30).
   He can be despised (Hebrews 10:29).
   He can be blasphemed against

(Matthew 12:31).

He can be ignored (Acts 19:2).

3. Actions performed by the Spirit are only possible for a Person.

There are some 160 passages in the Bible where the definite actions are mentioned, and language is meaningless, and absurd, if He is not a divine Person.

He can search – and what a Searcher! (1 Corinthians 2:10).

He can speak – and with what a Voice! (Acts 8:29; 1 Timothy 4: 1; Revelation 2:7).

He can cry – "no language but a cry" (Galatians 4:6).

He can pray – and what an Intercessor He is! (Romans 8:26, 27; 1 John 2:1).

He can testify – of God, of Christ, and of truth (John 15:26, 27).

He can teach – and who teaches like Him? (John 14:26; 16:12-14; Nehemiah 9:20).

He can lead – and always the right way (Romans 8:14).

He can command – and blesses obedience (Acts 16:6, 7).

He inspired Scripture – and speaks only through it (John 16:13; 2 Peter 1:21).

2. MANIFOLD NAMES AND TITLES GIVEN HIM AS FURTHER EVIDENCE OF HIS PERSONALITY.

The numerous designations given the Holy Spirit by Christ and His apostles seem to fall into five distinguishable groups, and taken together reveal, not only His personality but His Deity. Because the Three Persons comprising the Trinity are One, it is readily understood why He is associated with the Father and the Son in so many instances. First of all, then, we take –

Titles Combining Him With God the Father

The Spirit of God (Matthew 3:16; 12: 28).

He is thus named some dozen times in the New Testament. It was, of course, the first title given Him (Genesis 1:2), and reveals His preexistence and oneness with God in His nature. Coming from God, He functions for God – is God in action – existing to fulfill the divine will. He is consubstantial with God and therefore like Him in *person*.

The Spirit of the Lord (Luke 4:18; Acts 8:39; 2 Corinthians 3:17, 18).

Whether *Lord* used in some 15 passages refers to God the Father or God the Son, makes little difference. Both are named thus, even as the Spirit Himself is. As "The Spirit of the Lord" He claims divine authority and seeks to lead us to own the divine right of Lordship over all things. *Lord* here is given as *Jehovah* in the ASV, and is a title implying "The Covenant-Keeping One." As "the Spirit of Jehovah," He manifested all the attributes of Jehovah, and thus anointed Jesus to act as Jehovah's Representative, and as the Fulfiller of all Old Testament predictions of Him.

My Spirit (Matthew 12:18; Acts 2:4, 17. See Genesis 6:3).

Identifying Himself with Isaiah's prophecy of God's Servant (Isaiah 42: 1-4), Jesus quoted the phrase, "I will put *my* spirit upon him." Here we have the pronoun of personal possession, indicating the specific relationship existing between the Father and the Spirit who ever carries out the Father's will. At the Flood God said, "*My Spirit* will not always strive with men." But the Son, mantled with the same divinely possessed Spirit, never ceases to strive with sinners.

His Spirit (Ephesians 3:16; 1 Thessalonians 4:8; 1 John 4:13).

This title is the equivalent to the

above, the pronoun *his* referring to God in all three references. The Spirit was HIS, and His alone.

The Promise of the Father (Acts 1:4; 2:33).

The Promise of My Father (Luke 24: 49).

The Spirit of Your Father (Matthew 10: 20).

The Promise of the Spirit (Galatians 3: 14).

Here we have a quartet of titles akin in sentiment, because they are all related to the Holy Spirit as a promised Gift. He was promised by the Father – "I will pour out my spirit upon all flesh" (Joel 2:28, 29), which promise was fulfilled when the Spirit came in Christ's name (John 14:26). Then Christ Himself promised His disciples to send the Spirit, "I will send My Spirit" (John 15:26; 16: 7). At Pentecost, the dual, divine promise was fulfilled (Acts 2:16-21).

Because of all God is in Himself, He cannot break any promise He has made, and the testimony of Solomon is that "there hath not failed one word of all his good promise, which he promised" (1 Kings 8:56) – a tribute Paul confirms (Romans 4:21; 2 Corinthians 1: 20; Hebrews 10:23). Through Calvary and Pentecost we receive "the promise of the Spirit through faith" (Galatians 3:14), and such a promise is for all whom "the Lord our God shall call" (Acts 2:39). Jonathan Swift in *Dialogue* thinks that, "Promises and pie-crusts are made to be broken." But saints through the centuries have proved that no Scripture can be broken.

Then it will be noted that the Holy Spirit, as "the Spirit of Promise," is associated with God as Father. Jesus used the pronouns of Him – MY Father, YOUR Father – stressing thereby the privileged relationship in the redeemed

family of God (John 20:17). Further, as the Spirit of the Father, He manifested all the fatherly qualities of love, grace, mercy and provision (Psalm 103: 13). What a promise, full of comfort and strength, it is to realize that the indwelling Spirit is "that of our Father"! The pressures and problems of life may be trying, but He who came from the Father for our benefit, and shares the Father's sympathy and power is able to meet our need with His sufficient grace.

A striking feature of our Lord's parting word to His disciples, "I send the promise of my Father upon you" (Luke 24:49), is that in eight words it covers the Godhead – and the Church! With every believer there is the might of "God in three persons, Blessed Trinity."

> I take the promised Holy Ghost,
> I take the power of Pentecost,
> To fill me to the uttermost,
> *I take – He undertakes.*

The Gift of God (John 4:10, 14; Acts 10:45; 1 John 3:24).

The Spirit, as God's blessed Love-gift can be dealt with in this threefold way –

1. *He was given by the Father* (John 14:16, 26; Acts 1:4). Along with Jesus, He is an unspeakable gift, to be had without money.

2. *He was given by Christ* (John 15: 26). On that historic day of Pentecost, the Spirit came as the promised, empowering Gift of the ascended Lord.

3. *He came on His own initiative* (John 16:13). "When He . . . is come." Behind this statement are the willing, voluntary advent and activities of the Spirit.

That the well of water Jesus said He would give the woman of Samaria was the Holy Spirit symbolized, is found in His teaching concerning the Spirit who, at that time, "was not yet given, because Jesus was not yet glorified." From Pentecost on, the Spirit has been flowing from believers as "rivers of living water." The life-giving Spirit, then, came as the Gift of the ascended Lord to His redeemed people. And what a peerless Gift He is! How do we react to a gift from a loving friend? Why, in gratitude we receive it, highly value it, and use it to the full. A gift is freely bestowed, not bought. Simon the sorcerer, witnessing the power of the Spirit, offered Peter money, if he could arrange for the miracle-working power of the Spirit to be his. How scorching was the reply of Peter –

> "Thy money perish with thee, because thou hast thought that the gift of God may be purchased with money" (Acts 8:20).

Every believer, in the moment of his regeneration, was made the recipient of the Spirit. "If any man have not the Spirit of Christ, he is none of his" (Romans 8:9). Then, from the Gift Himself, the believer receives a gift or gifts to be used in the service of Christ. John's affirmation is most explicit –

> "Hereby we know that Christ dwelleth in us, by *the Spirit which He hath given us*" (1 John 3:24).

"As each has received a gift, employ it one for another, as good stewards of God's varied grace" (1 Peter 4:8-11 RSV). The writer of the epistle to the Hebrews speaks of "gifts of the Holy Spirit distributed according to His own will" (Hebrews 2:3, 4 RSV). That these gifts of the *Gift* are varied is evident from the teaching of Paul, the great expositor of "the things of the Spirit" (Romans 12:6-8; 1 Corinthians 12:4-11, 18-31; Ephesians 4:7-12). The important, personal question is, "Have I discovered my regeneration-gift received from the Spirit, and is He using it to the limit as I seek to be subject to His will?" Through grace, I possess the Gift of the Spirit, but whether He possesses me, flowing through as rivers of living water, is another matter.

> Great Gift of our ascended King,
>   His saving truth reveal:
> Our tongues inspire His praise to sing,
>   Our hearts His love to feel.

The Spirit of Him Who Raised up Jesus (Romans 1:4; 8:11; 1 Peter 3:18).

The apostles with united voice affirm that the life-giving Spirit was "the efficient cause of our Lord's Resurrection." What an authoritative declaration of Paul's this is – "The Spirit of him that raised up Jesus from the dead!" When Christ left heaven to become Man, born of a woman, the Holy Spirit was responsible for His conception in the womb of Mary, commencing the sacred life that ultimately was given as a ransom for many. The Spirit of the Conception was also the Spirit of Resurrection, for the Power imparting the antenatal life and bringing it to birth was the same who quickened that same body in the tomb, and brought forth the crucified Saviour, as "the first begotten of the dead." Peter says that Jesus was "quickened [made alive again] by the Spirit."

Surely this was the supreme effort of Him who came as the Giver of life for "by it He gave life to the dead body of Christ, but re-united the human spirit to its proper dwelling, not as a mere tenement, but as a home insusceptible of further death" (Psalm 16:10). Our blessed hope is that this selfsame Spirit is the Pledge of our final resurrection (Romans 8:23; Ephesians 1:13, 14; 4:30). His marvelous act in raising Jesus from the dead is the guarantee of our victory over death. *See* Revelation 11:11. An ancient creed refers to the Spirit as "The Lord, the Life-giver" and His power to quicken is not confined to raising those who are physically dead.

He can quicken us mentally and spiritually and physically –

> "The Spirit of him that raised up Jesus from the dead. . . shall also quicken your mortal bodies" (Romans 8:11).

Breathe on me, Breath of God,
So shall I never die,
But live with Thee the perfect life
Of Thine Eternity.

The Spirit Which Is of God (1 Corinthians 2:12).

The Spirit of Our God (1 Corinthians 6:11).

The Spirit of the Living God (2 Corinthians 3:3).

Here we have a triad of titles bound together by a common tie. Actually, the first title we dealt with under this section, namely *The Spirit of God*, should be linked to the three designations above. As "The Spirit of the Living God" and *"our God,"* He is a member of the "Godhead bodily," having a divine origin and nature, exerting divine power, and existing to fulfill the divine will. The term for GOD is *ELOHIM,* meaning "The Strong One," and as *Ruach Elohim* (Genesis 1:2) – His Creation name – the Spirit is identified with creative acts. "By his spirit, he hath garnished the heavens" (Job 26:13). Job also declares that the Spirit also had a share in the creation of God's masterpiece – Man! "The spirit of God hath made me, and the breath of the Almighty hath given me life" (Job 33:4).

The Spirit is God's Viceregent clothed with omnipotent power. The identity of God the Father with God the Spirit runs through Scripture. The two are One, just as there is no distinction between man and the spirit of man (1 Corinthians 2:11). All that God is, the Spirit is, in His character and attributes. As "the Spirit of the Living God," He manifests divine vitality in His ministry (2 Corinthians 3:3). As "the Spirit of our God" Paul implies by his use of this title, that He is one with God in the grace of His adaptability (1 Corinthians 6:11). The extremity of man's sinful case is met in the suitability of God's grace which the Spirit of Grace reveals and applies.

Spirit of the Living God,
Fall afresh on me.

The Holy Spirit of God (Ephesians 4:30).

As "The Lord Jesus Christ" is His full and reverent title, so "The Holy Spirit," used some 100 times in Scripture, is His expressive designation. In the above passage Paul is writing of those things that either please or pain the tender Spirit, and, being God the Spirit, He shares the grief of God the Father when the saints commit those things alien to the love and will of God and the Spirit. (*See* further under title *The Spirit of Love.*)

His Holy Spirit (1 Thessalonians 4:8).

The pronoun the apostle uses in this verse confirms the relationship between God and the Spirit, just as the phrase "His Son" proves the eternal relationship between Father and Son. Perfect holiness is an attribute characterizing the Trinity. In the narrative, Paul warns that all manner of uncleanness and unrighteousness cannot be tolerated either by God, the Giver of the Spirit, nor by the Spirit given. If the believer is to make spiritual progress, then all forms of sin must be consumed in the fire of divine holiness. (*See* under title *The Spirit of Burning.*)

Among the many occurrences of the title "The Holy Spirit" in Acts, there are these revealing His personality and character as the thrice Holy One –

Holy in testimony (Acts 1:5).

Holy in promise (2:33).
Holy in gift (2:38).
Holy in ministry (9:31).
Holy in endowment (10:45).
Holy in discretion (15:28).
Holy in authority (16:6).
(*See* further under *The Holy Spirit.*)

The Power of the Highest (Luke 1:35).

The term *highest* suggests superlativeness, superiority, nothing beyond, no further to ascend, and is used in many ways. For instance –

God is in the Highest, and the Highest of all (Luke 2:14).
Christ is "the Son of the Highest" (Luke 1:32).
The Spirit, is "the power of the Highest" (Luke 1:35).
John the Baptist was "the prophet of the Highest" (Luke 1:76).
The saints are "the children of the Highest" (6:35).

Luke, the beloved physician, reveals the mystery of how "The Son of the Highest" was made a little lower than the angels by "The Power of the Highest." The dominant feature of the Spirit's presence in Scripture is that of miraculous Power, and as God the Spirit nothing is impossible to Him, as the conception in Mary proves. As the Agent of the Most High God, the Spirit shares in His unlimited power. What must not be forgotten is that *Power* is never divorced from the *Person*. The Spirit is, in Himself, "*The Power* of the Highest." "Ye shall receive power, the Holy Spirit coming upon you." Power, then, is the manifestation of the Presence of the Spirit in any activity of His. Our danger is the craving for power, apart from the entire control of our being by Him who is the Power.

Titles and Names Expressing His Relation to God the Son

No one can read the gospels without being deeply impressed with the holy intimacy that existed between Christ and the Spirit. Christ could say, "I and my Father are *one*" (John 10:30). He could have also said, "I and the Holy Spirit are *one*," for they are in every way. When Christ said, "I, by the Spirit of God," the same is not to be confined to the casting out of demons (Matthew 12:28), but to our Lord's dependence upon the Spirit throughout His brief but dynamic ministry. Constantly filled with the Spirit, Christ fulfilled all that was predicted of Him as the One to have the Spirit of the mighty Jehovah resting upon Him (Isaiah 11:1-5).

René Pache, one of Europe's outstanding evangelical scholars in his work *Person and Work of the Holy Spirit,* says of the deep fellowship between Christ and the Spirit –

"The unity between the Son and the Spirit is marked by the fact that the attitude adopted by men toward one determines that which they maintain toward the other; he who rejects Christ resists the Holy Spirit; he who yields entirely to Jesus is used by the Holy Spirit."

This mystic union between the Holy Son and the Holy Spirit opens up several avenues of thought not too often dealt with by those handling the things of the Spirit. First of all, the rivers of the Spirit flowing through the Old Testament run into the sea of Christ in the New Testament (Ecclesiastes 1:7). In His varied operations before Christ came, the Spirit made possible for certain men, political wisdom, power of leadership, physical strength, artistic beauty, spiritual insight, prophetic foresight, and moral courage. But all the virtues of the Spirit were never found meeting in one person. For instance, Samson had the *power* of the Spirit, but not His *purity*. Moses had the wisdom of the Spirit to lead Israel through the wilderness, but not the qualification to take the people into the promised land. Christ, however, possessed all the gifts of the Spirit in their entirety and manifested them in His ministry. The sevenfold attributes of the Spirit which Isaiah predicted were evident in Christ's works, words and ways (Isaiah 11:2).

A further thought of great import is the way the Holy Spirit exclusively occupied Christ. Before the Saviour came, the Spirit had not found a permanent abode in anyone. But now, for the first time, He indwelt a human body, which He prepared for Himself, for over 33 years. Is it not a striking feature of Christ's relationship with the Spirit that after Christ's birth there is no record of the Spirit being associated with any other individual until He came at Pentecost as Heaven's Love-Gift for all believers. There had to be a Man, who was both able and willing to receive the fullness of the Spirit ere that fullness could be bestowed upon others, and that Man was Christ Jesus upon whom the Spirit concentrated all His energies (Acts 10:38).

As our *Meal Offering*, Christ was the "fine flour mingled with oil" (Leviticus 2:5), and the inseparable unbroken union between the *meal* and the *oil* is a merging, or incorporation, soul-inspiring to behold. For the student wishing to extend the idea of this beautiful blending, the following features could be developed –

> Christ was prophesied by the Spirit (Luke 24:26, 27; 1 Peter 1:11).
> Christ was born of the Spirit (Genesis 3:15; Isaiah 9:6; Matthew 1:18).
> Christ was justified by the Spirit (Isaiah 11:1, 2; Luke 2:20, 47; 1 Timothy 3:16).

> Christ was anointed with the Spirit (Matthew 3:16; Acts 10:38).
> Christ was gladdened by the Spirit (Luke 10:21 ASV).
> Christ died by the Spirit (Hebrews 9:14).
> Christ was raised by the Spirit (Romans 1:5; 8:11; 1 Peter 3:18).

> Christ gave commandments by the Spirit (Acts 1:2).

As to definite titles, connecting the Holy Son and the Holy Spirit, the following find mention –

The Spirit of Jesus (Acts 16:6, 7 ASV).

As previously indicated *Jesus* is the human name He received before His birth, and is associated with all He endured and accomplished in the days of His flesh. This Name above every name occurs almost 600 times in the gospels alone. Such a title indicates the heart-fellowship between the Holy Spirit and Jesus, particularly during His public ministry until His ascension on high.

What exactly constituted the ascension-gift of the Spirit? Jesus in His condescension became the *God-Man*, for within the womb of Mary, the Spirit fused Deity and humanity into one, and thus Jesus appeared as *God* in frail flesh. Because, therefore, He was conceived by the Spirit, and indwelt by Him from His birth, the Spirit was intimately connected with Jesus and understood everything from the divine and human standpoints. Indwelling the Man Christ Jesus for so long, He knew all about His human needs, trials, and emotions, and was able to succor accordingly. The Spirit of Jesus, then, came as the Spirit, both of God and man, and indwelling us can sympathize with all our human trials, needs, and feelings, and as the Spirit of God, He is able to succor us when we are tried.

Spirit of Jesus, glorify
    The Master's name in me;
Whether I live, or if I die,
    Let Christ exalted be.

The Spirit of Christ (Romans 8:9; 1 Peter 1:11).

When Paul used this title of the Holy Spirit, he did not imply the necessity of manifesting a Christlike spirit, but that no man is saved unless he has been born anew by the Spirit, and is indwelt by Him. Professor Warfield says that where this title, *Spirit of Christ,* occurs "most naturally it means the Spirit which proceeds from and represents Christ. As He is spoken of as having resided in the ancient prophets, the preexistence of Christ is assumed. Christ was in the prophets, and from Him came their inspiration."

The name *Christ* means Messiah, or the Anointed One (*see* under title *Christ*), and the Spirit is closely identified with all Messianic prophecies and activities, particularly with Christ reinvested with all glory and power. F. E. Marsh says that He is –

"*The Spirit of Christ* in the sphere of His testimony. He brings Christ to us in His revelation (1 Peter 1:11), and brings us to Christ by His association (Romans 8:9)."

How solemn is Paul's assertion, "If any man have not the Spirit of Christ, he is none of his" (Romans 8:9). If the Spirit is absent, so is Christ. The indisputable proof of our salvation is the presence of the indwelling Spirit, not as a mysterious influence but the divine Person who indwelt Christ for 33 years. This, then, is a most important title of the Spirit who is described as being *of* and *from* Christ –

He is the Spirit of *Christ* because He testified of Him (1 Peter 1:11); because He unites us to Him (1 Corinthians 12: 12, 13); because He is given by Him (John 1:33); because He acts for Him (John 14:16); because He will finally unite us to Him (Romans 8:11); because He makes us like Him (2 Corinthians 3:18).

The Spirit of Jesus Christ (Philippians 1:19).

The combined name *Jesus Christ* implies that the once humbled One, *Jesus,* is now most highly exalted, *Christ.* This double title, occurring only some 6 times in the gospels, was a favorite one of Paul who used it about 66 times. Peter and John employed it some 21 times. The Holy Spirit, then, is the One who knew all our Lord *was* as *Jesus,* and all He *is* as *Christ* exalted and alive forever, more. Paul speaks of "the supply of the Spirit of Jesus Christ" or, as Arthur Way translates it,

"Through the strength supplied to me by the Spirit of Jesus the Messiah" (Philippians 1:19).

There is no gauge checking the supply of the Spirit, although it would seem so by the meager supply of His strength many believers try to exist on! All He has, and is, and can do, is at the disposal of the humblest saint. The Spirit is ours, as it was with Christ, *without measure* (John 3:34).

The Spirit of His Son (Galatians 4:6).

This expressive title implies that the Spirit imparts right feelings, thoughts, and words Godward, and Christward. It is likewise a unique designation in that it emphasizes the Trinity – God, the Son, the Spirit, who is before us here in the relationship of His paternity. Further, as the Spirit of His Son, He produces in our hearts the language of a son, and assures us that we are sons in *His Son* and in Him, children of the Father. Through regeneration, the Spirit makes blessedly real the Spirit of Adoption whereby we cry "Abba, Father!"

and as the filial Spirit, His indwelling testifies to our sonship.

His Witnesses . . . So Is the Holy Spirit (Acts 5:30-32).

During their persecution for Christ's sake, some of the apostles testified to having seen Him slain and hung on a tree, and then made the outstanding claim that the Holy Spirit was also at Calvary to witness the bitter end. Thus, He is the only living Witness in the world to all that Jesus suffered for our eternal redemption. In His darkest hour, Jesus was consoled by the fact that the Spirit was there, just as His mother was, standing by His cross. As Dr. Elder Cumming in his volume *Through The Eternal Spirit* states it —

"There were human witnesses of the outward tragedy, but the Spirit who had been the lifelong companion of Christ's deepest and most secret thoughts, was the One solitary Witness of the infinite and eternal value which enforced and informed the sacrifice . . . Just as an attendant waited upon the steps of the sacrificing priest, who scrutinized the victim to be placed upon the altar, and was a sponsor for its unblemished health so the Spirit who had watched with unresting jealousy and vigilance over the life of the Son, mediated in His last offering, and as earth and Heaven became the sponsor for its spotlessness and soul-cleansing power."

It is because of the Spirit's association with the cross of Christ, that He ever blesses "the preaching of the cross" (1 Corinthians 1:18-21). Because He was there when it happened, He can illuminate all the cross means, to those who witness to the fact and efficacy of a crucified Saviour. What untold wonders the Spirit can accomplish in a world of sin, as those who are crucified with Christ, extol and magnify Him who died to take away sin!

Another Comforter (John 14:16).

Further on, under the title *The Comforter*, material will be found on the Spirit's mission as the divine Consoler of the saints. At this point, we are only dealing with the evident likeness to Himself Jesus indicated when He said that the Father would send *Another Comforter*. By the use of the word "another" Jesus implied that He was the *other* Comforter. In the original, *another* carries a twofold significance —

1. Another of the same kind.
2. Another of a different kind.

Which Greek term do you think Jesus used when He spoke of "*Another* Comforter"? Why, the first, of course — "Another of the *same kind*." Thus, actually He promised that the Father would send those He was about to leave, *another* like Himself. What a precious thought this is! In the Holy Spirit we have Jesus' other self, *His alter ego*. As "the Spirit of Christ" He is still to the saints all that Jesus was to His disciples.

Title and Names Expressing His Own Essential Deity

Yet once again let it be said that the Spirit of God is God the Spirit. Although He is referred to as "the Third Person of the Blessed Trinity," it is not in any sense of inferiority, for no one Person in the Trinity is inferior to another. All Three are co-equal, co-eternal. He is spoken of as *third* because of His manifestation and work.

In the Old Testament, God the Father is prominent; in the gospels, God the Son dominates the scene; since Pentecost, God the Spirit is the Agent between Christ and ourselves.

It was Hodge, the renowned theologian who coined the phrase, "The Holy Spirit is the Executive of the Godhead," which clear-cut conception and expression is indisputedly true. For, as Daniel Steele says –

> "Law emanates from the *Father*, mercy and judgment are committed to the *Son*, while the executive of both Persons is the ever-blessed *Spirit*. Here we have the three departments of government – the Legislative, the Judicial, and the Executive. Through the Holy Spirit the Father and the Son operate in human souls, reproving, regenerating, sanctifying and witnessing."

God the Father is the original Source of everything (Genesis 1:1). God the Son follows in the order of revelation (John 5:22-27). God the Spirit is the Channel through which the blessings of heaven reach us (Ephesians 2:18).

Thus the divine order is from the Father – through the Son – by the Spirit. As flowers and fruit form the last revealed part of a tree, so the Spirit is *third*, since His is the last revealed Personality. As it has been expressed, "He is *Third* not in order of time, or dignity of nature, but in order and manner of subsisting . . . There is but one source of Deity, the Father, from whom the Holy Spirit issues through the Son, whose image He is, and in whom He rests. The Holy Spirit is the link between the Father and the Son, and is linked to the Father by the Son."

> So God the Father, God the Son,
> And God the Spirit we adore,
> A sea of life and love unknown
> Without a bottom or a shore.

Paul was a great believer in the Trinity, as can be seen in the way he often unites the Three Divine Persons. For instance, he could declare with equal truth –

"Your body is the temple of the *Holy Spirit* who is in you" (1 Corinthians 6:19).
"Ye are the temple of *God*" (1 Corinthians 3:16).
"Christ in you" (Colossians 1:27).

In his epistle to the Ephesians, the apostle contrived to weave the Three Persons together in all six chapters, i.e., "The *God* of our *Lord Jesus Christ, the Father* of glory . . . *the spirit* of wisdom and revelation" (1:17).

The Scriptures do not stop to prove either the Personality or Deity of the Spirit. The truth of this is clearly expressed and constantly implied, and quite confidently "holy men of old" spoke and wrote of the Holy Spirit as God, knew Him as God, and rendered Him the position of equality with the Father and the Son. Paul's description of antichrist can be rightfully applied to the Spirit as "God that sitteth in the temple of God, showing himself that He is God" (2 Thessalonians 2:4). Let us endeavor then to classify the various evidences of the Deity of the gracious Spirit.

God (Acts 5:3, 4).

The Early Church accepted the Deity of the Spirit, and without hesitation ascribed divine names to Him. In his encounter with Ananias and Sapphira, Peter, confronting this pair with their deception, used two phrases – "thou hast lied unto *God*," and "lie to the *Holy Spirit*." There is no contradiction here for Peter believed the Holy Spirit to be God with power to smite the deceivers dead.

E. W. Bullinger reminds us that in Scripture the Holy Spirit is neither called nor spoken of as a *Person*, even thought He possesses the elements of personality. As He is spoken of as *God*, it is not correct to speak of Him as a Person apart from His being God Himself. Quite rightly we speak of Jesus as a Person, for He became one – "God manifest in *flesh*," and therefore individualized He is localized now on the Father's throne (Revelation 3:21), and when He returns to reign He will be seated "on the throne of His glory" (Matthew 25:31).

The Holy Spirit, then, is *God*, and the Spirit of the Triune God. As in Christ there dwells "all the fulness of the Godhead *bodily*" (Colossians 2:9), so, with reverence, we can say that in God the Spirit, there dwells the Godhead *spiritually*. Of Christ, as the *bodily* expression of God, we read, "Every eye shall see Him," but of the Spirit, the *spiritual* expression of God, it is written, "Whom the world cannot receive, because it seeth him not" (John 14:17).

Lord (2 Corinthians 3:17, 18 asv).

A further evidence of the Deity of the Spirit is found in the application of the august name of *Jehovah* to Him. We have already noticed that where the title Lord is printed in small capitals that consistently it implies *Jehovah* (Leviticus 1:1). Paul recognized the Spirit as Lord –

> "The Lord is the Spirit:
> Now where the Spirit of One Who is Lord is, there is freedom . . . Spirit that is Lord" (2 Corinthians 3:17, 18 Rotherham).

The first century church was so dynamic in her witness because of her recognition of the Lordship of the Spirit. This is why, throughout Acts we find not only the *presence* of "the Spirit of the *living God*" – a reference to God in the power of Resurrection – but also the *presidency* of the Spirit. Sovereignty infers complete power of dictation, and the apostles recognized this prerogative of Deity in the Holy Spirit. "Separate me Barnabas and Saul for the work

whereunto *I* have called them" (Acts 13:2-4). The same thought of Lordship is found in the repeated commanding phrase, "The Spirit saith unto the churches" (Revelation 2:7).

In several instances the tri-personality of Jehovah is clearly implied. Plurality is dominant in many combinations, but the unity of the Three Persons does not prevent each playing His own part. Here is an example of such tri-personality:

> "I heard the voice of Jehovah" (Isaiah 6:8-10 asv).
> "These things said Isaiah, when he saw his [Christ's] glory" (John 12:37-41).
> "Well spake the Holy Spirit through Isaiah" (Acts 28:25-27 asv).

Ancients believed that in the threefold Holy – "Holy, Holy, Holy, is the Lord of hosts" (Isaiah 6:3) – the three Holy Persons in the Trinity were meant. Scripture makes it plain that the Spirit shares the attributes of the Father and the Son, attributes implying those qualities and properties so conspicuous to Deity.

It is a prerogative of God alone to dwell *in* His creatures. So no other beings or persons are thus described in the Bible. The Spirit is never mentioned as being among creatures. When created spirits are enumerated, such as angels, archangels, thrones, dominions, principalities, powers, cherubim and seraphim, the climax never ends with the Holy Spirit, as we should expect if He is both a person and a creature. Jesus said of Him, that "He shall dwell *in* you," and that along with the Father and Himself (John 14:17, 23).

Eternal Spirit (Hebrews 9:14).

Rotherham translates this phrase, "Who through an age-abiding Spirit." *Eternity* is the property of Deity alone. As the *Eternal Spirit* He is uncreated, and uncreated is divine for ETERNAL means without beginning or ending of existence. In this arrestive title, then, the eternalness of the Spirit's being is emphasized, who never was any other than He is, and cannot be any other than He is, nor who can ever be any other than He was. It was through, or by, the grace and strength of the *Eternal* Spirit that Christ, the *Eternal* Son, offered Himself up to God as a ransom for sin. Some scholars affirm that this passage in Hebrews does not refer to the Holy Spirit, but implies the eternal spirit of Jesus Himself. But the Greek preposition rendered *through*, must be translated "by means of," and seems to point to the Spirit as being the active Agent at Calvary.

Omnipresent Spirit (Psalm 139:7-10).

The prefix *Omni* signifies "all," so an "omnibus" is a vehicle for all kinds of persons. *Omnipresence* implies the ability to be present everywhere at the same time. The Spirit, however, is in *all* believers everywhere. "Whither shall I go from thy spirit?" It is impossible to go anywhere where He is not present. Says F. E. Marsh, "In the Heaven of immensity, is the Hell of mystery, and in the Earth of secrecy, He is alike present."

Omniscient Spirit (1 Corinthians 2:10, 11; Romans 8:26, 27; Isaiah 40:13).

Omni – all; *science* – knowledge. Thus, omniscience means all-knowing, all-wise, and implies a knowledge of things past, present, and future. All that pertains to God, Christ, Satan, man, heaven, earth, and hell, is known to the Spirit who "searcheth all things." Only God can search the things of God. Man cannot see nor understand the things of God and of eternity, but the Spirit is cognizant of all. He is the *Custodian* of all God's secrets and *Revealer* of all He is (1 Corinthians 2:10).

Related to omniscience is *foreknowl-*

edge, or the ability to know the end from the beginning, and the knowledge of a thing before it comes to pass. Such a quality belongs alone to Deity. Peter testified to the Spirit's foreknowledge when he wrote that, some 1000 years before Judas lived, the Spirit inspired David to make the prophecy, "The Holy Spirit by the mouth of David spake concerning Judas" (Acts 1:16). Another evidence of the Spirit's foreknowledge can be found in Acts 11:27, 28.

Omnipotent Spirit (Romans 15:13; Zechariah 4:6).

From the first reference to the Spirit (Genesis 1:2), to the last (Revelation 22:17), He is before us as the Embodiment of Power, and as the Personification of Omnipotence. Christ declared that He cast out demons by the Spirit of God whom He called "the finger of God" (Matthew 12:28 with Luke 11:20). Scripture provides us with many symbols of the Spirit's almightiness (Micah 3:8; Romans 15:15-19).

Seven Spirits (Revelation 1:4, 5; 4:5; 5:6).

This repeated title implies the perfection of the Spirit's personality and power. There are not seven Holy Spirits, for Paul refers to *the one Spirit* – one in the bond of His unity (1 Corinthians 12:13). The Book of Revelation looks at all things from the divine standpoint seeing them perfectly as a series of *sevens*. The Lamb has *seven* horns – perfection of power; and *seven* eyes – perfection of knowledge. *Seven Spirits of God* is an allusion to Isaiah's prophecy of the Messiah who, when He came would receive the impartation of perfect power and knowledge by the Spirit, who would possess Him without measure (John 3:34). The seven manifestations of the Spirit are –

"The Spirit of Jehovah, of wisdom,

of understanding, of counsel, of might, of knowledge, of the fear of Jehovah" (Isaiah 11:1, 2).

There is only "One Spirit" then, but One who is a sevenfold manifestation.

> Come, Holy Ghost, our souls inspire,
> And lighten with celestial fire;
> Thou the anointing Spirit art,
> Who does Thy sevenfold gifts impart.

The Spirit performs tasks only possible to Deity, and His divine works are of a varied nature –

He can Create. Man may make, but only God can create. At Creation, the divine prerogative of creative power was exercised by the Spirit (Genesis 1:2). As a result of the Spirit's energy, the beauty of the earth, the glory of the sky, and wonders of oceans came into being. Thus, Cowper in *The Task* expresses it –

> One Spirit – His
> Who wore the platted thorns with
>   bleeding brow,
> Rules universal nature. Not a flower
> But shares some touch, in freckle,
>   streak or stain,
> Of His unrivalled pencil.

Inscribed upon John Ruskin's Memorial at Fraig's Crag, Keswick, England, are the words, so beautiful in their sentiment –

> "The Spirit of God is around you in the air you breathe.
> His glory is the light that you see, and in the fruitfulness of earth and joy of His creatures.
> He has written for you day by day His revelation, as He has granted you day by day your daily bread."

Scripture affirms that the Spirit of God –

> Created the world (Genesis 1:2; Psalm 33:6).
> Created man (Job 33:4).
> Beautified the world (Job 26:13).
> Brings death upon it (Isaiah 40:7).

Brings life into it (Psalm 104:30).

He can inspire. Man may enthuse another, but cannot inspire – a term meaning instruction by divine influence. Holy men who wrote Scripture had minds and pens controlled by the divine Author, the Spirit of Wisdom and Revelation. The word "inspiration" is made up of two Latin words, *in* or *unto,* and *spirare* meaning "to breathe." Thus to be inspired by the Spirit indicates that He has breathed into one the truth He desires the person to know and declare (2 Samuel 23:1-3).

> The Spirit inspired prophecy in general (1 Timothy 4:1).
> The Spirit inspired Scripture as a whole (2 Timothy 3:16; 2 Peter 1:21).

He can Regenerate. As the Spirit of Life, He can impart life, whether physical or spiritual (Romans 8:11; 2 Corinthians 3:6). He is the Personal Agent in regeneration (John 1:13; 3:1-8). Personal Agent in the unceasing sanctification and quickening of those He indwells (Romans 15:16; 1 Corinthians 3:16; Ephesians 5:18; Titus 3:5).

He can Resurrect. Man can kill and bury, but only God can raise the dead (2 Corinthians 1:9). The gracious Spirit is described as He who raised up Jesus from the grave (Romans 8:11). He will also have a share in the resurrection of saints. One bright day, He will lift them up from earth to heaven (Ezekiel 8:3; 1 Thessalonians 4:17).

The Deity of the Spirit is also proven by His identification with God the Father, and God the Son. Says Dr. C. I. Scofield – "There is no Biblical reason for believing in the Deity and Personality of the Father and the Son, which does not equally establish that of the Spirit." This blessed partnership of the Trinity is traceable in many directions –

1. The Work of the Cross.

Because the Redemption of the soul is precious, and none can redeem his brother, Deity alone can accomplish such a task. As the *Holy Three* are involved in the Cross, all must have the same nature (Psalm 49:7, 8; 1 Corinthians 1: 30). There is one passage bringing God, Jesus Christ and the Spirit together as one in this work of deliverance from sin, namely (Hebrews 9:14):

> There is the Godward Aspect –
> "without spot to God."
> There is the Christward aspect –
> "The blood of Christ."
> There is the Spiritual aspect –
> "through the Eternal Spirit."
> There is the manward aspect –
> "purge your conscience from dead
> works to serve the living God."

The three incomparable parables of our Lord – The Lost Son, The Lost Sheep, The Lost Coin (Luke 15), fittingly illustrate the work of God the Father, God the Son, and God the Spirit in man's redemption.

2. The Baptismal Formula.

In our Lord's great commission He instructed His disciples to baptize all who believed in "The Name of the Father and of the Son and of the Holy Spirit" (Matthew 28:18-20). He did not say "in the names," but *name* – the singular presenting one God in three Persons. All Three are One in Deity and accomplishment,

3. The Apostolic Benediction.

A further evidence of the Deity of the Spirit can be found in the much-loved benediction Paul wrote for the church at Corinth, and which is used to close church services today, and in which an outstanding quality is ascribed to each Person of the Trinity (2 Corinthians 13:14) –

> *"The grace* of our *Lord Jesus Christ"*

> – Medium of all blessing;
> *"The love* of *God"* – Source of all
> blessing;
> *"The fellowship* of *the Holy Spirit"*
> – Dispenser of all blessing.

4. The Heavenly Witness.

Many scholars feel that John's affirmation of the threefold heavenly witness is not authoritative, but that the verses have crept into the narrative. Nevertheless, the implied truth is precious.

> "There are three that bear record
> in heaven –
> "The Father, the Word, and the
> Holy Spirit, and these three are
> *one.*
> There are three that bear witness
> in earth, the spirit, and the water,
> and the blood; and these three
> agree in one" (1 John 5:7, 8).

5. The United Access.

Another proof of the Spirit's Deity is given by Paul when he unites the Three Persons of the Trinity in the composition of Jews and Gentiles as one body – "Through him [*Christ*] we both [Jew and Gentile] have access by one *Spirit* unto the *Father*" (Ephesians 2:13, 18). Whether it be for salvation or worship, the order is ever the same – to God, through the Son, by the Holy Spirit.

While we have endeavored to prove the Spirit's equality with the Father and the Son, it is necessary to indicate evidences of subordination on His part. Scripture certainly draws the clearest possible distinction between the Father, Son, and Spirit, giving to each their separate personalities, and outlining their mutual relation as they act upon one another.

Yet Scripture also teaches that the Spirit is subordinate to God and to Christ. Such subordination of the Spirit is brought out in that He does not glorify Himself but Christ, even as Christ

Himself sought, not His own glory, but His Father's (John 7:18; 16:12-15). As Bengel expresses it – "The Son glorifies the Father, the Spirit glorifies the Son." As for the believer, he must be found glorying all Three. One of the mysteries of our faith is that Christ, who thought it not robbery to be equal with God (Philippians 2:6), was yet subordinate to the will of His Father (John 6:29; 8:29, 42; 9:4). The practical aspect of such surrender to the will of God is that we must be as subject to His sway as the Son and the Spirit were.

Titles and Names Expressing His Character

There are a few designations of the Spirit that reveal His own essential nature. "As is His name so is He." Many a person bears a good name, but fails to live up to it. Nature and name do not agree. But all that is said of the Spirit, *He is.* For instance, take similar titles like these –

Holy Spirit (Romans 15:16 ASV).

Holy One (1 John 2:20).

The Spirit of Holiness (Romans 1:4).

Holiness, an emphatic mark of Deity, is attributed to the Spirit some 100 times in Scripture, and the titles used in this connection present Him in the character of His sanctity. As a member of the Godhead, He could not be anything but holy; and wherever He is without restriction, holiness is the evidence of His presence. It is because of this essential attribute that sin against Him is irremissible (Matthew 12:31, 32). Because the Spirit is the High and *Holy One* that inhabited eternity, we have to deal with One whose holiness cannot sanction sin. Sin indulged in silences His voice, and robs us of the sense of His presence.

Perfect holiness is attributable to each of the Three Persons of the Blessed Trinity, and is not therefore a quality peculiar to the Spirit, who bears the oft-repeated adjective of *Holy.* Such frequent references to His holiness may point to His distinctive office, in the redemptive scheme, *to make men holy.*

> Spirit of purity and grace,
>   Our weakness, pitying see:
> Oh, make our hearts Thy dwelling
>   place,
>   And worthier Thee.

Spirit of Love (2 Timothy 1:7).

Paul believed in "the love of the Spirit," as well as in the constraining love of Christ (Romans 8:35; Ephesians 3:19). Writing to the Romans, he entreated for them "the love of the Spirit," or as Arthur Way puts it, "All the love inbreathed by the Spirit" (Romans 15:30). Then, as the Personification of Love, He begets love in the saints as Paul indicates when he commends the Colossians for their "love in the Spirit" (Colossians 1:8). In writing to the Corinthians, the apostle has the union, "By the Holy Spirit, by love unfeigned" (2 Corinthians 6:6).

Not only does the Spirit unfold the God of Love and shed abroad such love in the heart, and cause love to become part of His fruit in Christian character (Galatians 5:22), He Himself is Perfect Love. As the heart is the seat of love, He possesses such a center of being, hence His grief over sins of the believer. "Grieve not the Spirit of God" (Ephesians 4:30). Grief is an element of the heart. Where there is no heart, there can be no sign of this human emotion. The early saints could walk "in the comfort of the Holy Spirit" (Acts 9:31 ASV). Where there is no heart, there is no comfort. Grief, then, reveals the personality and love of the Spirit. The lamentable absence of love among professing Christians is an evidence of the lack of the Spirit's control of their lives.

Spirit of Love, Thy best of gifts
    Upon Thy servant pour:
Love, which another's burden lifts
    And serves God every hour.

Good Spirit (Nehemiah 9:20; Psalm 143: 10).

What a precious testimony David gives the Holy Spirit in the phrase, "thy spirit is good" – not only does He manifest goodness, and provide such a quality in our lives as fruit (Galatians 5:22), but He *is* good, or as Nehemiah states it, He is God's *Good Spirit,* and therefore qualified to lead us and to cause goodness to follow us all the days of our pilgrimage (Romans 8:14; Ephesians 4:30). The ways of the Spirit are like the ways of the Father, and of the Son, ways of goodness and gentleness. The Spirit cannot act contrary to His character. *Being* good, He must do good, even as He inspired Jesus to go "about doing good" (Acts 10:38). He is the Good Spirit in the care of His actions, and thus – leads by His truth, feeds by His promises, prunes by His discipline, inspires by His love, instructs by His acts. May the *Good Spirit* enable us to be good, and do good at all times!

Goodness impart, that we e'en our
        foes may succour;
Faithfulness grant, to change our
        toil to song.

Titles and Names Related to the Saints

Although we have sought to classify the names and titles of the Holy Spirit under appropriate sections, there is nothing arbitrary about the divisions given, since the various designations identifying Him are related in some way or another to either saints or sinners. As the one Mediator between God and men is the man Christ Jesus (1 Timothy 2:5), so the sole Mediator between the Saviour and the saved is the Spirit (Ephesians 2:18). It was to the Spirit

that the sacred task was committed of convicting sinners of their lost estate, regenerating them by His power, and thereafter sanctifying them through the precious blood and the Word. Corporately, the Spirit is the Administrator of the affairs of the Church having control of her internal economy and external obligations as Acts so forcibly illustrates.

During an evangelistic mission in Minneapolis, U.S.A., D. L. Moody preached his remarkable sermon on the Holy Spirit. At the close of the service a man came up to the renowned evangelist and said, "Mr. Moody, you speak as if you had a monopoly on the Holy Spirit." Moody's reply was, "No, decidedly NO! but I do trust the Holy Spirit has a monopoly on me." That he had is seen in the way the evangelist was able to rock two continents nearer God. The titles we are now to consider reveal the blessed results we can expect if only we, too, are subordinate to the sway of the Spirit.

The Spirit of Truth (John 14:17; 15:26; 16:13; 1 John 4:6).

Each of these four references to the Spirit in relation to *truth* take on added significance when dealt with in the light of the context. For instance, John shows the distinction between "the spirit of truth" and the evil "spirit of error" (1 John 4:6). Jesus could claim, I AM THE TRUTH, and the Spirit not only testifies to Him as such but that He is, in Himself TRUTH, and therefore only associated with all that is true. As He is both "the Spirit of grace" (Hebrews 10: 29), and "the Spirit of truth" (John 14: 17), He especially represents Jesus in His twofold character – "full of grace and truth" (John 1:14). He convicts the world of the *truth* of its lost condition (John 16:8), and at the same time brings home to the heart of the sinner the *grace* that alone can remove his sin.

To those who are saved, the Spirit produces in them the fruits of *grace* while at the same time He guides them into all *truth* (John 16:13).

All *saving truth* is centered in the Person of Jesus who claimed to be "*The* Truth," and all *communicated truth* is centered in Him who inspired holy men of old to record Scripture truth (2 Peter 1:20, 21). Says Daniel Steele in his volume, *The Gospel of the Comforter* –

> "Truth is conformity to fact or reality. Eternal happiness is building on the granite of reality and laying every stone by the plumb line of truth. There can be no other destiny for a character thus constructed. . . . The designation Spirit of Truth might have been translated *Spirit of Reality.* He is thus called by Jesus because He works in human souls through the instrumentality of truth. He regenerates only through Christian truth. . . . The truth is the instrument; the Spirit is the efficient Worker. The stability of the new life consists in having the 'loins girt about with truth.' . . . The failure of many preachers arises from their dependence solely upon the saving efficacy of the truth without the Spirit's office to make it real" (2 Corinthians 3:6).

The Holy Spirit, then, is the Essence of Truth, and, therefore, its Author, and likewise its Communicator. In His own veracity He is "The Spirit of Truth" as John makes clear when he says, "It is the Spirit that beareth witness, because the Spirit *is* the truth" (1 John 5:7 ASV).

> Spirit of Truth, Thy word reveal,
>   Its treasure open wide;
> Lead me to see my Father's will,
>   And in that will abide.

The Comforter (John 14:16, 26; 15:26; Acts 9:31; 2 Corinthians 1:4).

Of all the names of the gracious Spirit this is one of the most precious and assuring to the child of God. How grateful to Jesus we are for bequeathing such a Consoler "with us to dwell"! His announcement that he would only be with His disciples "yet a little while" (John 13:33), left them distressed. How could they continue their witness without the One who had become their life, their all? Then He gave them hope in the promise, "I will not leave you comfortless: I will come to you" (John 14:18). The word for "comfortless" means desolate, or orphans, and the Spirit of Love was the One who would fill the vacant place in their hearts when Jesus came to leave them.

That the promise of "another Comforter" was amply fulfilled is evident from the way the apostles acted after He came at Pentecost for we read that they were found walking "in the comfort of the Holy Spirit" and consequently added to their numbers (Acts 9:31). They were conscious of His presence comforting with all divine encouragement in their trials (2 Corinthians 1:3-7). But what exactly are we to understand by "Thy best name of Comforter"? The Greek word for "comforter" is *parakletos* from which we have *paraclete,* composed of two words, *clete,* which means "called," and *para,* signifying "along with." Thus a *paraclete* is "one who is *called along with* another," or "one who is called to another's aid."

To fully appreciate, however, the work of the *Paraclete* we need to understand the position of the *clete.* A man called to appear before a court of justice to answer a charge made against him is the *clete,* or "called." But ignorant of the law, and unable to plead successfully before judges, another is called to help the *clete.* Knowing the case well, and able to state the case well, he was known as the charged man's *para-clete*

– a term corresponding in the Greek and etymology with the word *ad-vocate,* the word John uses of Jesus in heaven (1 John 2:1). The primary significance of *Comforter,* then, is "called to one's aid."

In the goodness of God, then, we have two divine *Paracletes,* One who had been the Paraclete of the disciples while on earth, but who is now in heaven, and the other Paraclete – the first Paraclete's *alter ego* who came at Pentecost as promised by Jesus.

O Source of uncreated light,
The Father's promised Paraclete!
Thrice holy fount, thrice holy fire,
Our minds with heavenly power inspire.

Each of the two Paracletes are specially fitted for the office He has to perform. Our Paraclete in heaven, Jesus the Righteous, is looking after our interests up there, and ever lives to advocate our cause (Hebrews 7:25). The Paraclete on earth, the Holy Spirit, is caring for God's interests, and pleads His cause before men (John 16:8-11). But not until the first Paraclete had died, risen again, and ascended on high, could the other Paraclete be given in His full power to apply the redemptive work of the Cross to sinners in their need of deliverance (John 7:38, 39; Romans 8:26, 27).

In us, for us, intercede,
And with voiceless groanings plead
Our unutterable need,
Comforter Divine.

Christ said that when the Spirit came He would quicken old memories of His life and teaching – which the Spirit did as the preaching of Christ and the Resurrection by the apostles proves! A. H. Vine in his hymn, *O Breath of God,* brings our two all-prevailing Paracletes together in the verse –

Christ is our Advocate on high;
Thou art our Advocate within;

Oh, plead the truth, and make reply
To every argument of sin.

(*See* further under title *Advocate,* and under *Another Comforter.*)

The Spirit of Life (Romans 8:2).

The operations of His vitality are varied. It was the Spirit who gave life to death at Creation (Genesis 1:2), and who quickens men mentally, physically and spiritually (Romans 8:1-13). He it was who raised Jesus from the dead for we read that "He was quickened by the Spirit." He is the Sustainer of life through the Word, and the goal of life in God. Israel, in her final restoration, will experience the power of "the Spirit of Life" when, as the Breath of God, He will breathe upon her that she may live (Ezekiel 37:1-10).

The Spirit of Adoption (Romans 8:15).

There is a sense in which this title and the previous one are two sides of the same coin. As the Spirit of *Life* in Christ Jesus, He sets us free from all our old relationships, while as the Spirit of *Adoption,* He brings us into new relationships. Those who have the Spirit of *Life* are free from the law of sin and death, which has no power over an existence that begins beyond the tomb on resurrection ground (Romans 8:2). Those who have the Spirit of *Adoption* can and do cry, "Abba, Father," having received the Spirit of sonship in their hearts (Galatians 4:4-7). He assures us that because of our acceptance of Christ as Saviour that we are God's children, and likewise assures us that, as we are obedient to God, we are pleasing to Him.

The term *adoption* itself implies that the act of taking officially the child of another to be one's own. This is what God does as the result of the finished work of the Cross. Through grace He takes a child of the devil and makes him His son, and the Spirit certifies the sonship. In Paul's use of the term, there is the contrast between the Spirit of Adoption – permanent security; and the spirit of bondage – the temporary relationship of slave to master (Romans 8:14-21).

> In us Abba, Father! cry;
> Earnest of our bliss on high;
> Seal of Immortality,
>   Comforter Divine.

The Spirit of Faith (2 Corinthians 4:13).

It may be felt by some that this is not a definite title of the Holy Spirit, but that the phrase means substantially the same as *faith* itself, namely, a believing sense or expression of truth, and is related to the same faith as David when he said, "I believed, therefore have I spoken" (Psalm 116:10 with 2 Corinthians 4:14). Too many try to speak for God without having first believed, or having accepted by faith, the saving truths of the Gospel. The particular aspects of Christian faith Paul mentions in the context are the resurrection of Jesus Christ, and the final resurrection of the saints.

Yet we are warranted in looking upon the words, "The Spirit of Faith," as another designation of the Holy Spirit, without whom saving faith is not possible. Seeing that *faith*, with all its implications, is one of His gifts (1 Corinthians 12:9), He Himself must be the Embodiment of such a gift. There are two aspects of Faith distinguished in Scripture.

1. *Personal Faith* (Mark 9:24; Ephesians 2:8; 1 Timothy 4:10).

When Paul said that if we believe with the heart we shall be saved (Romans 10:9, 10), he was not referring to the affections merely, but the sinner himself believing. The reason that the exercise of faith in the Saviour brings eternal life is not on account of anything in the faith, but because our moral nature is so depraved by the Fall that to

believe truly what God says about us and His provision for our need is a proof of the new birth. Personal faith, then, involves the acceptance of God's testimony (1 John 5:9-13), and it is the Holy Spirit alone who enables a man to accept God's testimony, and believe the truths of the Gospel. James reminds us that a body is dead without the Spirit, and faith, apart from the Spirit of Faith who is Love, and whose evidence is works, is dead. Paul confessed that if he had all necessary faith to remove mountains, but lacked the Spirit of Love in his heart he would be as nothing (1 Corinthians 13:2; James 2:17).

The apostle also speaks about "The faith *of God*" (Romans 3:3), meaning His fidelity to fulfill His promise. On our part, we are saved by grace *through faith* – our personal faith which the Spirit begets, accepting all God has declared. *Faith*, as with the *grace,* is a gift of the Spirit (Ephesians 2:8). The Spirit not only convicts us of our sin, presents the Saviour who died to save us, but constrains us to accept the Saviour by unreserved faith, and then assures us of pardon, justification, peace, union with the Saviour, and life forevermore.

2. *The Body of Faith* (Acts 6:7; 24:24; Jude 3. 20).

Jude's phrase about "*the* faith which was once delivered unto the saints" – which "holy faith" we are to build up ourselves in, is something very different from simply faith. *The faith* is what Paul calls "all the counsel of God" (Acts 20:21), or His plan and will in respect to the whole content of His redemption. Stephen, a man full of faith, because he was full of the Holy Spirit, witnessed a great company of priests becoming obedient to *the faith* (Acts 6:7). Felix sent for Paul that he might hear him "concerning *the faith* in Christ" (Acts 24:24). At Derbe Paul and Barnabas exhorted the disciples to continue *in the faith* (Acts 14:22). Such passages imply all the fundamental doctrines associated with their newly found faith. *See* Romans 1:5.

When Paul, in his farewell message to the elders of the church at Ephesus, spoke of not shunning to declare "all the counsel of God" to Jews and Gentiles alike, he likely had in mind the plan of God respecting their salvation, comprehending the two cardinal requisites of repentance and faith as emphasized in Acts 20:21. *Repentance toward God* every sinner owes to God as his rightful Sovereign, and *faith toward our Lord Jesus Christ* whose atoning work provided salvation, together constitute "the whole of practical religion, and comprise all the lawful and obligatory themes of evangelical instruction." J. A. Alexander, in his volume on Acts, goes on to say –

> "He who preaches the repentance and the faith here spoken of, in all their fulness and variety, will need to seek no other topics, and may humbly boast of having kept nothing back that was profitable to his hearers."

Jude's reference to *the faith* once delivered to the saints, "once" meaning *once for all*, never to be repeated, implies the whole body of revealed truth as found in Scripture. By *the faith*, we can understand, not only all features of Christianity found in the Gospel, but all God has manifested of Himself, and His purposes. Further, we are to contend – without contentiousness – for all manner of *truth*. It is called *faith* because this is the cardinal virtue in the whole system of religion, and because all depends on faith.

We return to our designation, *The Spirit of Faith*, for He it is who composed what the Church knows as *the faith*. Believing, as we do, that the Bible not only contains a divine revelation, but is a divinely inspired volume from beginning to end, which must be received in its entirety as such (Revelation 22:18, 19), we accept what the Bible affirms, that the Holy Spirit is the divine Author of Holy Writ. For the body of revealed Truth we call *the faith* we are indebted to *The Spirit of Faith*, for "holy men of God spake [and wrote] as they were moved [borne along] by the Holy Spirit" (2 Peter 1:21). As all Bible truth finds its center and climax in Christ, it was the Spirit within prophets and apostles alike who inspired them to give us the full revelation of Him who is the sole Object of saving faith (1 Peter 1:10-12).

> Come, Holy Ghost, for moved by Thee,
> The prophets wrote and spoke;
> Unlock the truth, Thyself the key,
> Unseal the sacred Book.

The Spirit of Praise (1 Corinthians 14: 15; Ephesians 5:19; Colossians 3:16).

This pleasant title is implied by what Paul has to say about the gifts the Ascended Lord, through the Spirit, gave to the Church. The phrase "spiritual gifts" (1 Corinthians 12:1; 14:12) means gifts of the Spirit, and the apostle unites two of them, namely, the gift of prayer, and the gift of praise.

> "I will *pray* with the Spirit . . .
> I will *sing* with the Spirit" (1 Corinthians 14:15).

The apostle also says, "Thou shalt *bless* with the Spirit" (1 Corinthians 14:16). While there is doubtless a reference to the spirit-part of the believer, the highest part of his being and the passive object of the Holy Spirit's operations, the translation of Arthur Way of these passages is most expressive:

> "I will by all means pray in the Spirit's rapture . . .
> I will sing in the Spirit's rapture . . .

Praising God in the Spirit's rapture."

Under the inspiration of the Spirit, the believer prays and praises intelligently, and others are consequently blessed. *Sing in the Spirit's rapture!* Is this not what Paul implies when he reminds us that one evidence of the unhindered Holy Spirit's infilling is the spirit of praise and thanksgiving? Let Way's translation help us again in the "Apostle's Hymn of the New Life on Earth" as found in Ephesians –

"As a special caution – do not, in your church-gatherings, drink wine to intoxication; that way debauchery lies; but *quaff deep of God's Spirit.* Speak out your thoughts to each other in psalms, in hymns, in chants inspired by the Holy Spirit. Let the sound of your singing, let the music of your hearts go up to the Lord in unceasing thanksgiving for all that He sends you, thanksgiving offered in the name of our Lord, of Jesus the Messiah, to God the Father" (Ephesians 5:18-20).

In his letter to the Colossians Paul reiterates this ministry of Him, whose fruit is JOY (Galatians 5:22).

"With psalms, with hymns, with chants inspired by the Spirit, be your hearts singing ever in thankfulness to God" (Colossians 3:16, 17).

The history of the Church proves that whenever there was a mighty demonstration of the Spirit's power in revival, there was always an outburst of praise. Some of our greatest hymns were written by Charles Wesley when his brother John and he were so marvelously used of the Spirit in the salvation of multitudes. David testified to the fact that it was by the inspiration of the Spirit

of Praise that he composed his matchless psalms. There was the particular song of deliverance he sang unto the Lord (2 Samuel 22). Then, as "the sweet psalmist of Israel" came to die, in his last words he attributed to the Spirit the ability to utter and write the majority of the songs making up the Psalter –

"The sweet psalmist of Israel, said, The Spirit of the Lord spake by me [spake to me] and his word was in my tongue" (2 Samuel 23:1-3).

Although many of us may not have a singing voice to chant David's psalms, the Spirit can make us the recipients of the singing heart. We can sing and make melody in the heart unto the Lord, or as Way translates it, "Let the music of your hearts go up to the Lord in unceasing thanksgiving for all that He sends you." An evident sign that we are living in harmony with the mind and will of the Holy Spirit is the way in which He can make us joyful – even when it seems there is nothing to sing about – "joyful in *all* our tribulation" (2 Corinthians 7: 4). The Spirit-endowed Master could go out to His bitter death singing a hymn – one of the Spirit inspired psalms of David.

Holy Ghost, with joy divine,
Cheer this saddened heart of mine;
Bid my many woes depart,
Heal my wounded, bleeding heart.

The Spirit of Wisdom and Revelation (Ephesians 1:17; 3:5).

In this title of the Holy Spirit Paul gives us two features of His operation as discernible and distinguishable, namely, *wisdom* and *revelation.*

As the *Spirit of Wisdom* He is the Initiator into the full knowledge of God and of Christ. He was associated with the Father and the Son in devising the plan of redemption, and ever seeks to extol Him who was made unto us *Wisdom.* It is the Spirit who makes the sinner wise unto salvation. And because His attribute is infinite wisdom, He works wisdom in the saints (Daniel 5: 14). It is by the Spirit we have the *word of wisdom* (1 Corinthians 12:8). In Him are hid all the treasures of wisdom (Colossians 2:3).

As the *Spirit of Revelation* it is His function to reveal to the saints the inner significance of spiritual mysteries (1 Corinthians 2:10-12). Our Lord promised that when the Spirit came He would show – unveil, reveal – all things to them (John 16:12-15). He it is who manifests the glories of Christ to the eye of faith (Revelation 1:1). He is the One John Bunyan describes as *The Interpreter*.

Further, these two attributes of the Spirit are related to the unfolding of Scripture, and to the illuminating of the mind of the saints. On that memorable walk along the Emmaus Road, two disciples talked together of all that had happened at Calvary, and they were disconsolate because their hopes of Messiahship had been dashed to the ground. Then a Stranger joined them who, unknown to them, was the Christ, whose body they thought had been stolen. What a marvelous surprise was theirs when their inner eyes were opened to see in the Stranger, the crucified, risen Saviour!

There are two phrases in that never-to-be-forgotten Bible exposition of Jesus we can bring together –

"He opened to us the *scriptures*" (Luke 24:32).

"He opened their *understanding*, that they might understand the scriptures" (Luke 24:45).

What would have been the use of Jesus opening the Scriptures if the eyes of those two saints had remained closed? Both actions were necessary if they were to know Him as the One around whom all Scripture revolved (Luke 24:27).

The Holy Spirit, as "the Spirit of wisdom and revelation," functions in this twofold way for our spiritual insight. As the Spirit of Wisdom He operates upon "the eyes of our understanding" (Ephesians 1:18), that we might understand the Scriptures. Thus we pray –

Open my eyes, that I may see,
Glimpses of truth Thou hast for me.

Then, as the Spirit of Revelation, He opens the Scriptures and makes clear truths that were hitherto beyond our comprehension. With opened understandings, we behold "wondrous things *out of* thy law." There they were all the time, but now they "shine out of" Scripture (Psalm 119:18).

Oh, send Thy Spirit, Lord,
    Now unto me,
That He may touch my eyes,
    And make me see;
Show me the truth concealed,
    Within Thy Word,
And in Thy Book revealed,
    I see the Lord.

The Spirit of Promise (Ephesians 1:13, 14).

As "the *Holy* Spirit of Promise" in the earnest of His glory, this pledge, along with all others, are certain of fulfillment because of all that He is in Himself. Because He is *holy*, He cannot lie. The Spirit came as "The Promise of the Father" (Acts 1:4; 2:33). God promised Him to Christ as a reward for His blood, sweat and tears, and Christ promised Him to His redeemed ones as the unfailing Source of their wisdom, power, and triumph (John 14:16, 26; 15:26). He is likewise "The Spirit of Promise," for it was He who inspired all the promises of the Bible (*see* the author's volume on *All The Promises Of The Bible*) and who enables the child of God to claim and inherit such promises.

The Spirit of Grace (Zechariah 12:10; Hebrews 10:29).

The Spirit of our gracious God is well-named "Spirit of Grace" because of His pleading ministry. He it is who acts in grace, communicates grace to saint and sinner alike, places us in the sphere of grace, and enables us to correspond to grace. (*See* more fully under *Spirit of Grace and Supplication.*)

The Spirit of Glory (1 Peter 4:14).

The apostle had remarked in a previous verse that all partakers of the sufferings of Christ would like to be partakers of His glory when He is revealed, and as "the Spirit of glory" He confirms such a joyful expectancy. At Pentecost, the Spirit came from Glory to dwell on earth, and He has been here now for well-nigh two millenniums, and will remain here until all the saints are in Glory. His indwelling is the assurance and pledge of our participation in Glory (Ephesians 4:30). He is the Guarantee of our eternal bliss. We are waiting to be with Christ, and He is waiting to have His own around Him (John 17:24), and the patient Spirit will soon effect the union.

The double divine name is in this title, "The spirit of glory and of God" implying that we are doubly secure, for both God the Father and God the Spirit are resting upon us. The word for *rest* here is the same Jesus said, "I will give you rest" (Matthew 11:28), and implies taking a rest or even finding satisfaction. What rest and satisfaction are ours as we await the moment when "the Spirit of Glory" will change the body of this flesh into a glorious body like unto Christ's (Philippians 3:20, 21)! (*See* under title *The Earnest*).

Unction From the Holy One (1 John 2:20, 27; 2 Corinthians 1:21).

The English word "unction," used only here in the KJV of verse 20, is the same word given as "anointing" in verse 27. The ASV reads "Ye have an anointing from the Holy One." The particular word used here for "anointing" is confined to sacred and symbolical anointings and is found in the unguent prepared for oil and aromatic herbs, and used in the anointing of priests for the service of the Lord. Thus, we have the phrases –

"Thou shalt take anointing the oil" (Exodus 29:7); and
"A holy anointing oil" (Exodus 30: 25 ASV).

Meatphorically, it is described as "the oil of gladness" (Hebrews 1:9), because of the inner joy the anointed one experienced in being set apart to minister unto the Lord. Two Persons of the "Mysterious Godhead, Three in One," are before us in John's assertion, namely *The Holy One*, and *The Unction*.

1. *The Holy One.*

While such a title can, with all propriety be applied to the Father, the Son, and the Spirit, the sense of the passage points to the Son whom even the demons acknowledged as "the Holy One." Peter also, in his exaltation of Christ, proclaimed Him as such (Acts 3:14). The anointing He received as a witness to His Holiness He now communicates to His own for He desires them to be holy ones, as He is *"the* Holy One." Thus the unction made them "holy as He is holy." The precious ointment poured out upon Him, as the Head, He desired to run down over all His Body, the Church.

The name *Christ* means "the Anointed One," and the term *Christos*, which Peter used, is rendered *His Anointed* (Acts 4: 26 ASV). The gospels show how He was anointed *above* His fellows. At the inauguration of His official ministry when "at last, the time had arrived when the bud should break into flower," Christ received the Divine Unction as a necessary preparation for all that awaited Him (Matthew 3:16; 12:18; Acts 4:27, 30; 10:38).

His anointing with the Spirit was an evidence of His claim. How were the people to know that this obscure Man of Nazareth was God's chosen One to become a "Light to lighten the Gentiles, and the Glory of His people Israel"? The Father's benediction and the Holy Spirit's descent upon Him indicated that He was indeed the One who should come (Isaiah 48:16; John 6:27).

His anointing with the Spirit was for victory over Satan. After the double attestation at Jordan there came the terrific contest with Satan in the wilderness (Matthew 4:1). Although angels ministered to His lower natural needs, it was the Spirit's unshared ministry to uphold and sustain Him during those forty days of testing. The first, direct outcome of Christ's unction then was not to cast out demons or to heal the sick, but to defeat the devil, both for His own sake and ours. He had to experience the full strength of the foe ere He could deliver those who were bound. After the Dove, there came the devil, and after Pentecost there came persecution (Acts 2:4).

His anointing was for service. Luke reminds us that "When the devil had ended all the temptation ... Jesus returned in the power of the Spirit into Galilee" (Luke 4:13, 14), where mighty things were accomplished. As the result of the marvelous and immeasurable endowment with the Spirit, His fame spread abroad (Acts 10:38). After the *Dove*, there came the *devil*, and after his defeat, there came the *Dynamic* with all power being His over demons, disease and death.

2. *The Unction.*
The great Gift of the Ascended Lord

to His Church was the selfsame Spirit who had been so intimately associated with Him before His exaltation to Heaven. Thus, as He left His own, He declared, "Ye shall receive power, the Holy Spirit coming upon you" (Acts 1: 8). John confirmed the fulfillment of this promise when he wrote, "Ye have received an unction from the Holy One" (1 John 2:20), for the Gift of the Holy Spirit was bestowed upon the saints as the all-sufficient means of enabling them, not only to possess a knowledge of the truth whereby they could expose the falsity of anti-Christian teaching, but witness for Christ in a mighty way in a world of sin. This *Unction* was to make the anointed ones holy in character, courageous in the defense of the truth concerning Christ and of all concerning the divine character and counsels. Through the *Unction,* they would "know all things" (1 John 2:20, 22, 23), relative to the prerogatives and rights of heaven, no less than divine purposes concerning earth. True knowledge of God and all His ways is only possible through the Unction of the Holy One for "the natural man receiveth not the things of the Spirit of God ... because they are spiritually discerned" (1 Corinthians 2:14). It is only "he who is spiritual" who knoweth and judgeth all things.

The only safeguard the believer of today has against the increasing agnosticism and apostasy surrounding him is "the Unction from the Holy One." Anointed, possessed, girded, and taught by the Spirit, he is able to discern immediately that which is not *the truth,* and reject it, even though the deviation may come from theological sources. The all-knowing theologian left to himself, without "unction from the Holy One," is apt to let some peculiar leaning, some personal bias or idiosyncrasy of his own prevail, exaggerating some one portion, or aspect, or feature of the divine plan, and raising many a cloud of lettered dust, such as may cause endless perplexity and doubt, and sadly mar "the simplicity which is in Christ." He is ignorant of the intimate connection with "the unction of the Holy One" and "the knowledge of all things spiritual" (Matthew 11:25, 26).

Thy blessèd unction from above
Is comfort, life, and fire of love;
Enable with perpetual light
The dullness of our blinded sight.

As we have reached the end of our meditation on the magnificent array of the definite names and titles of God the Spirit, we find ourselves in full agreement with Professor Beck of Tubingen who said that, "Theology without the Holy Spirit, is not only a dead stone, it is a deadly poison." My own heart has been strangely warmed in setting forth the various activities of the Spirit, the designations of Him suggest. What a difference there would be in pulpit preaching, if only all pastors would take a year to study nothing else save the revelation of the Holy Spirit as found in Scripture! Bishop J. Ryle says that —

"The place given to the Holy Spirit in the heart of most decided Christians is altogether out of proportion to that which it occupies in the Word of God."

Much of the barrenness and lethargy and powerlessness of the Church today is due to the lack of the knowledge of the Spirit's presence, presidency, and power in church life and work, as well as in personal experience.

2. SYMBOLIC DESIGNATIONS.

In the foregone aspects of divine names and titles which we have considered, attention has been drawn to the fact that the Bible contains the mind and will of God communicated to man in human, everyday language he can readily understand. By means of symbols, similes, metaphors, parables, emblems and types, it has pleased God to reveal Himself to our hearts. "I have . . . used similitudes, by the ministry of the prophets" (Hosea 12:10) – and how full Hosea is of them! Of Jesus we read, "Without a parable spake He not unto them" (Matthew 13:34).

Figures of speech abound to illustrate the work of the Father, the Son, and the Holy Spirit, as well as the Bible's own nature and ministry. In this, our final section of divine designations, we are classifying all that are relevant to the Spirit under the two general heads – Symbols From Natural Life and Symbols From Human Life.

SYMBOLS DRAWN FROM NATURAL LIFE

What a perfect reflection of the spiritual is the natural! How gracious and condescending of God it is to convey heavenly truth through the media of natural elements we are accustomed to! In this way infinity enlightens finity. The emblems used to convey the Spirit's attributes and activities are as windows allowing light to reach our minds so that we can more readily understand "the things of the Spirit." For the guidance of preachers and teachers we now tabulate the natural symbols.

Wind (John 3:8; Acts 2:2).

That the Holy Spirit is the secret of all life and vitality is evident from this forceful symbol describing His activity. As the natural wind is air in motion, so in the spiritual realm the Spirit is God in action, hence, the analogy between the circling winds and the movement of the Spirit in the lives of men. In the original, *Spirit* means breath, or wind. The wind is invisible, inscrutable, not amenable to human control, but manifest in its effects, and, therefore, a fitting emblem of the mysterious work of the Spirit in the work of regeneration as Jesus indicated in His conversation with Nicodemus —

"The wind bloweth where it will, and thou hearest the voice thereof, but knowest not whence it cometh, and whither it goeth: *so is every one that is born of the Spirit*" (John 3:8 ASV).

As by the breath of the Spirit the new man in Christ is created, so going back to Creation, God breathed upon Adam, and he became a living soul (Genesis 2:7). Job emphasizes the same truth in the phrase, "The breath [wind] of the Almighty giveth me life" (Job 32: 8; 33:4). In his prophecy of Israel as a resurrected nation Ezekiel prayed to the Spirit, "Come from the four winds, O breath, and breathe upon these slain, that they may live" (37:9). When Jesus came to send forth His disciples, He breathed on them saying, "Receive ye the Holy Spirit" (John 20:22).

Luke describes the coming of the Spirit on the Day of Pentecost "as of a rushing mighty wind" (Acts 2:2). *Mighty* speaks of power, and the Spirit, who came to impart power to witness (Acts 1:8), is all-powerful in Himself (Micah 3:8). *Rushing* suggests the approach, the irresistible action of the Spirit. Coming from above, He is sovereign, and is *the Wind*, the Breath of the Almighty because He is the manifestation of the divine presence and power, and able to energize and invigorate the saints in speedy and effective service.

Wind is varied in its manifestations. At times it is of hurricane force, yet can become "soft as the breath of even." Who, or what, can resist a mighty cyclone or a fearful tornado? The jailer needed the Spirit's power, as with earthquake power, and it took such a resist-

less force to save such a hard, cruel man (Acts 16:27-31). But no cyclone experience was necessary for Lydia, whose heart silently opened to the Lord as a bud to the morning sun (Acts 16: 14). If your conversion was not in tempest-fashion as the jailer in the prison at Philippi, don't criticize another Christian whose turning to Christ was of a radical nature.

O Wind of God, come bend us, break us,
Till humbly we confess our need;
Then in Thy tenderness remake us,
Revive, restore, for this we plead.

Another feature of the wind we can mention is that of its impetuous action. Not only can it pick up leaves and other light material and waft them gently along, but when it comes with hurricane force it can uproot trees and gather up other heavy objects and fling them a distance away. As "The Wind of God" the Spirit often engages in vehement action, as the following passages illustrate —

"The Spirit lifted me up between the earth and the heaven" (Ezekiel 8:3).

"The Spirit lifted me up, and brought me unto the east gate" (Ezekiel 11:1).

"The Spirit of the LORD fell upon me" (Ezekiel 11:5).

"The Spirit of the Lord caught away Philip . . . who was found at Azotus" (Acts 8:30, 40).

Acting as a sudden and mighty wind, the Spirit can control, and do as He deems best with those He desires to use. As with God, He doeth according to His will, and none can stay His hand saying, "What doest Thou?" No man knoweth the way of the Spirit, says Solomon (Ecclesiastes 11:5). Our obligation is to see to it that our sails are ever set to catch the wind as it "bloweth where it listeth."

> Come as the Wind! with rushing sound
> And Pentecostal grace!
> That all of women born may see
> The glory of Thy face.

Water (John 7:37-39; 4:14; Psalm 87:7).

Water is one of the most common of symbols used to describe not only the varied ministry of the Holy Spirit, but also the Holy Scriptures. We could not live without water, or rain. We need water to allay thirst, to give beauty to the flowers, and fertility to crops and harvests. But water is presented in many forms in Scripture.

There is *water*, "Whosoever drinketh of the water" (John 4:14). Clean water is one of the prime necessities of life, and in His conversation with the woman at the well, Jesus sought to show her how the Holy Spirit, as a Well of Water within her, was her only source of spiritual life and refreshment. The symbol of water is easy to understand. As Living Water, the presence of the Spirit in the heart quenches thirst and produces life where desolation reigned. He, alone, satisfies the soul's deep thirst. The waters of the earth have failed, and I am thirsty still. Aspects of water's beneficial usefulness can be traced thus –

> Cleansing (Ezekiel 36:25-27).
> Life, fertility, beauty (Ezekiel 47:1-12).
> Joy (Isaiah 12:3).

Without the Blood of Calvary, there would never have been the Water of Pentecost. Jehovah said to Moses – "Thou shalt smite the rock, and there shall come water out of it, that the people may drink" (Exodus 17:6). At the Cross, the Rock of Ages was smitten, and at Pentecost, Water flowed out of it (1 Corinthians 10:4).

There are *rivers*. "Rivers of living water . . . the Spirit" (John 7:37-39). Cast in the plural, our Lord's prophecy indicates the variety, abundance, many-sidedness of the Spirit's activities. What diversity there is in His dealings with men! There are many mighty rivers covering the earth, and no two of them are alike. Thus it is with the spiritual rivers. In the Spirit, there is water to swim in, a river that can not be passed over (Ezekiel 47:1-12).

There are *floods*. "Floods upon the dry ground" (Isaiah 44:3). Even though water may come as a cloudburst, or avalanche, it is still water. What a deluge flooded the earth with judgment in Noah's day. Yet a deluge of the Spirit is just as able to flood the earth with blessing (Revelation 21:3). Floods can stand for the copiousness and superabundance of the Spirit's supply. The trouble with far too many of us is that we drink just enough to keep us alive.

> O for the floods on a thirsty land
> O for a mighty revival.

There is *rain*. "He shall come down like rain" (Psalm 72:6). Absence of rain means famine, scarcity, and ruin as many hot countries experience. The Church is certainly suffering from spiritual famine, and is in sad need of hearing the sound of the abundance of rain. May He send upon her the latter rains of the Spirit for He alone can transform the desert, causing it to blossom as the rose (Isaiah 35:1; Joel 2:23)!

There are *springs*. "A well of water springing up" (John 4:14). Springs are not only reservoirs of pure, fresh water, but the source of great rivers. Said the psalmist, "All my springs are in thee" (Psalm 87:7), and this is true of the Spirit who is our "secret source of every precious thing." In Him is a perennial source of supply – a Spring that never ceases to flow. "Spring up, O well."

There is *dew,* "I will be as the dew" (Hosea 14:5). The Anglican Book of Common Prayer has a request for "the continual dew of Thy blessing," and this is what the Spirit waits to bestow upon every believer. Shakespeare has a phrase about "morning roses newly washed with dew." Secret, unnoticed through the night and early morn, the dew descends upon the earth and carries out its effective work. Can we say that the Spirit is our early Dew at the opening of each new morning?

> Come as the Dew, and sweetly bless
>   This consecrated hour;
> May barrenness rejoice to own
>   Thy fertilizing power.

Fire (Isaiah 4:4; Acts 2:3).

Twice over John the Baptist said of Jesus, "He will baptize you with the Holy Spirit and with fire" (Matthew 3: 11, 12; Luke 3:16, 17). The Spirit *is* the Fire, for He came upon the disciples at Pentecost as "cloven tongues like as of fire." *See* Luke 12:49; Revelation 4:5. *Fire* as a symbol is used of the holy presence and character of God (Deuteronomy 4:24; Hebrews 12:29), and also of the Word itself (Jeremiah 5:14; 20:9; 23:29).

Fire consumes what is combustible and tests that which is not so, and cleanses that which neither air nor water can cleanse. *See* 1 Corinthians 3:13-15; Mark 1:8. Its action is also life-giving, as is the warmth of the mother bird while she broods upon her nest. Fire operates in many ways.

1. It gives *light.* As Fire, the Spirit is the Source of spiritual illumination and knowledge. He it is who enlightens the eyes of our understanding (Ephesians 1:17, 18; Hebrews 6:4).

2. It *purifies.* As Fire, the Spirit exercises His power to purify, to judge and consume all impurity, and burn within us all that is not in conformity with His holy will (Leviticus 10:2; Malachi 3:2, 3).

> Oh that in me the sacred Fire
>   Might now begin to glow;
> Burn up the dross of base desire,
>   And make the mountains flow.

3. It gives *heat.* "I am warm, I have seen the fire" (Isaiah 44:16). How quickly fire can warm cold persons and things – symbolizing the Spirit's power to warm cold hearts. He it is who sheds abroad in our hearts the warmth of God's love (Romans 5:5). It was this warmth the Church at Ephesus had somehow lost (Revelation 2:4). In the days before the Chinese revolution a missionary asked a prominent educator what he thought was his country's greatest need. His reply was, "A company of devoted men and women with hot hearts to tell the story of Jesus."

4. It gives *power.* Fire generates steam and supplies the driving force to keep the wheels of industry running. In George Matheson's great hymn, "Make Me a Captive, Lord," he has the lines –

> My power is faint and low
>   Till I have learned to serve;
> It wants the needed fire to glow,
>   It wants the breeze to nerve;
> It cannot drive the world
>   Until itself be driven.

In the life and service of the believer, the Holy Spirit is this driving Power. He is the Fire in the boiler, so to speak, the energizing influence in our witness. *See* Levitius 9:24; 10:2; Acts 2:3, 4. If your power is faint and low let more of Divine Fire burn within.

Salt (Matthew 5:13; Mark 9:49, 50).

We have previously indicated that one reason the Bible abounds in symbols is the fact that it was written in the East where the language was very picturesque and people saw in natural objects mirrors of spiritual truths. This is why our Lord's illustrations are related to many of the ordinary things of life. His parables bear the stamp of His thirty silent years in Nazareth among the simple, ordinary, everyday life of humble people. Salt would be daily used in His home, and Jesus knew that there was no shortage of it in the country, that it was used in food and accompanied sacrifices (Leviticus 2:13). Jesus would also know from Old Testament Scriptures that newly born children were rubbed with it (Ezekiel 16:4), that fish, meat and fruit were pickled in it, that Israel entered into "the Covenant of Salt" (Numbers 18:19; 2 Chronicles 13:5).

Thus, in His matchless Sermon on the Mount Jesus used *salt* as the substance giving permanence to food which otherwise would rot, and if it lost its flavor it would be irreplaceable since salt has no substitute. He knew what He was talking about when He used it as a figure of speech to express the influence of the saint's spirituality in a corrupt world. From ancient times salt has ever been recognized as one of the most important elements in the seasoning and palatability of food. Job was asked by Eliphaz, "Can that which is unsavory be eaten without salt?" (Job 6:6). As salt seasons the food we eat and preserves it from going bad, so the Spirit seasons our spiritual food. How unsavory the Word of God is apart from the taste the Spirit gives it, and how He is able through believers to arrest corruption all around!

The declaration of Jesus concerning His Church is emphatic, "Ye are the salt of the earth." Dr. G. Campbell Morgan, in his most profitable volume, *The Parables and Metaphors of Our Lord* says of the illustration of the Salt and its Savor –

"The manifesto is the ultimate code of laws for the kingdom of God established upon the earth. . . . The function of the subjects of His Kingdom are so live that they give goodness its opportunity and hold in check the force of corruption.

"Our Lord emphasized this with words of satire, gentle, but clear and sharp as lightning: 'If the salt has lost its savor, wherewith shall it be salted? I like the Scotch rendering of that: 'If the salt has lost its *tang*.' That is a great word, *tang*, the pungent power of salt. Jesus says His people are to exercise that influence in the world. That is our responsibility, though men may not be pleased."

All who have been born anew by the Holy Spirit are to be used by Him to preserve the earth from corruption, to season its insipidity, to freshen and sweeten it. Scripture presents mankind as being entirely corrupt, and reminds us of those who sought, as the salt of the earth, to arrest such corruption. Noah was the man who walked with God and sought to warn the people of the coming Flood, but so festering was the wickedness of his time, that even his holy character could not preserve any, save those of his own family.

Then Jesus asked the question, "If the salt have lost its savor, wherewith shall it be salted?" If the salt loses its *tang*, or saline property, how can the unsavory be made palatable again? Of this we are confident, that the Holy Spirit never loses His saline property, but saints as salt can. We are the *salt* of the earth, because the Spirit indwelling us is *holy* and ever seeks to preserve us from deadly insipidity, imparting savor and pungency to our life and character, using us to arrest the decay all around us.

Our *saltness*, then, is Spirit-created spirituality, and if this goes we are "good for nothing." A living, vital Christianity is the only "salt of the earth," and if this is lost, *what else* can supply its place? Any church or professing Christian lacking such saltness is good, only to be "cast out" – a figurative expression of indignant exclusion (Matthew 8:12; 22:13; John 6:37) – "trodden under foot" is another figure, suggesting contempt and scorn. The want of spirituality in those whose *profession* and *appearance* were fitted to beget expectation of finding it, but failed to provide such saltness, is surely the tragedy of the Laodecian church Jesus described, which had lost its saline property to such an extent that He said, "I will spue thee out of my mouth" (Revelation 3:14-19).

We may lose our *saltness*, or *tang*, or the spirituality the Spirit supplies, through an impure mixture with the world. If we are to arrest its corruption, we must be free from any trace of it. "Come out from among them, and be separate" (2 Corinthians 6:17). Davis in his *Bible Dictionary* says that, "The impure salt of Syria, when exposed to rain or sun, or stored in damp houses, is apt to lose its taste and become useless." May grace be ours to ever retain our *tang!* May even our "speech be always with grace, seasoned with salt" (Colossians 4:6), and thus free from anything unsavory and unpalatable! "We must keep assiduously all good we have reached," says Richard Glover, "in order to keep others from evil."

Oil (Hebrews 1:9; Acts 10:38).

Under previous titles such as *The Anointed* and *Unction From the Holy One,* we discussed the use of oil in Bible times and of how it was used for various anointings, and is therefore beautifully symbolic of the manifold ministry of the Holy Spirit. The sick were associated with oil (James 5:14), and the Spirit alone can heal our bruised hearts. *Oil* was associated with food.

"Fine flour mingled with oil" (Leviticus 2:4, 5). Christ is the *Fine Flour,* and the Spirit is the *Oil.* Christ's utterance, "I, by the Spirit of God" reveals how the two were mingled together.

The further use of oil, not hitherto mentioned is that of *illumination.* For the lamps of the sanctuary "pure olive oil" was provided (Exodus 25:6). "Holy oil alone continually lighted the temple, where God was worshipped and where the person and work of Christ were wholly symbolized," says René Pache. "In the same manner, the Spirit illuminates and glorifies Christ, before our eyes, He gives us understanding of heavenly truths, and enables us to worship in spirit and in truth (Exodus 27:20, 21; John 16:14; Philippians 3:3)."

Jesus called His disciples lights, or lamps, and the indwelling Spirit as oil enabled them to shine and maintain an effective witness in dark days. Light comes from within, as does the spiritual illumination the Spirit makes possible, and is not to be confused with what men call "the light of reason," which can keep men in darkness as far as spiritual truth is concerned (Psalm 119:105). One duty of Aaron was to keep the lamps dressed, and filled with oil (Exodus 30:7, 8). How we need the continual dressing of the lamp of witness, to prevent it from smelling of neglect!

There is one other feature regarding the use of oil we can mention, namely, the pouring of it over the blood to sanctify the lepers and the priests of old (Leviticus 8:30; 14:17). *Blood* and *oil!* Do these not typify how we, as sinners, were saved and called to serve the living God? We are delivered from our spiritual leprosy by the blood of the Cross, and then, as priests, sanctified by the oil, or power, of the Spirit (Romans 8:2, 3). May the Oil of the Spirit remove all friction from our life and permeate and refresh every part of it!

Wine (Acts 2:13-15; Ephesians 5:18).

Such was the effect of the effusion of the Holy Spirit in the lives of the disciples on the historic day of Pentecost, that those around, witnessing the display of the Spirit's power through their lives and lips said, "These men are full of new wine." Their spiritual exhilaration and joy, and their amazing display of linguistic power, was mistaken for intoxication. "Wine maketh merry," said ancient writers (Psalm 104:15; Ecclesiastes 10:19), and the striking symbol of wine represents the refreshing, stimulating, gladdening influence of the Spirit in the life of the believer.

Our Lord Himself, Spirit-filled and ever full of rapturous joy, was taken for a wine-bibber (Matthew 11:19; Luke 7:34)). Paul would have us avoid all fleshly excitement produced by the excess of strong drink, yet "quaff deep of God's Spirit" (Ephesians 5:18). We can never drink of Him, as God's Wine, to excess. The more deeply and repeatedly we drink of Him, the more we desire. Infilled with Him, He creates a holy dissatisfaction over possession, for, satisfying our capacity, He increases our capacity, and thirst for Him never ceases.

Thou true life-giving Wine,
Let me Thy sweetness prove;
Renew my life with Thine,
Refresh my soul with love.

Seed (1 John 3:9; John 14:16).

As an emblem *seed* is used in many ways. The first symbolic use of this term taken from the realm of plants and flowers is in connection with Satan and the prophesied Saviour. "I will put enmity between . . . thy seed and her seed," said God to Satan (Genesis 3:15). In the fullness of time, Jesus came as the Seed of a woman – the Seed implanted within her by the Holy Spirit

when He overshadowed her, making her, thereby, the mother of our Lord (Luke 1:31, 32, 35); "to thy seed, which is Christ" (Galatians 3:16). The Scripture, which reveals Him, is also likened unto *seed* (Luke 8:5). Peter calls it "incorruptible seed" (1 Peter 1:23).

Isaiah, predicting the sufferings of Christ and how, as the result of the Cross, the Church born of the Spirit would appear, says of the Crucified One, "He shall see his *seed*," meaning, of course, all redeemed by His blood. In everyone born anew by the Spirit, Christ sees of the travail of His soul, and is satisfied (Isaiah 53:10, 11). From the original word for seed, we have our English term sperm, which, in the biological realm, is the male cell producing offspring.

John's use of this symbol perplexes many. "His seed remaineth in Him; and he cannot commit sin" (1 John 3:9). Although we are Christians, born of God, we know only too well that we do commit sin (1 John 1:8). Because this verse has been the source of erroneous teaching, a careful study of the true significance of its content is important. At the outset it must be clearly understood that those who are born of God have a dual nature, even though they are His children. This fact was realized by Paul who, as one deeply versed in the things of the Spirit, said, "When I [Paul, the new man in Christ Jesus] would do good, evil [old Saul of Tarsus] is with me." The strife between the two natures is apparent in the two laws the apostle mentions, "the law of God – the law of sin," and also in the confession "What I would, that do I not; but what I hate, that do I" (Romans 7:15-25). Paul further speaks of "the law of the Spirit of life" within his being delivering him from "the law of sin and death" (Romans 8:2).

The phrase "born of God" implies the

impartation of a new nature through the Holy Spirit, "that which is born of the Spirit" (John 3:5-8). At the moment of regeneration the Spirit enters the repentant, believing sinner, and becomes *His seed* – the Source of life, imparting life to him who was dead in trespasses and sin, making him a partaker of the divine nature (2 Peter 1:4). The Spirit then is the divine Seed, and because of His eternal holiness, cannot sin. But alongside of Him, as the Seed, is the seed of the serpent, the root, the germ of the satanic spirit and the satanic nature, for when we were born anew by the Spirit, our old nature did not cease to be. It co-exists with the new nature, and will, until our death or translation, when a glorious transformation into our Lord's unsinning nature will be ours.

The Spirit, as the Seed, "remaineth in him," says John, implying a permanent indwelling, and the divine nature He inhabits cannot sin. But if one born of the Spirit does sin, the sin arises from the old, corrupt nature which constantly strives after the lost dominion of the believer's life. His new nature cannot sin because it constitutes the newness of life from God the Spirit. When John goes on to say, "He . . . doth not commit sin," the present tense used here indicates continuous action, habitual practice, a manner of life. Those who are "the seed" of Christ of whom Isaiah wrote, and who have "His Seed," that is, the Spirit within, cannot practice sin. The product of his life corresponds to the nature of the Divine Seed. Born of the Spirit, which birth is permanent, the regenerated one cannot live in a state of sin.

What John teaches, then, in this difficult verse is not that the children of God do not *commit* acts of sin but that they do not lapse into sinners and *practice* sin. W. E. Vine says that the meaning suiting the context and the general tenor of the epistle is as follows –

> "The seed signifies the spiritual life as imparted to the believer, which abides in him without possibility of removal or extinction, the child of God remains eternally related to Christ, he who lives in sin has never become so related, he has not the principles of life in him."

In the believer, the Holy Spirit abides, or dwells, at the source of feeling and impulse, touching all springs of action and breathing on all the issues of life and where this God-planted *Seed* sends its roots into the depths and its branches into height and breadth of his nature, what desire or place is there for sin? May we be found assisting the Seed to reach full fruitage in our lives.

> Plant and root, and fix in me
> All the mind that was in Thee.

Seal (Ephesians 1:13; 4:30; John 6:27; 2 Corinthians 1:22).

Like his Master before him, Paul knew how to use what was around him to illustrate divine truth. His numerous military metaphors, for example, reflect his long and close association with the Roman army. While at Ephesus, a prosperous maritime city in the apostle's day, he came to know of its extensive timber trade, and noticed when the great logs and planks were brought in and sold that they were then sealed with burnt-in marks indicating ownership.

Under ancient Jewish law, the seal was a token of the completion of a transaction; and when the agreement was concluded, the act passed and the price paid, the seal was appended to the contract to make it definite and binding (Jeremiah 32:9, 10). The moment a person is born anew by the Spirit, he is sealed with the Spirit, and because *He* is the Seal, He cannot be broken. Sealed thus, we are no longer our own, for the Spirit, as the divine stamp upon us, marks us out as divine property until the day of final redemption, the redemption of the body (Romans 8:23). The Seal reads, on the one side, "The Lord knoweth them that are His," and on the other side, "Let every one that nameth the name of Christ depart from iniquity" (2 Timothy 2:19).

A seal was also used to convey to wax the design of the seal, and such monograms often implied a finished transaction when applied to documents in early-English times. It is said of Jesus, "Him hath God the Father sealed" (John 6:27), and He was "the express image of His person" (Hebrews 1:3), just as the wax bore the image of the seal. Perhaps the wax of our hearts is too hard – not soft enough to receive the divine image!

> Him from the dead Thou brought'st again,
> When, by His sacred blood,
> Confirmed and sealed for evermore,
> Th' eternal covenant stood.

Earnest (2 Corinthians 1:22; 5:5; Ephesians 1:13, 14).

The symbol of the *earnest*, relative to the Holy Spirit, is a most profitable one to explore, especially as Paul uses it three times in connection with the believer's redemption-inheritance. W. E. Vine's comment on the original word for our English *earnest* is enlightening –

> "*Arrabon*, originally meant earnest – money deposited by the purchaser and forfeited if the purchase was not completed, and was probably a Phoenician word, introduced into Greece. In general usage it came to denote a pledge or earnest of any sort. In the N.T. it is used only of that which is assured by God to believers: it is said of the Holy Spirit as the Divine pledge of all their future blessedness, particu-

larly of their eternal inheritance. See Genesis 38:17, 20, 28. In modern Greek, *Arrabona* is an engagement ring."

With us an *earnest* is a deposit paid by a purchaser to give validity to a contract. In Scotland, the word for earnest is *arle*. One farmer buying land from another would be handed a bag, filled with some of the earth bought, a part of his full purchased possession, or *arle*. It is in this sense that Paul uses the symbol, "Who hath . . . given us the earnest of the Spirit in our hearts." The Spirit is our *arle,* the pledge, the deposit on our complete inheritance. He is our solemn guarantee that we shall be effectively "filled unto all the fulness of God." Way's translation of Ephesians 1:14 reads –

> "The Holy Spirit, the Spirit that is the earnest of all that we shall inherit, the Spirit given to ensure the full redemption of what God hath claimed for His own, for the praise of His Majesty Divine."

What God has already given in part, He will bestow at last in perfection! In the Holy Spirit, as our Earnest, or Arle, we have Someone from heaven to go to heaven with. Now we have the firstfruits of the Spirit, and present possession of Him in our hearts is a pledge of future glory.

> In us Abba, Father's cry;
> Earnest of our bliss on high:
> Seal of Immortality,
> Comforter Divine.

Clothing (Judges 6:34; 1 Chronicles 12:18; 2 Chronicles 24:20).

The phrase "came upon" literally means, "The Spirit of Jehovah clothed himself with Gideon" (Judges 6:34 ASV margin). *Clothing,* as a verb, is frequently used in a figurative sense. See Isaiah 61:10. *Endued* implies, "clothed with power from on high" (Luke 24:49). The Spirit's empowerment is likened unto an act of clothing, or covering. In his most inspiring hymn, "O Worship the King," Sir R. Grant has a verse in which he describes the earth with its wonders untold and speaks of God as having –

> . . . 'Stablished it fast,
> By a changeless decree,
> And round it hath cast,
> Like a mantle, the sea.

Often the Spirit cast Himself like a mantle round those He sought to use for a specific purpose. Acting in free sovereignty He came upon men – and even a dumb animal – as He willed.

"*He clothed himself with Gideon*" (Judges 6:34). The name *Gideon* means, "He that bruises" or "cuts off iniquity" and for this warrior who bruised Israel's foes, the Spirit became the Mantle of Exhortation.

"*He clothed himself with Amasai*" (1 Chronicles 12:18). *Amasai* implies "The Burden of the Lord" which he was called to bear, and for his task the Spirit became the Mantle of Courage.

"*He clothed himself with Zechariah*" (2 Chronicles 24:20). Zechariah's name is suggestive. It means "Remembrance of the Lord," and the prophet sought to remind the nation of its sin against the Lord, and for him the Spirit was the Mantle of Rebuke.

Then there is the strong term about the Spirit who "came mightily upon" certain leaders. Literally the phrase implies that He attacked men, and as a greater Force compelled those He arrested to accomplish His task. Thus, we read that as the Omnipotent One, He

> "Came mightily upon Samson" (Judges 14:6, 19; 15:14).
> "Came mightily upon Saul" (1 Samuel 10:6, 10 ASV).

"Came mightily upon David" (1 Samuel 16:13 ASV).

Further, there is the softer, milder term *upon*, expressing a temporary divine enduement. Many illustrations of this action of the Spirit can be found in Scripture, e.g., Numbers 11:17; 24:2; 1 Samuel 19:20, 23; Isaiah 59:21; 60:1). We read that "The Spirit of Jehovah began *to move* Samson at times" (Judges 13:25). The word *move* means "cause to step," and the Spirit of Action can cause us to *stop* as well as *step*. Another gentle term is that of *rest*, used in connection with the mantling of the Spirit, and is associated with His dove-like character. The word *rest* signifies "to be at rest" as in Isaiah 57:2. "They shall rest in their beds." The Spirit of Peace and Serenity –

> "Rested upon" the seventy elders (Numbers 11:25, 26).
> "Rested upon" Elisha (2 Kings 2:15).
> "Rested upon" the Messiah (Isaiah 11:2).

How invincible we are when clad in the mantle, or whole armor, of the mighty Spirit! When He clothes the believer with Himself, protection is assured.

Seven (Zechariah 3:9; Revelation 5:6).

Representing "perfection," this numeral is symbolic of the Holy Spirit in the perfection of Deity, and also in the perfection of His mission and ministration. He is spoken of as having –

> "Seven Eyes" (Zechariah 3:9; 4:10; Revelation 5:6), possession of perfect insight, knowledge and understanding.
> "Seven Horns" (Revelation 5:6). *Horn* symbolizes power, and the Spirit is perfect in power and authority.

"Seven Spirits" (Revelation 1:4). We here have perfection of manifestation, as well as perfect obedience to the divine will.

"Seven Lamps of Fire" (Revelation 1:12, 13). Symbolic of divine holiness, these lamps suggest the Spirit's perfect holiness.

We sing of Him as "The Sevenfold Spirit," and so He is seeing that light, life, holiness, power, joy, love, and hope spring from Him. Further, as the "Sevenfold Spirit," He is intimately associated with the seven churches, and is revealed as having a separate message and ministry for each of the churches (Revelation 2:3).

SYMBOLS DRAWN FROM ANIMATE LIFE

There are at least five symbols related to life, and having life, used to emphasize the Spirit's omnipotent operation in our daily work, walk, and words. How good of God it is to aid our finite understanding by taking objects we can easily identify and using them as windows of truth!

Dove (Genesis 1:2; Luke 3:22).

This expressive emblem speaks of the Spirit's nature and office – His gentleness, tenderness, peace, beauty, innocence, patience, and sincerity. Not only is He "the Spirit of Might" and "the Spirit of Burning," but the Spirit of Love, of Grace, of Consolation. At His baptism, when Jesus was initiated into His public ministry, "the Holy Spirit descended in a bodily shape like a dove upon Him" (Luke 3:22). Such a semblance proclaimed two things, namely, the Spirit's own nature – loving, quiet, gentle, and the nature of the mission Jesus was to undertake – one of peace and sacrifice. The sixfold characteristics of the dove given in the Bible are applicable both to the Spirit and the saint. For instance, the dove is –

Swift in flight – "Wings like a dove" (Psalm 55:6).

Beautiful in plumage – "Wings of a dove covered with silver" (Psalm 68:13).

Constant in love – "The eyes of doves" (Song of Solomon 5:12).

Mournful in note – "Mourn sore like doves" (Isaiah 59:11).

Gentle in manner – "Harmless as doves" (Matthew 10:16).

Particular in food – "The dove found no rest for the sole of her foot."

The last reference, taken from Genesis 8:8-12, affords a striking image of the Holy Spirit who, on "this sin-laden and devastated earth, cannot find a pure place wherein to dwell, and comes back and rests upon Christ, represented by the Ark of Salavtion." René Pache goes on to say –

"When judgment is drawing to its close, the Spirit takes the Church away from the earth as the first fruit of humanity in the same way that the dove brought back an olive branch in her beak. Then when the time is fully come, the Spirit will be able to spread over all the earth which, during the Millennium, will be effectively filled with the knowledge of God, as the waters cover the sea. The raven which is an unclean bird feeding upon dead bodies, is an image of the flesh which delights itself in the midst of all impurities."

Theological discussions and church disputes often make those engaging in them hard, harsh, bitter, and acrimonious. In contending for the Faith, they become contentious in spirit and lose the radiancy of love, and sadly need the Holy Spirit to come upon them in the form of a dove. He alone can enable us to speak and defend the truth in love.

Yes, and the brutal world in which we live, and in which there are more cruel hawks than gentle doves, has need to seek out the olive branch of peace.

> Expand Thy wings, celestial Dove
> Brood o'er our nature's night
> On our disordered spirits move
> And let there now be light.

Porter (John 10:3; Acts 16:6-11).

As we have seen, there are very many direct, evident, and unmistakable symbols in Scripture of God the Father, God the Son, and God the Spirit. There are also *implied* symbols the preacher can use with profit, as Keach's monumental work on *Metaphors of Scripture* clearly proves. The occupation of the "porter" is one of these implied designations of the Spirit. In the original, our English word has a twofold significance. For instance, there is —

> *Porta,* meaning a "door-keeper," one who waits at a door to receive a message. "To him the porter openeth" (John 10:3). *See* Mark 13:34; John 18:16, 17). Rhoda's task was to open the door of Mary's house (Acts 12:13-16). David was content to be a doorkeeper (Psalm 84: 10).
> *Portare.* This second word implies "to carry," or, "a burden bearer." Those who take up our bags at railway stations are known as *porters*. We are invited to cast our burdens upon the Lord, and the Lord the Spirit is ever ready to assist us with our bags of trials and troubles. In fact, He is able to carry us *and* our burdens.

The Greek word our Lord used for *porter* was "porta," the one who opens doors. Some expositors see in the Porter Jesus spoke of, a reference to John the Baptist who, as His forerunner, came opening the door of the ministry of Jesus, or, in other words, prepared His way (Mark 1:1-8). The Holy Spirit, however, was the Divine Forerunner of Jesus, and opened the door for His entrance into the world. Now that He is here as the Good Shepherd, the Holy Spirit is His Porter, opening the door into the sheepfold (John 10:1-16). It is the function of the Spirit to open doors — and keep them open — for the Saviour. The *Shepherd* is likewise the *Door*, "I am the Door of the sheep." Contrast this with the phrase, "He that entereth in by the door is the Shepherd of the sheep."

Whenever the Spirit convicts a sinner of sin, and presents Jesus as the only efficacious Saviour, He opens a door for Him to enter into the sinner's heart. As the perfect Porter, the Spirit is ever at hand preparing souls for the entrance and reception of Christ (John 16:8-11; Acts 16:14). He likewise opens up the door of the world at large. The progress of missionary effort through the centuries is due to the Spirit's promptings, as the Book of Acts clearly illustrates. If He is found closing a door into Asia, He opens another into Europe (Acts 16:6-11).

Not only does the Spirit open doors, He also guards them so that strangers and hirelings cannot pass through. Further, are we not privileged in that we have been called to assist Him as the Porter? But are we allowing Him to open doors for the Shepherd to enter other hearts through our witness? As an under-porter, how many doors has the Head Porter enabled me to open for the King of Glory to come in? Am I in full sympathy with this necessary *doorwork* of Him who loves to open a door for straying sheep to enter the sheepfold? It is as true of the Divine Porter, as it is of the Divine Shepherd —

"He that is holy, He that is true...

He that openeth, and no man shutteth; and shutteth, and no man openeth" (Revelation 3:7).

Paraclete (John 14:16, 26).

Under previous titles attention was drawn to various aspects of the Spirit's ministry as the *Counsel for the defense*, as the word "paraclete" literally means. (*See* under titles *Another Comforter* and *Comforter*.) As a favorite designation for the Spirit, Christ used at least four times.

As the Paraclete, He is Christlike and abiding (John 14:16); He came as the Gift of the Father (John 14:26); He is represented as the Gift of the Son (John 15:26); He came as Christ's Ascension Gift (John 16:7). As we have often indicated in many of the names and titles considered, the Greek language is most pliable and gives to a word several meanings. Thus, we have three words for the English one of "comforter."

Comforter. "Walking ... in the comfort of the Holy Spirit" (Acts 9:31 ASV). Said Augustine, "The Holy Spirit on the Day of Pentecost descended into the temple of His Apostles, which He had prepared for Himself, as a shower of sanctification and a perpetual Comforter ... He is our sweetest Comforter." As such He is associated with our trials and sufferings.

Advocate. "We have an advocate with the Father" (1 John 2:1). This term, which John applied to Jesus as our Intercessor in heaven, and which He used of Himself while on earth (Luke 22:31, 32), is the same one translated "Paraclete." It is a term representing a pleader who comes forward in favor of, and as the representative of another. This idea is present in our two Advocates. The Holy Spirit *advocates*, Christ "pleads His cause." for the believer (Romans 8:26, 27). In heaven, Christ

ever lives to intercede for the believer (Hebrews 7:25).

Helper. "The Spirit also helpeth our infirmities" (Romans 8:26). *Helper* is another word resident in the original "paraclete." Among the gifts of the Spirit are *helpers*. "God hath set some in the church ... helps" (1 Corinthians 12:28). One wonders what churches would do without these more numerous gifts of the Spirit! *Helps!* Long may their tribe increase! But the Giver of these helps is the greatest Helper of all. Truly, God laid help upon His mighty Spirit! (Psalm 89:19). It was from Him Paul obtained help to continue his arduous and sacrificial labors (Acts 26:22). Yes, and all believers can find in the Spirit, "grace to help in time of need" (Hebrews 4:16). What a "Help of the helpless" is the Comforter Divine!

> Be with me when no other friend
>   The mystery of my heart can share;
> And be Thou known, when fears transcend,
>   By Thy best name of Comforter.

Witness (Romans 8:16; 9:1).

It was our Lord who said of the Spirit, "He shall testify of me" (John 15:26), and *testify* is the same word for *witness* in the original. Throughout Scripture the Spirit is before us as a true and faithful Witness for God the Father, and God the Son. *Witness* is related to an old English word, "witan," meaning to know. A witness in court is one brought there because of his knowledge of a case before the court, and much depends upon his testimony.

That Paul proved the Holy Spirit to be a perfect Witness is evident from passages like these – "The Spirit himself beareth witness" (Romans 8:16 ASV); "My conscience bearing witness with me in the Holy Spirit" (Romans 9:1). As a witness, the Spirit's testimony is always in harmony with His own just and righteous nature. He cannot act contrary to all that He is in Himself. He witnesses in, and to, the believer· in at least three ways –

In respect to pardon (Romans 5:1; 8:1).

In our lost estate we were sinners in the court of divine justice, guilty of transgressing the laws of God. But, pleading the atoning work of the Saviour, we were forgiven our criminality, and the Spirit entered as the Witness of our divine pardon, assuring us that we were no longer under condemnation.

In respect to adoption (Romans 8:14-17; Galatians 4:6).

The Holy Spirit witnesses with our spirit that we are now the sons of God. From the court of justice, we have been pardoned and acquitted, and go home to find ourselves brought into a divine family, with the Spirit as the continued Witness to our adoption as sons, and as sons, heirs of an eternal inheritance.

In respect to sanctification (1 John 4:13).

The indwelling Spirit is not only the evidence of our sonship, He is also the Source of our holiness, as saints. Pardoned in court, we become children in the Father's house, and then holy ones serving in His temple. As the Spirit of Holiness, He witnesses to our positional and practical and progressive sanctification. And the consciousness of the presence of an ungrieved Spirit within the heart is an evidence of our growing likeness to our holy Lord. One reason why the Spirit is called *Holy* is because it is His mission to enable us to perfect holiness in the fear of the Lord.

> Cheered by a Witness so Divine,
> Unwavering I believe;
> And Abba Father! – humble cry;
> Nor can the sign deceive.

Finger (Matthew 12:28 with Luke 11:20).

The early church fathers were wont to speak of the Holy Spirit as "The Finger of the Hand Divine." In Scripture, the oft-repeated designations, *The Finger of God* and *The Hand of God* are synonymous with omnipotence and occasionally with the added suggestion of the infallible evidence of divine authorship, visible in all God's works. The symbol of the *finger* is employed in a fivefold way –

1. *Of the Spirit of God.*

Combining what Matthew and Luke have to say about our Lord's miracle of casting out demons, we discover that the Holy Spirit is the Finger of God –

> "I cast out demons by the Spirit of God" (Matthew 12:28).
> "I with the finger of God cast out demons" (Luke 11:20).

Finger, as Christ's title for the Spirit of Power, fittingly describes Him as the indispensable Agent accomplishing the purpose of God. (*See* under title *Arm*).

2. *Of the Law of God.*

The two tablets carried the Ten Commandments "written with the finger of God" (Exodus 31:18; Deuteronomy 9:10). As Jesus named the Spirit "the finger of God," the implication is that He was associated with God in the framing and writing of divine truth. While human fingers actually penned the Scriptures as a whole, they were under the direct control of the Divine Finger. While they were the writers, the Spirit was the Divine Author. The forty or so writers responsible for the scrolls were inspired by the Spirit to set forth "the certainty of the words of truth" (Proverbs 22:20, 21). Peter declares that "holy men of God spake [and wrote] as they were moved [borne along] by the Holy Spirit" (2 Peter 1:21; 1 Peter 1:11).

3. *Of the Judgment of God.*

There are two references to the Divine Finger associated with judgment. First of all, when the magicians, in spite of their impressive enchantments, could no longer produce the same plagues with which God smote the Egyptians, they confessed to Pharaoh, "This is the finger of God" – and what an accusing finger it was (Exodus 8:19)! In *Julius Caesar*, Shakespeare asks the question –

> Shall we never
> Contaminate our fingers with false
>   bribes?

God's fingers were qualified to stretch out in judgment, for they were never contaminated with anything alien to His holy and just nature.

The second illustration of the divine fingers being connected with judgment is found in the sacrilegious feast of Belshazzar who shrank with fear as he saw "the fingers of a man's hand" write out on the palace wall the drunken king's condemnation (Daniel 5:5, 24-31). How apt are the lines of Edward Fitzgerald, of the 18th century, found in his *Omar Khayyám.*

> The Moving Finger writes, and,
>   having writ,
> Moves on: nor all thy Piety nor Wit
>   Shall lure it back to cancel half
>   a Line,
>   Nor all thy Tears wash out a
>   word of it.

4. *Of the Power of God.*

David, as a great lover of nature, considered the brilliant heavens above as the creation of the Spirit, and exclaimed, "... thy heavens, the work of thy fingers" (Psalm 8:3). Our first glimpse of the Spirit in Scripture is that of the Creator-Spirit (Genesis 1:2). *Firmament* implies a wide extent of space, and such an expanse was the production of the Executive of the Godhead, the Holy Spirit. He it is who seeks to create a wider expanse in our hearts that greater glory may be God's in and through our lives. The same

powerful Fingers fashioning the heavens are able to transform us into new creatures, or creations, in Christ Jesus (2 Corinthians 5:17; Galatians 6:15; John 3:6-8).

5. *Of the Saint of God.*

To ancient Orientals, fingers were essential in conversation because they were able to indicate what their mouths dare not utter in respect to concern or grave insult. Of a wicked person, Solomon wrote, "He teacheth with his fingers" (Proverbs 6:13). Isaiah speaks of "the putting forth of the finger, and speaking vanity" (Isaiah 58:9). But Paul has a more exalted conception of the Fingers of the Holy Spirit. Writing to the Corinthians in his second epistle, he reminded them that as a Christian church they were "the *epistle* of Christ ... written not with ink, but with the Spirit of the living God" (2 Corinthians 3:3). Moses wrote upon a tablet of stone, the Spirit writes upon the heart of the saint the laws of God (Hebrews 8:10; 10:16). Are we, as living epistles, proving to the world that the Holy Spirit is the Penman writing the story our lives?

> Write Thy new name upon my heart
> Thy new, best name of LOVE.

(See further under Appendices *Value of Book Study.*)

At last we have reached the end of our study of the divine names and titles of the Persons of the Blessed Trinity; and while we have sought to give such a rewarding study all necessary depth, some may feel that there are other designations that might have been included. We feel, however, that sufficient have been dealt with to prove what vast spiritual resources are suggested by the nomenclature of Scripture. George Meredith has the line, "Our souls were in our names." We have been discovering, that all the Father, and the Son, and the

Spirit are in themselves is manifested in their numerous names. As their names, so are they. Christ's condemnation of the church in Sardis was, "Thou hast a name that thou livest, and art dead" (Revelation 3:1). But all the divine names not only proclaim life, *they are life*. Magnifying Christ as the Son of God, John says that there is "life through his name" (John 20:31).

Lord Byron wrote of those who had "names that must not wither" – "Bright names will hallow song." Divine names are imperishable and hallow our soul, as well as our song. May we be found appropriating all that the divine names indicate in power and provision!

> "His name *through faith in his name* hath made this man strong" (Acts 3:16).

APPENDICES

1. The Nobility of a Name.

A striking feature emerging from a study of divine names in Scripture is the way writers had of using just the word *Name* as a channel of blessing or judgment without actually mentioning any precise, particular name. Because of all that was accomplished in and through "The Name," whichever definite designation was in the mind of the writer, a certain superiority and worthiness encircled it. Beyond the use of terms life, *Name, Thy Name, His Name*, there was the wisdom of all that they implied in the character, power and provision of its bearer.

Jesus often used the phrase, "in my name" or "my name's sake" (Matthew 10:22; 18:20; John 14:13; Acts 9:16). The precise names are not stated. Is it His name of *Jesus*, or *Christ*, or *Lord*, or any other of the titles given Him? When Peter and John were forbidden to "speak to no man in *this name*," the next verse expressly states what it is – "speak not at all nor teach in the name of Jesus" (Acts 4:17, 18). But when He says, "Ask in my name," which of His glorious names are we to employ? The answer is any, or all of them, for any name of His is effectual seeing that it represents all He is in Himself.

Conveying to Israel the divine conditions regulating her sojourn in the land of promise, Moses told the people to "fear this glorious and fearsome name," then stated the august name, THE LORD THY GOD (Deuteronomy 28:58). But in many instances injunctions are given as to honoring the divine Name without such an addition of the express name, although it can be found close at hand. David said of Zion, "They that love his name shall dwell therein"

(Psalm 69:36). What precise name were the saints of old to love? The previous verse says, "*God* will save Zion," thus the implication is the name to love is *Elohim* (Psalm 5:10). But every other name of His must be equally loved. The psalmist further declares, "His name shall endure for ever; his name shall be continued as long as the sun" (Psalm 72:17). What name? The next verse blesses *Jehovah*, and this is "the glorious name for ever" (Psalm 72:18, 19). But all divine names are glorious and everlasting.

Peter said of the lame man healed at the temple gate, "His name through faith in his name hath made this man strong" (Acts 3:16). In the narrative it refers to several names of the Divine Healer – *Jesus Christ, his Son Jesus, the Holy One, the Just, the Prince of Life* (Acts 3:6, 13, 14, 15). Any name of His is effectual to plead in the hour of need. David declared, "They that know thy name will put their trust in thee" (Psalm 9:10). This assurance is applicable to any of His names. But emphasis is on the phrase *they that know*. The mere repetition of a name, no matter how illustrious will never deepen trust in God. *Know* implies more than a mere superficial knowledge. It stands for *experiential* knowledge. When we have experienced all the power and authority and provision any divine name represents, only then can we trust and not be afraid, and tread down our enemies (Psalms 44:5; 63:4).

Recounting the deliverance of Israel from Pharaoh sacred writers wrote, "So didst thou get thee a name" (Nehemiah 9:10; Isaiah 63:12, 14; Jeremiah 32:20). Here *name* means not one by which the hearer is identified, but fame, honor, prestige. Among ourselves, if one accomplishes an outstanding achievement we say, "He made a name for himself." Thus, the miracle of parting the Red Sea for Israel's escape from the bondage of Egypt enhanced God's reputation.

Further, to say of a person, "I know thee by name," as Jehovah said of Moses (Exodus 33:12), meant more than a slight knowledge of a particular name. We know scores by their names, but have never had their acquaintance. When the ancients said, however, "I know thee by thy name," it indicated a distinction, a friendship, a particular familiarity. Thus, Jehovah not only knew the law-giver by his name, Moses, He spoke "face to face [with him], as a man speaketh unto his friend" (Exodus 33:11). Under grace, a similar privilege is ours for Jesus not only calls each of us by name (John 10:3), He likewise condescends to treat us as His friends (John 15:13-15).

2. Qualifying Attributes of Christ.

There is a legend to the effect that an artist tried to paint a portrait of Christ, but every time he tried, he failed. Disconsolate he went to Him and asked the reason for his lack of success, and Christ simply smiled and said, "No one can paint a picture of me for anyone else, for if he did, it would be said that the Christ was thus and thus; every one must paint his own picture." Is this not what every man does when he answers the question, "What think ye of Christ?" He challenges the world by His wonderful versatility, and presents an amazing revelation of qualifying attributes.

A remarkable feature of Jesus Christ is the way He fits into everyone's thinking. He is so many-sided each can find Christ in the mold of his own occupational life and day-by-day experience In this respect He challenges the attention of the world and meets the needs of all classes of men. As deep answereth

to deep, so Jesus responds to the movings of each soul of man. Life is varied, just as occupations are, and all, no matter what their round of duty may be, can find in Him the Saviour who is able to meet the particular need of each.

To the *Architect* – He is the Chief Cornerstone (1 Peter 2:6).

To the *Artist* – He is the One altogether lovely (Song of Solomon 5:16).

To the *Astronomer* – He is Sun, and Morning Star (Revelation 22:16; Malachi 4:2).

To the *Baker* – He is the Living Bread (John 6:35, 51).

To the *Banker* – He is Unsearchable Riches (Ephesians 3:8).

To the *Biologist* – He is the Life (John 14:6).

To the *Botanist* – He is the Plant of Renown (Ezekiel 34:29).

To the *Bride* – He is the Bridegroom (Matthew 25:1).

To the *Builder* – He is the Sure Foundation (Isaiah 28:16).

To the *Carpenter* – He is the Nail, and the Door (Isaiah 22:23; John 10:9).

To the *Christian* – He is the Son of the Living God (Matthew 16:16).

To the *Disconsolate* – He is the Comforter (John 14:1).

To the *Drifter* – He is an Anchor (Hebrews 6:19).

To the *Doctor* – He is the Great Physician (Matthew 8:17).

To the *Educator* – He is the Superb Teacher (John 3:2).

To the *Engineer* – He is a Polished Shaft, and a Living Way (Isaiah 49:2; Hebrews 10:20).

To the *Farmer* – He is the Sower, the Wheat, and Lord of Harvest (Matthew 13:37; John 12:24; Matthew 9:38).

To the *Florist* – He is the Rose and the Lily (Song of Solomon 2:1).

To the *Friendless* – He is the Friend closer than a brother (Proverbs 18:24).

To the *Genealogist* – He is the Name above every name (Philippians 2:9).

To the *Geologist* – He is the Rock of Ages (Isaiah 26:4 asv).

To the *Heavy-Laden* – He is Rest (Matthew 11:28-30).

To the *Herbalist* – He is the Cluster of Camphire and Root of Jesse (Song of Solomon 1:14; Isaiah 11:10).

To the *Horticulturist* – He is the True Vine (John 15:1).

To the *Jeweller* – He is the Precious Stone (1 Peter 2:6).

To the *Judge* – He is the Righteous Judge, Judge of all (2 Timothy 4:8).

To the *Juror* – He is the Faithful and True Witness (Revelation 3:14).

To the *King* – He is KING of kings (Revelation 19:16).

To the *Lawyer* – He is Counsellor, Advocate, Law-Giver (Isaiah 9:6; 1 John 2:1, 2).

To the *Lonely* – He is the Abiding Companion (Hebrews 13:5).

To the *Lover* – He is the Betrothed (Song of Solomon 2:16).

To the *Metaphysician* – He is Alpha and Omega (Revelation 22:13).

To the *Newspaperman* – He is Good Tidings (Luke 2:10).

To the *Oculist* – He is the Light of the Eye (Matthew 4:16; 6:22).

To the *Outcast* – He is the Friend of Sinners (Luke 15:1, 2).

To the *Philanthropist* – He is the Unspeakable Gift (2 Corinthians 9:15).

To the *Philosopher* – He is the Wisdom of God (1 Corinthians 1:24).

To the *Photographer* – He is the Exact Likeness (Hebrews 1:3).

To the *Pilgrim* – He is the Way (John 14:6).

To the *Potter* – He is the Vessel of Honor (2 Timothy 2:21).

To the *Preacher* – He is the Model Preacher, and Word to preach (Luke 4:18; Revelation 19:13).

To the *Ruler* – He is Ruler of the Kings of Earth (Revelation 1:5 asv).

To the *Sailor* – He is Master of ocean and sea (Mark 4:41).

To the *Sculptor* – He is the Living Stone (1 Peter 2:4).

To the *Servant* – He is the Good Master (Ephesians 6:9).

To the *Shepherd* – He is the Lamb (John 1:29), and Good Shepherd (John 10).

To the *Sinner* – He is the One born the Saviour (Matthew 1:21).

To the *Slave* – He is the Redeemer – One who buys back (Galatians 3:13).

To the *Soldier* – He is the Captain (Hebrews 2:10; Psalm 24:8).

To the *Statesman* – He is the Desire of all Nations (Haggai 2:7).

To the *Stormtossed* – He is a Refuge in storms (Isaiah 25:4).

To the *Student* – He is Incarnate Truth (John 1:14; 14:6).

To the *Theologian* – He is the Author and Finisher of Faith (Hebrews 12:2).

To the *Thirsty* – He is the Water of Life (John 4:10).

To the *Toiler* – He is the Rest-Giver (Zephaniah 3:17; Mark 6:31).

To the *Traveller* – He is the Guide (Psalm 48:14).

To the *Unclean* – He is the Fountain of Cleansing (Zechariah 13:1).

To the *Weak* – He is the Power of God (1 Corinthians 1:24).

To the *Widow* – He is the Husband (Isaiah 54:5; Jeremiah 49:11).

To the *Wise* – He is the Wisdom of God (1 Corinthians 1:24, 30).

To the *Zoologist* – He is the Lion of Judah (Revelation 5:5).

> O Hope of every contrite heart!
> O Joy of all the meek!
> To those who fall, how kind Thou art!
> How good to those who seek!

3. The Value of Book Summary.

Because of the wide range of truth embodied in Scripture there are various ways by which we can approach it, and it adds great zest and profit to Bible study when we pursue different methods of mastering the contents of such an inexhaustible storehouse of knowledge. Paul describes students of the Word as *workmen* who, if they are not to be ashamed of their work, must skillfully use every necessary tool at their command (2 Timothy 2:15).

As the Bible presents a progressive revelation of God and His purposes, one very serviceable system of arriving at what it teaches as to any theme is to seek our references to it from book to book, watching its development as you proceed. Those who are familiar with Dr. Elder Cummings' work on *The Eternal Spirit* will recall that this was his way of unfolding what the Bible teaches as to the personality and ministry of the Holy Spirit.

If we take a book like Ephesians as an illustration of book study, we find it saturated with the truth of the Holy Spirit who is mentioned some 14 times, in contrast to the demon-spirit against whom the Divine Spirit is in unceasing conflict (Ephesians 2:2). Grouping together what Paul had to say about the Spirit in his "Gospel of the Heavenlies" as Ephesians has been called, we had the following outline providing one with a profitable Bible meditation.

1. *Blessings of the Spirit* (1:3). This verse can be translated "the benediction of all blessings of His Spirit." Some dozen or more of these blessings are given in verses 1-14.

2. *Sealing of the Spirit* (1:13). He Himself is the Seal.

3. *Earnest of the Spirit* (1:14). He is the Pledge of all future blessings.

4. *Illumination of the Spirit* (1:17, 18). He opens Scripture and our minds.

5. *Access by the Spirit* (2:18). No entrance in any other way.

6. *Task of the Spirit* (2:22). Complete the one Body.

7. *Revelation of the Spirit* (3:5). Unfolds mystery.

8. *Power of the Spirit* (3:7). Opposite to energy of flesh.

9. *Unity of Spirit* (4:3, 4). He is the Author of unities.

10. *Grief of the Spirit* (4:30). Evidence of His personality and His love.

11. *Fruit of the Spirit* (5:9). Within and without.

12. *Fullness of the Spirit* (5:18). Evidences of Spirit-filled life.

13. *Sword of the Spirit* (6:17). Cuts both ways.

14. *Intercession by the Spirit* (6:18). Unfailing resource.

An extension of this particular method of book study is to be seen in the excellent outline Dr. W. Graham Scroggie gives us in his *Guide to the Gospels*. Pointing out that the chief source of Christ's teaching on the Holy Spirit was given by Him in His upper room discourse, this renowned teacher of the Word gives us the following summary as found in three chapters: John 14; 15; 16.

1. THE PERSONALITY OF THE SPIRIT. *Terms* of personality are employed of Him (14:16, 17, 26; 15:26; 16:7, 13).

   Qualities of personality are attributed to Him. He teaches, guides and communicates truth (14:26; 16:13).

Operations of personality are ascribed to Him. He leads, receives, glorifies, announces, assists (14:16, 26; 15:26; 16:14, 15).

2. THE DEITY OF THE SPIRIT.
Associations of Deity are His (14:16, 26; 15:26; 16:14, 15).
Attributes of Deity are His (14:17, 26; 16:7, 12, 13).
Actions of Deity are His (16:8-14).

3. THE CHARACTER OF THE SPIRIT.
He is the *Holy* Spirit, the Spirit of Truth, the Comforter (14:26; 15:26; 16:13; 14:16, 26; 16:7).

4. THE ADVENT OF THE SPIRIT, "When He Comes" (14:16, 26; 15:26; 16:7).

5. THE MINISTRY OF THE SPIRIT.
In the *World* (16:8-11).
In the *Church* (14:26; 15:26; 16:12-15).

BIBLIOGRAPHY

Bowman, Wm. Dodson, *What Is Your Surname?* (Faber and Faber, London, 1932).

Brownville, C. Gordon, *Symbols of the Holy Spirit* (Fleming H. Revell, New York, 1945).

Bullinger, E. W., *The Giver and His Gifts* (The Lamp Press, London, 1953).

Cottle, Basil, *Penguin Dictionary of Surnames* (Penguin Books, England, 1967).

Cummings, Elder, *The Eternal Spirit* (Drummond Tract Depot, Stirling).

Dolman, D. H., *Simple Talks on the Holy Spirit* (Marshall, Morgan, Scott, London, 1939).

Downer, A. C., *Mission and Ministration of the Holy Spirit* (James Clark, Edinburgh, 1909).

Figgis, J. B., *Emmanuel* (Partridge Co., London, 1885).

Foerster and Quell, *Lord* (Adam and Black, London, 1958).

Govan, H. E., *Studies in the Sacred Name* (Bright Words, Edinburgh).

Hill, Rowley, *Titles of Our Lord* (James Nisbet, London, 1935). 1935).

Holden, G. F., *The Holy Ghost – The Comforter* (Longman, Greens, London, 1908).

Hurlburt and Horton, *The Wonderful Names* (Grand Book House, Los Angeles, 1925).

Ingram, Winnington, *The Love of the Trinity* (Wells Gardner and Darton, London, 1908).

Jukes, Andrew, *The Names of God* (Kregel, Grand Rapids, 1967).

Kuhn, Harold B., *Names and Nature of God* (Christianity Today, Washington, D.C., 1970).

Kuyper, Abraham, *The Work of the Holy Spirit* (Zondervan, Grand Rapids).

L.H.S., *His Glorious Name* (Bible Warehouse, London, 1908).

Lockyer, Herbert, *The Breath of God* (Union Gospel Press, Cleveland, 1949).

Macbeath, John, *What Is His Name?* (Marshall, Morgan, Scott, London).

MacGregor, C. H., *Things of the Spirit* (James Clarke, Edinburgh).

Matheson, George, *Voices of the Spirit* (James Nisbet, London, 1905).

Marsh, F. E., *Emblems of the Holy Spirit* (Marshall, Morgan, Scott, London, 1911).

Marsh, J. E., *The Structural Principles of the Bible* (Pickering and Inglis, London).

Pache, René, *The Person and Work of the Holy Spirit* (Marshall, Morgan, Scott, London, 1956).

Pierson, A. T., *Knowing the Scriptures* (James Nisbet, London, 1910).

Redford, R. A., *The Doctrine of the Spirit* (James Nisbet, London, 1889).

Robson, John, *The Holy Spirit – The Paraclete* (Oliphant and Ferrier, London, 1894).

Rolls, Charles J., *The Name Above Every Name* (Loizeaux Bros., New Jersey, 1965).

Scott, Walter, *Bible Handbook* (G. Morrish, London).

Scroggie, W. Graham, *A Guide to the Gospels* (Pickering and Inglis, London, 1948).

Smith, Elsdon C., *The Story of Our Names* (Harper and Brothers, New York, 1950).

Sprunt, James, *Jehovah Titles* (George Stoneman, London, 1890).

Stalker, James, *The Christology of Jesus* (Hodder and Stoughton, London, 1899).

Steele, Daniel, *The Gospel of the Comforter* (The Christian Witness, Chicago, 1917).

Stevenson, H. F., *Titles of the Triune God* (Marshall, Morgan, Scott, London, 1955).

Stone, Nathan J., *Names of God – Old Testament* (Moody Press, Chicago, 1944).

Warfield, Benjamin B., *The Lord of Glory* (Hodder and Stoughton, London, 1907).

Webb-Peploe, *The Titles of Jehovah* (James Nisbet, London, 1901).

Whitelaw, Thomas, *Jehovah-Jesus* (T. and T. Clark, Edinburgh, 1913).

Wilkinson, W. F., *Personal Names in the Bible* (Alexander Strahan, London, 1866).

Withycombe, E. G., *Oxford Dictionary of Christian Names* (Clarendon Press, Oxford, 1949).

Profitable material was also gathered from *Ellicott's Bible Commentary,* published by Zondervan, Grand Rapids, Michigan; Jamieson, Fausset and Brown's *Critical and Explanatory Commentary,* also by Zondervan; *Fausset's Bible Dictionary,* also by Zondervan; contributed articles on "God," "Jesus Christ," and "The Holy Spirit" in *The International Standard Bible Encyclopedia* by Wm. B. Eerdmans, Grand Rapids. *Figures of Speech in the Bible* by E. W. Bullinger; *Dictionary of New Testament Words* by W. E. Vine; *Word Studies* by Marvin R. Vincent; *Dictionary of the Bible* by James Hastings; *The Emphasised Bible* by Rotherham; *Paul's Epistles and Hebrews* by Arthur Way. From all of these sources much wax was found to make our candle from which we trust some light has been received on divine appellations.

SUBJECT INDEX

A

Abba Father, 70, 71
Abraham, God of, 87
Adam, the Last, 107, 242
Adhon, 38, 192
Adhonay, 38
Adon-Adonai, 15, 16
Adonai Elohim, 15
Adonai Jehovah, 15, 191
Adoni-jah, 15
Adonis, 15, 93
Advocate, 99, 108, 109, 232, 314, 333
Aleah, 7
Almighty, 18, 87, 89, 109, 110
Almighty God, 7, 66
Alpha and Omega, 18, 96, 110, 111, 161
Amen, the True Amen, 111, 112
Ancient of Days, 74, 89, 136
Angel of His Presence, 112
Angel of Jehovah, 112
Anointed, 113, 319, 320
Apostle, 113, 114
Arm of Salvation, 116
Arm of the Lord, 115, 116
Ascension, 193, 201, 202, 224
Atonement, 184, 185, 205
Author, 117, 186, 263, 309
Author and Finisher of Faith, 100, 106
Authority, 15, 16

B

Banner, the Lord Our, 30-32, 52, 64, 87
Beelzebub, 102, 223
Beloved, the, 119
Beloved Son, 119
Bishop, 245, 246
    of Our Souls, 246
    Universal Bishop, 246
Branch, 121, 236
    of David, 121
    of Jehovah, 121
    of Righteousness, 89, 98
Bread, 122
    from Heaven, 123
    Living, 98, 103, 123, 213
    of God, 123
    of Life, 98, 103, 123, 213
    of Sacrifice, 123
Breath of the Almighty, 295
Bridegroom, 102, 103, 124-127
Bright and Morning Star, 127-130
Brightness of the Father's Glory, 130

C

Calvary, 23, 24, 26, 46, 49, 55, 136, 163, 222, 259, 278, 323
Carpenter, 131, 132, 278
Chief Cornerstone, 104, 105, 132
Chiefest Among Ten Thousand, 133-135
Child, 135, 274-280
Christ, 97, 101, 102, 104, 105, 107, 137, 138, 224, 277
    Jesus, 138
    of God, 139
    Son of the Blessed, 139, 140
    the Chosen of God, 139
    the Lord, 138, 139, 277
    the Son of God, 139
    Very Christ, 140
Comforter, 108, 109, 305, 313, 314, 333
Consolation of Israel, 140, 141
Counsellor, 88, 109, 141, 142, 218
Covenant, 142, 143
Covenant-Maker, 58
Covert, 76
    from storm and rain, 76
    from the tempest, 76
    of Thy Wings, 76
Creator, 6, 20, 45, 54, 82, 100, 207, 219, 249, 273
    of All Things, 89
Cross, 24, 26, 27, 29, 49, 56, 228, 310, 327
Crucifixion, 23

D

David, God of, 88
David, Perfect King (Christ), 143
Daysman, 205
Dayspring, 144, 208

SCRIPTURE INDEX

349